2007

Pastor Matthew Kiecker,

Best wishes,

Mary Utley

The
B I B L E
and the
W O R L D
T O G E T H E R

An Historical Guidebook

by

Mary Utley

Other books by Mary Utley:

PROGRAM NOTES: Making Music Together for 25 Years with the LaPorte Symphony
Orchestra, 1997

PROGRAM NOTES—THE ENCORE YEARS with the LaPorte County Symphony, 2006

MESSIAH, 2002

First Printing, 2006

Published in Michigan City, Indiana, by Abacus Print & Sign Solutions.

All quotations are from antiquity, objects or things found; and from classical writers.
Biblical quotations are from the Authorized, King James Version or the King James
Study Bible, Liberty University, and The Oxford Annotated Bible with the Apocrypha,
Revised Standard Version © 1965 by Oxford University Press.

ISBN: 978-0-615-13494-9
       0-615-13494-7

THANK YOU!

This book would never have come to be without the help, support and/or advice of some wonderful friends and family:

— The late Episcopal Bishop of Northern Indiana, the Rt. Rev. Walter C. Klein, who encouraged the germ of an idea; and whose classical library became my intellectual home.

— My parish priest for 25 years, the Rev. B. Linford Eyrick of St. Paul's Episcopal Church, LaPorte, Indiana, who taught me the faith as it was "once for all delivered to the saints," and who staunchly maintained that faith free of trendy, gimmicky innovations.

— The Rev. Clair Price who read the book when it was only a bare-bones skeleton . . . and didn't laugh.

— The Rev. Dr. Gerhart Niemeyer, Episcopal priest, head of the Department of Government and International Relations at the University of Notre Dame and staff writer for NATIONAL REVIEW magazine. Fr. Niemeyer came to my home to tutor me and recommend reading. Then, having studied Eric Voegelin's ORDER AND HISTORY at his behest, I submitted to him my re-written section on the CREATION OF MONARCHY. After reading it, he called me to say, "You have summed up all of Eric Voegelin on one page." (p. 55) I was too stunned to ask him to please put that in writing.

— The Rt. Rev. Stanley Atkins, Bishop of Racine, Wisconsin, Dean of Nashotah House Episcopal Seminary and one of the church's great scholars, tutored me by mail with what is still a file full of instructional letters. An authority on the New Testament and Roman Law, it was through his recommended reading, wisdom and concern that I was able to write about that aspect of the Roman period.

— Dr. Paul Maier, Professor of Ancient History at Western Michigan University is the author of many books including JOSEPHUS, the Essential Writings, THE FLAMES OF ROME, and PONTIUS PILATE; and is a frequent and familiar commentator in biblical documentaries on television. He called my book the "finest job of [reconciling] sacred and secular history" he'd ever seen. "It's hard to believe a lay person could have brought this off, but you certainly did!"

— The Rt. Rev. W.C.R. Sheridan, Episcopal Bishop of Northern Indiana was "awed" by my "amazing book." He had never seen "anything comparable," and asked if it could be used "as a text book?"

— The Rev. Howard Keyse, Rector of St. John's Episcopal Church. Elkhart, Indiana, was a true champion who "laboratory tested" the book in his class rooms. His unbounded enthusiasm and encouragement propelled the book into reality.

— Rev. Lester Kamp of Louisiana who, as the "little boy next door," I knew as "Sonny." His perspective and criticism from outside the Episcopal Church, was most helpful.

— My dearest friend, Marian Bistline, my role model, best "listener" and critic thought I could do no wrong.

—   Mrs. Phyllis Dolaway Nichols spent many long afternoons reading it together with me and correcting my careless construction.

—   My editor at the South Bend Tribune, John Miller, who hired me as an unknown quantity, trusted and nurtured me, than gave me wings and let me pursue visions and dream dreams.

—   The members of the various Bible Study classes who listened to "the whole thing" and made comments I will treasure forever, especially those of Father Jack Meyer.

—   My dear and valued friend, Merry Johnson, who is not only the first flute of the La-Porte County Symphony Orchestra, but a highly accomplished artist and sculptor. It is her painting that graces this books' cover jacket.

—   And finally, my dear, patient and generous husband, Jack Utley (Major John H. Utley, Jr. USAR) without whose help this book (nor the other two books) would never have come to be. He has been my advisor, supporter, consultant, patron, assistant and associate, colleague and factotum; who has put up with my "tunnel vision" and extravagance for so long, with never a word of complaint.

*   *   *

The illustrations in this book come from four sources: my own pen, the Dover collection, the Gustav Dore collection and the 1891 German Bible of my Grandfather whose devotion to our Lord was legendary. Only one picture (No. 1, pg. 1) is taken from a "modern" source and that one is from Michelangelo.

INTRODUCTION

Lucy in the Olduvai Gorge and Ignatius in the Roman Colosseum; Hannibal's armored elephants crossing the Alps and Silk Road caravans carrying gold, frankincense and myrrh; Helen abducted from Troy and Jezebel thrown to the dogs; godly Elijah and god-less Ahab; pharaohs and Caesars; masters and madmen; architects of Greece's golden age, King Tut's golden tomb and Herod the Great's golden temple; the builders and destroyers of Jerusalem, Carthage, Rome in flames and Pompeii under ash; and the creators of modern man: Homer, Plato, Aristotle and, of course, Moses, Jesus and St. Paul. Action and adventure, sex and violence, murder and mayhem; many a story contains little else. But how many have philosophy, faith, hope and love right beside, and a cast of characters that couldn't be invented . . . where faith, hope and love are the good guys?

Most people searching for a faith to live by resolve at some time or another, and with finest intentions, to "read the Bible through from start to finish." They (including myself, long ago) zip right through the first book, GENESIS, and rightly so; it is fast moving and exciting. The second, EXODUS, is awesome and gripping. But then come LEVITICUS and NUMBERS and the good intentions fall away. Repetitious ancient history, they seem useless to modern minds and lives. Hopelessly bogged down in only the third and fourth books, the reader gives up in frustration and lays down the Bible, never again to pick it up. And the glory, beauty, majesty, wonder, promise and inspiration of the World's Greatest Book is lost forever. And it needn't be, if something else had been read first; a guidebook, so to speak.

No sensible person would dream of undertaking a long, arduous journey to a foreign country without first having learned something about the country; read about it, studied road maps, guide books, etc. Reading the Bible is a journey, a very long journey, through thousands of years and many foreign lands. Because most people learn about the world in secular, public schools, the Bible world is often perceived to be almost a fantasy world, way back there . . . somewhere . . . a nebulous, far-away fairytale. In fact, the world of the Bible is a world of real-life, flesh and blood people acting out God's Great Drama, shaping world events. And a guidebook is needed that would take that Biblical world out of fantasy-land and put it together with the "real" world. That's what this book is trying to do; not to "teach" the Bible, nor interpret it, but to provide the stage setting from whence it came. For the Bible was not just "written" by someone who simply sat down and dreamed up tales; it was LIVED, experienced, witnessed, inspired by God, and then recorded, a chronicle of real people, events and nations. Most importantly, it is not just ancient history, past, dead, forgotten. The message of the Bible is as new today as ever, as fitting for modern man as for any other, and maybe, even, more so.

Nor is this book intended to be read INSTEAD of the Bible (just as a travelogue does not replace travel) but, rather, with it; so that the reader can visualize everything happening together and see the whole drama drawn out. And what a drama! In the time of Abraham men wore long flowing robes, sandals on their feet, and ate from earthenware dishes. If they went somewhere, they walked. Many, in the time of Jesus, did the same thing, and to many minds it would seem that the two men lived at the same time. And yet, EIGHTEEN HUNDRED years of history separated them; 1800 exciting, vivid, gorgeously colored years, some plodding slowly on and some fast moving and violent; years packed full of world-building events; years that are rarely placed side by side with the persons and events of the secular world. What was going on "out in the world" when Moses led the Hebrews out of Egypt, for instance, or when David fought Goliath; or when St. Paul was traveling about teaching faith, love and justice? (The Emperor Nero was trying to murder his mother, for starters.) What part did Biblical people play in the Glory that was Greece or the Grandeur that was Rome? And why do we know so little about Jesus from secular, historical sources? Didn't anybody else write about Him besides those who wrote the Gospels? (They did.) And how can we even believe the Gospels? Sometimes they don't even agree with each other.

The story of the Bible and the world TOGETHER is a fascinating one, full of "ifs." If Socrates had not been the teacher of Plato, and Plato the teacher of Aristotle, and Aristotle of Alexander the Great, the world would have been a far, far different place than it was when Jesus was born into it. If Alexander had not spread the beloved Greek *ethos* Aristotle had taught him far and wide, Saint Paul might have spoken nothing but Hebrew, and would not have been understood outside the boundaries of his own country. But Paul, a rabbinical Jew, was reared in a Greek world; he spoke Greek and he wrote it, and the world understood him.

And he traveled with the benefit of his Roman citizenship. If Julius Caesar had not been assassinated there would have been no Augustus Caesar, whose Pax Romana, or Roman Peace, made Paul a Roman citizen and allowed him to travel the length of the empire. For Jesus of Nazareth, it was the perfect time to be born. Any other, and the world would not only have rejected Him; it may simply never have heard of Him. (No, this is in no way a suggestion that the world was created and ordered solely to accommodate the Christian faith, that world history progressed along certain lines to conform to the Christian religion. Some Christian writers do, indeed, do that, beginning with St. Augustine in his CITY OF GOD which he wrote sometime around A.D. 400. But, while this text will try to show how certain secular events did, in fact, take such turns that encouraged the beginning and spread of Christianity, it does not presume to show "why." That Christianity could not have flourished and spread without Alexander's conquests or Augustus' Pax Romana is evident, but that does not suggest that those things occurred solely to accommodate the Christian faith.)

In this book I have drawn together the world's growth and the Bible's fulfillment into chronological perspective to show that the events of the Bible were not isolated and "otherworldly," but were, in fact, a part of the real world. I have taken the years the Bible was "lived" and "written," and put them together with what was going on "out in the world" at the same time. The format used is a chronological narrative count-down beginning "in the beginning . . ." to that one date by which all time is measured, the birth of Jesus Christ; and then a "count-up," so to speak, for the following 100 years to the completion of the writing of the Bible. The narrative also dramatizes several features that bring special meaning to the story: how, when and why the Old Testament prophecies were made, and how fulfilled in both the Old and the New; the many archeological artifacts unearthed which illustrate so vividly the Bible stories; and the many Bible passages which show why Judeo-Christianity is so important in the history of Western civilization, especially in America; how the American form of government and concept of humane civilization owes its very existence to God's Holy Word.

Every book in the Bible is summarized and placed in a boxed-in "capsule" where it was written or where it is most meaningful in history. Quotations are boxed in, also, all from classical, not modern, writers or sources, those who "were there" and saw events in the making, or helped make them: Plato, Livy, Tacitus, Caesar, Pliny, Josephus, Eusebius, Jeremiah, Paul, Matthew, Mark, Luke and John, the Law Code of Hammurabi, the Epic of Gilgamesh, the Rosetta Stone, the Septuagint, and, of course, the Bible (the Revised Standard Version for clarity of meaning, the King James for sheer beauty and familiarity.)

This book is NOT meant to interpret or explain the Bible, only to suggest how it may have come to be written; and it is, in no way, presented as definitive or authoritative. There are many other books for that. Rather, it hopes only to give a general idea of what might have, possibly or probably happened at "about" a certain time. Neither is it the purpose of this book to analyze, critique, prove or, especially, disprove the Bible. There are legions of other books, articles and TV programs all too willing to do that. Also, the very nature of the book depends on precise dating, but new discoveries are constantly being made, new theories formulated and new conclusions drawn, and while I strove for accuracy, there were times when all reference sources disagreed and I was forced to set my own arbitrary "average" dates. Finally, as you will see, the chronological text of the book is written in the present tense, not as past history that happened long ago, but as events that are happening now, today, whether the reader is at 1000 B.C. or A.D. 100. Thus, if the date reads, for example, 605 B.C. and the text reads "Three hundred years ago thus and thus happened . . ." it does not mean 300 years prior to A.D. 2006; it means 300 years prior to 605 B.C. or—905 B.C. The only place this does not apply is AFTER A.D. 100, because that is where the book ends; then, occasionally, it refers to dates in the future . . . two or three hundred years hence: "Such and such will happen" or "so and so will do this or that." But that will be evident in due time. That doesn't apply now. For now, every entry in the chronology is happening right now, today.

The great 18th century writer and lexicographer (or compiler of dictionaries) Samuel Johnson, once said: "There are two kinds of knowledge: either you know a subject so well it becomes your own, or you know where you can find information about it." When this project first began 30 years ago (I did not set out to "write a book," it just sort of happened), I knew precious little about this subject, but I did know where to find information about it; and doing that finding and learning and writing has been my own personal "wondrous journey," the most marvelous, fulfilling occupation I could ever have imagined.

TABLE OF CONTENTS

The Old Testament Years

Between the Old and the New

The New Testament Years

The BIBLE

The Holy Bible is not just one book, written by one man, but a collection of 66 books, all written by different people in many different times and in different languages and countries. Thirty-nine books in the "Old Testament" cover the time from Creation to about 400 B.C. (Before Christ), and 27 books in the "New" Testament continue from the birth of Jesus Christ to approximately 100 A.D. *(Anno Domini*—In the Year of Our Lord) when the last books of the Bible were completed. Fifteen other books, called the APOCRYPHA (which are included in some Bibles . . . and in this book) cover the approximate 400 years between the Old and the New.

The books of the Bible were written little by little over a period of a thousand years. They are the work of many writers, some who were really more like editors piecing together bits and pieces of earlier works. Some books were written specifically as "books" (histories, songs) and some were personal letters to friends by single, identifiable persons who would not then have thought that one day their letters would be included in the World's Greatest Book.

Whatever the purpose of writing and whoever wrote the books, one similarity applies to them all. They were not written by scientists or scientific historians, and should not be read to try to prove science or anthropology, but to learn about God and His relationship with His highest creation, Man. Likewise, secular history, science and anthropology will not prove or disprove God. Only the Bible is of value here, for it was written by men of faith, Godly men.

That the Bible is the Inspired Word of God is universally accepted by believers; but that should not suggest to them that God simply sat the writers of it down, took hold of their hands and guided them across a page without any thought on their own parts. Because, of all the gifts God gave man, foremost was free will, and the writers were free to write the word as they saw it; for they had *lived* these stories, they had seen and experienced the events as they happened, and although, as the great Paul said, "All scripture is God breathed," he also added that "the holy men of old wrote as they were moved." For God to simply "dictate" words to the writers as to puppets would mean He had taken back His own gift. It was the LIVING and EXPERIENCING that was inspired.

Differences in languages, translations and view points create problems in understanding the Bible, for it was not written in twentieth century English, nor in any modern-day language, but in ancient languages; and every word in it has been translated from the original Greek, Hebrew and Aramaic. Indeed, some parts of the Bible are written in more than one way with major discrepancies between each. But, just as a dozen people can witness an incident and each report it as honestly as he can, no two testimonies will be identical; so also, does the Bible have differences. The main point will never be how much of the Bible disagrees with itself, but the huge volume that does agree. No other book in the world, or in all time, has been more closely scrutinized or under greater attack as the target of those who would joyfully disprove it. And no other book has so staunchly withstood attack. Indeed, the more it is studied, the better it becomes; the more archeology finds, the more accurate it is proved to be; the truer its words, the more necessary to modern man. An enigma only when misused, it will always be treasured, loved and revered by those who accept it as the inspired word of God.

In the 19th century a movement which called itself "higher criticism" dominated biblical scholarship. It utilized a systematic "picking apart" of every line of the Bible, analyzing it and casting out everything that could not be verified with outside, secular sources (or coincide with scholars' pre-conceived opinions.) The Bible was all wrong, they concluded, on many points because no "outside evidence" could be found to support it. Moses didn't write the Torah; writing was unknown then. There were no Hittites as the Bible claims, no Assyrians, no Sargon, king of Assyria, no Pontius Pilate (he was invented for a scapegoat); no Roman census that required enrollment at one's "home town," no on-and-on. And the book of ACTS, Luke's "travelogue" of Paul's journeys, what a laugh, what nonsense! Those poor, misguided Christians; to be so gullible. So all that was left was a skeleton for scavengers to pick on: Karl Marx, who pronounced religion the "opiate of the people," and Friedrich Nietzsche, whose "God is dead" settled the matter and sealed the coffin. Of course, their new-age wisdom was eagerly seized upon by such as Adolph Hitler and Nikolai Lenin, and the years went by—terrible, bloody years, thanks to all their assorted God-LESS isms. But, little by little, another phenomenon occurred in those years: archeology-turned-Biblical archeology, that began, one-by-one, to show that every one of those Biblical assertions was factual and true. Thousands of artifacts proved writing way before Moses, even; all of Asia Minor covered with Hittite remains; whole cities of Sargon uncovered. (Every point will be dealt with later in this book, each in its own time.) "Higher criticism" still lives in many guises under many names, but the Bible survives with evidence of its truthfulness bulging the walls of museums world-wide, providing occupations for hundreds of archeology experts, buffs and beginners alike in all the Bible lands, and creating one of history's most fascinating disciplines.

The impact that the Bible has had on the development of history, not just as another book that somebody wrote, but as real, live people, places and events in relation to the revealed God, is incalculable, for it has been the prime mover in creating Western Civilization and a civilizing influence on the rest of the world. It has truly been said that "We cannot eliminate Judeo-Christian history without making nonsense of history in general." This volume, about the Bible, is not meant to be a theological treatise, or an unraveling of the mysteries of God, or an interpretation of His prophecies for I know nothing about those things, and would not presume. It is, rather, an attempt only at placing the Bible's books in their proper historical time slot to dramatize its interaction with, importance to and influence upon the whole world. It will tell the story of the people, the times, and the church that created THE BOOK, for it is, in fact, ONE BOOK.

And THAT is the unique thing about those 66 "books" that make up the Bible: the incredible, extraordinary, unparalleled and unrepeatable fact (and the only "proof" needed for those able to see the large picture rather that the little details) is that although it was written over a span of a thousand years by many different persons in different lands and circumstances, who had different reasons for writing and told their stories for different readers, who couldn't possibly have known what the others were doing, the end result is, in fact, ONE BOOK, that tells ONE story . . . and it begins with some of the most ancient writings in the world: the Hebrew Scriptures, that Christians call the OLD TESTAMENT . . .

The OLD TESTAMENT
(The HEBREW SCRIPTURES)

The "Old Testament" is the foundation upon which the "New" is built, without which the New is meaningless. By the same token the Old without the New is (according to Christians) simply unfinished. For the Old Testament lays out the plot and promises of God's Great Drama, and the New brings them to their mighty fulfillment.

The Old Testament—the Hebrew Scriptures—tells the story of the Jewish people and their God; their lives, loves, wars and tragedies, successes and failures, virtues and vices; and of HIS eternal presence and patience. It follows the long march of history from the creation of the world to the destruction of their first holy temple and their civilization, 587 years B.C., before the birth of Jesus Christ, or as the Jews themselves refer to it, B.C.E., Before the Common (or Christian) Era. The long chess game that was the history of ancient Israel, the power plays and intrigues between men and nations; all are drawn out in the Old Testament with an honesty and candor that lays bare their worst sins and immortalizes their greatest glories.

But the Old Testament is something else, also. Four hundred years after its close Jesus of Nazareth will make statements about Himself to friends and followers that, without an understanding of the Old Testament, make no sense at all: "EVERYTHING WRITTEN ABOUT ME IN THE LAW OF MOSES AND THE PROPHETS AND THE PSALMS MUST BE FULFILLED." (LUKE 24:44) . . . and . . . "THINK NOT THAT I HAVE COME TO ABOLISH THE LAW AND THE PROPHETS. I HAVE NOT COME TO ABOLISH THEM, BUT TO FULFILL THEM." (MATTHEW 5:17) Jesus of Nazareth can be ACCEPTED through reading only the "New" Testament, but for His claims and behavior to be fully UNDERSTOOD, one must begin in the "Old."

The Old Testament books were written in Hebrew, the language of Abraham, Moses, David and Isaiah. The books of DANIEL, EZRA and one verse of JEREMIAH are important exceptions written in Aramaic, the native language of Jesus of Nazareth. The men who wrote them were not methodical scientists sifting out indisputable facts; but were men of faith setting down in writing the concepts, beliefs and tenets of their people. The Old Testament is the testimony of a nation's belief in God, the only nation, then, that believed in only ONE God. Some events recorded in the Old Testament are, in fact, similar to "foreign" sources, as are the Biblical Creation story to the Assyrian ENUMA ELISH tablets and the Babylonian EPIC OF GILGAMESH to the Biblical Flood; an enhancement of the veracity of the Bible, showing the writers awareness of the world around them, its other cultures and beliefs.

Some of the Old Testament books were written at the time they occurred; others not until centuries later. Indeed, there was no form of writing when the VERY EARLIEST stories happened (GENESIS' first 11 chapters.) Some of the authors are known for certain, some only possibly; and others not at all. Even those books whose titles are the names of persons were often written by others to honor that person . . . a widely used custom in Biblical times. Hebrew literature did not, in fact, begin with the writing of the books of the Old Testament. Rather, there are numerous folk tales, songs and sagas that were known much earlier but are lost today, works which are mentioned and included in the Bible: decrees of Kings David and Solomon, prophecies and visions of Samuel, Nathan and Gad the Seer, the Deeds of Uzziah and the Song of Deborah, to name just a few.

The Old Testament is made up of several different types of books; Law, Prophecy, History and Sacred Writings. Each has its own purpose, rhythm and uniqueness, and yet, they are all inseparable. While modern skeptics argue the veracity of the Old Testament—who wrote it, when, where, why, was it God-inspired or man-created, one fact shines out crystal-clear. It was good enough, authentic enough, true enough for Jesus Christ. He never doubted its truth or its message, and He lived and died . . . and rose again . . . according to its teaching, tenets, precepts and promises. His life found its fulfillment in the LAW and the PROPHETS.

"Thou shalt love the LORD thy God with all thy heart,
and with all thy soul, and with all thy mind;
this is the first and great commandment.
And the second is like unto it,
Thou shalt love thy neighbor as thyself.
<u>ON THESE TWO COMMANDMENTS HANG ALL
THE LAW AND THE PROPHETS.</u>"

Jesus of Nazareth (MATTHEW 22:37–40)

The Law and the Prophets

The Law is that which was given by God to Moses twelve hundred years before the birth of Jesus Christ; and the Prophets are they who (among many other things) refined and defined that Law into the modern JUDAISM into which Jesus was born . . . and who prophesied His birth, life, death and resurrection six centuries before Him. Many times did Jesus refer in His teachings to the Law and the Prophets. Many times did He say, "You have heard it said by the men of old . . ."

The thirty-some years of Jesus' life before He began His ministry are almost totally unknown to us, yet one fact stands out clearly. In some way, that the Bible says was "astonishing" even to His parents, He had a thorough and penetrating knowledge of the Law and the Prophets. Indeed, the only event we do know for certain during those years, finds a twelve year old Jesus in Jerusalem with His parents at Passover, discussing with the teachers and scribes in the Temple the Law and the Prophets . . . and amazing them with His knowledge and wisdom.

The Law and the Prophets (the "Old" Testament to Christians, and more properly the Hebrew Scriptures) was the "Bible" of Jesus, and Paul and everyone who lived in their time. It was the only Bible they had, for Jesus, Himself, was to become the instrument of a "New."

The OLD

TESTAMENT

YEARS

* * *

The LAW . . .

The LAW

The first five books of the Bible are called the books of LAW; in Hebrew the TORAH, and in Greek, the Pentateuch, meaning "five scrolls." They contain the Law given by God to Moses on Mt. Sinai 3000 years ago which has been the foundation of the Jewish religion down through countless generations to this very day. GENESIS tells how God chose the people He wanted to serve Him and be His nation; EXODUS describes how He gave that nation the LAW; and LEVITICUS, NUMBERS and DEUTERONOMY catalogue the Laws for use. There are conflicting theories about how the books came to be written. Ancient tradition held that Moses, himself, wrote them, or at least part of them. But modernist theologians in the last century, and early in this, with their "higher criticism," scoffed at that idea, saying that they were mere folk tales written down little by little over the years, not by one man working alone, but by many, adding, deleting, revising and editing; that Moses could not have had the knowledge or skills to write them . . . in spite of the book of ACTS (7:22) saying: ". . . he was instructed in all the wisdom of the Egyptians."

And, in part, they were right. The first 11 chapters of GENESIS are, indeed, said to be primeval rather than historical, taking place long before there was writing, if indeed they actually took place; and it is true that not one trace of Moses has ever been found by archeology, nor of the patriarchs Abraham, Isaac and Jacob. But today, many scholars have returned to the Mosaic tradition deciding that with the vast amounts of empirical evidence of writing and scholarship found throughout all the Bible lands from his time, Moses COULD have written down his own story. Thousands of ancient artifacts—clay tablets, cylinder seals, papyrus scrolls, whatever—from Ur to Ebla, from Susa to Mari and from the Hittites to the Egyptians resemble, in many ways the form, content and style of the Hebrew LAW and prove that its literacy is, in fact, indigenous to their age and that of Moses, himself.

But even more surprising are the myriads of written artifacts about common, everyday things—bills of sale, receipts of payment, marriage and divorce decrees, requests for loans, school lessons, advice to children, complaints about too-strict teachers and worries about "juvenile delinquency"—all matters which prove that easily-learned alphabetic writing was widely used and commonly known, even BEFORE Moses' time. Indeed, one spectacular find at the Biblical Eben-ezer, dating to 1200 B.C., shows the entire Hebrew alphabet (missing only one broken-off letter) in the same sequence as today's, and easily readable by today's scholars, proving that writing was, by Moses' time, not only a secret, cryptic, jealously guarded mystery known only to the highly privileged and educated priests, as were Egyptian hieroglyphics, but a universally used skill and indispensible part of ordinary life. There is little question that a prince of Egypt would have had a superior education that COULD have enabled him to write what are, today, the first five books of the Bible, the Torah . . . the LAW.

In the beginning . . .

B.C.—Before Christ

??? In the beginning, God created the heavens and the earth, and he said, "Let there be light . . . and there was light . . .

" . . . and the light shineth in the darkness." (JOHN 1:5) And that was the first day.

— And God created a firmament and separated the waters below it from the waters above, and He called the firmament Heaven . . .

" . . . And without Him was not anything made that was made. . ." (JOHN 1:3) And that was the second day.

— And God let the dry land appear, that He called the Earth, and the earth brought forth vegetation, plants yielding seeds and trees bearing fruit . . .

. . . And continents rose from the seas, and slowly shifted on the waters and changed shape. Crashing mightily into each other, they heaved up the earth into towering mountains. Grinding earthquakes tore land from land; and boiling cauldrons beneath the earth spewed up fire and brimstone from flaming volcanoes. Then, stillness; and primordial mosses, ferns, pines and flowering plants. And that was the third day.

— And God put lights in the firmament so that there would be seasons, days and years. He made two great lights, the greater to rule the day and the lesser to rule the night; and made stars, also . . .

. . . The sun and moon shone down upon the earth, planets and stars without number; and beyond them constellations and far-flung galaxies. And that was the fourth day.

— And God commanded the waters to bring forth living creatures . . .

. . . so Trilobites and Ammonites, Crossopterygian and Archelon swam in the sea. Later, Brontosaurus and Tyrannosaurus Rex, Mammoth and Eohippus walked on the earth; and Archaeopteryx and Pteranodon flew in the air above it. And millions of years went by and they died out and were replaced by fish, birds and mammals. And that was the fifth day.

— And then God created Man in his own image, and gave him dominion over all the animals of the earth. And God called Man Adam, and gave him a wife whom He called Eve.

. . . Adam and Eve are Hebrew words: Adam meaning "man" (all mankind), and Eve (Hawwah), meaning "life." Thus, the beginning of the "life" of all "mankind." And that was the sixth day.

— And God looked on all He had done and saw that it was good. And so God rested.

. . . When God made man, He gave him something He gave no other animal. He gave him the ability to think and reason, to communicate with each other and with future genera-

tions, to remember the past and to look ahead and plan for the future, to become aware of a Being greater than himself, and to understand that he was endowed with the freedom to choose between right and wrong. But these were powers which had to develop slowly, very slowly . . . and so God gave man countless thousands of years to develop them. And that was the seventh day.

Now man had to learn to care for himself. He learned to build a fire, to chip away on stones to make tools to work and hunt with, and to live and cooperate with each other. And over those vast thousands of years man grew in knowledge, and developed his learning and skills.

All of history from the very beginning until 1300 B.C. is found in the time period of the book of GENESIS.

GENESIS

Book of LAW — Written in Hebrew,   c. ? to 600 B.C.

"In the beginning God created the Heavens and the earth." So begins the World's Greatest Book. "In the beginning God." Those few words state simply but eloquently that GENESIS is going to set the stage for the monumental drama to follow: that the Bible is going to be a record, not of man searching FOR "a" god, but of THE transcendent God revealing Himself TO man. GENESIS tells of the "beginning" not only of mankind, but of EVERYTHING: the world, life, love, laughter, sin, sorrow and suffering, condemnation and compassion, predjudice and forgiveness, envy, jealousy and generosity; pride, vice and virtue; and man's worldly occupations from farming, mining, shepherding, learning and writing to iron-, war-, and music-making. And most of all, it tells of the relationship between God and man, and the awesome and irrevocable fact that, because of God's gift of FREE WILL, man is not only responsible, but AC-COUNTABLE for his own actions.

The first 11 chapters of GENESIS are usually described as PRIMEVAL, not HISTORICAL, taking place long before man has learned to write and record his activities, thoughts and feelings; the origins of their stories lost in the mists of time. The drama begins in the "Fertile Crescent" of Mesopotamia (which means "between waters") between the Tigris and Euphrates Rivers of modern-day Iraq. Here, at the northernmost tip of the Persian Gulf, in the Garden of Eden, Adam and Eve came to life, and their sons, Cain and Abel whom Cain slew; and another brother, Seth, and all their descendants including Methuselah, who lived 900 years. Were these earliest people real, identifiable individuals, or personifications of ideas or tribes? Were these chapters meant to be scientific "history" as we know history today, specific in detail, or should not 20th century hindsight consider when they were written, by whom and for whom; why, how and what God was intending to reveal, and the writers trying to say? Or does it even matter? Neither science nor anthropology pose any threat to the Creation story, nor ask questions which weren't already addressed over 2000 years ago; for BOTH THE OLD AND THE NEW TESTAMENTS deal with the fundamental stumbling-block subjects of evolution and a seven day creation, each in one simple sentence, using the numerical conception of a thousand rather than a million or even billion: "FOR A THOUSAND YEARS IN THY SIGHT," reads Old Testament PSALM 90:4, "ARE BUT AS YESTERDAY WHEN IT IS PAST;" and the New Testament II PETER 3:8 echoes, "BUT DO NOT IGNORE THIS ONE FACT, BELOVED, THAT WITH THE LORD ONE DAY IS AS A THOUSAND YEARS, AND A THOUSAND YEARS AS ONE DAY."

The Bible deals, also, in GENESIS' very first chapter with another stumbling-block subject which will arise thousands of years hence with the development of Christianity and its basic tenet of a triune God, three in one: Father, Son and Holy Spirit. The second sentence in GENESIS (1:2) tells of the "Spirit of God" moving over the water before the heavens and earth were even formed; and later, when God made man, GENESIS (1:26) records God as saying, not "I will make man in MY image," but "Let US make man in OUR image, after OUR likeness." Thus, one God in plural aspect: a Trinity of Father, Son and Holy Spirit.

When the world's population grew large, God saw that it had, also, grown sinful. He regretted having made man and sent a great flood to make an end to him but, in God's first great covenant with man, He saved Noah, Noah's family and all kinds of animals . . . and the generations of Noah multiplied greatly and repopulated the earth. (CHS. 6–9) (Noah's Ark is thought by some to still lie encased in ice somewhere atop Turkey's Ararat Mountains.) Still, man had but one language—and much presumption—and built himself a tower so he could climb to Heaven and make himself a god. But Yahweh, the One True God, scattered the tribes of man over all the lands of the earth and gave them a "Babel" of tongues. (11:19)

Then, in chapter 12, at approximately 1800 B.C., GENESIS relates, the Lord said to Abram "Go from your country . . . to the land that I will show you . . . and I will make of you a great nation." (12:2) It was then the age of the great kings Sargon of Akkad and Hammurabi of Babylon, and the written word was a universal art. Thousands of impressed clay tablets and engraved stones still exist which bring back to life the time of Abraham, and make history accurately datable. Cuneiform tablets from Ur, Mari and Ebla name the same names as are found in GENESIS, describing in the same way the places GENESIS describes: a land of milk and honey, grapes, olives and grain, "where there is bread to eat . . . every day." Here Abraham lived, and his descendents Isaac, Jacob and Joseph for 200 years, their stories all told in GENESIS . . . real people in the real world, or mere figments of someone's—awesome, incomprehensible—imagination.

B.C.—Before Christ

B.C. ???   From Africa's Olduvai Gorge to Java and China: from the Levant of Mesopotamia to Anatolia's Konya Plain; and from the Steppes of Central Asia to the Hindu Kush, man is proceeding step by slow step through "periods, ages, eras and cultures" in a Stone Age the length of which will vary widely throughout the world.

c. 450,000 to 8,000.   Paleolithic (Old Stone Age) man is a nomadic hunter whose weapons are rocks, stones and huge hand axes, and whose prey are the great animals of the late Ice Age . . . mammoth, mastodon, saber-toothed tiger and giant bear. He has learned how to use fire to keep warm and to cook his food. He is clothing himself with skins of the wild animals he catches, using their splintered and carved bones and antlers to sew with and to make fish hooks, harpoons and implements. And he is burying with his dead things he believes necessary for a life after death.

Somewhere in the world someone stops what he is doing to listen to a sound coming from . . . somewhere. It is a soft, whistling sort of sound, pleasant to his senses. He searches here and there and finally finds a broken reed, hollow in the center, and he notices that each time a gust of wind blows over it, the sound starts and stops. He also notices that when the wind causes the reeds to hit each other it makes another—banging—sound. Finally he figures out that he, himself, can make the same sounds by blowing over the hollow center of the reed, plucking on the stringy ones or hitting one reed with another . . . and so music is invented. It will be one of the first of man's accomplishments mentioned in the Bible.

c. 20,000   With oil lamps and paint palettes made from stone, prehistoric artists are painting pictures of animals on cave walls in places that, today, are known as Lascaux, France, and Altamira, Spain. Using clay, charcoal and ochre, they portray huge, long-horned bulls, racing horses and wild beasts in bright reds, yellows, black and white. When the caves are discovered in our own time, clay sculptures and carved bones and antlers will also be found, indications, it seems, that even prehistoric man strove for artistic and spiritual expression and sustenance.

c. 16,000   Vast changes are taking place the world over with the melting of the great Pleistocene ice cap. On the continent that will someday be called North America, receding glaciers are leaving behind a gigantic waterway. Fifteen millennia more will go by before they take their present shape as the Great Lakes . . . and . . . many thousands of years from now, marine biologists in the "new world" will pull up a drilled core of ocean floor from the Caribbean Sea and learn millions of years of its history. The core will reveal a vast, sudden influx of fresh water into the normally saline sea at about this time. The biologists

will reason that gigantic chunks broke off of the ice cap, melted and surged down the Mississippi and Hudson Rivers (and on the other side of the world, down the Tigris and Euphrates into the Persian Gulf) of such enormous size and suddenness as to make the inundation universal, devastating and of such proportions as to fix itself in man's mind for many centuries to come . . . adding a scientific theory to the story of the great flood.

c. 16,000–9000.   The same changes in climate and shifting land masses creates a wide bridge or corridor from what today is called Siberia to Alaska, and great multitudes of Mongol peoples from Asia sweep across the "new world" continents. They will become the many tribes of American Indians.

c. 12,000–10,000.   The crowning glory of the Great Lakes is created as millions of tons of limestone riverbed gradually shifts under centuries of erosion, and Niagara Falls thunders into existence.

10,000 to 8000.   Mesolithic (Middle Stone Age) man lives in a changing world with the melting of the ice cap, a warming climate, the disappearance of large animals and the emergence of smaller, faster, modern-day animals. Following the new-growing forests northward, he now has need of distance weapons and more speed, so he learns how to use a bow and arrow. He is living in communal groups; on pilings in Swiss lakes and in tribes in the deserts. He knows how to plant seeds in the spring, harvest his crops in the fall and make pottery vessels in which to store his food, his oil . . . and his beer . . . which many scholars believe was what caused man to give up the pleasures of the hunt and shackle himself to the soil.

c. 8000–6000   Neolithic (New Stone Age) man is now clothing himself in fabric which he makes from one of his cultivated crops, flax. In Eastern Europe he is burning coal for fuel; he has domesticated sheep and goats and will soon begin keeping pigs and cattle. He is building rude dwellings from wood and (in Mesopotamia) mud bricks.

. . . at a place called Jericho in the middle-eastern Jordan River valley north of the Dead Sea, those houses are built in groups or communities. Jericho will exist, now, to our own time, the oldest—continuously occupied—walled city in the world.

. . . In far-away America, cave dwellers in "Alabama" are leaving charcoal behind from their fires, and in "New Mexico" hunters and warriors have, for a thousand years, been chipping out "Folsom" and "Clovis" points for their spears and arrows. Archeological names, they are the oldest spearheads in the "new" world.

c. 6000   No longer content with the drab necessities of life, Mesopotamian man, in the Fertile Crescent between the Tigris and Euphrates Rivers, begins to paint pictures on his pottery, to decorate himself and his surroundings. He also learns that there is an easier way to haul and pull than to use his own labors, so he tames the wild animals. He learns how to have the donkey carry his burdens and hitches the oxen to a simple wooden plow to break up the soil in his fields.

. . . The Aztec Indians in Mexico grow cotton for fabric . . . and, in far eastern Thailand, rice is cultivated for food, with metal and pottery tools and utensils used in its cooking.

c. 5000   Primitive villages housing farmers cover all of central Europe . . .

. . . In northern Africa the Egyptians have learned to live in harmony with their river, the longest in the world; sailing it in rude little dugout boats, and using the richness of its banks for farming. The Nile floods its banks every year and the silt left behind leaves the land fertile and renewed. As they bury their dead in the hot, dry desert sands bestriding the Nile, they notice that although inner parts of bodies rot away, the outer skin and flesh dries out and is preserved; so they begin to practice the art of embalming . . . and mummy making.

. . . At different times in different places man has learned how to work a shiny metal by pounding it into various shapes to create storage and cooking vessels and other implements. Their discovery ushers in . . .

. . . the COPPER AGE.

It will change many things . . . and bring both pleasure and pain . . .

c. 4500   The Egyptians have calculated, and divided, time into years of 360 days made up of twelve 30-day months and, by now, they, and the Mesopotamians, are making music with drums, flutes whittled from reeds, and harps (some of which can be found, today, in European museums.) They are using copper to create warlike weapons, also.

c. 4000   The fourth millennium B.C. finds dozens of cultures at many stages of development throughout the world, to which modern-day archeologists give colorful and descriptive names. There are the *Catal Huyuk* in Turkey, almost as old as Jericho—but not continuously occupied and forgotten for 6000 years; *Sesklo* in Greece and the *Starcevo* and *Veselinova* in Bulgaria; the *Danubian* in central Europe; *Windmill Hill* and *Long Barrows* in Britain; *Boian* in Romania, and the *Yang-shao* rice-farming culture in China. The *Impressed Pottery* culture in Italy gives way to the *Painted Pottery,* and in the Iberian Peninsula there are the *Capsian* in Spain and the Portuguese *Kitchen Middens*. All these cultures bring important advances in man's social affairs . . .

. . . He learns how to talk over problems and differences in a group, beginning the earliest forms of government; and; concerned not only with this life but one after death as well, the Egyptians have become skilled morticians, using sophisticated methods of preserving bodies as mummies.

3761   Many years from now when a people called Hebrews work out a calendar, this year—3761—will be considered . . . the year ONE.

c. 3500   Somehow, man discovers that connecting two round discs with a cross-piece, or "axle," makes it much easier and faster to carry himself and his goods from place to place, so the WHEEL is invented in the Fertile Crescent of Sumer in Mesopotamia. The Sumerians will be the ONLY PEOPLE to know of the wheel for another THOUSAND YEARS! With the invention of the wheel, comes the beginning of road building, irrigation and of oil production for greasing wheels and lighting lamps. With the use of water wheels, in the years ahead over 10,000 miles of irrigation canals will be built in Mesopotamia. Unlike Egypt's more predictable Nile River flood times, Sumer's Tigris and Euphrates are fierce and violent, their flood times never predictable. The land around them is sere and barren, life harsh, and the development of irrigation comes about through grave necessity. The wheel also brings more advanced methods of mining with beautiful objects being made from a gleaming, shiny metal called gold. For centuries man has known about gold, admired it and wanted to own more than other men, so they bring more and more out of the earth.

What had been primitive little villages in this mid-eastern part of the world have evolved into prosperous city-states, self-contained communities, each owned by its own god and ruled by that god's earthly administrator, or king. The cities unite occasionally for war or conquest, but even then each remains independent, and each builds its own temple to its own gods. And while these eastern civilizations are "evolving" . . .

c. 3100   . . . a unique phenomenon happens in Egypt; not thought to be a revolution, but a change, almost overnight. The many small villages and market-towns scattered throughout Egypt's upper and lower Nile Valley are united into one entity by a king named Narmer (or Menes in Greek.) Narmer combines the red crown of Lower Egypt (the Nile delta area bordering the "Great Sea, the Mediterranean) with the white crown of the Upper Lands (that half of the Nile closest to its source deep in Africa,) and builds a capitol city at Memphis. No one knows exactly how or why this unification came about, but it is the beginning of 30 kingly dynasties, which will rule Egypt for the next 3000 years.

c. 3000   The third millennium B.C. (Before Christ, or as non-Christians say, Before the Common Era) takes big steps forward, from far east to west, as man learns how to make a stronger, more durable metal by combining copper and tin, ushering in . . .

. . . the BRONZE AGE.

It also marks the beginning of

. . . RECORDED HISTORY.

Man has finally learned that he can draw curious symbols on a wet clay tablet, which mean the same things as the sounds he makes with his voice, and that another man can look at those symbols and know what he means. With this knowledge begins the dawn of recorded history as mankind begins to leave a written record of himself for posterity. What are thought to be the oldest written inscriptions in the world are in the wedge-shaped figures called CUNEIFORM, used by the Sumerians in the moon-shaped "land between the rivers" . . . the same place the Bible calls the GARDEN OF EDEN.

Over the next several thousand years the Fertile Crescent will spawn many other civilizations, and be known by many names: Chaldea, Assyria, Babylonia and Persia. Today it is called Iraq. Considered the "cradle of civilization," Sumer is more a geographical area, not a unified nation or society. Its city-states, including such wealthy, well-known names as Ur, Uruk, Eridu, Nippur and Lagash, are independent entities, each with its own god and its own king, each progressing at its own pace; possibly influencing one another, but in no way confederated. Sumer will leave behind much information about itself; not a composed,

chronological "history," but countless fragments of information; for Ur, Uruk, Eridu, Nippur and Lagash all have schoolrooms where writing is taught, and royal libraries where their engraved tablets are kept. Cuneiform figures are impressed upon moist clay with a stylus, and dried; and many thousands, still in existence today, tell of Sumer's laws, businesses, religions, medicine and astronomy. They tell how the Sumerians plan out their cities with mathematics, build them with sun-dried mud bricks and decorate them with gold, silver, copper and bronze . . . using 60 second minutes in 60 minute hours and 360° circles.

Early Sumerian Pictograph

The tablets include bills presented to debtors, and receipts for payment and include many of "the world's first," from a library catalogue to a legal precedent, a medical prescription, plagiarism and instructions for planting vital shade trees; love songs and accounts of a juvenile delinquent, a "sick society" and a political assembly; a two-house congress debating war or "peace at any price." The Sumerians carry on trade by caravan with the vast areas of Asia to the east, and Syria to the west. They use metal sickles, saws and plows for farming; and for sport, they engage in the world's oldest, boxing.

. . . Another civilization to begin writing is that of Egypt, along the beneficent banks of the Nile River. Unlike Sumer, Egypt IS a single entity, a kingdom united under one ruler since King Narmer united the Upper and Lower lands; and will remain so for the next 3000 years. While Egypt will go through numerous traumatic periods of crisis, unlike the repetitive rise and fall of Sumerian city-states, it will not break its one man rule. Egypt's complex, pictorial hieroglyphic writing develops at this time, also, apparently independently, unaware of others. Hieroglyphic writing, with its peculiar frame-like *cartouches*, mysterious, stylized animals and objects; wavy lines and staring eyes will be used now for almost 3000 years, then forgotten for another two, and finally re-discovered in our own time, the legacy of a fantastic civilization.

. . . Unlike Sumerian writing, on baked clay tablets, the Egyptians have developed something much more portable and use their skills to develop an efficient communications system up and down their river-dominated kingdom. Swift long-distance runners, guided on their way by obelisque shaped stone *stelae* engraved with hieroglyphic directions, carry their messages written on another new invention, called papyrus. Made from a plant that grows only in Nile swampland, papyrus is flexible and lightweight, making possible wide distribution of knowledge and information. It will be used now for almost 3000 years, until the invention of parchment in 190 B.C. Skilled in many crafts and trades, the Egyptians now develop the first full-bred dog, the Saluki, and are playing stringed instruments which will, eventually, evolve into guitars, lutes and zithers.

. . . The bountiful Indus Valley lying to the south of the mighty Himalaya Mountains of modern-day India and Pakistan gives birth to another great civilization, called the HARAPPA, after one of its largest cities. Now just a mud-hut farming culture, in just 500 years it will have grown into a model of urban sophistication.

. . . The first great civilizations of Europe are taking root now, bounding the Aegean Sea like the vertices of a triangle; three cities whose wondrous stories will capture the world's fancy forever. To the west, on Greece's *peloponnesus*, lies Mycenae that history will call "Golden;" north-east, across the waters at the western tip of Asia Minor, Mycenae's antagonist, legendary Troy; and to their south on the stretched-out island of Crete, fabled Knossos, center of a population so dense future archeologists will uncover 200 sites occupied by this time. The Minoan peoples living on Crete are the world's first sailors, navigating even the Great Sea, itself, the . . . Mediterranean.

. . . The Yang-shao villages of China are growing rice, millet and hemp, keeping dogs and pigs, and working pottery. Some 100 houses will, in future, be found in its principle village, Pan-p-o, located near modern-day Sian.

. . . and a tribe of nomads called Canaanites settle in what will come to be known as Israel. They will remain there, and in neighboring Syria, until conquered by the Hebrews 1900 years from now.

c. 2740   An Egyptian king, named Djoser, commissions an "architect" called Imhotep to design and build a great monument for his royal burial place. Imhotep uses a new, Egyptian invented skill, geometry, to design his monument in the shape of a pyramid, with a progression of level rises, or steps, around it. When Djoser dies, beautiful objects of alabaster, gold, silver and gems are buried with him. Imhotep is then deified as a god and is remembered as history's first architect, for his name is carved on the "stepped" pyramid. He and his monument usher in the great age of pyramid building.

c. 2700   A (possibly mythical) king named Gilgamesh rules the fifth dynasty of Uruk in Sumer, now, a man like those about whom the Bible's book of GENESIS speaks when it says, "There were giants [on] the earth in those days." For Gilgamesh is a giant in word and deed, believed to be "two thirds god and one third man." Gilgamesh is a man of brave deed and

Gilgamesh

deep thought; he sojourns in the land of the Living and of Death; is loved by, and rejects, the goddess Ishtar; confronts and confounds the scorpion people who guard the skies; overcomes the monster of the Cedar Forest and kills the Great Bull of Heaven. But Gilgamesh's beloved friend, Enkidu, dies, and the grieving king sets off on a lonely journey through "utter darkness," across the Waters of Death, to find a Mesopotamian Noah named Utnapishtim in the Far Distance, the only survivor of a great flood, from whom he seeks the secret of immortality.

The gods in the world of Gilgamesh are cosmological gods; persons, beings and things found in the cosmos. Each Sumerian city-state is owned by a god, and its king is that god's earthly administrator, appointed by the invisible forces behind that god in an orderly, hierarchical progression. Order on earth reflects the order in the heavens; sun, moon, stars and constellations, with their 12 zodiac figures. The Great Bull of Heaven that Gilgamesh kills is Taurus; and the goddess Ishtar, Virgo. The Monster of the Cedar Forest is the lion, Leo; the scorpion people he encounters, Scorpio; and the Great Flood which left only one survivor is Aquarius. Thus, in the adventures of Gilgamesh is found the germ of the "science" of astrology, as old and as primitive as Babylon, itself, the first city mentioned in the Bible.

Story tellers and singers of sagas will remember Gilgamesh, his adventures and the great flood for centuries now, and, little by little, write them down for future generations to read and wonder at. Almost 5000 years from now a British archeologist, excavating the city of Ur, near Gilgamesh's Uruk, will find an eight-foot deep layer of mud separating the ruins of the "old" city from the ruins of the "new." He will reason that it is, in fact, the remains of a flood . . . great enough to inundate the entire world of those who lived there.

Story tellers and singers of sagas remember King Narmer of Egypt, also, how he united the Upper and Lower lands into one kingdom and built a "capital" city at Memphis. A lengthy account of this sudden emergence of Memphis as Egypt's principle city can be read, today, on a carved stone (the extant copy dating to 700 B.C.) which claims that Memphis' god, Ptah, "gave life to all other gods"; being, therefore, the First Principal. He then gave all Egypt to Horus, god of the earth:

Thus this land was united, proclaimed with the great name . . . So it was that Horus appeared as king of Upper and Lower Egypt, who united the two lands in [Memphis] . . . the Granery of the God . . . The *Memphite Theology*, from the Shabaka Stone, No. 438, British Museum, London, one of the oldest written works in the world.

Egypt is a land of many gods, from cows to cats to croco-diles; some in human form, some animal, and some a combina-tion of both. Animals are eternal, the Egyptians believe, animal nature never changes; what they were yesterday they will be to-morrow. Like Sumer's, Egypt's gods are, also, "cosmological" gods, manifestations of beings and concepts found in the cos-mos. Although Egypt's gods are ranked on levels of importance from highest to lowest, the idea of a universal, transcendent God is as unknown to them as to the Sumerians. The cosmos, to the Egyptian, is two di-mensional; there are two givers of life, the sun and the Nile. The sun shines, or is dark. The Nile is either upstream or down stream. So, the gods have two aspects; the god, and its man-ifestation. Horus, god of the earth and lord of heaven, symbolizes life, and is manifest in the falcon; and Anubis, the god of death, is manifest in the jackal; and both go with the Egypt-ian kings to their golden graves.

Osiris and Isis, husband and wife, are the parents of Horus. Isis is the goddess of good things, especially children. Osiris represents the richness of the Nile; its drought and flood, or death and rebirth. Hathor is the cow-goddess of music and dance; Thoth (the moon) of wisdom; and Ptah is the personal god of the kings and their capital city, Memphis. Egypt and its gods are inseparable; one cannot be understood without the other.

c. 2600   High upon a desolate, windswept mountain peak in what will someday be called the White Mountains of California, USA, the seedling of a Bristlecone Pine tree takes hold and begins to grow. It will live through all the history in this book and another 1900 years more. Shaped more like an evergreen shrub than a single-trunk tree, today only part of it survives . . . but survive it does and now, in our time, the tree called "Methuselah" is the oldest living thing in the world.

. . . Egypt's Fourth Dynasty begins to rule, the dynasty of the greatest pyramid builders, Khufu (Cheops in Greek), Khafre (Chephren) and Menkaure. In an incredible building project still not fully understood to-day, King Cheops builds the mightiest monument of all time, the giant Pyramid of Giza, the first of the Seven Wonders of the Ancient World, and the only one still in existence. Constructed of almost two and a half million gigantic limestone blocks, it is 450 feet high and weighs close to six million tons. The wheel was invented 900 years ago and has drawn war chariots in Sumer for centuries, but it is still unknown in Egypt, and the pyramid(s) are built without the wheel's help. It has been said (some say wrongly) that the measurements of the great Pyramid's various corridors, hallways and chambers have many wondrous calculations worked into them: sophisticated knowledge of the earth, its size, weight and distance to the sun. Cheops' funerary boat, which takes his remains and his treasures up the Nile to the pyramid will be found 4400 years from now, and be finally placed in a museum near the monument. When the pyramid is already 1200 years old, a young Greek historian from Asia Minor, named Herodotus, will "travel the world over," visit Egypt and tell in his HISTORIES of the wonders of Egypt, greater than any other country on earth . . . but bought at a terrible price . . .

Up to [this time] Egypt was excellently governed and very prosperous, but . . . Cheops . . . brought the country into . . . misery . . . compelled [everyone] without exception to labour as slaves [on his pyramid]. The work went on in three-monthly shifts, a hundred thousand men in a shift . . . [it] took twenty years . . . it is square at the base, its height . . . equal to the length of each side; it is of polished stone blocks beautifully fitted, none . . . being less than thirty feet long . . . An inscription cut upon it record[s] the amount spent on radishes, onions and leeks for the laborers . . . said the (cost) was 1600 talents of silver. If [so] how much must have been spent . . . on bread and clothing . . . not to mention the time . . . to quarry and haul the stone, and . . . construct the underground chamber?

Herodotus, the HISTORIES

Modern scholarship disputes Herodotus and finds no evidence of slave labor, that he was taken in by local story-tellers and that the laborers were, instead, local conscripts. Whether slave or conscript (which nevertheless, is forced service) they had to eat and sleep, and in our own time, archeologists have found store-houses, barracks, bakeries, work-shops and even the quarries which supplied the stone blocks for the building.

But Herodotus continues . . .

Cheops reigned . . . fifty years . . . and was succeeded . . . by his brother Chephren [who] was no better . . . his rule was equally oppressive, and, like Cheops, he built a pyramid, but of a smaller size (I measured both of them myself). . . . Chephren reigned . . . 56 years . . . a period of 106 years all told, during which . . . the country was reduced in every way to the greatest misery. The Egyptians can hardly bring themselves to mention the names of Cheops and Chephren, so great is their hatred of them . . .   Herodotus, the HISTORIES, 2:126–7

During Khafre's reign, a great stone Sphinx is carved, also, near the Pyramid, another gigantic sculpture, almost 250 feet long and 70 high. Poised like a lion at rest, its sightless eyes stare out over the eternal sands of the desert. Carved with Khafre's face and a lion's form, the Sphinx will hold solitary vigil for centuries until, 4400 years from now (in A.D. 1801) soldiers of Napoleon Bonaparte's French occupation forces will use its face for target practice!

c. 2500   Far to the north of Egypt the Syrian cities of Ebla, Mari and Damascus are thriving now, great trading centers in the mid-east, linking northern Sumer with Egypt. They import goods from as far away as Afghanistan; lapis-lazuli and carnelian which they use to make jewelry, carved figures and pictured cylinders which they roll across soft clay to make seals and stamps. Worn on strings around their necks or wrists, the cylinders are used as identification, and to sign or label everything from legal documents to storage jars. Ebla dominates a huge area from the Mediterranean Sea to the Persian Gulf, the city's population, alone, numbering over 250,000 persons. Widely renowned for its learning, scribes trained in Ebla's academy are valued the "world" over. Their records are kept in a vast state archive, which eventually, will number over 20,000 clay tablets. Larger and more powerful than its neighbors, Ebla's military demands, and gets, tribute money from richer cities, including Mari.

Mari's 300 room palace and courtyard covers six acres of ground, and its own royal library holds many thousands of inscribed clay tablets. While Damascus will continue to grow and prosper as a hub of international trade for many centuries, Ebla and Mari will soon be conquered and destroyed, covered over by sand and time, completely forgotten, and not rediscovered until A.D. 1964. When they are uncovered, their archives baked as in a kiln by the fires of their conquerors, one large tablet from Ebla will astound a modern world. It is a Syrian story of the creation of the world, called the *Enuma Elish,* meaning, "when on high . . ."

When on high the heavens had not been named, firm ground below had not been called by name . . . their waters commingling as a single body; no reed hut had been matted, no marshland had appeared . . . then it was that the gods were formed . . .
The *Enuma Elish,* Tablets # 33014,6,7 The British Museum, London

The gods of the *Enuma Elish* do not create the world, they are the world: Tiamat, the sea; Apsu, the sweet water; and Mummu, cloud banks and mist. And they do not bring order out of chaos; the order is already there, and much valued. It is the younger generation led by Ea, the earth, that brings chaos. And then it is that the gods make man . . . and become angry with him, and seek to destroy him because he is noisey and "overbearing."

Their ways are verily loathsome to me. By day I find no relief, nor repose by night. I will destroy, I will wreck their ways . . .   The *Enuma Elish*

Except for its many spiteful gods and their capricious adventures, the *Enuma Elish's* story is similar to the Creation story in the Bible's book of GENESIS.

The harp

. . . Six hundred miles south-east of Ebla at the farthest reaches of the Fertile Crescent, the Sumerian city of Ur (the Bible calls it Ur of the Chaldeans) is also thriving as a great center of trade, artistry, wealth and learning. It is a royal city of paved streets and stucco houses, some with as many as ten rooms. Its people are rich, proud and peace loving, but enigmatic, also, and almost 5000 years from now, the ruins of Ur will reveal to astonished archeologists huge pits full of the remains of many people, sacrifice, apparently, to deceased royalty with whom they lay. The "Death Pits of Ur" will reveal, with much delicate brushing

B.C. 2500

The Ram caught in the Thicket

and scraping, marvelous works of gold; a royal lady's stunning headdress, a frightened ram caught by his horns in a briar thicket (perhaps like that the Bible mentions in GENESIS 22:13?) There is, also, an incredible, bull-shaped harp, and the so-called Standard of Ur, a shell and lapis-lazuli inlaid panorama of Sumerian man's activities in peace and war, complete with wheeled vehicles, carts and wagons, the first such evidence in history. All these things will find a new home in London's British Museum, while a troop of solemn little, hand-clasping votive statues, surrogate prayers who continue to pray while the householder is away, will find their way to the University of Chicago's Oriental Institute.

The Standard of Ur

The same digs will uncover libraries, schoolrooms and thousands, more, of clay tablets engraved with writings about many subjects: geography, geology, chemistry, surveying, mathematics, astronomy, politics, grammar, religion and medicine. They show that in their schoolrooms students study what modern language calls botany, zoology, penmanship and languages. The clay tablets on which the students write, tell what food they carry to school with them, what work they must do, what scoldings they receive from the headmaster . . . and often what beatings, for education is a serious business in Sumer.

Some of the tablets recount the story of King Gilgamesh's fabulous travels and his long-ago search for immortality after a great flood. Gilgamesh, one tablet reads, has heard of a man named Utnapishtim who lives far away, "beyond the waters of death," the only survivor of the flood, (the "Babylonian Noah" as he is called today.) So Gilgamesh begins a long journey to find him. Many adventures later, Utnapishtim tells Gilgamesh how the gods, weary of bothersome man, decide to destroy him with a flood but "Ea, the god of wisdom," warns him of the deluge ahead, and tells him to ". . . build a ship . . ."

. . . I did load aboard . . . The species of all living creatures . . . all my family and kindred; beasts wild and domestic . . . [then] did pour down the rain . . . it was fearful to behold . . . there arose a black cloud from the horizon . . . utmost darkness . . . even the gods were afeared . . . for six days and [seven] nights . . . the storm swept the land . . . [then] quieted the sea . . . the whole of mankind had returned to clay. I freed a dove . . . but [it] came back to me . . . a swallow . . . a raven . . . and he ate and flew about . . . croaked, and came not returning . . . I poured a libation and scattered a food offering . . . *The EPIC OF GILGAMESH,* Tablet #3375, The British Museum, London

Except that this Babylonian flood was caused by many gods, acting from spite and whim, this Epic of Gilgamesh closely parallels the account of the flood in the book of GENESIS; that of ONE, transcendent God, chastising a sinful world, and proved to a startled world that the people of the Bible were not the only ones who remembered a devastating event.

. . . The great Ziggurat of Ur is built by the Babylonians in Sumer. Ziggurats are temples to the gods of the Mesopotamian cultures, and this one (so near the Garden of Eden) is said to have been the greatest of them all, akin, perhaps, to the one the Bible calls the Tower of Babel. Newly restored and reconstructed on the ruins of the original, the Ziggurat stands again today in all its ancient arrogance. Very soon, now a man named Abram will be called out from Ur to find a new home and found a new nation. He and his family will carry with them, and pass down to their descendents, memories of the wonders of their homeland: towers and tales of floods and beginnings.

. . . Egyptians are importing cedar wood from that Eastern Mediterranean area the Greeks will call Phoenicia: wood that will soon become widely known and highly prized: Cedar of Lebanon. Expert Egyptian metal-smiths are creating works of great beauty with gold, silver, ivory and lapis-lazuli; and, observing the predictable regularity of the annual flood-time of their Nile River, they are—according to the historian Herodotus—". . . the first to discover the solar year and to portion it . . . into 12 parts . . ."

. . . The Harappa civilization flourishes now in the Indus Valley in India. From its great, busy seaports, merchant fleets carry ivory and cotton fabric as far away as Sumer. Its capital cities, Harappa and Mohenjo-Daro, are models of cleanliness, comfort, convenience and beauty. Larger in size than either Sumer or Egypt, the Harappa civilization will thrive peacefully for 1000 years, and leave behind no trace of warfare when it dies.

. . . and Canaanite peoples of Israel settle on a site that in future will become a most important city to a race called Hebrews. They will call it . . . Jerusalem.

c. 2450　The Pharaoh of Egypt is, at this time, King Izezi, about whom little is known, save that he had a very wise councilor, the Vizier Ptah-hotep. Ptah-hotep has served at court for many years, now, and has already designated his son as his successor, so he writes down all the wisdom he has learned over the years for his son to learn. It is called the Instruction of Ptah-hotep, and exists today in several manuscripts. Dotage has already come upon him, Ptah-hotep mourns in his opening lines, feebleness has arrived, his eyes are weak, ears deaf, strength disappearing, heart forgetful and to merely sit down or stand up is difficult. But his words reflect a keen mind, still (or rather, heart, for the Egyptians consider the brain useless and the heart the source of wisdom) . . .

> If thou art a leader commanding the affairs of the multitude, seek out for thyself every beneficial deed, until it may be that thy (own) affairs are without wrong . . . justice is great . . . it is fraud that gains riches . . . (but) the strength of justice is that it lasts . . .

Do not be covetous . . . do not be greedy . . . love thy wife at home as long as thou livest . . . How good it is when a son accepts what his father says! Thereby *maturity* comes to him. What I have done on earth is not inconsiderable . . . through doing right for the king up to the point of veneration . . .   The *Papyrus Prisse*, Bibliotheque Nationale, Paris, called the oldest "book." in the world.

Sargon of Akkad

c. 2350   The long history of Sumer comes to an end, as the world's first "empire" is created in Mesopotamia under the rule of Sargon of Akkad. Found as a baby in a basket of bulrushes (as will another little boy a thousand years hence) the Semitic Sargon overcomes his lowly origins, builds the city of Akkad and, using weapons new to warfare, the bow and arrow, goes on to conquer all of Sumer, displacing the Sumerians, and destroying the city of Ebla on the way. Then, taking control of modern-day Iraq, Syria and Asia Minor, he consolidates his power ". . . from sea to sea." Sargon's strong, central government will hold together through his 61 year reign and three more generations of his own family as well, for a total of 150 years, earning for Sargon the Great, the title of world's first emperor.

Sargon, king of Agade, rose (to power) . . . and had neither rival nor opponent. He spread his terror-inspiring glamour over all the countries . . .   Babylonian cuneiform tablet, British Museum, London

. . . In far eastern Korea, a man named Tangun rules, grandson (according to ancient legend) of the Creator and a beautiful earthly woman upon whom he breathed and transformed from a bear. His dynasty will rule a thousand years and, centuries from now, Korean legend will call Tangun the Father of Civilization.

. . . In China, the Yao, Shun and Hsai Dynasties rule, one after another. China's astronomers understand the equinoxes and solstices; its artists paint elaborate pottery, and its musicians play a five tone scale on hollowed-out bamboo flutes.

c. 2250   Having risen and fallen (under Sargon the Great and his successors) and risen again, the Syrian city of Ebla is totally destroyed by Sargon's ferocious, unsparing grandson, Naram-sin. After looting the city for every bit of treasure, Naram-sin burns it to the ground; but he leaves behind the greatest treasure of all, the vast royal library and its thousands of inscribed tablets, which bake like bricks in a kiln, and fall in a jumble to the floor when their wooden shelves burn and collapse in the fire. When the ruins of Ebla are found in A.D. 1968, its find will not be accidental, but the result of years of searching; for its name is found time and again on cuneiform tablets from many cities from Mari and Damascus to far-away Sumerian Ur.

The prospect of deciphering the strangely different Eblite language will promise to be a daunting one, expected to take years . . . until one tablet is found, considered today, the world's first dictionary which, happily, includes a comprehensive, bi-lingual translation of Eblite into Sumerian cuneiform. Then will come surprise after surprise, beginning with the creation story of the *Enuma Elish*. For, while the name, Ebla, is never mentioned in the Bible, many Biblical names ARE mentioned in Ebla's tablets: [Jeru-]salem. Hazor, Lachish, Megiddo, Gaza and Joppa, as well as the so-called "cities of the plain": Sodom, Gomorrah, Admah, Zeboiim and Bela, listed in the SAME ORDER as they are in GENESIS. 14:2 Biblical names of persons appear on the tablets, also: Eber, Esau, Ishmael, Israel, Abram/Abraham, Saul, Micaiah, Michael, and one found no where else in ancient writings than the Bible: Da-u-dum or David. Today, as this book, is written, the dig goes on at Ebla, with expectations of still more wonderful tablets to be found.

c. 2200   Shortly after Naram-sin's bloody reign, a strange barbarian hill people called Guti swarm down on Akkad from the northeast and wipe out both the city and empire, ending the dynasty of Sargon the Great. The fierce, destructive Gutian rule lasts nearly 100 years until it is overthrown by King Utu-hegal of Uruk. Little is known about Utu-hegal except that he is hailed as a liberator; and that it is during his reign that a most remarkable document, is carved on stone called the Sumerian King List, which enumerates the many Sumerian kings, telling how long each ruled. They are time-spans mind-boggling to modern readers: from 150,000 years to three months three and a half days! But the biggest surprise of the King List is the casual inclusion, almost as an afterthought, of a major world event that happened just after Sumer's eighth king!

When kingship was lowered from heaven, kingship was (first) in Eridu . . . Two kings . . . ruled it for 64,000 years. [Then] kingship was brought to Bad-tibera . . . [Then] to Larak . . . [then] Sippar . . . [then] . . . Shuruppak . . . These are five cities, eight kings ruled them for 241,000 years. (Then) the Flood swept over (the earth.) . . . After the Flood had swept over (the earth) (and) when kingship was lowered (again) from heaven, kingship was (first) in Kish . . .   The Sumerian
King List, trans. from ANET

The King List
British Museum, London

c. 2000   The turn of the millennium finds giant strides made in man's progress all over the globe . . .

. . . The Egyptians are using a key-operated wooden lock and carpenter's tools, including a level. An Egyptian "explorer" named Hennu sets sail in a little single-masted boat for a faraway land called Punt (possibly Ethiopia on Africa's Red Sea coast.) He brings back many things, including incense and myrrh, which Egyptians use in embalming. A carved stone telling of his trip exists today, making Hennu the first explorer known by name.

. . . The process of cheese-making is discovered by Asiatic nomads . . .

. . . North American Indians have tamed the dog; and Inca Indians are living in present-day Peru. Agricultural people, Indians throughout America are cultivating corn, pumpkins, beans, potatoes and peanuts.

. . . The inhabitants of the Syrian city of Mari have learned how to send code messages with fire signals, an important advance in times of war or internal upheaval, and . . .

Stonehenge

. . . The monument we know today as Stonehenge is built on the far-away island future generations will call England. Long thought to have been a place of worship for Druid priests, it is now considered a surprisingly sophisticated and effective, astronomical observatory with which they could learn the secrets of an orderly universe by timing eclipses, solstices and phases of the sun and moon. Although its thirty 28-ton stones come from Wales, almost 150 miles away, its builders are still Neolithic people, and Stonehenge, like the pyramids, is built without the help of the wheel.

1930   On that stretched-out island of Crete south of the Greek isles, the Minoan people have built the city of Knossos into a mountainous marvel. Its elegant, brilliantly painted, three-story palace covers six acres of ground, houses hundreds of people, and includes among its amenities, running water and flush toilets! Its sea-faring traders travel far and wide, carrying olive oil, honey, wine and pottery to many Mediterranean ports, and bring back gold, grain, linen and gems. The Minoans are a peaceful, placid people, skilled in the gentle arts of painted pottery, jewelry and elegant clothing; their tightly corseted ladies wasp-waisted and hoop-skirted. They write a complicated script archeology will call Linear A and B, and from it will come stories of the sea.

Another story of the sea comes from Egypt at about the time of King Senusert. It is an account of a ship-wrecked sailor named Sinuhe, a fugitive from a king's justice, stranded on a desert isle; made shiekh of a tribe of mid-east nomads (whom he calls Sand Crossers) and finally returned to Egypt from Syria, dressed as a bedouin, rich and famous, to be welcomed home by the successor king. Many centuries from now Sinuhe and his adventures will reappear as an Arabian Sinbad in A Thousand and One Nights.

c. 1900   Only 600 miles north of that young Bristlecone Pine tree, that is now 700 years old, stands a mountain, a volcano, in a land that will centuries hence be called Washington, USA. At approximately 1900 B.C. it heaves up a mighty eruption four times greater than it will unleash 3800 years later. It will THEN be called Mount St. Helens.

1800   Another volcano erupts almost half-way around the world, in a boot-shaped land hanging down into the Great Sea, the "Mediterranean," wiping out the bronze age villages around it. Almost 2000 years from now "Mount Vesuvius" will erupt again and bury in lava and ash the elegant Italian cities near it then, which will become famous to the world as Pompeii and Herculaneum.

c. 1800   One Babylonian god, called Marduk, is decreed Lord of Heaven, and granted ruler-ship over all other gods by his earthly manifestation, King Hammurabi, who rules Babylon now, and will for 43 years; and will guide it through "the golden age of Babylon," its high point of learning, literature and law. A leader of much skill, foresight and ability, Hammurabi involves himself in every aspect of his regime; every detail brought to him for final judgment. He codifies, updates or rewrites hundreds of laws, some very ancient, into a new CODE OF HAMMURABI. Nearly 300 of Hammurabi's legal provisions in thousands of words are carved, in the Akkadian language, on an eight-foot tall, polished black diorite *stela*. They cover everything from prices and wages to construction projects and military service; family disputes and fair taxes; false witness, kidnapping, murder, theft, incest, adultery and sorcery; inheritances, treatment of slaves, sale or purchase of property, prices, rents and interest. In an age of massive tribal retaliation, one family wiping out another for the sins of one member, it is the world's first known attempt to "make the punishment fit the crime." A "nun" caught drinking in a wine shop shall be burned; a woman accused of adultery (even though unproven) must throw herself in a river; one who murders her husband for another man shall be burned at the stake. Incest with a man's daughter shall drive him out of the city; with his mother will cause them both to be burned, and housebreakers will be killed and walled-in at the break.

[The] gods named me, Hammurabi, the devout, god-fearing prince to cause justice to prevail in the land . . . that the strong might not oppress the weak . . . If a son has struck his father, they shall cut off his hand. "If [a person] has destroyed the eye of [another], they shall destroy his eye." If he has broken (another's) bone, they shall break his bone . . . I, Hammurabi, the perfect king . . . overcame grievous difficulties . . . made an end of war . . . promoted the welfare of the land . . . May my name be spoken in reverence forever!   The *Hammurabi Stele*; the Law Code of King Hammurabi of Babylon

The eight-foot tall *Hammurabi Stele,* with the king's own image carved at the top, will be discovered at Susa in A.D. 1901, in perfect condition, and recognized as a most important find, an eloquent accounting of the customs, manners, mores—and laws—of the age. It stands, today, in the Louvre, Paris, France.

c. 1800   The city of Ur is one of those in Hammurabi's domain; wealthy, learned and worldly. It has flourished for hundreds of years, a major influence in international affairs. Now, Ur of the Chaldees becomes part of the first chronological, written "history" of the world . . . because of a man named Abram. . .

Scores of ages have gone by since Noah was saved from the flood, and since God said to him and his sons, "Be fruitful and multiply and replenish the earth . . ." And replenish they did, bringing forth sons and generations of sons, down through the ages and eras:

Gomer and Magog, Tubal, Meshech, Cush, Raamah and Sheba; Nimrod the mighty hunter and Asshur who "builded" Nineveh; Eber and Japeth, Peleg, Rehu, Serug . . . and Terah, who lived in Ur of the Chaldees. Now, Terah begat Abram, Nahor and Haran, and Haran begat Lot. Now the Lord said unto Abram, "Get thee out of thy nation, and I will bless thee and make thy name great." Abram, like his city, Ur, is a man of wealth and learning, and God promises him as many descendents ". . . as the sands of the earth." God offers to make Abram sire to a great nation in return for obedience; thus the COVENANT, or agreement, makes Abram the FATHER OF THE HEBREW PEOPLE, and begins the . . .

. . . AGE OF THE PATRIARCHS, Abram,

now ABRAHAM, ISAAC and JACOB, father, son and grandson. Abraham must not remain in Chaldea but must move to a new land far away. A man "very rich in cattle, gold and silver" (according to GENESIS) and probably knowledge and wisdom (according to the Hammurabic age in which he lives), Abraham takes all his household, family and 300 retainers to Canaan. His nephew, Lot, comes with him, but moves his own herds and flocks to the Jordan Valley close to the cities of Sodom and Gomorrah.

Abraham is "ninety years old and nine," and his wife, Sarah, 89, and the Lord appears to him and says ". . . I will make you exceedingly fruitful; and I will make nations of you, and kings shall come forth from you . . . and [your wife, Sarah] shall be a mother of nations . . ." And in one of the Bible's great examples of pure, earthy humor, ". . . Abraham fell on his face and laughed."

c. 1700 The Hittite peoples rule much of the Mid-east now, from Syria and Anatolia (Asia minor or, today, Turkey) to the Euphrates River of Mesopotamia. A most unusual people, their stone carvings reveal them to look and dress nothing at all like any of their neighbors. Although their civilization is considered not as sophisticated as Egypt's, it is generally given credit for one of the most important discoveries of ancient times, the smelting of iron. With this advance, which they will keep a closely guarded secret for many years, do the Hittites usher in . . .

. . . the IRON AGE.

The Hittite Empire will be short-lived but, in large part due to their superior iron weapons, extremely powerful, some of its royalty marrying, even, into that of Egypt. It is a society centered on religion and war, worshipping a vast pantheon of gods, and fighting with a war-machine that includes iron-armed cavalry capable of covering 50 miles in a single night. The Hittites will be part of the Mid-east for many hundred years, now, until the day when the Hebrew king, David, will fall in love with, and scheme for Bathsheba, wife of "Uriah the Hittite." When their civilization collapses, they will be forgotten BY ALL

BUT THE WRITERS OF THE BIBLE (who will, in fact, be mocked by scornful skeptics for their nearly 50 references to Hittites, whom they "knew" never existed. But the ruins of the Hittite civilization will be found in A.D. 1906, including another royal archive and thousands more inscribed clay tablets. When, with much difficulty, the tablets are deciphered, many questions will be raised, then answered, for the Hittite language is un-related to any other mid-eastern language; not Mesopotamian, nor Greek nor Egyptian, but Indo-European; its people derived, then, from migrant settlers from India and Europe! The find will include another law code, which many scholars consider even more enlightened than that of the great Hammurabi, for the Hittite Law Code stresses restitution rather than retribution.

. . . While Abraham dwells in Canaan, his nephew, Lot, "pitches his tent" and brings his herds and flocks near to Sodom, one of the "cities of the plain." But Sodom, and nearby Gomorrah, are exceedingly wicked cities, practicing every kind of evil; and God tells Abraham He intends to destroy them. But Abraham's relatives are there and he asks if God would destroy the good with the bad. "Will you save Sodom if there can be found 50 righteous?" God agrees and in a humorous, and very human, portrayal of the mid-eastern love of haggling over numbers, Abraham begins to bargain. "Suppose there are 40 righteous. Will you save it for 40?" Again God agrees. "How about 30? 20?" Each time God consents, and they settle on 10. But there are not 10 righteous, and when God destroys Sodom and Gomorrah, Lot and his family are the only ones saved . . . except for Lot's wife, who looks back and is turned into a pillar of salt. The story of Lot and the destruction of Sodom and Gomorrah, as fabulous as it may seem, and long written off as myth, are now believed to be based on historical reality by archeological findings of more than ample empirical evidence.

c. 1700   In his 100th year Abraham's wife, Sarah, gives birth to a son, who they call Isaac; and Abraham loves him greatly. But God test's Abraham's loyalty to Himself, and says, "Take your son . . . Isaac, whom you love, and offer him as a burnt offering." In perfect obedience Abraham builds an altar, binds and lays Isaac upon it and raises his knife; but God stops the sacrifice. His challenge had been made from neither whim nor brutal blood-lust, like that of mythical deities of ancient times. It was, rather, a revelation of His transcendence ABOVE all other gods, a manifestation of His clemency and compassion to a man who was no saint, but had shown that his loyalty would withhold nothing from Him, not even his own son. And ". . . Abraham looked, and behold, behind him was a ram, caught in a thicket with his horns, and he offered it as a burnt offering instead of his son," Isaac, who grows to manhood and becomes the father of Jacob and Esau.

. . . At about this time, Egypt is humiliated by a catastrophe, which will be as gall to the proud Egyptians, who have always scorned and disdained lesser "foreigners." For now, foreign invaders swoop down out of Asia and CONQUER the land of the Nile. "Sand-crossers," the Egyptians contemptuously call them, "wretched Asiatics." They are *Hegau-Khasut,* or Hyksos, meaning "shepherd kings," or "foreign chieftains." Semitic people from the mid-east area of Canaan (among whom can be found such Hebraic names as *Ya-Kob-har,* or Jacob) the Hyksos descend upon Egypt in horse drawn chariots, take control without war, and begin a dynasty of Hyksos kings. It is the first sight of wheeled vehicles the Egyptians have had . . . thundering machines screeching behind racing horses, churning up the desert sands in great clouds behind them.

> Now it so happened that the land of Egypt was in distress, There was no Lord. . .or King of the time. Distress was in the town *of the Asiatics.*   Papyrus from the British museum. ANET

The dominance of Hyksos kings over the once-proud Egyptians puts a new light on Egypt's relations with other peoples and countries. What was once undisguised hostility now becomes, through their Semitic rulers, a benign tolerance if not, even, a warm welcome. And although the Egyptians chafe under foreign rule, the Hyksos are considered by modern scholars to have been "knightly warriors" who share sovereignty with an aristocratic sort of feudal nobility . . . and life goes on in its slow, interminable way. Naturally suspicious of any change from old ways, Egypt gradually adopts new ideas and methods. Spinning and weaving techniques are improved; and the lyre, oboe and tambourine come into use as musical instruments. Egyptian ships are sailing beyond the mouth of the Nile, carrying on trade throughout the Mediterranean; and an Egyptian scholar named Ahmes uses algebra, the first mathematician know by his name and papyrus which is, today, in the British Museum, London. And the practice of medicine is studied . . . quietly . . .

> Everywhere he feels his heart because its vessels run to all his limbs.   The Secret Book of the Physician. Papyrus Ebers

Abraham's son, Isaac, lives a long and good life, obedient as a son to his father, Abraham, caring and concerned as a father to his sons, Jacob and Esau, and devoted to his wife Rebekah; not deserving of the ruse she and Jacob perpetrate upon him and Esau for a bowl of stew, a "mess of pottage." Jacob, in turn, is a man of contradictions: in his youth a devious schemer for his brother's birthright and his father's blessing, in later years he becomes a peaceable, productive man, a kind, gentle husband and father and an honest, devoted servant of God. He is also a man of great physical strength, and on the road to Jabbok outwrestles an angel in an all-night contest, letting the angel go only when he blesses him and says: "Thy name shall be called no more Jacob, but Israel; for as a prince thou hast power with God and with men, and hast prevailed." Thus, from Jacob do . . .

. . . the Hebrews become . . . *ISRAEL* . . . "He who struggled with God."

c. 1650   Jacob, now Israel, has twelve sons: Reuben the first-born, Simeon, Levi, Judah, Issacher, Zebulon, Benjamin, Dan, Naphthali, Asher, Gad and Joseph, the youngest and favorite. Their families are called the

. . . TWELVE TRIBES OF ISRAEL

To show his love for him, Jacob gives Joseph a "coat of many colors" (which, because of the many dyes used in its making, is a very expensive coat) and, out of jealousy, Joseph's brothers sell him into slavery in Egypt . . . a dismal prospect, for the Egyptian contempt for Semitic "sand-crossers" is well known. But Egypt is ruled at this time by the foreigner Hyksos kings, a Semitic people themselves, from the same mid-east area as Joseph; and when he is, in fact, imprisoned, it is a moral issue, not political, that puts him there . . . his rejection of a woman's unrequited love. But Joseph is a man of wisdom and unusual talent, and when his foresight saves Egypt from famine, he gains the attention of the Pharaoh, who appoints him . . . Prime Minister!

c. 1600   The Minoan civilization on Crete is flourishing now, its greatest palace complex at Knossos housing some 1300 persons in sophisticated luxury that includes indoor water, plumbing and sewage systems. The plastered walls of its 800 rooms are vividly painted with brilliant frescoes that show amazing things, including sports scenes showing some of the Minoans on Crete participating in the fearsome sport of bull-leaping: bulls with huge necks and chests, ferocious heads and fierce eyes. Minoan wall paintings show one acrobat grasp-

Fresco from Knossos

ing the huge horns in front, while another somersaults on its back and leaps into the open arms of the third. Minoan legend tells of (although archeologists have not yet found) an enormous, confusing *labyrinth* of hallways in which King Minos imprisoned his son, a fearsome Minotaur, half man and half bull . . . the product of an unholy dalliance of Minos' queen.

. . . Famine strikes all of the mid-east; seven years of drought following seven years of plenty, which had been squandered through ignorance of what was to come. But, in Egypt, Pharaoh's Prime Minister, the Hebrew Joseph, foresaw the disaster and had planned for it, and stored up grain. Now, his brothers travel to Egypt to buy food ". . . and Joseph knew his brethren, but they knew not him." Giving them corn and testing their honor and honesty, Joseph forgives his brothers, crying ". . . what ye did to me, ye meant for evil, but God meant it for good . . ." and they, and their father, Jacob now Israel, come to settle in Egypt's "land of Goshen" near the Nile delta. The Hebrews are well received, make a good life, and multiply . . . rapidly. And the years go by until, according to the last verse of GENESIS ". . . Joseph died, being an hundred and ten years old; and they embalmed him and he was put in a coffin in Egypt." And, as most of the graves of the Egyptians are not yet found, he could be there still. On the other hand, one coffin and mummy has, in fact, been found named Yuyah, which possibly translates into "Joseph." There is some speculation that it is, just possibly, the Joseph of the Bible.

But the foreign Hyksos rule grates on native Egyptians; there is continuous struggle, intrigue and rebellion, and the Egyptians learn from Hyksos war tactics the use of armor, bow and arrow, and the horse and chariot. One minor Egyptian king bewails his country's condition:

> Let me understand what this strength of mine is for! (One) prince is in Avaris, another is in Ethiopia, and (here) I sit associated with an Asiatic and a Negro! (sic. In some texts, Nubian.) Each man has his slice of Egypt, dividing up the land with me . . . No man can settle down, being despoiled by the . . . Asiatics. I will grapple with (them). My wish is to save Egypt and to *smite* the Asiatics!   The Carnarvon Tablet I from Thebes, which includes the first mention in history of the black race. ANET

1567   The Hyksos are finally driven out of Egypt with a war machine like their own and the true Egyptian line is restored to the throne, under a king called Ahmose. With Ahmose begins Egypt's great 18th Dynasty, the age of the mightiest pharaohs: Thutmose, Seti and the most famous woman pharaoh, Hatshepsut. It is a fabulous age of the building of an empire and its monuments. Egypt's victory over the Hyksos is widely celebrated.

> There was fighting on the water . . . his majesty made a great slaughter among them . . . There was no number to the prisoners . . . carried off. . .   Inscription on the tomb of a captain of a Nile vessel.
>
> . . . hundreds of ships of new cedar, filled with . . . countless battle-axes of metal . . . I *seized* them all. I did not leave a thing . . . so your wishes have failed, miserable Asiatic. Stone *stele* from Karnak. Both ANET

Egyptian papyrus listing semitic slaves

With the ouster of the Semitic Hyksos and the restoration of the true Egyptian monarchy, a "new king" senses that there is another power in the land that could become dangerous—the Hebrews. There are just too many of them. They are too dangerous; if they should become ambitious they could pose a serious threat; so the Egyptians take action to prevent that. All property of the Hebrews is confiscated, and they are pressed into . . . slavery!

> Now there arose up a new king over Egypt, which knew not Joseph. . . [that] did set over them taskmasters to afflict them with their burdens . . . and made their lives bitter with hard bondage, in mortar, and in brick, and in all manner of service in the field . . .   EXODUS, 1:8,11,14

. . . Another class of people is known to be in Egypt by this time, also, having drifted down from Mesopotamia where they first appeared centuries ago. Not kings or rulers, these, but wandering nomads called, in Egyptian, *'Apiru'* and in mid-east cuneiform, *Habiru*, a name startlingly close to what GENESIS 14:13 calls Abraham in Hebrew, *'Ibri*. The "Apiru" are a restless lot, referred to in many texts from Mesopotamia, Asia Minor, Egypt and Syria-Palestine. Citizens of nowhere, their only status is that of landless wanderers, and although scholars make no direct connection with the Hebrews, they believe there to be some relation. Egyptian wall paintings show these "Asiatics" strikingly different from native Egyptians, clad in one-shouldered, brightly striped, sarong-like dresses, with unmistakably Semitic

Egyptian wall painting of the "Asiatics"

faces" and hair styles. They show them, also, mixing mortar, filling frames and laying brick, just as described in the book of GENESIS.

1500   Halfway through the millennium the world is seething with activity:

. . . The Harappa civilization vanishes from the Indus Valley of India after flourishing for a thousand years . . . and leaves not a clue as to why behind. Part of it declined slowly over the years, and the rest died a swift, mysterious death. Its ruins will lie, covered over with time and totally forgotten for 3400 years, until A.D. 1922, when an archeologist will, by sheer chance, unearth some "interesting stones and bricks." The end of the Harappa civilization signals the beginning of the ARYAN which, modern scholarship believes, institutes the beginning of the *caste* system of social separation in India. The Aryans are given to constant warfare, but, over the next thousand years they will, also, raise Indian culture to a high level and produce some of India's greatest literature.

. . . Two primitive little villages begin to grow, now, in a rocky, mountainous—but beautiful—land that juts out like a hand with many fingers into the Aegean Sea. They are only dawning now, but their time will come: Athens on Greece's mainland, and Sparta on its Peloponnesus.

. . . The earliest MAYA Indians are living in Central America.

. . . The "General Sherman" Sequoia, or giant redwood tree, begins growth in southern California, one of the oldest things still alive to day, the tallest and largest living thing in the world.

. . . In China, the first great warlord dynasty begins, with the dawning of their Bronze Age. The Shang Dynasty will rule China for 700 years, its capital city full of great wooden palaces and pagodas. China's craftsmen are using pictographs for writing, a method that will evolve into their myriad written characters. "Writing" is, by now, almost a universal art, and. . .

. . . The Phoenecians invent the world's first true "alphabet." The race of peoples known, in Greek, as *Phoenician,* are thriving, now, in Lebanon and Syria, a most important people. Their greatness will not be like that of Greece or Rome in the years ahead, though, for Phoenecia will produce no great writers, philosophers or artists, generals or political leaders. But Greece and Rome could not become what they will without them, for Phoenecia has invented, and will give to the world . . . an ALPHABET. The Phoenician's *aleph-beth* will build them their own greatness as merchants, manufacturers, sailors, navigators, colonizers and traders. Their writing will keep their accounts, chart trade routes and further their influence and, together with one of the ancient world's greatest natural resources, the much desired wood of the fabled Cedars of Lebanon, will build them the world's first armed navy and merchant fleet to carry their goods and influence from their busy seaports of Tyre and Sidon to every corner of the ancient world.

Among Phoenecian imports are indigo and maddur plants from India which they use to make red and violet dyes. Their name, Phoenecia, stems from the Greek *phoinos,* meaning blood red or purple. Their exports include some of the earliest known dishes and vessels of glass. Another import their ships are bringing from India and Asia, and selling to Egypt, is having great impact on Egyptian life, religion. . .and entertainment; dwarves and sensuous dancing girls. Just as the ritualism of death is an important part of Egyptian life so, also, is the dance which accompanies it. Stiff and solemn, it has been performed by male priests invoking the gods or chanting the pharaohs to their tombs. That will change now. . .

. . . As will the burial of those pharaohs. Not for centuries have giant pyramids been built to house royal rulers in their after-life. They are not safe from grave robbers and no pyramid still holds its royal resident by this time. Now the pharaohs and their elaborate trappings are borne up the Nile in ornate funerary boats almost to the first cataract, to the remote, lonely, beastly hot Valley of the Tombs of the Kings. Here laborers carve long tunnels in the desolate, rocky cliffs hiding the valley; and the priests hide away their royal cargo in a maze of inner chambers. Many pharaohs are laid away here with fabulous fortunes in gold and gems to assure them wealth and luxury in their next life; and elaborate secrecy surrounds the locations of the tombs. Still, every tomb will eventually be found by grave robbers, and stripped of its precious store. Every one, that is, but one.

1490   One of the most remarkable of Egypt's pharaohs, Hatshepsut, rules now, a woman ruling not as a king's wife but as a king, herself, a condition for which hieroglyphics do not even have a word. Usurping the rightful throne of her stepson, Thutmose, she rules 20 years in peace, prosperity and expansion of trade. Hatshepsut affects the manner and dress of a man, but builds a temple to herself in the pink sandstone cliffs as graceful as it is gigantic.

c. 1470   Thutmose III deposes his stepmother after chafing under her long rule and immediately attempts to wipe out all memory and mention of her. His reign is one of conquest and war; and the far-flung boundaries of his empire stretch as far north as Syria and Canaan. Egypt, under Thutmose, will reach the greatest size and power it will ever know. Called by some the Alexander the Great of Egypt, he is brilliant in battle (where he wages eight campaigns, all successful) and ambitious as head of state. Thousands of slaves labor on his monumental building projects at Heliopolis and the magnificent Karnak, where hieroglyphic inscriptions record his wars, glories and victories. A massive black granite statue of Thutmose—young, strong and handsome, bare-chested and clad only in pyramid-shaped head-dress and loin-cloth, stands today in the

Egyptian Museum, Cairo; and New York City's Central Park is graced with one of his towering *obelisques.*

1450   A crescent-shaped remnant of what used to be a roundish island lies today just off the coast of Greece, with just a tip of a volcano jutting above the water of the bay. After rumbling threats for 10 years *Thera,* or Santorini, disappears in a mighty eruption at about this time; one of the world's greatest volcanic eruptions, called the loudest blast ever heard on earth . . . and leaves the remaining cliffs towering a thousand feet above the water. Eleven hundred years from now a Greek philosopher named Plato will write, about the blast, that a continent disappeared beneath the ocean ". . . in a single night and a day." He will call the "lost" continent . . . Atlantis. There is some speculation that Moses lived and the Exodus took place at this time rather than the traditional date three centuries hence, and that it was the eruption of Santorini that caused the many plagues of Egypt. The theory is hotly debated; but some researchers feel there is reason to believe the eruption had more effect on the civilizations just miles away. . .

. . . The development of the Aegean cities of Knossos, Mycenae and Troy is proceeding each in its own unique way. The Minoan culture at Knossos is nearing the end of its history, and its linear writing will not be deciphered until A.D. 1952. A buoyant people, the Minoans are life-loving, fun-loving and unacquainted with war or imperial ambition. Living the good life in their marvelous mountainside palaces, their main concerns are comfort, cleanliness and harmony. But their idyll ends (instantly and violently washed away in the tidal waves of Santorini?) . . . and a seagoing tribe from the north called Achean, moves in, warlike and plundering; ignorant of civilization and the architectural, engineering and plumbing marvels they find, which they lay waste and move into as squalid squatters. The Acheans will evolve, though, in due time into modern Greeks.

. . . Fabled "golden" Mycenae is glorying in its greatest age in northern Greece. Built high on a hill, the citadel's walls are 10 feet thick, and its main entrance is a massive sculpture that will become known as the "Lion Gate," an immense arch, framed by two great stone lions reared up on hind legs, face to face. The city's walls are richly frescoed, and Mycenae's unique and much desired pottery proves that Mycenaen ships sail far and wide, for many pieces will be found from Egypt to Ugarit, and from Phoenicia to Sicily. Mycenae is exceedingly rich, the epithet "golden" well used, for posterity will find gold everywhere; on clothing, utensils, decorations, and even as funeral wrapping for two small royal children. How did they get so rich? They rule the sea now, and history will blandly admit that their talents lie mostly in . . . piracy.

The Lion Gate

. . . "Wind-swept" Troy, happily situated in a most strategic location on Anatolia's south-coastal Plain of Argos, not four miles from the Hellespont, dominates that much-used waterway, collecting taxes and tolls from sea-going passers-by. Indomitable Troy will rebuild itself after adversity nine times before ". . . the day shall come, the great avenging day . . .

when Troy's proud glories in the dust shall lay." But it will never be forgotten for, 700 years from now, a blind bard named Homer will sing of "rosy-fingered dawns," "wine-dark seas," and great ships that "plough the watery deep."

. . . In the north Syrian city of Ugarit, the *Ras Shamra* texts are written down on clay tablets at about this time. Out of a pantheon of Mesopotamian gods and goddesses one god begins to assume prominence: Baal, who (according to the *Ras Shamra* tablets) ". . . destroys his enemies, the Sea and Flame, annihilates River, and muzzles the Dragon." Though he, himself, is slain, "Death is cleaved, ground on a millstone and sown in the field; and from there Baal rises and cries . . .

> What enemy rises up against Baal . . . What adversary against him who mounteth the clouds? For Baal the mighty is alive, for the Prince, Lord of the earth, exists.   The *Ras Shamra* texts from Ugarit. The British Museum, London

Ras Shamra Text

. . . Twelve hundred years have gone by since the great Sphinx was built at the foot of the pyramids; and now he lies buried beneath 40 feet of shifting desert sands. Legend tells that the Sphinx said to a young Egyptian prince resting in its shade, "Uncover me when you are king." And that he does, when he becomes Pharaoh Thutmose IV.

Egypt is an incredibly rich land, where there is as much gold "as the desert sands" but the wealth is only for the few. For the rest . . . they have their gods. The gods are important to the people, extremely important, for life is short and hard, with few rewards and little hope of anything better. But the gods promise health, happiness always and prosperity . . . if not in this life, certainly in the next. . .

1370   Amenhotep IV is king of Egypt, an odd-looking pharaoh, with a pear-shaped body, slit eyes and long, jutting face and chin that suggest generations of royal inbreeding. Amenhotep is a man ahead of his time, though, a prophet, almost, who sees much wrong in Egypt's religion. He sees only magic and superstition in the confusing maze of gods and goddesses, perpetuated by a vast, priestly bureaucracy's stranglehold over the minds of the Egyptian people. And so, his vision and driving desire is to do away with all of Egypt's many gods and institute the worship of only one god, Aten, the Sun. For the sun knows no favorites, he believes, but sends its blessings on everybody and everything, equally. The sun shines in the heavens; its rays are on earth. The king is the son of the rays, and therefore the instrument of Aten's will. So, under his new name, *Akhen-aten,* he will worship the Sun . . . AND THE PEOPLE WILL WORSHIP HIM!

Akhen-aten

> . . . beautiful on the horizon . . . O living Aten . . . Thou sole god, there is no other like thee . . . no other knows thee . . . save . . . thy son who came forth from thyself . . . the king of Upper and Lower Egypt, Akhen-aten   Akhen-aten's HYMN TO THE SUN, from an engraving at Tel-el-Amarna

With Akhen-aten in this enterprise, in startling contrast to his own strange appearance, is his wife Nefertiti, a most beautiful woman in any age of history. Together this unlikely pair moves Egypt's government from Thebes with its now obsolete chief god, Amon Re, north to a new "city of Sun" at Amarna (today's Tel-el-Amarna), and gangs of hatchet-men are dispatched throughout the kingdom to hack out all memory of the Amon Re of Thebes.

Nefertiti

Vast amounts of correspondence are carried out between Akhen-aten and his foreign "vassal" kings which will be found at Amarna's ruins and are known today as the *Amarna Letters*. They include references to that nomadic people called 'Apiru, or Habiru, which some scholars believe may have included the Hebrews. These 'Apiru are, apparently, in league with other governors against one Abdu-heba, governor of a city called JERUSALEM, and in letter after letter Abdu-heba begs Akhen-aten to . . .

An Amarna Letter

> Let the king, my lord, protect his land from the hand of the 'Apiru. If not, then let the king, my lord, send chariots . . . The 'Apiru plunder all the lands of the king and if there are no archers (here) the lands of the king, my lord, are lost!   Letters from Tel-el-Amarna. The British Museum, London

Whether the 'Apiru were actually Hebrews, though, or related to them, remains an unsolved question.

Akhen-aten's revolution is not only religious and governmental, but cultural as well, and now, at Amarna, he and Nefertiti begin to "modernize" culture and the arts, also. Dramatic changes are made in Egyptian sculpture as the stony stiffness of ancient statues are replaced by a soft realism, an almost living warmth, the most striking examples being stunning statuary busts of Nefertiti, herself, which make her sumptuous beauty come almost alive. This cultural part of the Amarna Revolution will succeed . . . but the religious brings about severe social upheaval, for it ruptures the entire religious bureaucracy which is the very essence of Egypt; and leaves its people feeling abandoned and deprived of the gods they need so much.

c. 1360   Akhen-aten dies and his young son-in-law succeeds him as pharoah. The boy is only 10 years old and rules under the regency of his grandfather. The priests of the old order force him to restore the worship of many gods, ending the Amarna Revolution; and there is great rejoicing that Egypt is back to normal.

The artists and stone-carvers have a field-day, and in no time his image appears all over the empire; hunting, fighting, riding . . . and sitting together with his wife. Master craftsmen create for him everything he needs with ebony, ivory, alabaster, lapis-lazuli and all manner of semiprecious gems. But it is the hand of the goldsmith that immortalizes the boy-king in the gleaming, indestructible metal. His lessons are written with golden writing reeds; he hunts with a lily-engraved golden harpoon and dagger from a gilded chariot, gleaming with golden scenes of himself as a mighty hunter. Intricate golden jewelry and collars adorn his gold-trimmed clothing and sandals; and he rules his kingdom from a golden throne, carved with a happy scene of himself and his pretty queen. He lives, as all pharaohs do, in a golden world, surrounded by golden images; but his gold cannot buy him a long life, and when Pharaoh TUT-ANKH-AMON dies, he is laid away in a golden tomb.

c. 1351   Only 19 years old, King "Tut" goes to live with the gods before he has lived as a man. He was only a boy and he performed no great deeds but he WAS pharaoh and, while he lived, the gods were restored to the people of Egypt!

> The good ruler, performing benefactions for his father (Amon) and all the gods . . . has expelled deceit throughout the Two Lands . . . the temples [had . . .] gone to pieces . . . shrines . . . became desolate . . . and the gods turned their backs upon this land . . . Then his majesty made monuments for the gods . . . of . . . fine gold . . . divine offerings . . . He surpassed what had been. . .   Engraved stele from Karnak, The Cairo Museum

A sorrowful Egypt is thrown into panic, for it did not expect the death of its young king. In only 70 days his body will be ready for burial and there is much to be done. Everything Tutankhamen needs for his journey to the other world must be ready when his mummy is ready.

The Valley of the Tombs of the Kings . . . barren, desolate, hot and craggy-cliffed. A slow journey up the Nile and a mournful procession over the desert has brought Tutankhamen to his lonely grave, an almost makeshift tomb carved in a hurry out of the cliff, not nearly so splendid as others all around. Down a long corridor he is carried; through an antechamber and into the large burial chamber where his coffins await him . . . and ev-

erything to make him happy and comfortable: his golden wine jars, lamps and jewelry, his golden fan for a cooling breeze, his golden chariot, boomerangs, and senet tables so he can play his favorite game. Every possession he had in life goes with him, now, in death. Four little golden goddesses will stand eternal watch around the shrine that holds King Tut's heart, the "source of life and all knowledge and wisdom," and other organs; and statues of Hathor, Anubis, Isis and Osiris all keep watch.

The oppressive silence of this valley of death is broken by the chanting of the priests and low sobs of the king's broken-hearted queen. Over her husband's head and shoulders lies a helmet made of 24 pounds of pure, beaten gold in his exact likeness, encrusted on the front with semi-precious gems and engraved on the back with hieroglyphic verses from the *Book of the Dead*. On this helmet the queen lays her own simple garland of fresh flowers.

Now the vizier gives the orders to begin closing the coffins; seven of them, one inside of the other. It is no small job, for just the first one, cradling the king's mummy in its fitted form, is a gleaming masterpiece of one full ton of solid gold! The rest are gilt wood, two inside of and three covering over, a granite sarcophagus. Finally the official seals are placed on the outer doors, the entrance-way is covered over with sand and the priests and mourners take their solemn leave. Tutankhamen is left to eternity. His silent, unknowing vigil will last through the lives of Moses, Alexander, Caesar and Jesus Christ. Constantine, Galileo, Columbus, Washington, Napoleon, Lincoln . . . all will live and die while King Tut lies hidden away. Not until an English archeologist scratches a hole in the door A.D. 1922 will a chink of light peep into the tomb and allow the world its first sight of the "glint of gold" in over 3000 years.

c. 1342   Soon after Tutankhamen's death Egypt's mighty 18th Dynasty comes to an end, and the empire begins its long decline. Not, however, until much is heard from a king named . . . Ramses.

c. 1330   Over 200 years have gone by since Joseph and his family came to Egypt, and his descendents are now in a pitiful condition; slaves of a system that knows and cares nothing about human beings as individuals of importance. Considered merely so many parts of a gigantic building machine, they either function or they die; they produce, or are punished until they produce more.

> And . . . Pharaoh commanded the taskmasters of the people . . . "You shall no longer give the people straw to make bricks, as heretofore; let them go and gather straw for themselves. But the number of bricks which they made heretofore you shall . . . by no means lessen . . .   EXODUS 5:6–8 RSV

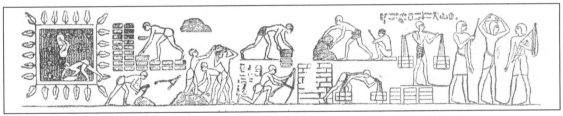

Making bricks from Egyptian wall paintings

Never have the Hebrews known what it is to have a land of their own, to be a nation to stand with other nations, to be done with servitude, free to serve and worship the ONE TRUE GOD of Abraham, Isaac and Jacob. Minds dulled by the last 200 years of slavery know only obedience through fear of punishment, and nothing about hope, courage, vision, faith, respect or loyalty through promise of greatness and love of God. They know one thing only, how to labor under the whip. And they have no leader, no man among them who could guide them out of Egypt; not one familiar with the royal court, its customs and procedures; how to get to the pharaoh and how to deal with him.

But in Pharaoh's OWN HOUSEHOLD there is one Hebrew who does not labor under the whip . . . the royal prince, Moses, found as a baby in a basket of bulrushes floating in the Nile, adopted by one of Pharaoh's, own daughters as her very own! Prince Moses' royal world is a world of luxury, wealth and absolute power, deeply ingrained and unquestioned over the centuries, a world concerned with monuments, not mankind. It is to this world that Moses finally realizes he does not belong and flees from it, eastward to the Sinai Desert and the land of Midian, a fugitive from Pharaoh's justice. Here he reconciles himself to his new condition; he is not an Egyptian prince, but a Hebrew, the son of Hebrew slaves. And here he remains among the descendents of Abraham. He lives their lives, learns their ways and worships their God; he raises a family and tends their flocks.

c. 1304   Ramses II is pharaoh, and his reign marks 67 years of glory for Egypt. It is the zenith of Egyptian history, the high point of its power and might. They are 67 gigantic years, for Ramses does nothing that is not gigantic: and it is as a builder that Ramses becomes a giant. Just as Cheops had been the mighty pyramid builder 1400 years ago, so now Ramses is the Temple Builder, his monuments lining the banks of the Nile for 200 miles, almost to the second cataract. The magnificent Abu Simbel is Ramses' creation, with its four 67-foot high statues of himself, seated, facing the Nile. Much of Luxor's engraved walls tell the story of his Hittite wars. The Ramesseum is a funerary temple to himself and to the god, Amon, where once stood the now fallen 75-foot, thousand ton pink granite statue. The overwhelming magnitude of Karnak includes a mile and a half Avenue of Sphinxes, gigantic pylons, courts, chapels, festival halls and the famous Hypostyle Hall, a virtual forest of 134 sandstone columns, each 65 feet high and 33 feet in circumference. Almost 300 years from now, the Greek historian, Herodotus, visiting Egypt, will write . . . .

Nowhere are there so many marvelous things, not in the whole world besides are there to be seen so many works of unspeakable greatness.   Herodotus, (See: 447 B.C.)

Ramses' statues show him in vigorous young manhood in the peak of condition, broad-shouldered, strong-limbed and slim waisted; and stone engravings throughout Egypt testify that Ramses does everything on a gigantic scale. They list, by name, 162 of his children!

c. 1290   Forty years have gone by since Moses fled Egypt to dwell in the land of the Midianites. He married Zipporah, daughter of the priest of Midian, and she bore him a son, whom he called Gershom for, he said, "I have been a stranger in a strange land." Moses tends his father-in-law's flock and, now, leading the flock in the wilderness west of Mount Horeb, Moses meets the Hebrew God . . . in the flaming midst of a fiery, burning bush. "PUT OFF THE SHOES FROM YOUR FEET, MOSES, FOR YOU ARE STANDING ON HOLY GROUND. I AM THE GOD OF YOUR FATHER, THE GOD OF ABRAHAM, ISAAC AND JACOB. I have seen the affliction of my people who are in Egypt. I know their sufferings and have heard their cry . . . AND I AM COME DOWN TO DELIVER THEM FROM THE HAND OF THE EGYPTIANS." Moses is in the presence of, not just any god, any one of Egypt's many cosmological gods; but THE God of creation, the transcendent, universal God; and Moses hides his face, for he is afraid to look upon God. "Come now therefore," God says to Moses, "and I will send thee unto Pharaoh, THAT THOU MAYEST BRING FORTH MY PEOPLE THE CHILDREN OF ISRAEL OUT OF EGYPT." But He has not a name, and Moses asks what He shall be called; and God says to Moses,

"I AM THAT I AM. . .

THUS SHALT THOU SAY UNTO THE CHILDREN OF ISRAEL, I AM hath sent me unto you. the Lord God of your fathers, the God of Abraham. Isaac. and Jacob; THIS IS MY NAME FOREVER, AND THIS IS MY MEMORIAL TO ALL GENERATIONS." But Moses is a reluctant servant, certain that nobody will believe him, a common man, slow of speech, with a stutter. Angry at being argued with, God says Moses WILL do His will; and Moses' brother, Aaron, will speak for him.

God warns Moses from the beginning that it will be no easy thing to convince Pharaoh to free 600,000 slaves* just for the asking. And, indeed, neither boils, frogs, locusts, hail, disease, flies nor blood in the Nile convince Pharaoh to part with his property . . . the Hebrew slaves. So God tells Moses, ". . . [a plague] will pass through the land of Egypt . . . and I will smite all the first born . . . both man and beast . . . on all the gods of the Hebrews will I execute judgement." But the plague "passes over" the homes of the Hebrews, for they had prepared for the night with sacrificial lambs and unleavened bread; and the Hebrews celebrate their first PASSOVER. God's instructions concerning the sacrifice had been detailed and explicit, for this sacrifice and ritual meal is to be a remembrance of Passover, a symbol of freedom for all time to come. The sacrificial lamb is to be the first born . . . without blemish, and . . .

Prophecy: . . . you shall not break a bone of it.   EXODUS 12:46 and JOHN 13:33,36 (See: A.D. 32, 3:00 P.M.)

c. 1290   The great king of Egypt, ruler of a mighty empire, concedes defeat, and Moses leads the Hebrews out of Egypt, past the ancient pyramids and up to the Red Sea (or 'Reed

(* NUMBERS 1:17–46. See also this book summary to NUMBERS, para. 1, 1290 B.C.) p.39

Sea," as modern scholarship believes it to have been.) Then God "hardens Pharaoh's heart" once more, so that "the Egyptians shall know that I am Lord," and Pharaoh and his army pursue the Hebrews. But ". . . the people of Israel go into the midst of the sea on dry ground," and Pharaoh's army is destroyed. And the Hebrews move on ". . . and the Lord goes before them by day in a pillar of cloud, to lead them the way; and by night in a pillar of fire, to give them light." On "the third new moon" after the Hebrews leave Egypt, they encamp in the wilderness before the mountain called Sinai, and Moses goes up to God on the mountain, and here God gives Moses . . . the LAW.

From this ragged mass of rabble, these wretched runaways from bondage and slavery, God announces that He expects much. He alone is their God, He alone will be worshipped, and HE WILL BE OBEYED.

EXODUS

Book of Law — Written in Hebrew,   c. ? to 600 B.C.

I AM THE LORD THY GOD . . . THOU SHALT HAVE NO OTHER GODS BEFORE ME. THOU SHALT NOT MAKE UNTO THEE ANY GRAVEN IMAGE . . . NOR BOW DOWN THYSELF TO THEM. THOU SHALT NOT TAKE THE NAME OF THE LORD THY GOD IN VAIN. REMEMBER THE SABBATH DAY, TO KEEP IT HOLY. HONOR THY FATHER AND THY MOTHER. THOU SHALT NOT KILL. THOU SHALT NOT COMMIT ADULTERY. THOU SHALT NOT STEAL. THOU SHALT NOT BEAR FALSE WITNESS. THOU SHALT NOT COVET.   EXODUS 20:1–17

With these words does the transcendent God usher in a new age in the world. Through all of history thus far, civilizations have (as in Mesopotamia) risen and fallen, risen and fallen, with no more meaning than one crop of grain replacing the one before, or (as in Egypt) with one pharaoh replacing another in a seemingly eternal monotony, one crisis after another, perhaps, but never serious enough to remake or replace the system. And the universal concept (found everywhere from what is today called "China" to "America")of mankind's role in the world order is the recognition, acknowledgement and worship of a vast pantheon of cosmological gods who function in an orderly cosmos.

In Mesopotamia, those gods are seen in the zodiac signs in the sky, the movements of the planets . . . sun, moon and stars, and in the invisible forces behind them in hierarchal regression down to earthly city-states which are owned by the gods and managed by the gods' earthly administrator . . . the king. In Egypt, the gods are "manifest" in cosmological things and beings: cows, cats and crocodiles, the sun disc and the moon; earthly animals and objects through which the god is seen. Out of death (the desert) the Nile brings life (its yearly flood and enriching silt.) And the gods' supreme earthly manifestation is Egypt's king, the pharaoh. All these cosmological gods are remote from mankind, uninterested in its fate or well-being, and perform their functions because the cosmos is an orderly place and their actions coincide and co-exist with that order.

Now, with the Hebrew experience of Moses and the Exodus, a new people emerge on the world stage, a new consciousness; a quantitatively higher spiritual order. For the Hebrew sojourn in the desert is not merely an end in itself, a simple running away, from one kind of misery to another; slavery in Egypt to . . . what? Starvation in the desert? It is, rather a giant leap forward, a forty-year refining of a crude ore. For it is in the in the desert that the Hebrews are transformed. Here their leader, Moses, meets, listens to, accepts and submits to the one, true, universal and transcendent God, the Creator of the World, the Father of all mankind and the source of all righteousness. Instead of worshipping created THINGS, the Hebrews will worship the CREATOR of those things. And this God is NOT remote from or unapproachable to man; but, rather, the opposite. He cares about His creation; takes part in their lives, acts His part in their history, listens and responds to them, and most of all, reveals Himself to them, His nature, His purpose and His being. And in Moses' acceptance of and submission to this God, He gains for the Hebrews a true freedom, to become a new type of people, His "chosen" people. Thus, while God will overlook the sins of their neighbors, He will not overlook theirs; for they, and they alone, are His CHOSEN PEOPLE, and they have been chosen, not only to receive, but to GIVE. Oh, they will not remain "pure," they very often will not live up to God's standards, and when they fall, just like other nations, they will fall with a mighty crash. But, by then, they will have recorded in detail, in order, and in fact, for all the world to read, the opening chapters of their *Historia Sacra*, their sacred history, their history-under-God, the first people in the world to do so.

Thousands upon thousands of impressed clay tablets, cylinder seals, engraved stones, papyrus manuscripts, tomb paintings and even pottery shards will be found in future years (and are still being found) which reveal in countless disassociated ways all sorts of information about every culture in the ancient world to those archeologists learned enough to painstakingly piece together their puzzles. But, of all the cultures, or civilizations, in the world to this time, Israel alone, because of Moses, the Exodus and the desert, will write and leave behind, an orderly record, a thought-out, chronological, year-by-year, event-by-event, person-by-person *Historia Sacra*, a history-under-God. And in the recording of these monumental events is the Chosen People's significance revealed; for the truth which they discover in the desert would soon die in the desert, as well, should they not produce that work which will become the first five books of the Bible, the TORAH, the LAW. And the backbone of that LAW, that gives it nobility and justification, that transcends every work of man, is that short section called the TEN COMMANDMENTS, which shall be, not merely a cultural guide-book for the Hebrews only, but a spiritual direction for all mankind forevermore. For, in a world in which human beings are mere expendable pawns in an elite power struggle amongst a cosmic hierarchy, the Ten Commandments teach the sanctity of every human life, that one must not be taken from another by murder, adultery or deceit; it teaches the blessings of family unity under the primacy of father and mother; it teaches the right to ownership of private property, that one person must not steal or covet that which another rightfully owns; and mostly it teaches that all of this must be observed under divine guidance and guidelines, honoring both His day and His name, for laws laid down by man can be rescinded by man, but laws ordained by God are eternal. Therefore, the Omnipotent God who created the universe must also be the sole author of its governance. The "chosen people," then, are to be that people through whom, eventually, God's Great Plan will be fulfilled.

The book of EXODUS belongs to that greatest of all Hebrews, Moses. It is his own personal story and the story of what he did for God and for the Hebrews. Born at a time when the pharaoh ordered the death of all Hebrew boy babies to slow down the alarming increase in their numbers, Moses was found by one of Pharaoh's own daughters and reared as an Egyptian prince. He was given an education as fine as any prince, instructed, according to ACTS 7:22, in "all the wisdom of the Egyptians." He was, then, a man of learning and wisdom, and understood the administration of justice. His high position at court undoubtedly brought him into contact with emissaries from other lands as well, including those cunieform-writing countries whose clay tablets tell of floods, arks and towers. Although some modern historians deny Moses' reality, and assign the writing of the LAW to a much later time, when there would "finally be writing," thousands of recent archeological discoveries bear out, beyond doubt, that alphabetical writing (as opposed to priestly hieroglyphic pictographs) was widely known by this time: which underscores the book of ACTS' assertion that this noble prince of Ramses' royal court was, indeed, highly skilled and broadly educated; and many other scholars believe that, not only was Moses a living, historical figure but, probably one of history's towering giants . . . who did exactly what the Bible says he did. Abraham was one of history's towering figures, the patriarch of his people; but Abraham's understanding of God was as a family God for their own clan to worship and serve. With Moses came the conception of God as UNIVERSAL; the God of the Israelites, yes, but of all mankind as well, and not only its God to worship, but its CREATOR from whom all blessings flow, all life and liberty and the "pursuit of happiness." With the Ten Commandments of Moses does the concept arise of God-given inalienable rights.

But the exact date of the Exodus from Egypt is not known, nor is it known with which pharaoh Moses had to contend. Most scholars believe it was Ramses II, the Great, the temple builder. Others say Amenhotep II, who ruled just after Thutmose; and still others say Ramses' son Merneptah; and, indeed, a carved stone from his reign, called the *Merneptah Stele* (see: 1230 B.C.) mentions "Israelites," the only Egyptian inscription to do so. Though Egypt, itself, apparently considered the exodus too unimportant to ever mention in writing, it would prove vastly different to the world at large without the Exodus. But then, the Egyptians were loathe to record their failures, which the ignominious loss of so many slaves would have been, and the *Merneptah Stele* refers to them, not as wandering runaways, but as "Israelites," an ALREADY SETTLED PEOPLE, an existing nation . . . which they are not at this time. One other interesting coincidence which points to Ramses II, concerns another of his giant building projects; the construction of a system of canals to join the Nile Delta with the north end of the Red Sea . . . at the very route the Hebrews would soon follow. Taking some part in the planning and/or carrying out of Ramses' canal project would certainly have required minds ". . . instructed in all the wisdom of the Egyptians."

Whoever Moses' pharaoh was then, Egypt—and that pharaoh—considered himself "son of god," son, that is, of Egypt's god, the chief god of many gods. But Moses had met the transcendent God, YAWEH, on the mountain; knew that he was meeting something infinitely greater than all of Egypt's gods; and that THAT God, who pronounced Himself "I AM THAT I AM," proclaimed that HIS son, HIS first-born was ISRAEL; and that He wanted Israel FREE . . . to serve Him.

c. 1290   God instructs Moses to ". . . speak unto the children of Israel, that they bring me an offering. And let them make me a sanctuary; that I may dwell among them . . ." an ARK, a very special Ark, to His own specifications, in which the sacred tablets of LAW are to be

kept, and which the Hebrews must carry with them wherever they go; a sanctuary in which He will reside, with a Mercy Seat from above which He will speak. It is to be the Ark of God's Covenant with the Hebrews. But having gotten them out of Egypt is only the beginning of Moses' many trials, his people proving faithless and fickle within the month, while he is still on the mountain with God. They had fashioned a golden calf (like the one pictured from the 2nd millennium of gilded bronze found at Byblos in our own time) around which they danced and sang, and "Moses' anger waxed hot and he brake the tablets beneath the mount."

The Byblos Calf

Moses' brother, Aaron, who had spoken for him before Pharaoh, is appointed the Hebrews' chief priest, and the family of LEVI is given its task:

LEVITICUS

Book of Law — Written in Hebrew,   c. ? to 600 B.C.

"And the LORD called unto Moses . . . saying . . . Speak unto the children of Israel . . ." Thus opens the book of LEVITICUS. One of the twelve "tribes" of Israel was that of Levi, whose family, or tribe, was set apart to be priests of God. Their role in the scheme of things, is clearly drawn out in LEVITICUS.

Many a good intention to "read the Bible through from front to back" has ground to a halt in the ponderous pages of LEVITICUS, for here is the nitty-gritty of the covenant. True, God gave Moses the LAW on Mount Sinai, but the fine points of its rewards and punishments, duties and strictures, do's and don'ts were drawn out in day-by-day confrontations. Time and again LEVITICUS (and NUMBERS, to follow) relates how 'God said to Moses, "Say to the people of Israel . . ." One by one God ordered what He wanted in sacrificial offerings and ceremonial blessings, and clean and unclean animals and people.

In chapter after chapter, the Hebrews' new way of life is drawn out for them in laws of behavior and offerings to God: health laws, childbirth laws, plague, leprosy, defilement and sacrifice laws; laws for sanctification, oaths and tithes. There are laws regulating the meat offering, the peace, sin and trespass offerings. There are instructions for the High Priest Aaron, and for his successors, what they shall do and what wear; for the Day of Atonement, the Holy Place, the Year of the Jubilee, and for keeping the Sabbath. In our time, many of these ancient laws seem coarse and even cruel, but they were given to an ignorant people who had no background but slavery; no education, no experience in ordering their own lives or governing the lives of others; and, mostly, no knowledge of how to worship God; and every last detail of behavior had to be drawn out for them.

God tells the Hebrews, "If ye walk in my statutes, and keep my commandments . . . I will have respect unto you . . . and establish my covenant with you . . . but if ye will not harken unto me . . . I will make your cities waste, and bring your sanctuaries unto desolation . . ." But even then, God says, He will not cast them off, utterly, nor break HIS part of the covenant, "for I am the Lord their God."

The original Hebrew language of the Old Testament calls God by several names, the most common being the unpronounceable YHWH, or Yahweh, later Jehovah. Another, "Adonai," means "Lord." "Elohim" resembles the Semitic EL, as in Isra-el and Beth-el, and means "divinity." "Shaddai" suggests a God who lives atop the mountains; and much later, in PSALMS, will there be found the Lord Sabaoth, or "Lord of Hosts." Parts of LEVITICUS (like GENESIS, EXODUS, and NUMBERS and DEUTERONOMY, to follow) are very ancient writings, dating back, possibly, to Moses himself; while portions are later additions which scholars know today as documents "E" for Elohist (those writings which call God Elohim), "J" or Jahwist (those that call Him YHWH or Jahweh), and "P" and "D" for Priestly and Deuteronomist (parts added much later by priests and historians.) The last chapters of LEVITICUS are called the Holiness Code for their Laws on justice and brotherly love . . . ideas new to mankind. Thirteen hundred years from now Jesus of Nazareth will draw His "Second Great Commandment" from LEVITICUS 19:18, *"THOU SHALT LOVE THY NEIGHBOR AS THYSELF."*

Nearly 3000 years from now a new nation called the United States of America, founded under God and upon His precepts, will ring out a song of freedom on a LIBERTY BELL engraved with these words from LEVITICUS:

> *Proclaim liberty throughout all the land unto*
> *all the inhabitants thereof. 25:10*

c. 1290–1250?   The exiles wander forty years in the wilderness before God allows them to come to the "Promised Land," and the older
generation, who had known nothing but slavery and submission, is
replaced by a new generation of freedmen and warriors. Now, the
first great census or numbering, is done in the wilderness, and
recorded in the book of NUMBERS.

NUMBERS

Book of Law — Written in Hebrew,   c. ? to 600 B.C.

The title NUMBERS refers to a census, or numbering, of the Hebrews which was
done soon after they left Sinai. The figures are awesome: 630,000 persons all set out together in a marvelously choreographed crusade. It makes a wonderful movie. But while
the Hebrew word, *elef,* used in the writing of NUMBERS does, indeed, mean "thousand,"
it also means "clans" or "families," so the 630 *elef* could mean 630 families or clans, a
more reasonable figure, understandably little noticed and never noted by the Egyptians.

Most of the book tells of the forty year sojourn in the wilderness; and, finally, of their
arrival in the Promised Land; of Moses' appointed spies returning from their mission to
report of a land "flowing with milk and honey, but with great cities, also, heavily fortified," and finally, of how the holy ARK of the Covenant was carried before them in their
journeying, and of the care it received from the Levite priests.

If LEVITICUS made tedious reading, NUMBERS is awesome, for its solemn recitation of the numbering of the Twelve Tribes: "The sons of Judah were . . ." and "The sons
of Benjamin were . . ." and "The sons of Dan were . . ." And yet, NUMBERS has lighter
moments also, as in the story of Balaam and his ass, and their encounter with a frighten-

ing, sword-wielding angel, which only the
ass could see and turn away from, while
Balaam beat it for its turning away. That
story is a good place to consider God's angels who appear so often in the Old Testament; imposing, masculine, militant beings
of "terrible countenance," wrestling and
brandishing swords, bringing death, destruction and judgement as often as they
bring guidance, protection, instruction and
deliverance. It is no wonder that the angels
who announce the birth of Jesus of Nazareth to shepherds in the field, 1200 years

Balaam's Ass

from now, will begin their announcement, "Fear not, for I bring you great . . . joy . . ." Not until Medieval/Renaissance/Baroque artists and architects remodel angels into chubby, curly-haired children, romantic little cherubs, will popular belief in these most important messengers of God be undermined.

NUMBERS also has some beautiful and familiar moments, well-loved for centuries. Six hundred years from now, at about 700 B.C. an unknown silversmith will etch some Hebrew words on to a tiny silver scroll, possibly a talisman of some sort, worn as a locket. It will somehow come to be buried in a mass grave in the Hinnom Valley just outside Jerusalem, and lay there for over 2600 more years until an Israeli archeologist finds it in A.D. 1979. Its translation will be awesome and amazing, for on the scroll are fragments of three verses from the book of NUMBERS:

The Silver Scroll

> The LORD bless thee, and keep thee: The LORD make has face shine upon thee, and be gracious unto thee: The LORD lift up his countenance upon thee and give thee peace.   NUMBERS 6:24–26

It is the oldest artifact ever found containing that word too sacred for the Hebrews even to pronounce: YHWH or Yahweh, the Hebrew word for God, or LORD.

By now, the Hebrews are doing little but grumbling and lamenting their supposed ill-fortune, having nothing to eat but manna every day, remembering ". . . the fish which we did eat in Egypt freely, the cucumbers, melons . . . leeks . . . onions, and . . . garlic." In frustration and anger at his complaining people, Moses offers himself and his life as an intercession between God and the mob of unruly ingrates, crying ". . . why hast thou dealt ill with thy servant . . . that thou dost lay the burden of all this people upon me?" But Moses is special to God who defends him, saying, "I make myself known to [others] in a vision, but with Moses I speak mouth to mouth, clearly." Not yet is it time for one man to sacrifice Himself for all people.

c. 1286   The Hittite empire covers all of Asia Minor and Syria, its capital city, Hattusas, the center of its thriving iron industry. Now, Pharaoh Ramses' expansionist ambitions bring his forces face to face with those of King Muatallish the Hittite at Kadesh on the north-Syrian Orontes River. It is an epic confrontation that brings devastating consequences. The Hittite forces alone, number 3500 three-man chariots and 8000 foot soldiers, who fight with a deadly arsenal of iron weapons. Both sides claim victory, and Ramses brags (on a carved stone, extant today) that he saved his army from disaster by winning the battle . . . single handed! Whoever won, the two kings eventually sign a peace treaty—the world's first—the Hittite copy engraved on a silver tablet, and the Egyptian on the temple walls at Karnak, maintaining that their peace . . . ". . . is better than the peace . . . which was formerly in the land . . ." Both copies begin with a preamble, and have sections relating to their former and present conditions, their renunciation of refugees and fugitives, and a defense alliance with each other against hostile outsiders:

> The EGYPTIAN copy: Behold . . . the Great Prince of Hatti, has set himself in a regulation . . . beginning from this day, to cause that good peace and brotherhood occur between us . . . Hostilities shall not occur between them forever.
>
> The HITTITE copy: [Ramses] the great king . . . of the land of Egypt, has entered into a treaty [written] upon a silver tablet with . . . the king of the Hatti land, [his] brother, [from] this [da]y on to establish good peace (and) good brotherhood be[tween us] forever. He is a brother [to me] and I am a brother to him and at peace with him forever.
>
> Pritchard: Ancient Near Eastern Texts (ANET)

1250   Both the Egyptian and Hittite empires are suffering major reversals, thanks, in part, to their mutual losses at that great, wasteful battle at Kadesh. Economies in chaos, manpower decimated, and energies drained, they are now faced with a new threat more grave than any before. Just as hordes of fearsome, plundering Viking Norsemen will swoop down in longboats out of a frozen north to terrorize Europe and England 2000 years hence, so also, do waves of invading foreigners come, now, from the east and north, from the farthest reaches of Asia Minor and the Aegean islands; primitive, warlike and conquering. So, now, down and across the Mediterranean, do the SEA PEOPLES begin to invade the pages of history.

. . . The book of DEUTERONOMY completes the Hebrew TORAH, the last of the five books of LAW.

DEUTERONOMY

Book of Law — Written in Hebrew, c. ? to 600 B.C.

"And it came to pass in the fortieth year, in the eleventh month, on the first day of the month, that Moses spoke to the children of Israel, according unto all that the LORD had given him . . ." DEUTERONOMY, or the "Second Law," is Moses' farewell to his people, and a final appeal to them to love God and each other, to obey the LAW and to expect discipline when they break it, ". . . as a loving father disciplines his son." He warns them not to put the LORD to the test. "You were chosen," Moses says, "not because you were many, for you are few; not because you are good, for you are stubborn and rebellious; but because He loves you, and He will not forsake you because He is faithful to His promise." Then Moses instructs them in that most important ceremony, Passover:

> When your sons ask you in time to come, "What is the meaning of all these testimonies, statutes and ordinances?" you are to answer: "We were Pharaoh's slaves in Egypt, and the Lord has brought us out with a mighty hand, and gave us the land as he promised, and commands us to keep His commandments." DEUTERONOMY 6:20, 21

The Jewish "Shema" is found in chapter six, also, that beautiful verse of Jewish litany which every Jew recites daily, and hopes will be his last words:

> Hear, O Israel, the Lord our God is one Lord.   6:4

DEUTERONOMY is written in the literary form of a speech given by Moses in his old age, to the Hebrews facing a new and intimidating age. It is a re-statement of all that had gone before, divided into three well-defined sections: the exodus, the desert, and the covenant. It finds the Hebrews encamped "beyond the Jordan in the wilderness," already preparing for their first assault on the Canaanite defenders of this "promised land." In his final address, Moses tells of future kings for Israel, a Holy Temple and a permanent sanctuary for God in a Holy City; indeed, the need for one centralized place of worship is one of his major concerns. He, also, warns the Hebrews not to be seduced by the Canaanite gods they will find in their new land . . . even while knowing it is sure to happen.

One copy of DEUTERONOMY is thought to have been the book found in the rubble of the Temple (ransacked and looted by the evil King Manasseh) during the time of the good King Josiah (See: 621 B.C.) and that it inspired him to a restoration of the true faith after many years of terrible abuse. It is also thought that much of DEUTERONOMY was actually written at a later time than this (perhaps in Josiah's time), although much of its material did, in fact, originate with Moses, himself, as many of its laws are elementary and primitive, as they would have been in Moses' time, governing a primitive people. In judicial matters, they let the punishment fit the crime, even as did Hammurabi's code; and in matters domestic, they teach the most elementary methods:

> . . . thine eye shall not pity; but life shall go for life, eye for eye, tooth for tooth, hand for hand, foot for foot. 19:21 * Thou shalt not sow thy vineyard with divers seeds lest [each of them] be defiled. 22:9 * Thou shalt not plow with an ox and an ass together. 22:10

Just as the "Holiness Code" of LEVITICUS commands love for thy neighbor "as for thyself," so does DEUTERONOMY command charity . . . in words easily adaptable to any age, including our own . . .

> When thou gatherest the grapes of the vineyard, thou shalt not glean it afterward: [that] shall be [left] for the stranger, for the fatherless, and for the widow.   24:21

Thirteen hundred years from now, confronted by the devil in the wilderness, Jesus of Nazareth will rebuke him, quoting from DEUTERONOMY:

> Ye shall not tempt the LORD your God.   6:16

And to a Pharisee's sly questioning in His last week on earth, Jesus will answer boldly that the First and Great Commandment is:

> THOU SHALT LOVE THE LORD THY GOD WITH ALL THINE HEART, AND WITH ALL THY SOUL, AND WITH ALL THY MIND.   DEUTERONOMY 6:5 (. . . this is the first and great commandment. And the second is like unto it, THOU SHALT LOVE THY NEIGHBOR AS THYSELF.   MATTHEW 22:35–39, from LEVITICUS 19:18)

c. 1250 Moses dies, whom "the LORD knew face to face," and Joshua becomes the Hebrews' new commander. God allows Moses to look across the Jordan River from Mount Pisgah to the Promised Land . . . as far as the eye could see. But warriors are needed now and, even though Moses' "eye was not dim, nor his natural force abated," he dies an old, old man, and is buried, not in a giant pyramid, nor in a gold-laden tomb . . . but in a private, quiet spot, ". . . a place that no man knows."

The

PROMISED LAND

The Promised Land

Israel, the land of the Jews, seems to many people a remote, far-away little dot of desert. Vitally important emotionally and strategically to the Jews—and, indeed, in its own way to the rest of the world—it has always been a "different" sort of land, and hardly the center of the world. This was strictly not so in the early Bible times, and especially not so now in the days of Joshua, the Judges, David and Solomon, and the succession of kings who will rule for the next 200 years. Indeed, Israel is now a most important little patch of land. In fact, it is the very center of the "world."

A quick glance at a map will tell why. It is, at this time, the ONLY ROUTE—a bridge, so to speak—between the two major civilizations in the awakening world. History's first great civilization, Sumer (in later years called Assyria, Babylonia and Persia; today Iraq) is flourishing to the north-east of Israel, and the second, Egypt, to its south-west. These two civilizations will contend with and make war on each other continually for centuries now . . . and Israel is strung out right in the middle.

On one side of Israel is the "Great Sea," the Mediterranean, impassable before the invention of great ships and hazardous even after. On the other side lies the great Arabian Desert—impassable (in olden ways) to this day. Thus little Israel is the lane used by all the traffic in the world, whether the traffic goes north or south, whether it passes in peaceful commerce or in warlike conquest, it passes through Israel. Much later, with the rise of Greece to the north and Rome far west, Israel's importance will dwindle to that of a desert outpost, but for now, he who holds Israel, holds the key to the world's transportation, trade, power and . . . wealth.

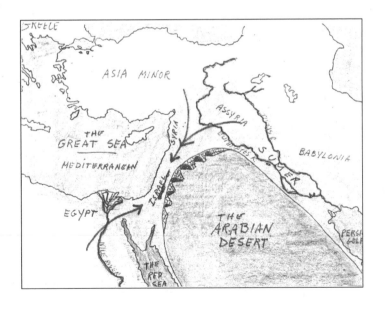

Joshua "fought the battle. . ."

c. 1250, on.   God now commands the able young warrior, Joshua, to lead this new generation of "Israelites" across the Jordan River to begin the conquest of Canaan. But the task is neither easy nor fast, and when Joshua "fights the battle of Jericho," and the "walls come a-tumbling down," it is only the beginning of many years of bitter struggle. Joshua suffers his first, and only, defeat in the battle for the city of Ai ". . . and rends his clothes, and falls upon his face . . . and puts dust upon his head." In a massive retaliation he burns the city and hangs the king. Then, city after city falls before his, and God's, might: Lachish, Gezer, Eglon, Hebron, Hazor and Azekah. And each one he smites . . . with the edge of the sword . . . and the kings thereof he utterly destroys. And Joshua takes the whole land . . . and gives it for an inheritance unto Israel . . ." (Modern archeology has found much evidence of Joshua's presence and his having done pretty much what the Bible says he did.) Then the land is apportioned to the twelve tribes. Even though the conquest is not yet complete, each tribe receives a specific area with set borders . . . all except Levi, whose sons are priests of God. They receive certain cities, among which are "cities of refuge" where accused persons may await judgement in safety. And the book of JOSHUA is begun . . .

JOSHUA

Book of History — Written in Hebrew,   c. 900–600 B.C.

Here, in the pages of JOSHUA, does the "great leap forward" make its mighty transformation, from the myriad cosmological gods of Egypt and Mesopotamia, to the reality of the Hebrew's One, True, Transcendent, Omnipotent God; for hardly can a page be turned without God's presence felt, His advice sought, His help given. "The Lord your God, he is the God in heaven above, and in earth beneath," Joshua tells his people. He acknowledges God's presence in making the sun to stand still and the moon to stay; and time after time the book says "The LORD spoke unto Joshua . . ." No more are animals and "things" to be worshipped, but only He who created animals and things, who created the universe, He who rules it and shall rule it forever.

The Hebrews' conception, at this time, of the God of Joshua is a god of war and conquest; leading them into battle, urging them on; indeed, even planning their strategy . . . a far cry from a God of mercy, charity and love. But that understanding will come in time. Now the Hebrews have to have their own land, and they have to fight for it. They need to learn that they will be winners when they are faithful to God and losers when they are not. While God does, indeed, appear in JOSHUA as a ruthless, avenging "commander-in-chief" so to speak, these very attributes point out dramatically that THIS God, Yahweh, the ALMIGHTY God, is a LIVING participant in history. Unlike the Egyptian and Mesopotamian gods, who merely "represent" or manifest things or beings, Israel's God speaks to His people, listens to them, directs them, rewards and punishes them, a concept totally new in the world. And He demands loyalty; He is a "jealous" God, and in spite of His wrathful aspect, a peace-loving servant, which He will remain from now on.

The stone altar
from Mt. Ebal

Before he died, Moses had charged Joshua (DEUT. 27:4–8) and the people that ". . . on the day when ye shall pass over Jordan . . . thou shalt set thee up great (uncut) stones [on] Mount Ebal, and . . . plaster them with plaster . . . and . . . build an altar unto the LORD thy God . . . and offer burnt offerings thereon . . ." And so they do. (JOSH 8:30,31) Thirty two hundred years from now, in A.D. 1982, an Israeli archeologist, uncovering a curious mound of rocks on Mount Ebal, will unearth just such an altar, matching exactly Moses' specifications, filled with earth, stones, the bones of sacrificial animals and a tiny Egyptian scarab, one Hebrew's momento from an earlier time in a far-away land.

Read as one, JOSHUA and the next five books (JUDGES, SAMUEL I and II, and KINGS I and II) make up a contiguous history of Israel from its first conquest BY the Hebrews to create for themselves a homeland, to the last conquest OF the Hebrews by a victorious Babylon, 600 years later. Joshua ruled Israel 40 years, and just before he "went the way of all the earth," he "made a covenant with the people," and charged them:

> Now therefore fear the LORD and serve Him in sincerity and in faithfulness; put away [all others.] And if you be unwilling to serve the LORD, choose this day whom you will serve, those of your fathers beyond the river or those in whose land you now dwell; but as for me and my house . . . WE WILL SERVE THE LORD.   24:14,15

c. 1230   Ramses' son, Merneptah, is Egypt's pharaoh, already up in years. His problems are enormous, as . . .

. . . great migrations of those new people, nomads of the water that the Egyptians call "Sea Peoples" swoop down and across the Mediterranean lands: Dorians, Ionians, Arkadians, Acheans, Sardinians, Sicilians, Philistines; by the thousands they come, primitive, warlike, destructive and conquering, to occupy Crete, Greece, Asia Minor, Syria and Israel. Where they come from or who they are is mostly unknown, but their coming will wreak havoc and destruction far and wide, and the "bridge" that is Israel makes it, once again, a battlefield, as the Sea Peoples move

Egyptian guard leading Sea Peoples & Semites,
from a Temple of Ramses at Medinet

down to face Egypt. After one confrontation, Merneptah gains a victory over the Sea Peoples—and over "Israel"—and a hymn of triumph is engraved on a black granite *stele* at Thebes. It is, today, in the Cairo Museum, the first mention of a SETTLED PEOPLE Israel in Egyptian hieroglyphics, and the foremost evidence for placing the Exodus before Merneptah's time—in the reign of Ramses.

> Great rejoicing has risen in Egypt . . . the victories . . . which Merneptah wrought. How beloved he is, the victorious ruler! Canaan is plundered, Ashkelon taken, Gezer captured, Israel lies desolate, its seed is no more . . . The *Merneptah Stele*, Cairo Museum, NO. 34025

Carved in low relief on an outer wall of the great Temple of Karnak at Thebes, on building blocks adjoining the Ramses/Hittite peace treaty, are scenes long thought to be of that famous battle of Kadesh. Some recent archeological study, however, suggests that the accompanying text had long ago been tampered with, and that the Pharaoh pictured is not Ramses, but Merneptah, and that the cities shown under siege are not Hittite cities but Canaan, Ashkelon, Gezer and ISRAEL! If the study is correct, the bas relief and the Merneptah *stele* are double—Egyptian—proof that there was a settled people, Israel, in the "promised land" by this time.

The Merneptah Stele

But Merneptah's success is short-lived and new waves of Sea Peoples advance . . . and drive out old kingdoms before them. The Hittite kingdom is one that falls before the onrush, and becomes totally forgotten by history . . . except for its inclusion in the Bible. It is replaced by one that will be remembered as . . . Trojan . . .

1194   Prince Paris of Troy goes to Greece to visit King Menelaus, falls in love with and carries away "the most beautiful of women," Menelaus' own wife, Helen. In a fury, Menelaus and the Greeks declare vengeance and their mightiest warriors set sail for Troy. Agamemnon, king of golden Mycenae with its fabled Lion Gate, and brother of the wronged king, becomes commander of the Greeks and leads a siege of the city. Achilles, "bravest of the brave," descendent of the "king of the gods," Zeus himself, is an unconquerable, deathless hero . . . but for one vulnerable spot on his heel. An arrow from Paris' bow will find that spot someday. Ajax, second in bravery only to Achilles, is handsome and bold. He will go mad when Achilles dies and kill himself in that madness; and Ulysses, king of Ithaca, a reluctant hero, will win the war with his wits.

For ten years the siege goes on and the men of Troy fight to hold their city: Prince Aeneas who will feature in another love story some day; noble Hector, greatest of the Trojans; Prince Paris, himself, whom neither side respects; wise old Nestor of Pylos, commanding from the sidelines; and Troy's own King Priam, venerable in age, but great of heart and courageous still. In future ages many tales will be told of deeds of valor and honor that the warriors perform . . . and of the tragedies they suffer as well.

1184   Finally, Ulysses designs a great wooden statue—a Trojan horse—and presents it as a gift to the people of Troy. During the

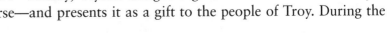

night he and his men emerge from a secret door, throw open the city gates and let in the conquering Greeks. The city is completely destroyed. History, or imagination? Apparently part of both. The ruins of Troy do, indeed, exist, unearthed in A.D. 1872, and appear to have been ruined, at least in part, by war. Nine successive cities of Troy have left remains on the hill now called Hyssarlik; the sixth apparently that of the Trojan War. The characters in the drama? Long thought only mythical, modern scholarship accepts many of them now as historical. The excavations of the many sites of the story are too convincing to be denied: Hittite cuneiform tablets mention the same names as those of the war; Nestor's Pylos was found the first day of the dig only inches beneath the soil; and Agamemnon's magnificent golden Mycenae has yielded up many secrets including a warrior's magnificent armor and breastplate just as described by Homer. Mycenae's unique beehive-shaped tombs possibly held the remains of the king himself, and his faithless wife, Clytemnystra. The beautiful Helen? No one knows. History concedes that the Myceneans were, in fact, little more than pirates, engaged frequently and profitably in raiding neighboring city-states for their riches . . . and their women, whom they put to labor in their fields, and call "women of Asia." Almost 400 years from now, the poet, Homer, will sing the exploits of the Trojan War in his sagas, the ILIAD and the ODYSSEY, and a thousand years hence, Ulysses' Trojan Horse will be remembered in a Roman AENEID, also.

> I fear the Greeks, even when bearing gifts.　　Virgil, (See: 30 B.C.)

c. 1160　The Hebrews are not alone in their fight for Canaan. The Sea Peoples called Philistines sweep down the eastern Mediterranean coast, plundering as they go, and settle along the Gaza strip. Ignorant, coarse and crude, the Philistines are talented in one thing: making money, lots of money, from trading, textiles, pottery and iron. Uncultured and scornful of learning, over the years the Philistine tendency to judge greatness by wealth and wisdom by riches, will gain them a reputation as money-grubbing illiterates. Almost 1300 years from now the Roman Empire, occupiers and ruthless destroyers of the "Promised Land" will, as a final insult and humiliation, brand the Jews with the Philistine name, and label a defeated Judea . . . Palestine.

On their way down the coast the Philistines had learned the secret of iron making from the Hittites and now guard it jealously. No other nation will learn how to produce weapons of war from THEM, and anyone else wanting iron tools for commerce and agriculture will pay dearly, iron sometimes bringing 40 times the price of silver!

As the nomad Israelites settle into their new land, albeit slowly and painfully, they begin to learn other things from their new neighbors, as well; the art of farming . . . and of worshipping the gods of fertility. The gods of the Philistines are the Babylonian Baal-zebub, or "master," Ashtaroth, goddess of love and war, and the chief Philistine god, Dagon. Those of the Amonites and Canaanites, in whose land Israel now dwells, are Dagon's son, the Storm God, Baal, his consort Ashtar, and numerous other separate-functioned household "baals." Baal worship is celebrated with weird rituals and sacrifices, including human; and that of Ashtar demands sexual license, her temples peopled

Egyptian
faience of a
Philistine Priest

with cult prostitutes, male and female. Temple prostitution is considered an obligation and an honor, for Baal worshippers do not expect morality or good examples from their gods. They expect fertility; fertile fields, rivers and orchards . . . and fertile women. In a world where one plague, drought or flood can wipe out entire peoples, how else can the race propagate and flourish? Baal worship began as a fertility rite intended to ensure a rich harvest of crops, cattle and sheep, but over the years has become lewd and lascivious, the unnatural acts of its cult prostitutes meant to inspire Baal and Ashtar to mate; and its worshippers commit acts of degradation and the sacrifice of children in flames. And the book of JUDGES says ". . . the people of Israel did what was evil in the sight of the LORD and forsook the LORD . . . and served the baals . . . and THE LORD RAISED UP JUDGES . . ."

JUDGES

Book of History — Written in Hebrew, c. 900–600 B.C.

"In those days there was no king in Israel; every man did what was right in his own eyes." Thus relates the second book of the history of the nation Israel. Near chaos with every tribe going its own way, unmanageable as a whole, Israel was beset at various times by the Moabites, Canaanites, Midianites, Amonites and the greatest threat of all, the Philistines. For almost 200 years after Joshua, in times of crisis "the LORD raised up judges." Religious leaders in a fashion, the judges were, also, military strongmen, folk heroes, almost, of the several tribes who appeared on the scene just long enough to "deliver" the Israelites from their current threat:

Othneil, renowned for his bravery, "brought them back to Yahweh," and "the land had rest for 40 years." Ehud, a "left-handed man" presented tribute to the king of Moab . . . and a two-edged sword in his fat belly. Deborah, prophetess and only woman judge, defeated "all the army" of Sisera the Canaanite, who fled and received for his reward a soft bed, warm cover, drink of milk . . . and a tent peg through his skull. Gideon's terrified people fled into the hills when the Midianites "came like locusts, with camels beyond number," the first ever seen in battle. But Gideon's select 300, armed with pottery, trumpets and a war cry, routed the horde ". . . and the land had rest for 40 years." Jephthah subdued the Amonites "with a very great slaughter" but paid the price of his own daughter because of a vow. And Samson, as naive as he was heroic, could outwit the Philistines with riddles, destroy their crops with foxes, kill them by the score "with the jawbone of an ass" and judge Israel for 20 years, but was no match for women, and his love for Delilah the Philistine brought about his own destruction as well as theirs.

Samson's Destruction

The writers of JUDGES made it very plain that Israel's setbacks happened when the people turned their backs on God, which they did, often, for the Philistine baals were actual, tangible objects that could be held and felt, and they promised plentiful crops and harvests; while Yahweh was invisible, inscrutable, remote and mysterious. The writers, also, made no effort to cover up the numerous dirty deeds of the judges nor apologize for their roguish behavior. Written down fragmentarily over the years as events happened, the book of JUDGES (like JOSHUA) is thought not to have been completed in present form until just before 600 B.C.

1100   Some progress and much expansion mark the Middle-east, as . . .

. . . The Egyptians increase their knowledge of physics, invent a siphon, and begin to use perfume . . .

. . . The Phoenicians are sailing their cedars-of-Lebanon ships on trading journeys as far south as the east coast of Africa . . .

. . . One group of the invading Sea Peoples called Dorians bring to a tragic end the "Heroic Age" and the brilliant civilizations that were Minoan and Mycenaean. Ignorant, unskilled and warlike, the Dorians destroy and burn everything before them; the fabulous palaces, cities and engineering marvels; drive out the unfortunate residents who flee in terror to places such as those someday to be called Athens and Sparta; and usher in a DARK AGE for Greece. While . . .

. . . The Philistine threat to Israel grows greater by the day, and the patchwork Israelite confederacy crumbles. Shiloh falls, "home" of the ARK and one of Israel's holiest towns, and is reduced to rubble. The Israelites meet the iron-armed Philistines in battle at Aphek, and lose it ". . . [with] a very great slaughter; for there fell of Israel 30,000 footmen. And the Ark of God was taken." The Philistines carry off the Ark and place it in their pagan temple of Dagon. The period of Judges has run its course; God's people are in grave, and very real danger of extinction, of being wiped out; and with them the Law of Moses and knowledge of Moses' God. And the people demand a king ". . . like other nations." But the prophet, Samuel, who has judged Israel ". . . all the days of his life," solemnly warns them what a king will do. He will ". . . take your sons to fight his wars and labor in his fields; your daughters for cooks and bakers; he will take all you own . . . and you shall be his slaves!" But the people do not listen; they insist, believing that a king ". . . will fight our battles for us." So lots are drawn and Saul, son of Kish, is chosen, a tall, handsome man ". . . like whom there is none other."   I SAMUEL 8

The CREATION of MONARCHY

The establishment of monarchy in Israel was an event of vast importance, as much as the Exodus, itself. For, while Moses' exodus from Egypt and covenant with God produced a great leap forward in spiritual understanding from the myriad cosmological gods of Egypt and Mesopotamia, the monarchy—in a circuitous and paradoxical way—also caused the downfall of that same kingdom, and itself, 400 years later.

The paradox lies in the effect that history and the monarchy had on each other; for, because of the establishment of monarchy (which unified the 12 tribes into one nation), Israel did, indeed, survive the Philistine threat but, in surviving, it betrayed the very God it sought to serve by serving its neighbors' pagan gods instead. On the other hand, without the monarchy, Israel could well have disappeared without a trace, taking with it the Law of Moses and all knowledge of God.

The writers of the books of history (JOSHUA, JUDGES, SAMUEL, KINGS and CHRONICLES) reveal another paradox, as well, for in their overriding concern to record Israel's SACRED history, they dismissed with cool contempt the monarchy's quite considerable SECULAR accomplishments. For, Israel's invention of a political system of government whose secular kings were independent of its religion, BUT ANSWERABLE TO ITS GOD was, in fact, a totally new concept in the world and a major stepping-stone to the idea of individual freedom—not for kings to rule rough-shod over voiceless subjects—but for EVERYMAN, "endowed by [their] CREATOR with certain inalienable rights."

Finally, the betrayal of God and His covenant by kings and commoners alike "going after" pagan gods and ignoring the military/political threat of the East, brought about a third paradox . . . the appearance on the scene of the Prophets who, in condemning Israel's sins, thereby clarified, refined and defined the Law of Moses into the Yahwism—and later the Judaism—that has survived the centuries. The narrow negativism that was the Mosaic Law, with its hundreds of commands, restrictions and prohibitions would not have evolved into a universal Judaism without the eloquent arguments of the Prophets. The Prophets would not have come upon the scene were it not for the sinfulness of Israel's people and kings, and the sins of the kings would never have been but for the creation of monarchy.

Samuel Anoints Saul the First
KING OF ISRAEL

c. 1050   "There was a man of [the tribe of] Benjamin whose name was Kish . . . and he had a son whose name was Saul . . . [and] there was not among the children of Israel a goodlier person than he . . ." An imposing, kingly figure, Saul towers head and shoulders above everyone else. Already a military hero before being crowned, two years afterward Saul begins his campaign against the Philistines. Saul's poorly armed forces are no match for the iron-armed enemy, though, and one confrontation is saved only through his son, Jonathon's stealth and surprise attack. But it is in these years that the Israelites wrest from the Philistines the secret of iron-making, and with the break-up of the Philistine monopoly begins the building of Israel's own war-machine.

"Now the philistines gathered together their armies to battle . . ." reads the first book of SAMUEL, on one mountain side, and the Israelites on another, with a valley between, and neither would start the fight. For forty days one Philistine soldier of formidable appearance, a giant of a man ". . . whose height was six cubits and a span," shouts a challenge to the Israelites to do battle. Only one hearer takes up the challenge; a shepherd boy, only a youth, "ruddy [with] beautiful eyes, and handsome." Armed only with stones and a sling, David fells Goliath with one shot to the head, and becomes a hero to all Israel . . .

I SAMUEL

Book of History — Written in Hebrew,   c. 950–900 B.C.

The two books of SAMUEL tell how Israel became a kingdom; how finally the wandering Hebrew nomads gained a nation of their own, and how the last judge, Samuel, anointed the young Saul Israel's first king, a commanding, inspiring leader . . . but tragic, also. A great warrior in his youth, he later lost his mind, threatening even young David, and ended his life pathetic and defeated by the Philistines on the Plain of Jezreel. The history of the future king, David, is told in I SAMUEL also, his battles with the Philistines; how, with only five smooth stones and his sling, he felled the giant, Goliath, causing the entire Philistine army to panic and flee, making David a legend in his own time. Although a simple tool, a sling-shot is no childs toy, but a highly accurate and lethal weapon in the hands of an expert, and David was certainly that. Sling-stones from this very time and place can be seen in numerous modern-day museums, including the Horn Museum, Berrien Springs, Michigan.

One of the most underrated and overlooked—but world-changing—events in the Bible is the creation of the Israelite monarchy, the beginning of the Hebrew kingship. It wasn't simply in the fact that monarchy began, but in HOW it began, by whose authority, and what it would mean to the future, not only of this little nation of ancient Israel, but to all of western civilization . . . especially that nation that will be FOUNDED AND

PREMISED on Biblical principles: the United States of America. The story is found in the eighth chapter of I SAMUEL.

When Samuel the judge became old all the elders of Israel said to him, "Give us a king to govern us." And Samuel prayed to the Lord [who said] "Hearken to the people for they have not rejected you, but . . . me from being king over them. Now, then, show them the ways of . . . kings." And Samuel said to the people, "A king to rule over you will take your sons for his chariot . . . horsemen, to plow his ground and reap his harvest; he will take your daughters for cooks and bakers; the best of your fields, vineyards and olive orchards, the tenth of your grain and your flocks AND YOU SHALL BE HIS SLAVES!" But the people refused to listen to Samuel, and said, "But we WILL have a king like all the nations, that he may govern us and fight our battles for us!" And Samuel repeated this to the Lord, who said, "then hearken to their voices . . . AND MAKE THEM A KING."   I SAMUEL 8:4–22

Thus it was only through God's permission and direction that a king was anointed in Israel, the first nation in the history of the world to create a secular government sanctioned by God. No Egyptian pharaoh or Sumerian god-king ever sought or received "permission" from the world's creator to rule; they "WERE" the gods and ruled by their own "divine right." Israel's king would be separate and independent from Israel's God . . . but ANSWERABLE TO HIM. The king would manage worldly affairs in worldly—or secular— ways, BUT he must do it MORALLY, also, according to God's commandments. Not for another 500 years will Greece conceive the idea of democracy, where every man speaks for himself in open forum; (See: Solon of Athens, 594 B.C.) nor Rome invent a republican government of elected representatives. (See: Roman Republic Established, 510 B.C.) And then, their systems will flourish only for an elite few, carried along on the back of slavery and brute force, based on the supremacy, not of individual freedom, but of an all powerful STATE, in whatever form: king, tyrant, dictator or emperor. But by this time, Israel's people already had their freedom, given to them by God when he commanded Moses to tell Egypt's pharaoh to . . . "LET MY PEOPLE GO," and to . . .

Proclaim liberty throughout all the land unto all the inhabitants thereof.   LEVITICUS, 25:10 (See: 1290 B.C.)

Now they have a king, but they also have a Higher Authority than the king to whom they can turn for redress when that king does not rule according to His will. Under that Authority, and by His instruction and permission the Hebrews have now invented (whether they know it or not) the world's first tripartite government of three separate branches: the LEGISLATIVE branch of Hebrew elders who, by their petition to Samuel—and through him to God—"legislated" into existence the EXECU-TIVE branch, or the king, who will "execute" the law of Israel, which will then be judged for its justice (or, obedience to God's will) by the JUDICIAL branch, Israel's Levite priest-hood. One day, soon, the prophet, Isaiah, will define the concept thus:

> For the LORD is our judge, the LORD is our lawgiver,
> the LORD is our King: He will save us.   ISAIAH 33:22 (See: 721 B.C.)

With variations only in its metaphysical composition, this tripartite EXECUTIVE, LEGISLATIVE and JUDICIAL concept will, many centuries hence, become the founda-tion of that nation whose Liberty Bell will someday, "Proclaim liberty throughout all the land unto all the inhabitants thereof." Philadelphia, Penn., USA, 1776

Written down little by little as events happened, it is believed that the actual compil-ing of the two books of SAMUEL was done by scribes in Solomon's temple (See: 950 B.C.) but not completed until much later. Scholars consider SAMUEL the first purely "histori-cal" book, written solely to relate "what happened," not "why." The judge, Samuel was also considered a "seer" or prophet, and when the historical books of KINGS and CHRONICLES are written at the time of the second temple, their author, or "chronicler," will often use the two books of SAMUEL for reference, and refer to them as the books of "Samuel the Seer."

1000   The first millennium B.C. (Before Christ) finds activity of all sorts in every corner of the world.

. . . The Great Lakes of North America have taken their present-day shape.

. . . In the Arabian city of Mecca, festivals are held which will evolve over the centuries into modern-day "fairs."

. . . According to legend, soap is discovered, by accident, on Sapo Hill near Rome, when fat from burning animals runs down a sacrificial altar, and mixes with wood ash in the fire below.

. . . The Shang Dynasty, rulers of China for 500 years, falls to a new power, and a Chinese "empire" begins to grow. Peking is thriving as a city, built with wooden temples, palaces and pagodas during this new Chou Dynasty. It will rule for 800 years.

. . . The Olmec Indians in Mexico establish the first civilization in the "new" world. Mean-ing in Aztec, "rubber people," the Olmecs carve fierce, vacant-eyed, gape-mouthed figures, some half human, half jaguar from jade . . . and some from stone nearly nine feet tall. They write with hieroglyphics which are little understood, even today.

. . . India's oldest collection of sacrificial hymns, the *RIG VEDA* is being written. From their worship of Agni and Varuna (fire and water), Vena and Soma (the mist-clouded sun and drug-clouded mind) comes the name for India's VEDIC Age.

. . . Phoenicians, sailing the breadth of the Mediterranean Sea, have established colonies in Spain and on the island of Malta. Phoenicia's coastal cities of Tyre and Sidon have grown into thriving seaports, water-way crossroads uniting the world's great trading centers.

Countless ships come and go, carrying tons of goods to an awakened world, hungry for whatever money will buy. But the Mediterranean can be fierce and unpredictable, churning up killer storms and high seas, and many a cargo ship does not reach its destination. One such ship found its rest just off the coast of Asia Minor/Turkey at about this time, and lay in the quiet blue depths for almost 3000 years, until A.D. 1982 when Turkish sponge divers happened upon its shadowy hull. The ensuing "treasure hunt" brought to light, once again, an incredible cargo headed by 60 tons of copper ingots, meant to be melted down, mixed with ingots of tin, also on board, and transformed into bronze. Part of its cargo was amber from the far-northern Baltic Sea, and ivory from southern Egypt . . . 3000 miles apart! Pottery from Myceneae, carved cylinder seals from Mesopotamia, ingots of blue glass, perfume-filled amphorae, fishing nets, bronze swords and arrowheads, all were aboard this—probably Phoenecian—trading vessel, the oldest shipwreck ever found.

. . . Semetic Bedouins called Arameans are occupying parts of Mesopotamia that will soon become Assyria. They have created a state centered around the great hub of transportation, Damascus, from which Aramean influence travels "the world over." Their language is called Aramaic. It will be used now for many centuries in the Mid-east and, a thousand years hence, will be the native language of a man called Jesus . . . of Nazareth.

. . . And DAVID SUCCEEDS SAUL AS KING OF ISRAEL. Under David the kingdom will become a large and powerful nation, one to be reckoned with in the world. Someday a nation called the United States of America will progress from walking across a prairie to walking on the moon in only 200 years. So, also, does little Israel go from rags to riches in the same length of time. And just as Israel is a bridge between two worlds, so also, is King David the bridge between the world of slavery and servitude in the time of Moses and that of sumptuous splendor in the days of Solomon to follow. For David is a "right man at the right time," a charismatic leader and political genius, who will take hold of a disorganized, patchwork kingdom and weave it into greatness.

The writers of the books of SAMUEL dwell heavily on David's military career, which is long and illustrious, for it is on the battlefield that David carves out his kingdom; and his moral character, which, they say, leaves much to be desired. They have little to say about his business acumen or his political expertise, but he certainly is generously endowed with both, for no one builds an empire without them. David will rule Israel forty years, only one year short of what Caesar Augustus will do in Rome ten centuries hence, but 28 years more than Alexander the Great . . . more than enough time to build an important kingdom. Thus, what had been a land of runaway slaves only 200 years ago, will now become under David's genius and during his reign, one of the important nations in the world.

David is a man of many talents; some would say a Renaissance man almost, had he lived in another time, another place. For not only is he a great leader, an empire builder; he is renowned as a poet, singer and musician. His love for the One True God of Israel is deep and sincere, and he composes many hymns in His name. They will be taught and sung in worship for many years and gradually written down. Five hundred years from now they, and many others, will be compiled into the book of PSALMS.

Some of the PSALMS of David

#19 The heavens declare the glory of God, and the firmament showeth His handiwork. 24 The earth is the Lord's and the fullness thereof: the world, and they that dwell therein. 27 The Lord is my light and my salvation: whom shall I fear? 51 Have mercy upon me, O God, according to thy loving kindness. 53 The fool hath said in his heart, there is no God. 30 Lord, thou hast been our dwelling place in all generations . . . a thousand years in thy sight are but as yesterday when it is past. 103 Bless the Lord, O my soul; and all that is within me, bless His holy name. 106 Praise ye the Lord. O give thanks unto the Lord: for He is good; for His mercy endureth forever.

David's Musicians

The twenty-third Psalm is among the most beautiful songs ever written, titled, simply,

---

A PSALM OF DAVID

The LORD is my shepherd, I shall not want; He maketh me to lie down in green pastures. He leadeth me beside still waters, He restoreth my soul. He leadeth me in the paths of righteousness for His name's sake. Yea, though I walk through the valley of the shadow of death, I will fear no evil; for thou art with me, thy rod and thy staff, they comfort me. Thou preparest a table before me in the presence of mine enemies; thou anointest my head with oil, my cup runneth over. Surely goodness and mercy shall follow me all the days of my life; and I shall dwell in the house of the LORD forever.

The singing of David's Psalms may have been accompanied by trumpets, cymbals, drums, psaltery, and David's own instrument, the harp, all musical instruments used in Israel by this time. David would probably have known an ancient Hebrew song called the SONG OF LAMACH. Written before the first books of the Bible, and the only portion still in existence is that included in the book of GENESIS   (4:32–24).

. . . The second book of SAMUEL picks up the narrative:

II SAMUEL

Book of History — Written in Hebrew,   c. 950–500 B.C.

The second book of SAMUEL tells David's story; how he mourned the death of Saul and Saul's son, his dearest friend, Jonathon. David built his little kingdom into an important member in the community of nations, put a final end to the Philistine threat and played a large part in wiping them out of existence. He captured the ancient city of Jerusalem, chose it to be Israel's capital, and it was called the City of David in his day. He made Jerusalem the Holy City, and brought there the Ark of the Covenant. After being carried about like a nomad since the days of Moses, it had been captured by the Philistines in the thick of battle, returned to Israel, and fallen into disuse. Now the Holy Ark had a permanent home.

In typical honesty and candor, the writers of SAMUEL made no attempt to gloss over some of David's ignoble behavior; his duplicity in dealing with the Philistines, and the shameful set-up of the killing of Uriah the Hittite so that he could marry Uriah's wife, Bathsheba. In fact, some modern-day critics, intending to discredit religion and the Bible, have accused him of such crimes as "extortion, conspiracy to do murder, consorting with the enemy" and "high treason," therein judging bronze-age behavior by 20th century standards. But David recognized his own iniquities, and questioned why God chose him for greatness: "Who am I, O Lord God," he prayed, "and what is my house, that thou hast brought me hitherto?" When king Hiram of Tyre built him a "cedar house," David questioned the justice of that, also, saying, "See now, I dwell in an house of cedar, but the Ark of God [dwells in a tent."] The writers of SAMUEL also dwell upon the fact that success "went to his head" and that David's latter years were far from the great early ones, and that his blind love for his scheming son, Absalom, even after Absalom led a revolt against him, nearly caused disaster. Still, David was Israel's greatest king, past or future, and under his guidance Israel was saved from extinction, and grew strong, large and important; and he "administered justice and equity to all his people."

961   At this point begins all the history found in the time period of the books of KINGS I and CHRONICLES I. Although David's son, Adonijah, contends for the throne, David passes the succession on to his better-loved son, Solomon.

The book of CHRONICLES I relates how David spent his last years designing a magnificent Temple to God. In his conquests, David had confiscated and stored away a great quantity of wealth with which to build a Temple: ". . . very much brass . . . for the brazen sea . . . the pillars . . . and vessels . . . iron in abundance for the nails," and ". . . 3000 talents of gold . . . and 7000 talents of refined silver, to overlay the walls . . ." Having planned even the Temple's music and divine services, David tells Solomon "in the sight of all Israel, to . . . take heed . . . for the LORD hath chosen thee to build [the temple."] Then, having prayed that Solomon would see his dream fulfilled ". . . in good old age, full of . . . riches and honor," David ". . . slept with his fathers."

Modern-day critics and skeptics, hoping to disprove the Bible, long have gloated that, since not one shred of empirical evidence has ever been found about a "King David," he obviously never existed, and was, therefore, only a myth invented by self-interested Jewish scribes . . . until July, 1993, when a basalt building block was uncovered at the Biblical (Tel) Dan, a well-dug site in northern Galilee, near Mt. Hermon by the Jordan River. Engraved with an easily readable inscription, the stone was once part of a carved stele celebrating a victory by an Aramean king of Damascus, and includes the words, "House of David" and "King of Israel." The news made headlines, not only in the archeological and biblical worlds, but the secular media as well, for the inscription had been carved, not by Jewish scribes in their own self-interest, but by Israel's enemies who were simply recording an historical fact. The stone proves that there was, indeed, not only a King David, but a kingly dynasty founded by him . . . a "House of David."

> . . . I slew of them . . . ___ [char]iots and 2000 horsemen . . . the King of Israel And . . . of the House of David . . .
>
> The KING DAVID Inscription from Tel Dan, now in the Israel Museum

House of David Inscription

961   Solomon becomes king at a time of peace and great prosperity, when there is "rest on every side, neither adversary nor misfortune." He rules 36 years, four years less than his father, David; and becomes renowned for his great wisdom, "greater than all the wisdom of the east or of Egypt." (I KINGS 4:30) People come from "all the world" to hear his words, songs, proverbs, opinions, and decisions; and he extends his kingdom's borders from the Euphrates River to the "land of the Philistines," to the border of Egypt. Solomon inherited his father's genius, but in different directions, for he is a shrewd political manipulator, and while David had won wealth in war, Solomon's genius lies in MAKING money . . . vast amounts of money.

David had built his kingdom directly in the path of the two great civilizations, Sumer and Egypt, and Solomon is well aware of the strategic importance of Israel's being the ONLY bridge between them. He knows who passes through his country, where they are going, how much they carry, and what is its worth. He knows his neighbors, uses them, trades with them, and allies himself with those who are valuable to him. He bargains with the Phoenecians for fleets of ships, and with Egypt in the south for horses and chariots . . . thousands of them . . . which he then sells to the Hittites in the north. He fortifies his cities, works copper mines, refineries, keeps a huge merchant fleet which brings wealth to the kingdom from far places, and maintains a standing army, all Israel's first. He contracts diplomatic marriages and treaties, and keeps the wealth of his own kingdom in mind. And under Solomon's financial genius Israel . . . and Solomon grow incredibly rich!

So Solomon sets about building his father, David's, dream: a holy house of God, so that the sacred Ark of the Covenant, carried about since the days of Moses and brought to Jerusalem by David, should be housed in a magnificent Temple!

c. 957–950   Under the direction of Phoenecia's King Hiram of Tyre, and using Hiram's navigators, architects and engineers, Solomon builds the Temple of Phoenecia's fabled Cedars of Lebanon, and of olivewood, and cypress. Obedient to David's wishes, he builds the brazen sea and the great pillars of bronze, and uses gold and silver beyond dreams. The altar, table and lampstands in the outer room—the holy place—are all pure gold and brass, as are all the vessels, utensils, dishes, basins and urns! In the center of the Temple—the Holy of Holies—two huge, golden cherubim crouch with out-spread wings; and there Solomon places the sacred Ark.

The Temple

It is thought by some that Solomon spent an equivalent of four billion modern-day dollars on the Temple! But "on the Temple" is not quite accurate; for the Temple, itself, is in fact, only a modestly sized building, a very small part of Solomon's main project: a royal complex which includes a palace for himself as fabulous as any other in the world. For Solomon lives like an oriental potentate, and takes to himself their powers as well. When he has finally depleted the treasury, he merely sells a few towns, as his personal property to sell. He marries the daughter of the Pharaoh of Egypt . . . but keeps a harem of a thousand other wives and concubines as well, who ". . . turn away his heart from God."

So Solomon ". . . [does] what is evil in the sight of . . ." the One True God whom David had loved and worshipped so simply and sincerely. Solomon "[goes] after" the pagan goddess Ashtar, she of the cult prostitution, and "build[s] high places" and pagan temples for his concubines to sacrifice to their gods. Solomon becomes famous, indeed, for his wisdom, so famous the Queen of Sheba travels from the south-eastern tip of Arabia (today's Yemen) to see him—more than a thousand miles—but he will, also, become infamous for his excesses, and for the unbearable tax burden to pay for them; and finally, for what he does to his own people. For Solomon's magnificent building projects are constructed . . . with slave labor . . . first that of other races, and then that of his OWN PEOPLE . . . 30,000 to labor in the cedar forests of Lebanon, 80,000 to quarry and shape wall and foundation stones, and 70,000 more to transport them. One hundred and eighty thousand men of Israel, FREE MEN, whom Moses had long ago led out of bondage are pressed, once again . . . into SLAVERY! Thus does Solomon sow the seeds of Israel's destruction!

. . . One of Solomon's many cities is Gezer, north-west of Jerusalem, given to him as dowry by Egypt's Pharaoh on Solomon's marriage to Pharaoh's daughter. Here, and at Hazor and Megiddo, will be found, in our own time, ruins of some of Solomon's Stables, which housed some of his 4000 horses. Something else will be found at Gezer, also, in A.D. 1908, a limestone tablet, small enough to be handheld, engraved in "Biblical" Hebrew and easily readable by modern scholars. Probably memorized by school children, the tablet is called the world's first calendar:

> His two months are (olive) harvest, His two months are planting (grain), His two months are late planting; His month is hoeing up of flax, His month is harvest of barley, His month is harvest and feasting. His two months are vine-tending, his month is summer fruit.
>
> The GEZER CALENDAR, now in the Museum of the Ancient Orient, Istanbul, Turkey.

The Gezer Calendar

926   Solomon dies, and his inept son, Rheoboam, becomes king. Before long, Jeroboam, one of the slave labor commanders, leads the ten northern tribes in REVOLT . . . and . . .

. . . the KINGDOM IS DIVIDED. . .
. . . and a united Israel is no more!!

Under Jeroboam the northern tribes of Reuben, Simeon, Zebulon, Levi, Gad, Issacher, Napthali, Asher, Dan and Joseph break away in revolt, but keep the name of ISRAEL. Lying directly in the path of the world's trade routes, Israel will be watched from the beginning by the greedy eyes of other nations, until it falls to Assyria in only 204 years. Israel's history from this time to its end will be a record of crime and corruption. Nineteen kings will hold the throne, gaining it most often, not by right, but by might, murder and intrigue. From the start the worship of the God of David is in jeopardy, for Jeroboam erects (with good but misguided intentions) two golden calves at Dan and Beth-el for worship, and every one of his successors will become a calf worshipper, save a few who will be even worse.

Under Solomon's son, Rheoboam, the two remaining tribes—Judah and Benjamin—keep the rest of the kingdom, but rename it JUDAH. Much of Judah is barren desolation, but it holds the jewel of the kingdom, its capital, JERUSALEM. Judah will struggle but, away from the beaten path, will last more than a hundred years longer than Israel. Nineteen kings and one usurper queen will rule Judah, a kingly dynasty of the family of the great David. They will include men of every sort of character, from good and wise to exceedingly evil; some whose love for God will be noble and heroic, and others whose pagan worship and practices will be an abomination to God.

Both nations will go through periods of prosperity and growth to disaster and ruin. They will play politics with each other and with the outside world . . . and both will eventually lose.

. . . The Phoenecians have built their seaport cities of Tyre and Sidon into the world's first important manufacturing centers. Their textile industry produces fine linen fabric and beautiful dyes, including purple which, because of the great expense of production, will always be called the "royal color." They have also perfected, and are producing, great quantities of glass; bowls, amphorae, and jewelry, beautiful works that rival gems in value. Their glass beads entrance more primitive peoples on their far-flung ocean journeys, and entice them into trading precious silver and gold for colorful baubles. More than just a few "merchant princes" make fortunes from glass trinkets.

Something else goes with the Phoenecians on their travels; graven idols, and the worship of the pagan gods, Baal and Ashtar. The Babylonian Baal worship, celebrated with human sacrifice, self-mutilation and bizarre rites requires many carved or cast statues for its temples. Ashtar worship is simply ritualized sex, her temples peopled with cult prostitutes . . . and lewd statues of them. Then there are the numerous household baals that every home must have. There are big profits to be made from the manufacture and sale of graven idols.

922, (Judah).   Rheoboam rules Judah 17 years and "increases the heavy yoke" his father, Solomon, had laid on the people. They are years that see the greatness of his grandfather, David, and the magnificence of Solomon brought low; the treasury that had once amazed the world, empty; and his people without hope.

(Israel).   Jeroboam rules Israel 22 years, the great golden calves he built at Dan and Bethel corrupting the worship of the Lord, Yahweh. In Solomon's last days, Jeroboam had sought asylum from him with Pharaoh Shishak of Egypt; had extolled to the Pharaoh the glories of Solomon's vast treasures . . . and now Shishak repays him . . .

Pharaoh Shishak

918   Having watched events in the north with a keen eye and lusting heart, Pharaoh Shishak knows the time is ripe. He invades Israel and Judah with . . . (according to the books of KINGS I AND CHRONICLES) 1200 chariots and 60,000 horsemen, ". . . and Shishak took away the treasures of the house of the Lord and the shields of gold which Solomon had made . . ." According to his own inscriptions on the walls of the great temple at Karnak, Shishak (Sheshonk in Egyptian) also raids and plunders 150 other towns, a severe blow to both Israel and Judah.

912 (J)   During a short reign, Abijam restores some Judean cities, then . . . because the next king of Judah, Asa, "trusted the LORD," during his 41 year reign, he defeats a "million" Ethiopians with half that number. But when he uses bribery and double-dealing against Israel, he is punished with a terrible disease.

900–876 (I)   Baasha, Elah and Zimri all gain the throne, and lose it, by murder . . . after which, King Omri takes the throne, whom the first book of KINGS labels, "wicked before all else." Aside from his religious shortcomings, though, Omri is an effective king, and founds an important "Omride" dynasty. He builds a capital city for Israel at SAMARIA (with Phoenecian expertise) and is mentioned in several ancient stone carvings . . . as is his son . . .

869   . . . the infamous Ahab, branded by Israel's chroniclers "the worst of all." Ahab transforms the kingly palace at Samaria into an ivory marvel: ivory, imported from Africa, on walls and floors, on furniture, chairs, beds and couches. (The ruins of the "Ivory Palace" have been found at Samaria, along with many scraps of ivory, left behind when the palace was sacked, stripped and destroyed in 721 B.C. Much of the beautiful, intricately carved ivory is, today, in the British Museum, London.) During Ahab's 22 year reign, he "[does] more to provoke the LORD . . . to anger than all . . . that were before . . ." Ahab marries a Phoenecian princess, Jezebel, worships her god, Baal, and builds pagan altars to it. Intending to make all Israel worship the false god, the treacherous Jezebel kills the prophets of Yahweh, the LORD, who speak against it.

873 (J)   During a peaceful 25 year reign, Asa's son, Jehoshaphat builds fortresses and store-cities in Judah, and grows "steadily greater . . ." But he marries his eldest son, Jehorem, to Athaliah, daughter of Ahab and Jezebel, and in so doing, brings Omride blood into Judah.

(I)   And now, a most remarkable man appears on the scene in Israel, from out of nowhere, clad in little else than loincloth, hairshirt . . . and conviction; a man whom the ravens feed, wild as the desert that nurtured him, and unafraid of the forces of evil. As fanatically opposed to Jezebel's pagan Baal as she is to his God, Elijah the Tishbite cries, "As the LORD . . . God of Israel lives, before whom I stand, there shall be neither dew nor rain these years except by my word!" And after drought and famine, Elijah confronts King Ahab who calls him ". . . troubler of Israel." "I have not troubled Israel," Elijah cries, challenging the king to a duel of gods; Baal against Yahweh. "You are the troubler of Israel, because you have forsaken the commandments of the LORD!" And in a mighty confrontation, 450 priests of Baal are defeated . . . and slain. Then Elijah prophesies a curse on the house of Omri and Ahab . . .

> . . . anyone belonging to Ahab . . . the dogs shall eat . . . they shall eat Jezebel . . .   I KINGS 21:23, 24

Modern archeology has uncovered burial jars from this, the time of Ahab and Jezebel, containing dismembered bodies of babies and small children, sacrificed to Baal and Ashtar. It has also uncovered the remains of pagan "high places" and "sanctuaries" in Samaria . . . and, in Jerusalem, a sanctuary complete with Baal statues, not 300 yards from Solomon's Temple to Yahweh!

But Baal worship is not the only threat to belief in the one true God, Yahweh. Far to the north, in modern-day Iraq, the Assyrian people have taken their very name from their god, Assur, or Ashur, as has their king, Ashurnasirpal. A ferocious and cruel people, religion and state are one to the Assyrians, and no merciless deed or atrocity is beyond what they will do to appease their god. Now, Israel and Judah join in confederation with other states, which stops Assyria for a while . . . but which, in time will only ignite their ferocity the more.

Now, a despairing Elijah goes to Mount Horeb (or Sinai, where Moses received the LAW) and searches in anguish for God. "I have been zealous for the LORD . . . he cries "[but] the people of Israel have forsaken thy covenant, thrown down thy altars and slain thy prophets . . . and . . . I only am left!" Then a "great and strong wind [rends] the mountains," and, after the wind, an earthquake, and after that a fire, but God is not in any of them. But then, a "still, small voice" tells Elijah that he is NOT alone, that there IS a "righteous remnant" left, about whom Elijah doesn't even know. "Yet I will have 7000 in Israel," God tells him, "all the knees that have not bowed to Baal." But for now, God says, ". . . anoint Jehu king of Israel, who will avenge the LORD . . . and destroy the evil house of Ahab!"

One of Israel's neighbors, the Moabites, have been subjugated under Israel's yoke since the days of Omri. Now Mesha, king of Moab, wins a battle over Ahab . . . and gloats over his brief victory by carving the story on a triumphal stone. The four foot high *Moabite Stone* has engraved on it the earliest extant writing in Hebrew/Phoenecian characters; and tells a story remarkably akin to that in KINGS I and II. On it Mesha attributes his success to HIS god, Chemosh:

The Moabite Stone

I am Mesha . . . king of Moab. Omri, king of Israel . . . oppressed Moab many days . . . his son succeeded him and he too said, "I will oppress Moab." I took (his) town . . . and slew . . . 7000 people. I took the altar hearth of David . . . and the vessels of Yahweh, and dragged them before Chemosh . . . and devoted the women and girls to Ashtar . . .   The *Moabite Stone*, which stands, today, in the Louvre, Paris, France

Legend says that at some unknown time in antiquity someone, believing the Moabite Stone hollow and filled with treasure, heated it red-hot on a fire then poured water on it to crack it open . . . but found it solid rock. Actually, that was done to it, but only after its find in 1868, by its Bedouin owner to spite his Ottoman rulers . . . but not before its entire text was recorded by Louvre representatives.

(I/J)   Kings Ahab of Israel and Jehoshaphat of Judah join together in battle against Syria. Ahab, mortally wounded, has himself strapped into his chariot, rides back into battle and dies a Hero's death; but just as Elijah prophesied . . .

. . . the dogs licked up his blood and the harlots washed themselves in it.   I KINGS 22:38 RSV

All history from the death of King David to the present time is found in the time period of the book of KINGS I.

KINGS I

Book of History — Written in Hebrew,   c. 900–500 B.C.

"Now the days of David drew nigh that he should die; and he charged Solomon his son, saying, I go the way of all the earth: be thou strong therefore, and shew thyself a man; and keep the charge of the LORD thy God, to walk in his ways, to keep his statutes . . . commandments . . . judgments, and . . . testimonies, as it is written in the law of Moses . . ."

The first book of KINGS opens with David's death, Solomon's accession to the throne and a vivid description of Solomon's reign; his vast building projects and his fabulous wealth. Considered by some to be one of the world's all-time great statesmen, Solomon brought David's rural, war-torn, isolated kingdom into the forefront of the international community of nations; thus Israel was, in reality, one of the important nations of the world at this time, and the story of how the Queen of Sheba traveled far to see the wonders of Solomon for herself shows how its fame had spread. But Solomon's excesses set his nation on a collision course with disaster and, after his death, it was torn with strife, divided by revolution and ruled by a long succession of, mostly, evil or incompetent men.

The writers of the two books of KINGS tell the story of the two nations—Israel and Judah—simultaneously, weaving back and forth between them. Their unsparing derision is brutally honest as they tell of the feats, foibles, failures and faithlessness of the kings, and of how they squandered their inheritance of both fortune and faith. But they tell, also, of that most important, enigmatic figure, the prophet Elijah, the personification of faith in the Hebrew Scriptures; and how he sought the word of God in the roaring of the wind, earthquake and fire, but heard it, instead, in a "still, small voice." It is a story that gives hope to the faithful even today, for God told him that no matter how bad things got, He would always be there, and even though it would seem that there was no one still faithful to Him, in fact, there would always be a "redeeming remnant" about whom Elijah would not even know, but who would carry on the faith.

The two books of KINGS were completed, in their present-day form, by writers who are known only as "Deuteronomists," or "Writers of the Law." They got their material from many sources, including other books then in existence, the archives of the Temple, itself, and mostly, the documents known today as "J" and "E." The "J" stands for Jahwhist, those portions of the text written by an unknown Judean writer who referred to God as JHWH: Jahweh, Yahweh or Jehovah. These are the roots of such words as Hallelu-JAH, which means Praise the LORD, and Eli-JAH, which means "Yahweh is my God." The "E" stands for Elohist, those portions written by an, also unknown, Israeli writer who used the name Elohim for God: EL as in Isra-EL, Beth-EL and EL-ijah; and can be found even in the pagan gods Bel and Ba-al. KINGS I ends with Elijah's calling of his successor, Elisha ("God is Salvation") and with the death of the evil king, Ahab.

850 (I)   During the reign of Ahab's son, King Ahaziah—who "provoked the LORD to anger"—Elijah the prophet, in a chariot of fire, is taken by a whirlwind to heaven . . . and Elisha inherits his mantle.

842 (I)   Elisha anoints Jehu, son of Jehoshaphat, king of Israel, a religious fanatic who begins a bloody purge to rid Israel of Baal. He deceives both kings Joram of Israel and Ahaziah of Judah into riding out to meet him . . . and slays them both. He has Jezebel

thrown from a window and, as Elijah had prophesied, ". . . the dogs ate her flesh." Jehu slays all that remain of the house of Ahab . . . and gathers their heads into baskets. Announcing, "Ahab served Baal a little, but Jehu will serve him much," he fills the house of Baal with its own worshippers and priests ". . . and wipes them out." But despite Jehu's blood-bath purge, Athaliah, daughter of Ahab and Jezebel, seizes the throne of Judah, holds it six years, a worshipper of Baal, then is herself slain, the usurper of the throne of David.

King Jehu of Israel is remembered in secular history, as well, the only Israelite king whose likeness exists to this day, although he would hardly like the way he is portrayed. In a carved picture panel on a seven-foot high block of black stone, Jehu is shown kow-towing on hands and knees before Shalmaneser III of Assyria, who . . .

The Black Obelisque

. . . received the tribute . . . of Jehu, son of Omri. Silver, gold, golden vase, golden cups, golden buckets, tin, a staff for the royal hand, puruhati-fruits. The *Black Obelisque*, now in the British Museum, London.

Panel from the Black Obelisque

(I)   During the reign of Jehu's son, Jehoahaz, Syria "brings Israel so low" its army is nothing more than a remnant . . . 50 horsemen, 10 chariots.

(J)   In Judah, the dynasty of David is restored through Ahaziah's son, Joash, who repairs the Temple, but pays a high price in tribute to ransom Judah's safety a while longer.

814   The city of Carthage begins to grow on the northern coast of Africa. Ancient legend says that a beautiful Phoenecian princess named Dido sailed the breadth of the "Great Sea," founded the city and became its first queen. Then the noble Greek prince, Aeneas, visits Carthage, he and Dido fall in love; but, when Jupiter tells Aeneas he is destined for greater things, Aeneas sails away and never learns that the firelight he sees on shore is the immolation pyre of the broken-hearted Queen Dido. Eight hundred years from now a Roman poet named Virgil will tell the tale in his epic saga, The AENEID.

800 (I/J)   Jehoash of Israel and Amaziah of Judah take their thrones at the lowest point in their countries' histories; their power gone, strength depleted, cities and countrysides a shambles; and their faith a mockery. They "look one another in the face" in battle, and a triumphant Jehoash seizes the Temple's treasures—and Amaziah's. But Amaziah outlives Jehoash . . . and then is slain for turning away from the LORD.

. . . The Etruscans are living in central Italy now, in the area today called Tuscany. Thought to be descended from one branch of the nomadic Sea Peoples, they still seem a mysterious people because their language has never been completely understood. They are skilled engineers, and build bridges, viaducts and canals (including a "grand canal" such as Venice will boast several millennia from now.) They are traders, also, and many fine imported products will someday be found in their ruins. Etruria is rich in crude ores, and its metal workers are highly skilled craftsmen, including goldsmiths who create fine dental bridges and inlays still in existence today, as are tweezers, razors, hairpins and combs. The Etruscans—of Tuscany—will flourish for several hundred years, now, but will be no match for Rome when that city begins to grow.

. . . A strange and wonderful thing is happening on those lands and islands of the Great Sea—the Mediterranean—today called Greece, as it begins, little by little to wake from its dark age. Two separate and distinct civilizations are growing, springing from two separate cities. Although they lie little more than a hundred miles apart, they will be very different from one another. For within just a few hundred years, the city of ATHENS, built around a fortified hill called the Acropolis, will burst into magnificent bloom, and become the most beautiful flower of "antiquity." The Athenians had fought off and repulsed the barbarous Dorian raiders years ago; welcomed the more worldly, learned refugees from golden Mycenae, and absorbed their knowledge and culture into their own. They believe that the cultivation of the mind ennobles the soul and body, so Athens will produce more great minds—philosophers, doctors, scientists, architects, inventors, sculptors, writers, historians and statesmen—than the world has yet seen; minds that influence our lives to this day.

The city of SPARTA, lying to the south, having welcomed the warlike Dorians and adopted Dorian ways, believes in austerity, stern, harsh and severe. Its military discipline is tough and rigorous, and the Spartans' most desired goal is death on the battlefield. Three classes of people live in—and are owned by—Sparta: citizens, those Spartans who are descendants of the Dorians; *perioeci*, free men, but not citizens; and the *helots*, the slaves, upon whom the Spartans declare war once a year to keep their numbers in check without technically committing "murder." Of those Spartan children who are not *exposed* to the elements of nature at birth, and left to die, the males are taken from their mothers at age seven to begin a grim "Spartan" existence devoid of culture, learning or emotion, and taught to care only for the cultivation of the body. While Sparta will become militarily triumphant for a while it will produce no great minds, nor will it leave great cultural works of art or literature behind them for posterity. Five hundred years from now when Alexander the Great is called a Greek, he will quickly point out that that means Athenian, not Spartan.

Homer

. . . The Greek alphabet begins to develop, based on the Phoenecian, thus, the Phoenecian *aleph* and *beth* become . . . *alpha, beta*.

. . . and, also in Greece (somewhere between now and 700 B.C.) the first "modern" poet, blind Homer, sings his epic poems, the *ILIAD* and the *ODYSSEY*. Homer, about whom nobody really knows anything for certain, bases his sagas on legends and folk tales, some real, genuine memories of past events and some myth, that, we now know, have been handed down by wandering bards for generations. For Homer lives in the iron age but never mentions iron; the armor of his heroes is silver-studded bronze, like that of Troy and Mycenae. But Homer's poetry breathes life into the ancient tales, and the Greeks take them literally . . . and worship as gods the many characters found in them; mighty heroes whose deeds are of heroic proportions. No ordinary mortals, when they live they live bravely and when they die they die nobly, to the majestic cadences of Homer's "rosy-fingered dawns," "wine-dark seas," and "wind-swept Troy."

The *ILIAD* tells the tale of the Trojan War, and its greatest hero, Achilles; of Agamemnon, king of golden Mycenae; Ajax, Nestor and Menelaus, who defend their ill-fated city from the wrath of the vengeful Greeks, furious at Prince Paris' abduction of their beautiful Helen. Homer's poetry is as heroic as those about whom he sings. In future years, when one Alexander becomes "great," it will be believing himself a modern-day Achilles. He will found a great city on Pharos Island at the mouth of the Nile River in Egypt because he heard a line from the *ILIAD* in a dream. Like himself, Alexandria will grow to greatness:

> An island there lies, where loud the billows roar. Pharos they call it, on the Egyptian shore.   Homer, the *ILIAD* (See: 332 B.C.)

The *ODYSSEY* tells of Ulysses' ten years wandering after the war, instigated by the spiteful promptings of Poseidon, god of the sea . . . and of earthquakes. It tells of his fantastic adventures in the land of the Lotus-eaters, and that of the Cyclops, where Ulysses cannily names himself Nobody, so that "nobody" will be blamed for blinding the one-eyed savage; and of his descent into Hades and consequent rebirth; how he resisted the irresistible Sirens and, finally, the happy reunion with his faithful wife, Penelope, who waited for him 20 years. The gods Zeus, Circe, Athene and Calypso all play parts in Ulysses' incredible "odyssey,"

Fragment of Homer from 2nd Century B.C.

> Like leaves on trees the race of man is found,
> Now green in youth, now withering on the ground;
> Another race the following spring supplies,
> They fall successive, and successive rise.   Homer the *ILIAD*
>
> It is not strength, but art, obtains the prize,
> And to be swift is less than to be wise.   The *ILIAD*
>
> Urge him with truth to frame his fair replies;
> And sure he will, for wisdom never lies.   The *ODYSSEY*
>
> O woman, woman, when to ill thy mind is bent,
> All hell contains no fouler fiend.   The *ODYSSEY*

The gods, they say, live on Mount Olympus, in the land called Hellas, and from Hellas come references to things Greek, or Hellenic. First, there was Chaos, and from it came heaven and earth. From a mighty race of Titans, Saturn came; and from him, Zeus, who rules the Heavens. Poseidon rules the ocean, and Pluto the lands of the dead. Ares is god of war; Aphrodite, love, Apollo, music; Athena, wisdom; and Vulcan rumbles the skies with thunder. Pan plays his pipes in Arcadian fields while the thread of human destiny is spun by the Fates. But then the first mortal is created, a woman named Pandora, whose curiosity causes her to open a forbidden box, and all that can happen to man is loosed—sin, suffering, misery, everything, save one thing only . . . hope.

The gods of Homer and Hellas are not cosmological gods like those of Mesopotamia and Egypt, things or beings found in the sky (the Zodiac) or on the earth (cows, cats and crocodiles). Greece's gods reflect, or duplicate man, himself. They are a society of aristocratic "Olympians" who do the same things humans do, who delight in their human counterparts, direct their affairs, enter into their lives (sometimes invisibly and sometimes in disguise) and even father semi-divine offspring. Every attribute man has, the gods have; they are wise and wicked, base and treacherous or noble, heroic and high-minded. As Hellas gets more and more involved in the world's affairs, Hellenism will become more imitated and emulated, the words "Hellenic" and "Hellenistic" meaning "to speak the language of the Greeks" or "in imitation of the Greeks."

785 (I)   Jeroboam II rules Israel forty prosperous years, and although he "did what was evil in the sight of the Lord," even the Chronicler of KINGS admits that "he enlarged the boundaries of" and "averted the wrath of the Lord from" Israel, and restored Israel to power.

783 (J)   King Uzziah rules Judah for 57 strong, prosperous years. He builds cities, towers on Jerusalem's walls, and fortifications. He hews out cisterns for water, encourages farmers and vinedressers "for he loved the soil," builds his army with "engines invented by skillful men, to be on the towers to shoot arrows and great stones." And his fame spreads far, for he is "very strong, and marvelously helped."

776   The Greeks all hold physical fitness in highest esteem, whether it is (for the Athenians) just one attribute of their many-sided personalities, or (for the Spartans) the sum total of their existence. Their love of competition leads them—commoners and kings alike—from near and far (but only men) to the Plains of Olympia, where they engage in sports contests called the *Olympics*. This is the first year the results of the Olympic Games are set down in record. They will be celebrated now, every four years (an *Olympiad)* for more than a thousand years before a Roman emperor calls a halt in A.D. 393. The games are so revered and respected that sacred truces between warring states guarantee safe passage for participants; solemn oaths are sworn to fair play and honest judgments, and the importance of grace and good conduct are judged equal with winning. And for those who do win: a simple olive wreath . . . and much honor. More than 300 years from now a Greek historian named Herodotus of Halicarnassus in Asia Minor, will write a monumental history of his time, and with one story will demonstrate just how highly the games—and the victors—are held. He tells of a man named Philippus of Croton.

This Philippus was an Olympic victor and the best looking man of his day; and . . . he received from the people of Egesta the unparalleled honor of a hero's shrine erected on his tomb, at which religious ceremonies are still held to win his favor.   Herodotus, RESEARCHES

Another story points up the awe in which Greece's enemies, the Persians, held men to whom honor meant more than money.

> . . . for when he learned that the prize was not money but [only an olive] wreath, he could not help crying out in front of everyone, "Good heavens, Mardonius, what kind of men are these that you have brought us to fight against—men who compete with one another for no material reward but only for honor!"   Herodotus, THE HISTORIES

753, June 15.   Babylonian astrologers have much to note and study, as the moon crosses between the sun and the earth in total eclipse. It is an event of much significance to future historians for it becomes a focal point for dating Biblical history, also. The glory days of the "Old" Babylonian empire are over and are being replaced by an arrogant young upstart called Assyria. Both nations speak the same language, Akkadian, but different dialects of it; and they date their history in different ways, as well. Babylon reckons its time by the regnal years of its kings—"the 15th year of the reign of Sargon the Great," or "the 20th year of Hammurabi." The Assyrian method is to assign one man to a special office for one year and then give that year his name. Both methods are confusing and liable to mix-up, but both note this date's eclipse of the sun, the date we call June 15, 753. It will become a most important focal point for noting the major events in the years ahead, years of passion, pain . . . and prophecy.

. . . and
the PROPHETS

. . . and the PROPHETS

It is nearly 200 years since the division of the kingdom. Israel and Judah have both gone through hard times and good. At the zenith of their existence they have been rich in territory and possessions beyond anything the ancient patriarchs could ever have imagined. And, from the depths of bad times, somehow manage to rise again. The little nomad theocracy that was, has become two kingdoms of luxury and wealth. Israel's capital, Samaria, is crowned with a fabulous ivory palace; and Judah's legendary Temple houses the Hebrew God . . . and a religious hierarchy to administer to Him, and to record the state of affairs. Never in their history has life been so good for the Hebrews . . . and never have they strayed so far from God.

And now, thoughtful, worried men appear on the scene with grave and dire warnings: "You have become sinful with your luxury," they cry, "and you will be destroyed!" For even now black clouds are gathering in the east and a new and frightful nation is gearing up its war machine, Assyria looms larger, and ever larger, on the horizon; but the Hebrews choose not to listen to the voices of warning, and continue their lives of licentiousness and idolatry that the . . . PROPHETS . . . say is an abomination to the Lord"

Notice: how Judah is set back from the sea; and Israel extends right up to it, offering a battlefield to any who want to fight from north or south.

c. 753   Amos, first of the LITERARY or WRITING prophets, begins to preach in the days of Kings Uzziah of Judah and Jeroboam of Israel.

AMOS

Book of Prophecy — Written in Hebrew,   c. 700 B C.

AMOS, the "herdsman of Tekoa," lived during a time of peace, prosperity and expansion, while Kings Uzziah of Judah and Jeroboam of Israel were ruling, statesmanlike rulers who expanded their kingdoms' borders, built up their military, and enriched their coffers . . . without interfering in each other's affairs. But it is also a time when the coffers of the already-rich overflow at the expense of the poor; and Amos is given the unwelcome duty of taking them all to task. A peace-loving man, Amos was a shepherd and forester, or woodsman, who wanted only to go about his own quiet business; but God chose him to preach the message of Israel's coming doom, destruction . . . and EXILE, because of the sinfulness and immorality of the people and the idol worship of their kings . . . and he obeyed. Amos' voice is the first to proclaim that God is a God for all people, not just the personal property of the Hebrews, and that worship of Him should not be just a ritual of burnt offerings. "I hate, I despise your feast days," he cries, "though ye offer me burnt offerings . . . I will not accept them."   5:21–2

Uzziah and Jeroboam are worldly kings, and carry on trade abroad, including Africa, from which they import large quantities of ivory, and when Jeroboam builds himself a magnificent ivory palace at his capital city, Samaria, Amos cries:

> "Woe unto them who build houses . . . and lie upon beds of ivory, and stretch themselves upon [ivory] couches . . . I will smite the winter house and the summer house: and the houses of ivory shall perish."   6:4 and 3:15

Many centuries from now the British Museum will house a vast collection of ivory found in the ruins of Samaria, which includes bits and pieces of broken furniture, walls and wall decorations, and an entire, intricately-carved headboard from an ivory bed!

The Ivory Headboard

> Prophecy: The high places of Isaac shall be made desolate and the sanctuaries of Israel shall be laid waste . . . Israel must go into exile.   7:9, 11 (See: 721 B.C.)

But gloom was not all he prophesied.

> I will restore the fortunes of my people Israel and they shall rebuild the ruined cities and inhabit them.   3:14 (See: 538 B.C.)

753   Far to the west in a land that hangs like a boot into the very heart of the "Great Sea," the Mediterranean, the first stirrings of life begin in a city that will soon dominate the

world. Three separate and distinct tribes of people, the Etruscans already mentioned, the Sabines and the Latin's dwell in an area covered by seven hills; the Palatine, Esqualine, Aventine, Viminal, Quirinal, Caelian and the Capitoline Hills. Little by little the three tribes

The Birth of Rome

unite in a loose federation and slowly merge into one city. Ancient Roman legend says that twin brothers, Romulus and Remus, sons of the Latin god, Mars, and a Vestal Virgin, were abandoned on the site, suckled by a she-wolf, and grew up to become the first rulers of the city of Rome. Romulus, the legend says, drew the boundaries of Rome with his plow; and the brothers ruled together for a while, but finally quarreled. Remus was slain, and Romulus became the first "King of Rome," a Latin, from the tribe of Latins, from which comes the name of their language. Just as the abbreviations B.C. (Before Christ) and A.D. *(Anno Domini—*In the Year of Our Lord) are used today to designate dates, so will Romans of this time designate this year, that we know as 753 B.C., as the "Year of the Founding of the City of Rome," or A.U.C., *Anno Urbis Conditae.*

Seven hundred and sixty-some years from now, a Roman historian named Titus Livius, or Livy, will publish his life's work, a 142 volume history of Rome from this time, of its founding, to his own. Thirty five volumes still exist today, from which this book will quote often. Livy believed that Rome was divinely ordained to rule the world . . .

(I . . . believe) it was already written in the book of fate that this great city of ours should arise, and the first steps be taken to the founding of the mightiest empire the world has known—next to God's. The Vestal . . . was raped and gave birth to twin boys. Mars, she declared, was their father—perhaps she believed it . . . neither gods nor men could save her or her babes . . . [she] was . . . flung into prison; the boys . . . condemned to be drowned . . . Destiny, however, intervened . . .   Livy, THE EARLY HISTORY OF ROME, 1:3, 4

750   The city of Corinth is, by now one of the richest and fairest in Greece. An important manufacturing city and trading center, it is a crossroads between Asia and Italy to whom it sells purple dyes and textiles, painted vases and bronze. Its *agora,* or marketplace, is graced with a porch, or *stoa,* as beautiful as any in antiquity.

. . . Assyria's war chariots scream into Judah on diversionary raids of harassment and plunder, and in Israel, the prophet HOSEA begins to preach.

HOSEA

Book of Prophecy — Written in Hebrew,   c. 750 B.C.

"O Israel, thou hast destroyed thyself . . . Ye have plowed wickedness, ye have reaped iniquity! ye have eaten the fruit of lies . . . FOR I DESIRED [LOVE] AND NOT SACRIFICE . . . KNOWLEDGE OF GOD MORE THAN BURNT OFFERINGS." (10:13 & 6:5) Thus, through the prophet, Hosea, does God now reveal this new, most glorious aspect of His nature. No more sacrifice and burnt offerings, but steadfast love and knowledge of

God, Himself; a striking and monumental departure from the old understanding, to a new, enlightened conception of the Almighty. But Hosea sees that the Israelites care not a whit about God or what He is, for Israel is in the depths of sin, and Hosea calls them ". . . a band of drunkards, they give themselves to harlotry . . . they break all bounds and murder follows murder . . . a vulture is over the house of the LORD, because they have broken my covenant, and transgressed my law . . . With their silver and gold they made idols for their own destruction. . ." But even as Hosea condemns them (and he condemns them bitterly) he speaks of love: "Come, and let us return unto the LORD . . . he hath smitten and he will bind us up," and forgiveness: "I will heal their backsliding, I will love them freely . . . for I am God, and not a man; the Holy One in the midst of thee."

The book of HOSEA is placed first in the section of the Bible called the Minor Prophets, the last 12 books of the Old Testament. Some are minor only in length, for their messages are extremely major, including HOSEA's. A native of Israel, Hosea preached to his own people already facing the threat of Assyria which, he cried, was "a vulture over the house of the LORD." Hosea prophesied to Israel that destruction and EXILE . . . were just ahead.

> For they sow the wind and they shall reap the whirlwind. 8:7 * They shall not remain in the land of the LORD . . . they shall eat unclean food in Assyria.   9:3 (See: 721 B.C.)

Hosea is the first Hebrew to preach the concept of God as FATHER, and is called the Prophet of Love, for he saw God as a God of love, whose "wife," Israel was a faithless harlot . . . whom Hosea forgave, and treated with love. Eight hundred years from now a new "Christian" Church will interpret as its own one of HOSEA's most touching and enigmatic prophecies about the birth of a child.

> When Israel was a child, then I loved him, and called my son out of Egypt.   11:1 (See: 1 B.C. and MATTHEW 2:15)

Assyria's very existence depends on its war machine, its lightning-swift cavalry and the terrifying ruthlessness of its troops. Their engineers float river bridges on pontoons of inflated animal hides, and assemble siege towers overnight with pre-cut timbers. Their mobile battering rams are iron-clad and their catapults hurl gigantic stones. Assyria teaches, by example, the futility of resistance. Horrible cruelties are inflicted on those who do resist; captives skinned alive, noses and ears cut off, tongues torn- and eyes gouged-out, and

Carved stone walls from Nineveh

heads piled up into great pyramids, to be counted by scribes. It is not history's biased verdict that condemns Assyria as cruel and brutal, but their own artists and stone-carvers who record, all too truthfully, their savage barbarism. Carved stone walls from Nineveh and other cities, hang today in European museums, showing these and other atrocities. Assyria's main target is Egypt, and to get there it must go directly through . . . Israel.

746 (I)   Jereboam II, the last strong king of Israel, dies; and the kingdom, thrown into chaos, collapses. Israel lies, doomed and helpless, in Assyria's bloody path.

Assyria is at the zenith of its power now; invincible in its strength, despised for its brutality and feared for the threat of the future. Its present king, Tiglath-pileser, has changed the ways of war. No longer will rape, robbery, looting, murder and mayhem be the only punishment of defeated countries, but—even as Amos and Hosea prophesied—EXILE will become the lot of entire peoples . . . dragged away in bondage, to fade away into oblivion.

c. 746   The prophet Jonah is sent by God to the Assyrian capital of Nineveh which he calls an "exceedingly great city, three days journey in breadth . . ."

JONAH

Book of Prophecy — Written in Hebrew,   c. 400–300 B.C.

"Arise, go to Nineveh . . . and cry against it; for their wickedness has come before me." Thus does God command Jonah in the opening lines of this allegorical book. But Jonah has other ideas and sails off in the opposite direction. What happens next is one of the Bible's most familiar stories; Jonah in the whale, or rather, the "great fish," which Jonah calls *Sheol*, the place of darkness and death. But the "reluctant prophet" is successful in spite of himself, and sulks all the more when God decides to spare the repentant Ninevites. JONAH's real importance, though, is to demonstrate God's love for ALL His creation; from sinful cities, to humble plants ". . . and also much cattle."

The book of JONAH will not be written until a much later time, but its events happened at this time. The historical book of KINGS II mentions Jonah at 14:25 by saying ". . . the word of the LORD God of Israel [was spoken] by the hand of His servant Jonah . . ."

---

745 (I)   After Jeroboam, King Menahem, the third king in one year, "rip[s] up women . . . with child," exacts a fortune from Israel to pay tribute to Assyria, and is mentioned on a stone carving of Tiglath-pileser:

I set my own official as district-governor over them . . . the tribute of Menahem of Samaria [and 17 other rulers] . . . gold, silver, tin, iron, elephant hides, ivory, blue and purple dyed embroidered cloth, ebony, walnut wood, everything precious, (fit for) royalty . . . cattle, mules and camels . . .   The ANNALS of Tiglath-pileser, king of Assyria

---

c. 740   Into the very midst of this time of political turbulence, treachery and intrigue appears, now, a young man of about 25 years named Isaiah, who tells a remarkable story: "In the year that King Uzziah died," Isaiah says, "I saw . . . the LORD sitting upon a throne, high and lifted up [and] seraphims . . . each [with] six wings . . . And one cried unto another . . . Holy, holy, holy is the LORD of Hosts: the whole earth is full of his glory. 6:3 [And] I heard the voice of the Lord, saying, whom shall I send, and who will go for us? Then said I, Here am I; send me." And God sends Isaiah to Jerusalem to preach His word, and to warn of disaster ahead, but tells him also, that the Hebrews will neither listen nor care, and that the disaster will not be stopped:

> And what will ye do in the day of visitation, and in the desolation which shall come from afar: To whom will ye flee for help? And where will ye leave your glory?   ISAIAH 10:3

753 (J)   An evil king Ahaz of Judah worships the pagan Baal and melts down the Temple's holy vessels to make graven idols. Ahaz sacrifices his own sons on a pagan altar, then bargains with Assyria for aid: but Tiglath-pileser "[brings] Judah low" and "afflict[s] instead of strengthen[s] him."

734 (I)   A king named Pekah murders his way to Israel's throne, and rules 20 years, a plotter and conniver who even wars against Judah . . . until Assyria invades, and . . .

733   Damascus falls to Assyria, and with that "buffer" state gone, Israel reels under the full force of Assyria's fury . . .

> . . . Pekah their king they deposed and Hoshea I set (as king over them . . .)   The Nimrud Tablet of Tiglath-pileser

732 (I)   A "treacherous" king, Hoshea rules nine years and pays tribute to Assyria, but plays politics with Egypt, so the "king of Assyria shut him up in prison." Israel's capital, Samaria, groans under siege for three long years by Assyria's new king, Shalmaneser . . . who is killed during the siege; and then by Sargon II, victorious and merciless in conquest. Sargon wastes no time finishing the job. In the first year of his reign . . .

721   . . . Samaria falls. Sargon II of Assyria conquers the northern kingdom and . . .

ISRAEL IS NO MORE!

Victorious Assyria brutalizes defeated Israel in the manner it knows best and is infamous for. Thousands of Israeliltes are tortured, maimed, dismembered, abused and murdered. Finally, the pitiful remains of the 10 northern tribes are herded away to Assyria's capital, Nineveh, and are never heard of again. They become known as the TEN LOST TRIBES OF ISRAEL. Sargon then re-populates Israel with foreign peoples, among whom are a tribe called Samaritans, who, for this reason will be much despised in the years ahead. The prophecies of Amos and Hosea have come true:

Assyrian Bas Relief

> ... the sanctuaries of Israel shall be laid waste, and Israel must go into exile.　AMOS 7:9
> (See: 760 B.C.) * They shall not remain in the land of the Lord ... They shall eat unclean food in Assyria.　HOSEA 9:3 (See: 750 B.C.)

Sargon II

Sargon II will rule Assyria only 16 years but—for him—they will be great years, and before he is murdered in 705 he will have conquered peoples from "... the four quarters of the world." He builds a capital city at Khorsabad and fills it with monumental stone carvings of mythical animals, defeated towns and kings. Khorsabad will live only as long as its founder, and when the ruins of its 180 rooms are excavated in the 19th century A.D. many of its wonders will find their way to the university of Chicago's Oriental Institute. There, standing today in splendid isolation, is one of Sargon's gigantic, human-headed stone bulls, 15 feet tall, and almost 40 tons in weight. "Sargon, the king of Assyria" is mentioned just once in the Bible, in ISAIAH 20:1, and that mention was mocked and derided for years (as was the frequent mention of Hittite peoples) by those who would discredit the Bible and expose it as mere myth, for they "knew" there had never been such a king, or people.

Sargon's Stone Bull

But Sargon had his victory over the Ten Tribes of Israel carved on a stone tablet, and it can also be seen today at the Oriental Institute:

> I besieged and conquered Samaria, led away as booty 22,299 inhabitants of it.　Cuneiform victory tablet of Sargon II of Assyria

Off the beaten path, the southern kingdom of Judah is spared for the time being, but the price comes high. A yearly payment of tribute money is exacted and, to get it, the Temple in Jerusalem is stripped of its treasure. It is sent to Assyria as ransom for Judah's precarious "freedom" and Judah is squeezed in a vise between Assyria and Egypt, for Egypt is the prize Assyria wants.

The prophet Isaiah is preaching now in Judah, and especially in Jerusalem to "... a sinful nation, a people laden with iniquity, offspring of evildoers ... who have forsaken the LORD, despised the Holy of Israel ... and are utterly estranged." A member of Jerusalem's higher class, Isaiah knows well the life of the city, and he sees much of its sinfulness in its women. "The daughters of Jerusalem are haughty," he cries, "and walk with outstretched necks, glancing wantonly with their eyes, mincing along as they go, tinkling with their feet ... they wear anklets, headbands, gauze, linen garments and veils." And he predicts woe to them, for "... they proclaim their sin like Sodom ..."

And Isaiah writes the first part of the book that bears his name:

ISAIAH

Book of Prophecy — Written in Hebrew,   c. 742–687 B.C.

"Come now, and let us reason together, saith the Lord," begins the book of ISAIAH, ". . . though your sins be as scarlet, they shall be white as snow; though they be red like crimson, they shall be as wool." Despite the dreadful prophesies Isaiah must preach, he is a reasonable man, begging his people to ". . . make you clean . . . put away the evil of your doings." But the faithful city has become a harlot, he mourns, "its silver has become dross." And, through Isaiah, God demands: "Shall I not, as I have done unto Samaria and her idols, so do to Jerusalem and her idols?"

ISAIAH is one of the most important books of the Bible, considered a "Major Prophet" partly because of the length of his book, but mostly because of the astounding significance of his message. For Isaiah's is the first and greatest book to prophesy the birth, sufferings, death and triumph of Him who will one day bring a "New Covenant." But the exact authorship of ISAIAH is in doubt to this day, as it is written from several perspectives. The first 33 chapters concern the present time, and the last 27 tell of events more than 100 years hence. Some scholars attribute the entire book to one man; most believe there were two Isaiah's living at different times; and still others say there may even have been three.

The "first" Isaiah was an aristocratic Judean nobleman of some importance at court and in the Temple for some 40 years. He was bitterly critical of Judah's foreign policy, getting itself tangled up in intrigue with Egypt while nervously existing in Assyria's shadow. As God's prophet, he could see that there was disaster ahead; Assyria was not armed for nothing; its methods were merciless, and its forces fierce and terrible fighters. Still, Isaiah's job was almost impossible for it was God's intention that he should be disdained and ignored by the idol-worshipping, pleasure-loving Judeans, and that only a tiny "Redeeming Remnant" (about whom Isaiah would not even know) would listen, believe, hold the faith . . . and someday rebuild, just as God had promised Elijah many years ago.

> Yet I have left me seven thousand in Israel, all the knees which have not bowed unto Baal . . .   I KINGS 19:18   *   The remnant shall return, even the remnant of Jacob, unto the mighty God . . . And in that day thou shalt say, O Lord, I will praise thee; though thou wast angry with me, thine anger is turned away, and thou comfortedst me. Behold, God is my salvation; I will trust, and not be afraid; for the LORD JEHOVAH is my strength and my song; he also is become my salvation.   ISAIAH 10:21 and 12:1,2

And, Isaiah says, the destroyer will be destroyed:

> And Babylon, the glory of kingdoms, the beauty of the Chaldee's excellency, shall be as when God overthrew Sodom and Gomorrah.   13:19

Many of Isaiah's prophecies have to do, though, not with the Remnant, but with a "Suffering Servant," an individual, a redeemer, a SAVIOR." Isaiah doesn't say WHEN He will come . . . but come He will!

> Prophecy: Therefore, the Lord himself shall give you a sign, Behold, a virgin shall conceive and bear a son, and shall call his name Immanuel. 7:14 (See: 3 B.C.) The people who walked in darkness, on them has a light shined. 9:2 (See: 23 A.D.) For unto us a child is born, unto us a son is given and the government will be upon his shoulder and his name shall be called Wonderful, Counselor, The mighty God, The everlasting Father, The Prince of Peace. 9:6 (3 B.C.) He will swallow up death forever, and the Lord GOD will wipe away tears from all the earth; for the LORD has spoken. 25:8 (A.D. 100) Then shall the eyes of the blind be opened, and the ears of the deaf unstopped; then shall the lame man leap like a hart, and the tongue of the dumb sing for joy. 35:5-6 (A.D. 23)

Twenty-five hundred years from now the government of a new United States of America will be organized; the first nation in the world to be specifically created on the "self-evident truth" that "all men are created equal," and that their right to "life, liberty and the pursuit of happiness" is "endowed by their Creator." The God-fearing, God-loving men who create the Constitution for this new nation will plan their government, not on the universal practice of ruler and ruled, king and commons, tyrant and tyrannized, but on free men governing themselves in a system of checks and balances; a "tripartite"—separate-but-equal three part—government of JUDICIAL, LEGISLATIVE and EXECUTIVE branches, acknowledging that it is "one nation under God" . . . just as that described by Isaiah 25 centuries before:

> For the LORD is our judge, the LORD is our lawgiver, the LORD is our king; he will save us. ISAIAH 33:22

c. 700   The prophet MICAH preaches, also, in Judah.

MICAH

Book of Prophecy — Written in Hebrew,   c. 739–700 B.C.

In sharp contrast to the aristocratic Isaiah, Micah was a commoner, a simple man come from a small village, with a philosophy that said, "What doth the LORD require of thee but to do justly and to love kindness and to walk humbly with thy God." But this was not what Micah saw when he came to the "Holy City" of Jerusalem. What he did see, he did not like, and prophesied that Jerusalem would fall:

> Hear this, rulers of the house of Israel, who build Zion with blood and Jerusalem with wrong. Its leaders give judgments for a bribe, its priests teach for hire, its prophets divine for money. Therefore because of you Zion shall be plowed as a field; Jerusalem shall become a heap of ruins. 3:9–12 (See: 587 B.C.)

But Micah promised something very different for the little village of Bethlehem, five miles south of Jerusalem, something wonderful . . .

> But you, O Bethlehem, who are little among the clans of Judah, from you shall come forth for me one who is to be ruler of Israel, whose origin is from old, from ancient days. 5:2 (See: 2 B.C.)

701   Assyria's new king, Sennacherib, invades Judah, and finds its king, Ahaz's son, Hezekiah, strong and defiant . . . and the story is told both in the Bible and on an Assyrian cunieform-carved stone prism found by modern archeologists:

> Now in the fourteenth year of King Hezekiah did Sennacherib king of Assyria come up against all the fenced cities of Judah, and took them.   II KINGS 18:13
>
> . . . as for Hezekiah, the Jew, who did not bow in submission to my yoke, 46 of his strong walled towns . . . I besieged and conquered . . . by battering rams . . . breaches, tunneling. He himself I shut up like a caged bird within Jerusalem . . .   The SENNACHERIB PRISM, now in the Oriental Institute, University of Chicago.

Hezekiah seeks the advice of Isaiah the prophet, and Isaiah replies: "Thus says the LORD, the king of Assyria will not come into this city . . . but will return . . . and fall by the sword in his own land."

Hezekiah repulses Sennacherib partly through payment of tribute . . .

> . . . the awful splendor of my lordship . . . made the over-bearing and proud Hezekiah . . . bow at my feet . . .   The SENNACHERIB PRISM

The Sennacherib Prism

. . . partly because of his brilliant defense of the city, which includes a vast engineering project: a great tunnel six feet high and almost 1800 feet long, carved out of solid rock, which brings Jerusalem fresh spring water . . . and of which the Assyrians are unaware . . .

> . . . he made the pool and the conduit, and brought water into the city.   II KINGS 20:20

The tunnel is begun at both ends and hewn out towards the middle, workman meeting workman at its conclusion:

> . . . while there were still three cubits to be cut through (there was heard] the voice of a man calling to his fellow, for there was *an overlap* in the rock on the right [and . . . left]. And . . . the quarrymen hewed (the rock), each man toward his fellow, axe against axe:
>
>
>
> and the water flowed from the spring toward the reservoir for 1,200 cubits, and the height of the rock above the head(s) of the quarrymen was 100 cubits.   The SILOAM INSCRIPTION, found in 1880 on the wall of the tunnel to the Pool of Siloam, still in use today. The Inscription is, today, in the Museum of the Ancient Orient, Istanbul, Turkey.
>
> The Siloam Inscription

But it is a plague, believed to be caused by field mice, that drives Sennacherib home . . . where he is murdered by his own sons.

c. 700   Not only in the East are empires in upheaval. In Greece, too, violence and lawlessness reign . . .

. . . and the Greek poet, Hesiod, takes note, and mourns: "Might makes right now. It is brother against brother, child against parent, all hard-hearted and no longer god-fearing."

Hesiod's ideal of beauty and grace was gleaming, golden Myceneae, gone now forever, alive only in his poet's mind. Son of a ship owner, Hesiod fears the sea and loves the soil, so becomes a farmer-poet, who wins a tripod for his poetry at the Chalcis games. In his *THEOGONY* he relates the genealogy of Greece's gods, beginning with Chaos, which produced Night and Day. He tells how Earth lay with Heaven and gave birth to the Hills and Seas . . . and Zeus, through whose line mankind appeared in the first mortal woman, Pandora. In his WORKS AND DAYS Hesiod writes about practical matters; how to live and farm, behave toward others, and when to plant and harvest. WORKS AND DAYS is called the first "farmer's almanac."

> Let it please thee to keep in order a moderate-sized farm, that so thy garners may be full of fruits in their season. * If thou shouldst lay up even a little upon a little, and shouldst do this often, soon would even this become great.   Hesiod, WORKS AND DAYS

. . . In the frozen north, wild Sythian tribes are invading what is, today, called Russia . . .

. . . and in the very far east, one war lord named Jimmu Tenno becomes Emperor of Japan, a "descendent of the gods," themselves. Japanese legend names him its first *Mikado,* beginning the age-old belief in the divinity of its emperors.

. . . The second king of Rome, after Romulus, is Numa Pompilius, of the tribe of Sabines. He re-organizes the Latin calendar, adding January (for the Roman god, Janus) and February; and fixes certain days of the week for working and others for holidays. While Romulus founded the political and military aspects of Rome, Numa establishes its religion. Unlike Mesopotamia's heavenly zodiac gods, Egypt's sun and creature gods, and Greece's human counterparts, Rome's gods come from the sea and the earth, the source of life, food and drink, and are most often abstract, like Health, Fortune, Hope and Virtue, having no outward form.

Faunus is god of fields and shepherds, and Flora goddess of flowers; Liber is god of wine, and Pomona of fruit trees; Diana is goddess of the hunt, and Lucina of childbirth. Every household has its Lares (souls of loving, watchful ancestors) and Penates (who guarantee a full pantry); and every man and woman has his Genius and her Juno, their spirit protectors. Juno Regina (meaning queen) is the special spirit of women, thus making June

the best month in which to be married. Every season has its spirit, as in Maia, or May; and earth, itself, is *Terra Mater,* Earth Mother. Rome's welfare is guarded by a sacred fire on the city's hearth, watched over and kept burning by Vestal Virgins, who must remain pure until age 30, or suffer beating and death. A *Rex Sacorum* is king of sacrifices and interprets the will of the gods, and the *Pontifex Maximus* or, High Priest, reigns over all. It has been said by latter-day scholars that, were they all counted up, Rome's gods would number in the thousands.

Although its first two kings were a Latin and a Sabine, Rome is hemmed in by Etruscans, with Etruscan settlements at what today are called Ravenna, Parma, Bologna, Verona, Rimini, Mantua and Modena. A highly industrious people, the Etruscans trade all across the Mediterranean, produce pig iron for weapons and create beautiful works of art with copper: coins, utensils, mirrors, fans, lamps and candelabra for peace, and chariots, shields, spears and helmets for war. They are a happy people, though, with a love of music and dance, which they accompany with lyre, pipes, trumpets and syrinx, or Pipes of Pan.

687   In Judah, twelve year-old Manasseh begins a 55 year reign, its "most evil" king; such evil that, according to II KINGS, Judah's punishment because of him will cause ". . . the ears of everyone who hears of it [to] tingle." His reign is an abomination to God, for he worships everything but God. He sets up idols and altars to Baal in the holy Temple and destroys the holy books! An irreparable loss to those Jews who still hold to the Law of Moses and of God, their destruction is an act of unspeakable evil. Magic and soothsaying, wizardry and mediums, all replace the worship of God, and ". . . he shed very much innocent blood." He burns his own sons as sacrifice on Baal's alter, and the Jewish TALMUD says that Manasseh ". . . executed the prophet Isaiah," ordered him ". . . sawn asunder, between two wooden planks." The book of CHRONICLES says that King Manasseh eventually repented, and the apocryphal PRAYER OF MANASSEH (See: 150 B.C.) bears that out, but it is not even mentioned in the book of II KINGS, which maintains that it was for Manasseh's sins that Judah would be destroyed. And the book of ISAIAH adds:

> For the nation and kingdom that will not serve thee shall perish; yea, those nations shall be utterly wasted.   ISAIAH 60:12

There is some modern scholarship which indicates that it was during Manasseh's bloody reign that Moses' holy Ark of the Covenant was spirited out of Jerusalem for safety; and through a tortuous and circuitous route, eventually ended up in deep African Ethiopia where, in unknown isolation, it remains to this day.

660   Assyria's ruler now is Ashurbanipal, a man of enigmatic personality, cruel and uncompromising toward conquered lands and peoples, but at home, a "patron of the arts." His capital city, Nineveh, is a vast, sprawling complex on the east bank of the Tigris River, a masterful collection of gardens, parks and temples. Assyrian art and architecture reaches its peak under Ashurbanipal . . . although much of it shows the bestiality of Assyrian warfare; its siege engines, battering rams, and the terrible atrocities committed against its unfortunate victims. With an avid interest in mythology, history and astrology, Ashurbanipal builds a huge royal library at Nineveh which holds thousands of clay tablets (many of which exist today.) Their writing covers many subjects; correspondence with foreign kings, including the age old "Amarna Letters" from Egypt's "sun king," Akhenaten, who ruled

Nineveh

before the time of Moses; and the even older Epic of Gilgamesh, also. Ashurbanipal's own written annals tell, also, of his harnessing defeated kings to his chariots to pull him through the streets of Nineveh.

> . . . as for those common men whose slanderous mouths had spoken . . . against my god Ashur, and plotted-against me . . . I tore out their tongues and abased them . . . their cut up flesh I fed to the dogs, swine, jackals . . . vultures . . . The RASSAM CYLINDER of Ashurbanipal

In the years since the last prophets, Micah and Isaiah, the little kingdom of Judah has been maintaining a precarious peace (while its late counterpart, Israel, is now no more than a bloody battlefield between Egyptians, Assyrians and even barbaric Sythian tribesmen who swoop down out of Russia.) Clamped in the vise between Assyria and Egypt, Judah engages in the dangerous stratagem of playing off one side against the other . . .

. . . In Italy, the third king of Rome is a Latin, Tullus Hostilius, whose name well describes his person, for he is a hostile ruler, and under him the city of Rome takes its first step toward expansion beyond its own boundaries. According to the historian Livy, Hostilius felt the hardy Romans were getting soft from too easy living. "Convinced that the vigor of the state was becoming enfeebled through inaction, he looked around for a pretext for war . . . [and] soon felt strong enough to declare war on the Sabines . . ." Legend (and Livy) also says that Hostilius was "struck dead by lightening as punishment for pride."

640   With the death of the evil King Manasseh, King Josiah begins a 31 year reign in Judah. The Bible says he "did what was right in the eyes of the Lord and turned neither right nor left." Josiah undertakes the rebuilding of the Temple, so badly abused by Manasseh, and . . .

630   . . . the prophet Zephaniah preaches in Judah . . .

ZEPHANIAH

Book of Prophecy — Written in Hebrew,   c. 630 B.C.

The prophet Zephaniah was a nobleman, a descendent of King Hezekiah, therefore familiar with the royal court and its condition. His book is an impassioned condemnation of the religious corruption running rampant in Jerusalem, which he calls "filthy and polluted," and he tells of the coming of the great and dreadful *Dies Irae*, the Day of the LORD.

> The great day of the LORD is near . . . a day of wrath . . . distress and anguish . . . of ruin and devastation . . . of trumpet blast and battle cry . . . because they have sinned against the LORD, neither their silver nor their gold shall be able to deliver them on the day of the wrath of the LORD.   1:14–18 (See: 586 B.C.)

The power struggle in the mid-east goes on. Assyria's strength is gradually declining and that of Babylon growing. Over-powered by the Chaldeans from the area of the Persian Gulf and the Medes from Iran, Babylonia slowly absorbs them both into itself, and now begins to flex its muscles and rattle its sabers.

628   In the 13th year of King Josiah's reign, the prophet Jeremiah begins to preach in Judah: "Faithless Israel has shown herself less guilty than false Judah," he cries. "You have polluted the land with your vile harlotry! Everyone from least to greatest is greedy for unjust gain . . . from prophet to priest deals falsely . . . and commits abomination. My grief is beyond healing. My heart is sick. Is there no balm in Gilead? [You have] forsaken the LORD your God when He led you in the way!" And in a prophecy fit for any age, including our own, Jeremiah cries, "Behold, says our God, I WILL FEED THIS PEOPLE WORM-WOOD!" While King Josiah's workmen are cleaning in the Temple, his secretary comes to him and says, "The high priest found a book of LAW in the house of the LORD, and has given it to me." (Today it is believed to have been a copy of DEUTERONOMY that was overlooked when King Manasseh destroyed the holy books.) And he reads it to Josiah:

> I am the LORD your God: you shall have no other gods before me . . . You shall not make for yourself graven images. Remember the Sabbath to keep it holy. You shall not kill. You shall not commit adultery . . .

Now does Josiah realize the horrible extent of Judah's sins, and cries aloud and rends his clothes. He has the whole city gathered together at the Temple and reads them the LAW; clears out the Temple of its pagan idols and utensils, and has them destroyed and burned. Following the book's instructions Josiah orders a great PASSOVER feast celebrated, the first since the long-ago days of the Judges; and all the people celebrate Passover.

> When your sons ask you in time to come, "What is the meaning of all these testimonies, statutes and ordinances?" you are to answer: "We were Pharaoh's slaves in Egypt, and the LORD has brought us out with a mighty hand, and gave us the land as he promised, and commands us to keep His commandments."   DEUTERONOMY 6:20, 21

The book of KINGS II says, of Josiah, that there was "no king like him, neither before nor after, for he turned to the LORD with all his heart, soul and might."

621   In Greece, an Athenian statesman named Draco holds the office of *archon*, now, and undertakes the immense task of codifying and putting into writing all of Athens' many heretofore unwritten laws. It is a much needed, welcome effort except, according to a Greek historian named Plutarch, who will write 600 years from now (See: A.D. 100) and from whom this book will quote much . . .

> . . . they were too severe . . . the punishment too great: for death was appointed for almost all offenses . . . those . . . convicted of idleness were to die . . . those that stole a cabbage or an apple to suffer even as villains that committed sacrilege or murder. [it was] said that Draco's laws were not written with ink but blood . . .   Plutarch, of Chaeronea, PARALLEL LIVES OF THE NOBLE GREEKS AND ROMANS

Asked why his "Draconian" laws are so severe, Draco responds. . .

> Small ones deserve that, and I have no higher for the greater crimes.   Plutarch, LIVES

620   Ancus Marcius is now the 4th king of Rome, like Hostilius a Latin, but unlike him a man of peace, who resorts to arms only in defense of Roman territories. As Romulus had established the noble Patrician class (the original founders of Rome) Ancus now establishes the Plebian, the common folk. The historian Livy says he reigned 24 years," and "his fame as both soldier and administrator was unsurpassed by any previous occupant of the throne."

> He well understood the value of . . . peace when Rome was young and her people still somewhat wild, [but] . . . Hostile peoples were . . . beginning to prick him to see how much he would stand . . . It was not enough, he thought, that wars should be fought; he believed that they should also be formally declared, and for this purpose he adopted . . . legal formalities . . .   Livy, THE EARLY HISTORY OF ROME. 1:32

. . . Babylonia has been growing larger and larger, gaining more and more power, conquering land after land, and now . . .

612   Babylonia conquers Assyria, and the Assyrian capital of . . . NINEVEH IS COMPLETELY DESTROYED! But not before all the booty Assyria exacted from the Jews is hauled off to Babylon. All the gold and silver vessels and ornaments that once graced the holy Temple are plundered once again.

> They made a strong attack on the citadel . . . the city was taken. They carried off much spoil from the city and temple area and turned the city into a ruin-mound and heap of debris . . .   A Babylonian cuneiform tablet, now in the British Museum, London.

And the prophet NAHUM is ecstatic over the fall of Nineveh!

NAHUM

Book of Prophecy — Written in Hebrew,   c. 612 B.C.

Assyria is conquered by Babylonia, and its mighty capital, Nineveh, is destroyed. The prophet, Nahum, from the village of Elkosh, is overjoyed and rejoices that "the mistress of witchcraft," that citadel of evil has fallen. He long believed it would happen and now it has! His entire poem is an exultation that it was the LORD'S judgment on a wicked city. "Woe to the bloody city," Nahum cries, ". . . chariots shall rage in the streets . . . (blood-red) . . . [and no] end of their corpses . . . Keep your feasts, O Judah, fulfill your vows, for never again shall the wicked come against you, he is utterly cut off."   1:15, 2:4, 3:4

But, situated at the very heart of the world struggle, Judah and its capital, Jerusalem, are battered and bruised by both Babylonia in the north and Egypt in the south, each lusting after the remnants of the fallen Assyria. King Josiah, knowing that an Egyptian victory would, also, mean Egyptian occupation of Judah, sets out to frustrate Pharaoh Necho's plans . . .

609   King Josiah, in a last vain attempt to drive out the Egyptians, takes on their armies at the hill of Meggido (later to be called Armageddon) . . . and dies a hero's death at the hand of Pharaoh Necho, himself. Jehoahaz is set up then, as king, but Necho has other plans. He exiles Jehoahaz to Syria in chains, sets up a puppet king over Judah, and levies upon him heavy tribute: one *talent of* gold and a hundred of silver.

605   But Babylonia takes control of Egypt's Sinai Peninsula, and is now the supreme power in the "Orient," and Nebuchadnezzar is its king. The Chaldean Nebuchadnezzar rebuilds its ancient capital, Babylon, as no city before, creating a fabulous collection of temples, towers, palaces, fortifications, bridges, inner walls, moats and outer walls. Even the fields between the walls are irrigated by water wheels and can feed the city should it come under siege. Babylon's city walls are 50 miles long and so wide four-horse chariots can race on them. The 130-foot main chapel to Nebuchadnezzar's god, Marduk, is gold plated, and the processional way that leads to the Ishtar Gate is lighted at night with oil lamps, and carved in relief with marching gods and lords. The enormous, brilliant blue, red and yellow glazed tiled facade of the Ishtar Gate, stands reconstructed today in the Berlin museum, with one left-over panel on display at the Institute of Fine Arts in Detroit, Michigan. The wood for the doors and roof is Cedar of Lebanon which Nebuchadnezzar brings back from raids into Syria:

The Ishtar Gate

I broke up towering mountains . . . ground up limestone . . . opened up . . . a straight way for the cedars . . . the canal [carried them] as though they were reeds . . . hardy, tall, stout cedars, of surpassing quality . . . solid products of Mount Lebanon . . .   Inscriptions carved in rock in a pass in the valley at Brissa Lebanon.

In Babylonia's libraries mathematics, astronomy and medicine are all studied, along with magic, astrology and the "black arts." Indeed, the movements and meanings of the stars are practiced to such an extent that the words "Chaldean" and "astrologer" will, in future, become synonymous with each other.

But Babylonia is not alone in its preoccupation with religion. King Josiah's religious reforms in Judah have brought about renewed interest, also. As the Temple priesthood begins to purge itself of the pagan practices of Judah's neighbors, it begins to realize anew that the God of Israel and the Jews' concept and acceptance of that God is unique in a world of hundreds of cosmological gods, and that they alone are to be the carriers of that truth down through the ages. So they begin to gather together the many legends, memories, customs, songs, documents, oral and written traditions and, of course, laws that, for centuries, have been part of their communal existence under the will of that God.

The compilers of all this material will research the history of King David in the writings of SAMUEL THE SEER (the same prophet Samuel who anointed Saul the first king of Israel), NATHAN THE PROPHET and GAD THE SEER (I CHR. 29:29); and find the history of David's son, Solomon, in the writings of NATHAN, the PROPHECY OF AHIJAH THE SHILONITE and the VISION OF IDDO THE SEER (II CHR. 9:29). IDDO THE SEER's writings also tell of Solomon's son, Rheoboam, after the division of the kingdom, as does also, the BOOK OF SHEMAIAH THE PROPHET (II CHR. 12:15). The SONG OF DEBORAH, which appears in JUD. ch. 5, is among the oldest Hebrew literature, and the BOOK OF JASHER, in JOS. 10:12, 13, tells how the sun stood still at Gibeon. Other ancient writings used are JACOB'S BLESSING OF HIS SONS in GEN. 49:3–27; THE SONGS OF MOSES (EX. 15 AND DEUT. 33), A WAR BALLAD (NUM. 21:27–30) and THE BOOK OF THE WARS OF YAWEH (NUM. 21:14,15). And now, there is the document King Josiah's workman found in the rubble of the Temple, which includes the LAW, the Ten Commandments and the instructions for Passover. This enormous undertaking will take nearly 200 years to complete before it finally appears in the finished form we know today.

. . . and the prophet HABAKKUK worries about the rise of Babylon:

HABAKKUK

Book of Prophecy — Written in Hebrew, c. 625–600 B.C.

Nothing at all is known about the prophet HABAKKUK except, through his own book, that he lived at this time; for in it he worries about the rise of Babylon. He understands that Judah needs—and deserves to be punished, but cannot understand why God would use a wicked nation like Babylon to do it. Habakkuk worries, also, over the age-old problem of why the wicked prosper. They will be dealt with by God, he decides, and the righteous shall live by his faith. And he concludes, "The LORD is in His holy temple; let all the earth keep silence before Him."   2:20

---

605   Judah's new king, Jehoiakim, levies a ruinous tax on the Judean people to pay the tribute set by Pharaoh Necho and, incredibly, in the face of impending doom, sets about to build himself a luxurious "vermilion" palace (JER. 22:14), and the voice of Jeremiah is heard again. "Woe to him," he cries, "who builds his house with unrighteousness and injustice, paneling in cedar, painting it vermilion . . . do you think you are king because you compete in cedar? Thus says our God, Israel and Judah have done nothing but evil in my sight from their youth. This city has aroused my wrath from the day it was built to this. Because of the evil they did to provoke me . . . kings and princes, priests and prophets . . . I will remove it from my sight." Modern archeologists have found the red-painted stones of Jehoiakim's "vermilion" house.

In the fourth year of the reign of King Jehoiakim, God directs Jeremiah to set down in writing everything he has preached; and Jeremiah dictates, to his secretary Baruch, the book of JEREMIAH:

JEREMIAH

Book of Prophecy — Written in Hebrew,   c. 627–580 B.C.

"Out of the boiling pot in the north," prophesies JEREMIAH in the beginning of his book, "shall evil break forth upon all the inhabitants of the land, and upon all the cities of Judah." A lonely, solitary man, Jeremiah disliked intensely having to preach his frightening message, which was that it was futile to try to resist the Babylonians because God was using them to punish His people, the Jews. He longed to return to his home in the country, but obeyed God and served Him as a prophet, warning the Jews of the coming devastation of their lives and destruction of their nation. He saw Nebuchadnezzar's bloody march through Judah, and recorded the ravage of its cities, one by one, unto the bitter end. But his greatest prophecy promises the Jews another chance, a renewal, a NEW covenant, replacing that made with Abraham so long ago. It will be a covenant of vast import . . .

> Behold, the days are coming, says the LORD, when I will make a new covenant with the house of Israel and the house of Judah, not like the covenant which I made with their fathers when I took them by the hand to bring them out of the land of Egypt, my covenant which they broke . . . says the LORD. I will put my law within them, and I will write it upon their hearts; and I will be their God, and they shall be my people.
> 31:31–33 (See: A.D. 32, Thursday)

Jeremiah is called a major prophet because both his book and message are long and important. (It is, in fact, the longest book in the Bible, with 52 chapters and more than 42,000 words.) Jeremiah dictated his book to his aide, or secretary, Baruch, and it contains one verse (10:11) written in Aramaic which was edited in at a later date. Jeremiah was a quiet, kindly, thoughtful man who stressed the importance of a close, personal relationship between every individual with God; and that that relationship—that person's life, sacred to God—began the very moment of conception . . . or even before . . .

> Then the word of the LORD came unto me, saying, Before I formed thee in the belly I knew thee, and before thou camest forth out of the womb I sanctified thee . . .   JER. 1:4,5

But he had stern warnings, also, for those shepherds of the flock, pastors of the church, who would use it for political reasons and destroy it in the process:

> Woe be unto the pastors that destroy and scatter the sheep of my pasture! saith the LORD. Ye have scattered my flock and driven them away . . . behold, I will visit upon you the evil of your doings.   JER. 23:1

Jeremiah's ministry was a long one, beginning in the time of King Josiah and lasting to the very end of Judah's existence, so he lived to see the rise of Babylonia and its eventual conquest of Assyria. It took only 41 years for his most frightening prophecy to come true . . . and Jeremiah was there to see it:

> . . . then shall this city be given into the hand of the Chaldeans, and they shall burn it with fire, and you shall not escape from their hand.   38:8 (See 586 BC)

Six hundred years from now the anger of another kindly, thoughtful man will be raised, in Jeremiah's words, against the abuses He finds in the Temple of His day:

> Has this house, which is called by my name, become a den of robbers in your eyes? Behold I myself have seen it says the LORD.   JER 7:11 & MATT 21:13 (See: A.D. 32 Monday)

Even as Nebuchadnezzar's armies draw near and one after another, the cities fall to Chaldean might . . .

604   Baruch reads Jeremiah's scrolls aloud in the public square. Instead of heeding the prophet's warnings, a furious King Jehoiakim burns the offending scrolls, and Jeremiah goes into hiding to begin to rewrite. And while disaster lies just ahead for Judah . . .

600   A new century finds new stirrings in distant lands, new inventions and new ideas:

. . . Masters of the seas, Phoenecian galleys sail regularly to Britain, may possibly have even crossed the Atlantic Ocean to South America and, now, under commission from Egypt's Pharaoh Necho (he who slew Josiah at the battle of Meggido) Phoenecian sailors successfully round the Cape of Good Hope and sail up and around the Western coast of Africa. The journey takes three years; a feat that will not be accomplished again—or at least recorded—for another 2000 years.

Stater

. . . The Lydians, in Asia Minor, are using coins for money, and soon the Greek *stater* the first coin made of silver, will be in general use.

. . . The symbol of the Star of David is beginning to be used, and one will many years hence, be found on a Jewish holy seal in Sidon.

. . . Four hundred years ago the Hindu holy hymns called the *Rig Veda* were composed in India and, now, commentaries on those Vedas are written, called the *Upanishads* and the *Brahmanas*, India's sacred writings. "Who are we," they ask, "why are we born, why live, and where do we go?" From the *Upanishads* come the mystic concepts of *karma, dharma* re-incarnation and the transmigration of souls. All these works are written in sanscrit which, like other languages, will eventually die out and be forgotten. Then the fanciful fairy stories of the *Vedas*, their fables, proverbs and romances will be lost for centuries and not re-found until the 19th century A.D.

. . . In Persia, Zoroaster is teaching a new philosophy, and says "all nature rejoices at his appearing." In the beginning, he says, were two spirits, the god of good and the god of evil, constantly in conflict. Whatever man does will aid one or the other, and at a last judgment he will be rewarded accordingly. Zoroaster's teaching will affect the fate of the Jews 62 years hence, through a king named . . . Cyrus.

. . . In China, Taoist philosophy teaches the simple life, repaying evil with kindness, and producing or rearing things without possessing them. Tao's vast pantheon of gods are aided with many superstitions and lucky charms.

. . . The Etruscans are firmly in control in central Italy, and one of their own, Lucius Tarquinius Priscus, the "Tarquin," is the fifth king of Rome, its first Etruscan king. His is a successful, prosperous reign of many accomplishments which will, many years hence be considered typically "Roman." Returning in triumph from a military campaign, Tarquin is borne in a great procession on a four-horse chariot, clothed in a purple and gold robe, or *toga*. Leading the parade are standard bearers, horn players, pipers and *lictors* who carry—and use—rods like "billy-clubs" as insignia of office . . . and to keep order. Next come the spoils of war, looted treasure, sacrificial animals and chained prisoners. The Tarquin's own magnificent chariot comes next followed by senators who have come from the city to greet him. Finally marches his triumphant army. The spectacle, called a *Triumph* will be repeated by victorious generals in Rome for centuries now. Tarquin, according to the first century A.D. historian, Livy, is the first ruler to have actively campaigned for the office he holds.

> He was the first who canvassed for the crown, and delivered a set speech to secure the support of the plebs.   Livy, HISTORIES 1:35

Under Tarquin Rome begins to grow as he builds a sewer system, lays out plans for a gigantic race course, a *Circus Maximus,* and institutes great public games with boxing, wrestling, discus and javelin throwing, pole-vaulting; wild, colorful chariot races and gory, hand-to-hand combats to the death by men called *gladiators.*

. . . The Celtic peoples of Europe are living in what modern archeology calls the *Hallstatt* period, their first iron age of farming and fighting. Having learned the process of iron-making from Mediterranean traders, they create their swords, utensils and jewelry from iron, gold, bronze, amber, ivory, ignite and jet in extravagant, stylized, geometrical patterns. They use hardware and tools we still use today; hammers, saws, pliers, pincers and shears; and forge iron bands to make wooden wheels longer-lasting. They have no written language so leave behind no written record of their activities, accomplishments or philosophy. Celtic homes are simply built of wood and thatch; and wooden walls enclose their villages . . . which will, many centuries hence, develop into Europe's great cities: Paris, Vienna, Prague, Munich, Brussels, Budapest . . .

Celts

. . . Even further north, one tribe of Celts, or *Brythony,* begin the invasion of the islands someday to be known as Britain.

. . . and the first, beautiful streaks of light across a Greek "dark age" little by little appear in the north, as . . .

the GOLDEN AGE OF GREECE begins . . .

and genius will flourish for the next 300 years. Something has come alive in the mind of man in this one tiny portion of the earth that makes him no longer content to merely shrug his shoulders and accept, without question "the way things are." Six little words reign supreme now, and they will be put to the test time and again in the years ahead. Of every thought and idea it will be asked who, what, when, how, where and, most of all, why? And the answers will teach the world to think, to ask, to reason and, on a stage, to laugh and to cry.

Made up of dozens of often inaccessible small islands, and a mountainous, difficultly traversed mainland, Greece's many "tribes" of people are, mainly, isolated into independent city-states, embodying the appearance of a city and the functions of an independent nation, each with its own governmental administration, religious priesthood and civic militia. These city-states are the center of every Greek, (male's) life–the *polis*—an entity to which he owes his allegiance and which he values beyond himself, Hesiod's "common good." Even the family home, itself, is second in a Greek man's life. The *polis* is his first concern.

The Greek cities on the rugged, coastal area of Asia Minor called Ionia have fostered much of the age's intellectual activity. Thales, who will become known to history as the Father of Philosophy, comes from the Ionian city of Miletus. He is the first scholar to conclude that the world is governed by natural, fixed laws, not by the whim of a multitude of capricious, cosmological gods. Twenty years old, now, he will study in both Babylonia and Egypt, and bring back *geometry* to Greece from Egypt. He will teach that the earth is a sphere) know the cause of lunar and solar eclipses; and through his mathematical/ astronomical calculations, will predict that there will be a solar eclipse in [what we know today as) . . . May, 585.

Thales' young pupil and associate, also from miletus, is Anaximander, a man of many interests. Studying geography, mathematics, astronomy and the cosmos, he has calculated the size and distance of the planets; created an astronomical globe and sundial; and drawn a map of the known world. He will succeed Thales as head of the Ionian School.

. . . A young woman named Sappho lives on the Greek island of Lesbos at about this time. She will become known and revered as Greece's greatest woman, poet, and maybe the greatest of all women poets. Of, possibly, nine volumes of Sappho's poetry, only a few fragments are known today, some of them thanks to some unknown scribe who copied out her work at about 600 A.D. His copies would then lay forgotten in the dry desert sands of Egypt for 1300 years until discovery in the 19th century A.D. much decomposed scraps of papyrus and vellum containing poetry simple in language, passionate in feeling . . . and perfect in form.

Aesop

. . . A freed slave of Iadmon of the Greek island of Samos, whom Plutarch calls "very much esteemed," is a master story-teller and tells his many tales which become known as AESOP'S FABLES. Each one has a moral to its story:

The gods help them that help themselves. * Familiarity breeds contempt. * We would often be sorry if our wishes were gratified. * Do not count your chickens before they are hatched.

> * We often give our enemies the means of our own destruction. * It is easy to be brave from a safe distance. * Please all, and you will please none. * Beware of the wolf in sheep's clothing. * sour grapes * Don't kill the goose that lays the golden egg.   Aesop, FABLES

Aesop could have been talking about the Jews in the years ahead, when he wrote, "The little reed, bending to the force of the wind, soon stood upright again when the storm had passed over . . ."

Judah, 598.   With King Nebuchadnezzar's mighty army at the very gates of Jerusalem, King Jehoiakim is assassinated and succeeded by his 18 year-old son, Jehoiachin. Terrified, the young king throws himself on the mercy of the invading king. But Nebuchadnezzar knows no mercy; casts him into chains and has him hauled away into exile in Babylon; he and the entire royal family, princes, judges, soldiers, craftsmen, smiths; all the "men of valor," 10,000 of Judah's best . . . and all the treasures from the king's house and from the house of the LORD.   II CHRON. 36:5–9

597, March 15/16   Nebuchadnezzar sets up Zedekiah as puppet king, who serves him loyally . . . for nine years . . .

> . . . in the month of Kislev, the Babylonian king . . . besieged the city of Judah, and on the second day of . . . Adar took the city and captured the king. He appointed therein a king of his own choice, received heavy tribute and sent them to Babylon.   From a Babylonian Chronicle, No. 21946, in the British Museum, London.

The Babylonian Chronicle

594   The widespread use of coined money creates economic problems in Greece, so now, the aristocratic Athenian lawmaker, Solon, is named sole *archon* or mayor, and given full authority to re-write Athens' legal code, that infamous "Draconian" code for which the sentence of death was so casually meted out. His reforms cover many areas from civil rights to seditious wrongs, and are so based on humanity and reason the Solon will be considered the "Father of Democracy." He devalues the *drachma*, adjusts weights and measures, exports, imports and land debts. His constitutional and judicial laws will, in fact, help move Athens toward democracy, as they are designed to make people aware of each other's needs and welfare, not just their own. Laws, he says, can be . . .

> . . . like spiders webs: if some poor weak creature comes up against them, it is caught; but a bigger one can break through and get away.   Diogenes Laertius, LIVES OF THE EMINENT PHILOSOPHERS 1:58

But the best laws, says Solon, by whose name politicians and lawmakers are often called to this day, are they . . .

> . . . that [encourage] those that are not injured [to] try and punish the unjust as much as those that are.   Plutarch, LIVES, quoting Solon, who also said, "Each day grow older, and learn something new."

593, on.   As Nebuchadnezzar's armies close in, three times the weak, indecisive king Zedekiah seeks out Jeremiah the prophet, asks for—and rejects—his advice. With a wooden yoke on his own neck Jeremiah warns the king that he is following a course of national suicide, but Zedekiah prefers the advice of those who say, "Impossible! God would never allow harm to come to his city and temple!" For his pains, Jeremiah is beaten, imprisoned and thrown into a cistern.

589   Zedekiah embroils himself in a revolt against Nebuchadnezzar in an alliance with Egypt, Moab, Ammon, Edom and the Syrian cities of Tyre and Sidon . . . and thereby seals his own . . . and Judah's doom.

Many centuries from now, in the earliest days of modern "archeology," the search will be for tangible treasure; gold, silver, gems, statuary. Such humble artifacts as broken pottery will be mostly ignored, disdained and discarded. Later, with archeology's transition to a "science," will come, also, the realization that even the smallest shard of pottery could BE a treasure. One such potsherd, found 12 miles from the fortified Judean city of Lachish is just that:

588   One by one Nebuchadnezzar demolishes and lays waste Judah's cities, towns and villages, and leaves them desolate. In his book, Jeremiah writes that THE LAST TWO CITIES TO SURVIVE ARE . . .

> . . . Lachish and Azekah: for these were the only fortified cities of Judah that remained.
> JEREMIAH 34:7

The Lachish Potshard

Now, what had been an effective line of signal fires from Jerusalem to town to village to desert outpost breaks down, and a desperate commander of an outpost beyond Lachish, searching in vain for the glow from the nearest fire, hastily scribbles on a broken potsherd:

> . . . we are watching for the signals [from] Lachish . . . [but] we do not see Azekah.   Hebrew potshard from Lachish, unearthed in the rubble, A.D. 1935. It, and the charred, fire-blackened city walls of Lachish can be seen today in the British Museum, London

In retaliation to the Jewish revolts, a furious Nebuchadnezzar reinvades Judah and sets up a siege of Jerusalem. The siege goes on day and night, for a year and a half, until . . .

587, July.

Babylonian Bas Reliefs

JERUSALEM SURRENDERS TO BABYLONIA . . .

> Prophesied: . . . a day of ruin and devastation, trumpet blast and battle cry . . . neither their silver nor their gold shall be able to deliver them on the day of the wrath of the LORD.   ZEPHANIAH 1:15,16 and 18 (See: 630 B.C.)

Nebuchadnezzar's retribution is terrible. A terrified King Zedekiah, attempting a night-time escape through a gate in his palace wall, is captured and haled before the Babylonian . . . and Nebuchadnezzar passes sentence. Zedekiah's two sons are slaughtered before his very eyes; then his own eyes are gouged out . . . and the succession of David is extinguished as Judah's last king is dragged away, chained, into exile. Having destroyed every city and village of Judah, Nebuchadnezzar turns loose his troops in Jerusalem. For an entire month they rape, pillage and murder. Thousands of Jews are slaughtered throughout all of Judah and left to lie where they fall under the hot summer sun. Finally, in August, 586, having stripped the city of anything of value . . .

JERUSALEM IS BURNED TO THE GROUND!

. . . and Solomon's magnificent Temple is left a pile of ash and rubble.   (JER., ch. 52.)

> . . . then shall this city be given into the hands of the Chaldeans, and they shall burn it with fire, and you shall not escape from their hand.   JER. 38:18 (See: 627 B.C.) * Therefore, because of you Zion shall be plowed as a field, Jerusalem shall become a heap of ruins. MICAH 3:12 (See: 700 B.C.)

In the early 1980's A.D., a tiny carved ivory pomegranate, not two inches high, somehow appeared for sale in a Jerusalem shop and caused a sensation among antiquities experts. Scientifically dated to just after King Solomon's time, its authenticity is so sure the Israel Museum paid more than a HALF MILLION dollars for it! Pomegranates are mentioned several times in the Bible, including an instruction in EXODUS of how they shall decorate the hem of the outer garment of the High Priest Aaron, Moses' brother, and his successors:

> . . . And . . . upon the hem of it thou shalt make pomegranates of blue . . . purple, and . . . scarlet, round about the hem thereof . . . a golden bell and a pomegranate, a golden bell and a pomegranate . . .   EX-ODUS 28:33,4

Not only is this little artifact thought to have been some form of decoration in Solomon's Temple, but it is identified as such by its own carved inscription around its shoulders: BELONGING TO THE TEMPLE OF YAHWEH, HOLY TO THE PRIESTS.

On display, today, in its own special room at the Israel Museum, it is thought to be the only relic to survive the destruction of Jerusalem and its holy Temple.

. . . Nebuchadnezzar orders his general to look after Jeremiah, treat him well and do him no harm, for he had tried to prevent the revolt. Jeremiah is allowed to choose whether to go to Babylon in "honorable" exile, or to remain in Jerusalem, and he chooses to remain. Whatever are left of the Jewish higher classes, 60,000 royalty and intellectuals, are hauled the hundreds of miles to Babylon. What survivors there are left in Jerusalem are the dregs of society, many of whom flee to Egypt, dragging with them the venerable old prophet, Jeremiah . . . whom they kill. Daniel, one of the young Jewish princes, becomes an exile, joining the prophet Ezekiel, taken away in the first deportation. The exiles are dumped into mud huts outside the city walls of Babylon . . . where they can either live or die.

585, May 28.   The sky blackens at noon; the sun is blotted out and is no more. But it is not a portent of even worse to come. It is the solar eclipse which Thales of Miletus had predicted 15 years ago.

c. 580   The book of LAMENTATIONS is written.

LAMENTATIONS of Jeremiah

Book of Sacred Writings — Written in Hebrew, c. 580 B.C.

1st Cen. BC Fragment of Lamentation

"How lonely sits the city that was full of people," mourns the writer of LAMENTATIONS. "Her gates are desolate . . . in the dust of the streets lie the young and the old . . . slaughtered without mercy . . . Mount Zion lies desolate . . . jackals prowl over it. My eyes are spent with weeping . . . my heart is poured out in grief." The short, 73 verse book (probably not actually written by Jeremiah, himself) is a collection of dirges and mournful hymns bewailing the destruction of Jerusalem, a destruction that was complete and terrible, with the Jews' holy Temple utterly burned to the ground. The poems in LAMENTATIONS were probably recited on days of public mourning.

LAMENTATIONS' sad message will have meaning for a faith called Christian, also, someday.

Look, O LORD, and behold for I am despised. Is it nothing to you who pass by? Behold and see if there be any sorrow like unto my sorrow.   1:12 (See: Thursday, A.D. 30)

The book of OBADIAH is also written.

OBADIAH

Book of Prophecy — Written in Hebrew, c. 580 B.C.

The shortest book in the Old Testament with only one chapter, OBADIAH rails at Judah's neighbors, the Edomites, for having given aid to Babylon at the time of the invasion of Judah. The last verses exult that the Jews shall return and ". . . the kingdom shall be the LORD'S."

c. 580   The books of KINGS and CHRONICLES conclude with the exile into Babylon.

KINGS II

Book of History — Written in Hebrew, c. 500 B.C.

KINGS II relates all the history of the Jews from 800 B.C. to now, the good years and the bad, good kings and evil, and the use and misuse of their religion; a religion of ONE GOD, unique in a world full of hundreds of strange gods. The time period covered by the two books of KINGS—over four centuries—were busy, "building" years of palaces and monuments, construction projects and official documents, and consequently, teem with myriad antiquities that illuminate the Biblical narratives; archeological gems that have put to rest the idea that the Bible is just a collection of folk tales and myths. Instead, tangible and dramatic artifacts bring back to life the characters and kings of Israel and Judah, and paint a picture of their feats and foibles with a vivid brush.

There are sling stones from David's time, and the foundations of Solomon's stables; a stone altar from the time of Joshua; ivory fragments from the palace King Ahab built and Jeroboam II enlarged: tiny burial jars with the remains of dismembered babies from Baal-worshipping sacrifices—the god of Ahab's wicked wife, Jezebel. The Moabite Stone of Mesha, king of Moab, gloats of a victory over King Omri of Israel, and the Black Obelisque of Assyria's King Shalmaneser shows a groveling King Jehu kow-towing to him on all fours. The ruins and monumental statues of Khorsabad prove that Sargon II really did exist, just like the Bible says, and did conquer Samaria. And whole cities full of Hittite ruins in Turkey prove their civilization extended far and wide. King Hezekiah's underground tunnel in Jerusalem saved the city once and still carries water to this day; and red-painted stones have been found of Jehoiakim's "vermilion house" that Jeremiah so bitterly denounced. The many engraved tablets of the proud Nebuchadnezzar boast of his victory over the Jews, the tiny pomegranate bears silent witness to it, and, of course, there are the wonderfully dramatic potshards from Lachish and Azeka which echo almost word for word the writings of Jeremiah. And these are only a sample; there are hundreds of others. Biblically oriented archeology today, is as exciting as any adventure and so far has only scratched the surface. All these wonderful artifacts have enlightened, illuminated and illustrated the Bible stories as true stories, about real people who lived real lives in the real, historical world.

Beginning with the death of the prophet, Elijah, and the exploits of the successor to his mantle, Elisha, KINGS II goes on to tell much of the venerable Jeremiah; and, in fact, it is through these writings—and his own—that more is known about Jeremiah than almost any other person in the Bible. But it tells, also, about the gory death of the wicked Queen Jezebel, of King Ahaz who practiced human sacrifice, and of Manasseh, who sacrificed even his own sons on a pagan altar. To these were the prophets speaking when they cried, "You and your sinful luxury will be destroyed!" Amos and Hosea had prophesied the fall of the northern kingdom of Israel to Assyria, and it happened, just as they said. Then Micah, Zephaniah, Nahum and Jeremiah all warned the Jews that (their southern kingdom

of) Judah and its holy city of Jerusalem would be destroyed as well. Even the reigns of the good and righteous kings Josiah and Hezekiah, could not stem the tide. When Nebuchadnezzar of Babylon moved in, it was all over. The monarchy was abolished, Jerusalem and its holy Temple burned to the ground and the Jews hauled off to captivity in Babylon. After only 434 years it was the end of the kingdom, and, to the Jews, the end of everything.

But was it? One prophet was already preaching the birth of a savior, a messiah, a "prince of peace." The other prophecies came true. Maybe this one would, also. It was one small ray of hope in a bleak, desolate world.

CHRONICLES I and II

Books of History — Written in Hebrew, c. 400 B.C.

The writer (writers?) of the two books of CHRONICLES is not known by name, and is referred to by historians simply as "the Chronicler." More like an editor, really, than a writer, he/they used many other sources for research, works which do not exist today but are mentioned, by name, in CHRONICLES. In addition to the books of KINGS, the Chronicler refers to THE WORDS OF SAMUEL THE SEER (that same prophet Samuel who anointed Saul the first king of Israel), of NATHAN THE PROPHET, of GAD THE SEER, the DECREES OF DAVID and of SOLOMON, the VISIONS OF IDDO THE SEER, and THE PROPHECY OF ABIJAH THE SHILONITE. While this book places CHRONICLES at this time, just after KINGS II, it is only for continuity of this narrative. The CHRONICLES were not actually completed until about 400 B.C.

CHRONICLES I begins its history from the very beginning with Adam, himself, through an immense genealogy of . . . everybody! Listing all the descendents of Adam and Eve, Noah and Abraham, the Chronicler (in Chapter I) recalls how GENESIS (Chapter 10) described the populating of the nations among their sons, and their sons' sons, and their . . . After the great flood Noah became the first "tiller of the soil" with his three sons, Shem, Ham and Japheth, who are considered the "ancestors of all the nations." Ham "begat" the Egyptians, Shem the Semites, including the Hebrews, and Japheth the Europeans and mid-eastern coastal peoples from the Caspian Sea to the Greek islands, his sons Gomer and Magog siring the Sythians, Madai the Medes of Iran, Jubal the Armenians and Javan the Greeks. Turkey began with Javan's son, Tarshish which became Tarsus (home, someday, to a man named Paul.) The lands inhabited by Ham's sons were named for them: Egypt, Canaan, Cush (the Cushites of Ethiopia) and Put (in east-Africa south of Ethiopia.) Ham's grandson, Heth, fathered the Hittites, and Nimrod "the mighty hunter before the Lord," founded mighty Babylon (in today's Iraq) with its ancient cities of Babel, Erech and Accad. Among the descendents of Noah's eldest son, Shem "the sire of all the Semites" were Elam (the Elamites of Babylonia), Asshur, who fathered the Assyrians and "builded Nineveh," and Aram, who sired the Arameans in Syria, relative to both Assyria and the Aramaic language. Shem is also called the "father of all the children of Eber," and Eber—descendent of Noah and ancestor of Abraham—is given special prominence in the GENESIS/CHRONICLES genealogies, for from it derives the very name Hebrew (or Habiru, "one who emigrates.") Modern-day scholars point out that differences between these peoples have more to do with languages, geography and culture than race; and modern-day politics should understand that the difference between Arabs and Jews goes back almost to the very beginning, to Abraham and his two sons, Jacob and Ishmael. For Jacob, legitimate son of Abraham's wife, Sarah, was re-named Israel—the-father of all Israel, and Ishmael, whose mother, Hagar, was Sarah's slave/servant-girl, begat the nomadic Arabian peoples. The CHRONICLES genealogy continues to the time of Samuel, Saul and David, and is so thorough it lists "the mighty men of the armies" and even "the sons of King David's music master."

CHRONICLES II picks up the story during Solomon's reign, through the division of the kingdom and the machinations of the kings of Israel and Judah, right through to the bitter end. Covering, as they do, thousands of years of history, CHRONICLES is understandably tedious . . . and not only for modern readers. The Bible, itself, tells in the book of ESTHER (6:1 See: 485 B.C.) that when Queen Esther's husband, King Ahasuerus, or Xerxes, could not sleep . . . "he had CHRONICLES read to him." (Some scholars say they weren't these Chronicles, at all, but those of Persia. But it makes a good story.)

The Chronicler tells essentially the same story the Deuteronomist told in the books of SAMUEL and KINGS, but in a different way. It is not history as we know history; detached, unemotional and non-judgmental. It is written, rather, almost as an object lesson of what SHOULD have happened, not what DID. He judges the kings of Israel and Judah not on their worldly accomplishments, which were considerable, but on their faithfulness to God; and most of them fell far short. He makes it very clear that Israel and Judah were destroyed, not because Assyria and Babylonia were aggressive and unstoppable, but because of their own sins and transgressions. It was the punishment of God on His own sinful people for their apostasy.

But the Chronicler did not end his book on a note of doom. His last two verses hint that a new day is coming for the Jews; that all is not lost, and that someday God will use a king named Cyrus to give them another chance.

The

EXILE

in

BABYLON

586 to 538   The Jews are in captivity in Babylonia.

The EXILE In BABYLON

580's   Nebuchadnezzar is a master builder and Babylon, a masterpiece, the "Glory of the Kingdoms." Its 200 square mile area is peopled by over 400,000 persons living in "modern" surroundings including buildings four stories tall; and the jewel of the masterpiece is the monument known as the Hanging Gardens of Babylon. Nebuchadnezzar built the 12,000 square feet of gardens for his queen, Amytis, lonely for the cool mountains of her homeland. He built her a mountain of her own, 269 feet high, on which he planted thousands of trees and plants, irrigated by water pumped from the Euphrates River. The hundreds of rooms inside are cooled by the sprays of water. The Hanging Gardens of Babylon will become the second of the Seven Wonders of the Ancient World.

580   Aesop's Greek fable of the Little Reed (See: 600 B.C.) well fits the Jews in exile, for while they had bent low before the storm, they manage to stand upright when it passes. Although they mourn for Zion and weep bitter tears, the Jews, far from languishing in agony, pick themselves up, fit themselves into Babylonian society, learn its language, Aramaic, and become merchants and traders. As it was mostly the higher classes—nobility and intellectuals—which had been taken captive, so they behave in Babylon, and over the years some rise to high position. Some, born in exile, will even remain when the rest return home. A young Jewish prince named Daniel is recognized by Nebuchadnezzar as an unusually bright and promising young man, and the king puts him into training to become one of his own pages . . . and . . .

c. 570   The prophet Ezekiel writes while in Babylon . . .

EZEKIEL

Book of Prophecy — Written in Hebrew,   c. 590–560 B.C.

Ezekiel was one of those Jews carried off to exile, probably with the first deportation of the 10,000 "men of valor" and the hapless King Jehoiakim; and he spent the remainder of his life in Babylon. He wrote his book just before and during his exile, entirely by himself, following ". . . the word of the Lord [as it] came to me," and it is, in fact, one of the few books of the Old Testament whose author is the same as the person in the title. His book is rich in prophecy, parables, oracles, allegory and visions shown him by God. Eighty seven times in his book does God call Ezekiel "Son of man," and tells him, "Son of man, speak to the elders . . .", "Son of man, propound a riddle . . ." and "Son of man, make known to Jerusalem her abominations." A stern, austere man, he was also enigmatic, and promised more than just humiliation for the Jewish remnant in exile . . . and has sometimes been called "The Father of JUDAISM."

Yes, the remnant will be returned home, EZEKIEL says, but not because of their repentance. It will be through God's grace alone. God's omnipotence and honor are not diminished because His people failed Him; their shame reflects on them, Ezekiel says, not on God, whose "wife," Jerusalem played the harlot to other nations, and who speaks again of Covenants, old and new.

> Yea, thus says the LORD God . . . who have despised the oath in breaking the covenant, yet I remember my covenant with you in the days of your youth, and I will establish with you an everlasting covenant . . . and you shall know that I am LORD . . . EZEKIEL 16:59–62

Ezekiel never returned home, but he "saw" Jerusalem again anyway, for he begins Chapter 40, "In the five and twentieth year of our captivity . . . in the visions of God brought he me into the land of Israel . . ." and the visions were of a new Temple that would soon be built, which EZEKIEL describes in detail in Chapters 40 through 47, details which match, exactly, archeological finds at Megiddo, Gezer and Hazor.

The Dry Bones

Ezekiel was apparently well acquainted with Babylonian literature for his own writing abounds in fanciful "oriental" imagery as in the tales of the "dry bones," the "wheel in the air" and "sour grapes," and his vivid, unsparing description and scathing indictment of Judah's corruption and repugnance are unequaled anywhere else. But his book is memorable in another way, also, for his is the first voice to stress individual worth and responsibility. Throughout history, it had not been uncommon for whole families to be punished for the sins or mistakes of one member, but Ezekiel maintains that God will judge each person on his or her own merit and not on another's. Moreover, He will not judge for past sins if they have been repented, but only for the present . . .

> . . . for I have no pleasure in the death of anyone, says the Lord God, so "turn, and live."
> EZEKIEL 18:32

562 Suffering fits of insanity, Nebuchadnezzar dies and is replaced by Nabonidus, sometimes called the world's first archeologist, for clay tablets still exist that tell, in his own words, how he restored a great ziggurat (possibly that of Ur.) Reading inscriptions on the original monument, built there 2000 years before, Nabonidus, in remarkable under-statement, says it had been ". . . built by a king before me . . ."

> I am a king who always . . . without interruption, is interested in the maintenance of the temples . . . I went to Uruk, Larsa and Ur and brought silver, gold . . . precious stones . . .
> Texts of Nabonidus, now in the Istanbul Museum, Turkey.

Hated, though, by the Babylonians, Nabonidus rules the empire from Taima and leaves Babylon to his son and co-regent, Belshazzar.

560   King Croesus rules in Lydia (Asia Minor.) His vast, legendary wealth will give rise to the expression still used today, "as rich as Croesus." Aesop the fable teller lives now at Croesus' royal court.

. . . Servius Tullius is the sixth king of Rome; the second Etruscan, and the first (according to a latter-day Roman writer/statesman, Cicero), "to hold the royal power without being chosen by the people." A census taken during this year shows 260,000 people in Rome, and Servius divides them into 35 tribes, and creates a new class of people, the *EQUITES*, meaning literally, "horsemen," men who can afford to *EQUIP* themselves with armor and a horse, *EQUUS*, and serve in the cavalry. Servius' major accomplishment is in forming an alliance with the Latins, creating a "Latin League" between Rome and the cities of Latium.

550   The pot continues to boil in the Middle-East, and the seething cauldron stirs up a new power, Persia. King Cyrus of Persia (southern Iran) overthrows the hundred year rule of the Medes (northern Iran) and begins his conquests.

. . . The ignominious end to which the once-favored Hebrew kingdom has come has reversed the Exodus and all it meant and took away Israel's uniqueness in the world community of nations. But the political catastrophe, far from being the "end of everything," has given the Jews, in fact, a new beginning; the realization that God does not merely "reside" in only one place, the temple, and that the worship of Him can have a universality not even dreamed of before. So now, far from home and without their Temple, the Jews begin to build *SYNAGOGUES* for houses of worship. From the time of Moses the Levite priesthood alone had had access to God; and from the time of Solomon that access had been in the Temple. Now the temple is gone and JUDAISM is born; and the Jews begin, each one, to worship in synagogues of their own.

. . . The Jews are not alone in their need for God . . . or for some faith to live by . . .

. . . Epimenides of Crete writes religious and poetical works, including a statement about God that, 600 years from now, a man named Paul of Tarsus will quote to the Greeks of his time in Athens:

> In Him we live and move and have our being.   Epimenides of Crete, quoted in ACTS 17:28 (See: A.D. 51)

. . . A Greek mathematician and philosopher named Pythagoras has traveled "the world over" from Egypt to India, from Persia to Gaul seeking knowledge. He knows that the earth is a sphere and that all heavenly bodies follow certain courses. He has formulated a geometrical *theorem* and created the first musical scale, called the *Pythagorean Scale*. He believes in the immortality, and transmigration, of the soul, and has gathered about himself a mystical "brotherhood" who share his knowledge and beliefs, one of which is that the mind is locked in the prison-house of the body and man's greatest challenge is how to set it free. Holding back a man from beating a puppy, he says:

> Don't strike him. He is a friend of mine . . . I recognize his voice.   Pythagoras

. . . and in the Far East, the roots of three new religions begin to grow:

. . . Confucius is living in China, and will become its most famous "sage."

. . . A Young Gautama Buddha is beginning his search for truth in India, and will become founder of the Buddhist religion. He believes that all life is suffering, and that man must learn how to deal with it.

. . . and Zoroaster's teaching of the conflict between light and darkness, truth and evil, and of man's duty to support the good, have gained wide acceptance throughout Persia. His is a rationalization of symbolism which forces man to choose between good and evil. Ahura-mazda, god of truth, light and peace is opposed by the evil power of lies, darkness and discord, Ahriman. Zoroaster's polytheistic "immanent logic" is taught by a sacred priesthood called . . . MAGI, who worship at desert Towers of Silence on Altars of Fire. Among the followers of Zoroaster, the "founder of the wisdom of the Magi," is King Cyrus, soon to be called, "the Great." The king, any Persian king, is the chosen tool of the gods, and embodies truth, light and good, therefore, whoever opposes him is evil, lie and darkness.

. . . and the unknown prophet called the "second" ISAIAH, living now, prophesies a memorable event for the Jews, through Cyrus . . .

Thus says the Lord . . . who made all things . . . "Cyrus . . . shall fulfill all my purpose . . . Jerusalem . . . shall be built and . . . the temple . . . foundation shall be laid." Thus says the Lord to his anointed, to Cyrus . . . I call you by your name . . . I gird you, though you do not know me . . . I am the Lord, and there is no other."   ISAIAH 44:24,28 & 45:4,5,6

One of the exiles in Babylon, Isaiah is an astute observer of the changing political scene, with a sharp and discerning eye. He sees momentous events ahead, and cries to Babylon . . .

. . . go into darkness, 0 daughter of the Chaldeans, for you shall no more be called mistress of kingdoms. I was angry with my people . . . I gave them into your hand . . . you showed them no mercy . . . now therefore hear this . . . in spite of your sorceries and . . . enchantments . . . disaster shall fall upon you . . . ruin shall come on you suddenly . . ."
ISAIAH 47:5–9,11

Then Isaiah cries his great affirmation of the One True God's omnipotence: "Thus says the Lord God:

"Have you not known? Have you not heard? . . . Have you not understood from the foundations of the earth? I am the LORD, I have called you in righteousness, I have taken you by the hand and kept you; I have given you as a covenant to the people, a light to the nations. Heaven is my throne and earth is my foot-stool . . . all flesh shall come to worship before me," says the LORD.   40:21, 42:6, 66:1,23

546   Cyrus of Persia defeats King Croesus in Lydia. Bitterly Croesus regrets his vain attempt to stop Cyrus' might and cries, "In peace sons bury their fathers, but in war fathers bury their sons." The Oracle at Delphi had told Croesus he would "destroy a great empire" and so he has: his own.

540   The prophet, Daniel, lives in Babylon, now, probably an acquaintance of the younger Ezekiel. The book of DANIEL that tells his story is, like REVELATION, a subject of much controversy, for modern critical scholarship maintains that DANIEL had to be written far later than this time (200 to 150 B.C.). Much of its history is mistaken, they say; much of its text does not fit this period. This king did not really exist; that one ruled at a different time than DANIEL says; the use of these words or that style doesn't fit this time; nor do Daniel's visions. But, as with other controversies in the Bible, time and archeology (the Dead Sea Scrolls and the Nabonidus Chronicles, for starters) are vindicating traditional viewpoints. So, because this writer is expert in neither escatology (study of the end times) nor apocalypse (revelation)—which is what DANIEL is all about—this book will leave the controversy to the experts and present DANIEL at its Biblical face value.

DANIEL

Book of Prophecy — Written in ARAMAIC,   c. 165–160 B.C.

Daniel was one of the princes of Judah brought into captivity years ago. Nebuch-adnezzar quickly recognized exceptional wisdom and promise in the young man and had him trained as a royal page. Brought to Babylon some nine years before Ezekiel, Daniel served in the royal court with great distinction for 70 years, long past the time when the Jews returned home, having won several kings' respect and support by his undaunted faith and trust in the Hebrews' One True God. The stories of that faith and trust are justifiably famous, for they are colorful, dramatic and vividly "oriental": Daniel saved from the den of lions, and his friends Shadrach, Meschach and Abednego saved, also, from the burning, fiery furnace. These testaments of great faith would aid and succor the Jews during many a latter-day persecution.

DANIEL'S 12 chapters are a wealth of symbolism, allegory and prophecy; the only "Old Testament" book to write of apocalypse, or revelation. It abounds in mystical dates, years, numbers, epochs, eras, mythical beasts and cryptic messages. Some think of DANIEL as a broad overview of the entire ancient world, embracing the long history of Egypt, Assyria, Babylonia, Persia, Greece, Rome the Empire, and finally Papal Rome, which takes it into modern times and possibly even . . . end times (maybe times like our own of jet planes and computers?)

But there shall be a time of trouble, such as never has been . . . those who turn many to righteousness . . . [will shine] . . . like the stars for ever and ever. But you, Daniel . . . seal the book, until the time of the end. Many shall run to and fro, and knowledge shall increase . . .   DANIEL 12:1–4

But in his apocalyptic night vision, Daniel describes the advent of a Messianic king . . . "one like the Son of Man . . ."

> I saw in the night visions, and behold, with the clouds of heaven there came one like a son of man, and he came to the Ancient of Days and was presented before him. And to him was given dominion and glory and kingdom, that all peoples, nations and languages should serve him; his dominion is an everlasting dominion, which shall not pass away; and his kingdom one that shall not be destroyed.   DANIEL 7:13,14 (See: A.D. 70)

Almost 600 years from now, in the last days of his life, Jesus of Nazareth will also speak of the Son of Man who will return . . .

> . . . in the clouds of heaven with power and great glory. And he shall send his angels with a great sound of a trumpet and they shall gather together his elect . . . from one end of heaven to the other.   MATTHEW 24:30–31

Daniel also prophesies the deliverance of the Jews from a Persian king by a young Greek king (named . . . Alexander) 200 years hence . . .

Fragment of Daniel c. A.D. 250

> . . . behold, there stood before the river a ram . . . and a he-goat came and he smote the ram . . . and cast him down . . . and waxed very great . . . the ram (is the king of) Persia . . . and the goat the king of Grecia.   DANIEL 8:3–8, 20,21 (See: 333 B.C.)

Serving in the court of Nebuchadnezzar and his successors, Daniel lived amid Oriental spendor such as legends are made of. But Babylon was no legend; its modern-day ruins in Iraq are still awesome, even without their ancient golden trimmings. But in Daniel's day Babylon was a city of gold, gateways, walls, pillars, golden altars and idols of human and animal gods, especially Bal (Baal) and Ishtar (Ashtar or Asheroth). But although Daniel served under six kings, he remained loyal and faithful to the LORD and was never tempted by their pagan gods.

The book of DANIEL was written in ARAMAIC, the Syrian/Aramean language the Babylonians had learned from the Assyrians, and that the Jews, living in Babylon for some 50 years, had learned from the Babylonians, eventually forgetting their own Hebrew. Aramaic would thus be spoken by the exiles even after their return to Judah and for another several hundred years, especially in the remote country villages, so that someday far from this time, it would become the native language of a man named Jesus, from Nazareth.

One of Daniel's prophecies came to pass before his very eyes, and his dramatic narration recounts how the Babylonian empire came to an end and the Persian began:

539   Nebuchadnezzar's grandson, Balshazzar, gives a great state banquet and, to impress his guests, orders out all the gold and silver vessels from the Jews' holy Temple . . . all that had been paid as tribute and all that had been sacked when Jerusalem fell; and all his lords and Satraps, wives and concubines drink wine from the holy vessels, a terrible profanity. To Balshazzar's amazement the fingers of a hand appear on the wall, writing mysterious words: "*Mene, Mene, Tekel, Upharsin* . . ." And Daniel is summoned to interpret them. "This, O king, is the meaning of the handwriting on the wall," said Daniel. "Counted, counted, weighed, divided. *Mene*: God has numbered the days of your kingdom, and brought it to an end. *Tekel*: You have been weighed in the balances and found wanting. *Upharsin*: Your kingdom is divided . . . and given to the Medes and Persians!"

539, October 12.   The army of Cyrus of Persia enters Babylon, "without battle," the Chaldean/Babylonian empire is no more, and the entire event is recorded on cunieform tablets:

His vast army, whose number like the waters of a river cannot be determined, with their armor held close, moved forward beside him.   The CYRUS CYLINDER, * On the 3rd of Marcheswan Cyrus entered Babylon and they waved branches before him. Cyrus proclaimed peace to Babylon.   The BABYLONIAN CHRONICLE Both in the British Museum, London

Balshazzar is executed. It is the end of Babylon. From the Indus River to the Mediterranean Sea, from the Caucassus Mountains to the Persian Gulf . . . Cyrus the Great is king of all Persia.

I am Cyrus, king of the world, great king, mighty king. I . . . entered Babylon . . . amidst jubilation and rejoicing. I did not allow any to terrorize the land. Their dwellings I restored. I put an end to their misfortunes.   The CYRUS CYLINDER

The Cyrus Cylinder

Not for Cyrus are the barbarian ways of Assyria and Babylonia. A benevolent and lenient ruler, enlightened by the teachings of Zoroaster concerning good and evil, Cyrus the Great issues an edict concerning the Jews in captivity. The EDICT OF CYRUS not only ALLOWS THE JEWS TO RETURN HOME but, also, to begin to rebuild their temple!

Prophesied: I will restore the fortunes of my people Israel and they shall rebuild the ruined cities and inhabit them.   AMOS 9:14 (See: 760 B.C.)

THE EXILE IS ENDED, AND . . .

538   THE FIRST GROUP OF JEWS RETURNS FROM BABYLON. Cyrus not only allows the Jews to return home, he even encourages them to rebuild their Temple, and to that end returns to them all the gold and silver vessels, censers, bowls and candlesticks—almost 6000 of them—which Nebuchadnezzar had taken from the Temple 50 years before. What a procession they make! They number 42,360 in a census, and in addition, there are 7,373

B.C. 538

servants and 200 male and female singers! They travel on 736 horses 245 camels and 6,720 asses! How great it is to be going home! They compose psalms and sing them on the way. But they are not prepared for the depressing and disheartening sight that meets their eyes. It has been, after all, 50 years. The Jews returning to Jerusalem are the GRANDCHILDREN of those who LEFT . . . a whole new generation! Fifty long years of abandonment and neglect piled on top of the rubble of destruction! The heaps of trash that used to be a Temple and palace, homes and shops, all overgrown with weeds and vines, Where to start? What to do? Many wish they had stayed in Babylon. And into their new time of crisis comes a voice of solace with a message of hope . . .

> Comfort ye, comfort ye my people, saith your God. Speak ye comfortably to Jerusalem, and cry unto her, that her warfare is accomplished, her iniquity is pardoned.   ISAIAH 40:1,2

530 . . . and the second half of the book of ISAIAH is written.

ISAIAH

Book of Prophecy — Written in Hebrew, c. 549–519 B.C.

> O thou that tellest good tidings to Zion, get thee up into the high mountains, O thou that tellest good tidings to Jerusalem, lift up thy voice with strength . . . say unto the cities of Judah, Behold your God! . . . arise, shine, for thy light is come . . . and the glory of the Lord is risen upon thee.   40:9 & 60:1, paraphrased, from George Frederick Handel's MESSIAH, autograph manuscript, British Museum, London

What wonderful words of comfort the "second" Isaiah has for the Jews, how vastly different from those of the "first." The writer whom some Biblical scholars call the "second" Isaiah lived and wrote at this time, about 150 years after the "first." He wrote the last 26 chapters of the book of ISAIAH during a long ministry that began just before the Jews returned from Babylon, and lasted a generation more. He may have lived in Babylon and returned home with the first group, as chapters 40 through 55 seem to look forward TO a return, and chapters 55 through 66 seem to suggest a return already accomplished. While the first Isaiah's tone was stern, strident and unbending in his condemnation of Judah's sins and apostasy, crying, "Woe unto them . . . woe to the crown of pride . . . woe to Jerusalem . . . and its rebellious children," time and again, that tone changes instantly with the opening line of chapter 40, as though the years that brought Judah so low are over and done. "Comfort ye," he says, "speak ye comfortably to Jerusalem." This Isaiah is more kindly and forgiving, and his message is transformed with promise:

> Every valley shall be exalted, and every mountain and hill . . . made low . . . the crooked . . . made straight, and the rough places plain. 40:1 Awake, awake; put on thy strength, O Zion . . . for thus saith the LORD, ye have sold yourselves for naught; and ye shall be redeemed without money.   52:1,3

116

Little by little, the archaic, restrictive—albeit necessary—Law that God, or YAH-WEH, gave to Moses so long ago, is being redrawn and defined BY HIMSELF, through the prophets, into a JUDAISM that is much greater in concept: the worship of a God who reveals Himself and His own many aspects and attributes. Amos had taught that God is a God for all people, not just the Hebrews, alone. Through Hosea, God proclaimed Himself a God of LOVE who wants no more of sacrifice and burnt offerings but, rather, knowledge and love of Himself. Jonah revealed God's love not only to mankind, but for ALL His creation, from plants to animals . . . and even 'sinful cities." Now, through Isaiah, God shows the magnificence of His universality, and His incredible plan for mankind's salvation.

> Heaven is my throne and earth is my footstool . . . all flesh shall come to worship before me, says the LORD.   66:1,23

The "first" Isaiah promised the coming of a Messiah, a Savior; and now, through the "second" Isaiah does God reveal the most awesome, astounding aspect of His being; one final, perfect and sufficient sacrifice, after which there need never be another. Yes, he will be a "Wonderful Counselor, a Prince of Peace," but a far different one than the Jews expect. They desperately want someone to lead them out of their plight, to build them back up again and beat back their enemies. But ISAIAH promises them, instead, a "suffering servant." Yes, He will save His people—and all people—but not with politics or an army. He will do it by offering himself up for a sacrifice; by suffering and dying for the sins of all mankind. Five hundred and fifty years from now, a carpenter from Nazareth, fully aware of His own destiny, will recognize Himself in the prophecies and know that He, indeed, must become ISAIAH's "suffering servant."

> Prophecy: The spirit of the Lord GOD is upon me because the LORD has anointed me to bring good tidings to the afflicted, He has sent me to bind up the broken-hearted, to proclaim liberty to the captives.   ISAIAH 61:1,2

He will be gentle and kind.

> He shall feed his flock like a shepherd; he shall gather the lambs with his arm, and carry them in his bosom, and shall gently lead those that are with young.   40:11

. . . but driven to fury by wrong and injustice:

> For my house shall be called a house of prayer for all people.   56:7

And, ISAIAH says, He WILL suffer . . .

The Good Shepherd from a 1st Century Painting in the Catacombs

Behold my servant whom I uphold; mine elect, in whom my soul delighteth; I have put my spirit upon him; he shall bring forth judgment to the Gentiles. He shall not cry or lift up [his voice] nor cause [it] to be heard in the street. 42:1,2 * I gave my back to the smiters, and my cheeks to them that plucked off the hair: I hid not my face from shame and spitting. 50:6 * He is despised and rejected of men; a man of sorrows, and acquainted with grief; and we hid as it were our faces from him: he was despised, and we esteemed him not. Surely he hath borne our griefs, and carried our sorrows, yet we did esteem him stricken, smitten of God, and afflicted. But he was wounded for our transgressions, he was bruised for our iniquities: the chastisement of our peace was upon him; and with his stripes we are healed. 53:3-5 * All we like sheep have gone astray, we have turned every one to his own way: and the LORD hath laid on him the iniquity of us all. 53:6 * He was oppressed, and he was afflicted, yet he opened not his mouth; he is brought as a lamb to the slaughter, and as a sheep before her shearers is dumb so he openeth not his mouth. 53:7 * He was cut off out of the land of the living; for the transgressions of thy people was he stricken. 53:8 * And He made his grave with the wicked and with the rich in his death: because he had done no violence, neither was any deceit in his mouth. 53:9 * For behold, darkness shall cover the earth. 60:2

The "suffering servant" prophecies: (See: A.D. 32, Friday)

And to herald the coming of the suffering servant, ISAIAH tells of

The voice of one that crieth in the wilderness, prepare ye the way of the LORD, make straight in the desert a highway for our God. 40:3 (See: A.D. 29 and MATTHEW 3:3)

Through the suffering servant, ISAIAH says . . .

The glory of the LORD shall be revealed, and all flesh shall see it together, for the mouth of the LORD hath spoken it. 40:5 (See: AD 30)

Later, a man named Paul, from Tarsus in Asia minor, will be sent on a great mission to teach the world about the suffering servant, with these words:

I have set you to be a light for the gentiles, that you may bring salvation to the uttermost parts of the earth. 49:6 (See: A.D. 47 & ACTS 13:47)

Almost 2300 years from now, a German *Baroque* composer will set these words of ISAIAH to music (and others, also, from both the "Old" and "New Testaments.") After 24 days of non-stop work in near-total seclusion, the shaken, emotionally drained, ailing and half-blind composer will tearfully relate how he created his immortal *oratorio*, MESSIAH . . .

I did think I did see all Heaven before me . . . and the Great God Himself! George Frederick Handel, A.D. 1741, September 12. The dated, autographed copy of the original score is, today, in the British Museum, London.

. . . Not all the Jews who leave Babylon, now Persia, go back to Judah. Thousands find homes in many other countries, taking with them their customs and their unique belief in

One god. With this "dispersion" of the Jews, begins the period of their history known, in Greek, as the DIASPORA.

. . . The legal reforms of the Greek lawmaker, Solon, have not worked, but left the aristocracy in control over the *demos*, or common people. The aristocratic *phratry* (from which come the English fraternize and fraternity) patronize the *demos*, twice leaving Athens in *anarchy* with no *archon*, or mayor/magistrate.) Now, a benevolent *tyrant* named Peisistratus (who usurped the office in 546) effects sweeping changes in the law. An aristocrat himself, he takes the aristocratic authority upon himself and transfers it to the "state"—the *demos*, the people, thus switching their loyalty from the aristocrats to . . . themselves and, thus, moves Athens another step toward DEMOCRACY. Then he, the state, takes the lead in cultural and civic improvement, and wins over and subsidizes Athens' two major "industries": its beautiful decorated pottery and its indispensable olive groves. He promotes religious and athletic festivals, making them not just local, but "national." He encourages recitations of Homer's ILIAD and ODYSSEY and, with great far-sight, causes them to be written down to be preserved for posterity.

521 Cyrus the Great, liberator of the Jews, whose memory the Persians cherish as "Father of the People," is killed in battle, and a great stone tomb is set up in the wilderness of Pasagardae (in today's Iran) where it stands to this day.

> Know O man, that I am Cyrus and I won for the Persians their empire. * The epitaph of Cyrus, as recorded-by Plutarch in his LIVES OF THE NOBLE GREEKS AND ROMANS. The times needed Cyrus, a man of great spirit, an excellent warrior, a lover of his friends, a bold and enterprising prince. Plutarch

The Tomb of Cyrus the Great

The son of one of Cyrus' governors takes the throne as Darius I, and now rules all of southwest Asia, Egypt and parts of Europe, the largest empire the world has yet seen. King Darius completely reorganizes the government, dividing the empire into 20 regions, or *Satrapys*, each ruled by a local *Satrap* (with Judea in the 5th Satrapy.) He builds a vast network of roads: mints coins called *darics*, and permits his dependencies to do likewise. He reorganizes taxation . . . and Persia's "postal" system, whose runners are famous for their speed . . .

> There is no mortal thing faster than these messengers: Neither snow nor rain nor heat nor gloom of night stays these couriers from the swift completion of their appointed rounds. Herodotus (See: 447 B.C.)

Darius undertakes a project like that of almost 800 years ago: the joining, by canal, of the Nile River delta to the Red Sea. Begun by Egypt's great Pharaoh Ramses, it was a project with which Moses, himself, might have been familiar. (See: 1290 B.C.) For the first time Persian *triremes* sail a direct route to the Mediterranean, and the East has access to the West.

The jewel in Darius' imperial crown is Persepolis, a magnificent city whose ruins exist today in southwestern Iran. A monumental double staircase at Darius' palace leads to a grand portal, guarded by gigantic winged stone lions. Carved on its walls are, not tortured victims writhing in pain as in former days, but dignified delegations of proud nobles bearing gifts to a regal king seated on a magnificent throne; his son, Xerxes, standing behind him. There are envoys from Media, Parthia, Cappadocia, Bactria and India; from as far south as Egypt, Ethiopia and Libya; and as far north as Ionia, Thrace and Macedonia. They carry gold, silver and ivory vessels, jars, lances and shields, and animal skins; and bring with them camels, bulls, a giraffe and a lioness with her cubs. Five hundred years from now a Jewish historian called Josephus (See: A.D. 64) will write this story about Darius of Persia in a massive history of the Jewish people:

Darius could not sleep and began to converse with his three bodyguards, promising riches and power to whomever could best answer a question. 'Tell me," he said, "which of these is strongest: wine, kings, woman or truth." In turn, each was defended . . . wine, because it makes the poor feel rich, the weak strong, and the sad happy. Kings for they can move mountains, and say who will live and who die. Then the third one, Zerubbabel, said "Woman is stronger, for man is not born nor can he live without her . . . BUT . . . the greatest of all is Truth, for everything else is mortal and short-lived. Only truth is immortal and eternal." Delighted, Darius awards the riches and princely power to Zerubbabel ". . . and anything else you want." "My request is this, O king," replied Zerubbabel. "Let me return to Jerusalem and rebuild the Temple of God." Darius not only did that, but sent to Phoenecia for Cedars of Lebanon to build it with; and sent letters forbidding any nation to hinder its building.   Josephus, ANTIQUITIES OF THE JEWS

521   THE SECOND GROUP OF JEWS RETURNS FROM BABYLON, NOW PERSIA.

Prince Zerubbabel leads home the second group of returnees from exile, 18 years after the first, who had cleared away rubble, made themselves homes, and tried to start work on a new Temple, but had been fiercely opposed, and stopped. Harassment from neighboring tribes, drought and famine; all have made the Jews' lives miserable, and given them time enough to think, not of a sumptuous temple, but only of survival. But now, two more prophets appear on the scene, preaching to the disheartened Jews that the temple to God MUST be built. An aged Haggai, carried away to Babylon as a boy, and a young Zechariah, born in exile, return now, also, and with the support of Cyrus and Zerubbabel, they preach and plead, coax and coerce until, finally (according to the book of EZRA) the Jews have a "renewed burst of activity. As one man" they go to work, and in the "seventh month" (our September-October) they set up an altar and sacrifice to God. The foundations of the new temple are laid and there are processions and celebrations, and the people cheer loudly . . . so loudly that "they drown out the weeping of the old, old folks" who remember what happened to the first temple.

520   The Etruscan people are firmly in control of the Italian city of Rome now, under Rome's seventh king, Lucius Tarquinius, called, by himself, Superbus. The Etruscans (in the

area today called Tuscany) are a highly talented people, and the 86 years (so far) under their rule have transformed Rome from a mud-hut village to a city of beauty and utility with architectural and engineering accomplishments from bridges, viaducts and canals, to public buildings and temples; and have made Rome safe by enclosing the city with a wall:

> Thus surely Etruria waxed strong. Thus Rome became the fairest of all things and enclosed her seven hills with a single wall.   Virgil, the GEORGICS (See: 27 B.C.)

The Etruscans are unique in the world in another way, one which shocks the staid, proper Romans who consider them "immoral" for the way they treat their women; not the Roman way, as chattel owned by husband or father, but as individuals of importance and independence, allowed to own property, socialize with men, attend dinner parties, and to study and practice mathematics and medicine. (Curiously, though, young women are also allowed to earn a marriage dowry by prostitution, a practice that will be joked about by future Romans as "marriage the Tuscan way." Later generations of Romans will far surpass Etruscan immorality.

But Tarquinius Superbus, Rome's third Etruscan king and the second Tarquin, is a heavy-handed ruler, a despot who began his reign by repealing many constitutional freedoms and putting to death senators who oppose him. The Latins and Sabines resent their oppression and even the Etruscans are becoming restless.

Tarquin

516   Five years hard work, frequent discouragement and sometimes grudging-self-sacrifice have brought the temple to completion. Although it is far less magnificent than Solomon's temple, it is built on the same plan—King David's plan—paneled with Cedars of Lebanon and, thanks to King Cyrus of Persia, the golden utensils and vessels once again have a home. But the Ark of the Covenant does not. for that disappeared with Nebuchadnezzar when the first Temple burned; and the Holy of Holies remains empty, closed off now, by curtains, a great, woven and embroidered "veil."

. . . King Darius puts down a conspiracy of rebellious Persian princes, and has his victory immortalized for caravan passers-by to see on a high cliff wall of an enormous rock called Behistun, in a Kurdish mountain pass 200 miles away from Babylon, about half-way between modern-day Baghdad and Teheran, Iran. Soaring over 300 feet above ground level, a huge *bas-relief* scene shows the victorious King Darius standing with his royal foot firmly planted on a prostrate rebel prince while nine others, duly chastised, line up before him, hands shackled behind their backs. Bow in hand, his son, the crown prince Xerxes, and a spear-wielding nobleman flank the king. It is a vivid depiction of Persian pride.

The entire story of the affair is carved on the rock, also; thousands of cuneiform words in three languages: Old Persian, Elamite and Assyrian. Almost 2300 years from now a British archeologist will labor four long, hot years, perched precariously on ladders, dangling in a rope swing from above, or clinging one-handed to the rock face from a narrow ledge, copying out the inscriptions . . . and then set about the enormous task of deciphering. The translation of the Behistun inscriptions will bring back to life the strange, wedge-shaped writing that will long ago have died away. The ancient laws of the great Hammurabi and Sargon; the Babylonian creation story and the adventures of Gilgamesh and the flood; the arrogant annals of Tiglath-Pileser, Nabonidus and Nebuchadnezzar; all can be read today because King Darius of Persia bragged to the world of his power and pride on the towering cliffs of Behistun Rock.

Lucius Junius Brutus

510   Rome's seventh king, Tarquinius Superbus, "the Proud," in power for 24 years now, is universally despised for his arrogance and excessive pride, his brutality, oppression and heavy-handed despotism; and the Romans are fed up with monarchy. All they need is an incident to overthrow him, and when it comes, it comes with tragedy. Lucretia, the beautiful wife of the Roman senator, Collatinus, is raped and, after telling her husband and father about it, stabs herself to death. The rapist is none other than Sextus Tarquinius, son of the king. Two men take the lead in revolt; the widowed Collatinus and his friend, Lucius Junius Brutus who had lost his own father and brother to the Tarquin brutality. The entire clan of Tarquin is driven out of Rome, and . . . THE MONARCHY IS ABOLISHED.

The stories of the seven kings of Rome are found in the writings of Greek and Roman historians, especially Plutarch and Livy. Whether or not they are just legend, Rome was, in fact, founded, developed, enlarged, king-ruled, misruled and overthrown, and so it may very well have happened as they wrote. After all, as Plato said, "Every myth has its truth," and the Etruscan presence and influence will, indeed, be felt for many centuries hence . . . down to our own day: the Etruscans' unique elevation of womens' status; marriage, funeral and religious rites; everything from sculpture, art, architecture, and their Latin language and "Roman" numerals. But while their manners and mores live on their cities do not, for the Etruscans build with wood, brick and terra cotta, so their remarkable engineering projects—bridges, viaducts, canals, public buildings and temples—erode away over the centuries and, in our time, are no more.

510   With the overthrow of the monarchy and the formation of a new government . . .

. . . THE ROMAN REPUBLIC IS ESTABLISHED

. . . a government of elected representatives, answerable to the people, or citizens, for their actions, and liable to be "voted out" if those citizens disapprove their actions. Lucius Junius Brutus and Collatinus become the first of two equally empowered CO-CONSULS of Rome, first in a long succession of heads of state, who rule for ONE YEAR ONLY and must "consult" together and, so, guarantee against one man gaining absolute power. So hated are the Tarquin kings by now that two of the first laws drawn up pronounce sentences of death to 1. any man who tries to make himself king. Punishable WITHOUT trial, it is the law that will be used to justify the eventual assassination of Julius Caesar; and 2. anyone attempting to hold office without having been "elected." And so prized is the status of citizenship that the third law gives any citizen who has been condemned to flogging or death the right to appeal to Rome's highest authority. Five hundred sixty years from now a Roman citizen named Paul, from the city of Tarsus in Asia Minor, will cite this law, and appeal to Caesar, himself, at Rome.   (See ACTS 25:10, A.D. 60)

Rome will have to wait a long time for its turn in the never-ending struggle for power but even now the sleeping giant is beginning to stir, and soon its hungry eyes will begin to peer about and spot tempting little prizes everywhere, just waiting to be plucked and gobbled up.

. . . An adventurous sailor called Hanno, from the fast-growing, Baal-worshipping city of Carthage, explores the west coast of Africa . . . and Carthage likes what he finds. Lying at the northernmost tip of Africa (in modern-day Tunisia), Carthage is also a sleeping giant with an ambition every bit as great as Rome's. Now it, too, begins to stir.

508   One last effort to restore the Roman monarchy is made by an Etruscan noble, Lars Porsena, who . . .

> . . . believing that it was not only a safe thing for the Etruscans that there should be a king at Rome, but an honor to have that king of Etruscan stock, invaded Roman territory with a hostile army.   Titus Livius, called LIVY, HISTORY OF ROME, Book 11:1–7 (See: A.D. 10)

One Roman soldier, Horatius Cocles, becomes the "bulwark of defense," who . . .

> . . . saw them as they charged down on the run . . . while his own people behaved like a frightened mob, throwing away their arms and quitting their ranks . . . [Horatius] commanded them to break down the (Tiber) bridge with steel, with fire . . . any[thing] . . . Then, striding to the head of the bridge . . . covered himself with . . . sword and buckler . . . confounding the Etruscans with amazement at his audacity . . . they cast their javelins from every side against their solitary foe . . . but he caught them all upon his shield . . . and held his ground . . . [with] the crash of the falling bridge [he invoked the Tiber to receive him. and] . . . leaped down into the river . . . under a shower of missles [and] swam across unhurt to his fellows . . .   LIVY, ibid.

Livy, himself, says that Horatius' incredible act of bravery would, "obtain more fame than credence with posterity." The Etruscans are driven back. The threat is ended, and the Republic prevails.

. . . Since Peisistratus' death 28 years ago, Athens has been ruled by the always bickering aristocracy and an occasional *archon,* and it is as tired of them as it is wary of another tyrant. So a brilliant young statesman named Cleisthenes takes control and, in the words of the "Father of History,"

> . . . he took the people into partnership.   Herodotus of Hallicarnasus

Where, before, a person's civic status was determined by the *phratry,* the family or clan from which aristocracy springs, now that is changed to the area or locality where one lives, be it in any one of three "districts": Urban/suburban, Inland or Maritime. Thus is every individual counted, and thus does the movement toward *democracy,* begun under Solon and nurtured by Peisistratus come to fruition under Cleisthenes

c. 500   From the Mediterranean Sea to the Pacific and Indian Oceans, the next 100 years are busy, building years . . .

. . . With work progressing on the Jewish temple at Jerusalem, the two "Temple Builders" set down in writing their experiences; the aged Haggai and the youthful Zechariah, both returned from Babylon.

HAGGAI

Book of Prophecy — Written in Hebrew,   c. 500 B.C.

Then came the word of the LORD by Haggai the prophet, saying, "Go up to the mountain and bring wood, and build the house; and 1 will take pleasure in it, and I will be glorified, saith the LORD." Haggai worked with the Jewish governor, Prince Zerubbabel, and the high Priest, Joshua, insisting that their most important work was getting the temple rebuilt. "Thus says the LORD," HAGGAI prophesied, "you busy yourselves each with his own house, while my house lies in ruins." Haggai said that all their troubles were due to the neglect of God's house, and that that should be their first responsibility; that it was necessary to prepare for the wonderful age ahead, when the Messiah comes.

> . . . thus saith the LORD of hosts; Yet once . . . a little while, and I will shake the heavens, and the earth, and the sea, and the dry land; And I will shake all nations, and the desire of all nations shall come . . .   2:6,7 (See: HEBREWS 12:26, A.D. 64)

ZECHARIAH

Book of Prophecy — Written in Hebrew,   c. 500 B.C.

"The LORD hath been sore displeased with your fathers," Zechariah says in the first chapter of his book. "Turn ye unto me . . . (and) Be ye not as your fathers." No sooner are the exiles returned home and already they are falling into "evil doings," and Zechariah says only if they turn to the LORD, will He turn to them. He felt, as Haggai did, with whom he worked, that the age of the Messiah was coming soon, and that the temple MUST be finished first, for He will usher in a time when "Jerusalem shall be called a city of truth," and children shall play in the streets. Even as Hosea announced that God wants no more of sacrifice and burnt offerings, so now Zechariah says, the long fasts and mournings of the exiles "even those 70 years," are over and done, and man's duty is to: "Execute true judgment, and shew mercy and compassion every man to his brother." 7:9

ZECHARIAH had a series of prophetic visions, explained to him by an angel: a vision of horsemen patrolling the earth, a man measuring Jerusalem, the "apple of his eye," filthy garments and a clean turban, a golden lampstand, a flying scroll, four chariots and a woman in a bowl. His fanciful Persian/oriental imagery recalls that of Ezekiel, but ZECHARIAH refers to a new presence in the world, also, just over the horizon . . . the Greeks. Then, in chapter nine, his tone changes to a Messianic hope, a Prince of Peace and a great and dreadful Day of the LORD. It will be a time both of jubilation and great sorrow, of simple faith and enigmatic mystery:

> Rejoice greatly, O daughter of Zion; shout, O daughter of Jerusalem; behold, thy King cometh unto thee: he is just, and having salvation; lowly, and riding upon an ass, and upon a colt the foal of an ass 9:9.   (See: A.D. 32, Sunday before Passover) * So they weighed for my price 30 pieces of silver . . . And I took the thirty pieces of silver, and cast them to the potter.   11:12,13   * and they shall look upon me whom they have pierced, and they shall mourn for him, as one mourneth for his only son. . .   12,10 (both, See: A.D. 32, Friday)

Almost 600 years from now an evangelist named JOHN will also write of ZECHARIAH's Day of the Lord:

> And the LORD shall be king over all the earth: in that day shall there be one LORD, and his name one.   ZECH. 14:9   * The kingdoms of this world are become the kingdoms of our Lord, and of his Christ; and he shall reign for ever and ever.   REV. 11:15 (See: A.D. 95)

And the prophet Joel preaches in the new temple . . .

JOEL

Book of Prophecy — Written in Hebrew,   c. 500 B.C.

Almost nothing is known about Joel except that he lived in Judah somewhere between now and 300 B.C. His book gives no hint, but it is apparent that he was somehow active in the life of the new temple. He experienced the horror of a plague of locusts and likened it to God's judgment and the coming Day of the LORD, that great and terrible day that will see "multitudes and multitudes in the valley of decision." Then, JOEL says, "your young men shall see visions and your old men shall dream dreams, and there will be wonders in the heavens above and signs on the earth beneath, but whoever calls on the name of the LORD shall be saved."   2:28 and 3:14

. . . in far-away China the now 51 year-old Confucius is teaching his moral principals of honesty and justice in a war-like age that will not listen. The suffering of the common people appalls Confucius; forced labor and war-making often waged just for the sport of rulers. His teachings are aimed at reform, and his conception of world order is: 1. The right to govern depends upon the ability of a dynasty to make the governed happy (the *teh*.) This *teh* can, however, wear out, and when it does, a heavenly decree, or *ming*, (2) ordains that the dynasty be overthrown, and (3) the *t'ien*, the power of heaven, will overthrow that dynasty and ordain a new *teh*. Five hundred years from now, and thousands of miles away, another teacher will express in a positive way what Confucius teaches in a negative:

What you do not like done unto yourself, do not unto others.   Confucius   *   Whatever you wish that men would do to you, do so to them; for this is the Law and the Prophets.
Jesus of Nazareth, MATTHEW 7:12

. . . Another teacher, now about 60, the son of an Indian Rajah, long ago rejected the Hindu *Vedas* and their vast pantheon of mythical gods, gave up his princely inheritance and, now, is striving for a "perfect condition" which he calls *Nirvana*. Everything (1) he says, "is pain. The cause of pain (2) is a craving of the passions. One must (3) work for the cessation of that pain with (4) right views, right effort, mindfulness and concentration." Someday a full third of the world's people will be followers of the "Four Noble Truths" of India's Gautama Buddha.

. . . In Greece, a writer named Thespis is writing dramas which are being acted out in "theaters," making Thespis the world's first dramatist, and marking the beginning of Greek theater. Well, not exactly the beginning. Greek theater actually began, some 200 years ago in a much different form than it has become by this time. It began with religious festivals in honor of Greece's gods, especially Bacchus, or Dionysus, the god of wine . . . and fertility. Celebrated four times a year, when vines are planted, dressed, harvested and, especially, when the wine is made, the festivals were accompanied by sacred songs and dances, hymns of praise and recitation of poetry and odes. But as the days wore on, Bacchus' much-loved liquid flowed ever more freely and passions rose, and the celebrations turned into wild, uninhibited *Bacchinalian* orgies, so frenzied and frenetic their reputation has not diminished to this day. Some of the scenes portrayed on Greek pottery are mind-boggling . . . and generally considered completely accurate. But over the centuries these festivals, while losing none of their passion, have evolved into certain set programs, performed before audiences. Now Thespis, an itinerant "playwright" from Attica, travels throughout Greece taking his festivals with him (timed, perhaps, by a water clock, invented by this time.) Thespis uses a *chorus,* and an *hypocrite,* or actor, who converses with the chorus and its leader in *dialogue*. The fertility orgies are only incidental to Thespis' "productions," his main work being the invention of *tragedy* which centers on the human condition. To our own day, actors are often called "Thespians."

. . . Heraclitus of Ephesus, known as the "Dark Philosopher" and most remembered for his statements that ". . . you cannot step into the same river twice," and that "nothing is so permanent as change," believes in a *rationale* of life, a *logos* or Divine Intelligence which he calls God, and heaps scorn on those who worship graven idols . . .

. . . and they pray to these idols, just as if one were to have a conversation with a house.
Heraclitus of Ephesus

. . . Far to the north the favored, fateful city of Byzantium begins to grow on the shores of the Bosporus, a most strategic waterway connecting the Aegean and Black Seas, where West meets East, Europe meets Asia. Past the Golden Horn and into its deep, fish-fertile harbor sail the largest ships now built, just as did tiny Argo when Jason and his Argonauts came, searching for Golden Fleece so long ago, after the Trojan War. Centuries of history will pass, now, before the very eyes of the Byzantines, years of both war and peace. For a thousand years Byzantium will play a major role in the Glory and Grandeur of both Greece and Rome, and at its greatest extent will rule one half of an empire as the Rome of the East.

. . . From the farthest reaches of Eur-asia, the Chinese are using hollow bamboo to pipe water, and are raising fish, particularly carp, domestically; and the Greeks have settled a colony at Lisbon, Portugal. But at home, the threat of Persian military might grows greater every day.

. . . The Persian Empire under King Darius, "the Great King," the "Mighty King," controls the greatest tract of land the world has yet known; five million square miles from North Africa to southern India, and from the Black Sea to southern Arabia, a vast, teeming conglomeration of hundreds of divergent ethnic entities, governed by 23 king-appointed *Satraps,* whose only duties are to carry out the king's wishes and collect his taxes in time of peace, and to raise and lead his armies in time of war. He, the Great King is the supreme, unapproachable sovereign whose mere nod of the head can mean instant death to anyone who comes too near or who uncovers a hand from inside his sleeve . . . which hand could hold a weapon. The oriental splendor that surrounds Darius is guarded by 10,000 highly trained and armed "Immortals," who are the elite core of his vast, uncountable armies, most of whom are green conscripts rounded up at the king's will. None of this is paid for by the king, though, from the staggering, unimaginable amounts of tribute money brought to him annually by his subservient nobles. That gold and silver is merely melted

A Persian Bowman

down into ingots, stored in his own private treasury and never again put into circulation. It is all paid, rather, by more taxes, and more . . . and more; and so, while Persia is an empire of gigantic proportions and wealth, it is, in many ways, only a shell. But Darius is ambitious and his goal is the conquest of Europe . . . beginning with Greece. He already has access to the Mediterranean at the Syrian/now Persian seaport cities of Tyre and Sidon, and has meddled enough in Greek aristocratic political intrigue to believe he can prevail. But underling kow-towing to an "all-perfect Great King" is bitter anathema to the freedom-loving, *demo-cratic* Greeks, and no two more disparate adversaries could hardly be imagined.

While the Greek city-states are fiercely independent, in no way a unified "Greece," they do, however, act in harmony at times: during their great athletic contests, on pilgrimages to their several oracles . . . and in their regard of barbarians which, to them, is anyone not a Greek. And the most dreaded "barbarian" is Darius. Now the Great King of

Kings demands "earth and water" from each Greek city, symbols of his world-wide sovereignty, and receives it from all but Sparta and Athens, whose envoys throw Darius' courier into a well where he should find both.

Some of the Ionian cities on the coast of Asia Minor revolt from Persian control, and the Athenians go to their aid . . . and burn the ancient city of Sardis in the process. So enraged is Darius on hearing of it that, obsessed with revenge, he retains one servant at his side whose only duty is to remind him . . .

> Sire, remember the Athenians.   Herodotus

490   Darius' navy sails the Aegean Sea to the Bay of Marathon, taking the Athenians by surprise, and a Greek soldier named Pheidippides runs the 150 miles to Sparta to get aid, which the Spartans promise, but delay to send because of poor omens. Still, the Athenians take on the Persians; they are perfectly drilled, fight as one man, armed with iron, and mostly, are free men, fighting for a free commonwealth, and each man for himself. The Persians fight in slavish submission to a despot, have no unity, no body armor and inferior arms, including . . . wicker shields! The Greek commander, Miltiades, executes a brilliant offense from his encampment in the mountains down to the low-lying plain . . .

> . . . when the Persians saw the Athenians running down on them without horse or bowman . . . scanty in numbers, they thought them a set of madmen rushing upon certain destruction.   Herodotus, THE HISTORIES 6:15

When the battle ends, Darius' dead number 6400, the Greeks 192. Pheidippides, having already run 300 miles to Sparta and back—and then fought in the battle—now races

"Rejoice, we conquer!"

another 26 to Athens, gasps only "Rejoice, we conquer!" and falls dead. Someone in the Greek ranks flashes a mirror signal to the Persians that Athens lies undefended, but the Greeks see the signal, also, fast-march to Athens, and are there when the Persian fleet arrives. The threat of an "Oriental" Europe is over . . . for now . . .

One of Miltiades' best generals at Marathon is a young genius named Themistocles, and in the years following the battle he becomes the dominant figure in Athenian politics. First elected *archon,* or mayor, 10 years ago, he has been carefully building up Athens' fortifications.

486   Darius I dies, and his son, Xerxes, is king of Persia, obsessed, as was his father, on revenge . . . punishment of the Greeks for the rout at Marathon. For six years he very carefully plans his campaign, building his army into the most formidable fighting force ever assembled in the East, with the select, specially trained and experienced Ten Thousand Immortals as its elite core. He stores provisions along the route he will follow, digs an

enormous channel to bypass a vulnerable isthmus, and builds an ingenious "bridge of boats" across the Hellespont near the site of ancient Troy.

Greek Silver Tetradrachm

483 A rich vein of silver is discovered on Mount Laurium, and many Athenians insist it should be divided amongst the population, everyone an equal share. But the astute, far-sighted Themistocles knows that the threat from Persia has only just begun and that Athens must defend itself . . . at sea! At Delphi, the Oracle tells him . . .

> "Build wooden walls!" The Oracle at Delphi to Themistocles, which he takes to mean . . . ships. Herodotus 7:140–43

Themistocles prevails, and the silver lode is used to build ships, 200 of them; sleek, swift *biremes* and *triremes* with two and three banks of oars, and deadly battering rams half hidden under the water. It is a time of great prosperity for Athens, for the building of its first navy provides thousands of jobs for the men who design and build the ships, those who provide the materials and those who man its oars. Themistocles will be remembered by history as the "Father of the Greek Navy."

480 Xerxes mighty Persian army of 200,000 men cross the bridge of boats over the Hellespont, and the Orient invades Europe! Three hundred of Sparta's best warriors, under Spartan King Leonidas, attempt to hold Xerxes off at the treacherous mountain pass of Thermopylae, inflict heavy damage on the invading Persians, but are wiped out . . . to the last man; and Xerxes marches on to Athens . . . which he burns . . .

Themistocles

> . . . at the last . . . the foreigners found an entrance . . . where . . . none would have thought . . . any man [could climb] . . . When the Athenians saw that [the Persians] had ascended to the acropolis, some of them cast themselves down from the wall and . . . perished, and others fled into the inner chamber. [The Persians inside opened the gates] and slew the suppliants; and when they had laid all the Athenians low, they plundered the temple and burnt the whole of the acropolis. Herodotus, THE HISTORIES 8:53

The Greek fleet retreats to the island of Salamis, and Themistocles begins to assert his authority and leadership. Knowing that Greek unity will quickly crumble if Persia prevails, and that the Persians will easily pluck off those cities not already capitulated, Themistocles addresses the navy commanders:

> Hear me now, and judge between two plans . . . If you . . . fight in open waters [our ships being . . . heavier and fewer] you will lose Salamis . . . lead their army . . . to the Peloponnese, and imperil all Hellas. But if you do as I counsel . . . engaging their many ships with our few in narrow seas, we shall win a great victory . . . Herodotus, *ibid.* 8:60

Then, posing as a traitor to Athens, Themistocles sends a servant to Xerxes with a message:

> I am sent . . . without the knowledge of the [others] . . . to tell you that the Greeks have lost heart and are planning flight and that now is the hour for you to achieve an incomparable feat of arms, if you suffer them not to escape.　HERODOTUS 8:76

Xerxes

"The Persians," Herodotus says, "put faith in the message," and take the bait; and Xerxes, against better advice, sails to meet Greece's "wooden walls" at Salamis. So that he can watch the entire battle and exult in his victory, Xerxes sits high atop a bluff, on a silver throne. But his fleet of over a thousand warships is boxed into a narrow channel by the heavier *biremes* and *triremes* of the much smaller Greek navy, and cannot maneuver. The only bravery Xerxes sees in his commanders is that of a woman, Queen Artemesia of Caria, and he cries, "My men have become women and my women, men." Xerxes is utterly defeated, and completely demoralized. . .

> . . . aware of the calamity that had befallen him, he feared lest the Greeks . . . might sail to the Hellespont and break his bridges, and he might be cut off in Europe . . . so he planned flight . . .　Herodotus 8:37

The threat of an oriental despotism in Europe is ended. Europe will not become "easternized" for another thousand years. History will call the battles of Marathon and Salamis, "The war to end all wars."

Xerxes leaves even his tent behind, and when the Greeks see its magnificence—gold and silver everywhere—its "embroidered hangings and gorgeous decorations" and the fabulous feast set out for him, the Spartan commander orders a typical "Spartan" meal brought in. Laughing, he shows it all to the Greek commanders, and says:

> Gentlemen, I asked you here . . . to show you the folly of the Persians, who living [like] this, came to Greece to rob us of our poverty.　HERODOTUS 3:82

Although Xerxes' European ambitions have come to naught, the last 15 years of his reign in Persia are years of accomplishment and glory. His empire still in good order, he gains renown as a master builder, adds another fabulous palace to the already beautiful Persepolis; and is even remembered in Hebrew history as a fair and reasonable king . . . (although, Herodotus says, it was under Xerxes that the Persians came to be called the "great drunkards of the ancient world," and that keeping a "harem" became important. He also recounts how Xerxes became entangled with courtiers, eunuchs and concubines in harem intrigues.) The Bible calls him Ahasuerus, and says one of his wives was a beautiful Jewess named . . .

ESTHER

Book of "Writings" — Written in Hebrew, c. 150 B.C.

". . . Ahasuerus . . . who reigned from India to Ethiopia over 127 provinces . . . gave a banquet for all his princes and servants . . . army chiefs of Persia and Media . . . and governors of the provinces . . . [to whom] he showed the riches of his royal glory . . . the splendor and pomp of his majesty for . . . 180 days. . . . [The] king loved Esther more than all the women . . . and . . . set the royal crown on her head . . ."

The book of ESTHER tells how the beautiful queen used her charms and wit to expose the plot of an intended *pogrom* against her people, the Jews, and helped them find favor with Xerxes the king—Ahaseurus in Hebrew. The book, itself, will not actually be written until about 150 B.C., in the time of Jewish persecutions by the Syrians. It will almost not be included when the "Old" Testament, or Hebrew Scriptures, are compiled because it is not, really, a religious book at all, never once mentioning, for example, the name of God . . . although the apocryphal ADDITIONS TO THE BOOK OF ESTHER, written 50 years later, will attempt to repair that oversight.   (See: 100 B.C.)

But ESTHER is a valuable book, historically, telling much about this time . . . even showing Xerxes having CHRONICLES read to him when he could not sleep. Two Jewish traditions begin with ESTHER; the feast of PURIM which celebrates her brave dead; and the modern-day Jewish women's organization known by Esther's Jewish name, Hadassah.

475   A Carthaginian naval commander named Himilco explores the west coast of Europe; those still unnamed lands that will someday be called Spain, Portugal and possibly even as far north as Britain.

472   One of the heroes of the battles of Marathon and Salamis (whose own brother died a hero's death in the fighting), was an aristocratic young infantryman named Aeschylus, to whom Athens has erected a plaque for his valor. He has, since then, made a name for himself in a field far removed from warfare. For Aeschylus' passion is the "theater" and under his inspiration and direction it has become something we, today—2500 years later—would still recognize as "modern." While Thespis had introduced an "actor" or *hypocrite,* Aeschylus now adds a *protagonist* and *dialogue.* A chorus leader recites *odes* between the *episodes,* and a *prologue* begins the *tragedy.*

Now Aeschylus produces his "historical drama," called THE PERSIANS based on his own first-hand, eye-witness experience in the wars, told as only a real-life participant could tell it . . . but told from the Persian point of view, a play unique for not being based

on mythology. He stages it in a *theatron* or "seeing place" (a seating area carved into the hillside) with an *orchestra* (or floor space/stage) at its base. Providing a backdrop to the *orchestra* is massive, painted *skene* or scenery, which can be moved and manipulated by a *mechane* or machine, so sophisticated it can conjure up ghosts and gods and all sorts of "special effects." THE PERSIANS features Xerxes' mother, Atossa, in *dialogue* with the *chorus* of Persian elders. Anxious about how the war is going, she asks just where is this "Athens" that her son is fighting for; and they tell her far to the west, beside the setting sun. "But why does my son want it so badly?" she asks. "Because when Athens is ours all Greece will be ours," they reply; and then comes a concept no Persian can begin to comprehend. "But who is the great Lord of Athens that can command such a host?" And the elders, in awe, tell her that the Greeks are free men . . .

> " . . . slaves to no man, subject to none."   Aeschylus, THE PERSIANS

Then a messenger arrives and recounts the whole dreadful story of the battle of Salamis with vivid, exciting action, a horrifying description of the dead and the humiliation of the king. After an appearance of the ghost of his father, Darius, the defeated Xerxes returns and he, and the chorus, lament:

> Chorus: On an evil day we joined the fray, With the brave Greek name; From Ionian ships a sheer eclipse on Persia came. Xerxes: With such an army, struck so dire a blow! Chorus: So great a power, the Persian power, laid low. Xerxes: I am the man! The father of shame! The fount of disgrace!   Aeschylus, THE PERSIANS

The *choregus,* or Chorus Leader who selects, pays and leads the chorus, in this production of THE PERSIANS is a young, aristocratic Athenian "politician" named Pericles, an ambitious young man who will go far.

470   The Olympic Games are not the only athletic contests in Greece. The Pythian Games at Delphi are important events as well, this year's chariot races especially exciting; and one chariot driver, in particular wins great renown. Twenty-three hundred years from now, archeologists digging in the ruins at Delphi will come upon a life-size, cast bronze statue of a young man lying face down, covered with dirt, but still standing proudly in victorious dignity, clothed in a traditional, protective, draped *chiton,* the reins of his chariot still in hand. It is a *Delphic Charioteer* created by one Polyzalus of Syracuse, so perfect in detail each eyelash is separately cast. The proud athlete stands again, today, in the Delphi Museum, Greece.

Delphic Chatioteer

. . . Much of the glory that goes with winning the games, whether they be Olympic, Delphian or other, is celebrated in the singing of odes in praise of the victor's name, family and his great accomplishments. The most famous singer and writer of odes is the aristocratic poet Pindar, from Boeotia, near Thebes. Having studied music and meter, and the adaptation of them to the dance, Pindar composes odes for male choirs which are accompanied by a lyre and flute and led by a choir director. His odes are so highly admired that Pindar, himself, is awarded many honors and money enough to make him a wealthy man. Famous all over the Mediterranean world, he is so well loved and respected that his house will be the only building left standing when Thebes is sacked and burned by Alexander the Great 135 years from now. Pindar believes that man has an immortal soul and will be judged after death.

> Forge thy tongue on an anvil of truth and what flieth up, though it be but a spark, shall have weight . . . for whatsoever one hath well said goeth forth with a voice that never dieth.   Pindar, *Isthmian Odes*

468   But sports contests are not the only Athenian love; the annual drama contests are events of much excitement, as well. The Athenians love the theater, and Athens considers it a vital part of every citizen's education. Everyone is encouraged to attend, and poorer people even have their admission refunded so they can afford to go. So that people in the farthest rows up on the hillside of the *theatron* can see better, the all male actors wear masks (their *persona)* reflecting either *comedy* or *tragedy;* and little megaphones inside the masks help the audience to hear. This year's contest is an event of much excitement, for the older master, 57 year old Aeschylus (he who fought at Salamis) is being challenged by a newcomer, young Sophocles, 27. (It is not known which plays they presented this year, for of the 30 plays Aeschylus wrote, only seven exist today, and only seven of Sophocles' 120.) Aeschylus has been Athens' master dramatist since he first won the contest 16 years ago, and his *trilogy* of bloodshed and revenge in the family of Agamemnon and Orestes—the *ORESTIA*—will win him first prize again 10 years hence. The world will have to wait almost sixty more years for *OEDIPUS REX,* the chilling masterpiece Sophocles will write when he is almost ninety.

The drama begins early in the morning, and all work stops as the entire city gathers at the theater. The great teacher, Anaxagoras, the man who brought *philosophy* to Athens, and young Pericles is with him, who will become Anaxagoras' most famous student. Another Anaxagoras student, young Euripides, born on the very day of the great battle (so legend says) is surely here, also, for his love of theater is already great, and he will someday become the third of Athens' three greatest dramatists. Pericles' good friend Phidias, at 22 already sculpting works of great beauty, will come with the promising young architects, Ictinus and Callicrates. All day the plays go on; 10 ap-

Sophocles

pointed judges listen, and the tension mounts. Aeschylus will win first place again, but this year belongs to . . . Sophocles!

> Silver and gold are not the only coin; virtue too, passes current all over the world. Sophocles, *OEDIPUS REX* * Though a man be wise, it is no shame for him to live and learn. Sophocles, *ANTIGONE*
>
> To see in advance is to suffer in advance. Truth comes with the light of day. Aeschylus, *AGAMEMNON* * God loves to help him who strives to help himself. Aeschylus, a fragment.

Sophocles is a serenely handsome young man, cultivated, refined and elegant, a "quintessential Greek." Born into a family of wealth and comfort, he is none-the-less a man of conscience, compassion and conviction, and during his long life will serve in the military, rising twice to the rank of general; and in his huge dramatic output, will explore human emotions to their fullest, dredging the very depths of misery, folly, passion and sorrow.

Zeus

465 The sculptor, Phidias, and the architects, Ictinus and Callicrates, are commissioned to create a temple to the god, Zeus, foremost of all Greece's gods. The site is the Olympian Plain, that same plain on which the Olympic Games are held. Phidias uses gold, ivory and precious gems to build his 40 foot statue of Zeus, and its ruby eyes gleam fire red. It will become the third of the Seven Wonders of the Ancient World. The foundations of the temple ruins, the playing fields, the starting lineup stones, the spectator area large enough for 20,000 persons, and Phidias' own cluttered workshop will be found A.D. 1870, as dramatic a find as any in archeology.

460 Athens has a new ruler and, with him in this Golden Age of Greece, begins . . .

The AGE of PERICLES

460 Pericles rules a city-state of 150,000 people. It is the world's first *DEMOCRACY,* wherein every man is encouraged to speak for himself and each is his own representative. Greatness flourishes in Athens, nourished by freedom, ruled by a great man.

> [Even, though] Pericles was of the . . . noblest birth on his father's and mother's sides . . . and had a considerable estate . . . and friends of great person . . . he took his side, not with the rich and few, but with the many and poor, contrary to his natural bent, which was far

from democratical . . . [but] in addition to his great natural genius, [he] attained by the study of nature, to use the words of the divine Plato, [the] height of intelligence . . . And so Pericles . . . let loose the reins to the people . . . and made his policy subservient to the people.   Plutarch, LIVES OF THE NOBLE GREEKS AND ROMANS

Pericles

Pericles appropriates or annexes subject territories and, to raise the Athenian standard of living, begins paying for public service . . . and for attendance at the theater, and is criticized by many for introducing a once sober, industrious and thrifty people to lives of luxury and excess; and for ruling, not a democracy, but an aristocracy. The comic writers and comedians lampoon him mercilessly, but Pericles' placid nature just ignores them, confounding his enemies and winning many friends.

. . . now all schism and division being at an end . . . the city brought to evenness and unity, [Pericles] got all Athens and affairs that pertained to the Athenians into his own hands, their tributes . . . armies, and galleys, the islands, the sea, and . . . wide extended power. Employing [his rule] uprightly and undeviatingly for the country's best interests, he was able, generally, to lead the people along . . . not [only by] his power of language . . . but his manifest freedom from every kind of corruption . . . [that all he did was] for the honor of the city . . .   Plutarch, LIVES

Pericles' greatest contribution to Athens, Plutarch says, that proves that Greece's greatest glory and ancient wealth are "no romance or idle story," was his construction of the public and sacred buildings; which, however, his critics decried as a "wanton waste . . . of a world of money . . ." as though ". . . to gild and adorn some vain woman." But his building projects also provide thousands of jobs.

The materials were stone, brass, ivory, gold, ebony, cypresswood; and the arts or trades that wrought and fashioned them were smiths and carpenters, moulders, founders and braziers, stone-cutters, dyers, goldsmiths, ivory-workers, painters, embroiderers, turners . . . merchants, mariners and ship-masters by sea, and by land, cartwrights, cattle-breeders, waggoners, rope-makers, flax-workers, shoemakers and leather-dressers, road-makers, miners . . . Thus, to say in a word . . . these public works distributed plenty through every age and condition.   Plutarch, LIVES

458   While democracy reigns in Greece, the REPUBLIC of Rome is growing in Italy, based on a representative, elected government of law. But a warlike tribe called Aequai threaten to bring it to an end. So a delegation of senators is sent to the small farm of a Roman general named Cincinnatus to tell him he has been named *dictator* for six months and given

absolute power to drive them out. This Cincinnatus does—in 16 days—and returns to Rome in triumphal procession with a great store of booty. He then surrenders the dictatorship and returns to his farm, a national hero and legend in his own time.

. . . Ever since the return of the Jews from Persia, Israel's neighbors—or adversaries—have done everything they could to hinder the progress of rebuilding Jerusalem, its temple and its walls. Now, in the reign of Artxerxes king of Persia, the prophet, Ezra, (a direct descendent of Moses' brother, Aaron, the first high priest) ". . . went up from Babylon; and he was a . . . scribe in the law of Moses, and the king granted him [a] request . . . and he came to Jerusalem . . . in the seventh year of the king." Ezra is sent on his mission to accomplish certain things: to inquire, for the king, about the status of the LAW, to carry back treasure to beautify the Temple, and to appoint scribes, magistrates and judges; and to this effect Artxerxes issues a decree that ". . . whatsoever Ezra the priest, the scribe of the law of the God of Heaven, shall require of you, it be done speedily."   EZRA 7:21   Artxerxes gives Ezra over six million dollars in gold, brass and silver talents, and Ezra presents it to the Temple heirarchy in an elaborate ceremony. Then he begins his attempt to purify the faith . . . by eliminating all foreign influence, particularly through marriage. ". . . now therefore separate yourselves . . . from the [foreign] wives." And the men of Israel do what is commanded them; the mass divorce takes two months, and they ". . . [make] an end with all the men that had taken strange wives."   10:17

454   Another delegation—of three patrician Roman senators—is sent to Greece, to study the law codes of Solon and others, and bring back a report to the Roman senate. They remain three years, until . . .

451   The report they present to the senate is approved, with revisions that break dramatically from the Greek, and create something totally new in the world, a written code for citizenship in a REPUBLIC. In all of history so far the laws of great civilizations were vested in the state and its gods, and dispensed TO THE PEOPLE. In Egypt, the Pharaoh's word was law, pure and simple; and in Babylon, the written code of Hammurabi prescribed punishments for particular situations. The Greek system (apart from Solon's laws) tries every case by jury, but each on its own merits, without reference to precedent or written principle, every Greek city-state having its own constitution. Now, with the Roman experience, a new concept begins, that Roman citizenship guarantees its holder certain inherant and well-defined RIGHTS and that these rights apply whether at home or abroad. Grown to fruition, this system of vested rights under the law will become Rome's greatest contribution to civilization.

Citizenship brings many privileges: the right to vote, hold office, own property and engage in commerce; and holds many responsibilities, also, for every citizen can be drafted into the army, and it is only after 10 years military service that elected office can be held. But few are privileged, for this new republic has created, not a society of equals, but an *aristocracy* headed by the "aristocratic" *patricians,* the nobility who are descended from the founding fathers. . .and who guard their privileges zealously. Below the *patricians* are the *equites* (or knights), the *equestrian* class, those wealthy-enough businessmen or merchants to *equip* themselves with arms and a horse *(equus)* for war . . . but cannot hold political power. These two, the *patricians* and the *equites,* make up the *SENATUS POPULUSQUE ROMANUS,* the SENATE AND THE PEOPLE OF ROME, the *S.P.Q.R.* that will soon fly from flags and be blazoned on public buildings all over the Mediterranean world. The lowest class of citizens are the *plebians,* or *plebs,* mostly small farmers, but citizens, still, and able to vote. Lastly, the slaves, with no rights at all. They are well-treated, though, and few in number, for they are still, at this time, expensive to buy and therefore, valued property.

Now, the laws are drawn up and engraved on 12 tables, or tablets, which are posted on the speakers rostrum in the Senate House where they can be seen at all times, by everyone (and where they will remain for the next 300 years). It seems, at this time, no world-shaking event, the posting of a short list of laws; but the Law of Twelve Tables will become the backbone of Roman law (and Rome will rule the world) and the foundation of Western civilization. So prized will the status of citizenship be held that one of the laws gives any citizen who has been condemned to flogging or death the right to appeal to Rome's highest authority. Five hundred-some years from now a newly-written book of ACTS will record how a Roman citizen named Paul, from the city of Tarsus in Asia Minor, will cite this law, and appeal to Caesar, himself, at Rome: "But Paul, speaking as a FREEBORN Roman citizen, said.

> "I am standing before Caesar's tribunal, where I ought to be tried; to the Jews I have done no wrong . . . If I am a wrongdoer . . . I appeal to Caesar . . ." Then [the procurator] Festus, when he had conferred with his council, answered, "You have appealed to Caesar; to Caesar you shall go."   ACTS OF THE APOSTLES, 25:10–12

Although the actual tablets are long since lost, their general intent is known; that, rather than merely listing certain punishments for certain crimes, the 12 tablets detail legal procedures and outline the RIGHTS of Roman citizens, be they high-born or low, and the numerous ways the state may not infringe upon those rights. Although a far cry from perfect, the posting of the Law of Twelve Tables is, in fact, a world-shaking event.

447   Pericles wants his city to be beautiful to the eyes of the Athenians and awesome to all who sail by at sea, and his building projects are transforming Athens into a gleaming marble vision. He now begins what will become his most famous monument, the

Parthenon. There is only one man with the vision and genius to oversee the project, his good friend, Phidias, who will create a great temple to the city's namesake goddess, Athena. Phidias is to make it the most beautiful temple ever built, so he appoints the job of designing it to the noted architects Ictinus and Callicrates. The three are already famous for their giant temple of Zeus near the playing fields at Olympia. The Parthenon will be built with marble from Mt. Pentelicus, which is rich with iron that will give it a golden glow; and it will sit at the very center of the city, high atop the rocky outcropping called the Acropolis. Work begins this year, 447.

c. 446   Pericles welcomes to Athens, and shows off the work being done on the Parthenon, to an already well-known traveler from Hallicarnasus in Asia Minor, born with an insatiable curiosity and longing to see the world. His name is Herodotus, and he intends to travel "as far as man can go," and does, from Macedonia to Egypt and from Babylon to West Africa, almost 1800 miles east to west and the same north to south . . . always writing about everything he sees, hears and learns. Attempting to report only that which is true, Herodotus often remarks:

Herodotus

> The following tale is commonly told . . . (but] my own opinion of these matters is . . .
> Herodotus, HISTORY OF THE PERSIAN WARS.

While Hebrew history is mostly based on man's relationship with God, and his keeping or breaking of God's covenants, Herodotus is the first to write history as investigative prose; how things happened, why, when and what was the cause and result? He is the first to recognize that war, like it or not, is usually the focal point of world events, that, for all its ugliness, war is usually what makes or breaks nations; and that each war has a cause and effect, a development and a conclusion. But Herodotus' writing is also readable and exciting, with the ability to conjure up in the reader's (or hearer's) mind vivid pictures of his many adventures. Thus, Herodotus' HISTORY OF THE PERSIAN WARS will earn him the title, Father of History, and reading his works aloud at the Olympic Games will win him an award of 10 talents of silver (a princely sum) from the appreciative Athenians. And yet, latter-day critics will contemptuously call him Father of Lies for wildly exaggerating the size of armies, for instance, and for reporting "un-critically" such absurdities as a bronze *krater* made by the Spartans for King Croesus of Phrygia, large enough to hold 300 gallons!

And yet, 2400 years from now archeologists will uncover in Vix, France, just such a *krater*, five feet tall, with horses, chariots and warriors marching around its neck, gorgons grinning evilly from its handles, and a stately female figure poised atop its lid. The *krater* will be found in the tomb of a Celtic lady, whether princess, priestess or prostitute no one knows. But her possessions, buried with her, speak of immense wealth gathered from far away: a cup from Greece, pitcher

The Krater of Vix

from Etruria, amber and coral from far-northern and southern seas, and a golden diadem from the Russian Steppes. Today the wealthy lady's treasures, and her *krater*, rest in glory at Chatillon-sur-Seine, France, silent testimony to the accuracy of an ancient historian.

. . . Far away from this Golden Age of Greece, the Hebrew/Jewish prophet Nehemiah is living a life of privilege and high position in the Persian court of King Artaxerxes, the king's own wine-taster, something only a most trusted subordinate could do. But word comes to Nehemiah that Jerusalem is in trouble, the people "in affliction" and the city walls not yet rebuilt—a dangerous condition, Judah being surrounded by hostile neighbors: especially Moabites and Samaritans (who had repopulated Samaria so long ago in 721 after its destruction by the Assyrians.) So, in . . .

444 . . . NEHEMIAH LEADS HOME THE THIRD GROUP OF JEWS FROM PERSIA, nearly 100 years after the Edict of Cyrus set them free. Not only does Artexerxes allow him to go (on condition that he would someday return) but sends with Nehemiah an armed escort, letters of safe conduct and orders that he be given timber from his own royal forest for building-beams. In spite of opposition from their enemies, in spite of an assassination attempt, and of rumors being carried back to Artaxerxes that Nehemiah is planning to overthrow him . . . the people of Jerusalem ". . . stiffen their hands for this good work," and every merchant builds a portion of the wall nearest his own shop."

> So the wall was finished on the twenty-fifth day of the month Elul in fifty-two days. NEHEMIAH 6:15 (Although 52 days seems incredible, subterranean portions of Nehemiah's wall have been excavated that show it to have been built in "great haste.")

Then Nehemiah and the people celebrate a great Passover feast; he restores the temple worship services and, together with the "princes . . . Levites, and . . . priests, signs "a firm covenant" to be true to God's house. And the rest of the people . . .

> . . . join with their brethren . . . and enter into . . . an oath to walk in God's law which was given by Moses the servant of God, and to observe and do all the commandments of the LORD our God and his ordinances and his statutes.   NEHEMIAH (9:38, 10:28,29)

Four hundred years ago God promised the prophet Elijah that no matter how bad things got, there would still be a "redeeming remnant" who would hear and carry on the faith. Ezra, like Nehemiah, sees himself as a prophet of that "remnant," and now, NEHEMIAH tells, in his book how . . .

> " . . . when the seventh month had come . . . all the people gathered . . . into the square before the Water Gate; and . . . Ezra the priest brought the law before the assembly, both men and women . . . And Ezra the scribe stood on a wooden pulpit which [the people] had made [and] he was above all the people; and when he opened [the book of LAW] all the people stood. And Ezra blessed the LORD, the great God, and all the people answered "Amen, amen," . . . and day by day, from the first day to the last . . . he read from the book of the law of God . . . [and] they kept the feast seven days . . ."   Nehemiah 8:1–6,18

EZRA

Book of Prophecy — Written in ARAMAIC,   c. 400–300 B.C.

It is a dramatic portrait, indeed, that the book of NEHEMIAH paints of the fiery prophet, Ezra, standing high on a pulpit, full of fervor and conviction, reading the Torah to the multitudes gathered in the street below him. Like Nehemiah, Ezra devoutly, even fanatically, believed that God belonged solely and exclusively to the Jews and to nobody else, and that they alone belonged to Him. The two prophets frowned on any dealings with Gentiles, and strictly forbade intermarriage. This concept of Jewish superiority would, in the years ahead, bring them much grief, but it was an understandable outgrowth of the traumatic exile in Babylon, when Judaism had come so close to extinction. Now the "Redeeming Remnant," of whom Ezra and Nehemiah saw themselves as spokesmen, must restore their religion to health.

Having lived his whole life in Persia, Ezra spoke the language of his captors and, so, wrote his book in Aramaic. It begins with the remarkable proclamation of that remarkable king, Cyrus of Persia, and the "Edict of Cyrus," which freed thousands of exiled Jews from their bondage. The first few chapters tell of the return itself, of Cyrus' edict, of how the exiles traveled; and itemize a census that was taken, listing how many people there were, how many animals, and what treasure (over $6,000,000,000!) then casually add that they also brought . . . 20 male and female singers!

Then, in chapter seven, Ezra tells his own story: how he returned home with the good will and protection of King Artaxerxes, and how he delivered a fortune in silver, gold and brass to the Temple. But it is in NEHEMIAH that the wonderfully vivid account of Ezra reading the law is found (which is one reason some scholars believe the two books were once one, or rather, were one with the two books of CHRONICLES, also, which all together tell the history of the Jews from the very beginning until now.) Ezra returned from his captivity in 458 B.C. and, with the Temple already built, probably became its first scribe (a highly honored position) as well as teacher or rabbi. The document which he read to the people is thought to have been an early form of the "P" or Priestly code upon which part of the "Old Testament" is based.

439   Once again, at the age of 80, the Roman general, Cincinnatus, is called upon to take the dictatorship and save his country, this time from civil war—a revolt of the plebes—and once again he does . . . and then willingly surrenders the dictatorship and returns to his farm. It is a precedent that will be followed and strictly enforced, for centuries, now, until it is broken by Cornelius Sulla and Julius Caesar. So honored is Cincinnatus' magnanimity

and greatness that 2200 years from now, when another general named George Washington voluntarily gives up his commission and refuses imperial power, he will be called the American Cincinnatus.

438   The building of the Parthenon is completed . . . Athens' most perfect temple, and Pericles' crowning cultural achievement. Approximately 2/3 the size of a modern-day football field, it is bordered by 46 graceful, fluted Doric columns that lean, ever so slightly inward to give the whole an illusion of perfect proportion. On its pediments and friezes, Ictinus and Callicrates have carved scenes from Greece's antiquity: battles with Amazons and Centaurs, caught in split-second actions: horses, humans and creatures so real they seem about to come alive. Standing in awesome isolation within her graceful marble-pillared temple is the giant, pagan mother-goddess of the city, itself, Athena, clothed in gold, ivory and gems, designed and built by the great Phidias; and in another room, that symbol of Greek freedom, the same silver-decked throne abandoned so hastily when Xerxes fled back to Persia after the battle of Salamis 33 years ago.

Athena

Pericles stands at the center of a circle of genius that orbits around him and around Athens, so great its like will not be seen again until the European Renaissance 1700 years hence. And those great minds who are not in the immediate Periclean age will spring from it, as will Plato from Socrates, Aristotle from Plato, and Alexander the Great from Aristotle. The long, illustrious list begins with Pericles' own wife (or mistress, because of an Athenian technicality . . .)

—   Aspasia, to whom he is devoted. Beautiful, brilliant and charming, she has made his home an intellectual center in Athens. The great and near-great are welcomed there, and she is the most influential woman in Athens in an age when women have little influence, and home life takes second place to the public "polis." Twenty-five years younger than Pericles, Aspasia (meaning simply "beloved,") was . . .

> . . . courted and caressed by Pericles upon account of her knowledge and skill in politics. Socrates himself would sometimes go to visit her . . . (Pericles) loved her with a wonderful affection: every day (going both in and out) from the market-place, he saluted and kissed her.   Plutarch, LIVES OF THE NOBLE GREEKS AND ROMANS

—   Anaxagoras, Pericles' own teacher, 62 years old now, believes in an orderly universe that was created and is governed by a supreme intelligence, a "mind" or "reason"—a *nous*—and that all matter is made up of an infinite number of particles. He believes that all the planets are made up of the same substance as the earth, that the features and shadows on the moon are hills and valleys, and that the sun is a flaming mass of rock. He believes that . . .

> All things were in chaos . . . when Mind arose and made order.   Anaxagoras

— Sophocles, the "quintessential Greek," army general and compassionate poet, whose plays reflect his belief in the inexorable power of the gods over man's fate, and the terrible justice they mete out to transgressors is, at 58, one of Pericles' closest friends . . .

— Euripides, now a master dramatist in his own right, feels that man's own passions are most often his downfall. In contrast to the wealthy, gregarious, out-going Sophocles, Euripides is a solitary man, quiet and contemplative, who, when not in Athens, lives in a cave on the island of Salamis where he was born on the very day of the battle that bears its name.

> Where two discourse, if one's anger rise, the man who lets the conversation fall, is wise.
> Euripides, PROTESTILAUS * The gods visit the sins of the fathers upon the children.   PHRIXUS
> * How oft the darkest hour of ill breaks brightest into dawn.   IPHEGENIA IN TAURUS *
> Those whom the gods would destroy they first make mad.   A fragment.

Euripides is the first Greek voice to speak out against the age-old practice of slavery, taken for granted since the beginning of time, which he calls . . .

> . . . that thing of evil, by its nature evil, forcing submission from a man to what no man should yield to.   Euripides

— The sculptor, Phidias, is another of Pericles' closest friends, he who created the Parthenon and that third "wonder of the world," the Olympic Temple of Zeus . . . as are . . .

— the architects Ictinus and Callicrates, who are creating wonderful works of art with marble, ivory and gold. Their Parthenon friezes—now called the Elgin marbles—are, today, one of the major attractions at the British Museum, London.

— Another sculptor, Polyclitus (the Elder) creates marvelous figures in motion, with the statues' weight resting on one leg, or an arm: a spear carrier and a wounded Amazon.

The Discus Thrower

— The sculptor, Myron's, Olympic athlete will become one of the world's most famous statues. Bent forward just before the throw, the DISCUS THROWER remains forever poised in that fraction of a second at the top of his arm swing. Myron's cast bronze original has long since been lost, but two latter-day Roman copies in marble stand today in the Vatican and British Museums. The Vatican copy, in Rome, stands in splendid isolation, befitting its importance; the British copy just one forlorn nonentity among many. A plaque at the base of the British copy explains the difference between the two. Its head was broken off way back in Roman days, the plaque reads, and the repairer did not know that a discus thrower would keep his eyes on the discus from the start of the throw to the end, as does the Vatican copy, and not, like the British, be looking straight ahead.

— Thycydides, at 22, is a keen-minded young military commander who will someday write a history of this time and of the terrible war looming just on the horizon. In his history, Thucydides records an oration of Pericles on the subject of democracy. Pericles is speaking in the agora, a commanding figure, and the people around him listen in awe . . .

> We are called a democracy, for the administration is in the hands of the many and not the few . . . when a citizen is in any way distinguished, he is preferred to the public service, not as a matter of privilege, but as a reward of merit . . . we are prevented from doing wrong by respect for authority and for the laws.   Pericles, quoted by Thucydides

Of Athenians, generally, he records Pericles saying:

> We cultivate the mind. We are lovers of the beautiful, yet simple in our tastes, without loss of manliness.

Thucydides, himself, has a somewhat less lofty view of the Athenians:

> Athenians invented the phrase, "make money." They seldom stop for quiet enjoyment, because they are always scheming for new profit.

Socrates

— Socrates, who "brought down philosophy from heaven to earth," is a young man of 31 now, already known for his manner of teaching by asking questions, causing his disciples to examine themselves and the human condition, as the Delphic oracle counsels: "Know thyself." A man like none other Socrates loves his city with a patriot's fervor, but is an unstinting critic of democracy. A man of piety and righteousness, he has a hearty sense of humor, always ready for good food, friends and drink. The most brilliant man of the age, he represents himself as the dullest. Believing that the Greek's pantheon of "foolish, immoral" gods are mere poetic inventions, he envisions the true God as an all-wise, all-good ruler of the world . . . who can still be worshipped the Greek way. A short, stout, ugly man, to his friends he is "all glorious within." Socrates will leave no written works but will be carefully written of by his students, Plato and Xenophon, and by the later Roman biographer, Plutarch:

> Socrates thought that if all our misfortunes were laid in one common heap, whence everyone must take an equal portion, most persons would be contented to take their own and depart. * The life which is not examined, is not worth living. * Nothing in excess. * Bad men live that they may eat and drink, whereas good men eat and drink that they may live   Socrates, quoted by Plutarch, LIVES

Up until this time of Socrates, philosophy has mainly concerned itself with things cosmological: the "natural" world, the nature and workings of the universe; the principles which control it and the knowledge man may gain from them. Socrates will change that, for he knows that knowledge, alone, can be used for ill as well as good, and his search is only for good, found in that part of a human being called the "soul." Mankind's principle quest in life should be "ethical conduct," the care of the soul: to make it "as good as possible," in short, "to make it like God." He feels that the exclusive cultivation of the body at the expense of the soul is a wasted life; health, wealth, knowledge and strength can all be used for "bad," but a soul cultivated for good is incapable of doing anything but good.

> Either death is a state of nothingness and utter unconsciousness, or, as men say, there is a change and migration of the soul from this world to another. Now, if death be of such nature, I say that to die is to gain: for eternity is then only a single night.   Socrates, quoted by
> Plato, in the APOLOGY

—   Hippocrates, a physician from the island of Kos, who will in future be revered as the Father of Scientific Medicine now, at 22, is beginning his long career, and will practice in Athens as well. He does not believe the ancient superstitions that disease is the "will of the gods," or punishment for sinfulness, so he studies everything "scientifically," testing, examining, assessing. He will teach the values of fresh air, sunshine, cleanliness and proper nutrition, and is a firm believer in the medicinal value of honey and vinegar. Hippocrates will someday write down his own code of behavior that will become known as the Hippocratic Oath, and be sworn by new physicians for centuries to come.

> I swear by Apollo Physician . . . that I will carry out, according to my ability and judgement . . . this oath. I will use treatment to help the sick . . . never with a view to injury or wrongdoing . . . whatsoever I shall see or hear in the course of my profession . . . I will not divulge.   The Hippocratic Oath

Two young boys are growing up in this heady atmosphere, and will soon make names for themselves . . .

—   Alcibides, now only 12, will become the man all Athens loves or hates. Handsome, brilliant and witty, he is, like so many young men of this age, totally unconcerned with religious or moral principles—or the opinions or good will of the older generation—and is, rather, cruelly cynical of Athens' values and virtues. Already he looks about him with a jaundiced eye and decides ". . . democracy is acknowledged folly." He will turn traitor to Athens in the future, desert to Sparta and win infamy for himself.

—   Aristophanes, now only 10, also studies his elders, but finds humor in all he sees. He will immortalize the great Greeks with his madcap comedies and riotous, raucus, ribald satires; frenetic tumults of burlesque and caricature that expose the stuffy, the pompous, the self-important and overblown: the philanderer, the scheming con-man, the errant aristocrat, the domineering wife and the sweet, innocent young thing. No one gets off Aristophanes' satirical hook. He lampoons their public piety and private charater, sometimes with a puckish narrator and an uninhibited song-and-dance routine by the chorus at skit's end. Nothing is sacred to him from the foibles of the most exalted philosopher to the sham and excess of the cheap politician. In short, the great slapstick comedians of our own time with their parodies and puns, wit and wisecracks, owe it all to Aristophanes, as do a goodly number of Periclean-age Greeks who would be completely forgotten today if they had not had their follies laid bare by his unsparing pen.

> Master, shall I begin with the usual jokes the audience always laughs at?
>
> | | |
> |---|---|
> | Come listen now the good old days, | This I know, the men of Sparta |
> | When children, strange to tell, | Whom we're cursing all day long, |
> | Were seen not heard, led a simple life, | Aren't the only ones to blame |
> | In short, were brought up well. | For everything that's going wrong. |
>
> I laughed 'till I cried!
>
> Aristophanes

These are the intellectual offspring of one city at one time, some whose greatness is on the wane, some whose stars have just begun to rise. But the orbit of genius around Athens extends much farther out than just the city, and there are great minds in other parts of Greece, also.

— Empedocles, now 50 and living in Greek Sicily, published when he was only 22, a work entitled ON NATURE, in which he theorized four elements of matter: fire, water, earth and air. He also studies blood circulation and atmospheric pressure.

— Democritus of Thrace (in Macedonia), now only 22, will be called the Father of Modern Science. His "atomic theory" proposes that everything is made up of atoms; and he believes that the Milky Way is made up of billions of stars. He theorizes about space, the universe, plants and animals . . . and the human condition:

> Poverty in a democracy is far better than wealth in a tyranny.
> Democritus of Thrace.

Democritus

Finally, there are now a whole "school" of "professional" educators called Sophists, who teach for pay, a scandalous innovation! They say that everything is relative: truth, morality and knowledge, that these things are simply what each person wants them to be: that it matters not so much what a man says, but how well he says it . . . in brilliant rhetoric. So, while they are learned men, the sophists are, mostly, more interested in clever, skillful and ingenious use of words and plays on words than in solid reasoning, more in winning arguments than in finding truth. The result of their artificial techniques of debate is usually deception, fuzzy thinking and quibbling over details. Seemingly refined and worldly, their dubius methods will have ill effect on man's search for truth for centuries to come . . . and from their name will come the modern terms sophistry and sophisticated.

432   Far to the east, the Hebrew prophet, NEHEMIAH RETURNS THE SECOND TIME TO JERUSALEM FROM PERSIA, only to find much of his religious reform undone, the Temple deserted most of the time and, on the Sabbath, a raucus market-place. Moreover, in it is living the very man who had tried to kill him! Now he must begin again. So, Nehemiah, whom scholars believe did, in fact, write much of his own book, begins with his duties in Persia:

NEHEMIAH

Book of Prophecy — Written in Hebrew, c. 400 to 300 B.C.

Cupbearer to the king

"Now I was cupbearer to the king," states Nehemiah proudly in the first chapter of his book. In the highly esteemed and trusted office of cupbearer, Nehemiah poured and sampled the wine of the king who was, at this time, Artxerxes, son of Xerxes, a good-natured, mild mannered king ruling over a declining kingdom. But Nehemiah was told of trouble "back home" and he wanted to return to Jerusalem and rebuild its ruined walls. Every word of Nehemiah's book echoes the strong, forceful personality that must have been his to deal so authoritatively with the king of all Persia and with the great task before him. Not only did King Artaxerxes allow him to go home (on condition that he would someday return) but he sent with Nehemiah an armed escort, letters of safe conduct and orders that he be given timbers from his own forests for building beams. So, Nehemiah leads home the second group of Jews from Persia. Nehemiah's task was not an easy one. The city walls were extremely important as protection from attack, invasion or harassment. The Samaritans who had repopulated Israel after it was conquered by Assyria so long ago in 721, and the neighboring Edomites were violently opposed to the Jews' return and rebuilding, and tried everything to stop the work, even carrying rumors to Artaxerxes that Nehemiah was hoping to overthrow him. So the reorganization and restoration of the LAW was fundamental, and if the laws were harsh and severe, they were also necessary, for Judaism had come perilously close to extinction. For his part in restoring to the Jews their unique "Jewishness" and purifying their religion, Nehemiah asked God, in the last words of his book, to "Remember me, O my God, for good."

Over the years the Athenian democracy has, in fact, become an empire under Pericles. The other Greek city-states each have their own constitutions, but their magistrates are Athenian, the Athenian navy rules the seas, and fully a third of the Athenian people remain in slavery, an issue whose time has not yet come. Still, Pericles' 30 year rule has been the pinnacle of Greece's Golden Age, and a beacon light for the intellectual brilliance to follow; but it has in it, also, the seeds of its own destruction, for it has bred the dark side of genius, wealth and glory, which is jealousy, envy and fear into the other city-states, particularly that one which is more might than mind, Sparta; and in due time, every notable Athenian will be banished, ostracized, persecuted, harassed or slain. Herodotus, Phidias, Anaxagoras, Euripides, Thycydides, Socrates and even Pericles, will all suffer in some way. Many grumbling voices claim that Pericles' love of liberty and democracy extends no further than Athens, itself, and that he has become, instead, the "enslaver of liberty." Now Sparta decides Athens must be stopped.

431   The Peloponnesian War begins . . . and will last for 30 years. Athens and Sparta, opposites to each other culturally and intellectually, now oppose each other militarily. Greek now faces Greek in mortal combat. But it is also a "world war" involving alliances and confederations. As the war gets under way and Spartans raid outlying areas preparing for larger battles, thousands of rural folk crowd into Athens hoping for safety behind the city walls, making the city dangerously overcrowded.

429   Athens is violently struck with an epidemic of plague which kills more than a fourth of the population, including . . . Pericles. Athens' greatest leader is stricken, a terrible blow for the city and its allied states, and the golden AGE OF PERICLES screams to a painful, sickened end.

> The course of public affairs after his death produced a . . . speedy sense of the loss of Pericles. Those who, while he lived, resented his great authority . . . readily acknowledged that there never had been in nature such a disposition as his . . . so great a corruption and such a flood of mischief and vice followed . . .   Plutarch, LIVES

419   The *DIASPORA,* or dispersion of the Jews following their return from exile, finds them in many countries besides Judea, including, of course, Egypt. A battered, torn fragment of papyrus exists today which tells the Jews on the Nile River island of Elephantine how and why they must celebrate Passover. A Jewish garrison there must have been returnees from Babylon, for the document is written in Aramaic . . .

> To my brother Yedoniah and his colleagues . . . Count the 14 days of the month of Nisan and observe the Passover . . . the feast of unleavened bread. Be ritually clean and take heed. Do no work nor drink beer, nor eat anything in which there is leaven . . . by order of King Darius . . . your brother Hananiah.   The PASSOVER PAPYRUS from Elephantine

The Passover Papyrus

414   When Pericles died moderation died, also, and now Athens's imperial ambitions have no cool head to check them. Already in actual control of the entire Aegean Sea and implicit control of almost all the cities of Greece and coastal Asia Minor, Athens now begins to lust after Carthage and Libya in North Africa, and the island of Sicily. Alcibides, whom history has called a perfect example of genius without principle, has long craved the island for his own and now plans the invasion of Sicily's Spartan stronghold of Syracuse with 134 galleys, 5000 men-at-arms and thousands more archers, slingers and bowmen. But the siege and nighttime battle turns into disaster and signals the beginning of the end for Athens. Alcibides is ordered home and instead turns traitor and deserts to Sparta taking with him much damaging military knowledge. While the war goes on, the general/writer Thucydides records its awful progress; its dreadful waste of both men and material, the confusion of issues, perversion of honor and possibly the worst development of all, the total breakdown of morality and decency: in short,

the destruction and dissolution of the Greek social system known as the POLIS that had been manifest in a mutual care and respect of Greek for Greek. The Athenian defeat at Syracuse will be remembered as another major turning-point of history, closing forever the door to an "Athen-ized" Europe, and opening it to the young Italian upstart to the north called Rome.

408   Throughout the 30 years of the war, life (for some) goes on as usual. Sophocles writes his two masterpieces about OEDIPUS REX just before his death at age 90 in 406. OEDIPUS THE KING tells a terrible story of a man who, innocently and unknowingly, kills his father and marries his own mother . . . and the horrible aftermath of it.

. . . The *Erecthion* temple is completed on the site of an ancient Mycenaean palace, near the Parthenon atop the Acropolis, the roof of its unique side porch upheld by six graceful Greek goddess pillars. Posiedon, himself, is said to have caused the crack in one stone block with a blow from his trident.

. . . and Socrates takes on another student . . .

406   Twenty-one year old Plato begins to study with Socrates. Plato's admiration for Socrates is boundless. He is with him continually, is there when Socrates debates with Protagoras whether goodness can be taught; with Philebus, whether pleasure or wisdom is greater; with Gorgias, the uses of rhetoric and the purpose of punishment; and with a sophist, the reality of ideas and truth. He is with him at an all-night banquet—a *Symposium*—where everyone speaks in praise of love (that finds Socrates the only one still holding forth in the morning after everyone else has either left or drunk himself to sleep.) Plato records every one of these sessions, and in future years, will gather them together in a volume called DIALOGUES. The Sophists are teaching that ". . . truth is that which is agreed on at the time of agreement, and as long as the agreement lasts." The Athenians are scandalized. No wonder the gods have turned away and no longer protect them. Although Socrates denies he is a sophist, they begin to look upon him with suspicion.

404   Having defeated the Athenian navy in a surprising move, Sparta moves in on Athens. The city is surrounded, its fields and orchards devastated, its vital olive groves destroyed. It is starved into submission, and the Athenians are humbled under the infamous rule of the "Spartan Thirty." It is the end of the Peloponnesian War. But the city, itself, is spared. The victors may be Spartan; but they are also Greek . . . and Athens was Greece's glory.

401   Thucydides dies, with his HISTORY OF THE PELOPONNESIAN WAR still unfinished. His commitment to accuracy in reporting, and his total lack of bias, have earned Thucydides honor as the first "scientific" historian.

> Of the events of the war, I have not ventured to speak from any chance information, nor according to any notion of my own. I have described nothing but what I saw myself, or learned from others of whom I made most careful and particular inquiry.   Thucydides, HISTORY OF THE PELOPONNESIAN WAR

. . . One former student of Socrates is a wealthy young Athenian farmer, horse-lover and cavalryman named Xenophon, who is more eager for fame and fortune in Persia than philosophy in democratic Athens. Xenophon leads the—now famous—"Greek 10,000" in a (futile) attempt to wrest the Persian throne from King Artaxerxes for Cyrus the Younger. But the effort comes to naught when Cyrus is killed in battle, and it begins, for the 10,000, a five-month retreat through the wilds of Kurdistan and the snows of Armenia until, decimated, snow-blinded and frost-bitten they reach safety 15 months and 4000 miles later, and give thanks to the gods. In his later years Xenophon will write:

> . . . the north wind blew full in their faces . . . parching up everything and benumbing the men . . . the depth of the snow was a fathom . . . [their shoe] straps worked into their feet, and the soles were frozen about them . . . some of the soldiers were left behind . . .
>
> Xenophon, *ANABASIS*

400   The turn of the century is a momentous one, in many ways. By this time Greek astronomers are recording positions of the stars, moon and sun; and the world's first lighthouse is built at Corinth.

. . . The Romans are gradually clarifying, refining and improving their republican government of law, under the paradigm of the Law of Twelve Tables, posted on the rostrum of the Senate House 50 years ago. The Twelve Tables will remain the backbone of Roman law for the next 300 years, and much of it will become, not the actual model, but the spirit and inspiration for its happy descendent of our own times, the United States Constitution and Bill of Rights. The founda-

tion of Roman law *(IUS)* rests on two sources: *ius scriptum* (written law) and *ius non scriptum* (unwritten law, or custom): and they govern two separate areas: *ius civile* (the law of Roman citizens) and *ius gentium* (the law of nations.) In the law courts cases are handled by *advocati* (advocates or trial lawyers), *iusconsulti* (consultants), and *iusprudentes* (jurists, from which: jurisprudence) The highest legal officials at this time are the Tribunes. Originally military representatives of various "tribes," the office has gradually evolved into civil or civilian Tribunes chosen in general election from the *plebian* (or lower) class to protect plebian rights from abuse by the *patricians*. The Tribunes' greatest power is that of *intercessio*, or *veto* (I forbid) which can call a halt at any time to unwanted actions or legislation by the Roman senate or local magistrates. Roman justice *(IUS)* will travel the "world" over for almost a thousand years now under the fear-inspiring banner of <u>*S.P.Q.R.—SENATUS POPULUSQUE ROMANUM*, the SENATE AND THE PEOPLE OF ROME.</u>

. . . But by no means is intellectual advancement or political activity confined solely to the Greeks and Romans. The Jews (home from Babylon for over a hundred years) now have their new Temple, beautifully decorated and securely walled, and it is attracting scores of intellectual and cultural patriarchs who are rapidly transforming it into a center of learning. Ezra and many other scribes labor long hours copying the five books of Moses into the form we know today—the Torah; as well as JUDGES, JOSHUA, KINGS and CHRONICLES, and composing new books, recording the Jews' long heritage. Like ancient Homer, Jewish singers and bards have sung psalms from memory for centuries and now begin to write them down, as are poets their proverbs and priests their collections of law. The wisdom of the ages and prophecies for the future, all are Israel's traditions: legal, spiritual, musical, proverbial and prophetic, to be remembered as "P"—or Priestly—writings. Together with the E, J and D (Elohist, Jahweh/Jahwist and Deuteronomist) they form the foundation of the Old Testament.

c. 400   The book of PSALMS is compiled.

PSALMS

Book of Sacred Writings — Written in Hebrew,   c. 400 to 300 B.C.

Scroll of Psalms from Qumran

"Praise ye the LORD. Praise God in his sanctuary; praise him in the firmament of his power. Praise him for his mighty acts, praise him according to his excellent greatness. Praise him with the sound of the trumpet; praise him with the psaltery and harp. Praise him with the timbrel and dance; praise him with stringed instruments and organs. Praise him upon the loud cymbals; praise him upon the high sounding cymbals. Let everything that hath breath praise the LORD. Praise ye the LORD."

"Hallelujah, Praise ye the LORD," echoes and re-echoes the 150th and last PSALM, the Jah or Yah of hallelujah being the first syllable of Yahweh, or LORD. The word PSALMS in Greek means songs, specifically songs to be accompanied by the *psalterion*, or psaltery, a stringed instrument probably akin to the lute or lyre. The collection of songs known as PSALMS was composed over the years since the time of kings David and Solomon, including those attributed to David, himself.   (See: 1000 B.C.) There are many songs of many subjects, their first lines reflecting many moods:

#1, Confidence: Blessed is the man who walks not in the counsel of the wicked. * 5, Anguish: Give ear to my words, O Lord: give heed to my groaning. * 9, Gratitude: I will give thanks to the Lord with my whole heart; and 107, O give thanks to the Lord for he is good. For his steadfast love endures forever! (118 . . . for his mercy endureth forever.) * 13, Grief and despair: How long, O Lord, wilt thou forget me for ever? * 34, Resolve: I will bless the Lord at all times: His praise shall be continually in my mouth. *

46, Faith: God is our refuge and strength, a very present help in trouble., and 121 I lift up my eyes to the hills. From whence does my help come? * 47, Joy: Clap your hands, all peoples! Shout to God with loud songs of joy! * 62, Trust: For God alone my soul waits in silence: from him comes my salvation. * 79, Horror: O God, the heathen are come into thy inheritance; thy holy temple have they defiled . . . * 93, Glory: The Lord reigns: he is robed in majesty. * 95, Celebration: O come, let us sing to the Lord; let us make a joyful noise to the rock of our salvation. * 114, Remembrance: When Israel went forth from Egypt, the house of Jacob from people of strange language . . . and 126, When the Lord restored the fortunes of Zion, we were like those who dream. * 119, Caution: Blessed are those whose way is blameless, who walk in the Law of the Lord! * 127, Vision: Unless the Lord builds the house, those who build it labor in vain. * 133. Contentment: Behold, how good and pleasant it is when brothers dwell in unity. * 150, Awe: Praise the Lord! Praise God in his sanctuary: praise him in his mighty firmament!

In some of the PSALMS are found strange and enigmatic verses about the same "Suffering Servant" of whom the two Isaiah's told, and other prophets will tell . . .

Prophecy: Yea, mine own familiar friend, in whom I trusted, which did eat of my bread, hath lifted up his heel against me. 41:9 * False witnesses did rise up; they laid to my charge things that I knew not. 35:11 * The kings of the earth rise up, and the rulers take counsel together, against the Lord and against his anointed. 2.2 * Thy rebuke hath broken his heart: He is full of heaviness. He looked for some to have pity on him, but there was no man, neither found he any to comfort him. 69:20 * They gave me gall to eat, and when I was thirsty they gave me vinegar to drink, 69:21 * My God, my God, why hast thou forsaken me? 22:1 * All they that see him, laugh him to scorn; they shoot out their lips, and shake their heads saying, he trusted in God that He would deliver him, let Him deliver him, if he delight in Him. 22:7-8 * A company of evil doers encircle me: they have pierced my hands and feet. 22:16 * They parted my garments among them and on my vesture they cast lots. 22:18 * Into thine hand I commend my spirit. 31:5 (See: Friday P.M., A.D. 32)

One of the Psalms promises that this will not be the end of Him, only the beginning . . .

But thou didst not leave his soul in Hell: nor didst Thou suffer thy holy one to see corruption. 16:10

And that the message of this event would be carried far and wide . . .

Their sound is gone out into all lands and their word unto the ends of the world. 19:4 (See: A.D. 80 and 100)

And justice will triumph after all . . .

The stone which the builders rejected is become the head of the corner. 118:22 (See: MARK 12:10)

400 The book of PROVERBS is compiled.

PROVERBS

Book of Sacred Writings — Written in Hebrew, c. 400–300 B.C.

"To know wisdom and instruction; to perceive the words of understanding . . . justice and judgment, and equity . . . to the young man knowledge and discretion . . ."   1:2–4
The writer of PROVERBS opens his book with a preamble explaining his intention: to teach wisdom and understanding to the young. Although one modern writer calls the author a "sententious old drone," PROVERBS' collection of pithy, perceptive precepts and maxims still vividly demonstrate that while we, today, may live in a high-tech world of overnight changes and split-second answers totally alien to the world of the Bible, HUMAN NATURE does not change—nor does the need for "family values"—and many of the proverbs, written some 2400 years ago are just as true and applicable and usable today as in the writers' own time .

The PROVERBS are attributed to the wisdom of King Solomon, but are more likely a potpourri of ancient Hebrew wisdom compiled by scribes, teachers and/or rabbis working in the new temple. They apparently were not intended just to be read casually as clever sayings, but were a serious part of the upbringing and education of young Jewish boys. There are many examples of good, common sense wrapped up in beautiful prose.

1:7 The fear of the LORD is the beginning of knowledge, but fools despise wisdom and instruction. * 3:5 Trust in the LORD with all thine heart: and lean not unto thine own understanding. * 3:11 Despise not the chastening of the LORD, neither be weary of his correction: For whom the LORD loveth, He correcteth. * 4:14 Enter not into the path of the wicked, and go not in the way of evil men. * 12:22 Lying lips are an abomination to the LORD, they that deal truly are his delight: * 15:1 A soft answer turns away wrath, but a harsh word stirs up anger. * 15:5 A fool despiseth his father's instruction, but he that regardeth reproof is prudent. * 17:1 Better is a dry morsel with quiet than a house full of feasting with strife. * 18:7 A fool's mouth is his destruction, and his lips are the snare of his soul. * 22:1 A good name is rather to be chosen than great riches, and loving favor rather than silver and gold. * 22:6 Train up a child in the way he should go; and when he is old he will not depart from it. * 24:1–2 Be thou not envious against evil men, neither desire to be with them. For their heart studieth destruction and their lips talk of mischief. * 27:2 Let another man praise thee, and not thine own mouth; a stranger, and not thine own lips.

Many of the PROVERBS appear to be private instruction from the writer to his own "son," and are summed up eloquently:

My son, if you receive my words and treasure my commandments . . . then you will understand righteousness and justice and equity, for wisdom will come into your heart.
2:1,9,10

c. 400   The SONG OF SOLOMON is written . . .

The SONG of SOLOMON

Book of Sacred Writings — Written in Hebrew, c. 400 B.C.

"I am the Rose of Sharon and the lily of the valleys," sings the Shulamite girl in the Song of Songs. "My beloved is mine and I am his: he feedeth among the lilies." Probably included in the "Old Testament" because of its attribution to King Solomon, the SONG OF SOLOMON is a collection of love songs thought to have been sung at Jewish weddings, about a lovely "black but comely" Shulamite girl, (1:5) about King Solomon who loves and desires her, and about her shepherd lover to whom she is faithful. The songs are unabashedly erotic and explicit; more so than some generations have liked to admit, and so have often been explained away as allegory and analogy. To the Jews they represented the love of God for his people and, to Christians, the love of Christ for His church. The most logical explanation, though, seems to be one that sees them for just what they are (the Old Testament being what it is: a totally honest and forthright record of one nation's existence and its peoples' progress, manners and mores): in other words, love songs both passionate and pure, neither sacred nor profane, devoid of either excess or perversion; a celebration of normal, natural physical love and devotion between a man and a woman. One of the most lovely and familiar verses is found in chapter two:

> My beloved spake, and said unto me, Rise up, my love, my fair one, and come away. For, lo, the winter is past, the rain is over and gone; The flowers appear on the earth; the time of the singing of birds is come, and the voice of the turtle is heard in our land.   2:10–12

The book of RUTH is written:

RUTH

Book of Sacred Writings — Written in Hebrew, c. 400 B.C.

RUTH is a short story which digresses for a moment back to the long-ago days of the Judges. Although, chronologically, it does, indeed, take place during the period of Judges (and is so placed in the Bible) it is generally thought not to have been written down until the time of the second Temple . . . possibly (some scholars believe) to soften the sting of the stringent decrees of Ezra and Nehemiah concerning the Hebrews' conduct toward Gentiles, especially those forbidding intermarriage. How can it be, the story seems to ask, that Jews cannot marry, or even associate with Gentiles when the great-grandmother of their own most honored king, David, was herself a Gentile? Ruth's story is a gentle, pastoral tale of a lovely Moabite woman and her faithfulness and love for her Hebrew husband, her

Ruth

mother-in-law Naomi, and YAHWEH, the one, true God of their people. As a young widow she gleaned corn in the field of Boaz, a distant kinsman. It was a custom as old as time, and a law since the days of Moses almost 800 years ago . . . as the book of DEUTERONOMY records:

> When thou cuttest down thine harvest in thy field, and hast forgot a sheaf . . . thou shalt not go again to fetch it . . . thou shalt not glean it afterward; it shall be for the stranger, for the fatherless, and for the widow.   DEUTERONOMY 24:19,21 (See: 1280 B.C.)

It is the last verse of RUTH that chronicles David's ancestry from her. Almost 500 years from now two Christian men, one a Jew called Matthew and the other a Greek named Luke, will compile genealogies of the man for whom their Christian faith is named. They will show how Jesus of Nazareth was descended, through two different lines, from David the king and then from the Moabite Ruth. When Ruth "found favor" in the eyes of Boaz, he married her and named their first child Obed ". . . and Obed begat Jesse and Jesse begat David," who became Israel's second king. 4:21,22 Ruth's beautiful confession of devotion and loyalty for Naomi appears in chapter one:

> Entreat me not to leave thee, or to return from following after thee: for wither thou goest, I will go: and where thou lodgest I will lodge: thy people shall be my people, and thy God my God. Where thou diest will I die, and there will I be buried: the Lord do so to me, and more also if aught but death part thee and me.   1:16,17

The book *of* JOB is written.

JOB

Book of Sacred Writings — Written in Hebrew,   c. 400 B.C.

"There was a man . . . whose name was Job . . . [who] was perfect and upright . . . feared God, and eschewed evil." So opens the book of JOB, the only book in the Bible written as a drama, with a "cast of characters," a plot and dialogue, a book that ranks in concept, content and construction with any of the greatest Greek dramas. JOB is a very ancient saga, known and sung throughout the middle-east for centuries, but brought to perfection by an unknown Hebrew scribe. Job was not only "upright," but wealthy, also, owning thousands of sheep, asses, a "great household" of servants and many children: seven sons and three daughters . . . the "greatest man of the east."   (1:3) And all was well until Satan appeared on the scene . . . not the personification of evil as he is seen today, but as an "adversary," an antagonist of both God and man, seeking always to goad man to commit sin and renounce God . . . but still, under God's control, who warns him just how far he can go in tormenting Job.

Satan sarcastically taunts God that it is easy for the rich and successful to be pious and God-fearing, and God allows him to take away everything Job possesses, including family and health. Job's friends then appear and challenge him time and again to curse

God for his misfortune. They accuse him of secretly being a sinful man, for aren't the age-old teachings true that you reap good things by doing good, and bad by bad? But Job insists that if we accept happiness from God, we must accept sorrow, also. Still his friends goad him on and finally, in the very depths of pain and anguish, Job demands of God HOW he has sinned that he should be so sorely punished. Has he lusted after women, worshipped pagan gods, not cared for his servants or the poor? No longer "patient" as in the old adage, Job rails at God that he IS faithful and worthy, and not deserving of such injustice. Then, out of the whirlwind, God thunders out His mighty reply . . .

Job

> . . . WILL YOU CONDEMN ME THAT YOU MAY BE RIGHTEOUS? WHERE WERE YOU WHEN I LAID THE FOUNDATIONS OF THE EARTH? Have YOU commanded the morning . . . that it take hold the ends of the earth? Can you make it snow . . . or hail, lightening, thunder, or cause it to rain . . . even where no man is? Who provides food for the raven . . . or decides how long animals carry their young? Did you give the peacock its beauty, or the ostrich its feathers? Does the eagle soar by your order, or the hawk fly by your wisdom? Gird up your loins now like a man . . . cast abroad the rage of thy wrath . . ." Chs. 38,39,40 (paraphrased.)

Overwhelmed by God's power, omnipotence, majesty . . . and His burdens, Job admits he had never even thought about those things before and, in sorrow and humility now, "repents in dust and ashes." Accepting then, that if man could understand God he would BE God, a pacified Job makes his magnificent statement of faith . . .

> I know that my redeemer liveth, and that He shall stand at the latter day upon the earth, and though worms destroy this body, yet in my flesh shall I see God. JOB 13:25–26

While the author of JOB is not known, nor the exact date of writing, it is certain that he was a master writer, every bit the equal of Aeschylus, Sophocles and Euripides, whose epic proportions of theme and content are equaled by the grandeur and beauty of his language. The book of JOB is beautiful proof of St. Paul's statement that "all scripture is God-breathed."

ECCLESTIASTES

Book of "Writings" — Written in Hebrew, c. 300–200 B.C.

'Vanity of vanities . . . all is vanity,' saith the Preacher, which is what Ecclesiastes means; a teacher or writer in an assembly or school (and not King Solomon, as some verses imply.) A reasonable, rational man, he can find neither reason nor rationale in life, and a life WITH religion seems no more rational to him than one without. Written between 300 and 200 B.C. at the heighth of the self-indulgent Hellenistic period following the era of Alexander the Great, the Preacher's philosophical musings are remarkably akin to the teachings of the Greek stoics whose philosophy taught a calm, tranquil acceptance of whatever comes, good or bad, as Divine Will which men cannot change. There is even a hint of the Epicurean belief that pleasure, tempered by moderation, should be man's goal. ". . . every man should eat and drink, and enjoy the good of all his labor, it is the gift of God."   3:13

ECCLESTIASTES is an extraordinary book, remarkable in that it is even IN the Bible, for its gloomy pessimism, doubt and even despair are contrary to every other Biblical book, and their messages. "We all die, the Preacher says, the righteous and the wicked . . . the clean and the unclean, he that sacrifices and he that does not, the good and the sinner; we can no more escape death than the beasts" (Ch 9) And yet, he accepts it philosophically: "For every thing there is a season," he muses, "a time to (live), and a time to die; a time to plant and a time to [reap] . . . a time to weep, and a time to laugh; a time to mourn and a time to dance . . . a time of war, and a time of peace . . ." 3:1–8 And he warns the reader to remember the Creator in the days of youth, for in old age you may not be able to. His expressions are used to this day: "There is nothing new under the sun," and ". . . everything in its own time." Having tried everything—wealth, power, wisdom—and not found the answer, he sums up "the whole matter" succinctly:

Fear God and keep his commandments, for this is the whole duty of man."   12:13

400   But enlightenment and learning seem to take second place to something else going on in the world, for not only in Greece are there wars and rumors of wars. All over the earth man is set upon man, from one continent to another . . .

. . . While the Spartans are great soldiers, they are not great leaders, and the Greeks suffer under their rule; first a reign of terror under the infamous Thirty Tyrants, and then the heavy hand of mismanagement, intrigue and repression. And while the political, cultural and social conditions of Athens and the other city-states stagnates, the arts and sciences languish, in far northern Greece a new militarism begins to emerge in an only half-civilized, primeval area called . . . Macedonia .

. . . In the far east the Chinese begin to build a giant wall to keep out marauding Huns and Mongols during this "Age of the Warring States." In later times it will be called the Great Wall of China.

. . . And those peoples who will become "Vietnamese" over-run the Red River Delta . . .

. . . The Celtic tribes of Europe are living in what modern archeology calls the *LaTene* period, trading with the Greeks and Etruscans south of the Alps. Living in the lushly forested, temperate-zone plains we know today as Spain, France, Germany, Czechoslovakia, the "Low Countries" (Holland and Belgium) and the Balkans, the Celts build their houses and town-walls of wood, hundreds of which have been found by modern archeologists. Their heavy iron instruments of war—and peace—daggers, knives, shields, spearheads, plowshares, jewelry and cooking vessels are decorated with distinctive Celtic swirls, loops, o's and s's.

. . . Barbarian Huns from far-away frozen Russia invade Europe and uproot its Celtic people . . . and other Celts from France invade Ireland.

. . . Deeply entrenched in an arms race, Rome and Carthage draw up a peace treaty on matters of commerce, armaments and territorial boundaries. Well they might, for both cities have the same thing in mind: expansion . . . and conquest. Only 375 miles apart, they lie face to face directly across the Mediterranean Sea. Carthage is a city built for war, an armed fortress with fortified walls and gigantic ship yards. It already rules much territory in northern Africa, but, taking control of the islands of Sardinia and Sicily, just off the Italian peninsula, is now moving closer . . . and ever closer . . . to Rome.

But, in Judea, the voice of a prophet named Malachi is heard, now, and he promises, something far different for mankind. His book is the last book of Hebrew Scripture, of what will come to be called the "Old Testament."

MALACHI

Book of Prophecy — Written in Hebrew,   c. 400 B.C.

It seems appropriate that MALACHI should be the last book of the Old Testament, for it is the herald of the New; the very name Malachi, in Hebrew, meaning, "my messenger."

Behold, I send my messenger to prepare the way before me.   3:1 (See: A.D. 29)

Most of Malachi's book is an indictment against unfaithfulness, neglect of religion and corruption amongst the temple priesthood; and he proclaims that the great and dreadful Day of the Lord is coming soon. But he talks of something else as well; the Covenant— that "agreement" between God and the Jews that had its beginning so long ago with Abraham. Six times in the books' four short chapters Malachi talks of the covenant, condemning those who break the Old, and prophesying a New. God will offer His people a New Covenant, MALACHI says, a Savior or Messiah, will come . . . but no one will know the hour or the day . . .

. . . the Lord whom ye seek, shall suddenly come to his temple, even the messenger of the covenant, whom ye delight in: behold, he shall come, saith the LORD of hosts. But who may abide the day of his coming? and who shall stand when he appeareth?   3:1–2 (See: 3 BC)

---

400   The LAW and the PROPHETS are now complete.* The foundation has been laid, the promises made, and the Jews are waiting for their Messiah to come. Many years ago AMOS and HOSEA, MICAH, ZEPHANIAH and JEREMIAH all prophesied that Jerusalem would be destroyed and the Jews would be carried away into exile; and that

---

* The reader should remember that several Old Testament books were, actually, NOT finished by now—or even begun—but that they are included in this section for continuity in telling the story.

someday they would return home and build a new city and a new temple. And it happened, just as they said; and the Jews hold the Prophets in very high esteem for it. Now there are Prophets promising a Savior, a Prince of Peace. ISAIAH says a child will be born and the government will be upon His shoulder. A leader! The Jews desperately want a leader. HAGGAI and MALACHI promise Him soon and ZECHARIAH says he will ride into Jerusalem on an ass . . . a very strange promise. But then, we will wait to see. After all, who SHALL stand when He appeareth?

BETWEEN

THE

OLD and the NEW

*   *   *

The Years of the

APOCRYPHAL

BOOKS

The APOCRYPHA YEARS and the WORLD

There will be 400 years between the close of the Old Testament and the beginning of the New. Four hundred fast moving, exciting years that will see, first, the final demise of the "oriental" empire of Persia; the brilliant lightening flash of Alexander the Great's Greek empire; and, finally, the awesome imminence of Imperial Rome.

For the Jews it will be the same old story; foreign domination, one conqueror after the other. First, the Greek—not so bad. Another, Syria—intolerable; and finally, Rome—fatal. So, for the Jews, these are years of watching, waiting, and hoping for their Messiah, the leader whom they hope will come to lead an army, build their nation into a great and powerful empire and beat down their oppressors.

It will be, instead, a time when the whole Mediterranean world is preparing—without even knowing it—for the coming of Christ. Alexander's conquering armies will make Greek a universal language, and the New Testament, to be written by Jews, about a Jew, will be written in Greek. The Romans soon will begin to build their modern roads all over the world, fifty thousand miles of super-highways that will carry trade, commerce and armies; but will carry, also, the Christian apostles and the Gospel of Christ. And Augustus Caesar's *Pax Romana* or Roman Peace, will make it possible for Paul, the Jewish apostle to the gentiles, to be a Roman citizen and travel freely on those Roman roads.

Should not all the events in the years ahead arrange themselves in order, the religion of Christ would have a very hard time getting past the outskirts of its own little country. God's great Plan for man is coming close, and the 400 years before its advent are fast-moving, exciting years!

The APOCRYPHA

Apocrypha: (WEBSTER) Greek: *apokryphos*. Hidden, concealed,
obscure, of doubtful authenticity or authorship.

The Biblical books on the pages you have just read make up the Jewish Holy Scriptures . . . the "Bible" which Jesus, Paul and the Apostles used, and all Jews will use to this very day. It is the only "Bible" there will be for the next 500 years. All the books ahead are not written yet, because the events about which they tell have not happened yet.

The writing of Jewish holy literature did not come to an end with the completion of the "Old Testament" books. Other books will be written by Jewish writers during the years ahead. In the near future are fifteen more short books, in particular; not nearly as important as the Old Testament books. Their authenticity is questionable but their value is not, for they are enlightening historically and entertaining as literature.

When the "Old Testament" is translated into Greek in the last years "B.C.," these books—the APOCRYPHA—will be included. So they are included in this book. They may not be included in the central *Canon* of the Bible, but they shed much light upon it, fill in some gaps and provide some enlightening details.

THE YEARS BETWEEN THE OLD AND THE NEW . . .

The "APOCRYPHA" YEARS

400   The focus of history shifts away, now, from Judea and the Jews, and a new scene opens in Greece . . . and, later . . . in Rome . . .

399   Socrates is condemned to death for "impiety" on two counts: "corrupting the youth of Athens," and "neglect of the gods" through "novel practices of religion." Socrates believes himself a "gadfly" given by God to the state to "stir it into life." His philosophical questioning has held up the Athenian conscience to a mirror, and some do not like what they see. Before Socrates, philosophical speculation had centered, mainly, on concrete, empirical matters, things that could be worked out and proved, physically: mathematics and physics, disciplines imported from Egypt, and astronomy from Babylonia. Socrates opened a whole new world . . . of the mind: abstract conceptions that can be discovered through "thought" and "reason": like goodness and truth, morality, beauty, happiness and freedom. Man is free, Socrates taught, when he is master of himself, not a slave to his desires. As for the State: it can rule with wisdom, courage, discipline and justice only when it practices self-discipline. Socrates could bargain himself out of the death penalty, but remains true to his own beliefs; and, as he drinks the fatal cup of hemlock, he tells his weeping students and disciples:

Do not talk about burying Socrates . . . say only that you are burying my body.

Socrates looks forward with joy to eternity for he fully expects to be reunited with other great persons of the past . . .

If death is the journey to another place, what can be greater . . . what would not a man give if he might converse with Orpheus and Hesiod and Homer? What infinite delight would there be in conversing with them . . . and in another world they would not put a man to death for asking questions . . .   Socrates, from. Plato's APOLOGY

Deeply embittered by his master's fate, Socrates' disciple, Plato, leaves Athens to study and teach in Italy, Sicily and Egypt. But Plato is disillusioned not only by Socrates' judicial murder, but by Athens, itself, its corruption and political machinations, the brutality of its dictators and the depths to which, its religion has sunk: the Bacchanalian festivals, for example, at which, he says he has seen the whole population of Athens drunk.

But Athens is drunk on other things, also; money and power. The Golden Age made a lot of people rich, and with the "community" or *polis* a thing of the past, it is now every man for himself. Stifled under alternately despotic and fascist dictatorships at home, many Greeks look abroad to expansion, especially north, to the fisheries and wheat-fields of the Black Sea area . . . so Greece begins colonizing as far north as Russia.

390 In that lush and beautiful area north of the Alps that is, today, called France, a new Celtic people appear, called Gauls. Their first major action on the world's stage shows them to be an enigmatic and unpredictable people, as a great army of Gauls march down through northern Italy, directly toward Rome, plundering and pillaging as they go. A terrifying sight, the Gauls cause the Roman defenders to panic in a rout at Allia, just outside Rome. They ransack, destroy and burn the city, all but the defensible capital. The terrified Romans pay them a huge ransom . . . and, to Rome's surprise, the Gauls simply turn around and go home . . . leaving the city to rebuild, its neighbors in fear for the future and its own people with this near-disaster forever ingrained in their memories.

Plato

c. 387 Plato returns to Athens to open a school which he calls the ACADEMY. It is the world's first university; and the fund he establishes to support it is the first "foundation." The ACADEMY teaches history, literature, mathematics, philosophy, music, logic, health, gymnastics, astronomy, politics, science, economics, sociology, city planning and business administration. The Academy will attract scholars for the next 900 years, until it finally closes in 529 A.D. Plato writes his DIALOGUES during his years at the Academy, that work which has been called the "starting point of modern science and philosophy," which makes "all modern thought but a footnote to Plato." They are written as casual conversations with Socrates in the leading role, guiding students and friends from idea to idea to idea. They are warm, human and even humorous. Plato, himself, never appears in the dialogues but his thought is evident throughout. Plato is a man of ideals and believes in an ideal condition for man; an ideal city, state, republic . . .

. . . societies fall when ignorance triumphs over wisdom, and freedom becomes license. LAWS The man who is slave to his appetites is master of nothing. The man who is master of nothing is the most miserable of men. * Until philosophers are kings or kings . . . have the spirit of philosophy . . . and political power and wisdom are united in one . . . the human race will never have rest from its troubles. Plato, the REPUBLIC

Plato believes there are two worlds; the spiritual, presided over by the "greatest of all ideas, the Idea of the Good, the Supreme One, the Father, God . . ." to which "man's immortal soul returns at death"; and the material, patterned on the spiritual, created by God.

> The universe must, have been created for it is a sensible thing. Plato, TIMEAUS

In this material world he envisions for man an Ideal City of perfect order; green and lovely, walled safely in, a haven of ideal wisdom, courage, justice, beauty and happiness. Six hundred years from now, in the very midst of the destruction of a great Roman Empire, a Christian scholar, teacher and writer whom the world now knows as Saint Augustine, will transpose Plato's ideal city into a City of God on earth that, with the reality of Christ, must be continued in the Christian Church. St. Augustine's CITY OF GOD will alter the course of western history.

Plato's speculations on the "idea" of God are another step in mankind's spiritual understanding. First there were the cosmological religions of Sumer and Egypt with their vast pantheons of nature gods (Sumer's being the zodiac figures in the sky, and Egypt's found in and on the "life-giving" earth.) They, in turn, were overshadowed and diminished by a "great leap in faith" when, the one, true, omnipotent Creator revealed Himself—and His LAW—to Moses. Over the years the myriad technicalities of that LAW, with its hundreds of negative restrictions and prohibitions, has been clarified and defined by God's "spokesmen," the Prophets, to reveal a God of understanding, love and compassion, a God who enters into history, takes part in it and in man's affairs; who is in control of the present every bit as much as He was at the Creation. And thus was born modern Judaism. Now Plato brings another dimension to spiritual understanding, a Greek concept totally unrelated to any before, or even to the Greeks' own mythological gods and heroes. For, in his attempt to understand the nature of God through a rationalization of principles, Plato combines loving *(philos)* and wise/wisdom *(sophos)* into *PHILOSOPHY*. But he knows, also, of the danger of philosophy INVENTING its own religion and so he creates a "study" *(logos)* of God *(theos)* to distinguish between true and false "*THEOLOGIES.*"

c. 367   A young man named Aristotle travels to Athens to study at the Academy with Plato. Aristotle comes from the Greek colonial town called Stagira on the shores of far-northern Macedonia, where his father is court physician to the king. (Both king and country are well to watch in the years ahead.) At only 17, Aristotle already displays an awesome intellect, and an insatiable curiosity about everything. Plato immediately recognizes genius, and the two become fast friends. Aristotle will remain at the Academy as both student and teacher, for 20 years.

Aristotle

> Cicero called Aristotle a river of flowing gold, and said of Plato's DIALOGUES, that if Jupiter were to speak, it would be in language like theirs. Plutarch, LIVES OF THE NOBLE GREEKS AND ROMANS

C. 360   Not everything is "golden" in Greece, however. The eccentric philosopher, Diogenes, goes about the streets of Athens with a lantern, ". . . looking for an honest man." The Athenian orator, Isocrates, however, doubts that there is one . . .

> The people fear their enemies less than their own fellow citizens. The rich would rather throw their property into the sea than give it to the poor, and the poor desire nothing more fiercely than to rob the rich.   Isocrates

Diogenes is a follower of the new "Cynic" school, founded by one Socratic student who took the Master's belief that virtue, not pleasure, is the supreme good in life, and radicalized it to hold that ALL pleasure is unnecessary, therefore, contemptible. A wise man neither wants nor desires anything, he teaches, and should owe allegiance to no-one and nothing; family, state nor society—for these can create ambitions and obligations which cannot be satisfied. Thus, the "cynics" reject the idea that men are motivated to good works by good intentions: rather, they believe, even the best actions are prompted by selfishness and self-seeking. So Diogenes searches, with his lantern, for an honest man, and in his rejection of life's pleasures or rewards, lives on crusts of bread by day and sleeps in a tub at night.

359   Philip II is king of Macedonia, son of that king for whom Aristotle's father was court physician. In far northern Greece, Macedonia is still partly primeval forest, almost barbarian and far removed from civilization. Philip is a warrior king with only one goal . . . conquest. But most of the Greeks feel he can best be dealt with through a policy of isolation and containment, and that an occasional minor concession will "pacify" him. They choose to ignore the fact that Philip is building up an enormous war machine, for which he has invented new methods of warfare, including heavy and light cavalry, and the fearful, spear-wielding *phalanx,* an impenetrable block of iron-armed soldiers who move together as a deadly juggernaut.

One Athenian orator, though, named Demosthenes, is well aware of the impending threat from the north, and speaks out against it forcefully and often. According to the historian, Plutarch, "The object . . . was noble and just, the defense of the Grecians against Philip; and in this [Demosthenes] behaved himself so worthily that he soon grew famous, and excited attention everywhere for his eloquence and courage in speaking . . . in the court of Philip [himself] no man was so much talked of . . ." His orations are called "Philippics . . ."

> Observe, Athenians, the height to which the fellow's insolence has soared; he leaves you no choice of action or inaction . . . he is always taking . . . more, everywhere casting his net round us, while we sit idle and do nothing.   Plutarch, LIVES OF THE NOBLE GREEKS AND ROMANS

Demosthenes

After his own considerable family inheritance was embezzled by one of its own trustees, Demosthenes studied law and oratory, and his self-discipline in learning was awesome to others. As a youth he suffered a severe stutter and put himself through grueling exercises to overcome it, running up hills and shouting above the roar of the sea.

> Demosthanes overcame his inarticulate and stammering pronunciation by speaking with pebbles in his mouth. Plutarch, LIVES

But his warnings will not save Athens . . . nor himself . . . who will be disgraced, exiled and finally take poison to avoid being captured. Eighty years from now, after the storm clouds settle, a statue will be carved of him (which stands, today, in the National Museum, Copenhagen) showing a toga-draped, sad-eyed, thoughtful man. An inscription at the base reads:

> Had thy strength been equal to thy will, Demosthenes,
> the war god of Macedon would never have subdued the Greeks.

353   In the kingdom of Caria, in Asia Minor, King Mausolaus dies, a good and wise king; and his widow, Queen Artemesia (she whose bravery won King Xerxes' admiration at the battle of Salamis 27 years ago) builds a fabulous tomb for him. The finest sculptors in the world are commissioned to work their stony magic on what will become the fourth of the Seven Wonders of the Ancient World, the MAUSOLEUM OF HALLICARNASSUS. The gigantic monument will stand a thousand years; and fragments of it remain, some in European museums. A sculptured frieze in the British Museum, London, brings to life wild chariot races and fierce hand-to-hand combat scenes of battle between Greeks, centaurs and Amazons. If the Museum's statue of Mausolaus is a true likeness, he was indeed, a handsome prince with strong features, noble brow and intelligent eyes. The works of the four master carvers of the mausoleum—Skopas, Timotheus, Bryaxis and Leochares—reflect the deeply passionate emotions of battle from anguish to agony to ecstasy; Skopas, the chief carver being remembered in history as the Sculptor of Passion. The size of the monument must have been mind-boggling, for just the friezes, themselves, measure almost a yard high.

. . . Another Greek sculptor, Praxiteles, is creating masterpieces of artistry in marble; a grinning satyr, and the gods Hermes (Mercury), Apollo and Aphrodite, the goddess of love. Praxiteles is total master of the "S" curve in the body that makes his statues graceful and pliant. Many still stand in modern museums, so beautifully real they seem almost alive, ready to move and breathe.

. . . The architect, Polyklitos the Younger, designs a magnificent open-air theater at Epidaurus. Carved into the hillside, its seating area, or *theatron,* plunges steeply down 55 rows to the round stage below, backed by gorgeously carved Doric and Corinthian columns. Epidaurus attracts theater lovers from far and wide to plays ingeniously staged and accompanied by the lyre and *syrinx* or Pipes of Pan, an ancestor of today's organ. Now restored to its ancient beauty, the theater once again echoes to the great Greek plays.

Praxiteles' "S" Curve

347 Plato dies at the age of 90, a teacher to the end, proudest, of all his works, of his Academy (that will produce great scholars for centuries after him.) His influence on all humanity is incalculable. To a world which gloried in the physical, he introduced the mind; that valued only action, he taught to think about the abstract, the unseen, the transcendant. Plato taught that man's ability to THINK is a spiritual attribute, not physical, and is related to—and can comprehend—another spiritual attribute, the IDEA; that no other part of the body can ever comprehend the IDEA except THOUGHT. But thought may be EXPRESSED by a WORD, an "expression," a *logos*, and when this *logos* is applied to the Divine Essence, or "God," *theos*, the result is a union of *theos/logos*, or *theology*, and that *theology* distinguishes between true and false thinking about Divinity

. . . At Plato's death, Aristotle leaves Athens for the island of Lesbos, off the coast of Asia Minor. Here he devotes himself to the research that will someday become a many-volume biological study of animals. Everything interests him and nothing is too insignificant to note. In the Aegean Sea he observes how the octopus uses his feelers and that dolphins sometimes snore. On the mainland he studies the habits of elephants and camels, bumble bees, spiders and the great horned owl. He writes of the bison on Mount Messipium, of hawking in Thrace, the wolves of Lake Meotis and the King of Sythia's mare. He delves into their histories, studies their bodily parts and motions, nesting, breeding and eating habits; he learns which ones shed their teeth and why they are born head first, and draws diagrams of their various organs. He tells how they mate and migrate, bear their young and change their plumage. Then he sorts them out, or "classifies" them, something no one has ever done before, so there are no guidelines to go by. He has, in fact, to invent his own methods and to invent an entirely new vocabulary to express his findings, to create "biology" and "pathology." He sorts everything according to *genus* and *species*, family, order and variety, the first person ever so to do. He is, in addition to his other greatness, the world's first systematic scientist

342, Macedonia.   Philip II has a son who is now 14 years old. The boy already shows remarkable promise as a soldier and leader; is fearless, imaginative, well-respected, has a brilliant mind and a driving ambition. He is convinced that he is destined for greatness. Gently and patiently taming an "untamable" horse, the young prince causes Philip to weep tears of joy and exclaim, "O my son, look thee out a kingdom equal to and worthy of thyself, for Macedonia is too little for thee." The boy's name is Alexander, soon to be called, "the Great."

> Whenever Alexander heard Philip had . . . won any signal victory, instead of rejoicing at it . . . would tell his companions that his father would leave him . . . no opportunities of performing great and illustrious actions.   Plutarch, LIVES OF THE NOBLE GREEKS AND ROMANS

Philip wants Alexander to have the finest education possible, so he invites Aristotle to Macedonia to become Alexander's tutor. Student and teacher become close friends, and Aristotle remains six years, instilling in Alexander a deep love and pride in Greek thought and culture, and a desire to carry this Greek *ethos* to all the world.

340   In Rome, the lower class, or Plebians, are gradually gaining more political power, although not without rancor, bitterness and class strife. In 367 the Roman constitution was amended to open the consulship to plebes, and the next year the first Plebian was elected Consul. Ten years later the first plebe was elected *dictator,* and now the law is re-written to say that one consul MUST be a plebe.

. . . Directly south of Rome, on the north coast of Africa, the city of Carthage is flourishing, the richest city on the Mediterranean Sea. Older than Rome, itself, Carthage is master of all of North Africa, the Balearic Islands, Malta, Sardinia, Corsica and half of Spain. A quarter of a million people live within its imposing city walls, as does a military force of 20,000 men, 4000 horses and a new, secret weapon, 300 armor-clad war elephants! Carthage's seafront is lined with 220 ship docks that accommodate thousands of immense galleys on trading missions to a hundred ports "world-wide," and military training missions to defend its use of the Mediterranean as its own private property, including exacting tribute from "trespassers." Carthage's vast, fertile African acres of irrigated grain fields, vineyards and orchards, and mineral deposits in Spain, are the envy of the world, and its beautiful marble-columned city one of its wonders. But its people are not, and are described by ancient historians as harsh, austere, graceless and gloomy; their Baal-worshipping, child sacrificing religion "savage," and their avarice disgusting, for whom "nothing" is disgraceful if it results in profit." Carthage and Rome hate, envy and mistrust each other and now wait only for sufficient provocation from the other.

340   Philip II wages a campaign against Byzantium and his son, Prince Alexander, is left in full control of the government. He is 16 years old.

In one of his *Philippics,* the Greek orator, Demosthanes, had called the Macedonians a "worthless pack of barbarians . . . not even . . . competent slaves." Now Philip, ruthless in politics but brilliant in battle, moves in on the Greek Peloponnesus to meet the combined forces of the ancient enemies, Athens and Thebes—and some other smaller states—in a major turning-point battle at Charonea. Philip's "new model army" of 30,000 Macedonian infantry with their newly invented weapons, formations and maneuvers, take on the larger but less imposing 35,000 Greek hoplites. Philip, himself, commands the right wing of the army, putting his own son, 18 year-old Alexander at the head of the left: and Alexander's brilliance and courage win the day and begin a legend. Both wings of the Greek force quickly collapse, and the center turns and flees. There is a minimum of bloodshed and the man whom Demosthanes had labeled "war god of Macedon" reigns supreme in Greece.

But Philip is magnanimous in victory, and organizes a congress of Greek states into a Hellenic League which acknowledges him, and his heirs, perpetual military commander of Greece. Philip convinces the Greeks to stop the eternal infighting amongst themselves, put first things first, and join him in an invasion of Persia.

336   Philip II is assassinated while planning the conquest of Persia, and Alexander becomes king of Macedonia. Twenty three hundred years from now, in A.D. 1977, Greek archeologists, having studied ancient writers, especially Plutarch, for clues, will dig deeply

Philip II

into a man-made, un-plundered mound of earth near Vergina in far-northern Greece, or Macedon, and find a classically designed burial shrine . . . and inside that, a masonry casket containing a solid gold ossuary, or bone box, decorated with a sunburst design, the symbol of Macedonian kings. In the box, undisturbed for 22 centuries lay the cremated bones of a person of great wealth and power, wrapped in purple fabric and covered over with a wreath of golden oak leaves, symbols of royalty. Also in the tomb are a magnificent golden armor, breast-plate, shield, helmet and a gleaming golden quiver with arrows, their wooden shafts still intact! A difference in lengths of a pair of shin-protecting bronze *greaves* reveal that their wearer had one shorter leg than the other. Although some scholars say there is no proof-positive, the evidence is overwhelming that this spectacular find is, indeed, the burial place of Philip II of Macedonia . . . who had walked with a limp form an old battle wound. The remains lie, today, in the Louvre, Paris.

. . . During these many years since the Jews' return from exile, their land has been under control of the powerful Persian Empire, in its Fifth *Satrapy*—a relatively benign condition, as the Persian kings have generally followed Cyrus the Great's lenient policies. Things are changing, though and there are hard times ahead, times like those of old, when they were batted back and forth between other nations. They have changed already, though, in one very important way . . . language . . .

. . . as the ancient language of the Jews, Hebrew, has slowly gone into disuse as a spoken tongue, replaced by Aramaic, which was learned by the exiles when they were captive in Babylonia. It will be joined very soon by another language . . . another culture, and new ideas in . . .

The AGE of ALEXANDER

336   Twenty year-old Alexander III is king of Macedonia, as remarkable a ruler as any in history. A man of average height and athletic build (according to Plutarch) he has "a white and ruddy complexion" and hair "like a lion's mane" on an aristocratic head which he holds "a bit aslant." Alexander inherited from his mother (a princess of Epirus) a half-wild, almost barbarian, visionary ferocity; and from his father, Philip II, a military genius, an intensely vivid imagination and driving ambition to unite what they saw as the enlightened and ennobled Greek race in the conquest of despotic, degenerate, oriental Persia. The heady splendor of his father's court, so highly charged with vaunting ambition had an "inter-

Alexander the Great

national" aura with foreign emissaries from both east and west coming and going. This, plus the incredible combination of classical idealism and scientific/metaphysical speculation of his teacher, Aristotle, have inspired the romantic young dreamer to lofty visions of bold enterprise. Now, Alexander begins his incredibly successful reign.

> Anaxarchus taught that the universe is made up of an infinite number of worlds . . . and Alexander grieved to think he had not yet conquered one.   Plutarch, LIVES OF THE NOBLE GREEKS AND ROMANS

The world about him having short-sightedly blinded itself to the massive Macedonian political threat and military build-up, now finds itself totally unprepared for the consequences; and within a year, Alexander controls territory from the Adriatic to the Danube. His teacher, Aristotle, leaves Macedonia and returns to Athens, to open a school of his own, which he calls the *Lyceum,* to teach art, politics, physics, natural science, logic and philosophy; and to gather together in written volumes "all the knowledge in the world."

335   Alexander puts down, with cool ruthlessness, an insurrection in the Greek city of Thebes; and Athens, and the other city-states, need no further persuasion. They capitulate peacefully; and all Greece is under his rule. Alexander destroys Thebes utterly, but spares the house of the ancient poet, Pindar, whose works Aristotle had taught him to love. He has no wish to be thought a barbarian.

334   On his way to carry out his father's plan to conquer Greece's ancient enemy, Persia, Alexander's army crosses the Hellespont on a bridge of boats, just as Xerxes' army had done 150 years before. At Gordium in Phrygia, a strangely twisted cornel-bark rope binds a wagon-yoke to a pole, and ancient legend says "*He who unties the Gordian knot shall be lord of all Asia.*" Without a moments hesitation, Alexander's sword slashes the knotted rope and wins, for him, an impressive psychological victory.

Alexander's first goal is Egypt, and to get there he and his army march south through Asia Minor where he visits the ruins of ancient Troy, retakes the Persian-held Greek cities of Sardis, Ephesus, Miletus and Hallicarnassus. He wins major battles at Granicus and Issus, forcing King Darius III to flee eastward where his forces get hung up in mountain passes, leaving Alexander in control of Darius' camp, his queen, his harem (which he frees) and his vast, uncountable riches. Down through Syria Alexander marches, and gets no resistance from Sidon, but Tyre is another matter. One of Darius' wealthiest seaports, it meets the Greeks with burning sulphur and red-hot sand catapulted over the city walls. A siege of seven months, the aid of 300 allied warships and floating battering rams gives Alexander the city . . . and its people . . . 8000 dead in battle, 2000 he executes . . . and 30,000 sold into slavery. The prophecy of the Bible's book of ZECHARIAH has come to pass:

> And Tyre did build . . . a strong hold, and heaped up silver . . . and . . . gold . . . Behold, the Lord will . . . smite her power into the sea . . . devoured with fire. Ashkelon shall see it, and fear; Gaza also . . . and [sorrow] . . . I will encamp about mine house . . . because of him that passeth by . . . and [raise] up thy sons, O Zion, against [the sons of] Greece . . .
> ZECHARIAH 9:3–5,8 & 13

Now between Alexander and Egypt lies just one more land to cross . . . the "bridge," —Judea. Ashkelon falls easily, Gaza holds out for five months . . . and is made a "desert." Then . . .

333   Jerusalem capitulates without struggle, and the Jews are under Greek rule. Alexander is already becoming a legend, and this story (apocryphal or not) is told by a latter-day Jewish historian, Joseph Ben Matthais, or Josephus, who was born just after the death of Jesus of Nazareth and died the year this book ends. In his HISTORY, Josephus describes Alexander's entrance into the city:

"In Jerusalem, the high priest, in 'agony and terror . . . not knowing how he should meet the Macedonians,' gathers the priests and a 'multitude of citizens' into a great procession out of the city to meet the Greeks . . .

> . . . when [Alexander] saw the multitude at a distance . . . the high priest in purple and scarlet clothing . . . mitre on his head . . . [carrying a] golden plate whereon the name of God was engraved . . . Alexander approached by himself, and adored the [God] and saluted the high priest. The Jews [then] did all together, with one voice, salute Alexander, and encompass him about . . . and he came into [Jerusalem] . . . and . . . went up into the temple [and] offered sacrifice to God, according to the high priest's direction, and magnificently treated [them all] . . . when the book of DANIEL was [shown] him, wherein Daniel declared that one of the Greeks should destroy the empire of the Persians, [Alexander] supposed that [he] himself was the person intended . . . and . . . was . . . glad . . ."
> Josephus, ANTIQUITIES OF THE JEWS, Book XI, Ch. VIII (See: A.D. 64)

This is the prophecy from the book of DANIEL that causes contemporary coin inscriptions of Alexander to show him with a goat's horn on his head, the symbol of a deliverer:

> Behold there stood before the river a ram . . . with two horns . . . and I saw the ram pushing westward, and northward, and southward . . . and [he] became great . . . and as I was considering . . . an he goat came from the west [across] the face of the whole earth . . . and had a [great] horn between his eyes . . . and [he] smote the ram. . . [and] . . . cast him down . . . Therefore the he goat waxed very great . . . The ram . . . having two horns are the kings of Media and Persia. And the . . . goat is the king of Grecia—Greece.   DANIEL 8:3–8, 20 & 21 (See: DANIEL, 539 B.C.)

332   Egypt welcomes Alexander as a deliverer, and he proclaims himself Pharaoh. At the mouth of the Nile River on Pharaos Island, Alexander founds the city of Alexandria, which will grow to greatness. It is the first modern, planned city, with laid-out, letter-named streets. His plans include building the greatest library and medical school in the world. Alexandria will soon rival Athens as the Greek center of intellectual and cultural life.

> For when he was master of Egypt . . . he resolved to build a large and populous city and settle a colony of Grecians there, and give it his own name. One night in his sleep a vision . . . said to him, "An island there lies where loud the billows roar, Pharos they call it on the Egyptian shore." Alexander immediately rose up and went to Pharos. For want of chalk, the soil being black . . . they laid out their lines with flour.   Plutarch, LIVES OF THE NOBLE GREEKS AND ROMANS

The quotation is from the ancient poet, Homer, whose sagas Alexander passionately loves and whose ILIAD he carries with him always and reads often, for, according to Plutarch, ". . . he saw himself as the modern Achilles." Understandably so, for Egypt looks upon him as a savior from the Persians. Some think that the oracle he visits—alone in the desert—may have told him just that.

Aristotle had encouraged Alexander to carry out scientific research projects everywhere he goes, such as the study of the annual flooding of the Nile River, and for that purpose Aristotle's nephew, Callisthanes, is with Alexander and his army, heading a team of scientists and researchers, who collect and send back all manner of knowledge; specimens and discoveries in such fields as geography, botany, minerology and meteorology . . . making this the world's first "scientific expedition." Aristotle uses the material in teaching at the Lyceum, and in compiling the world's first—*encyclopedia*.

While Plato (who had nick-named Aristotle "the Reader" because of his pupil's *encyclopedic* knowledge) believed in a mystical idealism, Aristotle uses observable phenomenon—such as Callisthanes sends him—combined with reason, common sense and *logic* to study the world. He delves into the finite and infinite, quantity and quality, substance, relation, evil and good, space and time; concluding—not always rightly—that "the earth is the center of the universe," and that the "Atomic Theory" is incorrect. He studies sleep and sleeplessness, memory, dreams and their interpretation, youth and old age . . . and the human soul or *psyche*. He compiles chronologies of the Olympic Games and studies the "customs of the barbarians." He compares 158 Greek constitutions to discover which form of government is best. He critiques Greek theater, composes guidelines for latter-day critics to follow, and lays the foundations of musical theory. In his works LOGIC, ETHICS, RHETORIC, POETICS, PHYSICS and METAPHYSICS he propounds thoughts and theories that will be held inviolable for centuries to come. He believes that man is ". . . a unity of body and soul . . ."

> . . . since man is essentially a rational animal, the good for man is activity of the soul in accordance with reason. The highest good for man is the contemplative life. * For man, when perfected, is the best of animals, but, when separated from law and justice . . . the worst of all, since armed injustice is the more dangerous, and he is equipped at birth with arms meant to be used by intelligence and virtue, which he may use for the worst ends. Wherefore, if he have not virtue, he is a most unholy and savage of animals, and full of lust and gluttony. But justice is the bond of men in states . . . the principle of order in political society.   Aristotle, POLITICS 1:2

Whether contemplating friendship, happiness, desire, justice or the search for truth, Aristotle time and again finds three plateaus, from the lowest, or "vulgar" (brutal, coarse, self-serving) to "moderate" (mutual pleasure and cultivation) to the "ideal" or "supreme" (desire of perfection through virtue, self-control, contemplation or philosophy.) This is Aristotle's search for the "good life" through a middle ground, or "Golden Mean," which is controlled by the soul. Aristotle uses logic to understand God, also . . .

> God is mightiest in power, fairest in beauty, immortal in existence, supreme in virtue; therefore, being invisible to every mortal nature he is seen through his works themselves.
> Aristotle, DE MUNDO

The contributions of Socrates, Plato and Aristotle to Western civilization and, indeed, to the world, are boundless, unending and incalculable, for they laid the foundations of everything modern man does, says or thinks. Our actions and reactions, feelings, hopes, desires, aspirations, forms of government, modes of behavior, methods, systems and processes, our interests in science, education and the arts were all thought out by them: how to make a speech, judge a play, get revenge, plan a city, raise a child. (How about this for today? ". . . youth should be kept strangers to all that is bad . . . especially to things which suggest vice or hate." POLITICS 7:17) . . . all were thought out by them. And yet, they were not perfect. Western (especially American) ideals of personal freedom and individual liberty for ALL PEOPLE do not come from Greek philosophy, but from the Hebrew (and later Christian) religion. Slavery, sodomy, infanticide, abortion, incest and communism/communal ownership of, not only property but families—wives and children!—were all justified or even advocated by some of them. The moral injunctions AGAINST those things are BIBLICAL injunctions, not philosophical Greek.

> The state is the . . . highest good . . . by nature clearly prior to the family and individual, since the whole is . . . prior to the part . . . Neither must we suppose that any . . . citizen belongs to himself, for they all belong to the state . . . are each part of [it] . . . [those su-

perior] in mind [are] by nature intended to be lord and master and [those inferior] by nature slaves . . . possessions . . . that some should rule and others be ruled is . . . necessary . . . from the hour of their birth, some are marked out for subjection, others for rule . . . [that is] both expedient and right. Socrates proposes in the REPUBLIC of Plato . . . [that] the citizens might conceivably have wives and children and property in common . . . [and] . . . [w]ould permit . . . familiarities between father and son or . . . brother and brother . . . As to the exposure . . . of children, let there be a law that [when there is] an excess number of children . . . no deformed child shall live, or, if the state law forbid this . . . let abortion be procured.   Aristotle, POLITICS 1:1,2,4,5; 2:1,4; 7:16 & 8:1)

Darius III of Persia

332   Now begins Alexander's long march through all those oriental lands whose ancient empires played so large a part in history: Sumer, Assyria and Babylonia, with their great, fabled cities of Ur, Nineveh, Babylon and Persepolis; his first goal being . . . the defeat of King Darius III and the final extermination of Persia.

331   On the night of September 20th, five years into his reign, under a lunar eclipse, Alexander's armies cross over the Tigris River; then march past the mounded-up ruins of Nineveh into the very heart of Persia. Darius expects him to head south for Babylon and intends to attack him from the rear, but Alexander knows what Darius expects and heads straight east to meet him face to face. The Persian army is a vast, formidable horde of rugged mountaineers, reckless, breakneck horsemen from the plains, reluctant conscripts from all across Asia: Afghans, Bokarans, Kurds, Turks, Sikhs, Bactrians, Babylonians, Medes, Parthians, Albanians and Sythians; and the back-bone of the fighting force is a "secret weapon" Darius hopes will slice though the Macedonians like a sword through meat: hundreds of sythe-bearing chariots. But they are facing the most mobile, highly motivated and modern army in history, armed with weapons and trained with tactics invented by Philip, himself, and perfected by Alexander . . . including the dreaded, spear-wielding *phalanx*, equipped, now, with razor-sharp pikes 24 feet long. And Darius' conscripts are facing something even more formidable: free men of Greece, and of every other country Alexander has come through so far, including Judea, men who look upon their leader as a champion of freedom, a fulfillment of prophecy, as a savior, deliverer, as Alexander . . . the Great.

Alexander the Great mosaic from Pompeii

331, October 1: The Plains of Arbela between the Tigris River and the mountains of Kurdistan. Expecting a night-time attack, Darius has kept his army up and at-the-ready all night; and morning finds them already weary. Alexander, his gold and silver-trimmed armor gleaming in the sun, leads the right wing and directs a battle plan so brilliant the

Battle of Arbela is considered, to this day, one of the most decisive in history. Darius' sythe-armed chariots charge the Macedonian *phalanxes*, but the precision-trained spearmen merely open ranks, letting the hapless chariots stream through and be cut down from their rear. When his own chariot driver is slain by a javelin, Darius, who had fought bravely and commanded skillfully early on, panics and flees to the hills on a fallen soldier's horse. Alexander, ecstatic with the love of battle and the "rapture of the strife," follows in hot pursuit. The Persian army is utterly defeated, Greece is avenged and Alexander the Great becomes a legend at the age of 25.

Now Alexander heads south for the great, fabled cities of Babylon (where he is hailed as Lord and Master), Susa and Persepolis which, in an evening of drunken debauchery, he allows to be burned in revenge for Xerxes' burning of Athens 47 years ago. Each city's royal palace yields up immense, uncountable, unbelievable treasure for Alexander to confiscate: tons of gold, silver, ivory and gems, that were paid in tribute, over the years, to Persia's kings by their submissive Satraps all over Asia.

330   Still pursuing the fleeing Darius, Alexander crosses the Zagros River into Media, only to find the king murdered by one of his own generals so that Alexander could capture . . . only a corpse. Now his opposition will come mainly from local tribesmen. On he marches as the years pass and the hundreds of miles turn into thousands, through Parthia and Bactria far north to Bokhara and Samarkand to the Jaxartes River, and then south-east, with China directly ahead.

327   Alexander the Great, king of all Persia, having passed through all of (today's) Iraq, Iran and Afghanistan, now crosses the formidable frozen waste of the three-mile-high Hindu Kush . . . where once again his temper gets the better of him, and, having adopted Persian dress, manners and attitudes, when Aristotle's nephew, Callisthanes, refuses to kow-tow to him in the eastern manner, on hands and knees as to a god, Alexander has the philosopher/scientist executed . . . causing Aristotle, back in Athens, to break off correspondence with him . . . forever.

History will find much besides this for which to condemn Alexander: a treacherous cruel streak in a hot temper: a liking for men as well as women, an insatiable thirst and weakness for debauchery, a grandiose desire to be worshipped as a god, and a tendency toward the very oriental despotism he so hated. Still, he is invincible, as the oracle had told him he would be, as he marches through all of Persia, losing not one battle. A brilliant strategist, utterly fearless, he, himself, is the first man into battle, every place at once, cheering his men, urging them on, collecting—and ignoring—many wounds to his body. The hardships Alexander's army suffers (and they are many) he suffers with them. When his men march afoot, he marches afoot: when they go without food or water, he goes without food and water . . . weakening himself more than he knows.

Down from the frozen Hindu Kush, Alexander's armies march through Pakistan with its fearful Gedrosian Desert and heat so terrible their armor burns flesh, forcing them to march 200 miles at night; then sail down the Indus River into India's Punjab. Of 20,000 footsoldiers and 15,000 horse only a fourth survive the heat, famine and disease. Here, their own suffering, Alexander's oriental affectations, and the Greeks' own disinterest in conquering India cause his generals to revolt and refuse to go on, so Alexander decides . . . return.

Alexander is at the height of his power and at the farthest limits of northern Asia. Everywhere he has reorganized local governments along Greek lines; trade, commerce, monetary systems and, of course, language, literature and culture. He has established a dozen Alexandrias all across Asia, and changed the face of the world. In just a lightening flash of 11 short years he has conquered and become undisputed master of an area the size of the United States of America. Now he plans to unite Europe and Asia, return to the west and bring Rome and Carthage under his control.

323, Early Spring.   Seven years and 7000 miles after he left it, Alexander, having retraced his route through Persepolis and Susa, arrives in Babylon, which he intends to make his capital city.

> At Susa, he married Darius' daughter . . . and celebrated the nuptials of (80 of) his friends, bestowing the noblest of the Persian ladies upon the worthiest of them. At this magnificent festival . . . there were no less than 3000 guests, to each of whom he gave a golden cup for the libations.   Plutarch, LIVES OF THE NOBLE GREEKS AND ROMANS

Alexander is famous the "world" over, believed to be superhuman, loved and revered by his troops and officers for all his many strengths, his bravery, vision, genius and undaunted, audacious spirit, and forgiven his weaknesses. Although many statues, coins and paintings of Alexander exist today, we still do not know his exact appearance because they are all stylized or exaggerated, especially those depicting him with horns; as in the prophecy from the Bible's book of DANIEL; and he is included in the folklore and literature of every land he passed through from Egypt to India . . . and some he did not, including England, in its CANTERBURY TALES. Four hundred years from now, during the reign of a Roman emperor, Hadrian, a Greek historian named Flavius Arrianus, or Arrian, will use the personal journals kept throughout this campaign by two of Alexander's generals—Aristobulus and Ptolemy—and write a history/biography of Alexander. About his "world-wide" fame and reputation, Arrian will write:

> I believe there was in his [own] time no nation of men, no city, nay, no single individual, with whom Alexander's name had not become a familiar word. I therefore hold that such a man, who was like no ordinary mortal was not born into the world without some special providence.   Arrian (c. A.D. 96–180)

323, early June.   Alexander receives tribute and honor from emissaries and delegations from "every country of the world" who regard him with "fear and wonder," but, his body weakened by privation and hardship on the long march, he is seized with a fever which worsens for almost two weeks. and, one by one, his officers walk slowly by his bed in a final farewell.

13, June, 323.   Alexander the Great dies at Babylon, not yet 33 years old, and is carried back to Egypt in a coffin of solid gold. Within ten short years his empire will have totally collapsed, but he has accomplished much of what he set out to do. He opened up the Far East and spread his beloved Greek *ethos* everywhere he went. Alexander was no liberator; he brought no freedom or liberty to the millions of people his life affected; he was a conqueror, imposing with force his views on all others. But his views were those he believed to be enlightened, and one of his greatest accomplishments was the creation of a "civilized" Greek world which did away with the boundaries between Greek and "barbarian." Three hundred seventy-one years from now (in the Year of our Lord, A.D. 48) a Greek speaking/writing Jew of Roman citizenship, named Paul of Tarsus, will write these words, that show how vast the influence of Alexander was on the world . . . and on a newly established "Christian" faith.

> For ye are all the children of God by faith in Christ Jesus . . . There is neither Jew nor Greek, there is neither bond nor free, there is neither male nor female: for ye are all one in Christ Jesus.   Paul to the GALATIANS 3:26,28

With Alexander's death begins the period of Greek history known as . . .

. . . the Age of HELLENISM,

from the Greek name for their own land, Hellas; which will see a flowering of beauty and culture in every part of the world he touched. Greek literature, architecture, music, dress and manners will be emulated, and those areas that are not genuinely Hellenic, will act Hellenic or Hellenistic, in imitation of the Greeks.

Ptolemy I of Egypt

Alexander's death also touches off a power struggle for his territories, some of which, like Athens and Sparta, revert back to their native rulers, and some are seized by Alexander's top generals to create three main divisions: 1. ANTIGONUS Cyclops, (so called for his having only one eye) becomes King of Macedonia; 2. SELEUCUS of Macedon (from whom a Seleucid Dynasty will take its name) claims all of Persia INCLUDING JUDEA IN THE 5th PERSIAN *SATRAPY*, beginning, for the Jews, a long, bitter ordeal; and 3, PTOLEMY SOTER (meaning "savior," takes control of Egypt as its governor, or Satrap. A man of letters (it was he and Antigonus who kept journals of Alexander's campaigns) and an able ruler, Ptolemy will leave Egypt a strong, secure kingdom when he completes a 38 year reign in 285. (His Ptolemaic Dynasty will rule Egypt for almost 300 years, now, until the death of its last, most famous Queen, Cleopatra.) Now, imbued with Alexander's vision of a Greek world, he sets about carrying out Alexander's wishes:

Ptolemy begins building the great library Alexander planned at Alexandria. It will eventually hold 700,000 scrolls, many original and many copied from originals borrowed from other libraries in many other cities. Much of Aristotle's work and that of the ancient Greek writers and poets will find their way to Alexandria, also, and scholars come from the world over to study. The library will, in time, grow to be the greatest in the world.

. . . The mathematician, Euclid, a native of Alexandria, will use and work at the library, and found there the first school of mathematics. Called the Father of Geometry, his textbook will be used until early in the 20th century A.D. and will be the basis for all geometry. Ptolemy once complained to Euclid that he wished there were an easier way to learn geometry, to which Euclid replied:

> There is no royal road to geometry.　　Euclid

Ptolemy also builds a vast, important museum (so-called from the inspiring Muses of Greek poetry) in Alexandria, which holds, among thousands of exhibits, many artifacts from Alexander's campaigns, including his great, golden coffin.

. . . One hundred years in the building, a magnificent Temple of Diana, or Artemis, is completed at Ephesus on the Aegean seacoast of modern-day Turkey, the fifth of the Seven Wonders of the Ancient World. Four times larger than Athens' Parthenon and covering two acres of ground, its hundred marble columns tower 67 feet high, and in it stands the gigantic monument to fertility, the graven, many-breasted goddess Artemis. Filled with marvelous treasures and wealth, it will still be very much in use when Saint Paul comes to preach Christianity to the Ephesians 375 years from now. (See: A.D. 52) From this time to that the silversmiths of Ephesus will reap great fortunes selling copies of the goddess and her temple worldwide, and they will demonstrate against Paul for the threat his God is to their business. To this day Ephesus is a much visited site of antiquity, although little of the "Artemision" remains. (More can be found in the British Museum, London.)

322　　Having fled Athens to escape a fate like that of Socrates, Aristotle dies one year after his greatest pupil, Alexander. A man of the world, equally at home in royal court or rural court-yard, he was a man of deep humanity as well, and provided in his will for everyone from family to slaves . . . whom he freed. Although Aristotle, himself, would have deplored it, not for 1800 years will his authority be challenged. He will be so revered in the years ahead that in the 12th century A.D., the Dominican monk-philosopher (Saint) Thomas Aquinas will refer to him simply as "the Philosopher."

. . . Alexander's withdrawal from India left a void in leadership there, also, that now is eagerly filled by Chandragupta Maurya, beginning a Mauryan dynasty of splendor and opulence. A man of many contradictions, Chandragupta maintains an army of three-quarters of a million men and some 3000 elephants, a tightly controlled bureaucracy, and a vast, highly sophisticated—and ruthless—spy network to ensure the stability of the empire . . . and his own safety. His public appearances are occasions of oriental pomp and glory; vivid, lavish collages of drums, bells and gongs, brilliant colors, gold and pearls adorning every-thing from emperor to elephants, dancing girls, parrots and peacocks. But he also works "tirelessly and unceasingly" for the well-being of his people, believing that a king's happi-ness lies in his people's happiness, and his welfare in theirs. Twenty-four years from now Chandragupta will abdicate his throne, enter a Jain monastery and, seeking Jainism's "supreme good," fast himself to death.

320   Ptolemy of Egypt raids Judea and captures Jerusalem. He will hold it nine years and transfer it back to Syria in 311.

. . . A Greek explorer named Pytheas sails the Atlantic coast to northwestern Europe where no Mediterranean man has been before. He sails from the Greek colony at what is today Marseilles, France, around Spain, up the Bay of Biscay, along the east coast of Britain past the Orkney and Shetland Islands. An expert astronomer, he is the first to fix latitudes, and the first explorer to near the Artic Circle. The British Celts tell him of a distant land "six days journey" north called Thule, or *Ultima Thule*, either Iceland or Norway. There he learns the secrets of the Artic lands; of long nights that never end; how the moon affects the tides; and how frozen water can crush the hull of a boat. Returning home he sails the northern coast of Europe, then walks the entire circumference of Britain, estimating its size at 40,000 *stadia*, or 4000 miles. There are those who doubt Pytheas' stories on his return.

c. 317   The writing of the books of the *APOCRYPHA* begins with, the LETTER OF JE-REMIAH.

The LETTER OF JEREMIAH

Apocryphal Book — Written in Hebrew,   c. 317 B.C.

A short book of only 73 verses, portions of which still exist, the LETTER OF JERE-MIAH claims to be a copy of a letter the ancient prophet sent to "those who were to be taken to Babylon as captive." It is a rambling discourse against false gods and graven idols ". . . made of wood and gold, decked out in the clothes of men. Do not succumb to them," he warns, "they can do nothing for themselves, so how can they help you?"

---

312   In several volcanic areas of Italy (near Rome, Naples and a little town near Naples called Pozzolani) can be found rich deposits of volcanic ash called pozzolana; and Roman technology has by now learned that mixing this ash with limestone produces a cement that will harden under water. This, and an equally important discovery of building a curved arch capped by a keystone (replacing the vertical/horizontal post-and-lintel construction of the past) now begins, for Rome, its incredible period of expansion. For now, a Roman patri-cian/politician/consul/dictator/censor . . . and builder, named Appius Claudius Caecus, be-gins the construction of two most important building projects . . . a road and an aqueduct.

Using the newly perfected pozzolana cement and the curved arch, Appius' aqueduct and highway arches straddle mountains and valleys, rivers and swamps. The 10 mile aqueduct is only the first that Rome will build in its long history; and within the next several hundred years the city will be supplied with over a hundred-million gallons of fresh mountain water every day. The first stretch of Appius' highway, 132 miles from Rome to Capua, is set on a base of crushed stone in concrete, then a layer of flat rocks cemented together, topped with fitted lava paving stones edged with cement curbsides and bordered by drainage ditches. It is a road meant to last . . . forever. Eventually it will extend 234 miles more to Brundisium, Rome's princi-

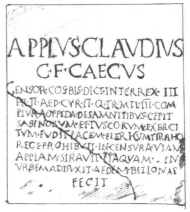

Plaque to Appius Claudius

pal seaport to the far east. Every mile along the way is marked by a marble columned milestone engraved with the bold letters *SPQR—SENATUS POPULUSQUE ROMANUS,* THE SENATE AND THE PEOPLE OF ROME. Appius takes the unprecedented step of naming both the aqueduct and the highway for himself, calling the road the *VIA APPIA,* or the APPIAN WAY. The most famous of Rome's highways, it will even be mentioned in the Bible, traveled by the man called Paul . . . from Tarsus.

. . . and so we went toward Rome. And from thence, when the brethren heard of us, they came to meet us as far as Appii forum [the forum on the Appian Way] . . . and The Three Taverns: whom when Paul saw, he thanked God, and took courage.   ACTS 28:14,15

The curved arch introduces Rome to a whole new world of architectural and engineering possibilities: vaulting, barrel vaulting, procenium arches, domes and arcades, that will build everything from monuments, mausoleums and monasteries to cathedrals and theater stages. Rome's arch-supported roads and aqueducts will someday be found all over the Roman world: from Spain to Romania and Britain to Africa, 50,000 miles of super-highways. The Old Silk Road will follow the path of Alexander and connect Rome with China; and the *Via Saleria,* for the transportation of salt, is still in use today.

311   Control of Judea is transferred from Egypt's Ptolemy to Syria's Seleucas, who intends to unify his multi-cultured kingdom with the Greek *ethos*. So he builds Greek style open-air theaters and elaborate *gymnasia* in which will be performed Greek dramas and public oration; physical and military education and training. But nudity in the *gymnasium,* and the worship of Greek gods is mandatory with these "benefits," and while some Jews welcome the new ways, many others have cause to fear.

310   In North Africa, Carthage wins a military victory over Greek forces, and sacrifices are made to Baal-Amon for having "saved the city." Centuries ago Baal worship was brought to Carthage by Phoenecians: (Queen Dido, herself, accompanied by 80 cult prostitutes to ensure the perpetuation of the race.) It flourishes there, still, a gigantic, bronze statue of Baal-Amon dominating his fantastic temple, fashioned as an old man with ram's horns, a sythe at his side, and arms folded as though holding a child. Now, for this occasion, with worshippers whipped into a frenzied orgy and mothers forced to watch without showing emotion, priests place infants—500 of them, one by one—into Baal's bronze hands, where they remain, just a second . . . before slipping down into a blazing fiery furnace.

305   Seleucus is crowned king of Babylonia/Persia, beginning a powerful, long-lived—and, for the Jews, ill-fated—SELEUCID Dynasty. And Ptolemy is crowned king of Egypt, the first pharaoh in the Greek *Ptolemaic* Dynasty, which will last for 300 years, until the death of its last and most famous queen, Cleopatra.

301   Now Ptolemy retakes control of Judea, and the Jews are, once again under the yoke of Egypt. But Ptolemy is not a pharaoh of ages past, intent on destroying their religion or forcing another on them. In fact, Greek/Egyptian rule is benign and quite tolerant and, while the great majority of Jews do retain their religious heritage, thousands of others migrate TO Alexandria, which is fast becoming the world center of intellectual, cosmopolitan Hellenism, more so by far than Athens, itself. Some scholars think that if this period of benevolent leniency had lasted, or if Alexander had lived many years and his influence had remained as pervasive, the Jews may have gradually become even more "Hellenistic" and less "Jewish."

. . . By the turn of the century, the cities of Rome and Carthage have become the West's two major powers. Carthage has geared up its war machine to perfect precision. Expansion to the south is impossible, for below it lies only the vast nothingness of the Sahara Desert; but, above it to the north, it sees rich reward. Because its ambition is as great as Rome's the two are set, now, upon a collision course.

300   Once again culture and progress, expansion and . . . war . . . vie for a century . . .

. . . Silver coins are being struck in Greece honoring Alexander the Great: *drachmas* and *tetradrachmas.*

. . . a Greek teacher named Epicurus founds an "Epicurean" school of philosophy in Athens, where he ponders the meaning of pleasure and pain, good and evil. Pleasure should be the main goal in life, he teaches, but pleasure of the mind, not the body; the lasting pleasure of morality, moderation, temperance, serenity and cultural refinement, not the temporary pleasure of excess and debauchery. What good is temporary pleasure if the end result is pain? We should eat well, live well, seek pleasant sensations, but in moderation, for over-indulgence can only lead to dissipation, and debauchery to grief. Epicurus is worshipped by his followers as the founder of an "Olympian" religion for he teaches that, although the Olympian gods are interested in governing neither the world nor man's affairs, a wise man can share in their divinity through the Epicurean ethos. In the future, some who follow Epicurus—who said, "It is not possible to live pleasantly without living wisely and right-eously" will forget that maxim and mistake hedonism for happiness, licentiousness for the good life, and gluttony for good taste so that, even to this day, we still use his name to speak of the abundance of an "Epicurean feast."

One of Epicurus' contemporaries, and perhaps acquaintances, is a handsome ladies man-about-town and successful poet named Menander, who has created a new form of the-ater . . . a "new comedy." Unlike Aristophanes' zany "old comedy," which used chorus and dance to lampoon current events, politicians and "celebrities," Menander's works could al-most be considered the forerunner of todays "situation comedies." In their more "sophis-ticated" plots are found stereotypes we recognize to this day: the giddy female and sweet young thing, the foppish dandy and the macho lover, the rich old miser and scheming fa-ther, milk-toast husband and harpie wife, the frustrated love affair and the long-lost off-spring who shows up at just the right moment. Menander maintains that "whom the gods love dies young." He "calls a spade a spade," marriage a "necessary evil," and says rather than "know thyself," we might better "know other people." Three hundred fifty-five years from now a man named Paul, from Tarsus in Asia minor, will write a letter to his Christ-ian converts in Corinth, and quote Menander as saying . . .

> Be not deceived: Bad company ruins good morals.   Menander.
>
> Saint Paul's first letter to the CORINTHIANS   15:33

On the other side of the world the Mayan Indian peoples are flourishing in Central America, influenced by the Olmec. They will continue, now, for many years, a vividly col-orful people much given to rituals, ceremonies and human sacrifice.

285   Succeeding his father's 38 year reign, Ptolemy II becomes Egypt's pharaoh, and for the next 45 years will maintain a court so intellectually brilliant and accompol-ished, so sumptuous and splendid . . . and so artificial, profligate and dissolute, it will be recalled in comparison almost 2000 years hence to that of Louis XIV at Ver-sailles before the French Revolution.

Ptolemy II

280   On the north side of the market place in Athens, there is a painted porch, a *stoa poikile*, that is used as a teaching forum by a Phoenecian philosopher named Zeno, from Citium on the island of Cyprus. Zeno came to Athens 34 years ago, becoming shipwrecked enroute, and losing every possession he had in the world. But Zeno was not devastated by the event, for he believes that it is man's duty to accept "stoically" whatever comes, good or bad, whether hardship, pain, poverty, persecution or death; for there is a *logos*, a reason, "word" or "cause" for everything. The world is not just a mindless machine with no purpose, he now teaches; there is a "divine

intelligence" that governs it and guides it, and that divine intelligence is one supreme God of boundless power and goodness. If man will simply understand and accept the will of God strongly, calmly and unmoved, he will find true happiness and peace, freedom from want and fear, and in perfect harmony with the will of God. Zeno's—Stoic—philosophy (or religion?) is named for the place where he teaches it; that painted porch or, *stoa*.

Almost 300 years ago a Cretan philosopher named Epimenides said, about God, "In him we live and move and have our being." Now Zeno enlarges on that idea. God is the Law of the world, he says, its ruler and up holder. He is not to be found or worshipped in temples or shrines made by man's hands, but in the shrine of the heart. Four hundred twenty-five years from now, one Paul of Tarsus will bring a new religion to Athens, and preach the Resurrection of Jesus Christ to the Epicureans and Stoics of his day on Mars Hill. His Christian "theology" will echo the thoughts of Epimenides and Zeno.

> . . . the Lord dwelleth not in temples made with hands: [for] he be not far from every one of us: "For in him we live, and move, and have our being," as certain also of your own poets have said, "For we are indeed his offspring."   Paul of Tarsus in ACTS 17:24, 27, 28

The Stoic philosophy will compete, now, with the Epicurean, the Cynic and with Greece's traditional mythologies. But the Greeks have been taught, for over a hundred years to consider life as did Socrates, Plato and Aristotle, questioning that, "While this or that MAY be true, then again it may NOT be." Not until Stoicism is carried to the earnest, practical, no-nonsense Romans will it flourish and find widespread acceptance. Even today, the Stoic virtue can be found in such creeds as this Serenity Prayer:

> God grant me the courage to change the things that can be changed,
> the strength to bear those which cannot,
> and the wisdom to know one from the other.

280   Chandragupta's son, Bindusara, rules India now, and, curious about the west, writes to Seleucus of Syria that he would like to sample some "Greek raisins, wine . . . and a Sophist." Seleucus sends him the food and drink "with pleasure," but adds that . . .

> . . . Greeks do not consider it good form . . . to trade in philosophers.

279   Most of the Italian peninsula is still independent from the city of Rome, its several states always squabbling and warring; the Sabines, Samnites, Umbrians, Campanians, the northern Gauls and that area in the "foot" of the Italian "boot" called Magna Graecia, where there are large colonies of Greeks. One Greek city appeals to Alexander the Great's second cousin, Pyrrhus, King of Epirus (in northern Greece, next to Macedonia) for help against the Romans; and Pyrrhus, adventurer and lover of war, is only too happy to respond. In 280 he sent 25,000 men and 20 elephants (which terrified the unsuspecting Romans) and won a major victory over Rome . . . but at tremendous loss to his own forces. Now, a year later, he wins another "Pyrrhic victory" over Rome . . . again suffering tremendous losses, and ruefully he comments.

> Another such victory and I am lost.
>
> Pyrrhus of Epirus, after the battle of Asculum

If Pyrrhus had had more help from the Greek cities of Magna Graecia, he may have nipped the rise of Rome in the bud, but now his "victorious defeats" leave Rome—almost—undisputed master of Italy.

264—241   Rome and Carthage now begin their long struggle for dominance. Meeting at Messina, Sicily, for a parley, the Roman commander seizes the Cartheginian, gaining the island . . . and a declaration of war. Most of it is fought at sea; naturally and logically for Carthage, built as a seaport, owing its very existence to the sea. But it is not natural for Rome, and 100,000 Roman soldiers—trained for land war—are lost just to storms alone. But the Roman character is indelibly marked by a "stoic" self-discipline, undaunted courage, tenacity, patriotism and a unique capacity for learning from others and from their own mistakes, of incorporating the best of other cultures into their own. whether in peace or war. The first PUNIC WAR now drags on for 23 years, the first of three wars . . . all of which Rome will win.

But something else lies behind the much-vaunted Roman courage; an ingrained, often primitive and even savage, cruel streak that, over the years, will manifest itself in many ways. Now, the first contest of gladiators to be recorded takes place to commemorate the funeral of a Roman nobleman. The "sport" (which the Romans learned from the Etruscans) will grow in popularity to the point where 2000 men will be killed in an 100-day "entertainment" during the reign of the Emperor Trajan in 100 A.D

250   No more are millennia or centuries the turning points of history . . . but decades . . .

. . . Chandragupta's grandson, Asoka, rules India now, a ruler unique among rulers. Eight years into his reign, with extreme violence and bloodshed, he conquered an area called Kalinga, on the Bay of Bengal. Now, horrified by the suffering he had caused—100,000 slain, 150,000 captives—he accepts the Buddhist faith; forswears any form of war or violence (including that to animals, ending the great big-game hunts the Indians love so well) and sets about ruling India with love, benevolence, humanity, charity and religious toleration. His missionary zeal for Buddhism will make it one of the world's major religions, and liken him, by some, to the Christian St. Paul. His "sacred and gracious majesty" Asoka diligently practices what he preaches:

> . . . to follow righteousness, to love [it] . . . and to give instruction in righteousness. If anyone does him wrong it will be forgiven . . .   Asoka Maurya, Ruler of India

During Asoka's reign, the Hindu holy books, the *Mahabharata* and the *Ramayana* are written, in India, having been passed down orally for many generations. They tell their tales of faith on a background of adventure and suspense.

. . . The *Laokoön* is carved on the island of Rhodes, an amazing statue of a man and his two sons entwined in a monumental death struggle with sea serpents; punishment, so the people of ancient Troy thought, for his (Laokoön's) having warned them that the great wooden horse left outside their city gates by the Greeks was a trap. The incredibly complex eight-foot high reminder of the Trojan War stands today in the Vatican Museum, Rome.

. . . The last two of the Seven Wonders of the Ancient World are attracting visitors from the world over, having been completed at about 275.

Coin of Ptolemy II

To thank Ptolemy of Egypt for having helped them win a victory, the people of the island of Rhodes commission the famous sculptor, Charis, to create a monument, a *Colossus of Rhodes*. Charis casts his "colossal" bronze statue of the sun god, Helios, bestriding the harbor 110 feet tall on 50 foot marble bases. It will stand only 56 years and be leveled by an earthquake in 224 B.C., but even in that time will be seen by thousands of sight-seeing world travelers.

The Seventh Wonder, the Lighthouse of Alexandria, is built on the island of Pharos, far out in the harbor of Alexandria, Egypt, another Ptolemaic achievement; begun by the first Ptolemy, completed by the second. Four hundred feet tall, it is the tallest lighthouse ever built. At its peak, a huge fire blazes day and night, backed by a gigantic rotating mirror to reflect the beacon light 20 miles out to sea. Hundreds of rooms in its foundation are used for storehouses and as a barracks for troops. The lighthouse will stand—and be used—for 1500 years until it, too, is leveled by an earthquake. Archeologists, today, believe they have found its sunken ruins.

The Lighthouse of Alexandria

The second Ptolemy of Egypt is not only a builder, but a scholar and patron of the arts and science; and Alexandria flourishes under his rule. Completing the lighthouse, he enlarges and enriches the great library, seeking out learned men to work and study there. One such is the Greek scholar, Archimedes, who will be remembered as the "Father of Experimental Science." He invents the lever, pulley and catapult; and his "Archimedian screw" is used by some to this day to raise liquid from a lower level to a higher. Working with gravity and the lever, Archimedes comments, "Give me a place to stand, and I will move the earth." The answer to a perverse puzzle about the displacement of water comes to Archimedes at the public bath when he steps into a tub . . . and it overflows. Up he bounds, forgetting to dress, and races joyously home, excitedly shouting:

> *Eureka!*—I have found it!

250   Another subject is being pursued at the Library . . . religion; in particular, the Jewish belief in ONE GOD. Three hundred years from now a Jewish historian named Joseph Ben Matthias, or Josephus (See: A.D. 64) will write a monumental history of the Jewish people called ANTIQUITIES OF THE JEWS. He will tell a fascinating story of how the Jewish LAW, or TORAH, (GENESIS, EXODUS, LEVITICUS, NUMBERS and DEUTERONOMY)

came to be translated into Greek and find a permanent home—and much honor—at a Greek library in Egypt. The work will be done by seventy *(septua)* Greek/Hebrew scholars, and called . . .

The SEPTUAGINT

The story, according to Josephus: ANTIQUITIES OF THE JEWS Book 12, Chapter 2

". . . when once Ptolemy asked (his library keeper) how many ten thousands of books he had collected, he replied, that he already had about 10 times 10,000; but that, in a little time, he should have 50 times 10,000. But he said he had been informed that there were many books of laws among the Jews worthy of inquiring after, and worthy of the king's library, but which, being written in characters and in a dialect of their own, will cause no small pains in getting them translated into . . . Greek . . . and Ptolemy wrote: 'King Ptolemy to Eleazar the high priest, sendeth greeting . . . as I am desirous to do [good to all Jews] I have determined to procure the interpretation of your law, and to have it translated out of Hebrew into Greek . . . to be deposited in my library . . . Thou wilt therefore choose out and send to me men of a good character, who are now elders in age, and six in number from every tribe. These, by their age, must be skillful in the laws, and of abilities to make an accurate interpretation of them.' "

Eleazar replies: "When we received thy epistle, we rejoiced greatly at your intentions. We have chosen six elders out of every tribe . . . and [have sent] the law with them . . ." When the 70 elders, all highly skilled in the law, arrive at the library, Ptolemy finds the books written in gold . . . on parchment scrolls so finely made even the seams could not be seen; and Josephus continues: ". . . when they were come to Jerusalem [with] the laws . . . [which were] written in golden letters . . . when they had taken off the covers wherein they were wrapped up . . . the king stood admiring [them] and [gave] thanks for coming to him . . . and still greater thanks . . . to that God whose laws they appeared to be. Then did the elders . . . cry out with one voice, and wished all happiness to the king. Upon which he fell into tears by the violence of the pleasure he had."

Ptolemy had gone to "very great expense" to make a proper—and magnificent—work place for the translators, and now comes himself to watch the work progress. In only 72 days the work is finished—with not a single major difference amongst them; and the law is read to Ptolemy, who is ". . . astonished at its greatness and the wisdom of the law-giver; wondering why it is that he has never been told of it before . . . then the priests and . . . elders . . . [recommended that] since the interpretation was happily finished it might continue in the state it now was, and might not be altered . . . that when [it] was judged to have been well done, it might continue forever."

In future years all the rest of the Hebrew scripture (the "Old" Testament), including the Apocrypha, will be translated and included in the *SEPTUAGINT,* and will become an important addition to the Alexandrian library. Copies of the *SEPTUAGINT* are still in existence in museums in Rome and the British Museum, London.

The great hunger for beauty, books and learning in the Hellenistic Age produces thousands of writers turning out works on many subjects: biographies, science, music, romance, everything. In ages past Greek life (for men) had centered, not around home and family, but around the *polis*, the community group for which Greeks worked, were proud of, and made beautiful. Now, under Hellenism, the *self* comes before the *polis*, personal achievement and enrichment more than community; and books and learning are the essential foundations for, not just an elite few, but for all. Schools of all sorts flourish and the *Cynics, Stoics*, the *Skeptics* and the *Epicureans* are all teaching values that we still recognize by their attributes: cynical, stoical, skeptical and epicurean.

The Phenomena of Aratus of Soli at the British Museum, London

. . . In Cilicia, Asia Minor (Turkey) Aratus of Soli writes a long poem called the *Phenomena*, one copy of which translated by Cicero, can be seen today in London's British Museum. The *Phenomena* is well admired and Aratus is much honored for it, especially in the royal courts of Macedonia and Syria. Three hundred years from now, Paul of Tarsus will quote from the opening lines while preaching Christianity to the Greeks in Athens. About God he will say:

> For we are indeed His offspring.   ACTS 17:28 (See; A.D. 51)

241, March 10.   A great naval battle off Aegates gives Rome control of the sea. Rome's military forte had been, mostly, that of a land-based army; but it has learned much about sea power during the first Punic War. Now, rejecting the long, narrow, high-speed battering-ram *triremes* and *quinquiremes* of Greece and Carthage, Rome builds battleships, huge galleys with grappling-hook gangways over which marines—more than a hundred per ship—charge the decks of the luckless enemy. Aegates makes Rome master of the Mediterranean, gives it the strategic islands of Sicily and (in 235) Sardinia, and ends the first Punic War.

240   Ptolemy III succeeds to the Egyptian throne and invites Eretosthanes of Cyrene to come to Alexandria and become superintendent of the Library. Mathematician, astronomer and geographer, Eretosthanes has written the first scientific treatise on geography. He knows the world is a sphere, and proves it by calculating its circumference to within just a few hundred miles; he knows the almost exact distance to the sun, and creates a map of the world complete with the lines of latitude and longitude. His contemporary Alexandrian, Aristarchus, believes that the earth orbits around the sun while rotating on an "axis." His calculation of a solar year will prove to be only five minutes off, and of the lunar month . . . one second!

. . . In China, astronomical observations are being recorded of eclipses and comets (including that which we know today as Halley's). Their mathematicians are using decimals and zeroes, and are familiar with the teachings, and musical scale, of the Greek philosopher, Pythagoras.

232   The Mauryan Dynasty collapses in India, less than 50 years after the death of the remarkable Asoka. His pacifistic, non-assertive policies have drained from the government, army and people their spirit, vigor and will to defend themselves from without or govern themselves from within, and left them prey to destruction. India's next period of greatness will not come for another 400 years.

226   Vast numbers of barbarian Gauls (from modern-day France) migrate southward over the Alps into Italy, looting and plundering the country-side and terrorizing the Italian people. They are ferocious fighters and the Romans have good cause to fear.

221   The Egyptians have enjoyed great prosperity under the Ptolemies, especially the intellectual Ptolemy III, whose reign was the high point of the dynasty and of Egypt's well-being. Now his son, Ptolemy IV rules, a miserable debauchee who begins his reign by murdering his mother, then wallows in every kind of vice and orgiastic religion, and allows himself to be manipulated by his mistresses, his male "favorites" and his sister/wife. And the magnificence of the royal court at Alexandria is brought low by unscrupulous wantons.

220   Once again, the world becomes one big battlefield, as . . .

. . . Gauls from Europe invade Thrace, Macedonia and an area of Asia Minor that will in future bear their "Gallic" name . . . Galatia. The Galatians will someday be visited by, and later receive a letter from, a man named Paul . . . of Tarsus.

. . . Judea takes the brunt again, as Syria moves down to battle the Egyptians on Jewish soil. Ill at ease, the Jews watch the machinations, intrigues and trade-offs between the neighboring powers. Some favor Egypt, some Syria. Under both they have had some good times . . . and bad. Although little is known about this period, it is thought not to have been too harsh for the Jews.

. . . With the marauding Gauls roving unchecked through northern Italy, Rome struggles to repel them and, now, takes the city of Milan with much bloodshed . . . and statuary carved at this time reflects the suffering and death that results. Today galleries in Rome show a defiant *Gallic Chieftan* escaping capture, gently easing his slain wife to the ground, sword point to his own chest; and a *Dying Trumpeter* sinking slowly to the ground in his own last agony.

. . . In China, Shih Huang Ti has waged war for years against the feudal lords and now becomes the first Emperor of China, a name derived from the dynasty he has begun—the Ch'in. His empire is put together with force, cruelty, destruction, and massive book burning, to wipe out memory of other times and ways. But Shih Huang Ti is a builder, also, and his handiwork stands to this day, a monument designed

The Great Wall of China

Soldier from
Shih Huang Ti's
underground army

to keep out the fierce hordes of invading Huns and Mongols—the Great Wall of China. A Chinese saying maintains that for every stone in the wall, a laborer died. Now the emperor decides he will need military protection after death, as well as before. So, instead of burying an army alive with him, he commands an army be built that will last forever; and 700,000 conscripts labor three decades to build it. Seven thousand life-size soldiers and horses are individually crafted of pottery and set up in military formation in a fantastic three-acre underground maze. Standing at the ready, they are discovered close to the Ch'in's burial mound in A.D. 1947, one of the most unusual archeological finds in history.

217   Weakened and demoralized by six long years of Gallic occupation and devastation, the Romans now hope for a period of respite . . . that does not come; for Hamilcar Barca, (meaning "Thunderbolt") the Carthaginian general of the First Punic War, had, before his death, caused his three "lion's whelps"—his sons, Hannibal, Hasdrubal and Mago, to swear an oath of eternal hatred against Rome and to bring about its destruction. Now Hannibal, 26, takes command of his father's forces in Spain, crosses the Pyranees into Gaul, then slowly, inconspicuously, so as not to alert the Romans, leads his incredible war machine—60,000 troops, 6000 horses and 37 African elephants—over the Alps, into Italy! It is a feat worthy of Alexander . . . but dreadful in its losses. According to a first-century A.D. Roman historian, Titus Livius, or Livy:

. . . they [suffered] a great loss both of men and baggage of every description . . . as the pass . . . was broken and precipitous . . . to an immense depth . . . the beasts of burden, with their loads, rolled down like the fall of some vast fabric . . . Hannibal . . . ordered the soldiers to halt on a certain eminence, whence there was a prospect far and wide [and] pointed out to them [the green plains of Italy below . . . which they should soon have in their] possession. [But] the [descent] proved [even] more difficult . . . being steeper . . . narrow and slippery . . . so that those who made the least stumble . . . rolled, both men and beasts of burden, one upon another . . . the beasts nearly perishing through hunger; for the summit of the mountains are . . . bare, and if there is any pasture the snows bury it . . .   Titus Livius, or Livy, HISTORY OF ROME, Book XXI

Carthaginian coin commemorating
Hannibal's crossing the Alps

For the next 10 years, Hannibal has almost free reign over all Italy, traversing the peninsula, trying—in vain—to convince city after city that he is there, not to conquer, but to "liberate" them from Rome. After a major battle at Cannae, where, by a brilliant ruse, Hannibal lured the Romans into open conflict, slaying 50,000, they refuse to take his bait again and, instead, merely watch his every move. But Hannibal's armies are mostly hired mercenaries, Spaniards, Celts and Gauls from Europe, Numidians from Africa and Corsicans, and are as treacherous to him as to the Romans; while Rome's strength, even when wounded and weary, lays in its indomitable patriotism and talent for fighting best in the worst of times. Knowing how badly crippled the army is, the Roman people mobilize; old men, women and children bring food and supplies, and wagons to haul away the wounded.

Now, even though Hannibal occupies Italy, Rome sends a young patrician, Publius Cornelius Scipio, to Spain to restore order in the ranks there and to retake Spain from Carthage, which he does spectacularly, enhancing an already glowing reputation earned in earlier campaigns. The handsome and aristocratic Scipio is a model officer, admired by his troops for his eloquence, skill, bravery and justice.

207   Hannibal's brother, Hasdrubal, leads his army—almost the size of Hannibal's—from Spain south into Italy, quietly and stealthily, through Gaul and over the Alps, just as his brother did, but with more skill and less loss . . . and Rome is surrounded by Carthaginians: Hannibal in the south, Hasdrubal in the north, only 200 miles apart. The Romans are petrified with fear and terror. Rome is in mortal danger of extinction, and Europe of going into history a mere possession of Baal-worshipping, child-sacrificing African Carthage.

The Roman consul/general commanding the armies facing Hannibal, Caius Claudius Nero (Claudian ancestor of a future Nero) intercepts a message from Hasdrubal stating where the two brothers should meet. Two hundred forty-four years before this, in 451, the Law of Twelve Tables was drawn up forbidding, on penalty of death, a Roman commander from marching beyond the boundaries assigned him by the Senate; but Nero cannot wait for formalities now, so sends the Senate a message saying, in effect, "I am doing this. Now you approve it," and immediately begins a fast march north. He quarters his men, under cover of night, in the tents of troops already stationed near the river Matauro, facing Hasdrubal, who suspects nothing. Not until Hasdrubal personally reconnoiters the Roman lines in the morning and sees great hordes of soldiers where the day before there had been few, does he realize how badly he is outnumbered. He retreats, and Nero follows, backing the Carthaginians into the river. Mataurus is another of the most decisive battles in history; Hasdrubal is slain, his forces utterly defeated and his head is flung into Hannibal's camp. Rome is saved; Hannibal returns to Carthage. He had fought 15 years and never lost a battle . . .

> You know, Hannibal, how to gain a victory, but not how to use it.   Plutarch, LIVES OF THE NOBLE GREEKS AND ROMANS

202   Hannibal's only defeat comes on the African battlefield of Zama, where he and Scipio meet face to face for the first— and last—time. Capturing some of Hannibals spies, Scipio has his tribunes show them all about the Roman camp, whatever they want to see, then sends them back to Hannibal, an act of audacious bravado calculated to inspire fear and trembling into the Carthaginians . . . which it does. Scipio and Hannibal . . .

Hannibal

> . . . met [on the field], each attended by one interpreter, being the greatest generals not only of their own times, but of any to be found. When they came within sight of each other they remained silent for a time, thunderstruck, as it were, with mutual admiration.
> Livy, HISTORY OF ROME, Book XXX

But their talks do no good, their words, Livy says ". . . bandied to no purpose," and they return to tell their soldiers that:

> Before tomorrow night . . . they would know whether Rome or Carthage should give laws to the world, and that neither Africa nor Italy, but the whole world, would be the prize of victory . . . and not for a single day, but forever . . . *ibid.*

Thus, says Livy, two generals, "by far the most renowned of any . . . belonging to . . . the most powerful nations in the world, advanced either to crown or overthrow, on that day, the many honors they had previously acquired." The battle is huge, and bloody. Scipio's victory gains for him the title, *Africanus Major*. Hannibal returns to Carthage to . . .

> . . . [confess] in the senate house that he was defeated, not only in the battle, but in the war, and that there was no hope of safety in anything but obtaining peace. *ibid.*

The victory at Zama ends the Punic Wars and opens a whole new age, as Rome breathes a great sigh of relief. Bloodied and battered, thousands of its best young men sacrificed, it begins to see the world in a different light, what it has to offer, how much and from whence. And so . . .

. . . The sleeping giant, Rome, comes wide awake, now . . . and is hungry. As it looks about, it sees vast lands on all sides, rich with all manner of good things, there just for the taking; fertile farmland and virgin forests in Gaul (France) and *Germania* (Germany), great fields of grain to the south in Egypt, citrus groves and vineyards in *Achia* (Greece) and *Hispania* (Spain) and beds of salt in *Germania*. Greece and Italy have marble that will make Rome beautiful, and Spain and Africa have gold and silver to make it rich. Beautiful amber will come from far northern Prussia, copper from Cyprus; gems, spices and drugs from Ceylon; mercenary soldiers from the Balearic Islands, and slaves from . . . everywhere. Oil from the near east will light Rome's lamps and torches, copper from Armenia will arm its soldiers, and ivory, perfumes and spices from Persia will charm its women. Iron from nearby *Dalmatia* (Yugoslavia) and tin in far-away *Brittania* will make it strong; art works and philosophy from Greece will enlighten its better nature; and, to entertain its worse, Africa will ship thousands of wild animals. And because Rome is lusting after all these good things it mints a new coin, the *denarius,* expands its great network of roads and builds up its merchant and military fleets that, already, sail galleys with 200 oars. But Rome will not

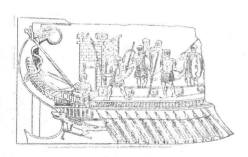

Roman Ship

trade for these things, or buy them; it will plunder and loot, and simply claim them as its rightful due; and immense fortunes await those who will be sent out to govern.

201   Having taken possession of Sicily and Sardinia after the First Punic War, Rome now annexes the next of its many prizes, that formerly had been held by Carthage: *Hispania*— Spain, with its vast gold and mineral deposits . . . and Rome's rape of the world begins.

. . . Despite their seeming natural severity, many Romans have a quick sense of humor. In his LIVES OF THE NOBLE GREEKS AND ROMANS, the historian, Plutarch, records several incidents:

> . . . a Roman divorced from his wife, being highly blamed by his friends who demanded, "Was she not chaste? Was she not fair? Was she not fruitful?" Holding out his shoe asked of them whether it was not new and well made. "Yet," added he, "none of you can tell where it pinches ." * Once Antigonus was told his son was ill, and went in to see him. At the door he met some young beauty. Going in, he sat down by the bed and took his pulse. "The fever," said Demetrius, "has just left me." "Oh, yes," replied the father, "I met it going out the door."   Plutarch, LIVES OF THE NOBLE GREEKS AND ROMANS

A former flour-mill worker named Titus Maccius Plautus is also recording the feats and foibles of the early Romans. His comedies are full of zany situations, mistaken identities and colorful characters: shrewish wives and hen-pecked husbands, innocent young things and rakes, swindlers and spongers. Sometimes coarse and rustic, many are also, in the words of Cicero, "*elegans, urbanus, ingeniosus* and *facetus*," or, "elegant, urbane, ingenious and facetious." But they are not bawdy; Republican Rome is still highly principled and clean moraled. Besides, Rome's *censors* would not allow bawdy plays to be produced;

they would close down the theaters. Plautus' plays are not produced in enormous carved, hillside *theatrons* like Greece's, but on makeshift wooden stages with painted facades and backdrops. Plautus borrows freely for plots from the ancient Greek writers, and will himself, be borrowed from in future, by such latter-day writers as Ben Jonson and William Shakespeare. Plautus will even find his way to Broadway and Hollywood when, someday, they re-tell how a "funny thing happened on the way to the Forum."

Tragedy and comedy

> Nothing is there more friendly to a man than a friend in need.   Plautus, *Epidicus*

But, if Rome hasn't fully learned the lessons of lust yet, it is learning—fast. Greece's Hellenism offers culture, art, sophistication . . . and self-indulgence; and Carthage's Baal-worship offers fertility rites and free-wheeling sex-orgies. The Roman soldiers returning from the Punic Wars have learned to live with violence and loose living, and the games of gladiators are an extension of that. The thousands of Carthaginian prisoners of war in Italy are pressed into slavery on Rome's farms; cheap, or even free, labor, where before there were independent, self-employed small farmers who had to earn a living and pay taxes. Far from the pastoral, provincial people they once were, the Romans are becoming worldly, their contacts with the outside world enormous, and growing, and they are learning to love the luxuries pouring into Italy and into their lives.

200   The next century will see activity of every sort.

. . . The *Winged Victory* is carved at Samothrace, Greece, an exciting statue, unlike the static beauty of olden times. Carved in victorious pose, she stands as though at the prow of a ship, the wind whipping her graceful gown, bird-like wings full-spread. Raised up in our own times from a forgotten grave in the watery depths, she is now without head or arms but is still—in the Louvre, Paris—a moving example of the sculptor's art.

. . . Ctsibius of Alexandria invents a *hydraulis*, the first pipe organ, powered with water, for use in the sports arena . . . so there is music while the gladiators fight.

The Winged Victory

The "Hydraulis"

. . . Since the long ago days of golden Myceneae and the age of Egypt's great pharaohs, the Mediterranean Sea has been infested with fierce pirates, or corsairs, who continue to plunder, terrorize and wreak havoc on commerce, trade and travelers, alike. All attempts to clear the sea of them have been futile . . . so far.

. . . The "bridge" which Judea forms between Syria and Egypt proves, once again, to be a burden, for with the impending threat of a fast-growing Rome hanging above them, the two embroil themselves in conflict, intrigue and war . . . much of it on Jewish soil, But the Syrian rule, under which the Jews find themselves at this time is, for the most part, tolerable. Antiochus III, successor to the Seleucid throne, issues a decree granting the Jews certain privileges which enable them to a "form of government in accordance with the laws of their country."

196   The Egyptian king, Ptolemy V, issues a decree, also, concerning the Egyptian religion, and his decree is carved on a black basalt stone. The date we call 196 B.C. is used in the decree, which is carved three times, in three different languages: Egyptian hieroglyphic, Demotic and Greek. Demotic is a newer, simplified form of writing being used in Egypt, now, replacing the ancient, complicated, pictorial hieroglyphics, which are used, now, only in secret by Egyptian priests. Hieroglyphic writing will soon be completely forgotten, and thousands of years of Egypt's greatness will fall into total silence. Almost 2000 years from now, an officer in Napoleon Bonaparte's French occupation forces will find the stone half submerged in the mud of the Rosetta mouth of the Nile River, and it will be recognized, im-

The Rosetta Stone

mediately, as an object of great value. After many years of study, the silence of centuries will be broken and the long lost language of ancient Egypt will be revealed when the *Rosetta Stone* is translated from Greek to Demotic to hieroglyphic. The 2 x 3 foot Rosetta Stone rests, today, in the British Museum, London.

190   In Pergamum, Asia Minor (already renowned for its beautiful tapestries and pottery) a new product called *parchment* is developed, which will find a very ready market. Up to now the material used for writing including every scroll of the "Old" Testament, was papyrus; but parchment is stronger, more durable and portable, and its use will spread rapidly.

186   Something else spreads rapidly in this year, that the Roman historian, Livy, calls one of Rome's greatest religious scandals, the *Bacchanalian* scandal of 186. "The trouble began," Livy records, "with the arrival . . . of a Greek of humble origin," who dealt, not with highminded Greek culture, but with "sacrifices and soothsaying," and "the mystic cult of Dionysus," god of wine and wantonness, known in Italy as Bacchus. Begun as a secret womans' "ecstasy," or orgiastic *bacchanalia*, conducted by female *Bacchantes*, after the Carthaginian wars, Livy says, men who "bore little resemblance to men" were admitted, also and "this evil, with all its disastrous influence, spread [throughout] Rome like an epidemic." The secret ceremonies are performed at night with gluttonous feasting, drinking and religious rites:

When wine had inflamed their feelings . . . and the mingling of sexes and ages had extinguished all moral judgment, all sorts of corruption were practiced. Not confined to one kind of evil or the promiscuous violation of [its members], the cult also supplied false witnesses, forged documents, perjured evidence, dealt in poisons and wholesale murders . . . and the violence was concealed because no cries for help could be heard against the shrieking . . . drums, cymbals, howlings, bangings, shoutings and [extreme noise that was part of the ceremonies] from frenzied devotees . . .   Livy, ROME AND THE MEDITER-RANEAN, Book 39:8–22 (paraphrased)

A Roman Orgy

The cult is finally exposed and, to make Livy's long story short, an investigation is conducted in the Senate, which outlaws and banishes the religion of Bacchus, not only from Rome, but from all Italy. From this time forward Rome, which had been lenient toward foreign religions, will hold them highly suspect until they have proven their worth.

184   One of Scipio's generals at the battle of Zama, Marcus Porcius Cato, son of an ancient plebian farming family, has risen over the years to high office, including the highest in Rome—Consul, in 195. Now Cato takes on the office of *Censor*. Shocked, scandalized

and sick at heart at the creeping decadence, immorality and corruption rampant in this "new age" he becomes its most outspoken opponent. Everywhere he sees the foundation of a healthy nation, the family, being undermined and degraded . . . much of it by the rising tide of "Greeklings" pouring into Rome with their "philosophy, rhetoric and sophism." A "nation of babblers," he calls the Greeks. He had quarreled bitterly with Scipio at Zama over Scipio's personal extravagance, his lavish distribution of spoils to his army . . . and his liking for (and flaunting of) Greek Hellenism, its "foreign customs and degradations." Called by some "the Last Roman," Cato mourns the decline of Rome's morality, dignity, virtue and honor, its self-discipline, thrift, hard work and moral religion; and now, as censor of public morality, he adopts policies and sets standards so strict and severe he gains more than a few enemies and is called, by his detractors, simply . . . Cato the Censor . . .

> I had rather men should ask why my statue is not set up . . .
> . . . than why it is. Cato the Elder

. . . but, apparently, no regrets . . .

> I regret only three things; having spent a day in idleness; having gone by sea to a place I could have reached by land . . . and having entrusted a secret to my wife. Cato

180   Far away from Rome, the book of ECCLESIASTICUS is written by Jesus ben Sirach, a scribe and teacher in Jerusalem for many years. "To fear the Lord is the beginning of wisdom," he says, and later adds, ruefully, ". . . but to devise proverbs requires painful thinking."

ECCLESIASTICUS, or, THE WISDOM OF JESUS, THE SON OF . . .
SIRACH

Apocryphal Book — Written in Hebrew,   c. 180 B.C.

SIRACH is the only Apocryphal book whose author is known . . . Jesus ben Sirach; a scribe, or teacher of LAW in the Temple. "Draw near to me," he says, "you who are untaught, and lodge in my school." After many years of teaching he now puts his wisdom into print. Almost 50 years hence, Sirach's grandson will translate the text into Greek and write a prologue to the book, which will commend his grandfather's great devotion to learning and the LAW.

"To fear the Lord is the beginning of wisdom," he says, "and in God's time he will give you your reward." So opens and closes Sirach's 51 chapter book. "Deprive not the poor of his living . . . [for] no good will come to the man who persists in evil . . ." Sirach's teachings range from talent to tribulation to table manners; how to act in poverty or prosperity; how to raise children, right or wrong; to be wary of counselors with self-interest, and especially how to maintain regular habits and respectability. He talks of spoiled sons and headstrong daughters, and says that "a good wife is a great blessing," but that he'd rather "dwell with a dragon" than with an evil one. But wisdom first and last; love learning and always seek wisdom. "Accept whatever is brought upon you, and in changes that humble you be patient . . . for even gold is tested in the fire. Forgive your neighbor the wrong he has done, and then your sins will be pardoned when you pray."

. . . Antiochus IV becomes king of the "Syrian" Seleucid empire, a man of much ability . . . and enormous vanity, calling himself *Epiphanes*—God Manifest . . . the "human manifestation" of the king of all the Greek gods, Zeus. Born and reared in Athens, he has a deep, even passionate appreciation for Greek Hellenism and a fanatical ambition to convert his entire kingdom to it. In Palestine, under Antiochus Epiphanes, the Jewish position of High Priest, hereditary for centuries, is sold for bribery to a Hellenistic Jew, and a concerted, vicious effort begins to totally eradicate <u>the religion of the Jews by declaring the Jewish God only a "local manifestation of Zeus."</u>

The head of Zeus on a coin of Antiochus Epiphanes

Antiochus has an elaborate Greek *gymnasium* built in Jerusalem, one of many indignities for the Jews, for, with use of the gymnasium comes the obligation to worship its pagan idols . . . and to bare the body for athletics (*gymnos* meaning, in Greek, naked) something the Greeks have always done, and that the Jews consider immoral. He profanes the Jewish Sabbath; his troops carouse in drunken orgy in the Temple, sacrifice pigs in mockery of Jewish law on the holy altar, tear up and destroy the holy books, and set up a statue of Zeus in the Holy of Holies. It is what the book of DANIEL calls the ABOMINATION OF DESOLATION." According to a soon-to-be-written history called MACCABEES. . .

. . . the king directed them to follow customs strange to the land, to profane the sabbaths and feasts, to defile altars, to make themselves abominable by things unclean and profane. They erected desolating sacrilege upon the altar, tore to pieces and burned the books of LAW; they put to death mothers who had their children circumcised . . . and hung the infants around their necks.   I MACCABEES 1

When conservative Jews rebel, 80,000 are slaughtered and 1800 talents of silver looted from the Temple. Not for centuries has a leader been so needed, and the one who does appear is another "right man at the right time."

167   A Hellenistic Jew is found worshipping a statue of Zeus in the city of Modein, and an enraged Mattathias kills him on the very altar . . . then flees into the hills with his five sons: John, Jonathon, Eleazar, Simon and . . . Judas, called Maccabeus, the HAMMER. "Like a giant Judas Maccabeus put on his breastplate," reads I MACCABEES, "like a roaring lion in his deeds." Claiming strength from Heaven, he urges on his few against many, and ". . . they were crushed before him." His fame spreads widely, even to King Antiochus. Exhorting his troops to . . .

Judas Maccabeus

"... REMEMBER MOSES AND THE RED SEA!!" ...

Judas takes on the heavily armed, highly trained enemy ... and defeats them! Judas' genius lies in guerilla warfare, using his own, and his allies' intimate knowledge of the land, to do by stealth and surprise, what he could never do on open field. I MACCABEES does not even try to list all his "wars, greatness and brave deeds" for, it says, "they were very many." Just once is Judas forced into open conflict and defeated; by 100,000 infantry, 20,000 cavalry, and a secret weapon the Jews had never fought before ... 32 wine-primed war elephants!

162   But Judas prevails and Syria sues for peace with the promise of religious freedom for the Jews; and Jerusalem accepts the terms. But Judas Maccabeus will accept no less than total independence ... and continues his guerilla war. He sends envoys to Rome, who appeal to the Senate to come to the aid of the Jews and help cast off the Syrian enslavement. Rome is only too happy to help weaken the mighty Seleucid empire, and sends back, graven on bronze tablets, a declaration of alliance with the Jews.

Judas the Maccabee is a member of a priestly family, the Hasmoneans, and this family will rule Judea, for good or ill, in the years ahead. Their alliances with Rome and with the Spartans will turn out to be a mixed blessing ... indeed, almost suicide. But for the time being Judea (or Palestine to the Romans, a mocking play on the name Philistine, (or "money—grubbing illiterates") enjoys a short period of precarious peace. To this day the Jewish holiday called HANUKKAH, the Feast of Lights, is celebrated commemorating the victory of Judas Maccabeus over the Syrians.

160   Judas Maccabeus is killed in battle, "and all Israel [makes] great lamentation for him," crying, "How is the mighty fallen, the savior of Israel." Judas' brother, Jonathon, becomes leader of the Jews and, with Antiochus of Syria now dead, also, and his sons battling for his throne, uses wit and cunning to play off one Seleucid faction against the other.

157   Over the years, the North African city of Carthage has healed and rebuilt itself, and grown large and powerful once again, proud, prosperous, beautiful ... and strong. Now, Cato the Elder, on a diplomatic mission to Carthage, comes to believe that it is, once again, a militaristic threat to Rome, and from now on, ends his every speech in the Roman Senate with the admonition ...

Cato the Elder

Carthago est delenda!—Carthage must be destroyed!

150   On the Greek island of Melos, a graceful statue of Aphrodite, or Venus, is carved. The "Autumn Days" of Greece's Golden Age have come, and this is among the last, but by far not the least, of great Greek sculptures. Discovered in our own century by a Melos peasant digging a well on his own property, today the armless *Venus di Milo* stands in the Louvre, Paris, a beautiful symbol of eternal beauty.

... In Judea, two more APOCRYPHAL books are written:

The PRAYER of MANASSEH

Apocryphal Book — Written in ?, c. 150 B.C.

Only 15 verses long, the PRAYER OF MANASSEH is a beautiful prayer which purports to be that of the evil King Manasseh of Judah (See: 687 B.C.) who, having repented his evil, begs forgiveness (although the book of KINGS, which tells Manasseh's story, does not say that it happened.) It is a prayer that could well be said even today, by any repentant sinner first coming to know God. It is not known for certain which language the book was written in, but it exists today in several. "For the sins I have committed are more than the sand of the sea," he confesses, but ". . . now I bend the knee of my heart beseeching thee for thy kindness."

TOBIT

Apocryphal Book — Written in Hebrew or Aramaic, c. 150 B.C.

The story of TOBIT is a fanciful tale which returns to the days of the divided kingdom after the fall of Israel, and the carrying away of the Ten Lost Tribes to Assyria. (See: 721 B.C.) A romantic adventure, it runs the gamut from domestic to fabulous, featuring both evil spirits . . . and the angel Raphael. It tells of Tobit, a good man, who loses his sight; of a beautiful Sarah possessed of a demon; and of Tobit's son, Tobias, who restores his father's sight, exorcises the demon and marries Sarah. It ends with their joy at the destruction of Nineveh which was captured but not, as the writer mistakenly says, by Xerxes or Nebuchadnezzar.

---

149   Cato the Elder dies, having preached the destruction of Carthage to the end . . . and finally, the excuse Rome needs comes. The peace treaty signed at Zama 42 years ago having expired, Carthage (subtly maneuvered by Rome) declares war on Numidia, its African neighbor . . . and Roman ally; and the second Scipio—Aemilianus—adopted grandson of the first Scipio, moves in on Carthage. The terrified Carthaginians mobilize every person, personal effect and building, melt down every statue to make arms for an heroic defense against a Roman siege . . . which lasts three years . . .

146   . . . but it is not enough. With extreme savagery and brutality, Rome takes Carthage. Fifty-five thousand Carthaginians surrender and thousands more are taken to become slaves on Rome's farms, those, that is, who are not executed by Carthage's own invention . . . crucifixion. The Roman troops are turned loose to loot, sack, rape . . . and level the city to the ground with a fire that takes two weeks to consume it. The troops carry out their duties with a ferocity that shocks even Scipio, himself. To insure it will remain barren and never grow again, the Romans plow the city with salt, and proud Carthage, the last and greatest threat to Rome's expansion is totally wiped out. The destruction of Carthage makes Rome the supreme power in the world, makes the Mediterranean Rome's private sea, and begins an era of degradation and immorality not even old Cato the Censor could have imagined.

When he retires from military life, the aristocratic Scipio—or *Africanus Minor,* to honor his victories—will become highly influential in the political and cultural life of Rome, gathering about him (as did his grandfather) a "Scipionic Circle" of intellectuals, men of letters and the arts, devoted to the spread of Greek learning, culture and cultivation within the Republic. But many Romans—and even some Greeks—fail to recognize the difference between CLASSICAL Greek culture (with its democracy, civilizing beauty, grace and profound thought), and self-centered Greek HELLENISM, which mistakes luxury for culture, excess for beauty and obfuscating rhetoric for philosophy.

One young talent who would surely have been in Scipio's elite circle had tragedy not overtaken him at only 26, was the remarkable African playwright, Publius Terentius Afer, or Terence. Born a slave at Carthage, he was sold to a Roman Senator who soon recognized his gift, granted him freedom and encouraged his genius. Terence's plays were successful from the first . . . among intellectuals. The commons thought them dull and boring, not like the great Plautus, who made them roar with laughter at his rough and rowdy slapstick. Transported to a different age, Plautus would write "Roseanne," Terence "Masterpiece Theater." But 13 years ago, Terence sailed for Greece to translate Menander's plays into Latin, and was forever lost to history, whether from misfortune while there or shipwreck *en route.* Terence's expressions are still used today: He wrote of "lovers' quarrels" in the "bloom of youth," of young men "sowing their wild oats" then "taking to their heels" because of "women who won't when you will and will when you won't." It isn't as though "the sky were falling," he wrote, so keep your "presence of mind," and remember "time heals all wounds." He "cared not a straw" that there are . . .

". . . as many opinions as there are people," because "nothing new can be said that has not been said before." Remember "fortune favors the brave," and that "from bad beginnings great friendships have sprung, so "take heed of others' experiences for your own advantage," and remember "nothing is so difficult it can't be had by striving."   Terence, from his six plays.

. . . The three Punic Wars won by Rome were bought with a terrible price: the population and countryside ravaged, resources exhausted or abandoned, the vigorous laboring *plebe* class (the foot soldiers) decimated, and an almost entire higher class of noble Romans (the *equites,* or mounted military officers) virtually wiped out . . . and with them all the old, honored Roman values of morality, dignity, temperance, honesty, honor and piety. In their place the returning veterans bring back to Rome the Roman ways of war: rape, ravage, looting and killing; and bring back, also, the religions of their vanquished foes, the wild, unrestrained drunken orgies of Bacchus, god of wine, and Baal, the Babylonian/Carthaginian god of fertility. Great fortunes were made on those wars; made or merely taken, and the new rich now buy up huge areas of land for great estates, and put into cheap slave labor on them the vast hordes of captives—Carthaginians, Spaniards, Gauls, Sicilians and Numidians—so that whatever small farmers there are left are forced off their land with no place to go . . . but to Rome to beg in the streets.

But, as with every war or upheaval, the passing of one class creates another. Rome acquired many new skills in the hundred years of the Punic Wars: road building, aqueduct-, bridge-, machine-, and ship-building. On its way to becoming the crossroads of the world, Rome now needs, not philosophers and artists, but engineers, architects, inventors, merchants and administrators, and while the Romans have lost their high moral virtues, they haven't lost their practicality. While the intellectuals may venerate Greek culture, to most Romans beauty is in bigness. If one temple or ship or monument is big, the next must be bigger, the bigger the better. And the Roman republic, as it is now, just isn't big enough.

With golden eagles and graven SPQR gleaming in the sun on its standards, triumphant Rome is on the march, and one after another the nations fall before its might. But Rome doesn't see itself as a conqueror; it is merely defending its borders, its military "pre-emptive strikes" one after another meant merely to defend and secure its own boundaries! Still its boundaries do continue to expand every time it fights—and wins—another border war.

146   Macedonia becomes a Roman province and, in a senseless act of sheer brutality, its most beautiful city, Corinth, suffers the same terrible fate as Carthage. Next, Sparta comes under Roman rule and, finally . . . Athens falls to Rome. Having bloomed in beauty for 300 years, the flower of antiquity closes its petals and becomes a mere province of a superpower. But it is not burned or destroyed. Aside from Carthage and Corinth, Rome does not want desolation and wasteland. It wants production, profit and . . . plunder. But like its treasures, much of Greece's knowledge will rub off on its captors; and Rome will adopt Greece's architecture, religion, science, literature, art and culture to the day when a Roman poet will say:

Captive Greece took Rome captive.   Horace, (See: 13 B.C.)

Much of Greece's knowledge and religion has rubbed off on the Jews in Judea, also, particularly one political group known as the SADDUCEES. Although few in number, they are the wealthier Jews, more educated and sophisticated . . . and more ready to adopt Hellenistic ways. Two hundred years from now the Jewish historian, Josephus, will write that the Sadducees "disavowed tradition in religion" and held strictly to the letter of the LAW, even when the results were severe or cruel; and that they believed that God is not concerned with man's conduct, neither good nor ill. Having come into being back in the days of Antiochus *Epiphanes* and Judas Maccabeus, the Sadducees now control the Temple, and have many members on the Sanhedrin, Judea's high court.

The opposition party to the Sadducees are the PHARISEES; outspoken, even fanatical, opponents to the Hellenizing influence of Greek culture. According to Josephus, the Pharisees believe that events are fore-ordained; that God DOES reward or punish virtue and vice; that religious tradition IS to be honored, and that the soul is immortal and the body will be resurrected. Like so many things, the Pharisee and Sadducee natures will change over the years, and what now is piety, idealism and faithfulness to God will become, with the passage of time, an often narrow-minded self-righteousness; to the time 160 years hence when Jesus of Nazareth will denounce them for their hypocricy, and John the Baptist will condemn them as a "generation of vipers."

141   The revolt that Judas Maccabeus began and carried out so successfully 25 years ago is completed now by Simon Maccabeus; and the last of the Syrians are expelled from Judea. The Maccabees will become among the most highly revered of Jewish heroes.

135   Simon Maccabeus is murdered and succeeded by John Hyrcanus. There is much intrigue among Jewish leaders themselves over the next years, as their own revolt for religious freedom turns into wars of conquest of their own, under bad leaders. Having gained their own freedom, they now force conversion to Judaism onto others.

. . . and the first book of MACCABEES is written . . .

I MACCABEES

Apocryphal Book — Written in Hebrew,   c. 140 B.C.

The two books of MACCABEES tell the story of the Jews from the time of Alexander the Great. MACCABEES I begins with Alexander's conquests and death, and the division of his empire amongst his generals. For the Jews that meant Syrian rule, from (Alexander's general) Seleucus to Antiochus Epiphanes, to the freeing of Judea from the Seleucid yoke by Judas Maccabeus and his family. The books of MACCABEES, written by a Jewish historian probably working in Jerusalem, are important ones for they tell of events in the mid-east in the years between the "old" Testament and the "new." The writer must have been right there throughout the whole campaign, for his work has a genuine, eye-witness military ring to it, as in the story of how one hero died . . .

And upon the elephants were wooden towers, strong and covered; they were fastened upon each beast by special harness, and upon each were four armed men who fought from there, and also its Indian driver . . . And Eleazar, called Avaram . . . gave his life to save his people and win for himself an everlasting name . . . One of the beasts was equipped with royal armor . . . and he supposed that the king was upon it . . . he courageously ran into the midst of the phalanx to reach it . . . killed men right and left . . . He got under the elephant, stabbed it from beneath, and killed it; but it fell to the ground upon him and there he died . . . [and the Syrians] . . . turned away in flight . . .

6:37, 43–47

135 Two books are written at about this time that tell of the long-ago last days of Nebuchadnezzar of Babylon.

I ESDRAS

Apocryphal Book — Written in Hebrew,   c. 135 B.C.

I ESDRAS (EZRA, in Greek) is a retelling of the history of the Jews just before, during and after the exile in Babylon. It tells of the last weak kings of the Hebrew kingdom; of the Persian king Cyrus, Artxerxes and Darius, and repeats the same story Josephus relates of the puzzle Darius posed, "Which is stronger; man, woman, wine or truth?" (521 B.C.) And it tells of the great Passover feast held by the good King Josiah, and how he told the priestly Levites to . . .

"Put the holy ark of the Lord in the house which Solomon the king, the son of David had built. You need no longer carry it upon your shoulders. Now worship the lord your God . . . in the Temple."   1:3, 4

JUDITH

Apocryphal Book — Written in Hebrew,   c. 135 B.C.

JUDITH is the story of one woman's courage in saving her people from Nebuchadnezzar's general, Holofernes, at the time of the Babylonian occupation of Judah. It tells how Holofernes lusted after the beautiful widow, Judith; how he planned to have her before he destroyed her land; how Judith's "raiment ravished his eyes, her beauty captivated his mind . . . and her sword severed his neck."

Nebuchadnezzar was not king of Assyria, as the story reads, nor was he still alive and ruling after the exile, but some scholars believe those errors were included intentionally to make the point that the story is fictional.

Rome on the march is looked upon by other nations with awe and wonder . . . and fear and dread. Drunk with success, it now owns Sicily, Spain, Macedonia, Greece, Carthage and Sardinia, and everything they possess. Now, just by reputation alone it acquires an eighth possession, half of all Asia Minor, as the last king of Pergamum dies and leaves all of his country to Rome . . . in his will!

But, inside, the Republic is sick and getting sicker. Old Cato the Censor was totally right when he foresaw trouble ahead. With the nation getting rich on plunder, greed and brute force, its people do the same. Political corruption has been honed to such a fine art, the joke of the day is that a man can get rich enough in one year as governor of a province to pay the bribes that got him the job, in two years to bribe his way out of a trial, and in three to live a life of luxury from then on. Murder by gladiator as sport is commonplace, and slaves who were once few and expensive to buy—therefore highly valued and well treated—are now free booty from conquered lands. Beastially treated, they labor on land once owned by proud Roman farmers . . . who now beg in the streets of Rome. Even those remedies that are tried by the Senate to right a nightmare of wrongs, do not work: the poor of Rome, resettled in new colonies elsewhere . . . can't manage themselves, and returned veterans given free land, don't know how to farm. And a young aristocrat named Tiberius Gracchus, grandson of Scipio Africanus, sick at the sight of foreign slaves tilling fields once tended by freemen, speaks to the Romans:

> The savage beasts of Italy have their . . . dens . . . for refuge and repose . . . You fight and are slain to maintain the luxury and wealth of other men. You are called masters of the world . . . but have not one foot of ground to call your own . . .   Plutarch, LIVES OF THE NOBLE GREEKS AND ROMANS

133   Elected one of Rome's 10 tribunes, Tiberius proposes a number of well-intentioned reforms, but in carrying them out takes upon himself the powers of a king, that hated office the ancient Law of Twelve Tables forbade, and the Romans so abhor . . . and is murdered.

132   The grandson of Jesus Ben Sirach, working in Egypt—possibly in the Alexandrian Library—translates Sirach's book, ECCLESIASTICUS (See: 180 B.C.) from the original Hebrew into Greek. It is a very difficult job, he says in his prologue, now part of the book, for ". . . despite diligent labor in translating, what was originally expressed in Hebrew does not have exactly the same sense . . . in another language."

130   The city of Nicea in Asia Minor, or Bithynia as Rome calls it, will one day become famous as the site of a great Christian Church council and namesake of the Nicean Creed. Now it is the home of and experimental site of a Greek mathematician and astronomer . . . and genius . . . named Hipparchus (who, perhaps, also works at the Great Library). About 50 years old, now, Hipparchus is the first to use trigonometry (some say he invented it) for astronomical purposes. He has catalogued over a thousand stars, noting their latitude, longitude and magnitude of brightness; uses latitude and longitude to divide the world into "climates"—temperate, torrid, frigid—and to measure distances of localities for mapmaking. He has invented an "astrolabe" (a precursur of the sextant) for measuring the distance from earth to the sun and stars. He is a man far ahead of his time, a great inventor and pioneer, but his own writings will be lost in the years ahead, and he is remembered only through the writings of other ancient writers,

. . . With the great hunger for knowledge in this Hellenistic Age, many people are traveling to see, not only the world, but the man-made beauties in it as well; and one form of book in demand is the "travel guide." One such guide is compiled by Antipater of Sidon (in Phoenecia) and includes those sights he considers (and we accept to this day) the "Seven Wonders of the World": the Great Pyramid at Giza, the Hanging Gardens of Babylon, the Temple of Zeus at Olympia,. the Mausoleum of Hallicarnassus, the Temple of Diana at Ephesus and the two latest, the Colossus of Rhodes and the Lighthouse of Alexandria.

. . . Rome's business is not Hellenism, though; it is too busy with the business of conquest. Now, Rome seals its domination of the Mediterranean with the conquest of the Balearic Islands just off the coast of Spain. Rich with potential for citrus groves, the Romans introduce the cultivation of olives, also. A strange, barbaric people, the men are expert stone-slingers, and the Romans conscript them into the army . . . and

From a Roman Mosaic

take, also, thousands of indigenous pack mules and tons of pitch for road and shipbuilding.

124   Rome's "tax base" is now plunder and slavery. Big time speculators, slum landlords, contractors and slave traders all get rich on the labor of slaves and the importation of cheap, slave-grown corn from Sicily. In the city, slaves replace Romans as clerks in stores,

The Gracchus brothers

laborers in factories, artisans in shops and servants in homes, and thousands of destitute Romans sit idle. Now young Gaius Gracchus follows in his brother, Tiberius', foot-steps, and is elected Tribune. Where Tiberius had been gentle, quiet, correct and temperate, Caius is passionate and impetuous, and his orations to the people and Senate are vehement and blood-stirring. Caius sets about promoting a broad range of reforms, from public works projects like road-building, to restoration of Tiberius' land laws, free uniforms for the army, reform of the jury system and . . .

122   . . . free distribution of corn to the masses, a DOLE, until he can get them resettled in new colonies elsewhere. But Caius begins making mistakes, going too far. He runs for, and wins, a second—unprecedented—term as Tribune, "packs" the Senate by doubling its size, and proposes citizenship for all of Latium . . . that the Romans see as a threat to their superiority. For the first time ever the Senators appear at the capitol in full battle dress, and Caius flees . . . but is captured, and slain. When it is learned that the Senate has offered ransom for his head—worth its weight in gold—it is brought back to them filled . . . with molten lead . . . while the people he sought to serve busy themselves looting his house. Over 3000 of his supporters are slain—without trial—and the pattern is drawn for government by violence and bloodshed.

121   Rome conquers southern Gaul, the Mediterranean coast of France; and when Jugurtha, king of Numidia (near what was Carthage) displeases Rome, it begins a war there, too.

114   Rome's swelling bureaucracy holds many a political plum, and many fortunes are made at the public expense. With graft and corruption a way of life, it does not go unno-

ticed in the provinces. Jugurtha, brought to Rome from Numidia in a bribery trial after the "Jugurthine" war . . . bribes his way out . . .

> "At Rome, all things are for sale." Jugurtha, quoted by Sallust in his *Cataline*

"Incarcerated" in a Roman prison, the *Carcer Tullianum,* Jugurtha dies, according to Sallust, ". . . of starvation, rodents and lice in underground darkness and irremovable filth."

113   Rome remembers only too well the devastating invasions of Italy by the Gauls from France and Hannibal's Carthaginians. Now comes another frightful invasion, and it proves as terrifying as any before; thousands of blond-headed barbarians from far-northern Germany who wipe out legion after Roman legion.

> The accounts at first exceeded all (belief), as to (their) number and strength . . . but in the end report proved much inferior to truth . . . as there were 300,000 effective fighting men, besides a far greater number of women and children . . . seeking new countries to sustain (them) . . . They were of invincible strength and fierceness . . . Several of the greatest Roman commanders with their whole armies . . . were ingloriously overthrown . . .
> Plutarch, LIVES OF THE NOBLE GREEKS AND ROMANS.

The German (Cimbri and Teutone) tribes wander Italy at will then cross over to ravage Spain. Rome desperately needs a leader, someone who can restore order and pride in its decimated and demoralized army, and one man comes forward who earned fame and triumph in the war against Jugurtha in Africa.

107–101   . . . Caius Marius, elected consul, takes on the challenge and sets out to train, almost from scratch, a whole new army; and succeeds beyond expectations . . . but succeeds, also, in giving it powers that eventually will do a great deal more harm than good. Having formerly been made up of Roman CITIZENS who owed their allegiance to Rome, it becomes, now, open to anyone, most of whom care nothing about a Republic and owe their loyalty and allegiance to which-ever general promises the richer reward. Marius succeeds, also, in making another change, equally as devastating to the Republic. Ignoring the ancient Roman Law, and a dying constitution, he runs for, and wins, the office of consul—the highest office in Rome—over and over again, opening the door for dictatorship and . . . civil war. Finally defeating the Germans with a massive slaughter of 100,000 men at Aix la Chapelle and Marseilles, Marius runs for consul—and wins—a fourth, fifth and sixth time . . .

> . . . he sued for his sixth [term] in such a manner as never . . . before . . . courted the people's favor and ingratiated himself with the multitude . . . derogating . . . the dignity of his office . . . [and] became very odius to all the nobility . . . distributing vast sums of money among the tribes.   *ibid.*

100   With a world in turmoil, the last century before Christ begins . . .

. . . The corn dole is standard practice now in Rome, with thousands of people believing that "the government" OWES them a regular handout; that that is better than hard work and poor pay on a farm. In his LIVES OF THE NOBLE GREEKS AND ROMANS, Plutarch says that, by this time, Roman citizens who own their own property number no more than . . . 2000.

. . . The first school for gladiators is in operation in Rome, where condemned prisoners are trained in all the grisly . . . and ingenious . . . methods by which men—and even some women—kill each other for sport in the arena.

. . . Not only in the west is there war and conquest. Expanding its own borders in the far east, China conquers Indo-China, modern-day Viet Nam.

. . . and there is progress and invention. Heron of Alexandria, a Greek geometer invents all sorts of mechanical contrivances: fire engine, water-driven organ, coin-slotted gadgets, and a practical, workable steam engine, which he uses to propel a sort of antiquarian merry-go-round. But its vast potential is never realized and, so, eventually forgotten. It will not be re-invented for almost 2000 years and, then, will become the principle of modern-day ocean liners and jet

A gladiator from the British Museum

engines. Some of Heron's hand-sketched note-books exist today, some in Greek, one in Arabic translation, in European libraries.

. . . The Great Silk Road is now in use; not a road, really, but a vast network of caravan trade routes that brings together Rome and the farthest reaches of Asia, opened up by Alexander the Great 200 years ago. The Han Dynasty rules in China now, and is eager for trade with the West.

The Silk Road begins in Antioch in Syria, that great hub of world trade; and continues through today's Bagdad and Teheran, passing directly beneath that great cuneiform-carved Behistun Rock of kings Darius and Xerxes. Skirting the towering Altai mountains, it swings deep under the great Gobi Desert of Mongolia. Down into China it plunges, and stretches across the vast expanse from Kashgar (or Turfan) to its final destination at Ch'ang-an (today's Sian), six thousand miles from Rome! Relay journeys take years to complete, and on the way the Steppes of Central Asia yield up emeralds, furs and copper, and the Black Sea sturgeon bulging with roe. Thousands of camels in caravans miles long, bring back tons of beautiful silk—worth its weight in gold—from China, along with ebony and other exotic goods; and, in exchange from the Romans, the Chinese learn the pleasures of the grape-vine. Persia, in between, is a jealous middle-man so most Romans are not even aware that there is a China, but noble Roman ladies wear Chinese silk, and fortunes are made from east to west.

But it is a dangerous route, frought with many perils; from treacherous mountain paths to quicksand and river rapids; from terrible frozen winters and searing summers with desert hurricane sandstorms that can bury a caravan in one hour, to wild barbarian hordes that swoop down from the north. So other routes are used to the south, by water, in Rome's many-oared, slave-manned galleys, from Damascus down the Euphrates River and the Persian Gulf (rich with pearls) to India. There the traders get cotton, ebony, spices and drugs. Lapis-lazuli and sapphires come from the Kashmir, rubies from Burma and turquoise from Tibet. From Arabia comes intricately tooled leather work, woven goods, beautiful oriental carpets and exotic perfumes, and for the wild races in Rome's arenas, gorgeous, high-spirited Arabian horses. Something else comes from Arabia, also, something that symbolizes royalty, diety . . . and death. For, from the teeming bazaars in the crowded cities surrounding the vast Arabian Desert, the caravans bring back . . . gold, frankincense and myrrh.

. . . In Judea, another religious group is formed in addition to the Pharisees and Sadducees . . . or maybe *because* of them, but their energies are directed a different way, for many pious Jews are convinced the Messiah is coming soon and that they must prepare themselves for his advent. The order of ESSENES is a militant brotherhood with a leader called the Teacher of Righteousness, who preaches that only they, the Essenes, can be saved. They have built themselves a sprawling monastic complex in the bleak, desolate, lunar-like wilderness of Qumran, bringing water from distant mountains through conduits to underground cisterns. Their mission is to copy and preserve all the Hebrew holy books (the "Old Testament") on parchment scrolls. This they do, laboriously by hand, every one except ESTHER, (including parts of the Septuagint and Apocrypha), wrapping them in leather and packing them into clay jars. The sect will remain in their Dead Sea hide-away, and thrive, for another 170 years.

. . . The turn of the century also finds much activity by other Jewish writers as those scrolls are copied out in the desert; and six more Apocryphal books are written:

II MACCABEES

Apocryphal book — Written in Greek,   c. 100 B.C.

"All . . . which has been set forth by Jason of Cyrene in five volumes," writes the author of II MACCABEES, ". . . [I] shall attempt to condense into a single book." Whoever he was, Jason's large work is long gone and only the 15 chapters of II MACCABEES remains. They tell much the same stories as MACCABEES I, but passionately; exhorting the reader to remember always that, in spite of all the terrible tragedies which continually befall the Jews ". . . though [the Lord] disciplines us with calamities, he does not forsake his people."

Antiochus IV, *Epiphanes,* of Syria, he who called himself the "human manifestation of Zeus" and sacrificed swine on the holy Altar of the Temple, receives a scathing indictment from the writer who accuses him of ". . . insolence . . . superhuman arrogance . . . who thought he could touch the stars of heaven." The writer may have been a Hellenistic Jew, working at the great Library of Alexandria. He hopes his story is ". . . well told and to the point, for it is the best that I can do."

BARUCH

Apocryphal Book — Written in Hebrew,   c. 100 B.C.

Baruch was friend and secretary to the venerable old prophet, Jeremiah who had warned the Hebrews of the coming destruction of Jerusalem by Nebuchadnezzar of Babylon. Baruch had written down Jeremiah's words and read them aloud in Jerusalem to the people and to the king, himself. This book was not compiled until much later than Baruch's time, though. It contains prayers and poems meant to be read at worship, on behalf of the exiles, and on the nature of wisdom. It says that although the children of Zion have "traveled rough roads" and strayed far from God, yet He will ". . . bring you everlasting joy with your salvation."

Several "additions" are written for the Old Testament book of ESTHER; in an arguable time and language:

Additions to the book of
ESTHER

The book of ESTHER was almost not included in the "canon" of the Old Testament for it is in no way a religious book, never once, for example, mentioning the name of God. These "additions" are an attempt to correct that oversight. They are very pious and religious, and show that because of Esther's piety and devotion to Him, God saved the Hebrews from the wrath of her husband Ahaseurus, King Xerxes of Persia.

Finally, three delightful short stories are written about the Old Testament prophet Daniel. The writer intended them to be included in the book of DANIEL. Like ESTHER, all are Apocryphal Books, probably written in Hebrew at about 100 B.C.

The PRAYER OF AZARIAH and the . . .
SONG *of the*
THREE YOUNG MEN

This short book is a hymn sung by the Hebrew exiles Shadrach, Meshach and Abednego as they walked unharmed in Nebuchadnezzar's "burning, fiery furnace." It is a beautiful litany of blessings to the Lord for the sun and moon, rain and dew, light and darkness, cattle, springs, hills, mountains and all who worship the Lord, ". . . for his mercy endures forever."

The Fiery Furnace

SUSANNAH

The young Daniel is the hero of this story as he executes a clever bit of "detective" work, successfully defending the beautiful and virtuous young Jewish matron, Susannah, from false charges of adultery by two lecherous old men who wanted her for themselves. Daniel examines them separately, and easily exposes their plot, to the relief and joy of all.

BEL and the DRAGON

The Babylonian graven idol, Baal, is called Bel in this delightful little tale of intrigue in which Daniel again executes a clever bit of investigative work, and so destroys the pagan temple of a false god. By the footsteps in the flour he had strewn about Bel's temple, he proved it was not the god eating and drinking the sacrificial offerings. The second half of the book re-tells the famous story of Daniel in the lions den; how the ancient prophet Habakkuk miraculously fed him; and how the king worshipped the Hebrew God when he saw Daniel safe.

The Jews are not alone in their preoccupation with religion, but that of Rome is far different. What had, once, been a whole pantheon of native gods that encouraged patriotism, strong family life—childrens' respect for parents and parents' devotion to children—the unique Roman self-discipline and innate peasant common-sense, has, over the years, given way to foreign mystery cults and superstitions. The vacuum created by the lessening of respect for the traditional values is only too eagerly filled by new sensational indulgences. Cynicism and self-gratifying Hellenistic philosophies compete with voluptuous, amoral, sense-gratifying, hedonistic religions from the east. A sure sign of decadence, worry those Romans who still care for their country, are the weird aberrations in dress, manners, entertainment and . . . religion. Many of Rome's new gods are merely borrowed from conquered peoples and transformed into Latin deities. Thus, the Greek chief of the gods, Zeus, becomes Jupiter in Rome; and Venus, goddess of love, is Aphrodite. Wild, drunken "Bacchanalian revels" are held in celebration of Greek-Dionysus/Roman-Bacchus, god of wine. (That infamous Bacchanalian scandal that caused the Senate to arrest 7000 frenzied adherents and execute hundreds more, was nearly 90 years ago, but the cult and its lewd practices still thrives.) The Vestal Virgins and the Sibylline Oracle are still consulted for advice that is followed "religiously," but the worship of Cybele, a fertility goddess whose name came from the Sibylline Oracle, is also celebrated with wild orgies. The worship of Mithras a masculine religion, comes from Persia; and finally, that of the Egyptian Isis, whose brother and husband are one—Osiris—long forbidden in Rome, is given sanction, and conservative Romans (what few are left) worry that it will open the door to even more abuse.

97   In Rome, an engineer (and former consul) named Sextus Julius Frontinus, is appointed Superintendent of Waterworks, and begins cleaning out the graft and corruption he finds already there; and prosecutes many who have illegally tapped into the system. During his administration, alone, nine aqueducts are built, which carry 85,000,000 gallons of fresh mountain water into Rome every day. They will become models for many more that the Roman "empire" will eventually build in scores of far-flung Roman cities. It is an accomplishment of which Frontinus is extremely proud, and his own published records about them still exist telling of their building and value to Rome. They are greater, he says, than . . .

> . . . Egypt's idle pyramids and other useless, though renowned, works of the Greeks.
> Frontinus, AQUADUCTS 2:75

91   But Rome's republic is falling apart; its Senate manipulated, its civil laws ignored, and corruption and graft replace good government. Its two political parties—the patrician *optimates* and the plebian *populares*—carry on a "social war" that rapidly disintegrates into civil war. Much of the Italian peninsula attempts to secede from Rome and call itself "Italia," and is defeated. Attempting to pacify the secessionists, Marcus Livius Drusus, tribune, suggests granting citizenship to all cities of Italy . . . and is assassinated.

89   All Italy is granted Roman citizenship.

88   A poor-born patrician named Lucius Cornelius Sulla, general under Marius, uses battle and bloodshed to work his way to the top and is elected co-consul. Called the "most ruthless Roman" he is an enigma and a contradiction. A cold-blooded butcher of thousands he is, also, called *Felix*, meaning "happy," for his love of (his own) life, laughter, wine, women and song, good food and great luxury. But, in the army, he lives the life his soldiers lead and shares their hardships and triumphs. Marius' military reforms of 106 (B.C.) had changed the army from temporary militia, or citizen soldiers loyal to ROME, to long-term, career professionals loyal to their own general. Now, bad blood and conflicting ambitions between Marius and Sulla cause Sulla to lead his own—personal—army to Rome . . . and Marius flees to Africa. It is the first time ever a Roman general leads Roman troops against Rome.

87   Rebellion against Roman rule in Greece, and the slaying of all Roman/Italian colonists in Asia Minor by King Mithridates of Pontus, now cause Sulla to have himself named proconsul (in effect, consul/general/governor all in one) and march off to the East, leaving Rome in the care of co-consuls Octavius and Cinna . . . who immediately resume the civil war. With Sulla gone, Marius returns from Africa with his personal army of 6000 men, kills Octavius and . . .

86   . . . campaigns for—and wins—his SEVENTH term as co-consul (with Cinna). Three weeks later, at 71, he dies of exhaustion. Cinna, now in sole leadership, declares the absent Sulla a public enemy, and uses his four year consulate to govern the republic as a dictatorship.

86, March, at Athens.   Sulla has a vehement and implacable desire to conquer Athens; its ruling tyrant having provoked him daily upon the city walls "with foul words, scurrilous jests and unseemly gesticulations . . ." According to Plutarch, when Sulla finally takes the city . . .

> . . . the blood . . . shed about the market-place . . . spread over the whole [city] . . . and . . . overflowed the suburb.   Plutarch's LIVES

But Sulla is, also, a lover of Greek art, and loots the city of everything that can be carried away, including the still mostly unpubliched writings of Aristotle, for his own personal collection.

85   At Pontus, Sulla makes peace with King Mithridates, quarters his troops in private homes and orders each householder to pay, feed, entertain and provide civilian clothing for his "guests." When he returns to Italy, Sulla brings with him enormous amounts of wealth for the Roman treasury . . . and art works for himself. The Latin/Roman experience of government will have a vast influence on future generations and nations, and often some of the best lessons learned will be from Rome's "bad examples." This is one. Eighteen hundred years from now the Founding Fathers of a new American republic, all well educated in Roman history and mindful of the lessons of the past, will remember Sulla's excesses when writing a new United States Constitution:

> . . . No soldier shall, in time of peace be quartered in any house, without the consent of the Owner, nor in time of war, but in a manner to be prescribed by law.   Article III, The U.S. Bill of Rights

83   Sulla slaughters the republican senators in their seats at the Senate House and appoints his own . . . who eagerly accede to his claim as absolute dictator for an indeterminate time, and his infamous "proscriptions" begin . . .

Sulla

> Sulla being thus wholly bent upon slaughter, [he filled] the city with executions without number or limit.   Plutarch, LIVES

Every day Sulla has hundreds of names *proscribed*, or listed, for execution, persons who may receive no legal defense and whose property is confiscated. But Sulla hopes to end the revolution and rebellion, and restore the authority of the senate in the Roman constitution; so he begins to propose a vast and comprehensive program of constitutional reforms. His *leges Corneliae*, or Cornelian laws (so-called from his clan name, Cornelius) cover every aspect of government: the size and terms of office of the senate and army, legal justice, duties of and restraints upon magistrates, *praetors*, *tribunes* and provincial governors. Some historians believe that Sulla's reforms might have saved the republic had Rome wanted to be saved; but, to everyone's amazement . . .

80 . . . Sulla retires from public life. He dies a year later, and his "Cornelian Laws" die, also, without ever having been given serious trial by a spineless senate.

. . . A young Roman nobleman, scion of an ancient patrician family, is taken captive by the Mediterranean "corsairs" while returning from his studies (and refuge from Sulla) in Greece, and afterward, claimed to have "lived like a prince" among the pirates until he was ransomed:

> When (they) demanded . . . twenty talents . . . ransom, he laughed at them for not understanding the value of their prisoner, and gave them fifty. When he had a mind to sleep he would . . . order them to make no noise. He wrote verses and speeches . . . and those who did not admire them, he called to their faces illiterate and barbarous.   Plutarch, LIVES OF THE NOBLE GREEKS AND ROMANS

The lusty bragadoccio is that of an untamed, profligate young man, interested only in sport, gaming, good times and the private rooms of the noblest Roman ladies, married or not. His name is Caius Julius, of the family called Caesar.

73 A Greek soldier named Spartacus, captured by the Romans at Thrace and trained as a gladiator at a great gladiator school at Capua, escapes his captors, raises an army of 70,000 rebel slaves and begins a major slave revolt. His hideout is on a volcano named . . . Vesuvius.

72 Spartacus' army, grown to 120,000, and armed with weapons they make themselves, capture much of southern Italy and begins to march on Rome. The Romans—and all Italians—are mad with fear, for these are not men born into slavery, with submissiveness inbred, but captured freemen from other lands filled with hate and resentment for their captors.

71 Marcus Licinius Crassus, scion of another leading patrician family, in command of eight legions, utterly defeats Spartacus . . . whom he crucifies, along with 6000 of his followers. Their crosses line the Appian Way from Rome to Brundisium, as a warning to other slaves. The warning is effective. There are no more slave revolts in Rome.

Crassus, at 44 a financial genius and heir to a banking fortune is, according to Plutarch, the "richest man in Rome," with only "one vice of avarice . . ." Though kind to his servants, hospitable to strangers and generous to the poor, it is partly off the poor that he makes his money . . .

> . . . [taking] advantages of . . . public calamities . . . he made it his practice to buy houses that were on fire and those in the neighborhood for little or nothing . . . so that the greatest part of Rome, at one time or another, came into his hands.   Plutarch, LIVES

Pompey

70 Crassus and 36 year-old Gnaeus Pompeius, or Pompey, some-day to be called "the Great," are elected co-consuls of Rome. Having risen to prominence during the reign of Sulla, Pompey is a man of gentleness and dignity, temperate, eloquent and a general of infinite skill, courage and resourcefulness. Surrounded and near capture or death in one battle, he simply dismounted his beautifully and richly adorned horse, turned it loose and made his escape while the enemy fought amongst themselves for the horse and its gold and silver trappings. He was awarded his first *triumph*, or triumphal procession into Rome, even before he was old enough to be a senator before (according to Plutarch) ". . . he had scarcely yet fully grown a beard."

67 Pompey is given the task of clearing the pirates out of the Mediterranean, allowed three years to accomplish the task and granted 500 ships, 120,000 foot, 5000 horse and 24 military-experienced senators or lieutenants. Moreover, a "decree granted Pompey not only the government of the seas as admiral, but . . . sole . . . sovereignty . . . absolute power and authority at sea and 400 furlongs inland . . ."

> . . . whilst the Romans were embroiled in their civil wars . . . the seas lay . . . unguarded . . . so that now . . . with these pirates [were] men of wealth . . . noble birth and superior abilities as if it had been a natural occupation . . . They had arsenals . . . harbours . . . watch towers and beacons, all along the seacoast . . . and fleets . . . with the finest mariners . . . one thousand [ships] and they had taken no less than 400 cities . . . and would often go inland up the roads, plundering and destroying villages and country-houses.   Plutarch, LIVES

It takes Pompey only THREE MONTHS to clear the sea of the "corsairs" that had been its plague since the days of Egypt! Taking 90 men-of-war and 20,000 prisoners, he then re-settles them on farms in colonies far inland, to make honest farmers of them . . . and marches off to settle matters in the east with Mithridates of Pontus (Asia Minor) who had been aiding and abetting the pirates against Rome . . . and then to Palestine, where two brothers—Aristobulus II and Hyrcanus II—are fighting a dynastic war for the Jewish throne.

66 Pompey conquers Pontus and becomes master of all Asia Minor, Bithynia having been willed to Rome in 74, Crete taken in 68 and Cilicia the next year.

65 Julius Caesar is elected to his first public office, three years older than Alexander the Great was at his death, a fact he recognized and mourned.

> Do you think I have not just cause to weep, when I consider that Alexander at my age had conquered so many nations, and I have all this time done nothing that is memorable?
> Plutarch, LIVES

Caesar's ambition, now aroused, becomes insatiable (supported by that arrogant flair that returned him, 15 years ago, to those captor pirates, to take back his ransom and . . .

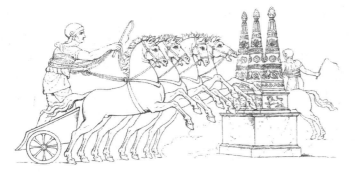

Julius Caesar

crucify the lot). Now *quaestor,* he is elected to an office guaranteed to win the love of the masses—Director of Public Works and Games—which it does, as he is a big spender and shrewd manipulator. His greatest project in this office, is the planning and beginning of the *Circus Maximus,* the greatest of many arenas the Romans will eventually build to entertain the masses. The gigantic, oval-shaped race course will, when completed, seat some 200,000 *spectators* (itself a Latin word). Five and six chariots abreast, teams of four horses each will scream down the mile long *circus* and, at each end, be urged on by whips in the hands of *agitators.*

65–62   Pompey the Great, general of all the armies in the East, wins victory after victory for Rome: Thrace, Galacia and Phoenecia, Syria and the island of Rhodes. But there is no destruction, burning or desolation. Rome wants its territories in good—profitable—working order . . . and Pompey is a beneficent conqueror . . .

> . . . the concubines of King Mithridates . . . Pompey sent . . . all away to their parents and relations. At Rhodes he attended the lectures of all the philosophers. At Athens . . . he gave fifty talents towards repairing and beautifying the city.   Plutarch, LIVES

63   Finally, Pompey's Roman legions march into Judea; first as mediators, to call a halt to the infighting between its Maccabean rulers, and then to bring all of Palestine under Roman rule. Pompey's battering rams make short work of one city wall, and 12,000 Jews die in the fighting, but Jerusalem is taken, and . . .

. . . JUDEA BECOMES A ROMAN PROVINCE.

> . . . the city was taken on the third month . . . upon the hundred and seventy-ninth Olympiad, when Caius Antonius and Marcus Tullius Cicero were consuls . . . those that have written [about] Pompey [Strabo . . . and . . . Titus Livius (Livy), the writer of Roman history] will bear witness [to] this thing.   Joseph Ben Matthais, or, Josephus, ANTIQUITIES OF THE JEWS

But Jerusalem is only occupied, and will still maintain a precarious peace with a vestige of self-rule for 69 more years, a client state and servant of Rome. Pompey enters the Holy of Holies in the temple on horseback, but he touches nothing and destroys nothing, wanting only to see for himself what it is, so great, that these stiff-necked Jews fight and die for, so obstinately. And the mystery is only made more so, when all he finds . . . is an empty room.

> . . . so Pompey went into it . . . and saw all that which was unlawful for any . . . man to see [except] the high priests . . . yet did Pompey touch nothing . . . on account of his regard [for] religion; and in this point also he acted in a manner that was worthy of his virtue. The next day he gave order to those who had the charge of the temple to cleanse it . . .   Josephus, ANTIQUITIES OF THE JEWS

Built 500 years ago by Haggai and Zechariah after the Jews' return from exile, the Temple is now a creaking, decrepit old relic. Ignored or abandoned by many Jews, abused by the Greeks and Syrians, it is now just a sad reminder of times past. A new temple is needed, and the Jews will get it . . . but they won't like it.

Cicero

The Marcus Tullius Cicero mentioned in Josephus' ANTIQUITIES OF THE JEWS, is a 43 year-old philosopher/statesman dedicated to saving the republic . . . but too astute to believe it can be saved. A brilliant trial lawyer, he studied rhetoric, oratory and philosophy while in Greece, a self-imposed exile from Sulla's bloodbath. Asked, there, to declaim a speech in Greek as one of his hearers did not understand Latin, he complied, thinking he could benefit from their criticisms, but was told:

> You have my praise and admiration, Cicero, and Greece my pity and commiseration, since those arts and that eloquence which are the only glories that remain to her, will now be transferred by you to Rome.   Appolonius of Rhodes, quoted by Plutarch, in his LIVES

A man of justice, clemency, virtue and duty, Cicero sees the insanities of his day, the avarice, immorality, cruelty and bloodshed as the result of *furiosi,* madmen, "wild beasts in human form." His ideal of a humane government is *imperium et libertas*—order and freedom, under a system of enlightened law: public law, *Res Publica,* and private law, *Res Privita,* governing citizens who accept and adopt the moral virtues of "temperance, wisdom, justice and fortitude." But this is not the reality of this day whether it be politician or practitioner, trader or toiler, all are infected with the *libido dominandi,* the lust for dominance, and an *appetitio principatus,* an appetite for power.

One such man is Lucius Cataline, whom Cicero defeated in his run for consul. Accused of, among other things, "deflowering his virgin daughter and killing his own brother," he has won over the "profligate citizens" of Rome by paying for their endless debaucheries. Being "the head . . . of some that endeavored to . . . subvert the [republic] not from any good motives, but for their own private gain, he had resolved to kill Cicero in a tumult at the elections. But Cicero takes on the challenge with a series of powerful orations to the senate, and so brilliantly do Cicero's *Philipics* condemn Catiline's conspiracy, that the senators walk away from where Cataline sits, shout him down when he tries to speak and order him out of the city . . . only to be hunted down and slain.

> Cataline had plotted a dreadful and entire subversion of the Roman state by sedition and open war, but [was] convicted by Cicero . . . [the other conspirators] resolved to set the whole town on fire . . . [and rouse] whole nations to revolt. Plutarch, LIVES

The entire incident in the senate is recorded . . . in shorthand . . . invented by Cicero's dearly loved freedman/secretary, Marcus Tullius Tiro, to keep pace with Tiro's prolific employer.

> . . . for Cicero, the consul, had dispensed in various parts of the senate house, several . . . expert and rapid writers [using what] we call . . . shorthand. *ibid.*

But, "intemperately fond of his own glory," Cicero often puts down others with jests and puns, as he does the oldest man in the senate who opposes a certain bill, saying it would never pass whilst he lived. "Let us postpone it," says Cicero, "Gellius does not ask us to wait long." And when Sulla's son publishes bills of sale after wasting his inheritance, Cicero, hinting of Sulla's infamous bills of proscription, said he "liked these bills much better than those of his father." Thus was Cicero also hated, by some.

> . . . the desire [for] glory has great power in washing . . . philosophy out of the souls of men . . . and politicians. *ibid.*

62   The political career of Julius Caesar is on the rise. He governs as *praetor* in Spain . . . and returns a wealthy and famous man.

> There was nobody of any rank that did not go some day's journey to meet Caesar on his return from Spain . . . but [Marc Antony] was the best received, admitted to ride the whole journey with him in his carriage. *ibid.*

Born in Alexandria, Egypt, Antony, at just 20 years old, has already wasted an inherited fortune on drink, dissipation and bad company. Bold and masculine in appearance, he has a noble look that people compare to Hercules, but is fond of ostentation and has a "vaunting temper." Still, he is also a brave soldier and shows promise as a leader; and Caesar welcomes his courage, energy and shrewd military instinct. And Antony, a true child of these Hellenistic, revolutionary times, recognizes greatness in Caesar . . . and opportunity for himself.

Marc Antony

There are some, though, who have no liking for Caesar, including Cicero, who feels he is too "ambitious . . ."

> Cicero was the first who had any suspicions of [Caesar's] designs upon the government . . . and detected [his] ambition for absolute power. *ibid.*

61   Having put Rome's affairs in order in the East, General Pompey returns to Italy, and in his LIVES OF THE NOBLE GREEKS AND ROMANS, Plutarch writes, with awe, of his spectacular triumphal procession into Rome . . . thousands of people and animals, both conquered scuffling miserably in the dust, and conquerors, their burnished armor

gleaming in the Roman sun. With horns blaring fanfares and drums beating measured cadence, every legion, every cohort carries its own standard and S.P.Q.R.-engraved emblem—*SENATUS POPULUSQUE ROMANUS*—THE SENATE AND THE PEOPLE OF ROME—while long trains of wagons groan under great loads of loot and other countries' treasures. Pompey, himself, stands high in a golden chariot drawn by four of Arabia's most perfect horses.

> The splendor and magnificence of Pompey's triumph . . . took up the space of two days . . . there were the tables (tablets on standards) carried, inscribed with the names . . . of the nations over which he triumphed, Pontus, Armenia, Cappadocia, Paphlagonia, Media, Colchis, the Iberians, the Albanians, Syria, Cilicia, and Mesopotamia, together with Phoenecia and Palestine, Judea, Arabia, and all the . . . pirates subdued by sea and land . . . 1,000 fortified places . . . 300 cities . . . 800 ships of the pirates . . . where Rome's revenues [had been] 50 millions, [they were now] 85 millions. Among his prisoners of war in the triumph are kings and princes, royalty and rulers of all sorts. So Pompey's first triumph was over Africa, his second over Europe, and this last over Asia; so that . . . he seemed in these three triumphs to [hold] the whole world captive.   Plutarch, LIVES OF THE NOBLE GREEKS AND ROMANS.

60   Pompey, Crassus and Caesar form an alliance and rule Rome as the First Triumvirate, a "masterful blend" (according to Plutarch) of Caesar's "youthful vigor," Pompey's long lifetime of experience, honor and renown, and Crassus' great wealth . . . and another Cato, the young great-grandson of old Cato the Censor, cries out that "By their own vote [the people are] placing a tyrant in their citadel." And Cicero calls them the worst of the *furiosi*, the madmen. Cato is imprisoned and Cicero banished. The three ". . . had formed a design," Plutarch says, "to take to themselves the greatest provinces . . . and [simply] parcel [them] out . . ." The republic is divided into three parts: Pompey will govern the east, Crassus the west, and Caesar "who has so won over the people and rabble by his hand-outs" all of Gaul, "with an army of four legions."

Like his great-grandfather, this Cato—the Younger, is intensely devoted to preserving the republic, and "amidst corruption and disorder, he showed such a love of discipline, so much bravery, courage and wisdom in everything . . . it appeared he was in no way inferior to the old Cato." Inheriting a fortune, he turns it into ready cash to loan to friends at no interest. A man of true virtue, austerity and resoluteness, he has already won renown in the military, and, before accepting political office, makes it a point to learn everything there is to know about it. He considers public service "the proper business of an honest man," and says any thanks given him should be given to the commonwealth. He will be called, "the Last Noble Roman."

Now does Caesar begin his conquest of Gaul. Through all the centuries, history has concentrated on those peoples and nations from the Mid-east to the Mediterranean who have recorded their affairs and left written records behind them; and given only slight attention to those people from whom many years hence will emerge that most important group of nations called Europe. North of the Alps from Spain to Bohemia and from Scotland to the Balkans, the many tribes of Celtic people have flourished for five centuries in a culture rich in farming, fighting and folk arts. But they will always remain something of a mystery, for the Celts do not yet have writing and, so, pass none of their history or philosophy on to posterity. Although constantly on the move fighting each other off or searching for new land, the Celts have generally settled certain areas; the *Nervii* in Belgium, the *Boii* in Bohemia, the *Celtiberi* in Spain, the *Helvetii* in Switzerland, the *Venetii* and the *Aedui* in Brittany and central France, with the *Parisii* along the Seine, founding the city now called Paris. The *Scordisci* and *Eravisci* have settled Transylvania and Budapest along the Danube, and the *Dardani* occupy the Balkans (and the Dardanelles) to the Black Sea.

The Celtic peoples

Theirs is an iron culture; chariots, weapons, utensils, but they trade with faraway countries (as did the lady of Vix 400 years ago) for silver, gold and other riches. Their clothing is woven of tartan plaid; leggings wrapped with rope, trimmed with golden collars and cuffs. Phoenecia and Greece long ago colonized parts of Gaul, and established beautiful cities at such places as Marseilles, Antibes and Nice, complete with temples, theaters and gardens, but most Gauls mistrust and resist Mediterranean "civilization" and retain their own ways. Gaul is an area of the world rich in beauty and natural resources; and Rome desires it greatly.

59   Totally lacking in military experience, Caesar, with Marc Antony at his side, begins his Gallic campaign. His military genius soon becomes apparent, and his pursuit of the Gallic Wars wins him glory in the field . . . and the love and respect of his soldiers.

> He was . . . master of the good will and hearty service of his soldiers . . . the love of honor and passion for distinction were inspired into them by Caesar himself . . . his contempt of danger was not wondered at . . . for they knew how much he coveted honor. But his enduring hardship beyond his natural strength astonished them . . . for he was a spare man, had soft and white skin . . . and was subject to an epilepsy . . .   Plutarch, LIVES

Caesar, himself, meticulously records every detail of his Gallic Wars, and of Gaul, itself . . .

> Gaul is divided into three parts, inhabited by the Belgae . . . the Aguitani . . . and the Celtae. There are two classes of persons [in addition to the common folk who are treated almost as slaves] . . . the druids and knights . . . the knights are [continuously] making wanton attacks [upon] themselves or repelling such. The druids are concerned with . . . worship . . . sacrifices; they decide disputes, determine rewards or penalties. The druids meet in conclave . . . once a year . . . they commit nothing to writing . . . and their training requires twenty years.   Julius Caesar, COMMENTARIES ON THE GALLIC WARS

The Druids meet in sacred groves of oak and mistletoe which they cut by moonlight and use for medicine.

Druids

Their cardinal doctrine is . . . that souls do not die, but after death, pass from one to another . . . and that for a man's life a man's life be paid . . . employing the Druids as ministers for such sacrifices . . . [They build cages] woven of twigs [in human shape] and fill them with living men . . . and set on fire. They worship Mercury, Apollo, Mars, Jupiter, Minerva. Into funeral pyres they cast everything, even [wives, children, slaves] that had been dear to the departed in life.   Caesar, THE GALLIC WARS

Two thousand years from now, farmers digging peat from a bog in northern England's Cheshire village of Lindow, will uncover a most startling object, the well preserved body of a man. They, and the local authorities, will believe him to be a modern-day murder victim, but carbon dating will place him to approximately this time. A handsome, healthy, aristocratic young man, he was no soldier or slave, for his body bears no wounds of battle nor wear and tear of labor; and his skin is unblemished. But there is one fatal wound at the back of his neck, and a "last meal" in his stomach; and authorities now believe him to have been a Druid; the wise men and sages of Britain and Gaul, a privileged class: judges, poets, physicians and magicians who, Caesar says, studied ". . . the stars and their movements, the size of the Universe and the Earth, the nature of things, the power of the immortal gods." Lindow Man is thought to have been a Druid sacrifice, and his new home, the British museum, considers him a most sensational find, the first tangible, empirical proof of Druidism.

55   Having pushed up into Germany, Caesar resolves to cross the Rhine River, to demonstrate Rome's superiority to the Germans and warn them of its invincibility; and he does it in a most spectacular way, not in unsafe, undignified little boats, but by building a timber bridge over which his legions can march, in triumph! The incident becomes one of the most famous chapters in his COMMENTARIES ON THE GALLIC WARS, which he writes, always, in the third person.

Caesar . . . had resolved to cross the Rhine [on a wooden bridge, which presented] the greatest difficulty . . . on account of the breadth, rapidity, and depth of the river . . . he . . . [sank pilings] each a foot and a half thick . . . at [distances] of two feet . . . by means of engines . . . and kept them firmly apart by beams two feet thick . . . in addition to . . . buttresses [which] sustained the force of the stream . . . within ten days the . . . whole work was complete . . . and the . . . army led over . . .   *ibid.*

Germans

Those Germans who sue for peace, Caesar treats in a "courteous manner" and returns to their territory, those who resist, he . . .

> . . . burned down their villages and houses and cut down their corn . . . when . . . [all he had resolved] was accomplished . . . namely to strike fear into the Germans . . . having spent . . . eighteen days beyond the Rhine, and . . . advanced far enough to serve both honor and interest—he returned into Gaul, and cut down the bridge.   Caesar, THE GAL-
> LIC WARS

As for German customs, Caesar writes that . . .

> The Germans differ much [from the Gauls] . . . have no Druids, but worship the sun, the Fire god and the Moon; their whole life is composed of hunting and [fighting] . . . they are zealous for toil and hardship . . .   *ibid.*

Back in Gaul, Caesar takes town after town, wooden walled-in fortified villages or settlements that will someday grow into France's great cities: Lyon, Bourges, Reims, Orleans, Limoges, LeHarve and Calais. He defeats the *Venetii* in Brittany and the *Nervii* in Belgium—a battle immortalized by William Shakespeare in Marc Antony's great oration. There ambassadors of the *Nervii* "recount the calamity of their state" to Caesar that their senators are reduced from 600 to three and their warriors from 60,000 to 500. According to Plutarch, Caesar . . .

> . . . drove [himself] so rapidly . . . and disciplined himself so far as to be able to dictate letters [while] on horseback and to give directions to two who took notes at the same time . . . he had not pursued the wars in Gaul full ten years when he had taken by storm above 800 towns and subdued 300 states.   Plutarch, LIVES OF THE NOBLE GREEKS AND
> ROMANS

All Gaul becomes a mere Roman province . . . save one tribe, the *Arverni* (in the vicinity of modern-day Auvergne), led by an "aristocratic, but headstrong" young man of "boundless energy," called Vercingetorix. Familiar with Latin manners, mores and military tactics, the handsome, polished Vercingetorix is no barbarian chieftan, and deals Caesar his only defeat in all Gaul. But his victory is short-lived for the Romans cannot be stopped, and Caesar takes Vercingetorix captive. The gallant Gaul will be held captive for six years, displayed in Caesar's *triumph* back in Rome, and die in a Roman prison. But his courage and gallantry will not be for-

Vercingetorix

gotten, and France, to this day, considers Vercingetorix its first national hero.

55   Eager to know more about the great island off Gaul's west coast, Caesar takes two legions and crosses the English Channel to Brittania, but is repulsed by the fierce, valiant Britons, who fight from shrieking-wheeled chariots which dart every which way amongst the Roman ranks, seemingly out of control .

> Caesar's ships . . . because of their size, could not be run ashore . . . the troops . . . loaded down with [weighty] arms . . . had to leap down from the vessels, stand firm in the waves, and fight the enemy [at the same time] . . . the enemy . . . with limbs free . . . hurled missiles . . . spurred on their horses . . . it frightened our troops . . . the Britons . . . dye themselves with woad, which produces a blue colour, and makes their appearance in battle . . . terrible. Caesar, THE GALLIC WARS

54 A second crossing—with five legions and 2000 cavalry—is more successful. Landing at Deal, only a few miles from today's Canterbury, they fight their way across Kent and up into Middlesex, crossing the Thames River near a fortified British town now known as London. In Book Five of his GALLIC WARS, Caesar describes Britain as . . .

> . . . triangular, one side opposite Gaul, the second towards Spain . . . [and] the third . . . has no land confronting it. Inland . . . Britain is inhabited by tribes . . . indigenous to the island, the maritime part by [booty-seeking Belgians of an earlier age.] The population is innumerable . . . farm buildings . . . close together . . . very like those of the Gauls . . . there is timber of every description . . . and . . . a great store of cattle . . . most Britons do not sow corn, but live on milk and [meat] and clothe themselves in skins. *ibid.*

Caesar returns to Gaul from Britain. He will leave its conquest to a later time. Some historians believe that Caesar painted the Britons and Druids blackly to justify Rome's—and his own—actions, and that, in truth, one need look for cruelty no farther than Rome, itself.

52 With Caesar away for 10 years, and Crassus just killed in battle in Parthia, Pompey the Great becomes sole consul of Rome, a man of whom Plutarch writes:

> Never had the Roman people's good-will and devotion been more zealous in all changes of fortune; more early in first springing up, more steadily rising with his prosperity, or more constant in his adversity . . . when he gave it was without assumption, when he received it was with dignity and honor. Plutarch, LIVES OF THE NOBLE GREEKS AND ROMANS

But . . .

> . . . while Caesar [now great and famous with his wars in Gaul] in appearance . . . seemed far distant from Rome, entangled in the affairs of the Belgians . . . and Britons, in truth he was working craftily by secret practices in the midst of the people, [under]mining Pompey in all political matters of importance. (And) . . . the city now . . . began to roll and swell, so to say, with the stir of the coming storm. *ibid.*

Cicero and Cato the Younger, both returned from exile, are not ignorant of what is happening. Cicero calls Caesar a "prince of scoundrels who has never seen the shadow of honor [or] right." And Cato (who, as *praetor* in 54, was stoned in the Forum for pushing a bill in the Senate to require all political candidates to disclose their financial status and campaign contributions) says that Caesar ". . . is the only one of the revolutionaries to undertake, cold-sober the subversion of the republic."

51   The Macedonian family of Ptolemy has been ruling Egypt for almost 300 years, since the death of Alexander the Great; and now its most famous member becomes queen, at 18 years of age. Cleopatra will rule Egypt for 20 years, one of history's most famous women. Her co-regent is her dimwitted brother/husband—whom she will murder. Cleopatra's fame is deserved for she is not just a figurehead, but cultivated, intelligent and accomplished; able, according to Plutarch, to speak "seven and more" languages, including Latin, Hebrew, Greek, Syrian and Arabian . . .

Cleopatra

> It was a pleasure to hear the sound of her voice, which like an instrument of many strings she could pass from one language to another . . . Her actual beauty . . . was not in itself so remarkable that none could be compared with her . . . but the contact of her presence . . . was irresistible . . . the attraction of her person, joining with the charm of her conversation . . . was . . . bewitching.   Plutarch, LIVES

Another ancient writer, the Jewish historian, Josephus, tells of another side, however, to the nature of Cleopatra, whom he calls a "wicked creature . . ."

> She was . . . very covetous . . . and if there were . . . any hopes of getting money she would violate both temples . . . sepulchers [and holy places] . . . a slave to her lusts . . . she wanted everything she could think of and did her utmost to gain it . . .   Joseph Ben
> Matthias or Josephus, ANTIQUITIES OF THE JEWS

Rome, meanwhile, is in the throes of a most miserable, corrupt, violent period of its existence, with no trace left of the ancient Roman uprightness or morality. Instead are every form of degradation, evil and dissolution. The society that once valued honest labor now lives on government hand-outs; the few poor who could work prefer the bribes to be had from vote-buying, blackmail, false witness, assassination and the public dole. Political campaigns are won by whichever candidate can get the most dirt on the other. Gang wars rule the streets and crimes of every kind abound; the only defense against them, for those who can afford them, are hired gladiators. As much as he dislikes him, Cicero says that the times need a Caesar.

49   Caesar returns to Italy from Gaul only to learn that Pompey, allied, now, with the republicans, has persuaded the senate to declare him a public enemy and order him to disband his army and give up his command.

> Caesar had long ago resolved upon the overthrow of Pompey, as had Pompey, for that matter, upon his . . . Crassus having been killed in Parthia . . . if one wished to make himself the greatest man in Rome, he had only to overthrow the other.   Plutarch, LIVES

49, January 10.   The order for Caesar to surrender his legions reads: ". . . the other side of the Rubicon." Instead, he crosses the small river . . . and begins a civil war.

> . . . when he came to the river Rubicon, which parts Gaul within the Alps from the rest of Italy . . . he wavered much in his mind . . . [considering] the greatness of the enterprise . . . how many calamities his [crossing] would bring upon mankind [and how it would be remembered by] posterity . . . [At last] using the proverb frequently in their mouths who enter upon dangerous and bold attempts, *Iacta alea est*, "The die is cast" . . . he took the river.   Plutarch, LIVES

Marching unresisted south to Rome, Caesar makes himself "master of all Italy without bloodshed in the space of 60 days," plundering nothing and forgiving all. Pompey, whose idle troops would be no match for Caesar's seasoned veterans, leaves for Greece to build up his forces and meet Caesar elsewhere.

48, June 7.   Pompey the Great and Julius Caesar meet in battle on the plains of Pharsalus in Thessaly to decide who will preside over what remains of the Roman republic. According to Caesar's own figures, Pompey's losses number 15,000 killed and 24,000 taken prisoner. Caesar's dead include 200 soldiers and 30 centurions.

> . . . how mad a thing human nature is when once possessed with . . . passion . . . they could no longer be induced to spare their country . . . their own glory or [that] which till this day both had . . . of having never yet been defeated. [Pompey] lost in one hour all [his many years of] glory and power.   *ibid.*

Pompey flees to Egypt and Caesar pursues him to Alexandria, only to find him . . . murdered. Cleopatra's brother, Ptolemy X, afraid to either aid him or let him go, had Pompey the Great stabbed to death as he stepped off his boat. On being shown Pompey's severed head and given his signet ring, Caesar bursts into tears.

Caesar sets up his command headquarters in the palace of the Ptolemies, and summons Cleopatra to meet with him, secretly, to discuss the fate of Egypt. Her ingenuity becomes apparent from the start . . .

> Cleopatra was at a loss how to get in undiscovered, till she thought of putting herself into the coverlet of a bed and lying at length, whilst (her servant) Appolodorus tied up the bedding and carried it on his back through the gates to Caesar's apartment.   *ibid.*

The Library in flames

Caesar is enchanted, and sets her up as his mistress although she is 30 years his junior. In due time she will bear him a son and call him Caesarion.

48   The great library at Alexandria, Alexander's dream and Ptolemy's accomplishment, is (partially) destroyed at about this time. Nobody knows for certain what actually happened, but it is thought that some of the Roman troops set it afire, whether accidentally or otherwise.

What is certain is the dreadful loss to mankind; the knowledge and wisdom of centuries of man's progress stored in its million-some scrolls, 40,000 of which probably went up in smoke in this single night.* There had been stored in Ptolemy's library the work of, literally, thousands of writers of Hellenistic Greece; in a building, itself a work of art, that displayed magnificent works of art. There had been the great philosophical and theatrical works of ancient Greece; the many sciences explored throughout the last 300 years; books of medicine, music, poetry, history, geography, biographies of great people now unknown; the wisdom, languages, legends and lore of far-away countries; to say nothing of romance, mythology and adventure, and the original Septuagint, itself. The world will survive many upheavals in its long progression from this age to our own; wars, revolutions, dark ages and light, ravages, pillages and elementyal eruptions, erosions and withering away. Today it is pure speculation whether the great writers and philosophers who have survived the centuries were really the greatest, or that those who do exist are, perhaps, really the great survivors.

c. 48   The WISDOM *OF* SOLOMON is written in Alexandria.

The WISDOM OF SOLOMON

Apocryphal Book — Written in Greek,   c. 48 B.C.

This long poem is not Solomon's wisdom at all, but that of a Hellenistic Jew who lived in Alexandria at about this time. Of course, there is no way of knowing, but it is interesting to speculate whether he had ever worked or studied in the Great Library. Living in the very heart of Greek Hellenism, his wisdom is both Hebrew and Greek: ". . . there is for all mankind one entrance into life, and a common departure," he says, "but the souls of the righteous are in the hand of God." Wisdom is a "kindly spirit," he writes, "a holy spirit. Wisdom is radiant and unfading . . . giving heed to her laws is assurance of immortality, and immortality brings one near to God . . ." Thus, "the love of wisdom is the keeping of her laws." These "laws" are Old Testament laws, which the writer is attempting to express in ways attractive to "modern" Greek philosophical minds used to the teachings of Plato and Aristotle, the Greek word *philosophy*, itself, meaning "love of wisdom." In his latter chapters, he effectively dismisses the futility of a world of pagan gods and graven idols:

> . . . men who were ignorant of God . . . supposed that . . . fire or wind . . . the circle of the stars . . . or the luminaries of heaven were the gods that rule the world . . . through delight in the beauty of these things [they] assumed them to be gods . . . let them know how much better than these is their LORD . . . the author of beauty [who] created them

---

* The final destruction of the Alexandria Library will not come until A.D. 642 when conquering Muslim Arabs will confiscate and haul away its contents to their own libraries in Baghdad and Damascus. Then will follow the great, Golden Age of Muslim enlightenment, so highly praised in contrast to Europe's wallowing in its own "Dark Age."   (See: J.H. Ellens, BAR, Jul/Aug 2003)

> . . . yet [they] are little to be blamed . . . for . . . they trust in what they see, because the things that are seen are beautiful.
>
> But miserable, with their hopes set on dead things, are [those] who give the name "gods" to the works of men's hands . . . gold and silver fashioned with skill . . . a useless stone [shaped by] an ancient hand . . . a [sawn] down tree [carved] like the image of a man . . . or [made] like some worthless animal [and set in] a niche . . . in the wall . . . an image a lifeless thing . . . for health [they] appeal to a thing that is weak, for life [they] pray to a thing that is dead.　　Chs. 13 & 14

II ESDRAS was not actually written at this time but, rather, some 150 years hence, about 100 A.D. It is included here, though, to keep it in the APOCRYPHA YEARS.

II ESDRAS

Apocryphal Book — Written in Hebrew/Aramaic,　c. 100 A.D.

Like the book of DANIEL and that which will become the last book of the Bible, REVELATION, II ESDRAS is an *apocalypse* . . . prophetic revelation. The writer or writers of ESDRAS (Ezra in Greek) had strange, frightening visions of the end of Israel, the fall of Rome and the end of the world. Like the writer of REVELATION, he disguises Rome as Babylon, and cries, "Woe to you, Babylon," for the destruction it will (by A.D. 100) have wrought. There shall be "wars and rumors of wars," he warns, "calamities, death and destruction," But the "elect" shall be tested as gold is tested by fire, and ". . . you who keep my commandments and precepts will be delivered."

The Jews are faring well at the hands of the Romans, well-liked and appreciated by Caesar for their rulers' friendship and co-operation in supplying troops for his legions, and he issues a decree posted in brass at Rome:

> Gaius Caesar [imperator, dictator, high priest] and consul the fifth time, decreed that the Jews shall possess Jerusalem, and may encompass that city with walls and that Hyrcanus . . . the ethnarch of the Jews retain it in the manner he himself pleases . . .　　Josephus, ANTIQUITIES OF THE JEWS

Hyrcanus, Judea's Hasmonean ruler, is of the Maccabee family, which has ruled Judea now for 116 years, since the heroic Judas Maccabeus and his family freed it from Syrian rule. It is a family that Josephus calls "splendid and illustrious" both for "the nobility of their stock . . . and the glorious actions they preformed for our nation." But in these latter days there have been nothing but "dissension" among them, jealousies and maneuvering for the throne. Now, an Idumean (or Edomite) politician and political opportunist named Herod, the son of Antipater, schemes with the Romans, and is made governor of that area of Judea called Galilee. He is, Josephus says, "of no more than a [common] family and of no eminent extraction," but he has winning ways, has spent many youthful years in Rome and has friendships and ties with many important Romans. The Galileans mistrust him, though, and resent an alien Edomite having power over them. Herod is just 25, mightily ambitious and, according to Josephus, a "youth of great mind and courage."

Julius Caesar

48   Caesar wins another major victory over the republican forces at Thrapsus, and it is all over. The Roman republic, begun 500 years before this time when Persia was still a power, before the glory that was Greece, before Pericles and Alexander, is dead, slain by ambition, lust for power, contempt for constitutional law, political corruption and manipulation of the masses. Cato the Younger, the "last noble Roman," having believed passionately in a Roman republic, who worked and fought for it, then seen it die, dies with it. After an evening with friends and his son, good food, wine and conversation, a stroll around camp and orders to his officers, he calmly, quietly reads Plato's dialogue on the soul . . . and stabs himself to death. Caesar later says, "I begrudge you taking your life, Cato, even as you begrudged me the chance to spare it."

Julius Caesar returns home in triumph, and is named dictator for 10 years. Cleopatra and her son, Caesarion, join him in Rome. Caesar's enemies are not enchanted with Cleopatra, though, and condemn him for having taken up with a "shameless, oriental whore" who, they believe, will scheme for control of Rome. There is no aspect of life that Caesar does not now control; military, governmental, bureaucratic, financial, religious, all are under his control. It is said he was born to do great things, and he has. He works for many reforms in the government and accomplishes much, while pardoning his enemies. He establishes colonies outside Italy where the poor of Rome can move to better their lives; re-organizes city and provincial governments, and commissions the drawing up of a new calendar, which begins the use of a leap year. The "Julian" calendar uses his name for the month of July. A far cry from the dictator/butcher, Sulla, Caesar's nature is never vengeful, spiteful or mean, but rather, giving, forgiving, and generous in wealth and benevolence. When once he could not pay his troops for lack of funds, they took up a collection to give to him. He burned Pompey's vast correspondence—unread—so that nothing damning could be learned from it. And yet, while designing a new Rome, he has destroyed the old; the republic 500 years in the building, now gasping its final hours. And those Romans who had hoped to preserve it are afraid of his naked power-grab. Among the many actions that cause resentment against Caesar is a high-handed manner of treating the senate as a mere yes-man. His co-consul not being active one year, wags called it the "consulate of Julius and Caesar." He is overheard to say that "the republic is merely a name, without form or substance," and to quiet his critics he appoints one Caninius co-consul for the last day of the year 45, which causes Cicero to quip that "Caninius is a most vigilant magistrate, for during his term of office, he never slept."

44   Caesar is appointed Dictator for Life by an accommodating Senate, and a conspiracy against his life is organized. On one of Rome's many holidays, the Feast of the Lupercal,

JVLIVS CÆSAR

Marc Antony, Caesar's co-consul, offers him a laurel diadem—a king's crown—and three times Caesar declines. But the conspirators believe that he is not sincere; that the day will come that he will make himself king, that position so hated by the Romans that its forbiddence was the first item written into the Law of Twelve Tables 500 years ago after the overthrow of the Tarquin kings: "Any man who tries to make himself king can be killed . . . without trial." So Cassius, Casca and Marcus Brutus continue their plans, all free men, and alive, since Caesar pardoned them for fighting against him in the civil war. Marcus Junius Brutus is the scion of one of Rome's most illustrious and ancient families, a direct descendent of that Lucius Junius Brutus who helped oust the Tarquins to become one of Rome's first two co-consuls. He has inherited all of the first Brutus' good qualities.

> Brutus, for his virtue, was esteemed by the people, beloved by his friends, admired by the best men, and hated not [even] by his enemies . . . For he was a man of singularly gentle nature, of a great spirit, insensible of the passions of anger . . . or covetousness . . . Antony, himself, [said] that Brutus was the only man that conspired against Caesar out of the apparent justice of the action . . .   Plutarch, LIVES

Brutus (whom Caesar believed was his own son from a long-ago love affair) is an unwilling conspirator, but his love of the republic is great and his intentions are honorable and genuine. Not so Cassius, though, the originator of the plot . . . whom both Plutarch and William Shakespeare say had a "lean and hungry look . . ."

> What was barbarous and cruel was Cassius . . . a man of fierce disposition [who] hated Caesar . . . out of private malice rather than love of the republic . . . [indeed, all of them save Brutus, alone, plotted] . . . from private envy and malice . . .   *ibid.*

44, March 15.   Caesar's wife, Calpurnia, begs him not to go to the senate as she had a terrible dream in which she saw him with bleeding wounds, but the conspirator sent to escort him prevails. A soothsayer had told Caesar to "Beware the Ides of March," and on his way to the senate . . .

> . . . Caesar said to the soothsayer, "The Ides of March are come," who answered him calmly, "Yes they are come, but they are not past."   *ibid.*

Julius Caesar is stabbed to death on the Ides of March in the senate chamber by the daggers of 23 conspirators and, according to Plutarch, "falls dead at the foot of Pompey's statue." Marc Antony, with Caesar's bloody toga in hand, delivers an impassioned funeral address to the people of Rome on the senate steps, saying that the conspirators—"honorable men, all, all honorable men"—did what they thought was right . . . and then reads them Caesar's will, in which he left 75 drachmas to "every Roman citizen." Playing their emotions like an instrument, Antony's oration leads to anarchy . . . and civil war . . .

> There was no man of his time like Antony for addressing a multitude or for carrying soldiers with him by the force of his words.   Plutarch, LIVES

Marked men now, the conspirators flee Rome for their various provinces, and Cleopatra flees to Egypt. Cicero, who had taken no part in the conspiracy, but did not condemn it, becomes leader of the Senate, lamenting that to kill a monarch does not kill the monarchy; and three men struggle for control of that . . . and the nation: Marc Antony, Marcus Lepidus, consul and son of a consul, and Gaius Julius Caesar Octavianus, great-nephew of the first Caesar. Born in the year Cicero was consul, Octavian is only 18 now, a serious and austere youth, and he leaves his schooling in Greece and hurries back to Rome, where he learns that Caesar had adopted him his legal heir. Now Octavian, believing that he is destined to save Rome, returns to claim his inheritance. Mostly he is paid little heed, and Cicero calls him a "praiseworthy youth" who should be "rewarded . . . and removed." That remark numbers Cicero's days.

43, November 27.   Antony, Lepidus and Octavian take joint power as a second "triumvirate" for five years, and retire to an off-shore island for a parley. The first order of business: punishment of the murderers.

> . . . the conference lasted three days. The empire was soon determined of . . . being divided amongst them as if it had been their paternal inheritance. That which gave them the most trouble was who should be put to death, each bargaining for his own friends or family . . . in the end . . . Octavian sacrificed Cicero to Antony, Antony gave up his uncle . . . and Lepidus yielded his brother to them. I do not believe anything ever took place more truly savage or barbarous than this . . . for, in this exchange of blood for blood, they were equally guilty of the lives they surrendered . . . and those they took.   *ibid.*

By the time the proscriptions are ended the dead will include 300 senators and 2000 knights. Now Antony and Octavian head for Asia Minor to do battle with Cassius and Brutus. Plutarch says that "never [before] had two such large Roman armies come together to engage each other."

42   According to Plutarch—and Shakespeare—the conspirator Brutus, in his military headquarters in Asia Minor, ". . . working very late all alone in his tent, with a dim lamp burning by him," receives a visit from an "unnatural and frightful body" standing by him. It says only . . .

> Thou shalt see me at Philippi

At two huge battles at Philippi, in Greece, Brutus and Cassius are defeated by Antony and Octavian. Both men die by their own swords, the same that helped slay Caesar. Octavian returns to Italy where, for the next 15 years he will slowly, but very surely, build up a strong political power base. Marc Antony returns, Plutarch says, "back to his old ways."

Antony is as much disliked in civilian life as he is well liked in the military . . . and for the same reasons: a coarse, crude, free-wheeling camaraderie with his troops, encour-

Marc Antony

aging—and sharing—their various escapades, sexual and otherwise. A true personification of sophisticated Hellenism, Antony epitomizes its self-indulgence, trusts too much in its people and promises, and repents its betrayals too late. Cicero had called him a "wretched, insignificant subordinate of Caesar's," a "toy captain," who publically flaunts his debaucheries, and Antony, to his eternal disgrace, will prove him right.

. . . Herod of Idumea, tetrarch of Galilee, is back in Rome, having fled Jerusalem to escape political intrigue. A friend of the Romans, he closely allies himself with—and bribes—Marc Antony to persuade the senate to declare him king of the Jews.

> . . . Herod offered (Antony) money to make him king, as he had formerly given it to him to make him tetrarch . . . So a senate was convocated . . . and Antony informed them . . . that it was for their advantage . . . that Herod should be king. This seemed good to all the Senators; and so they made a decree . . . when the senate was dissolved, Antony and Caesar went out of the senate house, with Herod between them . . . to offer sacrifices, and to lay up their decrees in the capitol . . . Antony also feasted Herod on the first day of his reign. And thus did this man receive the kingdom . . . on the hundred and eighty-fourth Olympiad.   Josephus, ANTIQUITIES OF THE JEWS XIV, 14:4–5

40   Antony leaves Rome, traveling through Asia Minor—to take control of his third of the empire, the Eastern provinces, including the land of his birth, Egypt. In the years ahead, Asia Minor's city of Tarsus will become famous as the home of a man named Saul. For now, its fame rests on other foundations. At Tarsus now, Antony summons Cleopatra to answer charges that she gave aid to Cassius, and gets no response. He summons her again . . . and again . . .

> . . . at last . . . she came sailing up the Cydnus in a barge with gilded stern and out-spread sails of purple, while oars of silver beat time to the music of flutes and harps. She herself lay . . . under a canopy of cloth of gold dressed as Venus . . . come to feast with Bacchus. Antony was . . . captivated . . . [She awoke and kindled to fury his passions, stifling the last traces of sound judgment. Her love with Caesar was when just a girl, but with Antony in the time of life when women's beauty is most splendid, and intellects in full maturity.]
> Plutarch, LIVES

Antony and Cleopatra form a political, military and romantic alliance that makes a great love story . . . today. But it was not that to Rome, for there she is called "that oriental whore," and there it is feared that she and Antony intend to unite Rome and Egypt and rule both from Alexandria and the fears are well founded.

37   "King" Herod returns to Judea from Rome with Antony's backing and, according to Josephus, takes Jerusalem by force, kills the last Maccabean ruler and becomes, in political fact, King of the Jews.

> [Herod] made an assault upon the city, and took it by storm . . . and all parts were full of those that were slain . . . as if (his troops] were a company of madmen, they fell upon persons of all ages, without distinction . . . Herod was afraid lest [the true, blood-line ruler] Antigonus . . . should be carried to Rome . . . he might get his cause to be heard by the senate, and might demonstrate [that] he was himself of the royal blood, and Herod but a private man, that therefore it belonged to his sons . . . to have the kingdom . . . Out of Herod's fear of this it was that he, by giving Antony a great deal of money . . . persuad[ed] him to have Antigonus slain . . . And this is what history tells us was the end of the [Hasmonean] family.   Josephus, ANTIQUITIES OF THE JEWS XIV, 16:2,4

It is the end of the dynasty of Judas Maccabeus, Israel's great hero who overthrew the Syrians 126 years before. And it is the end of true Jewish rule in Israel.

36   Antony is back in Rome, where Octavian, all this while, has been working tirelessly and skillfully to win back the good will of the Roman people after the blood-baths that followed Caesar's assassination. Rome, now demoralized, devastated and drained of energy from hundreds of years of social and civil wars and conquests, is sunk in crime, corruption and chaos, and universally despised for its beastial rape of the world. Now Octavian begins to see himself as a healer, a restorer and a champion of what was good in "the old days," and that includes defending the Latin/Western spirit against the wiles of the effeminate Hellenized east. Now, to scotch Cleopatra's ambitions, and to seal the alliance between the two wary allies, Octavian gives his much-loved sister, Octavia, in marriage to Antony. In due time they have a child, and for a while all is well. But Cleopatra's blood is in his veins, his soul no longer his own but hers, and so Antony leaves wife and child for the East. On his arrival, his first action is to give Cleopatra a present: Phoenecia, [Syria], Cyprus . . . Cilicia . . . [part of Arabia] . . . and "that side of Judea which produces balm."

32   Antony sends a letter of divorce to Octavia, marries Cleopatra, and wills all of his third of the empire to the twin children she has borne him. In a fury, and with the approval of the senate, Octavian, now an implacable enemy, declares war; and in a brilliant move, declares it, not on Antony, which would make it just another wearisome, draining civil war, but against Cleopatra, which makes it a "world" war, "enlightened," pragmatic Rome against decadent, obsolete Egypt.

King Herod of Judea makes no effort to support Antony. In fact, Herod is preoccupied elsewhere, happily unable to help the man who made him.

31, Sept. 2.   Octavian and his best general—and best friend—Marcus Agrippa, defeat Antony and Cleopatra in a great naval battle at Actium, off the coast of Greece. Antony's troops far outnumber Octavian's but his ships are heavy galleys and Octavian's triremes are sleek and swift. Antony's shore-based foot-soldiers and horse are greater than Octavian's, also, but Cleopatra wanted a naval battle, so Actium is fought at sea. Still, Antony commands his navy brilliantly and courageously, sailing from ship to ship in a small boat, encouraging his men and bidding them to stand as firm as they would on land. And then, the incredible happens:

> . . . on a sudden Cleopatra's sixty ships were seen hoisting sail and making out to sea in full flight . . . with a fair wind . . . [and] here . . . Antony showed . . . the world [that he was no longer commander of his own judgment . . . For, as if he had been born part of her, and must move with her . . . he abandoned all that were fighting and spending their lives for him . . . to follow her that had so well begun his ruin and would hereafter accomplish it . . . Those who were [later] told of it could not . . . [believe] . . . so incredible a thing as that a general who had 19 entire legions and 12,000 horse . . . could abandon all and fly away, and he, above all, who had . . . in a thousand . . . battles been inured to [misfortune.] Plutarch, LIVES OF THE NOBLE GREEKS AND ROMANS

Reality comes to Antony quickly, though, and in miserable, disgraced seclusion, he hears that all his allied princes and kings have deserted him and gone over to Octavian; while Cleopatra spends her time testing various poisons on condemned prisoners to see which are least painful. Antony kills himself with his own sword, so that he falls, "not ignobly, but a Roman by a Roman overcome." Cleopatra, last of the Greek Ptolemies who had ruled Egypt since the death of Alexander the Great in 323 B.C., commits suicide with the sting of an asp brought to her in a basket of figs. As Octavian's prize possession, she had no wish to be taken prisoner to Rome to suffer the humiliation of being put on exhibition in his triumphal procession. Octavian graciously allows them to be buried together . . .

> The thing had been quickly done. Opening the doors they saw her stone dead, lying upon a bed of gold, set out in all her royal ornaments. [With her last breath] her maid-servant said it was "extremely well done" of her lady ". . . as becomes the descendant of so many kings," and fell dead by her. *ibid.*

Octavian prevails, the most powerful man in Rome, the only contender for the throne. One hundred years of civil strife and civil war are ended, and Egypt is secured for Rome.

Actium was far more than just a battle between two Roman factions seeking power; for its symbolism went much deeper, even into the very psyche and spirit of Rome, through its religion. For, the possibility of "Egyptizing" Rome with Egypt's assorted animal and creature gods, was just as repugnant to the Romans as "Orientalizing" Greece by the Persians had been to the Greeks (that the battle of Salamis ended.) That the high-minded, intellectual wisdom of the Greeks and the practical, stoic pragmatism of Rome could be perverted by the demeaning worship of cows, cats and crocodiles was unthinkable, and made Actium not only a "world" war, but a holy war as well. Thus, even though the Roman republic was dead, the Latin spirit was still alive, regenerate in one man, its champion and savior, Octavian Caesar . . . soon to be called Augustus.

And King Herod of Judea quickly declares his allegiance to the victor.

It was no small thing for history that the path of Octavian Caesar should cross that of Cleopatra; for with her death THREE THOUSAND years of empire have come to an end; while his life, the most glorious years ahead, will begin another empire . . . larger and mightier than any before.

29   Octavian Caesar returns to Italy and is awarded a three-day *triumph* into Rome. With him is his greatest general and best friend, Marcus Agrippa, the hero of the battle of Actium. And with Octavian in his *triumph,* also, comes the entire, vast, unbelievably huge Egyptian treasury of gold, gems and antiquities to enrich the coffers of Rome. Octavian is universally hailed as the "restorer of peace," and the savior of Rome and the Roman people; and is awarded the title, *PRINCEPS CIVITATUS,* the First citizen of Rome.

28   The Roman senate awards Octavian another title, the *PRINCEPS SENATUS* or, First on the Roll Call of the Senate. He has based his right to leadership on *Imperium legitimum,* or, legitimate authority, as the true and rightful heir of the "Divine Julius"; and on the personal standards of leadership he has set for himself: *virtus, clementia, justitia* and *pietas*— virtue, clemency, justice and loyalty, or piety, devotion and patriotism. All this in a man who began his mission as an amoral bloodletter. He is now, in his own words, "the Master of All Things."

27, January 13.   Octavian's first decision as sole ruler of Rome is among the most important he will ever have to make: how to maintain a delicate balance. The republic, as it used to be, is dead; he knows that, but he also knows that dictatorship is too dangerous, and he has no desire to meet his great uncle's fate. The question, then, is how to build a new republic without rebuilding into it the very weaknesses that destroyed the old. So, in a remarkably shrewd, dramatic, far-sighted—and amazing—political move, he resigns his office and relinquishes his power announcing that the republic is restored. The flabbergasted senate, reacting in shock, also resigns, begging him to reconsider; and Octavian agrees . . . on condition that everything be done within constitutional limitations. He places his own office—now *Imperator,* or Emperor—under the authority, jurisdiction and scrutiny of the senate, liable to regular re-election and accountability in all matters . . . save only a few: he is to have sole control over foreign affairs and the military: complete freedom of action for what he believes the best interests of the empire. Under Octavian's *Nova Concordia* or New Deal, he is to be recognized, only, as *Princeps Senatus* or, roughly, Principal Senator, and his government a *Principate,* a principality.

The terrible civil wars had left Rome, and all Italy, a devastated shambles, economy non-existent, the countryside in neglected ruin; roads, aquaducts, bridges, towns and cities, all in ruin; and its peoples' spirits demoralized; morality a thing of the past, fear of the future the only reality. People don't care, any more, whether they can vote; they worry whether they can walk a street in safety. They don't care about their responsibilities; they want to be taken care of. And now they have, for a leader, one of the ablest, cleverest, subtlest, most devious and infinitely patient rulers in history . . . as evidenced by his own motto of *Festina lente* or "Make haste slowly," and the figure of the inscrutable Sphinx on his signet ring. He is a genius at presenting his case, at making people believe they want what he wants them to have. Everything he speaks, he writes out and reads, so he can't be mistaken or misquoted. And in crafting his *principate,* this "prince" combines the best ideas of the right wing (Cato, Cicero and Brutus) with those of the left (Caesar, Sulla and Marius) to found a workable middle way.

Octavian had brought back to Rome with him, the vast fortunes of golden Egypt, and now he puts the great horde of wealth into circulation, and overnight money is available for loans to start new businesses, repair neglected aquaducts, and re-build ruined roads; to buy farm implements and potter's wheels and school books. He promises no more confiscation of property or person, and no more blood-bath or vendetta; and hope begins to return to the Roman people.

27, January 17.   In a great, solemn ceremony, the senate, rejoicing in its restored powers, bestows upon Octavian the title *AUGUSTUS* (the Exalted), so, using his family name, Caesar, he becomes CAESAR AUGUSTUS, the first Emperor of . . .

... *the* ... *ROMAN EMPIRE. It begins* ...
the AGE OF AUGUSTUS ...

27 ... and he is, according to a later Roman historian, Cornelius Tacitus (See: A.D. 100) "... thwarted by no man."

> ... after the fall of Brutus and Cassius, there remained none to fight for the commonwealth ... no leader even [of] the Julian party ... he (Octavius) began by gradations to exalt himself over them; to draw to himself the functions of the senate and ... magistrates, and the framing of the laws; in which he was thwarted by no man ... Neither were the provinces averse to that condition of affairs; since they mistrusted the government of the senate and people ... and the avarice of the magistrates ... Cornelius Tacitus, ANNALS OF THE ROMAN PEOPLE, Book I

Augustus

And Augustus' proclamation goes out: that the world, sick of war, is to be blessed with peace, a ROMAN peace, a *PAX AUGUSTA*. All the many countries which now make up the Empire will be protected by Rome in exchange for their loyalty and allegiance to Rome. Those provinces which are secure to Rome and do not need military supervision, may govern themselves. Those, like Egypt, which would bolt from Rome if they could, Augustus puts under military governorships. They will all be granted free trade amongst themselves; rapid communication and transportation; and prosperous commerce. To this end, he organizes a vast system of civil service (including various "fringe benefits") and more equitable taxation. He appoints successful businessmen to administrative positions, and allows Roman cities to govern themselves. Roman citizens may travel unhindered throughout the empire, and any Roman citizen, in any part of the empire suffering injustice under the law, may appeal as a last resort, to Caesar himself, in accordance with the ancient Law of Twelve Tables. Soon, now, a Jewish Roman citizen, named Paul, will make use of the last two benefits.

Augustus plans great things for the capital city. He will restore Rome's old temples and build many new. He will carry out vast urban renewal projects, tear down tenement slums and build new public housing. He divides Rome into political wards and precincts, appoints a city *prefect* (mayor) and organizes fire and police departments, all the world's first. And to ensure his own safety, Augustus creates an elite *Praetorian* Guard—three *cohorts* of a thousand men each—as his personal body guard; and six more *cohorts* stationed around the city. It will, in time, become strong enough to make—and overthrow—emperors.

Augustus hopes to bring back morality to his sin-loving land, and supports a series of strict laws which include provisions that allow young people to attend certain functions only "... when accompanied by an adult." Supporting him in this, as in everything, is Augustus' second wife, the aristocratic Livia Drusilla, who will become renowned

Livia

for her steadfast devotion to her husband; and her modest, matronly ways which, historians say, are the perfect model to other Roman women of what an ideal wife should be. With a heritage, not only of the Claudian family, but Livian and Julian also, Livia's nobility is highly exalted and among the most ancient in Rome, going back to the first king, Romulus, himself. As Augustus' own personal tastes are extremely simple—a few bites of food and maybe one glass of wine—Livia often cooks many of his meals herself, and weaves the homespun for his togas with her own hands.

Augustus has a genuine, deep and abiding interest in culture and the arts; those fashioned both by hand and mind; and three of Rome's greatest writers will, each in time, enjoy his patronage and friendship; the historian Livy, and poets Horace and, for now, Virgil, who some scholars consider as important to Rome as any emperor. Just as Homer's ODYSSEY was a saga of the sea, Virgil's GEORGICS sings the praises of land and the dignity of laboring on the land. Aristotle had taught the Greeks that the highest good for man is the contemplative life—thought, wisdom and philosophy; but Virgil says there is nothing wrong with work; that it is good honest labor that makes a life worthwhile, the concept that made Rome great in the days of its building the republic; that concept Augustus now hopes to restore. Virgil is happiest on his small farm near Naples, and his GEORGICS tell of essential things: the cultivation of fields, how heavenly bodies affect the weather and how to read their signs; how to breed horses, raise herds and flocks, dress grape vines, trees and olives and to keep bees. Virgil had read the GEORGICS to a delighted Augustus in 23, and now he becomes the emperor's *poet laureate,* and spends the rest of his life writing what some will call the "Roman Bible." Rome is a city/nation unique in history, he writes, divinely destined to bring civilization and peace to the world, a new age, a Roman Peace; and Augustus was divinely appointed to be that bringer of peace. The glory of Rome is to shine upon the world through the empire; its mission unlike any ever before; and he bases his poem on a story as old as Rome itself:

> I sing of arms and the man who first from the shores of Troy came destined an exile to Italy . . .   Virgil, the AENEID, 1:1

The man Virgil sings of is Aeneas who, in obedience to his divine destiny of founding the city of Rome, so long ago left a heart-broken Queen Dido to perish on an immolation

pyre at Carthage. But it is not only Aeneas of whom the poet sings, but Rome's second founder as well, the divinely decreed Augustus; and Virgil's injunction to him and to his successors of what their mission and destiny are . . .

> Others shall shape bronzes . . . shall mold from marble living faces, shall better plead their cases in court . . . name the stars as they rise: you, Roman, make your task to rule nations by your government (these shall be your skills), to impose ordered ways upon a state of peace, to spare those who have submitted and to subdue the arrogant.
> Virgil, the AENEID, 6:847

Virgil

In another of his writings, the ECOLOGUES, Virgil makes a most enigmatic statement about a child soon to be born, who will usher in a new age for mankind:

> Now too the virgin goddess returns, the golden days of Saturn's reign return, now a new race descends from high heaven . . . Begin, baby boy, to recognize your mother with, a smile.   Virgil, the ECOLOGUES, 4:1

Some scholars think it is Augustus, himself, pictured as savior; but others, in years ahead, will see the child far differently, and venerate Virgil as a Christian prophet. Thirteen hundred years from now a Florentine writer named Dante Alighieri, will be guided in his own long poem, The DIVINE COMEDY, through purgatory and hell, on his journey to paradise; and conversing together, Dante and Virgil will agree that that savior was, indeed, born . . . but not in Rome . . .

> The world is all renewed; Justice returns and man's primeval spring . . . and out of Heaven descends another brood.   Dante, *La DIVINA COMEDIA, PARADISO*. Canto 22, line 70, suggesting the birth of Christ and His Christian Church.

Thorough and methodical as he is in everything, Augustus is already considering an eventual successor to his throne, and his choices are: Marcellus, husband of his only daughter, Julia. Now 20 years old, Marcellus shows much promise of intelligence and administrative ability. Or Drusus, younger son of his wife Livia, by her first husband. Now a bright young man of 17, Drusus is quick-witted, much interested in military and civic affairs, and Augustus loves him as a son. In no case does Augustus want Livia's older son, Tiberius, to gain the succession. Although he is an admirable young man in many ways, and appears headed for a brilliant military career, Augustus sees, also, disturbing signs of a moody, suspicious nature. Tiberius is, however, Livia's favorite . . . and Livia is an ambitious woman.

23   The first of his many grief's to come, Augustus' son-in-law, Marcellus, dies at the age of 20.

21   Augustus arranges a marriage between Marcellus' widow, his daughter, Julia, and his trusted friend and advisor, the famous general, Marcus Agrippa—he who defeated Antony and Cleopatra at Actium. Born the same year, they have been lifelong friends, and Agrippa's expertise, loyalty and wisdom have been invaluable to Augustus. An exceedingly wealthy man, his generosity has helped make Rome the gleaming marble vision it is; and he will, himself, build its most beautiful temple, the *Pantheon*. A man of many accomplishments, Agrippa is now Augustus' choice to be his successor to the throne.

Agrippa

Julia will bear Agrippa five children, including two sons, Lucius and Gaius; but give him, also, pain and humiliation, for Augustus' only child races with the fastest crowd in Rome, deceives Agrippa repeatedly, and makes little effort to conceal her wantonness.

19   The poet Virgil dies unexpectedly, his AENEID not yet polished to his own satisfaction, and he has ordered it destroyed . . . an order Augustus, happily for the world, sees is not carried out. The former republican partisan and military tribune, Horatius Flaccus, or Horace, becomes Augustus' *poet laureate,* whose ODES and EPODES are admired and emulated by poets to this day.

Horace

Horace writes his ODES about anything that comes to mind: why an old woman should act her own age and not that of a sweet young thing, to advising a shy young lover to break loose from mama; from hoping to pass his old age in style, with a sound mind, to correct behavior at a drinking party. Having risen in the military to tribune, he recalls his service—and defeat—of the republican cause under Brutus and Cassius, and his subsequent pardon by Octavian, and asks whether any Roman streams were untainted by the civil wars, and what sea was not dyed incarnadine. But that is over now, and he opposes empire no more; rather, sees Augustus as the savior of Rome; and he extols his glories as a "Herculean Caesar," saying, "I will fear no insurrection nor violent death while Caesar keeps the world." The great landed estates that the Punic Wars created by the importation of thousands of enslaved prisoners of war, thereby ousting other thousands of tax-paying small farmers, has changed the whole makeup of Italy, he writes, and . . .

> . . . now regal villas . . . leave few acres for plowing . . . [and] ornamental ponds and beds of violets [replace] olive groves . . . [but] no ivory or gilded panels gleam in my house . . . my Sabine farm . . .   Horace, ODES 2:15,18

Well acquainted with luxury, Horace describes eloquently everything from elegant estates to fabulous feasts; but much prefers and loves his small farm in the Sabine Hills, one of the most famous farms in history, and he is content to live there until he dies, an event of which he has no fear, since ". . . pallid Death kicks impartially at the doors of hovels and mansions." Rather, he warns, "avoid speculation about the future [and] count as credit the days chance deals." Enjoy your life and . . . *CARPE DIEM!* Seize the day!

> Do not inquire, we may not know, what end the Gods will give . . . The better course is to bear whatever will be . . . be wise, decant the wine, prune back your long-term hopes. Life ebbs as I speak—so seize each day, and grant the next no credit.   Horace, ODES 1:2

18   King Herod has been ruler of far-away Judea for 21 years, now, and can easily be called "the Great." Shrewd, calculating and clever, Herod is a consummate politician and diplomatic genius. He may be only a client king to overlord Rome, but he is, also, another of history's great, indefatigable builders. His fortress-palaces are everywhere; Samaria, Bethlehem, Jericho's magnificent Winter Palace and mountain-top Masada near the Dead Sea. His gigantic race arena at Jerusalem is built to please—and rival—Caesar's Circus

Maximus at Rome; and his brand-new seaport city, Caesarea, is built from scratch in the wilderness, a marvel of modern engineering with break-waters, sluice channels, aqueducts and inner and outer harbors. Its ruins, both out of and under water, can be seen to this day. Herod learned much during his early years in Rome, and Caesarea is built in Roman style with a forum, government buildings, baths and, dominating the whole, a great temple to his friend, Caesar Augustus.

Herod the Great

But Herod the Great is also unscrupulous, cunning and cold-blooded, incredibly cruel and merciless to any who might pose a threat to his power or safety . . . and the Jews of Judea despise him . . . for all that, and for being an Edomite, of that hated race who aided and abetted Nebuchadnezzar's destruction of Judah 500 years ago. Early in his reign, Augustus had awarded Herod the title *Amicus Caesaris,* Caesar's Friend, and the Jews hate him even more for his subservience to Rome than for his Hellenistic pretensions. Now, to placate them, Herod undertakes his most grandiose project: restoration of the Jews' Holy Temple. It will be, as Josephus will later record, the "most prodigious work ever undertaken by man . . . the expenditure . . . incalculable, and its magnificence never surpassed . . ." He will surround it with luxurious public gardens and trim it everywhere with precious metals and gems; and it will be not only his greatest work, but the greatest work ever. But he needs the support of the people, which he does not have, and so, delivers a speech to them:

> I think I need not speak to you, my countrymen, about such other works as I have done since I came to the kingdom, although I may say they have been performed . . . (more) to bring . . . security to you than glory to myself . . . and I imagine that, with God's assistance, I have advanced the nation of the Jews to a degree of happiness which they never had before.   Josephus, ANTIQUITIES OF THE JEWS, 15:11:1

Herod tells them "our forefathers" built the second temple after their return from Babylon, but were not able to build it as great as its founder, Solomon, intended because of restrictions imposed by kings Cyrus and Darius of Persia. But, he continues . . .

> . . . since I am now, by God's will, your governor, and . . . have had peace a long time, and . . . gained great riches . . . and (most importantly] am at amity with and well regarded by the Romans, who, if I may so say, are the rulers of the whole world . . . I will do my [best] to . . . make thankful return [in] the most pious manner to God [for] giving me this kingdom [to rebuild His temple] as complete as I am able.   *ibid.* 15:11:1

The Jews are not impressed; his ambition mere pandering to the Romans, his piety, self-serving. But Herod promises to proceed in everything according to Jewish law and, according to Josephus ". . . as he promised them beforehand, so he did not break his word." A thousand wagons, ten thousand skilled workmen, stonecutters and carpenters are brought in just to "take away the old foundations," and then the work on the new proceeds. Over the next 11 years, 18,000 persons will labor, just in the building of the Temple alone! The entire temple-mount complex will take many more! It is nothing short of mind-boggling. Taking shape, the outermost, walls—800 feet long and 100 high—seen from the outside, present a formidable, impregnable, prison-like aspect to an approaching pilgrim; awesome and daunting to friend or foe in its bleak, barren immensity. Six furlongs—three quarters of a mile—across, it is so high the bottom of the ravine it overlooks on one side cannot be seen. But, once inside, those formidable outer walls are lined, all the way around, with serenity; a graceful, Corinthian-columned, open cloister, its 162 gleaming marble pillars each carved of a single, solid block of stone 25 cubits—38 feet—high, and thick enough in girth for three men to surround one, touching hands. "The stone was white marble," Josephus says, "of natural magnificence and excellent polish" which "afforded a very remarkable prospect." Entry gates are on every side, nine of them, and every one covered over with gold and silver ". . . as were their jambs . . . and lintels." Each gate has two doors, 30 cubits in height and 15 in breadth . . .

> Now the magnitude of the . . . gates were equal one to another, but that [one made of Corinthian brass called] the Corinthian gate, which opened on the east [facing] the holy house itself, was much larger . . . and adorned after a most costly manner . . . much richer and thicker plates of silver and gold . . .   Josephus, THE JEWISH WARS

Facade of the Temple on a coin
struck in AD 135

Josephus' description of the Temple is famous . . . and awesome:

> Now the outward face of the temple [lacked nothing to amaze] men's minds or . . . eyes: for it was covered all over with plates of gold of great weight, and, at the first rising of the sun, reflected back a very fiery splendor, and [forced those who] look upon it to turn their eyes away . . . as at the sun's own rays. But this temple appeared to strangers . . . at a distance, like a mountain covered over with snow; for . . . those parts of it that were not gilt . . . were exceeding white.   *ibid.* WARS, 5:5:6

"As to the holy house itself," Josephus says, "the most sacred part of the temple, its . . ."

> . . . front [was] covered with gold all over . . . [making it] . . . appear to shine . . . [the gate] had golden vines above it, from which clusters of grapes hung as tall as a man's height. [It was] divided into two rooms, between them [an immense double] door . . . but before these doors there was a veil [of tapestry] of equal largeness with the doors. It was a Babylonian curtain, embroidered with blue and fine linen, and scarlet and purple, and

of a . . . texture that was truly wonderful. Nor [were these] colors without . . . mystical interpretation, but . . . a kind of image of the universe: scarlet for fire, flax earth, purple the sea; also the heavens . . . three things [were in there] very wonderful and famous among all mankind: the candlestick, the table of shewbread, the altar of incense. Now the seven lamps signified the seven planets . . . In the inmost part of the temple was nothing at all. It was inaccessible and inviolable, and not to be seen by any; and was called [the] Holy of Holies.   Josephus, THE JEWISH WARS, 5:6:4

At the north-west corner of the outer courtyard, Herod builds a most imposing structure, awesome in its appearance, menacing in its purpose, symbol of every aspect of the Jewish/Roman existence: the mighty, military Antonia Fortress, named for the man who made him, his patron Marc Antony.

Now as to the tower of Antonia . . . situated at [the] corner of two court cloisters . . . [It was in the] size and form of a palace [with] courts, baths, camps: insomuch that, by having all conveniences that cities wanted, it might seem to be composed of several cities, but by magnificence it seemed a palace . . . There always lay in this tower a Roman legion . . . in order to watch the people, that they might not attempt to make any innovations; for the temple was a fortress that guarded the city, as was the tower of Antonia a guard to the temple.   *ibid.* 5:6:8

Crowning the outer wall directly opposite the Antonia Fortress is the Royal Stoa, an opulent, exquisite basilica-like walkway that Josephus says equals in beauty and magnificence any other, any where. At the far end of this stoa is a vaulted apse where the Jewish "supreme court" the fabled—and dreaded—Sanhedrin meets to debate and hold in their hands the fate of accused trespassers of the LAW.

But, building his monument, Herod makes one monumental blunder that will set in motion the gears to grind out its own destruction . . . and that of the Jews. For at the top of the temple, Herod places a graven idol, an enormous, golden, Roman eagle, and the Jews find his blasphemy . . . intolerable.

17   The great Jewish teacher, Hillel (the Elder), a prince of the Sanhedrin and its president, opens a school in Jerusalem for the study of the LAW. An outstanding scholar of Jewish law, one of his major achievements is in cataloging the many hundreds of laws under a few categories, making them much easier to understand and study. Someday his grandson, Gamaliel, will serve on the Sanhedrin, also, and will become the teacher of a young Jewish scholar named . . . Saul. (See: A.D. 26) The Sanhedrin is the highest Jewish court and governing body, and consists of 70 members and a high priest. It administers Judea's laws and justice (within the allowable framework of Roman rule), collects taxes, and has power to arrest . . . holding their sessions, now, in the far-eastern apse of the Royal Stoa of Herod's new temple mount. More will be heard from the Sanhedrin in the future.

. . . One of Rome's many festivals, discontinued during the Civil War, were the Secular Games, a three-day celebration of Rome's birth and existence, held just once every hundred years. Now Augustus re-institutes the games in a celebration of the Preservation of the State, three days and nights of athletic contests and sacrifices to the gods of the first fruits of harvest; wheat, barley and beans, rams, pigs and pure white cattle and oxen. Rome's *poet laureate,* Horace, considers Augustus its "second founder," descendent of Aeneas, himself, and writes a special poem for the occasion. On the Games' last day a chorus of young boys and girls sing his newly composed "hymn to the Gods who love the Seven Hills . . . may (they) view nothing greater than the city of Rome . . ."

> Now Faith, and Peace, and Honor, and pristine Modesty, and Manhood neglected, dare to return, and blessed Plenty appears with her laden horn.   Horace, THE CENTENNIAL HYMN

Horace is well aware of the beauty and value of his ODES, for they have won him much fame amongst ordinary people, and the highest praise from Augustus, and he sums up his life's work with pride . . .

> I have achieved a monument more lasting than bronze, and loftier than the pyramids of kings . . . I shall not wholly die (but) be renewed and flourish . . . spoken of as . . . the first to have brought Greek song into Latin numbers . . .   Horace, ODES, 3:30

16–13   Despite almost continuous ill health, Augustus is an inveterate traveler and intends to visit every province in the Roman Empire, strengthening ties and securing his *Pax Augusta.* Five years ago he visited Greece and was wildly cheered as "Bearer of Glad Tidings," "savior," and "God the son of God." Now he travels to Gaul and Spain, and receives equal adulation, but his people, back home, miss him, and Horace writes . . .

> . . . since you promised the sacred council of the Senate an early return, return. Give back the light, dear leader, to your country . . .   *ibid.* 4:5

12   Augustus' dearest friend, son-in-law—and heir to the throne, Marcus Agrippa—dies suddenly, at 50 years of age, and a bereaved Augustus is again without an heir; so he adopts his two young grandsons (sons of his daughter Julia and Agrippa), Lucius, now eight, and

Gaius, six. Augustus loves the boys for they are sturdy, serious and intelligent young lads, and he personally undertakes their education to inherit the throne of Caesar. Livia's son, Drusus, is still in Augustus' consideration too, though, for he is a noble young man, away now on military campaign in Gaul, as is his older brother, Tiberius, already one of Augustus' best generals.

. . . With great ceremony before throngs of spectators, the title and office of *Pontifex Maximus* is bestowed upon Augustus, a position all future emperors will inherit automatically. Rome's innumerable religions and religious laws are overseen and prescribed by a sacred college of priests, a *collegium* of *pontifices,* who administer the *ius divinum,* the "divine law." At the head of the college is the high priest chosen, from earliest times, from amongst its own members, by them; but conferred, since the "Divine Julius" held it, upon Rome's supreme head of state. Always a superstitious people, the Romans have gods and goddesses for . . . everything, from tangible, physical properties to abstractions: ideas, emotions and feelings; hundreds of powerful, capricious deities, often spiteful and cruel, always unpredictable. To understand life and appease the gods, the

Augustus

Romans rely on astrologers, magicians, seers, conjurers and sorcerers to read the omens and auspices in everything from flights of birds to the entrails of sacrificial animals. And the foremost intercessor between vulnerable humanity and malicious, malevolent fate is the *Pontifex Maximus,* the high priest, who alone has the power to appease wrath, mediate injustice and communicate intentions. Now, the emperor—already sole, undisputed leader of the secular state—also becomes the supreme religious authority, creating a UNITY of church and state, a marriage of politics and religion whose effects will be felt—for both good and ill—throughout the ages, now, to our very own.

For the emperor has become more than a mere man: he is now the indispensable mediator, the living link, between man and god: secular, political ruler and sacred cultic priest one and the same, with no higher appeal for either one for any injustice from the other. The Roman conception of *LEX REGIA.* "The king is the law speaking," applied to both church and state in one entity, gives both, untrammeled, unquestionable power over . . . the people. In just 600 years the Romans have come full circle: from voiceless subjects of a king in a monarchy, to free citizens in a republic, to servile dependents of a super-state in an empire. Augustus did not intend to deal a death blow to the republic and spawn an empire. He meant to rescue the republic and restore it, healthier than before, to the Roman people. But, somehow, the years have passed, prosperous, peaceful years, and it has often been more . . . practical . . . to just do things himself, or let the State do them, than to wait for the people to bumble along on their own . . . and they like the security that has brought. But in giving the Romans security, he has made them wards of the state; and in protecting them from the gods, he has transferred godly power to himself . . . the Emperor!

. . . One of Augustus' responsibilities, as Pontifex Maximus, is the welfare of the sacred sisterhood of Vestal Virgins, among whose duties is the safe-keeping of Rome's sacred fire. In primitive times fire was hard to come by and, once made, carefully guarded; so the Vestals are now a very important cult. He, also, takes upon himself the "purification" of Rome's religions, cleansing them of immoral foreign influences; so he formally bans the gods of Egypt and the East . . . but sanctions that of the Jews, for the Jews have been good friends to Rome—and grants religious toleration in the provinces. His actions win great popularity with the people.

. . . Livia's son, Drusus (Augustus' step-son and heir to the throne) is thrown from a horse in Germany, and badly injured. He lingers a month in terrible pain but, although Livia sends her own personal physician, with her own special medicines, Drusus cannot be saved. Tiberius, wild with grief, having raced 400 miles from Gaul, arrives just in time to hold his brother in his arms as he dies; then walks ahead of the funeral procession the entire distance from Germany to Rome.

5   The Jewish sect of Essene brothers is flourishing at their greatest number, now, living in their wilderness community by the Dead Sea, where they labor diligently at copying all of the Jewish holy books (the "Old" Testament) onto parchment scrolls. Since the Romans first occupied Judea, the Essenes have been putting their precious scrolls into clay jars and hiding them in remote desert caves for safe keeping. They expect the promised Messiah to come soon.

4   Always playing politics, Augustus' old friend King Herod of Judea makes a serious political blunder which brings down upon him Augustus' wrath. His title *Amicus Caesaris* (Caesar's Friend) is stripped from him and he is relegated to the rank of subject, a humiliation from which he will not recover. (This is not conventional wisdom. It is thought by most historians that 4 B.C. was the date of Herod's death, but some new research believes that date actually to have been this political demotion.) Now, to counter an imagined plot against himself, the paranoid Herod has two of his own sons murdered. Hearing of it, Augustus, aware of Jewish restrictions against eating pork, comments with wry humor, that he would ". . . rather be Herod's pig than his son."

3   Since Agrippa's death Augustus' daughter, Julia, has lost all restraint on her self-conduct. Her wantonness and vices have made her the laughingstock of Rome. A forced marriage to Tiberius (Augustus forcing him to first divorce his own much-loved wife) stems the tide for a while but soon turns into disaster. Julia has become a hopeless, amoral harlot. A broken-hearted Augustus, immune apparently, from no tragedy, and complying with his own morality laws, exiles her from Rome . . . forever.

. . . Almost a quarter of a century has gone by since a young Octavian, in only his early 30's, became emperor, which means that next year will be Augustus'

. . . *silver jubilee!*

Twenty-five years of peace for Rome; no civil, social or world wars, no internal strife; the empire basking in a glorious *Pax Augusta!* The Romans long ago forgave and forgot Augustus' ruthless and bloody rise to power; his massive retaliation of his great-uncle's—

and his own—opponents; his rough shod ride over any view but his own to the glorious destiny he saw for Rome. Nine years ago Rome named him *pontifex maximus,* high priest, and now, to honor him again, they intend to celebrate, and—true to the Roman nature—celebrate big. So work begins on the gigantic celebrations in honor of the man all Rome now loves and respects. There will be religious observances in the gleaming marble temples of Jupiter Capitolinus (king of the gods) and of Venus and Roma (mother goddess of the Romans.) Orations and speeches of praise will be given in the *Forum Romanum,* especially in the *Curia*—the Senate House. New temples will be built, and old ones refur-

Caesar Augustus

bished. Feasting and banqueting will go on for days, and guests will come from all over the empire. The beautiful theater of Marcellus, which Augustus had built in honor of his late son-in-law, will echo to the sound of Greek plays, musical events and performances of tribute. There will be parades and triumphal processions, and the gigantic *Circus Maximus* will pack in many thousands of people for the wild chariot races the Romans love so well. And, of course, there will be contests of gladiators, for the Romans are more and more wanting the bloodshed and violence of the arena, rather than the drama and comedy of the theater.

Augustus himself, a sober and austere man, full of the sorrow of his years, will take little part in the spectacle but will sit back and tolerate it; for these are his people, and if the celebration will make his people happy, so be it. One honor he will surely relish, though, and certainly not refuse: he is to be awarded the title . . .

. . . *PATER PATRIAE*—FATHER OF THE COUNTRY!

When the ceremony is held (so some recent studies say) he will be presented with a list of names, an enrollment (RSV), of the inhabitants of his empire, in a declaration of their loyalty and allegiance. Citizens and non-citizens, everyone must enroll, must witness their congratulations to Caesar's accomplishment and anniversary; and those with royal blood must enroll at the city of their royal ancestors, therefore . . .

"... a decree went out from Caesar Augustus that all the world should be enrolled. This was the first enrollment . . . and all went to be enrolled, each to his own city." (LUKE 2:1-3 RSV)

And so, in far away Judea, a young couple named Joseph and Mary begin a seventy-mile journey from Nazareth to Bethlehem; for that is the city of their mutual ancestor, the great King David. A simple, unlearned man (so it is believed) Joseph speaks no Greek nor

Latin, only Aramaic, the language of the Jewish peasant, brought back by the exiles freed from Babylon 500 years ago. He is an obscure carpenter from an obscure little village in an obscure corner of the empire. His life revolves around the skill and patience with which he uses his chisel, awl and saw, and he knows little of world affairs. Still, he knows it is not right for the Romans to be in his country . . . but, also, that he cannot change things, so . . . if they must enroll, they must enroll.

Very little do Joseph or Mary, or anyone else (except He whose Great Plan this is) realize how important it is for them to enroll, to sign this "pledge of allegiance" to Caesar Augustus. For Mary and Joseph both have royal blood in their veins, both descended, through different lines, from King David,* heirs to the throne of Israel. Should the Jews ever be able to throw off foreign domination and restore their own true monarchy, both Mary and Joseph would be in line (however far!) to the Jewish throne; and any child of theirs would have royal blood in his veins from (as far as the world knows) BOTH his parents. A king for Judea? Who better could give a king to Judea than these two descendents of its greatest king? Is this a journey, then, merely to pay taxes, as supposed for so many years; or is it part of a Greater Plan, of which even the players are not fully aware? For all his lack of worldliness, Joseph has a soul that believes in God and a heart that trusts Him, and he has been told that these days' events have been entrusted to his care; so his rough, strong hands are gentle as a mother's as he helps Mary onto his donkey to begin their long journey south.

Even farther away in that ancient land now called Persia, the Chaldean *Magi*—or "wise men"—still practice their ancient art, studying the movements of the heavenly bodies. Well they might for (according to the same recent studies) unusual things are happening in Leo, said to be the constellation of the Jews. Several of the most prominent heavenly bodies seem to pull together, cross paths or meet in close conjunction: Jupiter, king of the planets; Venus, the goddess of love and mother goddess of Rome; Regulus, the king STAR named for the Latin Rex, the largest star in Leo; and even Mercury . . . the Messenger. Romans, Jews, king, mother; what does it all mean? The Magi know the Jews expect a Messiah. True, they already have a king, but Herod is not a Jew; he is an Idumean and hated by the Jews. So the Magi watch the night skies over Judea. Finally, what appears as one huge star hovers just above the horizon, a phenomenon dazzling in its beauty. It remains all evening, then slowly settles behind the desert palms . . . directly over far-away Judea. Seeing this, the Magi set out on their own long journey.

---

* MATTHEW 1:1–17 traces Jesus' Jewish lineage back to King David and Abraham; and LUKE 3:23–38 shows the universality of His origins through David back to Adam, common to all humanity. Footnotes in THE KING JAMES STUDY BIBLE, Thomas Nelson, 1988, Liberty University, say that: "By tracing Jesus' ancestry back to King David, through the line of Davidic kings [he is connected] with His royal heritage. The geneology [in MATTHEW] is that of Joseph, Jesus' legal father, whereas the geneology in LUKE is that of Mary, His actual parent, showing His bloodline back to David."   p. 1403 1:1,2

Late 3   Bethlehem is crowded with people, some here for the same reason as Joseph and Mary. It has been a terribly long and exhausting journey, for Mary's pains have started, as she is soon to deliver a child. But Mary is strong, and Joseph has already been told (MATTHEW 1:20) that she is someone very special. Finding no room in the inn, they remain at the stable, the humblest of dwellings, with animals all about, and shepherds nearby in the fields. It is a crisp, clear night; and the millions of stars in God's firmament are shining brightly . . . especially one very large star, so close . . . one could almost reach up . . . and touch it.

> Prophesied: The Lord, whom ye seek shall suddenly come to his temple: even the messenger of the covenant whom ye delight in: behold, He shall come, saith the Lord of Hosts. But who may abide the day of his coming, and who shall stand when he appeareth?
> MALACHI 3:1,2 (See: 400 B.C.)

The

NEW

TESTAMENT

YEARS

The NEW TESTAMENT and the WORLD

The religion of Jesus Christ is an historical religion, founded upon actual historical persons and events; not upon philosophical theories or abstract values. We worship Christ born, crucified and resurrected because historically (Christians believe) He was. We celebrate communion with God because Jesus did it Himself, and commanded us to follow suit. The New Testament Gospels are not mere biographies. The men who wrote them did not intend simply to tell the story of a man's life. They meant, instead, to convince the reader of the nature and being of that man, that the reader should BELIEVE not only what He did, but who He was, and is to this day, and forevermore will be . . . and be SAVED by that belief.

The twenty-seven "books" of the New Testament tell the two greatest stories ever told. The first is the GOOD NEWS, or GOSPEL, of the birth, life, death and resurrection of Jesus of Nazareth, the Christ, or Messiah the Jews have waited for so long, whose birth forevermore divided time into "before" and "after."

The second story tells about the establishment and growth of the faith that bears His name, by the disciples who befriended and believed in Him, or were converted to that belief. As apostles, they traveled "the world over," and some wrote letters (epistles) to friends and to the churches they had founded. These letters became the first "literature" of the Christian faith. Later, many years after Jesus death, four Christian men (three who had known Jesus and one who was too young and did not) set down in writing, in different times and places, His story as each knew it. Each had a different reason for writing and a different audience that he hoped would read his story. These books are called Gospels— Good News—and together with the Epistles, make up the New Testament.

Every one of the New Testament books was written in Greek, a language that was unknown in the Middle East until Alexander the Great brought it with him three hundred years before Christ. And three different dialects of Greek were used in the writing:

— A cultured, educated dialect such as that spoken by Luke and in which his two books, LUKE and ACTS, and the epistles of JAMES and HEBREWS were written . . .

— "Koine" Greek, the everyday vernacular of the uneducated, common man; Peter, Jude and John.

— and the dialect that could be anyplace in between, a Greek spoken by Paul, who was reared in a Greek world but was Jewish to his very core, a Pharisee, son of a Pharisee, with a Hebrew education. Since the ancient "classical" Hebrew language had gone into disuse long ago with the exile into Babylon, those Jews who did not speak Koine spoke Aramaic— which they had learned in Babylon—or a mixture of both. The Assyrian/semitic language called Aramaic is that which was spoken by Jesus of Nazareth, His family, friends and most of the people to whom He preached. (He is thought to have had knowledge of other languages also, though, as witness His responses to the questioning of the Roman praefect,

Pontius Pilate.) Prophesies, wars, conquests, tearing down of nations and rebuilding, languages dying and new ones born; thus have all these events that happened hundreds of years before this time shaped the events that are about to happen. For, had not the apostles had the support of the centuries, and only their own ancient language of Hebrew, they would have been understood in their own little country and no place else.

The "Glory that was Greece" had been that of a highly cultivated people whose thinkers provided wisdom and knowledge that is the foundation for Western civilization to this day. Moreover, Greece had developed something the world had never seen before—democracy—where every citizen had a voice in the government and each man spoke for himself . . . but, it was a system borne on the back of slavery, abortion, infanticide, incest, sodomy and communism, all with the approval of its greatest thinkers.

The "Grandeur that was Rome" lasted a thousand years, five hundred in the building and five hundred in its decline. In it's building, Rome developed the concept of republican government, with elected representatives. During the years of Empire, its strength lay in its genius for organization and in unadulterated brute force. Indeed, its organization was honed to such fine precision it survived (for a while) debauched, inept, and even insane emperors. But the Romans never understood the more sophisticated sensibilities of the Greeks. Indeed, the emperor, Nero, would have been admired for his artistic talent in Greece but, in Rome, it was that, as much as his cruelty, for which he was hated. Rome's theaters echoed only to the cries of gladiators, the clash of swords and the screams of victims.

Rome's religions were a conglomeration of "imports" from Greece, Persia and Egypt; gods, goddesses and creatures that were not only unacceptable to many but embarrassing, as well. And so, Judaism's rationale of ONE God looked more and more attractive. Indeed, some of Greece's greatest thinkers held that concept long ago. Socrates had speculated about the human soul; Plato said that it is immortal and imperishable, and Aristotle professed a belief in a "*logos*" or, controlling principle in the universe. Not too many years from now, Paul of Tarsus will quote TO the Greeks statements about God by two of their own writers.

But because of the exile in Babylon, some of Judaism's leaders, hoping to keep their religion alive, are preaching that ONLY the Jews are God's people, and He is theirs alone. Oppressed for centuries, the Jews are looking, now, for the coming of the Messiah who will free them from those oppressors and build them once again into a great and powerful nation. But great kings, and Messiahs, are not born in stables, nor do they live as carpenters, nor die with criminals on a criminal's cross. Instead, the Jews look for a king mightier than David, more magnificent than Solomon, nobler than Josiah; and they have forgotten that their own most revered prophets have promised, not a glorious monarch, but a Suffering Servant, and when Jesus of Nazareth refuses to accept the role of military revolutionary, and offers instead, repentance and redemption, He will be "despised and rejected" and crucified.

ANNO DOMINI
(IN THE YEAR OF OUR LORD)

The birth of Jesus Christ has been calculated, for some centuries to have occurred between 7 and 4 B.C. based, in part, on the 300 year-old astronomical theories involving a lunar eclipse of the 17th century mathematician Johannes Kepler, a situation somewhat akin to relying on Isaac Newton for advice on space travel. The theories are based upon clues found in two of the four Gospels, MATTHEW and LUKE, the only two that mention Jesus' birth. The clues involve the star of Bethlehem, the governorship of Cyrenius, the taxing or enrollment of the empire, the magi from the east and the killing of the boy babies by King Herod. There are also clues in Josephus' HISTORIES and in ancient Roman and Jewish documents and carved inscriptions: a lunar eclipse, the burning at the stake of two rabbis and the date of the death of Herod, himself; the Varus war and the dates of the priestly "courses." "Cyrenius was governor of Syria now," the arguments go. "No, it was then. The star was this phenomena. No, it was that. It was this lunar eclipse. No, it was that one." And that's only for starters. It is not the purpose of this book, or this writer, to debate or expound on those complicated issues; they are all moot questions, important questions, wide open to debate with learned partisans on both sides, with new evidence found and new theories put forth all the time.

Unfortunately, the scientific, astronomical/astrological speculations and calculations result in a Jesus who was born between 4 and 7 B.C. and, therefore, began His public ministry when He was between 34 and 37 years old; which is completely at odds with the evangelist Luke who says He was "about" 30 . . . and Luke's frequent use of "about" never means "give or take a few years or even months." It is, rather, "nearly, almost" or "approaching." (LUKE 1:56, 9:14, 19:7, 22:59 and 23:44) The only historian to record the events immediately surrounding the birth of Christ, Luke tells his story with such remarkably intimate detail it has been thought for centuries that he got his information directly from the one person in the world who was there and would know, Jesus' mother, Mary. Luke also wrote the book of ACTS, that remarkable "travelogue" of the 10,000 miles of the Apostle Paul's journeys. He addressed ACTS to a "most excellent Theophilus," apparently a Greco/Roman official of some rank who would have required accurate documentation; and a concern for historical accuracy is a hallmark of Luke's writing. Some years ago a bitter foe of Christianity set out to disprove ACTS by retracing Paul's steps and, as that would be "impossible," debunking Luke's accuracy. He ended up a Christian, himself, when he found nothing to debunk. If, then, Luke's historical record in ACTS is accurate and irrefutable, it seems likely his Gospel is also accurate. Indeed, some modern scholarship has put forth theories in agreement with Luke convincing enough to cause many modern planetaria to adapt their Christmas exhibits to Luke's dating.

Luke wrote his story in a time of deadly hostility to the fledgling faith when he could easily have been proven wrong and/or denounced as a fraud . . . but he wasn't. The writings that still exist today of some of the early church's bitterest enemies, including Celsus and Porphry, say nothing against him; and many of the greatest early church fathers agree with him: Origen, Eusebius, Irenaeus, Clement, Jerome and Tertullian. Luke says that Jesus began His public ministry "in the 15th year of the reign of Tiberius Caesar" (3:1) when Jesus "was about (nearly or almost) thirty (30) years of age (3:23)," which implies that He could even have been 29. In fact, the historian Epiphanius states, unequivocally, that Jesus was "29 years and 10 months of age when he began his ministry." (DIALOGUE WITH TRYPHO, 88) The 15th year of the reign of Tiberius Caesar began on August 19 A.D. 28 and ended August 18. A.D. 29. By Luke's reckoning, then, Jesus was born between late 3 or early 2 B.C. So, because it is not the purpose of this book to join in the esoteric, scientific or mathematical controversies, and because Luke's dating fits with Roman history, I am going to let all those moot questions remain for the experts to argue and for time to either confirm or confound, and take the evangelist, Luke, at his word.

The Years

JESUS LIVED

ON EARTH

The YEARS JESUS LIVED on EARTH

> Prophesied: Therefore the Lord Himself will give you a sign. Behold, a virgin shall conceive and bear a son, and shall call his name Immanuel. ISAIAH 7:14 (See: 739 B.C.)

Late 3.   During the night, Mary's child is born and named Y'shua (or Yeshua: Joshua) which means "Yahweh is my help," and translates to Jesus in Greek. But angels who sing His praises to shepherds in the field proclaim Him "a Savior, which is Christ, the Lord!"

> For unto us a child is born, unto us a son is given: and the government will be upon his shoulder, and his name shall be called Wonderful, Counselor, the Mighty God, the Everlasting Father, the Prince of Peace. ISAIAH 9:6 RSV (See: 739 B.C.)

Joseph and Mary take Jesus to Jerusalem, five miles north of Bethlehem, to present Him to the Lord in the Temple, and to offer sacrifice according to the Law. There a very old man called Simeon takes the boy in his arms, and in a voice strained with emotion blesses God and prays, "Lord now lettest thou thy servant depart in peace . . . for mine eyes have seen thy salvation . . ."

2, Feb. 5.   In conclusion to a year of celebrations for his Silver Jubilee, the Roman Senate, united to the man as never before, awards Caesar Augustus the title, *PATER PATRIAE . . . Father of the Country*; and Augustus records it in his journal or "register . . ."

> While I was administering my thirteenth consulship the senate and the equestrian order and the entire Roman people gave me the title Father of My Country. Caesar Augustus,
> *RES GESTAE*, 6:35

. . . For many months the Chaldean Magi have been following their enigmatic star from Persia to Judea in search of a newborn "King of the Jews." Now the star appears to halt in its westward course and hang motionless just south of Jerusalem . . . above a little town called Bethlehem . . .

> But you, O Bethlehem . . . who are little . . . among the clans of Judah, from you shall come forth for me one who is to be ruler in Israel, whose origin is from old, from ancient days.
> MICAH 5:2 (See: 739 B.C.)

Having learned the location from Herod, the Magi find Jesus in a house in Bethlehem, and present Him with their gifts: gold, because they believe him a king; frankincense because they believe Him God; and myrrh, because they know he must die. This "showing" of Jesus to Gentiles for the first time will be celebrated in years ahead as the feast of the "EPIPHANY."

Insanely jealous of his throne and afraid of the rival king whom the Magi were seeking, the paranoid Herod orders all boy babies murdered . . . and Joseph and Mary take Jesus, and flee to Egypt.

1   Sickened by Herod's intolerably evil deed, two Jewish rabbis climb to the top of the Temple and, in patriotic defiance, pull down Herod's golden Roman eagle and smash it to bits on the ground; and, according to the Jewish historian, Josephus, a lunar eclipse on the night of January 9/10, 1 B.C., leaves the city of Jerusalem in blackness, the only light for miles being the horrible red glow of fire, in Herod's courtyard, two rabbis . . . burning at the stake.

Having ruled all Palestine for 36 years, Herod the Great dies on January 28, 1 B.C. and the Jews breathe a sigh of relief. The relief will not last long.

. . . The Holy Family returns from Egypt to settle in the remote northern village of Nazareth where they will be safe from Herod's successors.

> Prophesied: Out of Egypt I called my son.   HOSEA 11:1 (See: 750 B.C.)

A.D. — ANNO DOMINI
In the year of our Lord

1   For 753 years Rome has dated its history A.U.C.—*Anno Urbis Conditae*, the "Year of the Founding of the City of Rome." The birth of one child will change that. Almost 700 years from now, an English Christian scholar named Baeda, called the Venerable Bede and The Father of English History, will put into use an entirely new method of calculating time. No more will "the 10th year of Hammurabi's rule" or "the 15th year of the reign of Augustus," be the only—confusing—clues to history. From then on, one simple rule will settle the matter. For Bede will divide time into B.C. (Before Christ) and A.D. (*Anno Domini*— In the Year of Our Lord.) He will call this year, the year ONE.

Almost 2000 years from now, when a brand new nation calling itself the United States of America, writes its governing constitution, it will date it to ". . . the year of our Lord one thousand seven hundred and eighty nine." In wording the article in which this phrase appears, the delegates to the convention will not be referring to "the year of our Lord King George III," or "our Lord Napoleon," or "our Lord Julius Caesar." They will be referring to "the year of our Lord Jesus Christ,"—this year, and the birth of this child—and the Constitution will be approved, unanimously, "in the year of our Lord," 1789, by every one of its 39 signers, including its author, James Madison, and the nation's future first president, George Washington.   (Article VII, para. 2)

. . . King Herod's double crime of killing the babies and burning the two Jewish rabbis has inflamed all Judea, and riots break out which increase in violence as their repression under Herod's son, Archelaus, increases. Roman troops, Jewish troops, zealots and commoners, all are involved in riot and rebellion. The Temple is stormed and looted, Herod's summer palace at Jericho burned . . . and Judea races recklessly toward anarchy.

. . . Augustus' grandsons are now grown to young manhood; Lucius is 22 and Gaius 20. They are the pride of his life. He is proud of their good minds, their accomplishments and the promise they show. Both are in the army now, Lucius in Gaul and Gaius in the eastern provinces.

2 Lucius Caesar dies in Marseilles.

4 Gaius Caesar dies in far-away Armenia.

> . . . Lucius Caesar, as he was on his way to our armies in Spain, and Gaius while returning from Armenia, still suffering from a wound, were prematurely cut off by destiny, or by their stepmother Livia's treachery.   Tacitus, *ANNALS*

Augustus is totally bereft and bereaved. Of five men and boys whom he had chosen as heir, not one survives. He is left no choice. Livia's favorite son will become heir and next emperor. Caesar recalls Tiberius to Rome.

> Inexorable wrath shall fall on Rome: A time of blood and wretched life shall come. Woe, woe to thee, O land of Italy, great, barbarous nation . . . and no more under slavish yoke to thee, will either Greek or Syrian put his neck, barbarian or any other nation. Thou shalt be plundered and shalt be destroyed for what thou didst, and wailing aloud in fear, thou shalt give until thou shalt repay.   The *Sibylline Oracle*, A.D. 6, prophesying the fall of the Roman Empire.

Judea has been in a constant state of upheaval and tumult, ever since King Herod's death, with his sons, Archelaus, Antipas and Philip conspiring in plot/counter-plot for the throne and the eventual division of Judea—by Caesar in Rome—amongst them. There have been riots ever since Herod's burning of the two rabbis, with a resultant killing of 3000 rioters by Archelaus' troops; and, later, the crucifixion of 2000 more. Augustus had warned Archelaus to go easy on the Jews after his father's atrocities, but his warnings fell on deaf ears for Archelaus is every bit as evil and cruel as Herod, and his beastialities are more than the Jews can take. Augustus, always a friend to the Jews—and to the Herods until now— has tried patience and fairness, but finally has had enough. When a delegation of 50 Jews arrives in Rome to plead with him to remove Archelaus from power, and are supported by 3000 Jews of Rome, Augustus deposes him, exiles him permanently to Gaul, and institutes direct Roman government in Judea. According to the Jewish historian, Josephus . . .

> Coponius . . . a man of the equestrian order, was sent . . . to have the supreme power over the Jews . . .   Josephus, ANTIQUITIES OF THE JEWS

6 The supreme power is that of *praefect*, now Judea's highest ranking official, its chief magistrate, empowered to maintain peace and order. It is the end of Jewish independence, as . . .

ROME RULES SUPREME IN JUDEA UNDER A ROMAN PRAEFECT.

8 Augustus has tried for years to bring about moral reform in his sin loving state, a restoration of the sanctity of marriage, a halt to the spread of licentiousness and vice, and a return to the religion of old Rome. But he has fought a losing battle and the poets who

extol the virtues of vice meet with an enthusiastic audience. Publius Ovidius Naso, called Ovid, is first among them, and his work, THE ART OF LOVE, finds its way even into Augustus' royal household. Agreeable women are easy to find, he says, especially at the theater, where . . .

. . . they come to see . . . and come to be seen. * In the fields of our neighbor, the grass forever is greener. * Always the other man's herd offers the richer reward. * Even suppose you guess wrong, it costs you nothing to try. * If they say yes or no, they're pleased with the invitation.   Ovid, ADVICE TO MEN from THE ART OF LOVE

At 35, Ovid is the darling of Rome's wealthy, fast-and-loose crowd, whose only concern is pleasure, sex and Hellenistic self-indulgence. Born to old wealth, he is Athens-educated, well-traveled (including ancient Troy) and so clever as a lawyer, he delivers his courtroom arguments in poetry and satiric verses . . . to the enormous delight of his hearers. In his ADVICE TO MEN, Ovid assures his readers that his book is based on experience, that he is preaching only what he has, in fact, practiced. "Let the soldier bare his breast to an arrow," he says, "or the merchant make one voyage too many." He wants to die . . . "on the job." A man must adapt his methods to his "quarry," he writes, "some fish are trawled, some netted, some caught with line and hook yet none are uncatchable. After all, Troy fell late, but fall it did. "What is softer than water," he asks, "what harder than stone? Yet with persistence the soft-dripping water erodes away the stone . . . But first, get acquainted with your quarry's maid," he advises, "corrupt her with promises, corrupt her with [gold] . . . Today is truly the Golden Age; gold buys honors . . . love . . ." And he sums it all up: "When you've [won your catch] write on your trophy *Ovid was my guide.*"

IN HIS ADVICE TO WOMEN, Ovid says to have fun while you can, in your "salad days," for the years glide past and what's gone can never be recovered. "We men are a cheerful breed," he says, "it's bright girls who best charm us . . . elegance. But don't yield too soon to a lover's entreaties. Pleasure too [quickly] enjoyed lacks zest . . . still, don't overdo those stubborn refusals." One of Ovid's admirers, who has followed his advice only too well, is Augustus' own granddaughter, Julia, the very image of her mother in more ways than just in name. With bed partners beyond counting, her wantonness is common knowledge . . . to everyone but Augustus, who is the last to learn. When the whispers joining her and the middle-aged Ovid become pervasive, Augustus banishes the two far from Rome . . . and from each other.

9   Born in northern Italy's Padua, 22 miles from Venice, the son of a freed slave, the Gallic/Roman historian, Titus Livius or Livy, like Virgil, writes under Augustus' patronage and friendship and, like Augustus, is deeply worried about the depths to which Roman morality has fallen. A devoted family man and loving father, he is the empire's first historian, devoting his whole life to his monumental 142 volume *HISTORIAE AB URBE CONDITA,* HISTORY FROM THE FOUNDING OF THE CITY OF ROME, a work that covers 700 years. In the 35 volumes that have survived the centuries are found all the marvelous stories that make up the vision of Rome which we have, today; the romance of a kingdom turned republic turned empire: of Prince Aeneas sailing away from Carthage and his Queen

Dido, to fulfill his destiny of founding the city; the twin brothers Remus and Romulus, who became Rome's first king and gave it his own name; Pompilius who founded its religion, Hostilius its army; Marcus Ancus who set it on a path of conquest; and the Tarquins who made the kingdom great . . . and brought it down to ruin. Livy tells of the first Brutus who overthrew the monarchy and established the republic; of the posting of the Law of Twelve Tables in the Senate and the creation of citizenship; of Horatius at the bridge, the gallantry of Cincinnatus who twice returned his dictatorial power when it was twice thrust upon him, and of Hannibal crossing the Alps; the Gracchus brothers who worked for reform but created a welfare state by starting the corn dole; Sulla the butcher who ruled through blood and fear; Pompey the Great who doubled Rome's size and whom Livy idolized; the first Caesar who, in designing a new Rome destroyed the old; and finally Augustus, architect of the Empire; all live and breathe in Livy's vivid prose and matchless style.

Modern-day critics find fault with Livy's scholarship; accuse him of erratic use of references and his using history to "sell" his own beliefs but Livy explained in his own Preface to his work that his mission in writing the history was twofold: to "do my duty to the memory of the deeds of the chiefest people in the world"—the character of the Romans what made them good and great and strong, and what made them fall into the moral degradation of "these latter times when [they] are working their own decay. And secondly, he says, to hold up these things as a monument for his readers, as good and bad examples of what "for yourself and for your country . . . you should imitate [and] . . . what . . . avoid." For the rest, Livy says:

> . . . either my love for the task which I have undertaken deceives me, or there has never been a state . . . richer in good examples . . . into which avarice and luxury made their entrance so late . . . where thrift [was] honored . . . so long . . . [But] riches have introduced avarice, abundance of pleasures has brought to men the desire by way of luxury and lust to ruin themselves and to ruin all.   Titus Livius, *HISTORIA AB URBE CONDITA*, History from the Founding of Rome

Over the years Augustus has spent much time away from Rome in various parts of the Empire, principally in Germany, seeking to make the borders secure. He is particularly fond of the Germans, their staunchness, their hardy fearlessness and their blond, Teutonic good looks; but now, far to the north, the Germans under the command of Arminius (or Hermann, Germany's first national hero) deliver his legions a crushing defeat in the battle of Teutoburg Forest, and Rome never again advances beyond the Rhine River. Fifteen thousand men, three entire legions—the 17th, 18th and 13th—under General Quintillius Varus are betrayed and led into ambush in the primeval forest by the savage Teutonic tribes . . . and annihilated. It is the worst massacre in history. Their heads are nailed to trees, and their bodies left to rot where they fall. Officers are butchered for sacrifice on pagan altars. The blow is especially galling, for Arminius held Roman citi-

zenship and had even been awarded the equestrian rank. Augustus is inconsolable, crying, "Varus, give me back my eagles!"

Although the battle itself has been described as a relatively minor skirmish that the first Caesar, Julius, could have won easily, many modern historians consider Teutoburg Forest second only to Waterloo as the most important (pre-World War II) battle in European history, for it did two things: it guaranteed that Germany would remain "German" and never be "Romanized," and it taught the Germans—and the world!—that, in fact, Rome was NOT invincible.

10, Passover.   Joseph and Mary of Nazareth make their annual pilgrimage to Jerusalem for the Passover celebration, and take with them their young son, Jeshua (or, in Greek, Jesus), now 12 years old. The return trip becomes a nightmare when Jesus is discovered missing from the caravan. Jerusalem is a big, bustling, wicked city, full of dangers for a country lad, and a frantic Mary and deeply worried Joseph search three long days through the streets and market place. After all, the same slave trade which sold the first Joseph, the patriarch, centuries ago, still flourishes now, more than ever. But Jesus is found in what He calls "His Father's house,"—the Temple of God, discussing with the teachers there the LAW and the PROPHETS; discussing and debating, questioning the teachers and answering their questions, .and amazing them with His knowledge and wisdom.

. . . Asia Minor, today's Turkey, bounded on north and south, by the Black and Mediterranean Seas, and lying partly in both Europe and Asia, has played a major role in history over the years. Here flourished the great Hittite civilization, later displaced by the enigmatic, wandering Sea Peoples. At its far east towers Mount Ararat where, some think, Noah's Ark came to rest, and at its far west, ancient Troy, celebrated in the sagas of Homer. Across its plains and over a bridge of boats on the Bosporus, armies, first of the Persian Xerxes, frustrated in his hope of conquering Europe; and then Alexander, triumphant in winning not only vast lands, but minds and souls, too, to his beloved Greek *ethos*. Now Asia Minor is divided, by the Romans, into provinces with names familiar to modern-day readers of the Bible's book of ACTS: Galatia, Cappadocia, Pamphylia, Phrygia, Bithynia, Pontus, Cilicia, Asia on the Aegean Sea, and Thrace, the European province, bordering on Greece's Macedonia. Asia's great, venerable cities include Pergamum, where parchment was invented; Smyrna, as old as Homer; and Ephesus, world center of the worship of Artemis or Diana, in her magnificent temple, the Fifth Wonder of the Ancient World. Here silversmiths make fortunes fashioning models of the many-breasted fertility goddess for tourists from the world over. In Pontus' city of Amasia, an Asiatic Greek named Strabo visited Arabia, Greece, Gaul, Spain and Egypt, and studied at the Great Library of Alexandria before its destruction in 48 B.C. He has written a 47 volume work entitled GEOGRAPHY which, even today, is a rich source of knowledge about this time. One of the great cities of Asia Minor about which Strabo wrote is Tarsus in south-coastal Cilicia, which he calls . . .

> . . . first city of Cilicia, not merely material wealth, but intellectual. One of [the] great university cities of the Roman world.   Strabo

The universities Strabo speaks of are not all Greek/Hellenic, however, for Tarsus has a large Jewish population, also, and their rabbis are men of great learning. Into this Greco/Roman/Jewish atmosphere another Jewish boy is born at about this time. It is not known whether his path and that of Jesus of Nazareth will ever cross while they both live, for nowhere in history either sacred or secular is it mentioned. But, together, through one's judicial murder and the other's testimony to it, they will change the course of history. No one knows for certain, either, when Saul of Tarsus was born, but as the man, Paul, he will die at about A.D. 67 in middle age, so his birth may well have been around 10 or earlier.

14   Throughout the 41 years of his reign, Augustus has become renowned for his vast building projects, as were the mighty Ramses of Egypt and noble Pericles of Greece. In Rome alone he has built or restored 52 temples as well as countless monuments, auditoria and government buildings. The city has grown, in size and splendor, and become the greatest city in the world, and, according to the Roman writer, Gaius Suetonius Tranquillus (who will be court librarian and archivist to a latter-day emperor at the turn of the century) Augustus "once boasted that he had found Rome brick and left it marble." So far as he knew, Suetonius adds, Augustus inspected every province of the empire, except Sardinia and North Africa, being prevented of sailing there by a series of gales. And, in spite of all this, "he wanted no special privileges," was appalled at being called "my lord," and was "unmoved at being contradicted in the Senate." Augustus did not intend to hold office this long but somehow the years have just passed by and, now, having never been blessed with good health, he is, at 77, nearly an invalid. He has written a sober document of his life and works, a "register," called the *RES GESTAE* or "things done," but, broken-hearted because of his

personal tragedies . . . and the Roman peoples' subservient dependence upon government and its welfare handouts that the years have brought about, he considers himself and his rule a failure. Suetonius records history otherwise:

Augustus conquered, either as commander on the spot or commander-in chief . . . [many new provinces . . . and tribes] . . . Yet never invaded wantonly, nor desiring to increase Rome's boundaries or his own glory . . . Such was his reputation for courage and clemency . . . [that some] nations then known only by hearsay, voluntarily sent envoys to Rome, pleading for friendship and [peace] . . . He fought no battle or campaign unless hope of victory was greater than fear of defeat . . . Only twice did he think seriously of restoring the Republic: immediately after the fall of Antony, and once when he could not shake off a long illness, but realized that to divide government would only jeopardize his own life and national security . . . then published his intentions:

> "May I be privileged to build firm and lasting foundations for the Government of the State. May I also . . . (be) known as the author of the best possible Constitution, and of carrying with me, when I die, the hope that these foundations which I have established for the State will abide secure."   Suetonius, LIVES OF THE TWELVE CAESARS

Augustus is not unhappy that the end is near . . . nor is his ever ambitious wife, Livia. It comes, finally, in the month named for him, August, A.D. 14. In his ANNALS OF IMPERIAL ROME, Cornelius Tacitus says:

> . . . Livia had carefully beset the palace, and all the avenues to it, with vigilant guards; and favorable bulletins were from time to time given out, until . . . in one and the same moment were published the departure of Augustus, and the accession of Tiberius.   Book I, Tacitus, The ANNALS

Augustus' genius produced a monument greater than marble or gold, a living thing, a vital reality: the *PAX ROMANA,* the Roman Peace, and it will last for 200 years. It will outlive inefficiency and bureaucratic bungling, and it will outlive . . . the several madmen who will succeed him on the throne.

> In profound tranquility were affairs at Rome . . . the younger sort had been born since the battle of Actium, and even most of the old during the civil wars: how few were (now) living who had seen the ancient free state. The character of the government thus totally changed; no traces were to be found of the spirit of ancient institutions. The systems by which every citizen shared in the government being thrown aside, all men regarded the orders of the prince as the only rule of conduct and obedience . . .   Tacitus, Book I, the ANNALS

14   Tiberius Claudius Nero* becomes the second Caesar of Imperial Rome, a member of the Claudian family through both his father, one of Julius Caesar's top officers, and through his mother, Livia, Augustus' second wife; one of the oldest, noblest families in all Italy, tracing its lineage back to Romulus, himself. Livia's ambition is finally realized. Wife of the first emperor, she is now mother of the second. In September, Augustus is named one of the gods of Rome. Jesus of Nazareth is now, approximately, 17 years of age.

Tiberius

Factual history, both sacred and secular, is totally silent concerning Jesus' activities during these and the 15 years ahead. It is almost universally assumed that He is following His father as a carpenter of Nazareth. However, He appears in the folklore of several peoples far removed, from Tibet to Nepal, and from Egypt to England where, according to legend surrounding the Abbey ruins at Glastonbury on the beneficent Isle of Avalon—far removed from Greek influence, Roman harassment or Jewish restrictions, He could study, pray, meditate and

---

* This is not "the" infamous Nero. He comes later: A.D. 54. This is the emperor Tiberius.

commune with His heavenly Father in preparation for His future ministry and final passion. The Glastonbury legends say that an uncle, Joseph of Arimathea, a tin merchant, took Jesus with him on his trading journeys.

. . . Livia's favorite son, Tiberius, becomes Emperor of Rome at 55 years of age, a bitter man at having had to wait so long, and had others preferred so often before him. With a naturally suspicious mind and morose nature, Tiberius will become a ruler whose depravity of mind and body will overshadow his considerable administrative abilities, and whose brutality will outweigh his many accomplishments. The New Testament writer, Luke, mentions him in his Gospel but doesn't comment on his conduct.

. . . General Germanicus, son of Drusus and nephew of Tiberius, a man of noble character and excellent reputation, is stationed with his legions in Germany. In a humanitarian errand of mercy, he returns to the Teutoburg Forest, scene of the defeat of Varus eight years ago. Germanicus proceeds to give a decent burial to the bleached bones, still lying where they fell, of the thousands of soldiers massacred there. Germanicus' little son, Gaius Caesar Augustus Germanicus, is with him in camp and the scene of carnage leaves a lasting impression on his mind. Only three years old, he marches about camp wearing soldiers' boots, or *caligae,* and the troops affectionately nickname him "Little Boot" or . . . Caligula.

15   Tiberius begins his reign in a quiet, unassuming manner with a real interest in the welfare of his people and the empire, offering, sincerely, to resign the throne and restore the republic. But a restored republic is the last thing the Romans want: let Tiberius bear the burdens of government, not them. One of Augustus' best generals, Tiberius came up through the ranks: *quaestor* at 18 years of age, *consul* at 23, an *ovation,* a *triumph,* and the titles *Imperator* and First Soldier of the Empire . . . all before he was even old enough

to qualify for them. Now, in agreement with Augustus' political and moral reforms, he works to maintain them with an almost "superstitious reverence" for Augustus' constitutional measures. He works to reverse a tendency in the courts to protect the criminal rather than the victim. He is a careful steward of the empire's treasury, keeping taxes low by keeping spending down; and writes to one provincial governor who wants to raise taxes in his province, "A good shepherd shears his flock, he does not

Silver tetradrachm with laureate head of Tiberius & radiate head of Augustus, minted in Egypt

flay them." He has a military dislike for courtly fawning and flattery, and a general's respect for blunt honesty, and while he shows much courtesy in dealing with the senate he is also repulsed that so many senators have become toadying, kowtowing flunkies and sycophants, and is heard to walk out of the senate chamber muttering under his breath, in Greek, "Men fit to be slaves!" The lowly and unfortunate fare better:

> It happened once that . . . he . . . expressed a wish to visit the local sick. His staff misunderstood . . . [and] all the patients (were) carried to a public colonnade and there arranged in groups according to their ailments. Tiberius was shocked; for a while he stood at a loss, but at last went to see the poor fellows, apologizing even to the humblest . . . for the inconvenience he had caused them.   Suetonius, The XII Caesars

Not that Tiberius is popular with the people, well loved or even liked; he is not, for he has been, from his youth, gloomy, morose, inscrutable, close-mouthed and slow to speak; and people mistrust and even fear him. But he is an able administrator, a serious and brilliant student of Greek and Latin literature, and a tireless worker for the good of the empire . . . and some historians even call him a great emperor.

The High Priest

18   In Judea, or Palestine as the Romans call it, Joseph Caiaphas is appointed High Priest of the Jewish Sanhedrin, one more member in a family dynasty to hold the exalted position. A cunning, crafty man, Caiaphas will feature much in events just ahead. Almost 2000 years from now, in November, A.D. 1990, a burial ground will be found underneath a road south of Jerusalem. One of the most spectacular artifacts in one of the chambers will be an ornate, intricately carved "ossuary" or bone box, containing the bones of several people, including a 60 year-old man. On the outside of the box, carved twice, will be found the name "Yehosef bar Qafa," or, Joseph son of Caiaphas. Today, there is almost no argument that these are, in fact, the remains of the High Priest, Caiaphas, who will play so large a part in the fate of Jesus of Nazareth.

19   The Jews in Rome have for years, been fairly treated by Augustus, and Tiberius agrees that in a free country there should be free speech and thought (and he even tolerates slanders about himself) but now, wanting to purify the Roman religion, he abolishes . . .

> . . . foreign cults at Rome, particularly the Egyptian and Jewish, forcing all citizens who had embraced these superstitious faiths to burn their religious vestments and other accessories. Jews of military age were removed to unhealthy regions [that, if they should succumb, their loss would be of small moment] and others of the same race or similar beliefs were expelled from the city and threatened with slavery if they defied the order.   Suetonius, The TWELVE CAESARS

. . . Tiberius' nephew, the noble General Germanicus, dies suddenly and mysteriously in Antioch, Syria, and all sorts of strange and sinister artifacts are found in his room: spells, curses, charred and bloody ashes and "other malignant objects," . . . and the rumors fly. Was it Gnaeus Piso, his second in command? Or Tiberius eliminating a rival? Or the aged Livia (who is known to have visited a professional poisoner,) The entire empire grieves and mourns the loss of this most well-loved and honored general . . . but his eight year-old son, Caligula, is strangely unmoved . . .

> Contradictory rumors have raged around it . . . Some believe all manner of hearsay . . . others twist truth into fiction; and both sorts of error are magnified by time.   Tacitus, The ANNALS

22   "The year," Tacitus says, "was peaceful abroad." But the emperor, and senate, have many matters to consider, including all sorts of "current extravagance . . . The sums," Tacitus adds, "spent on gluttonous eating were widely discussed . . ." One very rich Roman spends, according to a contemporary, "*myriads* of *drachmas* on his belly." Marcus Gabius Apicius, famous as a gourmet—and gourmand—lives in the Italian province of Campania, south of Rome, which surrounds the seaport city of Naples, where hundreds of sea-going vessels bring foodstuffs and other luxuries from around the "world." Apicius' culinary delights show great skill and ingenuity, and the cookbook that bears his name will live for centuries. His recipes range *ab ovo usque ad mala,* or roughly, "from soup to nuts." There are appetizers, relishes, casseroles, soufflés and omelets; simple boiled dinners to exotic stuffed capons and flamingo, roast parrots and partridges. He tells how to preserve foods with vinegar, honey and wine, and even dry sawdust for mushrooms; and how to make delicate or pungent sauces like today's Worcestershire, tartar, chutney and mayonnaise. Apparently his book will travel widely in the years ahead, for his recipes for fish in white wine, egg and vegetable pie, chopped goose liver, marinated beef and salt fish balls live on today as French *Sole au vin blanc,* asparagus *quiche, pate de fois gras,* German *sauerbraten* and Norwegian *Fiske bollen.* Apicius makes them all, blending fine wines with herbs and spices as common as parsley, garlic and mint, to exotica like juniper and thyme; fenugreek from Africa, coriander from India, cardamom from Ceylon and ginger from China. Citron, chervil, mustard, caraway, sage, oregano and even fleabane and catnip are included in Apicius' cookbook which exists today in several museums, the oldest cookbook in the world.

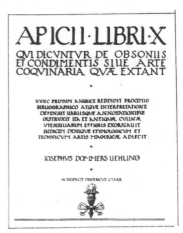

Apicius' Cookbook

Apicius is not the only one spending "myriads of drachmas" on his belly, for all over the empire the "new rich" indulge in orgies of gluttony and, as Tiberius' "old-fashioned austerity" is well known, according to Tacitus, "when the matter [is] raised in the senate, it [is] referred without discussion to the emperor," who writes a letter. "Matters of great moment," he says, "the welfare of all the people, the security of the empire, these are an emperor's concerns, now how much rich people eat . . .

> . . . and where should I begin my prohibitions . . . with the vast mansions, or cosmopolitan hordes of slaves . . . gold and silver plate . . . pictures and bronze work . . . men's clothes indistinguishable from women's . . . or the export of our currency to foreign or enemy countries for precious stones?"   Tiberius, quoted by Tacitus, The ANNALS

"If you want to try to abolish these things," Tiberius adds, in effect, "good luck, but when you make enemies, don't blame it onto me." The matter is dropped.

23   It is nine years since Tiberius became emperor and while he may not have been a popular ruler, or one without blame for numerous extreme eccentricities, he has kept the em-

pire sound and stable, keeping order in the cities with swift action by the Praetorian Guard and on the highways by decreasing the distance between military posts. Where Augustus had striven to serve only as "first senator" of Rome, Tiberius has become a true emperor and sole ruler. His two principal biographers differ widely in judging him: Tacitus says he could be very generous (matching with his own personal funds a huge amount of government aid to 12 Asian cities badly "overwhelmed" by earthquakes), but Suetonius says he is a dreadful penny-pincher, a close-fisted miser . . . and, in fact, the 100 million *sesterces* left in the treasury at Augustus' death has multiplied into TWO BILLION, 700 million, keeping taxes and spending down. But Tiberius has a dark side, and while Suetonius suggests that he always was evil but just hid it, Tacitus says that his cruelty and debaucheries began with the appearance of Sejanus on the scene . . .

> Tiberias now began his ninth year of national stability and domestic prosperity . . . But then suddenly Fortune turned disruptive. The emperor himself became tyrannical—or gave tyrannical men power. The cause and beginning of the change lay with Lucius Aelius Sejanus, commander of the [Praetorian] Guard.   Tacitus, The ANNALS

The son of a Roman knight, Sejanus "increased his income . . . by a liason with a rich debauchee . . ." then attached himself to Augustus' (great) grandson Gaius Caesar, called Caligula, and insinuated himself into Tiberias' confidence . . . and began his "criminal attempt on the throne."

> To Sejanus alone the otherwise cryptic emperor spoke freely and unguardedly . . . Of audacious character and untiring physique, secretive about himself and ever ready to incriminate others, [Sejanus was] a blend of arrogance and servility [and] concealed behind a carefully modest exterior an unbounded lust for power.   *ibid.*

25   Sejanus' goal is to get Tiberius out of Rome and out of his way: Tiberius is too conscientious, too hard-working, finding "comfort" in his work. So Sejanus begins, very subtly, to denounce to Tiberius all the negatives of Rome: the crowds, noise and smells, and the drudgery of being emperor. And then there is his mother, Livia, the "Augusta," nagging at him all the time, bossing, interfering in his life and work. Sixty-five years old and Emperor of Rome, and his mother is still on his back.

26   Tiberius leaves Rome for the Isle of Capri, taking with him just a few people; a senator, jurist, knight, a number of Latin and Greek scholars for intellectual companionship. He is fascinated by Capri, and the privacy it affords . . .

> . . . having only one small landing-beach—the remainder of its coast consisted of sheer cliffs surrounded by deep water. However, a catastrophe at Fidenae recalled him to the mainland almost at once.   Suetonius, the TWELVE CAESARS

A catastrophe, indeed. During the years of the republic, Romans had enjoyed the great works of the Greek theater, and later their own writers, such as Plautus. But their tastes have coarsened and they demand, and get, gladiators and wild animals instead of drama and comedy. To satisfy the Romans' bloodlusts for human and animal butchery, huge arenas are built all over the empire where thousands of people cheer on their favorites and turn thumbs down on the rest. Most of the arenas are well built and will last for centuries but others are the shoddy work of labor bought with graft and corruption. One such arena is that at Fidenae (today Castel Guibileo, a few miles north of Rome,) which collapses under the weight of an excited crowd during the games. Twenty thousand people are crushed to death under the thundering mountain of rock and cement! It is the worst disaster since the massacre in Germany!

> It began and ended in a moment . . . [the builder] neither rested its foundations on solid ground nor fastened the wooden superstructure securely . . . for sordid profits. Those killed at the outset . . . at least escaped torture . . . More pitiable were [the 10,000 more] . . . mangled but not yet dead.   Tacitus, The ANNALS

Tiberius does all he can to alleviate the suffering, distributing money "in proportion to losses incurred" with total disregard to status or position; everyone in need is treated equally, given to generously. All Rome is grateful, and the senate awards him a vote of thanks. But, while Tiberius is occupied with Fidenae, the *Pax Romana* is under the care of his trusted lieutenant, Sejanus.

The *Pax Romana* has brought a new order of things to the world, much of it beneficial. But the hand that holds out the Roman Peace is also clenched in a fist, and wears a glove of iron. "Peace," it says, "you shall have peace, as long as you do what I say. I will give you . . . certain concessions, if you are peaceful, that is, if you submit quietly and obediently . . . and don't make trouble." But there is one nation whose people just don't know how not to make trouble . . . Palestine. God's "stiff-necked" people, the Jews, have been trouble for Egypt, trouble for Assyria and Babylonia, and they will be trouble for Rome! Seven years ago Tiberius expelled the Jews from Rome and now . . .

26   Tiberius appoints Pontius Pilate Roman *praefect* or, military commander of Judea/ Palestine. Pilate is, judging from his name, from the *equestrian* (middle class, mounted cavalry) rank. A surprising amount of information is known about Pilate from sources other than the Bible, (which says very little) such as the Jewish writers Philo Judaeus and Josephus. The Hellenistic Philo (of Alexandria) writes that Pilate is "rigid" and "stubbornly harsh," with a "spiteful disposition . . . [a] wrathful man." Josephus' writings show Pilate to be willful, proud and interested only in keeping order and carrying out the will of Rome, rather than maintaining an even balance, understanding Jewish interests or the Jews, themselves. (A surprising amount of misinformation, also, has one modern source calling him "the most vicious man ever, alone responsible for the crucifixion of thousands," for which there is NO documentation.) But there is irrefutable documentation literally "carved in stone," linking together the names of Tiberius and Pontius Pilate, the *"praefectus Judaeus,"* which puts to rest forever the idea that Pilate never really existed, but was only invented for a scapegoat at a "treason trial." A limestone building-block from the theater at Caesarea, found in 1961 (today in the Israel Museum, Jerusalem) bears the engraving:

TIBERIEVM
ponTIVS PILATVS
praefCTVS IVDA

| TIBERIEVM –TIVS PILATVS * |
| TIBERIUS –TIUS PILATE |
| PRAEFECTVS IVDA – Praefect of Judea |

From the beginning Pilate begins to antagonize the Jews. With his official residence at Caesarea, Pilate marches into Jerusalem with several *cohorts* of his "army of occupation" his soldiers carrying golden eagle standards bearing the Roman *S.P.Q.R.* and the graven image of Tiberius Caesar, breaking the Jews' Second Commandment (Thou shalt not make unto thee any graven image.) And the Jews come ". . . in multitudes . . ."

. . . to intercede with Pilate . . . that he would remove the images . . . on the sixth day he gave a signal to his soldiers . . . and threatened immediate death unless they would leave. But they threw themselves on the ground, and laid their necks bare . . . rather than [transgress the law] . . . deeply affected . . . Pilate . . . commanded the images be carried back to Caesarea.   Josephus, ANTIQUITIES OF THE JEWS (See: A.D. 80)

Pilate is not so accommodating with the tumult that follows his second transgression: the looting of funds from the Temple treasury to build an aquaduct—and puts down that rebellion with bloodshed and brute force.

28   Under Sejanus' subtle prodding, Tiberius' suspicious nature inflames and he begins to see everybody as a threat, including his own family. He has violent scenes with his mother, Livia, for meddling in his affairs, and has his grandsons declared public enemies . . . and starved to death. He becomes more and more inaccessible, except through Sejanus, and while he is still sole ruler of Rome, entrusts more and more authority to his cunning and cruel lieutenant. Finally, sick of Rome, sick of his bullying old mother, sick of being emperor and sick of himself, Tiberius leaves the city and returns to the Isle of Capri, where he spends his last 11 years, according to Tacitus and Suetonius, sunk into a mire of sin and scandal. Rome is left to a reign of terror under his alter ego, Sejanus . . . and the Praetorian Guard.

. . . what attracted him was the isolation of [Capri], separated from [the mainland] by three miles of sea . . . Harborless . . . sentries can control all landings . . . In winter the climate is mild . . . in summer . . . delightful . . . the bay it overlooks . . . [is] lovely . . . On this island then, in twelve spacious . . . villas, Tiberius took up residence. His former absorption in state affairs ended. Instead he spent the time in secret orgies, or idle malevolent thoughts . . . his abnormally credulous suspicions . . . unabated. Sejanus, who had encouraged them . . . at Rome, whipped them up . . . the only access [to him] lay through Sejanus, and only crimes secured Sejanus' good will.   Tacitus, The ANNALS * . . . having found seclusion at last, and no longer feeling himself under public scrutiny, he rapidly succumbed to all the vicious passions which he had for a long time tried, not very successfully to disguise . . . on retiring to [Capri] he made himself a private sporting-house, where sexual extravagances were practiced for his secret pleasure. Some aspects of his criminal obscenity are almost too vile to discuss, much less believe.   Suetonius, THE TWELVE CAESARS

29   The Greek-speaking city of Tarsus, far away from Rome in Asia Minor, is famous for having been the fateful meeting place 70 years ago of Antony and Cleopatra. It is one of the "free cities" of the Roman Empire, and so its citizens are Roman citizens, including its large Jewish population. It ranks with the best of the empire in education and culture, and the Jewish community has an excellent rabbinical school there. From this school now comes one of the greatest men of his time, who will alter the course of religious thinking forever. Raised a Jew in a Greco/Roman world, he is a man like none other. He believes as a Jew, behaves as a Roman and bespeaks himself in Greek and Hebrew. The Greeks call him Gaius and the Romans, Paulus. To the Jews, he is Saul . . . of Tarsus. Born into the tribe of Banjamin, he is a Pharisee, the son of a Pharisee, trained in the LAW and the PROPHETS, and hidebound in his beliefs. Still, he lives in the world of Alexander, a Greek world. He speaks Greek and he writes it and is acquainted with its great written works . . . indeed, will quote those works in Athens someday.

Even as the teachings of Socrates affected Aristotle's thought through their intermediary, Plato, so also may the teachings of the old scholar, Athenodorus, have filtered down to Saul, a fascinating thought for Athenodorus knew and worked with the orator Cicero and the geographer Strabo, was teacher, friend and advisor to Caesar Augustus, himself; tutor to young Claudius (who will be Caesar someday), resident for years of the imperial court, and witness to the building of an empire. In his old age Athenodorus returned to his home, Tarsus, a respected elder from the big city. He died at 81 in A.D. 7, probably before Saul was born, or just after, but his influence would still have been great. What tales the young Saul may have heard about the elder man, and about Greece, Rome and Spain that fired his imagination, no one knows, but the possibility was there. Now, as fine an education as Saul received in Tarsus, he still thirsts after more knowledge, and so travels to Jerusalem to study with another great teacher, Gamaliel.

29   "In the fifteenth year of the reign of Tiberius," according to the Bible's Gospel of LUKE, a Jewish ascetic and prophet named John, called the Baptist, begins preaching in the wilderness of Judea that ". . . the time is at hand," that the Jews have waited for so long . . .

... the MESSIAH IS COME!"

> Prophesied: The voice of him that crieth in the wilderness, prepare ye the way of the LORD, make straight in the desert a highway for our God.   ISAIAH 40:1–3 (See 530 B.C.)   *
>
> Behold, I send my messenger to prepare the way before me.   MALACHI 3:1 (See: 400 B.C.)

A strange man, dressed in camel's hair and leather girdle, who lives on locusts and wild honey, John is the "living link" between the prophecies made and fulfilled, the last prophet, and the messenger of the words of Isaiah, Jeremiah, Micah, Malachi and the Psalms; of a Messiah promised and the Messiah proclaimed. Whether John is a member of the Essene brotherhood will be much debated in future years, but he does have much in common with them; his poverty and rejection of worldly goods; his solitary, half wild way of life in the wilderness, and his belief in the imminent coming of the Messiah. However, to the Essenes baptizing is a daily ritual, and John baptizes once only. Now, at about 30 years of age, Jesus of Nazareth seeks out John, his cousin, and John hails him, "The Lamb of God, who taketh away the sins of the world." (JOHN 1:29) When John baptizes Him, the Spirit of God descends upon Jesus like a dove, and a voice from Heaven is heard to say:

> *THIS IS MY BELOVED SON IN WHOM I AM WELL PLEASED.*   MATTHEW 3:17,
> MARK 1:11, LUKE 3:22

Just as Moses and the Israelites wandered 40 years in the desert, so Jesus goes alone to the desert for 40 days to prepare Himself for His mission. He is tempted by the devil with food, wealth and power, but replies, from the LAW:

> Thou shalt not tempt the LORD thy God.   DEUTERONOMY 6:16 (See: 1290 B.C.) & MATTHEW 4:7

Herod the Great's son, Herod Antipas, friend of the Roman royal family and now King of Judea, has John the Baptist arrested for his criticism of him and his wife; and Jesus "withdraws" from Nazareth for Capernaum, the "Galilee of the Gentiles."

> The people who walked in darkness have seen a great light; those who dwell in a land of deep darkness, on them has light shined.   ISAIAH 9:2 (See 739 B.C.)

Back in Nazareth, Jesus goes, on the Sabbath, to the Synagogue (which has been found by archeologists), and, ". . . as his custom was," (according to LUKE 4:16) He begins to teach and is handed a book of the prophet Isaiah; opens it to chapter 61, and reads . . .

> The spirit of the LORD God is upon me; because the LORD hath anointed me to preach good tidings unto the meek; he hath sent me to bind up the broken-hearted . . . and . . . to proclaim the acceptable year of the LORD . . ."   ISAIAH 61:1,2 (See 530 B.C.)

Then, as "all eyes are fixed on Him," He closes the book, gives it back to the attendant, and says, "Today this scripture has been fulfilled in your hearing." And all "spoke well of Him and wondered at His gracious words . . ."   LUKE 4:16–22

Even as there were 12 tribes of Israel, so does Jesus choose 12 to be His disciples. His choices are not made lightly for in each man He will find something unique and significant; a talent, an attribute, a capability. For each one there will be a specific mission; they are being called, not for worldly glory or honor, but for Godly labor, endurance, sacrifice, travail and suffering. All 12 are men, and Jesus chooses them after a full night's prayer and communion with God.

And it came to pass in those days, that he went out into a mountain to pray, and continued all night in prayer to God. And when it was day, he called unto him disciples; and of them he chose twelve, whom also he named apostles.   LUKE 5:12,13

First century mosaic from Migdal (Magdala)

Walking by the Sea of Galilee, He calls to Simon Peter and his brother, Andrew, fishermen casting their nets: "Follow me and I will make you fishers of men." So strong is His personality and so sure His authority, He has but to say, "Follow me!" and they do. A second two brothers, James and John, mending their nets with their Father, Zebedee, leave their boat and follow him, also. The fiery tempers of these two causes Jesus to affectionately call them "Sons of Thunder." He chooses another James, a kinsman, called the Lesser for his younger age; Thomas, who must always have things proven to him; and Matthew, a tax collector for the Romans, whose job is so hated by the Jews. In Galilee he finds Philip of Bethsaida, and Philip finds Nathaneal (or Bartholomew) and says to him, "We have found Him of whom Moses in the law and the prophets, did write . . ." Nathaneal is "an Israelite in whom there is no guile" who Jesus sees "under a fig tree," and comes, questioning, "Can anything good come out of Nazareth?" Thaddaeus and Simon the Canaanite come to Jesus "eagerly." All are from Galilee . . . all but the last, the group's "treasurer," Judas Iscariot, from Kerioth. All will love and serve him . . . and one will betray Him.

In Cana of Galilee, Jesus attends a wedding with Mary, His mother, for whom He performs the "beginning of miracles," making wine from water; and from now on the miracles happen often, astonishing even His disciples. Most are miracles of healing, for everywhere he goes there are people in need, suffering people for whom His love and compassion know no bounds.

Then shall the eyes of the blind be opened, and the ears of the deaf unstopped, then shall the lame man leap as an hart, and the tongue of the dumb shall sing.   ISAIAH 35:5,6 (See: 739 B.C.)

He cleanses lepers, heals the deaf, dumb and blind, makes cripples whole and restores epileptics and paralytics. He heals a man of dropsy another with a "withered hand," a woman "bent over," and drives out demons from those possessed, unclean spirits whose names, and numbers, are "legion." Accused of being Satan, He replies, "Can Satan drive out Satan? A house divided against itself cannot stand." News about Him travels fast, and the crowds that follow Him begin to grow. They want a miracle worker, and here He is.

> He shall feed his flock like a shepherd, and shall gather the lambs with his arms and carry them in his bosom, and gently lead those that are with young.   JOHN 10:14 and ISAIAH 40:11 (See: 530 B.C.)

30   Jesus is now recognized as a person of supernatural power and authority, to whom people listen, and so, He begins to preach the kingdom of God and to call sinners to repentance. From a mountain-side He teaches the people gathered below, and from a low-lying plain and sometimes offshore in a boat, so He won't be crushed by the crowd. Almost 2000 years from now, in A.D. 1968, a thoroughly water-logged, but still intact, skeletal hull of an ancient fishing boat will be found in and rescued from a drought-dried Lake Galilee. Dated by its construction features to somewhere between the first centuries B.C. and A.D. it is immediately dubbed by the news media, "the Jesus boat." The speculation runs wild: could it have been the (or "a") boat Jesus set foot upon? No one knows. Does it resemble one He MIGHT have used? Yes, indeed, it does. Twenty-six feet long and 7–1/2 feet wide, it would hold 15 people including a crew of five, more than enough room for Jesus and His twelve disciples. The Galilee boat rests, today, painstakingly preserved in a specially-built water bath in the Yigal Allan Museum on the shore of Lake Galilee, not 600 yards from where it had lain for 2000 years.

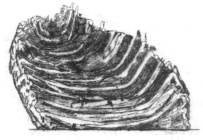

The "Jesus" boat from Lake Galilee

Believing Jesus' Miracles to be the work of God, one Pharisee, named Nicodemus, comes to Jesus secretly, at night, asking, "how can a man be born when he is old?" And Jesus tells him, "That which is born of the flesh is flesh, and that which is born of the spirit is spirit;" that he "must be born of water and the Spirit" or he cannot enter the kingdom of God, "for God sent not His son into the world to condemn the world, but that the world through Him might be saved."

Passing through Samaria, Jesus asks for a drink of water from a woman at the ancient well of Jacob, amazing her, for the animosity between Jews and Samaritans is ancient, indeed, going back hundreds of years to the conquest of Israel by Assyria . . . the days of the Ten Lost Tribes. But Jesus says that had He given her water, she would never thirst again, for it would be water of eternal life. Puzzled, she says she knows the Jews expect a Messiah—as do the Samaritans—who will explain all things, and Jesus states, openly for the first time, and to a woman, "I who speak to you am he."   JOHN 4:26

The woman of Samaria from the Roman Catacombs

The Samaritan woman is not the only one surprised by Jesus' actions. In most of the world's cultures to this time, women have been considered inferior beings, chattel to be bought and sold, ruled and dominated, even in those cultures with women goddesses. But Jesus' relationship with them is warm, close, loving and sympathetic. He shows them honor and respect, and treats them as equals; and they, in turn, show Him a devotion and loyalty equal to any man . . . and beyond some. Even in not choosing a woman for His "first circle" of disciples does He do them honor, for the disciples live together, travel together, spend most of their time in close company . . . a closeness that would bring dishonor to a woman in their midst. Still, regardless of ancient restrictions, scandalous or no, women are among His most valued friends and followers, who both receive from His ministry and minister to Him. Indeed, His own mother; Mary, was given the greatest honor any mortal will ever receive . . . to carry and bear the Son of God.

Jesus gathers His disciples together on a mountain top, and begins to teach them, privately. "Blessed are they," He says, "who are meek and poor in spirit, who mourn, who are merciful, pure in heart, who hunger after righteousness or make peace; and especially blessed are they who will be persecuted" for His sake. Knowing that there are many doubts and fears that He intends to corrupt the Jewish religion, He tells them,

"THINK NOT THAT I HAVE COME TO ABOLISH THE LAW AND THE PROPHETS. I HAVE NOT COME TO ABOLISH THEM, BUT TO FULFILL THEM."
MATTHEW 5:17 rsv

No longer shall it be "an eye for an eye," as in the past, though, for "I say unto you, love your enemies, bless them that curse you, do good to them that hate you and pray for them . . . that persecute you . . . for if you do good only to those who are good to you, what credit is that to you? Forgive them 70 times seven times, and judge not that you be not judged. Take the log out of your own eye before you criticize the speck in your neighbor's; and be not anxious about tomorrow but be like the birds of the air. And when you give alms, or fast, or pray, do it not as the hypocrites who do it for glory. They have their reward. But do it in secret, and the Father, who sees in secret, will reward you openly. And when you pray, do not heap up empty phrases, but very simply say:

The Sermon on the Mount

Our Father, which art in heaven, Hallowed be thy name. Thy kingdom come, Thy will be done in earth, as it is in heaven. Give us this day our daily bread. And forgive us our debts, as we forgive our debtors. And lead us not into temptation, but deliver us from evil. For thine is the kingdom, and the power, and the glory for ever. Amen.   MATTHEW 6:5–13

Our FATHER, Jesus said. He addressed God as FATHER and, as though to seal the matter for all time, added, ". . . hallowed be thy name." Again and again He addresses God as FATHER. In fact, when those four books are written that will tell His story—MATTHEW, MARK, LUKE and JOHN, they will quote Jesus 170 times addressing God as Father or, once even, on a night of despair like a frightened child to his "Daddy," as "*Abba*." "I was begotten," He is saying "not made. I have an earthly mother, Mary, but a Heavenly Father, God.

Naming by name the false god of greed and avarice, Jesus tells His disciples not to ". . . lay up treasures on earth; you cannot serve both God and *mammon*—money. For moths and dust can ruin treasures on earth, and thieves steal. But lay them up in Heaven; for where your treasure is, there is, also your heart. And give not that which is holy unto dogs, neither cast your pearls before swine; but beware of false prophets, wolves in sheeps' clothing. Believe in my name. Ask and it will be given you, but ask the Father in my name." IN MY NAME, Jesus said. Incredible statement! Astounding words! Is He really suggesting what it sounds like?

Back down from the mountain, crowds of people await Jesus with questions, requests, pleas. Asked about the ancient restrictions on "unclean" food, He replies, "All foods are clean. What goes into the mouth cannot defile you, but what comes out . . . slander, pride, foolishness, covetousness, wickedness, murder, adultery, licentiousness, envy." He tells them not to be smug and self-righteous, praying, "God I thank you that I am not like other men," but pray with humility, "God be merciful to me a sinner. Love your enemies, and *DO UNTO OTHERS WHAT YOU WOULD HAVE OTHERS DO UNTO YOU.*" "But what must we do," He is asked, "to be doing the works of God?" "This is the work of God," Jesus replies, "*BELIEVE IN HIM WHOM GOD HAS SENT.*" A centurion believes, and gains Jesus' admiration and praise, who tells him, "Surely, in all Israel I have not found such great faith."

Jesus now has a huge following, the crowds who come to listen and be healed number in the thousands. But He has enemies, also, bitter, resentful and afraid of the threat He is to their official authority. Although He observes proper Jewish tradition in most ways He associates, also, not only with women, but with sinners and riff-raff, all strictly forbidden by the stringent Pharisaic legalism that has turned the Law of Moses into a moral straitjacket. Now, on a Sabbath day, IN THE SYNAGOGUE at Capernaum, Jesus heals a man's "withered hand," thus "working" on the Sabbath, and the angry Pharisees "straightaway [take] counsel with the Herodians . . . how they might destroy him."

Now Jesus begins to teach about Himself, not as a mortal Rabbi, but something far greater, almost beyond belief. "I am the light of the world," He says, "and the bread of life. He who follows me will not live in darkness, but in light, and eat the bread of life. I AND THE FATHER ARE ONE. YOU BELIEVE IN GOD, BELIEVE ALSO IN ME." The disciples are astonished at His teaching, "for His word was with authority."

To tell them what the kingdom of heaven is like, Jesus speaks in parables, allegorical stories: he tells of ". . . a merchant in search of fine pearls," or a man who sows seed in his field, whether in rocky, shallow or good ground. It is "like a net thrown into the sea" or a "grain of mustard seed." He likens the kingdom to the "wise and foolish maidens," a king settling accounts, treasure hidden under a bushel. He tells them of the compassion of a good Samaritan, the return home of a repentant son; the vaunting pride of a Pharisee and the humble prayer of a tax-collecting Publican. He reminds them that good sense would not sew new cloth onto an old garment, nor fill old skins with new wine; and tells them about a rich fool, a faithful steward, laborers in a vineyard, lost sheep and a barren fig tree. He describes an unjust judge and an unmerciful servant, a shrewd manager and a watchful porter; and everything He tells them has deep and profound meaning. Each parable teaches His listeners something about life, truth, morality, God . . . or about Himself, that they would reject if He merely preached at them, or that His enemies would pounce upon if He spoke them outright. Then He scolds the crowd for not understanding His message; they are able to predict the weather by a rising cloud in the west or the blowing of a southerly wind. If they can do that, He demands, "Why do you not know how to interpret the present time? Ask and it will be given you; seek, and you will find; knock, and it will be opened to you." And, like a woman's joy at finding a lost coin so, he says, is there "joy before the angels of God over one sinner who repents."

Salome with the head of
John the Baptist

Jesus hears of the grizzly death of His cousin, John the Baptist, beheaded by a lust-crazed King Herod Agrippa to satisfy a vow to his stepdaughter, Salome. Sick at heart, Jesus "retires to a lonely place," but a "great throng" awaits Him there, so He teaches . . . and then feeds them— all 5000 of them—on five loaves of bread and two fishes! Then is a clamor raised among the 5000 to seize Him and MAKE HIM KING . . . on the spot! Here is their Messiah, their provider, their protector, who will feed them, take care of them, grant all their de-

The loaves & fishes mosaic from the
Church built on the site of the miracle
at Jerusalem

sires! So Jesus "withdraws" with haste to the hills, to be alone and pray. But then the wind rises, and at "the fourth watch of the night" He walks out to His disciples, whose boat is in peril from one of Lake Galilee's fierce winter storms . . . which ceases at His presence. Many eyewitnesses to these miracles look upon Jesus as their "manna from heaven," their welfare, their savior from worldly woe, but Jesus says, "Your fathers did eat manna in the wilderness, and are dead . . . I AM THE BREAD OF LIFE: HE WHO COMES TO ME SHALL NOT HUNGER, AND HE WHO BELIEVES IN ME SHALL NEVER THIRST."   JOHN 6:35

Jesus often "flees" for safety, or quiet contemplation and prayer, to a "far place," away from crowds and harassment; and now goes north, near the Syrian seaport cities of Tyre and Sidon (the Bible doesn't say why); and from there to Caesarea Philippi, named for both Caesar, in Rome, and Herod the Great's son, Philip, whose territory it now is. On the way, Jesus asks His disciples, "Who do men say that I am?" Hesitantly, almost timorously, they offer, "Elijah, Jeremiah, John the Baptist, returned from the dead." Then Jesus asks that question which will echo down the centuries, the question every human being who hears His name, and the WORD, must answer some day, one way or another.

"But who do YOU say that I am?"

A prophet? A good man? A compassionate healer, or a charlatan? Somebody's invention? Or simply a wise teacher? But wise teachers do not claim to be Messiahs . . . or the "Bread of Life." Who do YOU say that I am?" Then Simon Peter answers, without hesitation, "THOU ART THE CHRIST, THE SON OF THE LIVING GOD." And on the rock of that faith, revealed to Peter not by flesh and blood but "by my father which is in heaven," does Jesus say that He will build His church ". . . AND THE GATES OF HELL SHALL NOT PREVAIL AGAINST IT."   MATTHEW 16:16–18

Now does Jesus talk of His own future, how He will suffer, in Jerusalem, at the hands of the elders, the chief priests and scribes, and be killed and on the third day raised. "And," says the book of MARK, "HE SAID THIS PLAINLY." 8:31,32 "God forbid, Lord," Peter cries, "not you!" and Jesus tells him "Get thee behind me, Satan . . . you are not on the side of God." And He adds that whoever would follow Him must take up his cross, also, for whosoever would save his life must lose it, and whoever loses it—for His sake—will save it. "What does it profit a man," He asks, "to gain the whole world and lose his soul?"

Again Jesus takes His disciples aside and privately teaches them their own mission: how they must go out into the world and tell the world about Him. "All things have been delivered to me by my Father," He begins. "No one knows the Father save the Son and anyone whom the Son chooses to reveal Him to. He who receives you receives me, and HE WHO RECEIVES ME, RECEIVES THE FATHER. MATTHEW 11:27 Also, I say unto you, whosoever confesses me before men I shall confess before the angels of God, and he who denies me before men will I deny; and he who blasphemes against the Holy Ghost shall not be forgiven. But, fear not little flock, for it is your Father's own good pleasure to give you the kingdom. And be not concerned for what you will eat or drink, but be like the lilies of the field, for your Father knows what you need." Jesus' own life and dress manifest that trust. Artists in later generations will portray Him appearing perpetually ethereal, meek and mild, in immaculate white robes and ever present halo. But His "biographers" don't mention that. Rather, His garments are more than likely the coarse, natural homespun common to a working man, just as apt to soil, and the quiet and cool of the mountains where the air is fresh and crisp offers Him a chance to shake the dust of the highways and the heat

of the towns from His clothes. Only once do the gospels describe Him as the artists show
. . . in the mountains . . .

Jesus often goes up into the mountains to pray, where His Father's presence is close and comforting, and His prayers fervent and intense. And there it is that one of the major events in His life occurs, when He goes there with Peter, James and John, to pray . . .

> And as he was praying, the appearance of his countenance was altered, and his raiment became dazzling white. And . . . Moses and Elijah . . . appeared in glory and spoke of his departure which he was to accomplish at Jerusalem . . . And a voice came out of [a] cloud, saying, "This is my son, my chosen, listen to him!"   LUKE 9:28–35

It is an event of enormous significance, for God to reveal His son Jesus, the fulfillment and perfect expression of the Law, in company with Moses, God's instrument in the crafting of that Law, and Elijah the fore-runner of the prophets who would refine it. The Law and the Prophets; Moses, Elijah and Jesus originator, harbinger and incarnation.

> And the glory of the LORD shall be revealed and all flesh shall see it together, for the mouth of the LORD hath spoken it.   ISAIAH 40:5 (See: 530 B.C.)

"Tell no man of the vision," Jesus tells them, "until the Son of man be raised from the dead."

Raised from the dead! What does He mean? This man not only talks in parables, He talks in riddles. What does He mean, "Take up your cross and follow me?" What has this kind and gentle man to do with a cross? And whatever did He mean when He said He would spend three days and three nights in the heart of the earth? "You will weep and lament," He said, "but the world will rejoice. You will be sorrowful but your sorrow will turn to joy, for unless a grain of wheat falls into the earth and dies, it remains alone. But if it dies, it bears much fruit." Whatever does the man mean? Jesus' disciples do not *understand* Him yet, but they *believe* in Him, that He is the Son of God, the Christ, the promised Messiah! Not yet, though, are they the strong soldiers of God they will someday be. Now, they are still simple men, anxious for themselves, eager for a place in Heaven nearest Jesus and He tells them that "everyone who exalts himself shall be humbled, and those who humble themselves shall be exalted."

Jesus praises the humble generosity in the giving of a poor widow's mite, more, for her, than all the rich together who give little of their abundance; and He protects an adulteress from stoning, challenging her accusers that only he who is without sin should cast the first stone; then says to her, "Go, and sin no more." Knowing that she need only touch His garments to be healed of her disease one woman causes a "sudden surge of power to go forth" from Jesus; and when He learns the cause sends her away healed, because of her faith. But "many others," including Joanna, the wife of Herod Agrippa's steward, Susanna and Mary Magdelene, are among His closest companions and "minister to Him of their substance;" Mary, who may have been that "sinner" who washed His feet with her tears, dried them with her hair and anointed them with ointment from an alabaster box . . . much to a Pharisee's indignation.

Jesus spends much time with the humble and makes no effort to cultivate the wealthy or influential, from whom He could profit in worldly ways. Rather, He tells a "rich young ruler" that "it would be easier for a camel to get through the eye of a needle than a rich man into heaven . . . and yet, with God all things are possible." He eats and drinks with publicans and sinners . . . and is roundly criticized. He replies, "They that are whole need not a physician but they that are sick. I am come to call not the righteous, but the sinners, to repentance." And to those sinners . . . and the sick, suffering, weary, bereaved, lonely, sick at hearty and downcast . . . in fact to everyone, does Jesus say . . .

> "COME UNTO ME, ALL YE THAT LABOR AND ARE HEAVY LADEN, AND I WILL GIVE YOU REST. Take my yoke upon you, and learn from me . . . and you will find rest for your souls."   MATTHEW 11:28:29

Not only do His friends not understand Him, but His townspeople, also, who have known His parents and people, now wonder, as though He is new to them, where He got His wisdom, His authority . . . and they "take offense at Him." Twice is He rejected at Nazareth, but Jesus replies, "My teaching is not mine but His who sent me," and adds, wryly, "A prophet is not without honor . . . save in his own country."

> The stone which the builders refused is become the headstone of the corner.   PSALM 118:22, MATTHEW 21:42, MARK 12:10

Jesus' most constant companion is John, the "beloved apostle." He is with Him at almost every major event in Jesus' life, and so, sees and hears things the others do not . . . and remembers and understands them in ways the others would not. He was with Jesus when He accepted a drink of water from the Samaritan woman, saying "Whoever drinks of this water shall thirst again, but whoever drinks of the water I give will never thirst . . . the water of eternal life." John will someday be the only disciple to write about Jesus' miracle at the wedding at Cana, and of His long discourse on the "Bread of Life"—Himself, who "came down from heaven, not to do mine own will, but the will of him that sent me." He heard Jesus tell the Jewish official, Nicodemus, "Truly I say to you, unless one is born again, he can not see the kingdom of God." Confused, Nicodemus questions how a man already old can be reborn. But Jesus is not teaching the rebirth of the flesh, but of spirit, that, "the Son of man must be lifted up, so that whoever believes in Him may have eternal life . . . FOR GOD SO LOVED THE WORLD THAT HE GAVE HIS ONLY BEGOTTEN SON, THAT WHOSOEVER BELIEVETH IN HIM SHOULD NOT PERISH, BUT HAVE EVERLASTING LIFE." (JOHN 3:16) Someday John will write a book in which he will tell all these things that it was given only to him to tell, that will include Jesus' unequivocal description (in the face of angry listeners ready to stone Him) of His own place in God's Great Plan. "Truly, *verily*, I say unto you BEFORE ABRAHAM WAS, I AM." (JOHN 8:58)

32   Jesus' friends, Mary and Martha, send for Him to tell Him their brother, Lazarus, is sick, hoping Jesus will heal him. Their house has been home for Jesus on every trip through Bethany, and the two women have served Him often, Martha with practical household duties, Mary with attentive devotion. But Jesus arrives too late, His dear friend, Lazarus, is dead. Deeply grieved, Jesus weeps . . . and restores him to life. "I AM THE RESURRECTION AND THE LIFE," He says, "HE WHO BELIEVES IN ME SHALL NEVER DIE." (JOHN 11:25-26) News of the miracle travels fast and results in many new believers. Fearful that "everybody" will believe, the High Priest, Caiaphas, tells the Jews that Jesus' death would be "expedient," so "from that day on they took counsel how to put Him to death." (JOHN 11:53)   The most powerful man in Palestine, hundreds, if not thousands, of people owe Caisphas their very livelihoods for, as the Jewish historian Josephus says in his HISTORY OF THE JEWS, "Running the temple is the biggest business in Palestine." There are teachers, clerks, scribes and musicians, servants, cooks, butchers, cleaners and potters; every one to some degree dependent upon Caiaphas' good graces, subordinate to his orders. Whether high-placed associates and administrators or lowly sycophants, minions and flunkies, when Caiaphas wants something done, they do it. And now, Caiaphas wants Jesus dead.

The Caiaphas Ossuary

One of the most spectacular—indeed, almost unbelievable—finds in modern biblical archeology will occur over two thousand years from this time when, in November, 1990, a bulldozer working south of Jerusalem, will accidentally uncover a cavern in which were buried 12 ossuaries—bone boxes like little coffins for burying bones after the dead person's flesh had "aged" away. (This was a Jewish custom used only for about 100 years, in only this part of the world at only this time.) One of the boxes contained the bones of several people, including one 60 year-old man, a man of great wealth and much influence judging from the beauty of the box's decoration, intricately carved with ornate swirls and rosettes. On the outside of the box is carved twice, the name "Yehosef bar Qafa," or Joseph, son of Caiaphas. Today, there is almost no argument that these are, in fact, the remains of the High Priest, Caiaphas, who is now playing so large a part in the fate of Jesus of Nazareth . . . an archeological find that SHOULD have made headlines around the world!

The ruins of the High Priest's palace, the "house of Caiaphas" have long been known near the Pool of Siloam in Jerusalem's upper city on the Western Hill. Several churches have been built on the site since Byzantine times, but it is the three levels of excavations beneath them that tell Caiaphas' story. For there have been found the ruins or evidence of vast corn and oil storage areas, a grist mill, stable, a "treasury" with weights and measures which were used only by the temple priests court of justice and a guard-room complete with a whipping block.

Another fabulous archeological find is the entire white limestone and marble Greco/Roman city of Sepphoris just three miles away from Jesus' "home town" of Nazareth. Built by Herod Antipas after his father, Herod the Great's death, it replaced a city destroyed in the riots that followed Herod's slaughter of the babies and burning of the rabbis during Jesus' infancy. Sepphoris is not mentioned in the Bible, but Josephus tells its story and its existence is not questioned. Under construction during Jesus' youth and young manhood, and only an hour's walk from Nazareth, Sepphoris offered all kinds of employment opportunity for master carpenters, for its sophisticated ruins have yielded up colonnaded streets, markets, fountains, pools, public baths, grain silos, wine cellars, elegant villas, a public forum, gymnasium, a 4000 seat hillside theater (that once had a great, wooden stage) and Antipas' own royal palace. Once called "the most beautiful city of the region," the "ornament of all Galilee," the discovery of the long forgotten city puts to doubt the idea of Jesus as a back-woods rustic from an isolated village with no knowledge of urban life, for Sepphoris also offered all kinds of other contacts, as well: city officials, architects, construction workers, money lenders, shop keepers, athletes . . . and actors whom Jesus would refer to, often, in his teachings. For when He denounced those who flaunt false piety as "hypocrites," Jesus was using the Greek word for "actor." Is all this just idle speculation? The Gospel of JOHN suggests not; its last verse reads:

> And there are also many other things which Jesus did, the which, if they should be written every one, I suppose that even the world itself could not contain the books that should be written.   JOHN 21:25

Jesus' disciples turn aside some children whom they think will be bothersome and an "indignant" Jesus rebukes them, takes the children in His arms and blesses them. "Let the children come to me," He says, "for to such belongs the kingdom of God. Truly I say to you, whoever does not receive the kingdom of God like a child shall not enter it." It is a truly provocative, revolutionary message in a world of evil, intrigue, brute force and false gods like Baal for whom children are torn asunder and burned for sacrifice. "Love your enemies, turn the other cheek, FORGIVE," Jesus says, "and suffer the little children." Simple, trusting faith that could cure the ills and abuses of the world—His own and ours, today—better than all the socio-therapists put together. "Whoever causes one of these little ones who believe in me to sin, it would be better . . . a great millstone were hung round his neck and . . . thrown into the sea."   MARK 10:13–16 & 9:42

"Love one another," Jesus tells His friends, "as I have loved you. I have chosen you, my friends, that you should go and bear fruit. If you keep my commandments you will abide in my love, and remember, greater love hath no man than this; that he lay down his life for his friends." JOHN 15:13 Lay down their lives they will; and Jesus tells them they will be persecuted for Him, and will suffer; but, also not to fear. "Take up your cross and follow me, and have no fear of them that kill the body, but only them that kill the soul; for he who loses his life for my sake, will gain life everlasting. Temptations are sure to come, but woe to him by whom they do come . . . for I have not come to bring peace, but the sword . . . for the Son of man came not to be served, but to serve, and to give his life as a ransom for many."

What a strange thing to say, "I have not come to bring peace but a sword." Again His disciples are baffled and, indeed, later ages will try to turn Him into a political revolutionary, out to overthrow governments, their own included. But Jesus' sword will cut the good from the bad, virtue from evil, absolute standards from relative rationale. Those things that were true and good yesterday, are true and good today, and will be tomorrow and a thousand years hence, and Jesus' "sword" will cut them off from social manipulating and cultic "enlightment."

32   It is three years now since Jesus began His ministry, three years in which He has gained the love of the common people, the enmity of the official class, and the envy of the die-hard revolutionaries. If only THEY could have the power over a mob that He has, they could raise an army against Rome in no time. The Zealots still hope they can persuade Him to take up the revolutionary sword and . . . TAKE ON ROME! Once again Jesus makes the journey to Jerusalem, knowing that this time it is dangerous for Him, but knowing, also, that He must do it. On His way to Jerusalem, Jesus stays again with Mary, Martha and Lazarus in Bethany, and Mary anoints Jesus' feet with an expensive ointment, causing the disciple, Judas, to complain that it should have been sold and the money "given to the poor." Jesus replies, "Let her alone . . . she has done a beautiful thing to me. For you always have the poor with you, and whenever you will, you can do good to them; but you will not always have me . . . where-ever the gospel is preached in the whole world, what she has done will be told in memory of her."   MARK 14:6–9

32, Sunday before Passover.   Jesus enters the city riding on a donkey, and the friendly crowds along the way—hundreds of Jewish believers—wave palm branches like flags, cheering Him triumphantly into Jerusalem as their king. The message to those who know the Law and the Prophets is clearly that here, indeed, is God's "Suffering Servant" come to fulfill His mission.

> Prophesied: Rejoice greatly, O daughters of Zion, shout O daughters of Jerusalem. Behold thy king cometh unto you, triumphant and victorious is he, humble and riding on an ass . . . He is the righteous savior and he shall speak peace unto the nations.   ZECHARIAH 9:9,10 (See: 521 B.C.)

The suffering servant knows full well what is ahead. "The hour is come," He says, "that the Son of man should be glorified," for, as He said, a grain of wheat must die and be buried to be reborn to produce new life. But, for this mortal man, at this moment, it is small comfort. "Now is my soul troubled," Jesus ponders, "and what shall I say? Father save me from this hour? But for this cause came I unto this hour . . . And I, if I be lifted up . . . will draw all men unto me." This he said, the book of JOHN records (12:27,32,33) "signifying what death he should die." Once again Jesus weeps . . . for Jerusalem, and its own dreadful fate, just ahead.

Up to this time Roman customs, political, religious or civil influence and especially Roman law, have affected Jesus' life relatively little, for the Galilee of His three year ministry is not yet under Roman jurisdiction, being still one of the *Civitates Liberae,* the Free States, and will continue to be self-governing for 12 more years. But now, on "Palm Sunday," the scene changes to Jerusalem, administered by the Emperor Tiberius' Judean *praefect,* Pontius Pilate, within the legal requisites of Roman *provincia:* Roman military occupation, taxation and supervision of public order. Jerusalem is, unmistakably, a Roman *provincia,* or province; and Jesus' last days are to be spent under Rome's jurisdiction.

The charge is often made that the Gospel writers of the "New Testament," those four who told Jesus' story, told it the way they did merely to prove and justify ancient prophecy. And that it does; but their stories do something else besides. Matthew, Mark, Luke and John were not lawyers expert in Roman law; they were fishermen and a tax collector. They had no idea of, no interest in the legal subtleties of Roman law; their only interest was in telling the Good News of God in the story of one man. And yet scholarly examination, in recent years, of Roman law in comparison with the Gospels show that they are perfectly in accordance with Roman law OF THIS TIME, A.D. 32, not a hundred years earlier, or later, or a decade or a year. Just as modern law is constantly amended and rewritten, so was Roman, and the Gospel writers could not have understood, nor written into their accounts the many subtleties of change from, say, late republican law, to early empire, to late empire. Had Jesus' life just been invented and the writing of the Gospels a mere fabrication, someone's invention a hundred years after the fact the story would have reflected Roman law of THAT time, not this. No, the writers told the story as it happened; and, as it happens, the recording of the events of the last days of Jesus' life reflect unmistakably the framework of Roman law in the first century, A.D., just when the Gospels say they did.

Charges have also been made, throughout the centuries, that the entire Jewish race, collectively, should be held responsible for Jesus' death, and Jews have often been terribly persecuted for it, but the following events show something far different.

Palm Sunday, afternoon.   Jesus goes to the temple, and what He sees He does not like. It is more like a market place, an oriental bazaar then a temple of worship; money changers haggling over prices, raucous cries of bargaining, and big money being made on sacrificial animals. Only Jewish money is accepted in the temple, and Jerusalem's far-flung commerce is carried on with coins of many kinds: Roman *denarii* and *quadrans,* the Greek *drachma* and *stater*; while Asian payments are weighed out with *minas* and *talents.* Long forgotten is the ancient admonition of the prophet Hosea:

> For I desire steadfast love and not sacrifice, knowledge of God rather than burnt offerings.   HOSEA 6:6 (See: 750 B.C.)

Jerusalem is a motley hodge-podge of Asiatic mysticism and idolatry, Hellenistic sophistication and self-indulgence, Roman arrogance and brute force, and Jewish frustration and political intrigue. The wealthy and more worldly Jewish Sadducees long ago came to grips with the harsh facts of life, reconciling themselves to a foreign presence in their land, and grudgingly working out a "peaceful co-existence" with both Greeks and Romans. Some, like the tax-collector, Matthew, and the high priest, Caiaphas, went so far as to openly collaborate with the Romans and the Sadducees who are now the dominant power on the judicial Sanhedrin. The Pharisees ("they who have separated themselves") are the religious/political reactionaries, staunchly nationalistic and anti-Roman; whose unbending, implacable adherence to the very letter of the ancient Hebrew LAW—and their own Pharasaic restrictions—make them appear ostentatious and hypocritical. There are more than 600 commandments and restrictions in the ancient Law, and the Pharisees observe them all; from wearing their beards square cut, not rounded off, to crossing the street to avoid looking upon a woman.

And then there are those fanatical Zealots, fiercely militaristic and hell-bent on ridding Palestine of the scourge of Rome, come what may. One of their breed, in prison at this time, is a man convicted of murder and insurrection, called . . . Barabbas. Jesus leaves the city, sick at heart, and stays the night with His friends in Bethany.

32, Monday.   Jesus returns to the Temple, openly and unafraid, teaching and preaching. Then he takes the fateful step that antagonizes the authorities, scribes and priests. Driven to fury by wrong and injustice, He drives the money-changers out of the temple . . . as one who has Godly power to do it, crying, "Is it not written my house shall be called a house of prayer for all nations, and you have made it a den of thieves!"

Has this house, which is called by my name, become a den of robbers in your eyes. Behold, I myself have seen it says the Lord,   JEREMIAH 7:11 (See: 627 B.C.)   *   ". . . for my house shall be called a house of prayer for all people.   ISAIAH 56:7 (See: 530 B.C.)

32 Tuesday and Wednesday.   Jesus returns to the temple to teach; and the scribes, Pharisees and Sadducees all question Him with loaded questions, trying to trap Him. The Sadducees ask about marriage after death, and the scribes challenge Him to name which commandment is the greatest. Without hesitation, Jesus quotes both DEUTERONOMY and LEVITICUS and replies:

Thou shalt love the LORD thy God with all thy heart and with all thy soul and with all thy mind. This is the first and great commandment. And the second is like unto it. Thou shalt love thy neighbor as thyself. On these two commandments hang all the law and the prophets.   DEUT. 6:4 and LEV. 19:18; MATTHEW 22:38–40

Then the Pharisees ask Him whether it is lawful to pay taxes to Caesar. If He says yes or no it will condemn Him with some group. "Yes," will mean that He approves of the Roman occupation of Judea, and "no" will give the zealots their leader. With one short, succinct statement, Jesus seals His fate with the zealots and closes forever the question of whether He will lead a revolution against Rome. Taking in his hand a Roman denarius with the image of Tiberius imprinted on it, Jesus replies:

> Render unto Caesar the things that are Caesar's, and unto God the things that are God's.   MATT. 22:21, MARK 12:17 and LUKE 20:25

Render unto Caesar

Jesus now has the better of them all, and they know it. Now does he level his attack upon them. "Woe unto you hypocrites," He cries, "because you shut the kingdom of heaven against men. You care nothing for law, justice, mercy or faith, but only tithes, gifts and sacrifices!" And woe to Jerusalem as well, Jesus tells His disciples as He prophesies:

> Jerusalem shall be trodden down [by] the Gentiles.   LUKE 21:24

The Judas coin

32, Wednesday.   Judas Iscariot, the disciple who has been in charge of the group's meager finances from the beginning, goes to meet with the chief priests . . . and comes away with 30 pieces of silver . . .

> And they weighed out as my wages, thirty shekels of silver.   ZECHARIAH 11:12 (See: 521 B.C.) MATTHEW 27:9 (See: A.D. 80)

32, Thursday.   In the evening, Jesus and the twelve meet together for the Passover meal. Before they eat, Jesus turns quietly to Judas and says, "What you are going to do, do quickly." After these days' business is finished, Judas will hang himself in remorse and regret . . . and be buried in a potter's field.

> . . . and the LORD said unto me, Cast it unto the potter. And I took the thirty pieces of silver, and cast them to the potter.   ZECHARIAH 11:13 (See: 521 B.C.) MATTHEW 27:9,10 (See: A.D. 80)

Jesus has many weighty matters on his mind and, finally, it is time to share them. "Now," He begins, "is the Son of man glorified, and in Him God is glorified. The scripture must be fulfilled in me: 'He was numbered with the transgressors.' (ISAIAH 53:12. 530 B.C.) Little children, yet a little while I am with you . . . and where I am going you cannot come. Nevertheless, I tell you the truth, it is to your advantage that I go away for if I do not, the Counselor will not come to you." Simon Peter protests, "Lord, I would go with you. I would lay down my life for you!" "Would you?" Jesus asks. "Before the cock crows, Peter, you will deny me three times."

"But let not your hearts be troubled," Jesus tells them all. "In my father's house are many rooms. I go to prepare a place for you." "But how will we know the way, Lord?"

asks a doubting Thomas. "I AM THE WAY, AND THE TRUTH, AND THE LIFE: NO ONE COMES TO THE FATHER, BUT BY ME," (JOHN 14:6) "Abide in me. I am the vine and you are the branches. Because I live you will also. As the Father has loved me, so have I loved you. By this will all men know that you are my disciples. The hour is coming when whoever kills you will think he is offering service to God. I did not say these things from the beginning for I was with you then. I have yet many things to say to you but you cannot bear to hear them now. When the Spirit of Truth comes, He will guide you into all truth; the Comforter, the Holy Spirit will teach you. In the world you have tribulation," Jesus concludes, "but be of good cheer. I HAVE OVERCOME THE WORLD." (JOHN 16:33) And Jesus asks His Father to watch over His "little flock." "Now I am no more in the world," He prays, "I am coming to Thee, but they ARE in the world. Holy Father, keep them in Thy name that they may be one, even as we are one."

"Do this in rememberance of me."
From a 3rd Century wall painting

In communion together, Jesus serves them the Passover meal, which for a thousand years has looked back, commemorating delivery of the Hebrews from slavery in Egypt: and He speaks more enigmatic words: "This is my body. Take, eat, do this in remembrance of me." And, giving them wine to drink, He says, "This is my blood of the new covenant which is poured out for the forgiveness of sin." (MATTHEW, MARK, LUKE) The NEW COVENANT! There, He has said it! The old covenant God made with Abraham (GEN. 12:1–3) so long ago, at the very dawn of history, is replaced with a new and greater covenant, just as Jeremiah prophesied more than 600 years ago; and as Malachi promised 400 years ago!

> Behold the days are coming says the Lord, when 1 will make a new covenant with the house of Israel and the house of Judah. (JER. 31:31, See: 605 BC) * The lord whom ye seek shall suddenly come to his temple, even the messenger of the covenant, whom ye delight in: behold, he shall come, saith the LORD of Hosts. (MALACHI 1:1, See: 400 BC)

No longer need man look backward to mourn or commemorate wrongs suffered under ancient oppressors! The sin and suffering of ages past is being atoned for and WILL BE atoned for in future, for Jesus will, Himself, become the instrument of a . . . NEW COVENANT! When he writes about this night many years hence, Jesus' friend, John, will explain that the flesh and blood of this "LAST SUPPER" are, in reality, Spirit and Truth:

> God is Spirit, and those who worship Him must worship in spirit and truth. JOHN 4:24

At midnight, Jesus goes to pray in the Garden of Gethsemene with some of the twelve. "My soul is sorrowful," He says to them, "even unto death. Remain here and watch with me." And they promptly fall asleep. A lonely, desolate mortal man, He asks His Father if the "cup" before Him can be removed. Dreading what He knows is ahead, Jesus' prayer, now, is not to a formal, divine Father, omnipotent creator of the universe,

The Garden of Gethsemene

but to His *Abba Father,* in his native Aramaic, His "Daddy," a name He alone can use. It is the cry of a frightened child to his own loving, caring, familial father, close, personal and comforting. He does not want to go through this. "Nevertheless," He prays, "not my will but thy will be done."   (MARK 14:36)

Behold and see if there be any sorrow like unto my sorrow.   LAMENTATIONS 1:12 (See: 530 B.C.)

Betrayed by one of His own, Jesus says to him, "Judas, betrayest thou the Son of man with a kiss?"

Yea, mine own familiar friend, in whom I trusted, which did eat of my bread, hath lifted up his heel against me.   PSALM 41:9 (See: 400 BC)

Jesus is seized by the guard from the temple and His terrified disciples "forsake Him and flee." He is taken to the house of the high priest, Caiaphas, who quickly assembles members of the Sanhedrin. And Jesus defends Himself. "I have taught openly in the synagogues," He says, "and nothing secretly. Why did you take me now and not then?" They try Him that night, illegally, charging Him with blasphemy; that He claimed He could destroy and re-build the temple in three days: but their witnesses disagree, leaving the charges unproved . . .

We heard Him say, I will destroy this temple that is made with hands, and within three days I will build another made without hands. MARK 14:58 * False witnesses did rise up; they laid to my charge things that I knew not.   PSALM 35:11

They re-charge Him with claiming to be the Messiah. This will prove to be as serious a charge before the Roman governor as before the Jews, for it is generally believed that with the coming of the Messiah will come, also, the end of Roman rule. Asked by the council if He IS the Messiah, Jesus condemns Himself with six short words. "I am," He replies, "You have said so." Finding Him guilty of blasphemy, the Jews hedge that the *Pax Romana* disallows them passage of the death penalty, so Jesus is held until morning, early in the morning, during the *praefect's* period of *labores,* before Pilate begins to observe his *salutario,* a two hour uninterruptible leisure.

Word of his arrest spreads fast, and little by little a crowd gathers and grows all night, quietly at first, out of curiosity. These are not the same people who welcomed Him into the city with joy and anticipation; not the scores of Jewish believers who were witness to His love and kindnesses. This is a hired claque rounded up by the temple bureaucracy, the result of that day when Jesus raised up Lazarus from the dead and the high priest, Caiaphas, decided that Jesus' death would be "expedient . . . and from that day . . . took counsel how to put Him to death." These are the people who, the historian Josephus says, make running the Temple the "biggest business in Jerusalem," Caiaphas' sycophants, minions, flunkies, merchants, moneychangers, associates and administrators who owe their livelihoods to the High Priest, obeying him now that he wants Jesus dead. The zealots in the crowd know their cause is lost; Jesus will not lead their revolution . . . but, maybe, if they can get him free, the prisoner, Barabbas will! So, they begin to whisper the word, "crucify."

32, Early Friday A.M.   Before the break of dawn Jesus is taken before the Roman *praefect* Pontius Pilate, the mind, voice and authority of Rome in Judea, and the two meet in history's most decisive confrontation: INCARNATE GOD WITH INCARNATE ROME! Pilate's *praetorium* is set up in the huge court-yard of the Antonia Fortress, before a massive, polished *pavement*, upon which Jesus stands (and which has been found by archeologists in our own time). Pilate sits upon the official *bema*, the judgment seat, while the *delatores*, the accusers (in this case the chief priests and elders) present their *cognitio*, their evidence. "He is perverting the nation," they charge, "forbidding the payment of tribute to Caesar, claiming to be Christ, the king, stirring up the people through all Judea from Galilee to here in Jerusalem." The charges are an attempt to shift the onus of responsibility from the high priest to Pilate, himself, and to Rome.

But to their chagrin, Pilate adheres strictly to Roman law—first century Roman law. If Jesus has committed these "crimes," they were committed in His (Jesus') own *forum domicilii*—His home area, Galilee, not under Roman rule, not in a *forum delectii* (away from home, in Jerusalem) and therefore punishable—if at all—there, not here. Thus, acting entirely within his *Provincia imperium*, Pilate pronounces an acquittal . . . with a warning: "Take him and judge him according to your law." The change in *venue* is a diplomatic coup nothing short of brilliant. He symbolically "washes his hands" of the matter, and sends them, and Jesus, to King Herod Antipas, the Jewish ruler. Executioner of John the Baptist, son of that Herod who had been king when Jesus was born, Antipas has long wanted to see Jesus for himself.

> The kings of the earth rise up, and the rulers take counsel together, against the LORD and against his anointed.   PSALM 2:2 (See: 400 B.C.)

With the chief priests and scribes "vehemently" shouting accusations, Antipas looks Jesus over and questions Him at length, but gets no answer, Jesus pleading, by his silence, *nolo contendere*. He will not admit guilt nor defend himself.

> He was oppressed and he opened not his mouth: he is brought as a lamb to the slaughter, and as a sheep before her shearer is dumb, so openeth he not his mouth. ISAIAH 53:7
> (See; 530 B.C.)

Antipas and the elders mock Jesus and clothe him in "kingly" apparel, a "royal purple" robe is hung about Jesus' shoulders, a mocking crown of thorns pressed into His head, and He is sent back to Pilate. Having sealed His fate with the Jews, Jesus now declines to do so before the *praefect,* who asks Him, "ARE you the king of the Jews?"

We do not know, today, what language they spoke together; probably neither Aramaic, Jesus' native language, the common tongue of most Judean provincials, nor Pilate's Roman Latin. Most likely it was Greek, for Greek speech and influence had been pervasive, if not dominant, in that part of the world since Alexander, and it is more probable that Jesus understood it, than not. Moreover, it was then the language of diplomacy all over the Middle East, the *Lingua franca,* that Pilate, as Roman diplomat, would have been required to know and use.

Jesus replies, "My kingdom is not of this world." The crowd, now large, is uneasy . . . and so is Pilate; that is not the response of a political revolutionary. He takes his prisoner out to them that they may "know that I fine no fault in him. *Ecce homo,*" he tells them, "Behold the man." Behold the man, indeed. Jesus is that same man they have heard so much about, and nothing bad. But crowds are easy to manipulate, and the manipulators are busy. All it takes is the din of repetition, a catchword over and over, "crucify, CRUCIFY, *CRUCIFY!!*"

So far, the chief priests have charged Jesus with religious "crimes," saying, "We have a law that he ought to die because he made himself the Son of God." The inference to the widespread belief that with the coming of a Jewish messiah will come, also, the end of Roman rule, is not lost on Pilate, the worldly *praefect,* and makes him "the more afraid." Confused and trying to be fair, Pilate, back in the judgment hall away from the crowd, asks Jesus, "Who are you? From whence do you come?" But Jesus gives him no answer. Frustrated, Pilate says to Jesus, "You do not speak to me? Do you not know that I have power to release you, and power to crucify you?" And Jesus answers him:

> You could have no power at all against me, except it were given you from above. JOHN 19:11

Except it were given you from above. The whole broad vista of Jewish history and the thousand year panorama since the creation of its monarchy is summed up in Jesus' one short sentence: how the disorganized, demoralized Hebrews in the long-ago days of the Judges demanded of the last judge, Samuel, that he "make them a king . . . like other nations . . . to fight our battles for us . . ." It sums up how Samuel spoke for God and warned them what a king would do to enslave and make them serve him. And especially it sums up God's revelation of Himself as the ultimate—and only—source of moral governmental power over free peoples, by saying to Samuel, "All right, then, they won't listen. They want a king . . . so . . .

> Hearken, to their voice, and make them a king. (I SAMUEL 8.6–22)

Finally, Jesus' reply sums up how Israel's, and Judah's, long lines of kings misused and abused their God-given power for un-godly gain and were destroyed: they, their countries and their people. Thus it was then, is now, and will be in the future for nations yet unborn.

The book of JOHN, which alone records this incident, between Godly power and Roman, doesn't say whether Pilate understood Jesus' enigmatic statement "You would have no power were it not given you from above." It says only that "from henceforth, Pilate sought to release him." And so, he refuses a conviction on their religious charge. So the claque shrewdly switches strategy to practical politics, and puts the pressure on Pilate with the threat, "If you let this man go, you are not Caesar's Friend, *Caesaris Amicus*," that same demoted condition a mortified Herod found himself faced with 36 years ago. But Tiberius Caesar, now at his worst, is no rational, fair-minded Augustus, and the LAST thing Pilate wants is to lose his good will . . . so he "brings Jesus forth" and sits down on the judgment seat "in the place that is called the Pavement, but in the Hebrew *Gabbatha*," (which has been found by modern archeologists.) And Pilate says unto the Jews, "Behold your King! Shall I crucify your king?" The chief priests answer, "We have no king but Caesar!" No king but Caesar! That wasn't always so. Seven hundred years ago Isaiah spoke eloquently and emphatically about the king of the Jews:

> The Lord is our Judge, the Lord is our Lawgiver, the Lord is our King. He will save us.
> ISAIAH 33:22 See: 700 B.C.

But the chief priests have, long ago, forgotten that and continue their trumped-up trial. The crowd is now a murderous mob, loud, ugly and menacing, demanding the release of the prisoner, Barabbas, a custom in keeping with the time. The anti-Roman Zealots will have their revenge on Jesus . . . and their revolutionary as well. And so, Pilate makes the fatal decision. He cannot risk alienating a vicious Herod on one side and a crazy Caesar on the other for one troublemaking provincial, so he accedes to the demands of the angry mob and, acting within his *imperium*, his imperial authority, Pilate frees Barabbas, sentences Jesus to death and decrees . . . crucify . . . and Jesus is led away to be scourged by the Roman soldiers. Of the three degrees of beatings Rome administers to convicted criminals—*fustus*, a "slap on the wrist," as it would be called today; *flagella*, warning and punishment, and *verbera*, Jesus is beaten to the severest limit, *verbera*, as required for those condemned to the cross . . . 39 or more lashes. The whip used has sharp bone shards and splinters braided into its thongs that cut and tear skin until it hangs in bloody ribbons from its victims' backs. Those skeptics, in future years, who will say that Jesus survived the crucifixion, and faked a resurrection, forget about this scourging. The ghastly devastation that was Jesus' body by now would hardly have presented to the disciples the image of glorious, triumphant victory over death.

> I gave my back to the smiters, and my cheeks to them that plucked off the hair: I hid not my face from shame and spitting. ISAIAH 50:6 (See: 530 B.C.)

The Via Dolorosa

Acceding to another Jewish demand, Pilate orders the accusation against Jesus hung on His cross that reads in Hebrew, Latin and Greek: JESUS OF NAZARETH, KING OF THE JEWS. The claque protests, loudly. They want it to read, "He SAID he was king of the Jews." Pilate's only reply: "*Quod scripsi, scripsi.*" "What I have written, I have written." Below in the courtyard Simon Peter, he whom Jesus called "the rock," denies three times to passersby that he knows Jesus, and Jesus turns to look at him as a cock crows the dawn. Jesus, given His cross, is led down the street known today as the *Via Dolorosa*, the Way of Sorrows, and a great multitude follows the grisly procession, weeping and mourning the man they love.

> And there followed him a great company of people, and of women, which also bewailed Him. LUKE 23:27 * All we like sheep have gone astray, we have turned every one to his own way: and the LORD hath laid on him the iniquity of us all. ISAIAH 53:6 (See: 530 B.C.)

This is not that noisy claque that demanded His death. Their evil deed is accomplished. These are His mostly-Jewish friends, followers, those whom He healed, fed, befriended, forgave; those whom He inspired, to whom He gave hope and love. Jesus' death, laid at the proper doorstep, is not the work of the Jewish race, but of the stiff necked temple bureaucracy, jealous of their power, position, influence and wealth, unwilling to accept the fulfillment of their own prophecies.

Jesus, seeing His mother, says to the women, "Daughters of Jerusalem, weep not for me but for yourselves and your children, for the days that are ahead." Three times He falls under the weight of the cross and the Roman soldiers seize a bystander, one Simon, from Cyrene in northern Africa, to help carry the cross. It would not do for Jesus to die of exhaustion on the way. At the hill called *Golgotha*, the Place of the Skull, He is stripped of His clothing; His hands and feet nailed to the cross, and in spite of the pain, rejection and humiliation, Jesus prays: "Father, forgive them, for they know not what they do."

> All they that see him laugh him to scorn, they shoot out their lips and shake their heads, saying, "He trusted in God that he would deliver him; let him deliver him, if he delight in him . . ." A company of evildoers encircle me: they have pierced my hands and feet.
> PSALM 22:7,8 and 16 (See: 400 B.C.)

At "the third hour" (about 9:00 A.M.) His cross is raised between those of two thieves, one who challenges Him to save Himself and them, and the other who knows Jesus is guiltless, and asks His forgiveness. "Truly, I say to you," Jesus tells him, "today you will be with me in Paradise."   LUKE 23:43

> He was numbered with the transgressors, and bore the sins of many.   ISAIAH 53:12
> (See: 530 B.C.)

Hanging from a cross of shame in the white heat of morning, Jesus is mocked, reviled and challenged: "If you are the Son of God, come down from the cross," and the chief priest, scribes and elders laugh, "He saved others; he cannot save himself."

> Thy rebuke hath broken his heart, he is full of heaviness. He looked for some to have pity on him but there was no man, neither found he any to comfort him.   PSALM 69:20
> (See: 400 B.C.)

Roman law allows an executioner's squad to share out whatever worldly goods the victim may possess, and the Roman soldiers gamble for Jesus' robe, a game like dice.

> They parted my garments among them, and for my clothing they cast lots.   PSALM 22:18
> (See: 400 B.C.)

Jesus sees His mother standing desolate, grief-stricken and transfixed with horror before Him. Despite the agony of his own suffering, His compassion and love for her entrusts her into the care of His closest friend, John. "Woman, behold thy son," He whispers, and to John, "Behold thy mother." In these, His final torture-wracked hours on the cross, Jesus is not debating theological issues on the nature and gender of God, but crying from the very depths of His soul to those two beings He knows best and loves most, His earthly mother, Mary, and His heavenly Father, God.

Friday, 12:00 Noon.   Now begins an awesome phenomenon, as the books of MATTHEW, MARK and LUKE, with eloquent simplicity, report that ". . . from the sixth hour there was darkness over all the land unto the ninth hour."

> For behold, darkness shall cover the earth.   ISAIAH 60:2 (See: 530 B.C.)

3:00 P.M.   Entering His final agony, Jesus cries "with a loud voice:"

> *ELOI, ELOI, LAMA SABACHTHANI?* which is to say, "My God, my God, why hast thou forsaken me?"   PSALM 22:1 (See: 400 B.C., and MARK 15:34)

It is the opening of the 22nd Psalm. Written 400 years before this time it is a long psalm which describes some of His suffering on this day. Jesus knows the psalm well, and knows it ends in triumph and exultation.

Only once does Jesus breathe a word about His own suffering, as excruciating pain wracks through His arms and body, pain so devastating many who suffer it are driven mad, and He barely manages to whisper, "I thirst." He is offered "wine mingled with myrrh" (such as was given Him by Magi at His birth) to help ease the pain, but He refuses it.

> They gave me gall to eat, and when I was thirsty they gave me vinegar to drink. PSALM 69:21 (See: 400 B.C.)

That word so casually used in our own time, "excruciating," comes, literally, from this beastial act of punishment: the Latin *ex-* meaning "out of (the)" and *cruci-*cross, crucify: "out of the cross." It is a death that horrified the Roman consul, Cicero:

> It is a crime to put a Roman citizen in chains, it is an enormity to flog one, sheer murder to slay one; what, then, shall I say of crucifixion? It is impossible to find the word for such an abomination. Marcus Tullius Cicero, *IN VERUM* 1:11:4

But Jesus is not a Roman; He is only a Galilean provincial, a Jew, and a convicted felon, and crucifixion is good enough for Him. The Romans have crucified many thousands of people and, in the years ahead, will crucify thousands more; and countless millions of people throughout all history have and will suffer painful deaths of all kinds. But Jesus has taken upon Himself "the sins of the world," and His pain is not the pain of one man's crucifixion, but the pain of . . . Everyman. Many centuries hence, a well-meaning Christian hymn will be written beginning "Gentle Jesus, meek and mild" that will impart forever the image of a pale, weak creature who somehow just accidentally got caught up in the tumult of His times. Gentle Jesus, meek and mild? He wished child abusers thrown into the sea with millstones around their necks, physically whipped money-changers out of the temple; and finally performed the greatest act of courage in all history—when he could have opted out—and died on the cross for—Everyman.

3rd century drawing of Jesus from the Roman catacombs

Now, his mission complete, the prophecies fulfilled, mankind given a NEW COVENANT with God, Jesus cries out, with a loud voice, "IT IS FINISHED." Hanging broken and bloodied from a criminal's cross, Jesus of Nazareth, just 35 years old, breathes His last prayer as a mortal man: "Father, into thy hands I commend my spirit," and dies. LUKE 23:46

> He was cut off out of the land of the living; for the transgressions of thy people was he stricken. ISAIAH 53:8 (See: 510 B.C.)

The land already in darkness, now the earth shakes, rocks are split, graves opened, and the curtain of the temple torn in two. A terrified centurian below the cross whispers in awe: "Surely this WAS the son of God." The Jews ask Pilate to have Jesus' legs broken with a club to hasten His death by shock; they do not want Him on the cross the next day, the Sabbath. The legs of the two thieves are, indeed, broken but Jesus is already dead, and the soldiers "pass-over" Him. Thirteen hundred and twenty years before this at the first PASSOVER God gave instructions to Moses and Aaron that, of the sacrificial lamb required . . .

> You shall not break a bone of it. EXODUS 12:46 (See: 1290 B.C.)

But one of the Roman soldiers thrusts his spear into Jesus' side, and those who love Him weep for Him.

> . . . and they shall look upon me whom they have pierced, and mourn for him, as one mourneth for his only son. ZECHARIAH 12:10 (See: 518 B.C.)

One Joseph of Arimathea, privately a follower of Jesus, publicly an important member of the Jewish council and therefore a man of authority, asks for and is given, Jesus' body which is laid, wrapped in a new linen shroud, in his own tomb.

> And he made his grave with the wicked, and with the rich in his death because he had done no violence, neither was any deceit in his mouth. ISAIAH 53:9 (See: 530 B.C.)

Ossuary ankle bone with spike still intact

In later years biblical revisionists and destructionists, hoping to disprove the Gospel story, will point to this incident as "proof" that this whole story is a myth. Crucified criminals, they maintain, were not laid in tombs but in common paupers' graves, or left on the cross for predators. But, in 1968, another ossuary, or bone box, was found near Jerusalem containing the bones of a crucified man, a young man, whose name, Jehohanan, was carved on the box. His legs had, indeed, been broken and his heel bones, together, were still pierced by the seven inch spike that had held him on the cross. He had, indeed, been laid in a tomb until his flesh "aged" away, and his bones—with the spike still intact—then re-buried in the ossuary. It, and the ossuary containing the bones of the High Priest, Caiaphas, reside today in the Israel Museum, Jerusalem.

Pilate orders the sepulchure sealed and a guard posted. Though his grief-stricken, guilt-ridden, heart-broken and humiliated disciples do not yet know it, Jesus of Nazareth has become the very embodiment of the LAW and the PROPHETS. The Suffering Servant has fulfilled His mission. His life has been the ultimate tragedy and His death the ultimate sacrifice; for in His life did the LAW gain nobility, and in His death did the ancient PROPHETS find their fulfillment.

> For God so loved the world, that he gave his only begotten Son that whosoever believeth in him should not perish, but have everlasting life. JOHN 3:16

The Years

That Remember

Jesus' Earthly Life

The Years That Remember Jesus' Earthly Life

Every nation has its own particular genius, something in which it excels beyond all others. For the ancient Phoenician sea farers, it was adventure, trade and business; the Greeks art, science, architecture, culture and philosophy; the Romans government and organization. The Jews' special genius was religion and religious law. They had no talent for art because their God forbade it: "Thou shalt not make unto thyself graven idols." Their likenesses appeared on no coins, in no self-made portraiture or statues. For the faithful Jew, it would have been blasphemy; for the rest, it just wasn't their "genius." There is, in fact, out of all the years of the Old Testament, only ONE likeness of an Israelite King (still in existence) which shows a kowtowing King Jehu groveling on hands and knees before a victorious Assyrian invader, carved by an Assyrian on an Assyrian "Black Obelisque."   (842 B.C., p. 70)

But, apart from physical likenesses, hundreds of artifacts do, indeed, exist, some included in this book, which testify in other ways to the accuracy of the Old Testament writers, artifacts of gold, ivory, stone, iron, bronze—hard materials that last for millenia. There are far fewer from New Testament times, although some of the new finds are not only dramatic but spectacular. The reasons are many. The time frame of the Old Testament was several thousand years, that of the new less than 100. Jesus' mission, and that of His followers, was not to conquer nations, win themselves glory or memorialize themselves in worldly ways, but to save souls and bring a message to man from God. They built no monuments of stone, carved no marble statues, struck no gold nor silver coins, and engraved no treaties on granite stelae. Wooden benches, tables and chairs hewn in a carpenter shop do not last 2000 years, especially when made by an obscure peasant, born in a stable and executed as a criminal. Nor do fish nets woven by the sea; and parchment upon which fishermen write rots away in a very short time. Two thousand years of weather, wars, fires, natural disasters, "dark ages" and hostile "enlightenment" separate Jesus' age from our own. It is remarkable that as many artifacts exist as do.

For a perspective comparison one might consider an interesting parallel, one small but vital part of the mid-east, a place St. Paul knew well and traveled through many times, for it is near his home town of Tarsus in Cilicia. It is a mountain pass high in the Taurus Mountains, and Paul had to travel through it on every journey to the Holy Land. The pass is called the Cilician Gates, a very famous name and place, one of the most traveled mountain passes in the world. Through its narrow, hundred-yard gorge marched the armies of Assyria's Sennacherib, Macedonia's Alexander the Great, Rome's General Pompey and Emperor Hadrian, thousands upon thousands of troops, horses and pack animals over 700 years of campaigns; and yet, not one suit of armor, not one helmet, breastplate, horse shoe, cooking pot, button, buckle or sword has ever been found. Not one bit of evidence to prove they'd ever been there, and yet, there they were, and no one disputes the fact.

The Cilician Gates

In A.D. 1906 the scientist/physician/musician and much admired Albert Schweitzer began an intellectual "quest for the historical Jesus," and in 1910 published a book with that name; concluding that an historical Jesus was not to be found. Believers would just have to accept Him on faith. And that conclusion has been used to Christianity's detriment ever since, although Schweitzer, a devout Christian himself, was probably correct then; but that was in 1910, NINETY-SIX YEARS AGO! And how things have changed! Today it would be like Abraham Lincoln expounding on space flight or Florence Nightengale on open heart surgery. Since 1910 modern, scientific archeology has changed the whole picture . . . not even trying to do so. For archeology did not set out to "prove" or "disprove" the Bible; and it has not done that; it's purpose is to search for and study mankind's past. But the more they found and learned the more astonished they became at how closely their findings corresponded with what the Bible says . . . and still does as the years go on, (although the minimalists deny this.) For in any given season archeological digs are under way at many different sites, utilizing the efforts and intellects of dozens of persons, from renowned professional archeologists to student volunteers.

Ancient cities which had gone out of existence, been forgotten and finally considered only mythical have been found (or evidence of them), one of which is Migdal, home of Mary Magdalene (of Migdal), which has yielded up not only a mosaic reproduction of a first century wooden boat such as Jesus would have known and used but, incredibly, from a drought-dried Lake Galilee, a real, honest-to-goodness INTACT skeletal remains of a first century boat, exactly like the mosaic, big enough to hold a crew of five, and twelve others besides! The remains of houses have been found matching the descriptions in the gospels of Peter's house in Capernaum, and the house that had a hole in the roof where the man with palsey was lowered down to be healed by Jesus. Inscriptions have been found naming New Testament names, especially one carved with both the names of Pontius Pilate and the Emperor Tiberius. Two ossuaries have been found, bone boxes like little coffins where bones were placed after the flesh was gone; one of a crucified man with the spike still piercing the ankle bone, and the other, intricately carved of ivory, that of an important, wealthy man, with the name, carved on it, of Josef Caiaphas, the chief accuser and plotter against Jesus of Nazareth. Even the pavement Jesus stood on to be condemned has been found, as has an anti-Christian wall graffiti showing Him with a horses head! And the list goes on . . . and on!

And yet, even in the face of all this empirical, tangible evidence with its seductive, siren call to believe "on the evidence" (even as doubting Thomas did), that temptation must be resisted. Jesus wanted no part of it. Faith, He said, we must believe on faith . . . such as that of a child, faith that could move mountains. The years ahead are years of faith . . . that did more than move mountains. It changed a world.

HE IS NOT HERE . . .

Prophesied: For thou wilt not leave my soul in hell; neither wilt thou suffer thine Holy One to see corruption.
PSALMS 16:10

HE IS RISEN FROM THE DEAD!

32   So announces an angel on the third morning to the two Mary's who come to anoint Jesus' body with myrrh and other spices.

I know that my Redeemer liveth, and that he shall stand at the latter day upon the earth, and tho' worms destroy this body, yet in my flesh shall I see God.   JOB 19:25,26
(See: 400 B.C.)

"Why do you seek the living among the dead?" the angel asks. "Remember how He said the Son of man must be delivered up, crucified and on the third day rise?" Then Jesus appears and says to the weeping Mary Magdalene, "Mary," and she turns and cries, *"Rabboni!"* (which means Teacher.) Hearing of this the disciples take it for so many "idle tales." But on the road to Emmaus Jesus questions two of them, and they, not recognizing Him, cry, "Are you the only visitor to Jerusalem who does not know what has happened there these last two days?" "O foolish men and slow of heart to believe all the prophets have spoken," Jesus responds. And ". . . beginning with Moses and all the Prophets HE INTERPRETED TO THEM ALL THE SCRIPTURES CONCERNING HIMSELF, (LUKE 24:27) . . . and they hurried back to tell the rest."

While they are together, Jesus appears among them and asks, "Why do questionings rise in your hearts? These are my words I spoke while I was among you: *EVERYTHING WRITTEN ABOUT ME IN THE LAW AND THE PROPHETS AND THE PSALMS MUST BE FULFILLED."* Then he "opened their minds to understand the scriptures, that repentance and forgiveness of sins should be preached IN HIS NAME to all nations." "ALL AUTHORITY IN HEAVEN AND ON EARTH HAS BEEN GIVEN TO ME," the living Lord tells them. "Go, therefore, and make disciples of all nations, baptizing them. . .

. . . in the name of the FATHER, and of the SON, and of the HOLY SPIRIT . . . teaching them to observe all that I have commanded you; and lo,

. . . I AM WITH YOU ALWAYS, EVEN UNTO THE END OF THE WORLD."
MATTHEW 28:19,20

Jesus tells His disciples, "AS THE FATHER HAS SENT ME, EVEN SO I SEND YOU," and He breathes on them and says, "RECEIVE THE HOLY SPIRIT . . . *WHOSOEVER SINS YOU FORGIVE, THEY ARE FORGIVEN, AND WHOSOEVER SINS YOU RETAIN, THEY ARE RETAINED."* *JOHN 20:23*

Finally, they begin to realize the full meaning of Jesus' death, that burdened with the sins of all mankind, He HAD to die—not peacefully, in ripe old age, signifying nothing, but cruelly and unjustly, knowingly and willingly—to be resurrected, the fruition of God's Great Plan, the ONE, PERFECT and SUFFICIENT SACRIFICE. Now do they realize that He was not a VICTIM of His time born, by chance, into an unfriendly age, unable to control events or choose His associates or successors; but the MASTER of it, that He, Him-

self—God incarnate—CHOSE the time and place to live and die, to physically enter human history . . . and leave it; that He could, at will, suspend those same immutable laws of nature which He, Himself, had created. Now do they understand that the omnipotent God who created that world and those laws, and man and all things would not, after that creation, cease to care, turn a deaf ear, and leave him alone and unaided. But, loving His Creation would, Himself, return to be mankind's friend, advisor, companion, healer, lover, solace, inspiration, joy and SALVATION. No longer need man search and grope for God, wondering what He is, why He is, how He acts and thinks; no longer need he read stars or tell fortunes, carve idols or invent theories; for GOD HAS NOW REVEALED HIMSELF PERFECTLY, FULLY, His mind, body, purpose, message and meaning. *ONE NEED ONLY KNOW CHRIST TO KNOW GOD.*

He that believeth on me, believeth not on me, but on him that sent me. And he that seeth me seeth him that sent me. JOHN 12:44,45

He is the image of the invisible God . . . [in whom] all the fullness of God was pleased to dwell . . . the mystery hidden for ages and generations, but now made manifest to his saints. COL. 1:15,19,26

Only Thomas still doubts, until he touches the wounds but Jesus says, "Blessed are they who have NOT seen and yet believe." Then Jesus "parted" from them, and they return to Jerusalem "with great joy and (are) constantly in the temple blessing God." It is the first ASCENSION DAY. There are now, according to the book of ACTS, "about 120 brethren." That there should once again be 12 disciples, the remaining 11 pray together and cast lots, and the lot falls upon Matthais. On the day of Pentacost, when they are all together, "a sound comes from heaven like the rush of a mighty wind . . . and there appears . . . tongues as of fire, resting on each one . . ." And the Holy Spirit fills them all and makes these . . .

. . . WEAK MEN STRONG, TIMID MEN BOLD, SIMPLE MEN WISE . . . AND CREATES . . . APOSTLES OF A FAITH . . . where, before, there were only fishermen

. . . and a tax collector. It is the first "WHITSUNDAY."

A newly emboldened Peter, "filled with the Holy Spirit," preaches eloquently and quotes the Prophet Joel's promise that "Your young men shall see visions and your old men shall dream dreams," and says, "This Jesus hath God raised up, whereof we are all witnesses . . . and have received the promise of the Holy Ghost." And he tells the Jews of Jerusalem to "repent your sins for having murdered the righteous and Holy One," and 3000 more souls believe and are baptized.

> And they continued stedfastly in the apostle's doctrine and fellowship, and in breaking of bread, and in prayers . . . and many wonders and signs were done [and they found] favor with all the people . . .   ACTS 2:42,47

After Peter's sermon, he heals a lame man, an act that is witnessed by the high priests and Sadducees who admit ". . . for that indeed a notable miracle hath been done . . . is manifest to all . . . that dwell in Jerusalem; and we cannot deny it." But they threaten Peter and John, anyway, telling them to ". . . speak henceforth to no man in . . . the name of Jesus." But the apostles are undaunted, perform many "signs and wonders," teach openly in the Temple, and win another 5000 to the faith (many, who are pilgrims to Jerusalem for Pentacost, will carry the faith back to their homes far away.) Now the priests and Sadducees begin seriously to plot against them. But the rabbi, Gamaliel, warns them to "take care what you do with these men. There were [false prophets] before who [came to naught.] Leave them alone, for if it is of God you will never be able to overthrow them . . . AND YOU MAY EVEN BE OPPOSING GOD!" One of the early converts is a man named Steven, now "deacon" Steven, who preaches with fervor and conviction . . . and raises animosity . . . especially in the man named Saul . . . from Tarsus, in Asia Minor, a Jew and strict Pharisee. Saul's fiery, passionate nature will not allow him to heed the warning of his teacher, Gamaliel and, as he hears more and more about this sect of "Nazarenes" who claim this Jesus, who was crucified like a common criminal, is the Son of God and is "risen from the dead," his fury and rage know no bounds. Perverting Judaism's sacred tenets is, to him, the vilest perfidy, and its adherents must be wiped out. Like a man possessed, he takes on the task.

Now the deacon, Steven, "full of grace and power," is haled by the Jews before the council "with false witnesses." Preaching passionately of the Jews' long history, he accuses the "stiff-necked people" of "always resisting the Holy Spirit," In a rage, they "rush together on him," cast him out of the city and stone him . . . and the witnesses "laid down their clothes at a young man's feet, whose name was Saul . . . And Saul was consenting unto his death." Then, according to the book of ACTS, a "great persecution arose against the church in Jerusalem." Saul "made havoc" of the church, laid it waste . . . and dragged off men and women . . . to prison. Those who escaped Saul's wrath ". . . scattered abroad throughout the (region] . . . and went every where preaching the word."

How far the brethren "scattered" and to what far-away regions will probably never be known for certain, but apparently some traveled very far, indeed, as far as can be gone, for two centuries from now, two great Christian "fathers of the church"—scholars and teachers—will write that . . .

. . . some . . . passed over the ocean to those which are called the British Isles . . . Eusebius, Bishop of Caesarea * . . . [the] power of God our Savior is even with them in Britain, who are separated [by water] from our world. Origin of Alexandria (For both, See: A.D. 100) Trans. from Andrew Gray

Within the grounds of the beautiful Abbey ruins at Glastonbury, England, stands a flowering thorn tree believed for centuries to have been planted by Joseph of Arimathea, in whose own tomb Jesus was buried. The legend there is ancient that Joseph, a merchant trading in tin with Britain, and possibly even Lazarus, whom He restored to life, were among those who "scattered" abroad, Joseph making his way back to *Brittania,* to found England's first church, older even, than the church at Rome. The "Holy Thorn," as it is called, today is only a salvaged cutting from a gigantic, gnarled original destroyed during a latter-day English civil war. The legend says that the tree was Jesus' own walking staff which took root and grew when Joseph thrust it into the ground. It thrives today, *Crataegus Monogyna Praecox*, the only thorn tree to

bloom twice a year, and the only one in England native, not TO England, but to the mid-eastern Mediterranean Levantine, of which Israel is a part. The legend further says that Joseph brought with him for safe keeping, and buried at the foot of Glastonbury Tor, that cup—the Holy Grail— from which Jesus and the 11 drank at the last supper. Two hundred eighty two years from this time, to settle certain church disputes in A.D. 314, the then Roman emperor, Constantine, will convene a council of Western bishops at Arles, France. Written records will list the attendance there of three British bishops (York, London and Lincoln) among a total delegation from all Europe of only 33, a large proportion from such a far-removed corner of the empire; three British bishops who could minister to a flock only if, indeed, a flock were truly, already there.

Whatever happened to the "clean linen cloth" in which Joseph wrapped Jesus' body, no one knows for certain, but there is kept safe to this day in the cathedral of Turin, Italy, a 14 foot-long linen cloth, imprinted—somehow—with the image of a man, both front and back. He was a victim of crucifixion, brutally abused, blood stains on wrists and feet. But more than that, the almost six-foot image, thin dark face serene in death, shows blood stains on the head, also, like a crown, vicious whip mark scourges and a sword wound on body and side. In our own time, although a (possibly ill-done) carbon-dating process has shown the Shroud of Turin to probably date from A.D. 1400, other comprehensive scientific tests have not been able to explain a number of questions, including why the Shroud nail holes are not in the palms as all art work of that age depicts, but rather are in the wrists as we know today it was actually done in Roman times; and why the fabric, itself, and microscopic pollen particles in it, are such as those used or found only in the mid-east in the time of Christ.

35   The apostle Philip goes to preach in Samaria and wins many converts . . . including a local magician, or sorcerer, named Simon Magus, who claims his magic, which "amazes" the Samaritans, is "the great power of God." After his baptism, Simon remains with Philip, Peter and John and, awed by their power to heal, offers them money, saying, "Give me also this power, that any one on whom I lay my hands may receive the Holy Spirit." It is the first known Christian "heresy," an attempt to buy God's grace, and Peter acts quickly: "Your silver perish with you," he warns Simon, "because you thought you could obtain the gift of God with money! . . . Repent . . . this wickedness . . . that the intent of your heart may be forgiven . . ." ACTS 8:20–22. Simon's attempted bribe of church office will be remembered through history as "simony," and himself as the first Christian heretic. Almost 300 years from now a great Christian scholar will write a history of these times (and those to come) and tell a most fascinating story; one that is supported by several other early church historians:

> Our savior's marvelous resurrection and ascension into heaven were by now everywhere famous . . . the subject of general discussion all over Palestine, [and so] was accordingly communicated by (Pontius) Pilate to the Emperor Tiberius . . . It is said that Tiberius referred the report to the senate, which rejected it . . . the old law still held good that no one could be regarded by the Romans as a god unless by vote and decree of the senate . . . but Tiberius made no change in his attitude and formed no evil designs against the teaching of Christ.   Eusebius of Caesarea, The HISTORY OF THE CHURCH 2:2 (See: AD 100)

Eusebius adds that "these facts were noted by Tertullian, an expert in Roman law . . . in fact one of the most brilliant men in Rome." In his DEFENSE OF THE CHRISTIAN FAITH, Tertullian added:

> Tiberius . . . communicated [the report] to the senate, making it clear to them that he favored the doctrine. The senate however, because they had not examined [it] themselves, rejected it; but Tiberius stuck to his own view, and threatened to execute any who accused the Christians.   Tertullian of Carthage, quoted by Eusebius in HISTORY OF THE CHURCH 2:2–3 (See A.D. 100)

"Heavenly providence" says Eusebius, "has purposefully put this in the emperor's mind, in order that the gospel message should get off to a good start and speed to every part of the world."

. . . The persecution of Jesus' followers in Jerusalem, though, is severe and cruel, and the believers, after many "scattered abroad," are disorganized and sorely in need of secular leadership, and the historian Eusebius tells this story:

> [after the murder of Steven] . . . James . . . the [step] brother of the Lord . . . whom the early Christians surnamed the Righteous because of his outstanding virtue, was the first, as the records tell us, to be elected to the episcopal throne of the Jerusalem church.
>
> Eusebius, HISTORY OF THE CHRISTIAN CHURCH

He goes on to say that neither Peter nor the brothers John or James (the elder) claimed the office of bishop "because the savior had specially honored them, but were content that James (the younger) should serve because of his great righteousness."

35 Saul of Tarsus continues his assaults on the followers of Jesus, and by his own admission, shuts them in prison, forces them to blaspheme, condemns them to death and, "in raging fury . . . persecutes even foreign cities." Still "breathing threats and murder" he seeks and receives permission to travel to Damascus, where there is a large congregation, to wipe them out there. But on the way, at about noon, he is stricken blind by a brilliant light . . . "brighter than the sun," felled to the ground and questioned by a voice which leaves his stunned companions "speechless" with amazement: *Saul, Saul, why do you persecute me?*" "Who are you, Lord?" Saul asks, in another of history's great confrontations: and the voice replies:

5th century mosaic of Paul from Ravenna

"*I AM JESUS OF NAZARETH WHOM YOU ARE PERSECUTING* . . . rise and go to Damascus . . . and you will learn what to do." Saul neither tears his hair nor rends his clothes in the ancient Jewish manner but, blinded by the light, has himself led into the city to await further orders. But Saul's reputation has gone before him, ". . . how much evil he has done . . . at Jerusalem." Then the Lord speaks to one Ananias, a believer in Damascus, "Rise and go to the street called Straight . . . to the man of Tarsus named Saul . . . FOR HE IS MY CHOSEN INSTRUMENT TO CARRY MY NAME BEFORE THE GENTILES AND KINGS AND THE SONS OF ISRAEL: for I will show him how much he must suffer for the sake of my name." Sight and health restored, "immediately" Saul begins to proclaim Jesus, that "HE IS THE RISEN SON OF GOD." All who hear him are confounded, and now he has to convince the same Nazarene Jews who first he persecuted, including Peter and James in Jerusalem, that he is now, in fact, one of them.

35 While all these things have been going on, much has been happening in Rome . . . and on the Isle of Capri . . . nothing good. Tiberius' mother, the aged Livia, died in 29 and, having been estranged from her for years, Tiberius made no effort to attend her funeral. The

man he left in charge in Rome, the Praetorian Guard commander, Sejanus, proved himself a bloody tyrant and assassin, killing Tiberius' heirs and plotting to overthrow him and seize the throne for himself. When Tiberius finally realized, in 31, that Sejanus was, in fact, conspiring for the empire, he had him arrested in the senate house, and executed. Tiberius' vengeance was incredible:

> Frenzied with bloodshed, the emperor now ordered the execution of all those arrested for complicity with Sejanus. It was a massacre . . . without discrimination of sex or age, eminence or obscurity, there they lay strewn about—or in heaps . . . Until his mother died there was good in Tiberius as well as evil . . . as long as he favored (or feared) Sejanus, [his] cruelty . . . was detested, but his perversions un-revealed. Then fear vanished, and with it shame. Thereafter [there was] only . . . unrestrained crime and infamy. Tacitus, THE ANNALS OF IMPERIAL ROME

Even though Tiberius has always been gloomy, moody and inscrutable, Tacitus says in his ANNALS that the only reason he can give for what began with the emperor's self-imposed exile to Capri was that his mind must have come completely unhinged: that nothing else could explain his unbelievable atrocities and debaucheries. He uses plunder, confiscation, harassment and violence to force suicides, making sure first that he is made heir to the victim's fortunes. Rather than be summoned before him to suffer unspeakable cruelties, men open their own veins, and take poison in full view of the assembled senate. He has certain rooms in his villas decorated with paintings and statuary that leave no doubt of what their occupants are supposed to do. "He was fascinated by beauty, youthful innocence and aristocratic birth," Tacitus says, "new names for types of perversion were invented. Slaves were charged to locate and procure his requirements . . . it was like the sack of a city." One young woman of high birth commits suicide in her husband's and father's presence after having been forced to join Tiberius in his chamber, and two young brothers, who plead with him not to use them, have their legs broken. And the long litany of perversions that historian Suetonius recites is even worse. Writing his LIVES OF THE TWELVE CAESARS some 75 years from now, Suetonius tells of Capri's "sheer cliffs of great height . . . and deep water . . ."

> In Capreae they still show the place at the cliff top where Tiberius used to watch his victims being thrown into the sea after prolonged and exquisite tortures. Suetonius, LIVES

Tiberius' great-nephew, the young Gaius, or "Caligula," has been living with him on Capri since the sudden, mysterious death (which many believe he caused) of his father, Germanicus, the most honored, loved and mourned man in Rome. Caligula, now 23, is well aware of what goes on at Capri and, instead of being repulsed, enjoys it immensely.

> . . . even in those days [Caligula] could not control his natural brutality and viciousness. He loved watching tortures and executions; and, disguised in wig and robe, abandoned himself . . . to . . . gluttonous and adulterous living. Tiberius . . . indulg[ed his] passion . . . for theatrical dancing and singing on the ground that it might have a civilizing influence on him. *ibid.*

Tiberius is not so mad he does not recognize something even worse:

> With characteristic shrewdness, the old emperor . . . would often remark that Gaius' advent portended his own death and the ruin of everyone else. "I am nursing a viper for the Roman people" he once said.　Suetonius, LIVES

Tiberius recognizes his own depravities, also and, according to Tacitus ". . . his criminal lusts shamed him . . ." and in the depths of self-disgust, he admits as much in a letter to the senate:

> ". . . may all the gods and goddesses in Heaven bring me to an even worse damnation than I now daily suffer!"　*ibid.*

Only once does Tiberius consider returning to Rome, and crosses the bay to Italy, but loses courage and begins to return to his "secluded sea-cliffs . . ." but fate—and Caligula—have other plans . . .

> On March 16th the emperor ceased to breathe, and was believed to be dead . . . but . . . recovered . . . asked for food . . . [Caligula] stood in stupefied silence, his soaring hopes dashed . . . [but Macro, the new commander of the Praetorian Guard] ordered the old man to be smothered with a heap of bed clothes . . .　Tacitus, ANNALS

37　Caligula ascends the throne of Caesar with the good will and wishes of the people of Rome. The army remembers fondly its "little boot," and the citizens remember his great and good father, Germanicus, with love and respect. He has only to be half the man Germanicus was and all Rome will rejoice, and he begins his reign by playing up his inherited popularity with great emotional show. He gives Tiberius a magnificent funeral, honors his father by renaming the month of September "Germanicus," chooses his uncle Claudius as co-consul, recalls exiles, restores free elections and reinvests magistrates with their rightful authority. He publishes the accounts of the empire, which Augustus had done and Tiberius halted, encourages good deeds with generous rewards, and re-establishes good relations with distant kings. He even refuses to read a threatening note, saying there is "no danger," because "nobody hates me." And he builds. Oh, does he build.

Caligula

Caligula's building and spending projects are incredible . . . all done at great speed as the penalty for delays is death. Where there is flat land, he builds a mountain, and then tunnels through, over or around it. Where there is a mountain, he levels it. He goes miles out of the way to cut through the hardest rock, avoiding softer that could easily have been dug. At banquets he feeds favored guests golden meat and golden bread, and he, himself, drinks pearls dissolved in vinegar. And In just his first year as emperor, Caligula impoverishes himself, and squanders the two *billion,* seven hundred million sesterces he inherited from Tiberius. But he is "wickedly ingenious" at finding more. Traveling through Italy he stays at private homes and villas—then loots them of their valuables; in Greece he plunders art works; and in Egypt steals—for himself to wear, right out of the coffin—the golden breastplate of Alexander the Great, entombed there for almost 400 years. Finally, his biographer breaks off his narrative to tell of another side of Caligula:

> So much for the Emperor, the rest of this history must deal with Caligula the Monster.
> Suetonius, LIVES OF THE 12 CAESARS, IV:22

The monster is incredibly evil and depraved, with not one trace of conscience or morality. Believing himself a god—a supreme god—he "converses" with Jupiter and Olympia, and on bright, moonlight nights, invites the moon goddess to his erotic bed. He has incest with all three of his sisters, encouraging his male friends to join him and do likewise. (He has sex with them, too, any one, any age. And then he exiles them and seizes their wealth.) He dresses in fantastic, elaborate costumes: golden beards and ladies' gowns; tridents and diadems, and has a life-size golden idol of himself dressed identically to him, every day. For amusement at the public games, in the worst heat of the day, he has the arena's shade canopy pulled back, and forbids anybody to leave; and, needing more meat for the wild animals, gives the order, giggling:

> Kill every man between that bald head and the other one over there!   *ibid.*

Everything and anything can make him jealous enough to kill for: someone better looking, or with more hair or a more beautiful garment, and his contempt for people causes him to cry, "I wish all you Romans had only one neck!" He openly deplores the state of the times, because they have been marked by no public disasters, nothing to make his reign memorable . . .

> . . . like the Varus massacre [in Germany] under Augustus, or the collapse of the amphitheater at Fidenae under Tiberius . . . his own [prosperous] reign . . . would . . . [be] wholly forgotten, and he often prayed for a . . . famine, plague, fire or earthquake.
> *ibid.*

Caligula loves to drive up prices at auctions. When one rich old senator dozes off, he has the auctioneer acknowledge every nod:

> Before the bidding ended Aponius had unwittingly bought thirteen gladiators for a total of 90,000 gold pieces.   *ibid.*

Coin of Caligula

Everyone suffers from Caligula's mad wrath, and the Jews are a special target, for he hates them above all, with an insane hatred that would exterminate the entire race. In his ANTIQUITIES OF THE JEWS, the Jewish historian, Josephus, tells a remarkable story of a certain tumult between the Jews and Greeks of Alexandria. A Greek ambassador tells Caligula that while all nations have built altars and temples to his godhood, only the Jews refuse because their god forbids it. Caligula, furious, takes their refusal "very heinously." He sends one Petronius to raise an army and wipe them out.

> But there came many ten thousands of the Jews to Petronius . . . to offer . . . petitions . . . that he would not compel them to transgress . . . the law of their forefathers.   Josephus, ANTIQUITIES 18:8

Petronius sympathizes but says he MUST obey the emperor's orders. "So be it," say the Jews, "we won't fight you, but you will have to kill us, everyone, for we will not violate our God. Petronius is so impressed, he sends them home, saying . . .

> . . . if Gaius [Caligula] . . . turn the violence of his rage upon me I will . . . undergo . . . that affliction . . . [rather] than see so many of you perish, while . . . acting in so excellent a manner.   *ibid.*

Now there had been a drought for a whole year and although this was a clear day, Josephus says, Petronius had no sooner finished his speech than it began to rain, heavily, leaving Petronius in awe that the Jews' God should so take care of them. Meanwhile, in Rome, the Jews' (Idumean) King Herod Agrippa had been entertaining Caligula with a most magnificent feast and Caligula, pleased, tells him to ask for something—a country or some cities—anything, and it shall be his. But Agrippa asks only that Caligula no longer think about setting up statues in Jewish temples. "Thus," says Josephus, "did Agrippa cast the die," and Caligula, in a rare moment of sanity, knows enough not to go back on his promise. But it is the last boon the Jews—or anyone else—will receive, and Caligula plans to seize the holy Temple in Jerusalem as his own, to be called the temple of Jupiter the Glorious, the Younger Gaius."

No form of evil is too base for Caligula and, to gain more funds, he sets up a brothel in the imperial palace, "stocking it" with married women and young boys. Inviting all Rome to come and enjoy themselves, he charges high interest rates on the money he loans them for their admission. His one military expedition is an unbelievable farce: his hostages, school-children; his prisoners of war, branches lopped from trees; and the bounty brought back, sea shells plundered from the ocean. Everything he does, he says is his right as a god; his murders, lying, cheating and adulteries . . . often with new brides, which he later describes in detail, to others. And while indulging himself, he whispers, ". . . this beautiful throat will be cut whenever I please." His great love is his horse, Incitatus, who . . .

> . . . owned a marble stable . . . ivory stall, purple blankets . . . jeweled collar . . . a house . . . slaves, and furniture . . . It is said that he . . . planned to award Incitatus a consulship.
> Suetonius, LIVES, GAIUS, 55

Caligula is well aware of his mental infirmity and thinks of going into retirement to "clear his brain." Instead, men who had vowed they would gladly give their own lives to save his during an illness, are killed so their vows will be kept; and he seldom has anyone put to death "except by numerous small wounds." Asked at a banquet by Rome's two co-consuls, why he has suddenly burst out laughing, Caligula replies:

> What do you think? . . . I have only to give one nod and both your throats will be cut on the spot." Suetonius, LIVES 4:32

41   Finally, Rome has had enough. At age 23, after ruling less than four years, Caligula is ambushed and slain by his own Praetorian Guard. So fiendish had he been that nobody even dares rejoice, thinking it just another of his tricks to trap them. And so abhorred by now is the name Caesar, that many declare that everyone so named should be slain with him.

It is no wonder, then, that the Praetorian Guard, searching the palace, should find his uncle, Claudius Caesar, cowering in terror behind an arras, clinging to the drapery with trembling hands, frightened out of his wits. But the guard knows Claudius, believes him harmless, and lifts him onto their shoulders, proclaiming him on the spot, the Emperor of Rome. And with this act does the army begin to assert its authority over the civil government.

Grandson of Marc Antony by his mother Antonia, and of Livia by his father (Tiberius' brother) Drusus, Tiberius Claudius Drusus Germanicus is, by birth, eminently qualified to be emperor of Rome but, by nature a most unlikely candidate. A multitude of childhood diseases has left him with a stutter, a head that wobbles, an ungainly body and an awkward limp; in short, an appearance that embarrassed his step-grandfather, Augustus, and is cause for jest amongst every other relative. Polio, malaria, measles and colitis have left him partially deaf and in constant pain, but they have not damaged his brain; and thanks to his own instinct—and the good advice of important friends and men of letters, including Livy—he has been shrewd enough to use his doltish appearance to escape his nephew, Caligula's mad wrath.

But Claudius is no fool. He is, in fact, a scholar, historian, biographer, playwright, scientist and linguist. He has written a history of Carthage, of the Etruscans and of Rome, and is working on a history of his own family (all of which, unfortunately, are lost to posterity), and has added three new letters of his own invention to the Latin alphabet. His teacher and mentor was that same Athenodorus who was Augustus' friend and advisor. Now Caesar at 50, Claudius begins to restore, reorganize or improve every area of government, intending to be as good a ruler as he can. He sets up a cabinet with such offices as Secretary of State, Treasury and Attorney General; and to insure his decisions he restores the ancient office of Censor, holds that office himself, and simply "censors out" his opposition. He is . . .

Claudius

> . . . a most conscientious judge; sitting in court even on his own birthday and those of his family, sometimes actually on ancient . . . holidays or days of ill omen. Instead of always observing the letter of the law . . . let himself be guided by his sense of equity . . . when . . . punishments prescribed were . . . too lenient or too severe, changed them accordingly.
> Suetonius, LIVES, Claudius: 14

Claudius' motive in doing these things is not self-interest: he hopes to restore the Republic, to put government back into the hands of the people. It is not a popular ambition. Many men have been killed for aspiring to it. But Claudius is, in essence, a good man and he begins his—unwilling—reign in good faith and conscience. Thus does Claudius the Fool bring back sanity to the empire . . . for a while.

But Claudius has an unfortunate weakness . . . women. Oh, not like Tiberius or Caligula; Claudius is a moral man. But he is a passionate man, and while his first two wives were chosen for him, he chooses the last two and they will prove his undoing.

If the emperors of this period are cruel and inhuman (excepting Claudius) so, also, are their women monsters of depravity. No evil is unknown to them, no sin a stranger. Augustus' own wife, Livia, has been kindly treated by history as a paragon of aristocratic virtue. And yet, some historians admit that she schemed ruthlessly for years to get her son Tiberius on the throne. The Roman Tacitus strongly suggests that there is good reason to suspect her of foul play in the deaths of several who stood in his way . . . including her own husband, Augustus, himself. Augustus' only daughter and granddaughter, both named Julia, were immoral harlots who caused him much grief and forced him, with broken heart, to banish them from Rome. Eighteen years from now an emperor will murder his own mother . . . a woman so vile and sinister, some will say of her death, that no woman deserved it more. Now, Claudius must suffer, married at this time to Messalina, his third wife. Her unceasing debaucheries will scandalize Rome and disgrace Claudius . . . and his fourth wife will murder him and put a hoodlum on the throne.

Among Claudius' early actions is the restoration of good relations with the Jews, who had been brutally misused by Caligula, and he sends an edict to both those fractious Jews and Greeks in Alexandria and Jews all over the empire:

I will, therefore, that the nation of Jews be not deprived of their rights and privileges on account of the madness of Gaius [Caligula] but that those rights and privileges, which they formerly enjoyed, be preserved to them, and that they may continue in their own customs on account of their fidelity and friendship to the Romans . . . since they were preserved to them under the great Augustus . . . it will therefore be fit to permit the Jews, who are in all the world under us, to keep their ancient customs without being hindered so to do.
Josephus, ANTIQUITIES OF THE JEWS, 19.5.2

43   Almost a hundred years ago Julius Caesar made two incursions into far northern *Brittania,* and now Claudius Caesar intends to undertake its conquest. One of the kings of the many tribes of Britons is Caractacus, a man whose valor and courage are known throughout the empire. His domain includes the area known today as Hampshire and Gloustershire, in the west of England, near Wales. He is proud, bold, brilliant, successful in war and a "descendent of illustrious ancestors." Claudius is anxious to bring his domain under Roman rule, and travels to Britain with his legions . . . and returns to Rome in glory.

The senate had already voted him triumphal regalia, but he thought Britain was . . . where the real triumph could be most readily earned . . . Sailing from Ostia . . . he marched

> through Gaul . . . crossed the channel from there; and was back in Rome six months later. He had fought no battles and suffered no casualties, but reduced a large part of the island to submission. His triumph was a very splendid one . . . Suetonius, LIVES OF THE XII CAE-SARS, 5:18

While Claudius is away his ever-evil wife Messalina—at her lover's urging—competes with one of Rome's most notorious prostitutes in a contest of endurance, to see which one can last the longest and service the most. It is the joke of all Rome, but no one is brave enough to tell Claudius, who loves her dearly and suspects nothing. When Messalina presents him with a son he only loves her the more, and names the boy Brittanicus in honor of his British campaign.

44   Almost ten years have gone by since Saul the Christ-hater became Paul the Apostle, years that have seen him in Arabia, Cilicia and Syria. His departure from Damascus was one of history's great ironies; having come threatening lives, he fled it on threat of his own . . . ignominiously, in a basket lowered over the city wall. Since then he has been assistant to Barnabas at Antioch, which is becoming an important center for the new faith, the "Nazarenes." Peter and James the Younger still lead the followers in Jerusalem, James having become their first "bishop," but others of the original twelve are missionaries far a field . . . and every one of them will learn what Jesus meant when He said, "Take up your cross and, follow me." (MATT. 16:24) The two broth-ers, John and James the Elder (sons of Zebedee) are be-lieved to have gone separate ways; John (taking with him Jesus' mother, Mary) to Ephesus in western Asia Minor where he is building strong congregations in seven coastal cities; and James (according to a latter-day tradi-tion) to Spain in the area of Santiago de Compostela, be-fore he returns to Jerusalem. Tradition has Thomas the doubter teaching in India and Persia, Philip of Bethsaida in Hieropolis, Greece and Ephesus; Simon, the Zealot in Persia, also, and Bartholomew, now in India, will later go north to Armenia where, for his faith, he will be . . . skinned alive. Matthew will teach in Ethiopia and later Persia, where he will hear more of those eastern Magi who saw a star so long ago. Andrew will teach the "back-ward and ruthless barbarians" of Sythia (the Russian Steppes) and then go to Achia where he will be hung on

an X-shaped cross. Very little is known of Thaddeus or Matthias who replaced Judas Is-cariot, except that they, like the others, will lose their lives for the faith they so strongly believe.

Every one of these apostles has taken with him to those far places not only a FAITH IN Jesus Christ, but the PRACTICE OF that faith, what to do and how to act as faithful followers. They have been teaching, not only what to believe, but how to behave because of that belief, what "rites" and rituals are to be observed and performed in remembrance of what he said or did; what was done to Him or what He, Himself, instituted and commanded to be continued in His name. Living in a hostile age of a cruel world, they hold their secret services in caves, cellars, attics or "upper rooms," using oil, lamplight, (frank) incense and vestments. The Psalms are recited or sung; lessons and prophesies of the Hebrew scriptures read; the works, words, wisdom and wonders of Jesus are told and re-told; baptisms and marriages are performed, healings from sickness and absolutions from sin. But most of all, foremost of their rituals and central to their very existence is the reenactment and commemoration of Jesus' last supper before His "one, true, perfect and sufficient" sacrifice on the cross . . . a "holy communion" with the LORD, Himself. And with these "gatherings together" of the followers of Jesus, this *ekklesia,* has a . . . this ekklesia, has a catholic (small "c"—meaning universal) "church," a kyriakon, taken . . . "church," a *kyriakon,* taken root and begun to grow.

> Thus. . .the whole world, was suddenly lit by the sunshine of the saving word . . . and its inspired . . . apostles went forth into all the earth, and their words to the ends of the world. In every town and village . . . churches shot up bursting with eager members. Men who through the error they had inherited from generations of ancestors were in the grip of . . . idol worship, by the power of Christ and . . . the teaching of His followers . . . were freed . . . turned their backs on devilish polytheism in all its forms, and acknowledged that there [is] one God only, the Fashioner of all things.   Eusebius, HISTORY OF THE CHURCH

Now Paul and Barnabas return to Jerusalem with a gift. There has been a widespread and severe drought which, according to ACTS (11:28) "came to pass in the days of Claudius Caesar," and the church in Jerusalem is impoverished because of it. With money he collected for them at Antioch, Paul now returns to prove that his generosity is great, his faith is true and his constancy unshakable.

44   Judea's King Herod Agrippa, grandson of Herod the Great, named for Augustus' best friend and general, was Claudius' boyhood companion, educated in Rome, and the two have remained close friends . . . until Herod involves himself in a plot against Rome. Now, according to ACTS (12:1) ". . . Herod the king-stretched forth his hands to vex certain of the church." His first victim is none other than James the Elder who, together with his brother, John, Jesus had called "sons of thunder." Agrippa has James "beheaded with a sword," the first of the twelve disciples to die a martyr's death. In his HISTORY OF THE CHURCH, Eusebius tells about the murder and quotes another early church father, Clement. He relates how . . .

> . . . the man who brought [James] into court was so moved when he saw him testify that he confessed that he, too, was a Christian: so they were both taken away together, and on the way he asked James to forgive him. James thought for a moment; then he said, "I wish you peace," and kissed him. So both were beheaded at the same time.   *ibid.* 2:3

The shrine of Santiago de Compostela, Spain, is dedicated to James, and thought, by tradition, to hold relics of his remains, as he had served there earlier. Then, Eusebius continues, when Herod ". . . saw it pleased the Jews, he proceeded . . . to take Peter also." but, despite chains, locked gates and guards, Peter miraculously escapes ". . . and makes his way to the house of Mary, the mother of John . . . whose surname was Mark." These criminal acts of Herod set off riots in Judea that will spread far and wide and not soon end. But Herod is stricken with disease soon after, and dies; and Barnabas and Paul, their mission in Jerusalem complete, return to Antioch . . . and take John Mark with them.

c. 46   Among his many responsibilities the new emperor, Claudius, is also concerned with Rome's religions, and one of his actions is to abolish completely the "savage and terrible" Druid cult, and to take steps to put an end to certain public disorders caused by another. Ever since the murder of the Apostle James there have been riots amongst the Jews and the followers of Jesus, not only in Jerusalem, but in Rome as well, to the extent that "Christus" is mentioned by the secular Roman writer, Suetonius, in his secular history, the LIVES OF THE XII CAESARS:

> Because the Jews at Rome caused continuous disturbances at the instigation of Chrestus, he expelled them from the city.
> Suetonius, LIVES, Claudius: 25

Suetonius' mention of "Chrestus" or Christus/Christ is among the first by a non-Christian writer, and is a significant historical fact.

Paul is getting more and more frustrated at the Jews' indifference and hostility toward the message of Christ that he preaches, and finally says that since God has called him for a specific mission, he will obey that call:

1st century drawing of St. Paul

> Prophesied: I have set you to be a light for the Gentiles that you may bring salvation to the uttermost parts of the earth.   ISAIAH 49:6, 530 B.C., and ACTS 13:47   *   And when the Gentiles heard this, they were glad and glorified the word of God . . .   ACTS 13:48

THE

MISSIONARY

JOURNEYS

OF

PAUL

The MISSIONARY JOURNEYS of PAUL

For so the Lord has commanded us saying, I have set you to be a light for the gentiles, that you may bring salvation to the uttermost parts of the earth. ISAIAH 42:6 (See: 530 B.C.) and ACTS 13:47

47 With these words in a vision at Antioch is Saul, now called by the Roman Paul, sent into the world, accompanied by Barnabas and John Mark (who, to Paul's bitter disappointment, leaves before journey's end.) Their travels take Paul and Barnabas, by sea, to Cyprus where they "proclaim the word of God in the synagogues of the Jews" (ACTS 13:5) and, after rebuking a sorcerer, make a believer out of the Roman governor of Cyprus, Sergius Paulus, a major triumph! The Proconsul Sergius Paulus' name appears only once in the Bible (ACTS 13:7), but is well attested in secular ancient writings and archeology. Both Pliny (the Elder) and the 3rd century physician, Galen, mention him and, not just one, but two engraved stones have been found with

Paul's 1st journey

his name carved on them. One was found at Rome, where he lived in retirement, and the other at Paphos, the very city where Paul converted him to the faith.

Sergius Paulus stone from Paphos

SERGIUS PAULUS . . . PROCONSUL . . . [of Cyprus]
The Paphos Stone.

Leaving Cyprus they travel overland into Asia Minor where they establish churches in Galacia, Phrygia, Pamphylia and Psidia. They have much success converting new believers, but are also driven out of one city and stoned in another, Lystra, where they are believed to be the Greek gods, Zeus and Hermes. Sailing back to their "home base" of Antioch, they gather their church together and declare all that God has done with them, how he "opened the door of faith to the Gentiles." After a stay of "no little time," they leave, again, for Jerusalem.

48 The Empress Messalina, having gotten away so easily with uncountable crimes and vices, and fooled Claudius so completely, now does something that causes the historian Tacitus to say, ". . . I am not inventing marvels. What I have told, and shall tell, is the truth." In an outrageously brazen attempt to usurp the throne from Claudius while he is away at Ostia . . .

> . . . on an appointed day and before invited signatories, a consul designate and the emperor's wife [were] joined together in formal marriage . . . assumed the wedding-veil, sacrificed to the gods . . . taken their places at a banquet, embraced, and finally spent the night as man and wife.   Tacitus, ANNALS 11:27

Finally Claudius' advisors find courage enough to inform him of the whole incredible truth, and Messalina is captured fleeing from an orgy-like wedding party . . . and executed. The stricken Claudius doesn't even ask how . . .

> In the days that followed, the emperor gave no sign of hatred, satisfaction, anger, distress, or any other human feeling . . . even when he . . . saw his children mourning . . . The vengeance on Messalina was just. But its consequences were grim.   *ibid.* 11:36

Claudius vows never again, but within the year marries again . . . an even poorer choice. His new wife is his own niece, Agrippina, sister and once lover of her brother, Caligula. Having already been married twice, Agrippina is a beautiful, rich widow who has worked her wiles on a helpless, passionate Claudius for just one reason: she wants her own son to someday be emperor and intends to stop at nothing to see it happen. At his birth the boy's father, knowing Agrippina's background, and his own which was just as bad, had commented that ". . . no good man could possibly be born" to the two of them. The boy's name is Lucius Domitius Ahenobarbus, later to be called . . . Nero.

Peter & Paul

49   Paul returns to Jerusalem for a confrontation, a council—the first church council—with Peter and the other elders . . . and especially with James, called the Just, the kinsman of Jesus. James had, according to the early church historian, Eusebius, "been elected by the apostles to the episcopal throne at Jerusalem," and is, therefore, its first "bishop."

> [James] was universally regarded as the most righteous of men because of the heights of philosophy and religion which he scaled in his life . . . He alone was permitted to enter the Holy Place . . . He used to enter the Sanctuary alone, and was often found on his knees beseeching forgiveness for the people.
> Eusebius, Bishop of Caesarea, A.D. 313–339, THE HISTORY OF THE CHURCH, 2:23

The subject of the council is circumcision; whether this ancient Jewish practice is required of a follower of Christ. Paul feels that it is not and he meets strong opposition, but then James speaks, and quotes the ancient prophets Amos, Jeremiah and Isaiah, as he says:

> Brethren, listen to me, [Peter] has related how God first visited the Gentiles [and said] "I will return and . . . rebuild the dwelling of David . . . that the rest of men may seek the Lord, and all the Gentiles who are called by my name . . ." Therefore my judgment is that we should not trouble those of the Gentiles who turn to God.   ACTS 15:13–19

The matter is settled; Gentiles need not first become Jews to become a Christian. Now Paul is brought word that some of his new converts in Galatia have already fallen away from the faith he just taught them, and writes them a letter. It (or I THESSALONIANS) is probably the first written work of what will become the New Testament.

GALATIANS

Epistle of Paul — Written in Greek,   c. 48 A.D.

"O foolish Galatians! Who has bewitched you?" Paul cries in this, possibly his first letter. "I am astonished that you are so quickly deserting him who called you in the grace of Christ . . ." GALATIANS has been called both the Magna Carta and the Declaration of Independence of Christianity, for with this letter does it cease to be a Jewish sect and become a universal religion for all mankind. For here Paul puts to rest the need for the age-old Jewish requirement for circumcision, having won the decision at Jerusalem. No, it is not necessary for a new Christian to first become a Jew, he maintains, "there is neither Jew nor Greek, neither slave nor free, male nor female; for you are all one in Christ Jesus." And he warns, "Do not be deceived, God is not mocked." Paul stoutly maintains that salvation comes solely through faith in Jesus Christ, but adds that there is still a moral way of living. He condemns "immorality, licentiousness, sorcery, idolatry, dissension, carousing, envy and the like," and says that the way to the kingdom of Heaven is through "love, joy, peace, patience, kindness, faithfulness and self-control."

GALATIANS is the ideal book for a new Christian to read, as it lays out the faith simply, clearly and concisely. Not all scholars agree that the letter was written this early; some date it to Paul's third journey, but most feel his reaction to the Galatians' "falling away" would not have been so passionate some years hence.

There also exists a letter which purports to have been written by Paul's fellow missionary, Barnabas, which also maintains the independence of Christianity from Judaism. In the years ahead when the "New Testament" is compiled, the church fathers will decide it is not authentic and, therefore, not include it in its canon, but the letter is, nevertheless, an interesting testimony of these times.

> Bring no more [burnt] offerings of rams or goats . . . these things therefore hath God abolished, that the new law of our Lord Jesus Christ, which is without the yoke of any such necessity, might have the spiritual offering of men themselves.   The apocryphal EPISTLE OF BARNABAS 2:5,7,8

50   Paul begins his second missionary journey, again from Antioch, traveling, this time, with Silas and Timothy. The church is healthy and thriving in Antioch by this time, more so than in Jerusalem. And here, according to ACTS (11:26,) they are first called (some think in mockery and derision) . . .

. . . CHRISTIANS.

Paul's "base of operations," Antioch and his "home town," Tarsus, lie like big and little sisters, only 80 miles apart on the southern-most edge of Cilicia, Asia Minor, separated by the jutting finger of the Gulf of Alexandretta. They are in the very heartland of the territory conquered by Alexander the Great 300 years before this time, and have been under

Greek influence ever since. Antioch, the Jewel of the East, is beautiful to both the eye and the mind. Three miles of vine-laden arcades cover its marble main street which shoppers can use at any time, for the streets are lighted at night, an accomplishment not even Rome can boast. More important, it is, by this time, a renowned center for culture, education and progress. Its Greek and Latin schools are among the finest in the empire. The works of Plato and Aristotle have been taught here for 300 years, and no educated person can be unaware of them. Its medical school ranks with any in the empire, and from it has come a young Greek doctor who, together with Paul, will change history.

Traveling overland through Asia Minor Paul, Silas and Timothy revisit the churches Paul had founded on his first trip, and then, "come down" to Troas near to the ruins of ancient Troy; and it is here that Paul meets the young Greek doctor, Loukas. Paul is impressed with his knowledge and skill, respects his character, faith, gentleness of spirit and "way with words," and invites him to accompany them the rest of the way, and they become close companions. Loukas has a habit of writing down everything they do and see, and his record of their travels will someday be known as the book of the ACTS OF THE APOSTLES. Thus, from Tarsus has come the apostle (Saint) Paul, and from Antioch, his protegee and biographer (Saint) Luke*.

Crossing the Aegean Sea, they reach Macedonia, birthplace of Alexander the Great, whose conquests made it possible for Paul the Jew and Luke the Greek to talk together and understand one another; and the fabled cities of Thessalonica and Philippi, that battlefield

---

* Some sources say Luke was not a Greek, nor a doctor. Either way is debatable.

where the slayers of Caesar were bested by the future Augustus, whose Roman Peace now gives Paul and Luke the freedom to travel. Here, at Philippi, they are arrested ". . . for troubling the city" and "teaching customs which are not lawful . . . to receive . . ." They are beaten with rods (local magistrates were usually accompanied by *lictors* who carried—and used—rods, like "billy-clubs." They are cast, publicly, into prison; but during the night an earthquake tears loose the doors and they are told to leave town, quietly. "They beat us publicly," Paul retorts, angrily, "uncondemned Romans, and now they cast us out secretly? No! Let them come themselves and free us publicly!" Paul's reputation and knowledge of his Roman citizenship goes before them, and at Thessalonica they are called "These men who have turned the world upside down." (ACTS 17:6) Upside down, indeed! Paul and Luke in Greece! What a momentous event! Men of faith and conviction bringing their message of Christian salvation to the very heart and soul of learning and culture. The course of Western civilization will change because Paul has come to Greece . . . and because Luke is with him to record it.

Finally, Athens! How Paul must have looked forward to seeing Athens and now must want to be successful in spreading the Lord's message in this citadel of paganism. He preaches wherever and whenever he can; in the Agora from one end of the marketplace to the other; and makes the rounds of the city, like any tourist, going from temple to temple. Much of what he sees angers him, as does that great, golden idol in the Parthenon— the goddess Athena, worshipped for her pagan beauty and riches. Then, one temple catches his eye and excites his mind. Engraved on its altar are the words, TO THE UNKNOWN GOD. Inspired, Paul preaches eloquently about this to the Stoics and Epicureans at the Areopagus, the supreme court of Athens, its highest tribunal. To them he pleads, "What you therefore worship as unknown, this I proclaim to you:

Paul in Athens

"In him we live and move and have our being," as even some of your poets have said, * "For we are indeed his offspring." Epimenedes of Crete (See: 550 B.C.) and Aratus of Soli (See: 250 B.C.)

Paul the Jew, a Roman citizen, quoting Greek poetry to the Athenians! What an incredible event! "Being then God's offspring," he says, "we ought not to think that the Deity is like gold, or silver, or stone, a representation by the art and imagination of man." As he tells them of the resurrection, "some mocked," but others believe, and one becomes an important link in the Christian chain:

. . . there was the Areopagite, Dionysius by name, who was, as Luke related in the ACTS, the first convert after Paul's address to the Atheneans in the Areopagus. He became the first Bishop of Athens. Eusebius, THE HISTORY OF THE CHURCH 3:4

50 In Rome, the Emperor Claudius appoints Lucius Junius Novatus, called Gallio as *proconsul*, or governor, of the senatorial province of Achaia, the southern portion of Greece. A native Spaniard, born in the Andalusian city of Cordoba, Gallio has risen through the ranks, a man whom contemporary historians refer to as charming, fair-minded and just; with a resolute courage and stoical fortitude like that of his younger—and eventually more famous—brother, Seneca. Also born in Cordoba, Lucius Annaeus Seneca is a lawyer, politician, writer and Stoic philosopher, recalled, now, from political exile on the island of Corsica to become the private tutor of Claudius' step-son, Nero. Each in his own way, Gallio and Seneca will play large parts in the history of this tine.

51–52 The administrative center of Achaia is the beautiful, worldly city of Corinth, and here Paul stays for a year and a half, founding one of his most important churches. He wins some important Jewish converts, among whom are fellow tent-makers, Priscilla and Aquila, and Crispus "the chief ruler of the synagogue" who "believed on the Lord with all his house," but is "opposed and reviled" by many more, and in disgust and frustration Paul cries, "FROM NOW ON I WILL GO TO THE GENTILES!" Arrested, then, by "the Jews," he is taken before the Roman *proconsul*, Gallio, who tells them that if it were a criminal case, something serious, he would hear it. "But you are just arguing about words and names, so see to it yourselves!"

Gallio's decision and final statement as recorded in ACTS (18:14, 15) matches perfectly with Roman law of this period, that he found the *cognitio* (evidence) *extra ordinem* (beyond the usual or ordinary) within his *arbitrium iudicantis* (his arbitrative jurisdiction.) Gallio's final action in the matter is also typically Roman for this time, before persecutions; a tolerant, live and let live attitude with Christianity as with other religions. The Greeks beat up Paul's principle accuser right in front of the Tribunal . . . but "Gallio paid no attention to this." ACTS 18:17

Whether Paul and Gallio would become better acquainted and even friends after this meeting has long been a subject of speculation with the likelihood in favor, for each man would have recognized in the other an intellectual like-mindedness, and this hearing would certainly have provided the opportunity.

. . . It is eight years since the emperor Claudius traveled to Britain, eight years of continual uprising and rebellion by the undaunted Britons against the Roman invaders. Finally the valiant British general Caractacus, is betrayed—not conquered—and brought to Rome in chains. The triumphal procession is immense; all Rome wants to see this proud Briton humbled. But the historian Tacitus, says that even though huge crowds lined the streets, "Rome trembled when she saw the Briton, though fast in chains!"

> . . . the Praetorian cohorts were drawn up . . . then . . . the royal vassals, the ornaments and neck chains and the spoils which the king had won in other wars . . . next were his brothers, his wife and daughter, last of all Caractacus. All the rest stooped in fear to abject supplication . . . not so the king! Tacitus, ANNALS 10:33–37

Head Up and back straight, Caractacus defends himself before Claudius at a tribunal:

> . . . equal to my noble birth and fortune I should have entered this city as your friend rather than your captive: and you would receive me . . . a king descended from illustrious ancestors. If you Romans choose to lord it over the world, does it follow that the world is to accept slavery? Neither my fall or your triumph [will] become famous . . . [but] if you save my life, I shall be an everlasting memorial to your clemency.   Caractacus, quoted by Tacitus

Caractacus

Claudius is so impressed he goes against all precedent and grants Caractacus and his family full pardon, but they must remain in Rome. Some students of English antiquity believe Caractacus and his family were converted to Christianity during their years in Rome; that his son, Llyn, took the Roman name Linus; his daughter became Claudia (the emperor's own family name) and married Rufus Pudens Pudentia. Fifteen years from now the apostle Paul will conclude a letter to his friend Timothy with this message: "Eubulus sends greetings to you, as do Pudens and Linus and Claudia and all the brethren," (II TIMOTHY 4:21) but whether there is any connection with Caractacus will probably never be known.

51   While in Corinth, Paul writes two letters to the church he founded in Thessalonica, in far-northern Macedonia.

I THESSALONIANS

Epistle of Paul — Written in Greek,   c. A.D. 51

Exactly how many letters Paul may have written in his lifetime is not known; 13 (and maybe 14) are included in the New Testament. If GALATIONS, which many believe to have been the first, was, in fact, written at a later time, I THESSALONIANS would then be his first. He wrote it to his friends in the church he helped found at Thessalonica (today's Salonika) to calm their fears about some Christians who had died before Christ's second coming, which they expect soon.

". . . that you may not grieve as others do who have no hope," he reminds them, ". . . believe that Jesus died and rose again [and through Him) God will bring with him those who have [already] fallen asleep . . . as to the times and seasons . . . you know the day of the Lord will come like a thief in the night [which need not] surprise you, for you are the sons of light and day . . . put on the breastplate of faith and love, the helmet of hope and salvation . . . whether we wake or sleep, we live in Him. Rejoice . . . pray . . . give thanks always . . ."   4:13–5:16

A second letter is sent to them a few weeks later:

II THESSALONIANS

Epistle of Paul — Written in Greek,   c. A.D. 51

Paul wrote this letter to clear up some erroneous ideas the Thessalonians had gotten elsewhere. ". . . do not be shaken in mind, or spirit . . . that the day of the Lord has [already] come . . . let no one deceive you. Do you not remember what I told you? . . . stand firm and hold to the traditions which you were taught by us . . ."

Learning that some had simply stopped work to wait for the "last day," Paul rebukes idleness or laziness: "If any will not work, let him not eat." 3:10 Paul is a firm believer in paying his own way. As a teacher he could expect the congregation to support him, but his injunction to "let him not eat who will not work," includes himself, and he practices his tent making trade wherever he goes.

Their work finished for the time, and a strong, flourishing church established, Paul and his companions leave Corinth, crossing the Aegean Sea to Ephesus, then the Mediterranean to Caesarea, to Jerusalem and back to Antioch where they spend the winter. Paul's second missionary journey is over. Meanwhile . . .

52   . . . the Empress Agrippina has kept up a constant assault on Claudius to adopt her son, Nero, and make him his heir, even over Claudius' own son, Brittanicus. Her influence on the trusting Claudius is enormous, and he finally consents. Claudius' always poor health is failing and Agrippina grasps power, turning his last years into another reign of terror: killing for estates, for fortunes, imagined insults, flatteries, jealousies. Agrippina will do anything, no matter how evil, to promote her son to the throne . . . even to offering herself to him. And Nero is as evil as she.

But Claudius' unspoken hope, secret ambition and great desire has been the restoration of the republic, the return of self-government by the people; but he has been a "good" emperor, and his very goodness has pacified the Roman people and reconciled them to an emperor and an empire. All their needs satisfied by a benevolent state, why should they not want it to continue? Why take upon themselves again the burden of governing when an emperor will do that for them? Another "good" emperor and the republic will never be restored . . . but, just maybe, another evil one . . . Claudius agrees to adopt Nero, removing his own son from succession . . .

53   There is a major thorn in the side of the *Pax Romana*, far away to the east, in Judea. Almost every day there are reports of outbreaks of sedition and revolt, and the historian, Eusebius, tells of one incident:

While Claudius was still on the throne, during the Passover Feast so riotous a tumult broke out in Jerusalem that of those Jews alone who were forcibly crushed together round the temple exits 30,000 trampled each other to death. Thus the feast ended in distress to the whole nation and bereavement to every household.   Eusebius, HISTORY OF THE CHURCH 2:20:1

Claudius, himself, sums up in a letter to the Alexandrines, his objections to ". . . certain political actions of the Jews . . . including this new religious sect who are . . . stirring up a universal plague throughout the world." Now he sends another legion to Judea, and appoints a new Procurator, Antonius Felix, a man he feels will be "sympathetic" to the Jews. Historians (the Roman Tacitus and Jewish Josephus) accuse Felix, though, of ruling with a heavy hand, of many crimes, instigating trouble for personal profit, reveling in cruelty and lust and acting like a king . . . with the ability of a slave.

53, Antioch.   Paul and Luke set out on a third missionary journey, retracing many previous steps ". . . strengthening all the disciples." It will take them four years. Passing through Syria, Cilicia. Galatia and Asia, they arrive at Ephesus, where they take up residence . . . ". . . and God did extraordinary miracles by the hands of Paul . . . so the word of the Lord grew and prevailed mightily."
ACTS 13:11, 20

Paul's third journey

Ephesus is a magnificent city of a quarter-million persons, many of whom make vast fortunes in commerce and banking as it is a great trading hub on the Imperial Highway from Rome to the far-east. Much of it gleams shiny-new for many of its attractions have been built during and since the time of Augustus: its colonnaded main street, agora, gymnasia and baths; its 24,000 seat theater and many hundred-thousand book library (all of which have been uncovered in our own times and some restored to their former glory.) But they alone are not what makes Ephesus a world famous tourist attraction in Paul's time; for just outside the city stands the gigantic temple to the fertility goddess, Artemis—or Diana—completed in 320 B.C. and counted as the fifth of the Seven Wonders of the Ancient World. Four times the size of Athens' Parthenon, it covers two acres of ground and took 220 years to build. The enormous many-breasted statue of the fertility goddess is the model for another—and possibly the largest—of the city's industries; silver graven images of her; amulets, statuettes and charms sold to tourists as souvenirs. The silversmith's guild that makes them is well organized, powerful, wealthy and jealous of its power and wealth . . . and the cult prostitution that accompanies the worship of Artemis is also big business in Ephesus. They all stand to lose a lot if Paul is successful.

54   In disgust and misgiving at his evil, scheming wife and her toadying son, Nero, Claudius moves to restore his own son as his heir to the throne and, according to Suetonius . . .

> . . . meeting Brittanicus, embraced him with deep affection. "Grow up quickly, my boy," he said, "and I will explain what my policy has been." With that he quoted in Greek from the tale of Achilles. "The hand that wounded you shall also heal."   Suetonius, The XII CAESARS

He will "at last provide Rome with a true-born Caesar." But, Tacitus says, he is too late . . .

> Agrippina had long decided on murder. Now she saw her opportunity, but she needed advice about poison. A sudden drastic effect would give her away. A gradual, wasting recipe [would give Claudius the time he needed . . . so . . .] the poison was sprinkled on a particularly succulent mushroom . . .
>
> The senate was summoned. Consuls and priests offered prayers for the emperor's safety. But meanwhile his already lifeless body was being wrapped in blankets and poultices. Agrippina, with heart-broken demeanor, held Brittanicus to her as though to draw comfort from him. [But] by various devices she prevented him from leaving his room, blocking every approach with troops.
>
> Claudius was voted divine honors, and his funeral was modeled on that of the divine Augustus—Agrippina imitating the grandeur of her great-grandmother, Livia . . . But Claudius' will was not read . . .   Tacitus, THE ANNALS OF IMPERIAL ROME 12:65–66

Nero

Agrippina has won her unique place in history: daughter of one of Rome's greatest men, Germanicus, she was sister (and lover) of one emperor, Caligula, wife of another, Claudius; and now the mother of a third, Nero, who takes the throne at 16 years of age. The Spanish philosopher, Seneca, has been Nero's tutor and is now his chief advisor, along with Burrus, commander of the Praetorian Guard and a good man, so the empire is in safe hands for the time being. But while they are able to guide Nero in matters of state, they are helpless in matters of his person. So devious is Nero that when he wants he can turn on some of the polish Seneca has tried to instill in him over the years, but underneath he is nothing more than a hoodlum . . . common, low and cheap. Disguising himself, he roams the streets at night with gangs of hoodlums, committing all sorts of foul crimes against men, women and little children. Those who try to defend themselves are murdered . . . or worse. Now Rome has, for an emperor . . . a gangster.

Born at Cordoba, Spain, the 58 year-old Lucius Annaeus Seneca has already been exiled twice—by Caligula and then Claudius—and recalled by Agrippina to become Nero's tutor. A stoic philosopher of great wisdom and learning, and a statesman of infinite skill and ability, he is now, in effect, the Prime Minister of the Empire, leading it through what a later emperor named Trajan will say is, governmentally, the finest period in the history of Imperial Rome. Seneca has been plagued all his life with many illnesses, especially asthma which he considers the worst, for he is constantly gasping his last breath, explaining, he says, why the doctors have nicknamed it "Rehearsing Death." Seneca carries on much correspondence with many friends

Seneca

and with his older brother, Lucius Junius Novatus, called Gallio, the Proconsul of Achia (who appears in a major role in the Bible's book of ACTS, 18:11–17).

Seneca's LETTERS FROM A STOIC cover everything from his asthma (You will not die because you are sick but because you are alive. That end awaits you [even] when you have been cured), to which of the liberal studies is best (the pursuit of wisdom,) to wondering if there was anything he couldn't be persuaded to do after having been persuaded into making a trip by sea. His disgust and loathing for the public "games" cause him to warn against mass crowds that make people go home more selfish, self-seeking and self-indulgent, crueler and less humane. Are these really games, he asks, when you hear such things as, "Lets have some throats cut . . . so there's something happening." 7:3 He says there is a big difference between living a retiring life and a spineless one, and, as it is with a play so it is with life—what matters is not how long the acting lasts but how good it is . . . or how bad. "Whenever you see a corrupt style," he says, "you know that society is going downhill," whether clothing, architecture, literary style, whatever; and the corruption is not just among the common people, but the cultivated, as well. It was "not philosophy that taught the world to use keys and bolts on doors." The noble spirit trusts to fate, he says, and the other side is the "puny degenerate" who "sees nothing right in the way the universe is ordered, and would rather reform the gods than . . . (him)self." But he also brings philosophy to task, and complains that one philosopher says there is nothing certain in the universe; another, that there is one certainty, that nothing is certain. And, again, one says that only one thing exists; another, not even one . . .

> It is difficult to say which of these people annoy me most, those who would have us know nothing or the ones who would not leave us even the small satisfaction of knowing that we know nothing. * . . . the gods have given no one the knowledge of philosophy, but everyone the means to acquire it. What would it be worth if it were [simply] handed out.
> Seneca, LETTERS FROM A STOIC 88–40

While Seneca and Burrus control the empire wisely, they are unable to control Nero, who now has his step-brother, Brittanicus, poisoned . . . Claudius' last hope for a restored republic. With his only rival eliminated, Nero now has only one obstacle to unbridled license, his mother. Agrippina knows this and for the first time, she also knows fear. So, she begins taking small doses of poison, to build up immunity.

54   Paul and Luke are still in Ephesus, but Paul's mind is on his church in Corinth just across the Aegean Sea in Greece, and he writes them a most beautiful, profound letter.

I CORINTHIANS

Epistle of Paul — Written in Greek,   c. A.D. 55

Paul founded the church in Corinth and always had a deep affection for it, but the city itself was, in fact, a hot bed of sin and sodomy. A cross-roads on the Imperial Highway to the east, it was a trading center, not only for silks and spices, but for human favors as well, and Paul heard that some of his converts had back-slidden to their old ways. He implored them to return and (in chapter 7) told them how they must behave in

Corinth

language that, taken out of context, makes him sound anti-woman and, at times, even anti-marriage. But Paul, like all early Christians, still believed that Christ's second coming was to happen in their lifetime and that the world could end any day. Why waste precious time with marital concerns when you could be praying and preparing for the end? Besides, there was Corinth, itself, a den of iniquity; enough reason to give "love" and sex a bad name, and Paul quotes the Greek poet, Menander, as he warns:

> Do not be deceived: "Bad company ruins good morals."   Menander of Attica (See: 300 B.C.)
> & I CORINTHIANS 15:33)

But first CORINTHIANS is also a much beloved letter, and Paul's greatest Christian dictum is found in it: "Christ our Passover is sacrificed for us. Therefore let us keep the feast." 5:7,8 Chapter 13 is possibly the most beautiful paeon to Christian love ever written:

> "If I speak with the tongues of men and angels but have not love, I am a noisy gong or a clanging cymbal. If I have all faith so as to remove mountains . . . if I give away all that I have . . . and deliver my body to be burned . . . but have not love I gain nothing. Love is patient and kind . . . not arrogant or rude . . . love bears all things, believes, hopes, endures all things. Love never ends . . . prophecies, tongues, knowledge, they will pass away. When I was a child, I spoke, thought, reasoned like a child, but when I became a man I put away childish things. Now I know in part, then I shall understand fully, even as I have been fully understood. So faith, hope, love abide, these three; but the greatest of these is love."   13:1–13

Paul's great exultation over death is in chapter fifteen.

> "For as in Adam all die, even so in Christ shall all be made alive. Lo, I tell you a mystery. We shall not all sleep, but we shall all be changed, in a moment, in the twinkling of an eye, at the last trumpet. For the trumpet shall sound and the dead will be raised incorruptible and . . . this mortal . . . must put on immortality . . . then, O grave, where is thy victory? O death, where is thy sting?"   15:22,55

55   Through scheming, treachery and murder, Agrippina has given Nero half the world. Now he intends to repay her. He arranges to have his mother's food poisoned, but Agrippina's foresight in building up immunity is effective and his murder plot is foiled.

Paul and his fellow-workers have been very successful in Ephesus winning many souls for Christ, but they have been successful in raising animosity, also, and now, the book of ACTS says: ". . . there arose no little stir concerning 'the Way.' " For 400 years that fifth Wonder of the World, the Temple of Artemis, or Diana, has meant big business to the Ephesians, its silversmiths enjoying a lucrative practice supplying tourists from the world over with silver idols of the goddess. Now Paul is preaching that "gods made with hands are not gods," and the city is up in arms. They "(rush) with one accord into the theatre," shouting, "Great is Diana of the Ephesians." But cooler heads prevail, saying that Paul is "neither sacrilegious nor [a] blasphemer of our goddess," and that they, themselves, are in danger of "being called into question for this day's uproar." Warned that "the [courts] are open and there are proconsuls; let them bring charges," the mob leaves the theater. 19:23–38 "After the uproar ceased," ACTS continues, Paul "took leave of them and departed for Macedonia."

. . . Nero arranges to have a device built that will cause the ceiling in his mother's bedroom to fall in on her, and crush her to death in bed. Agrippina learns of the scheme and is not in the room when the "accident" occurs.

. . . Paul's hot temper and autocratic "stiff-necked" ways often cause trouble between him and his churches. Corinth, closest to his heart is such a one. Now in Macedonia, Titus brings him good news from the Corinthians (after having had a "painful visit" there) and in joy and relief he writes this letter:

II CORINTHIANS

Epistle of Paul — Written in Greek,   c. A.D. 55

Paul says he regrets if his first letter grieved anyone, and yet he doesn't regret it because their grief made them repent and return to the faith, and in that he rejoices. He talks much of hurting others, and the need for forgiveness; and for generosity in giving to others, as in the money he is collecting for the impoverished church in Jerusalem:

> The point is this: he who sows sparingly will also reap sparingly, and he who sows bountifully will also reap bountifully . . . not reluctantly or under compulsion, for God loves a cheerful giver.   9:6,7

Many times Paul had to defend his own sincerity and faithfulness and, in this letter, tells of his many sufferings: "Five times have I received at the hands of the Jews the forty lashes less one. Three times . . . beaten with rods; once . . . stoned. Three times I have been shipwrecked; a night and a day . . . adrift at sea; on frequent journeys, in danger from rivers . . . robbers . . . my own people . . . from Gentiles . . . in the city . . . the wilderness . . . at sea . . . from false brethren; in toil and hardship, through many a sleepless night, in hunger and thirst . . . without food, in cold and exposure. Who is weak, and I am not weak? Who is made to fall, and I am not indignant? If I must boast, I will boast of the things that show my weakness. The God and Father of the Lord Jesus, he who is blessed for ever, knows that I do not lie."   II CORINTHIANS 11:24–31

. . . Nero invites his mother to a great banquet at his island villa, and sends a luxurious pleasure boat to bring her. The boat is so constructed that it will fall apart and sink. One servant is killed but Agrippina suffers only a cut and swims to shore.

57   But the business of the empire goes on in spite of the insane activities of its head of state (thanks to Seneca and Burrus behind the scenes.) Every day sees delegations of diplomats from all over the empire . . . Armenia, Parthia, Belgica (that will someday be called Belgium) and finally, from Germany, itself! What a sight to see these furskin-clad descendents of the savage massacre at Teutoburg Forest sitting amongst the pristine togas in the senate house trying to figure out what makes Romans tick.

Paul is worried about the Romans, also, but his concerns are the Christian Romans and they, living in the very heart and core of wickedness, need very special attention. Now, back in Greece, at Corinth, Paul writes a long letter to the Romans, takes many pains with it and explains the meaning of Christ in great detail.

ROMANS

Epistle of Paul — Written in Greek,   c. A.D. 57

"Christ being raised from the dead will never die again," Paul writes in this most thorough dissertation of Christian doctrine, "death no longer has dominion over him. He died unto sin once for all, but the life he lives, he lives to God. You also must consider yourselves dead to sin and alive to Christ Jesus. If we live, we live to the Lord, and if we die, we die to the Lord, so then whether we live or . . . die, we are the Lord's."   6:9–11

Paul's letter to the Romans is a profound spelling out of the meaning of Christ and the Christian faith. It is not a Christian treatise, as such, nor a moral guide-book, but a practical, personal letter to a community of believers in a particular city, Rome, the only letter Paul wrote to a church he, himself, did not found.

"All people are sinners," Paul says, "both Jew and Gentile; the Jew for transgressing the Law and the Gentile for immorality and idolatry. Therefore, all who have sinned without the Law will perish without the Law, and all who have sinned under the Law will be judged by the Law." BUT, he rejoices, ". . . now the righteousness of God has been manifested APART from the Law, although THE LAW AND THE PROPHETS BEAR WITNESS TO IT: the righteousness of God THROUGH FAITH IN JESUS CHRIST FOR ALL WHO BELIEVE! We know that the whole creation has been groaning in travail until now," he says, but adds that " . . . in everything God works for good with those who love him . . . What then shall we say to this? If God is for us, who is against us? He who did not spare his own son but gave him up for us all . . . Is it Christ Jesus who died, yes, was raised from the dead, who is at the right hand of God, indeed intercedes for us? Who shall separate us from the love of God? Shall tribulation, distress, persecution, famine, nakedness, peril or sword? No, in all these things we are more than conquerors through him who loved us. For I am persuaded that neither death, nor life, nor angels,

3rd century fragment of Romans

nor principalities, nor things present, nor things to come, nor powers, nor height, nor depth, nor anything else in all creation, will be able to separate us from the love of God in Christ Jesus our Lord."

"I am telling the truth in Christ," Paul stoutly maintains, "I am not lying . . ." and adds proudly, "I am not ashamed of the gospel. It is the power of God for salvation to everyone who has faith." It is not the word of God that has failed, he reasons, but we who have failed the Word. "How are men to call upon Him in whom they have not believed? And how are they to believe in him of whom they have never heard?" Every person who knows the Gospel, he says, must work, each in his own way, according to his own talents, to spread it. "Let us cast aside the works of darkness and put on the armor of light!" And never think of yourself as alone, he says, but remember Elijah, to whom God promised a faithful redeeming remnant. "So too," says Paul, "at the present time there is a remnant, chosen by grace."

Of the atrocities and insanities of his age, Paul speaks comfortingly: "I consider that the sufferings of this present time are not worth comparing with the glory that is to be revealed to us. But," he warns, "let every person be subject to the governing authorities . . ." The severity of those "governing authorities" in Jerusalem has left the church there in abject poverty, and Paul has been collecting money for them throughout Greece and Asia Minor.

Paul had a many-faceted personality: tenacious, volitile, high-strung and "stiff-necked," that peculiar quality which has characterized the Jews from the time of Abraham. He suffered, gladly, swift to anger, swift to forgive. A driver, he was also driven, and having driven himself this far, he intended to go farther. Determined to make the trip back to Jerusalem and then to Rome, he determined to go, also, to Spain . . . and maybe beyond! "Since I no longer have any room for work in these regions, and since I have longed for many years to come to you, I hope to see you in passing as I go to Spain, and to be sped on my journey there by you, once I have enjoyed your company for a little. At present, however, I am going to Jerusalem, with aid, for the saints."　15:23–25

At the end of his letter to the Romans, Paul sends greetings to the many new Christians in Rome from his friends and disciples in Corinth, where he wrote the letter, among whom are ". . . Timothy, my fellow worker . . . Gaius, who is host to me and to the whole church . . . [and] . . .

. . . Erastus, the city treasurer."　ROMANS 16:21,23

The office of city treasurer or *quaestor,* was a necessary step on the political ladder for any Roman interested in attaining higher office; and another step up was that of *aedile,* or superintendent of public works (the same office that launched the career of Julius Caesar.) Paul's friend, Erastus, "the city treasurer," apparently received that promotion eventually, for the evidence exists to this day. In A.D. 1929 a limestone pavement was found in Corinth, including one paving block which must have been very impressive in its day, its message chisled out and the spaces filled in with gleaming bronze letters. They read, in Latin:

> *ERASTUS IN RETURN FOR HIS AEDILESHIP LAID [THE PAVEMENT] AT HIS OWN EXPENSE.* *   The Erastus inscription ASCS, Athens

Erastus, the city treasurer

Many scholars think that Paul's interest in carrying the Word to Spain may have been stimulated by his acquaintance with the Spanish-born *proconsul,* Gallio who dismissed charges against him in Corinth five years ago, and that he also intends to visit Gallio's brother Seneca on his stop in Rome. Now unofficial "Prime Minister" of Rome, Seneca has surely heard of him by now for Paul is known throughout the empire, and Christ's followers can be found even in the royal house. Moreover, whether or not they ever do meet (and neither secular nor sacred history records it anywhere) they have a philosophical like-mindedness that is remarkable. In several of his letters to other people, Seneca writes:

> Philosophy has taught men to worship what is divine, to love what is human, telling us that with the gods belongs authority, and among human beings fellowship. That fellowship lasted for a long time intact, before man's greed broke society up . . . LETTER 90:3 *
> . . . there resides within us a divine spirit, which guards us and watches us in the evil and the good we do. As we treat him, so will he treat us. No man, indeed, is good without God . . . He it is that prompts us to noble and exalted endeavors . . . 41:1 * we should, indeed, live as if we were in public view, and think, too, as if some one could peer into the inmost recesses of our hearts—which someone can! For what is to be gained if something is concealed from man when nothing is concealed from God?   SENECA 83:1

And in his first letter to the CORINTHIANS, Paul wrote:

> Do you not know that you are God's temple and that God's spirit dwells in you? If anyone destroys God's temple, God will destroy him. For God's temple is holy, and that temple you are. I COR 3:16,17 * This is how one should regard us, as servants of Christ, and stewards of the mysteries of God, [and His servants must] be found trustworthy. 4:1,2 *
> If anyone imagines that he knows something, he does not yet know as he ought to know. [For] "knowledge" puffs up, but love builds up . . . if one loves God, one is known by him. 8:1,2 * [So] do all to the glory of God . . . [but] be imitators of me, as I am of Christ.
> I CORINTHIANS 10:32, 33 & 11:1

With every atrocity Nero commits he gets bolder and more outrageous. Seneca and Burrus are slowly losing control as Nero listens more and more to other, more reckless, advisors. Tacitus is not the only historian awed by the enormity of Nero's incredible follies and crimes. Suetonius, too, records his sordid and disgusting story, how he "practiced every kind of obsenity," dressing up in the skins of wild beasts to attack the private parts of persons tied naked to stakes, auctioneering off his own stolen goods from the very steps of the imperial palace, and admiring his late uncle Caligula because he, too, believed that "fortunes were made to be squandered . . ."

> Nero never wore the same clothes twice . . . [and] seldom traveled . . . with a train of less than 1000 carriages . . . He built a palace, stretching from the Palatine [Hill] to the Esqualine . . . [which he called] "The Golden House . . ." The entrance hall . . . [contained] . . . a statue of himself, 120 feet high; and the pillared arcade ran for a whole mile . . . The main dining room was circular, and its roof revolved, day and night, in time with the sky. [When it was completed] Nero dedicated it [saying]: "Good, now I can at last begin to live like a human being."   Suetonius, LIVES OF THE TWELVE CAESARS. Nero:30

His work finished in Greece, Paul heads home. At Miletus his friends, fearing they will never see him again, beg him not to go to Jerusalem . . . "and they wept . . . embraced . . . and kissed him . . . and brought him to the ship . . ." After crossing the Mediterranean, his friends at Caesarea do the same, and Paul cries, "What are you doing, weeping and breaking my heart? For I am ready not only to be imprisoned, but even to die . . . for the name of the Lord Jesus." When Paul's friends see that "he would not be persuaded" they cease, saying, "The Lord's will be done;" and Luke records, simply and succinctly that, "after those days we took up our carriages and went up to Jerusalem . . . and when we were come to Jerusalem, the brethren received us gladly. And the day following Paul went in with us unto James; and all the elders were present . . ."   ACTS 21:14–18

The apostle, James, called "the Just," has long been the head of the church in Jerusalem, according to the Christian historian, Eusebius, its "first bishop." The Epistle of JAMES is thought to have been written by him, and if so, it would have been written by now, for James' days are numbered.

JAMES

Epistle of James — Written in Greek,   c. A.D. 60

According to the third century historian, Eusebius, James had very early been "elected by the apostles to the episcopal throne at Jerusalem," (BK 2:23) and is now universally regarded as "the most righteous of men." His authority has been deferred to many times over the years: after Peter's miraculous escape from prison following the murder of the "elder" James by Herod Agrippa in 44, when he told those in the house of Mark's mother, Mary, to "Tell [about] this to James and the brethren . . ." And at the first council five years later which decided the question of circumcision and the need for Gentiles to become Jews first and then Christians. Luke says in ACTS that after Paul and Barnabas told their side, James said, "Brethren, listen to me . . . my judgment is that we should not trouble . . . the Gentiles who turn to God."

James

Scholars do not agree whether JAMES was written very early by James the "brother" (step-brother, according to Eusebius) of the Lord, or very late by a Hellenistic Christian, or, in fact, by James the Just; because on one hand the writer makes reference to Christians still worshipping in "synagogues" rather than later "churches." On the other hand, the Greek used in the writing is much more polished and articulate than they feel a Galilean Jew would probably have known. They argue, also, whether the letter's teachings (faith without works is meaningless) brought James and Paul (faith alone justifies) into conflict. Most feel James and Paul respected and co-operated with each other, and that they are actually, teaching the same thing with only slightly different words.

Whatever the answer to those questions, JAMES is a beautiful letter, rich in wisdom and encouragement for the new Christians: ". . . testing of your faith produces steadfastness . . . be quick to hear, slow to speak, slow to anger . . . be doers of the Word, not hearers only . . . He who doubts is like a wave of the sea that is driven and tossed by the wind . . . As a great ship is steered by a very small rudder, so is a man steered by his tongue, a restless evil full of deadly poison . . . If any thinks he is religious but does not bridle his tongue, his religion is in vain." James' stricture against complacency is almost menacing: ". . . you believe that God is one; you do well . . . Even the demons believe and shudder. But," he concludes, "we all make mistakes," and a sinner's repentance "will cover a multitude of sins." Chs. 1–3

58   Desperate to save her life and even maintain some semblance of power, Agrippina (who Tacitus calls an "always terrible woman") pulls out all the stops with her equally terrible son:

Agrippina's passion to retain power carried her so far that at midday, the time when food and drink were beginning to raise Nero's temperature, she several times appeared before her inebriated son all decked out and ready for incest . . . Tacitus, The ANNALS 1.1:13:62

But he wants no more of that now, for Nero is in love . . . with one of Rome's great beauties, Poppaea Sabina; rich, "clever and pleasant to talk to" in fact, Tacitus says, "Poppaea had every asset except goodness . . ."

While married to a knight . . . she was seduced by Marcus Salvius Otho, an extravagant youth who was . . . particularly close to Nero. Their liason . . . quickly [became] . . . marriage. Otho praised her charms and graces to the emperor . . . either a lover's indiscretion or a deliberate . . . idea that joint possession of Poppaea would be a bond reinforcing Otho's own power . . . he was often heard saying he was going to his wife who had . . . what all men want and only the fortunate enjoy . . . Tacitus, the ANNALS 11:13:47

Nero is smitten on first sight and when, one day, Otho locks him out of their mutual bedroom, Nero banishes him to Lucitania/today's Portugal. (Given the rank of Governor, Otho will, himself, become emperor 11 years from now for all of 95 days.) But Poppaea is not happy; she wants to be empress, and Nero is still married to his first wife, the virtuous and well-loved Octavia, and besides, Agrippina opposes the idea. So Poppaea taunts Nero that his mother is still alive, and begins to put on the pressure.

58   Paul is, indeed, singled out by the mob in Jerusalem while telling his story in the temple. When he tells of taking the faith to the gentiles, "certain of" the Jews riot against him and demand scourging but, bound with thongs, Paul asks a centurion nearby if it is lawful to beat an uncondemned Roman citizen? Amazed, the "chief captain" says HE paid a great price for HIS citizenship, and Paul replies, "I was free BORN!" A hearing before a council of Pharisees and Sadducees ends in "great discension" and "fear lest Paul should be pulled in pieces," and he is taken in protective custody to the fortress at Caesarea. During a long, black night, Jesus appears to Paul, to say, "Take courage [Paul] for as you have testified about me at Jerusalem so, also, you must bear witness at Rome."   ACTS 23:11

Paul is taken before the Roman *praefect*, now called *procurator* or governor, Antonius Felix, who begins a preliminary hearing, a procedure called *provocatio*, in which he will gather evidence and leave the trial to the emperor. He says to Paul, "I will hear you when your accusers are also come," proper procedure under first century Roman law, a statute called *destitutio*. But Paul knows Roman law, also, from his early education in the great schools of Tarsus, and he knows that when accusations of guilt are made and the accusers fail to show up at the trial they, themselves, are then guilty of *calumnia*, a crime that carries stiff penalties for the defaulting accusers. Neither is the governor, Felix, ignorant of "The Way," the faith which Paul preaches, and Felix listens with interest. A prosecutor named Tertellus calls Paul a "pestilent fellow, a mover of sedition and a ringleader of the sect of Nazarenes." But Felix agrees with Paul's legal position and has him held for a later hearing . . . and possibly a bribe for Paul's freedom?

A coin of Felix

Many years from now, in the declining years of the Roman Empire, the procedure for a trial will be handled much differently. *Provocatio* will give way to a procedure called *appelatio* (from which comes our own "appellate" court, wherein the local magistrate, himself, tries the case and renders a verdict, which can then be "appealed" and taken to a higher court (or, then, to Caesar, in Rome.) The book of ACTS, which tells Paul's story, has Roman law exactly right.

. . . Nero always wants everything done "in good taste," so he appoints his friend, Petronius Arbiter as *Arbiter Elegantiae*, and refers every matter of propriety to his "Arbiter of Good Taste." Petronius, Tacitus says:

> . . . spent his days sleeping, his nights working and enjoying himself. Others achieve fame by energy, Petronius by laziness. Yet he was not . . . regarded as dissipated or extravagant, but . . . a refined voluptuary . . . [a man of] unconventional . . . sayings and doings . . . to the blasé emperor nothing was smart and elegant unless Petronius had given it his approval.   Tacitus, The ANNALS, XVI:17,18

Petronius' most famous work is the infamous *SATYRICON*, a satirical fable which, more than any other book shows the depths of depravity to which Rome has sunk by this time. His writing, like the people and incidents he writes about, range from sophisticated, refined and elegant to vulgar, coarse and barbarous. He races non-stop from debauchery in a brothel to luxurious country estates, city slums and public baths to the incredible "dinner at Trimalchio's" (or is he thinly veiling "dinner at Nero's?") Whatever, the *SATYRICON* is a remarkable book and Petronius a remarkable character to have preserved for posterity one of the most splendid yet savage, brilliant and inhumane periods in history; scenes of degradation and brutality enacted on a stage setting of inspired Roman grandeur and magnificence. In his writings, Petronius uses phrases we still use today: "My heart was in my mouth," and "Not worth his salt."

59   Wild in his desire to marry Poppaea, Nero is frustrated by her "conditions," one being the death of his mother. She is relentless in her barrage of invective against Agrippina, so Nero has his mother charged with conspiracy . . . and assassinated. Tacitus says, "This was the end which Agrippina had anticipated for years . . . But Nero only understood the horror of his crime when it was done."

> One good turn deserves another. * Beware of the dog.
> Petronius, Arbiter of Good Taste

Nero adopts a gloomy demeanor as though sorry . . . and [in] mourning for his parent's death . . ."

> Then he plunged into the wildest improprieties, which vestiges of respect for his mother had hitherto not indeed repressed, but at least impeded . . . There was no stopping him . . . scandalous publicity did not satiate Nero . . . indeed, it led on . . . he shared his degradation . . . brought on to the stage members of the ancient nobility whose poverty made them corruptible . . . in the wood which Augustus had planted . . . places of assignation and taverns were built, and every stimulus to vice was displayed for sale . . . never was there so favorable an environment for debauchery as among this filthy crowd . . . every form of immorality competed for attention, and no chastity, modesty, or vestige of decency could survive. The climax was the emperor's stage debut. Meticulously tuning his lyre, he struck practice notes to the trainers beside him.   Tacitus, The ANNALS OF IMPERIAL ROME XIV:12–14

60   Far to the north, Roman armies are still pounding at a resisting Britain. Tacitus describes one invasion from the sea. The wild, undaunted Britons' defense of their homeland is frightful, even to the despised Roman invaders:

> The enemy lined the shore in a dense, armed mass. Among them were black-robed women with disheveled hair like Furies, brandishing torches. Close by stood Druids, raising their hands to heaven and screaming dreadful curses. This weird spectacle awed the Roman soldiers into a sort of paralysis . . . [presenting] themselves as a target.   *ibid.* XIV:29

The massacre, destruction and rapacity by both sides, Briton and Roman, is horrendous: slaughter, sacrifice and terror . . . and only leads to the inexorable Roman advance.

One tribe of Britons is the Iceni, led by their queen, Boadicea or Boudicca, who leads a ferocious, but futile assault on the Roman merchant community of Londinium (today's London) nearly wipes it out and does, in fact, take some 80,000 Romans . . . whom she crucifies . . . leaving traces of red ash in the soil that can be seen to this day. But Rome's might cannot be stopped, and like another queen (Cleopatra) of a century ago, kills herself rather than be captured and taken a prisoner to Rome.

. . . Gaius Plinaeaus Secundus, called Pliny (the Elder) is working on a monumental study of nature, called *HISTORIA NATURALIS*, the most comprehensive encyclopedia of ancient times. When finished, it will contain 20,000 topics in 37 volumes. Pliny's nephew (whom he will adopt as his son) says that not an hour any day was spent by his uncle other then in reading and writing, even during meals (and Pliny is a big man.) His works are written in the "minutest hand" on both sides of a page; the bibliography for the NATURAL HISTORY listing as references 146 Latin and 329 foreign writers and their works. Much of his natural science Pliny learned from Aristotle; about the heavens and the earth, man and animals, plants, birds, insects, stones and precious gems. But he lists, also—uncritically—a strange assortment of weird beings, monstrous humans, unicorns and flying horses . . . which casts doubt on his scholarly credibility. Some other of Pliny's books are on subjects that range from how to throw a javelin from horse-back, to lessons in oratory, to the German wars. Pliny feels that man himself, not nature, is the cause of most of man's troubles, although . . .

> It is far from easy to determine whether she [Nature] had proved to him a kind parent or a merciless stepmother.   Pliny the Elder, HISTORIA NATURALIS, 7:1

But Pliny has not, yet, heard the last from nature. That will come just 13 years from now.

60   During Paul's imprisonment at Caesarea, he has been allowed visitors and certain other liberties, but now, the *procurator* Felix's "mismanagement" of Judea and his "seeking favor with the Jews" has come to Nero's attention in Rome, and Nero has him recalled, tried and banished from Rome. Nero then appoints Porcius Festus *procurator,* and one of the first matters brought before him is that of the Apostle Paul.

Unlike the procrastinating Felix, Festus is a man of action, taking up his responsibilities with firmness and resolve. He goes to see Paul at Caesarea, and asks him if he wants to return to Jerusalem—under his own *Imperium,* or sovereignty, for trial by the Jewish Sanhedrin. This is the last thing Paul wants, and he speaks boldly to Festus: "I stand at Caesar's judgement seat, where I ought to be judged: to the Jews I have done no wrong. [Therefore] I appeal to Caesar." Thus, as a Roman citizen Paul invokes a provision of the *Pax Romana,* a law as ancient as the Law of Twelve Tables, first posted in the Roman Forum 500 years ago at the birth of the Roman Republic. Festus meets with his *consilium,* or cabinet of advisors, for their "consensus." The *consilio* must be decided et *animus* (by wisdom and courage), et *pudentia* (with prudence), and *non impetu* (not by impulse). But the *imperium* is his, alone, and Festus tells Paul, "You have appealed to Caesar; to Caesar you shall go."   ACTS 25:10–12

Paul appealing to Agrippa

But first, the Jewish King Herod Agrippa II and his sister/wife, Bernice, come "with great pomp" to welcome Festus to Palestine, and Festus tells them about Paul. Paul respects Agrippa as a fair man, and Agrippa justifies that respect by giving Paul a fair hearing. Paul begins at the very beginning and tells the whole story: his "manner of life" from youth, his fanatical opposition to the Nazarene sect of Jesus, and his complicity in the murder of Steven; his conversion on the road to Damascus and his activities ever since. As he tells them of Christ risen from the dead, Festus cries out, "Paul, you are mad; your great learning is turning you mad." "I am not mad, noble Festus," Paul replies, "but . . . speaking the sober truth . . . and the king knows these things . . . for they were not done in a corner." Then he asks Agrippa, ". . . do you believe the prophets? I know [you do]," and Agrippa replies: "In a short time you think to make me a Christian?" Leaving Paul, they all agree that he is guiltless and should be acquitted, and Agrippa concludes the matter, saying, "This man could have been set free if he had not appealed to Caesar."   ACTS, chs. 24–26

After having languished two years in captivity in Caesarea, Paul is sent, a prisoner to Rome. Six years ago, when he was arrested in Corinth, Paul was taken for trial before the Roman proconsul Gallio, the great Seneca's elder brother, who recognized trumped-up charges and dismissed the case. It is thought that, being intellectual, like-minded men, a friendship of some sort might have sprung up between the two and that, now, Paul's appeal to Caesar may actually be an unspoken appeal to Seneca, himself, that with his vast influence over Nero, he might intercede. At any rate, the trip that Paul wanted to make for years finally comes about, but not the way he planned. His protégé and "biographer," the Greek physician, Luke, has kept a journal of all their travels, and now records the dramatic and perilous journey to Rome:

Paul is put under the guard of a centurion named Julius of the Augustan cohort stationed in Syria. Putting to sea from Sidon, they sail "under the lee" of Cyprus and then up to Myra in the south coast of Asia Minor, where they find "a ship of Alexandria sailing for Italy." Paul is, by now, a seasoned veteran sailor and astute weatherman, having sailed thousands of miles on his three missionary journeys. Sailing next under the lee of Crete at Fair Havens, he reads ominous signs in a gentle south wind, and he warns the captain not to sail, but is ignored . . . and they are blasted by one of the Mediterranean's infamous, fierce "tempestuous winds, called the northeaster," which blows for days until, Luke writes, "all hope of our being saved was at last abandoned." But Paul is visited by an angel who says to him, "Do not be afraid, Paul; you must stand before Caesar; and lo, God has granted you all those who sail with you." 27:24. For 14 days they are tempest-tossed, starving and lost at sea, their only courage coming from Paul who tells them to "take heart," not one soul on the ship (ACTS 27:37 says there were 276) will be lost, for God has told him so. The ship will go, yes, and its cargo, but not one person. Then, striking a shoal, they know not where, the "vessel runs aground." Some swim to shore, some cling to a piece of wreckage, and not one soul is lost. The island is Malta, just south of Sicily, and the Maltese people "show them unusual kindness," and kindle them a fire. Paul gathers firewood and . . .

> . . . a viper came out because of the heat and fastened on his hand. [Seeing] the creature hanging from his hand . . . the natives perceive him a murderer receiving justice, having escaped it in the storm . . . but Paul] shook off the creature into the fire and suffered no harm. They waited, expecting him to . . . fall down dead [and when he didn't] they said that he was a god.   ACTS 28:3–6

They wait out the winter on Malta/with Paul curing illnesses and winning souls and, after three months, in a ship with a "figurehead of the Twin Brothers," (Castor and Pollux, patron gods of seamen and travelers, from their having sailed with Jason and his Argonauts,) they sail for Italy. After one seven-day stop at Syracuse, where Paul visits the Sicilian Christians, they dock just south of Naples at Puteoli (Or Pozzuoli, where pozzolana cement was invented that built the Roman Empire.) And in one of the Bible's great understatements, Luke writes . . .

> And so we came to Rome.   28:14

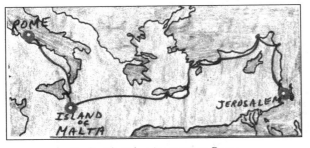

Paul's 4th & last journey—to Rome

The Christians in Rome expect Paul's arrival and come south on the Appian Way 43 milestones to meet him at the Forum of Appius, and at 33 milestones, to the Three Taverns; and "On seeing them Paul thanked God and took courage." Paul is put under house arrest, but, in the closing lines of the book of ACTS, Luke records, "He lived there two whole years at his own expense and welcomed all who came to him, preaching the kingdom of God and teaching about the Lord Jesus quite openly and unhindered."   ACTS 28:30–33

During his imprisonment in Rome, Paul writes three letters to the Christians of the churches he had founded at Philippi, Ephesus and Colossae, and one to his friend, Philemon. The four are called the "Captivity letters" and are all written between A.D. 61 and 63.

The Appian Way

COLOSSIANS

Epistle of Paul — Written in Greek, c. A.D. 62

Paul heard of a heresy of the faith and acted quickly to see that no one should "make a prey" of the Christians at Colossae "by philosophy or empty deceit." He stressed that "Christ is the image of the invisible God, the first born of all creation . . . in him all the fullness of God, was pleased to dwell . . ." The gospel, Paul says, is "bearing fruit in the whole world" and asks them to lead lives "fully pleasing to, and worthy of, the Lord."

> He is the image of the invisible God, the first born of all creation, for in him all things were created, in heaven and on earth, visible and invisible . . . He is before all things . . . the head of the body, the church . . . the mystery hidden for ages and generations but now made manifest to his saints.   1:15–17 & 26

THE MYSTERY HIDDEN FOR AGES . . . BUT NOW MADE MANIFEST! Thus, in one short phrase has Paul summed up all of history, all the religions that ever were, all the questions about the meaning of life itself. Jesus Christ is the mystery hidden for ages and generations but now made manifest to those who believe in him, the "saints." Therefore, Paul says, "let the peace of Christ rule in your hearts . . . and be thankful."

As he often did, Paul signed COLOSSIANS "with my own hand," and sends them greetings from Luke "the beloved physician." He also mentions another of his letters: "When this letter has been among you, have it read in the church of Laodicea." Paul's letter to the Laodiceans will not be included in the canon of the Bible when the New Testament is compiled, but it is interesting and important anyway, for once again he warns against heresy:

3rd century fragment of Colossians

> Let not the vain speeches of any trouble you who pervert the truth that they may draw you aside from the truth of the Gospel which I have preached . . . be steady in the doctrine of Christ . . . and peace shall be with you.   The apocryphal epistle of Paul to the LAODICEANS.

Certain other ancient documents suggest that Paul and Nero's advisor, Seneca, brother of the proconsul, Gallio, who dismissed the case against Paul 11 years ago in ACTS (18:12–17) may have met, become friends and corresponded. In the apocryphal EPISTLES OF PAUL AND SENECA they discuss Seneca's desire to read Paul's letter to Nero:

> Seneca: "[I] was delighted with your book of epistles . . . wonderful instructions for moral conduct . . . sublimity of these doctrines . . . their grandeur . . . I am determined to read them to Caesar . . ."
>
> Paul: "I reckon myself very happy in having the judgment of so valuable a person (Seneca) . . . esteemed censor, philosopher . . . tutor to so great a prince . . ."

> Seneca: ". . . the Emperor . . . was surprised to find such notions in a person who had not a regular education . . ."
>
> Paul: ". . . a very dangerous attempt . . . to declare [to him] that which is so very contrary to his religion . . . a worshipper of heathen gods . . ."
>
> The apocryphal epistles of Paul and Seneca, 1:14, 7:5 & 8:2

Although the Paul-Seneca letters are, in fact, very old (being mentioned in the writings of both St. Jerome and St. Augustine about A.D. 400), they are generally considered not to be authentic. Still, there is a germ of truth in them. Paul's appeal to Caesar after his trial in Jerusalem was, very likely, a tacit appeal, not to Nero, but to Seneca through their brother/friend Gallio. And although they lived in different "worlds," (Seneca in Nero's and Paul in Christ's) their literary and philosophical like-mindedness could well have been a bond. Moreover, Seneca and Gallio were Spaniards and it could well have been they who planted in Paul his desire to go to Spain.

Seneca

Some Christians believe that Paul is interested in going even farther than Spain . . . to Britain; that among those whom Paul won for Christ during his captivity was the British King Caractacus and his family, freed now to return home, encouraging Paul to include Britain in his missionary work. Now Paul writes a letter to a close friend and fellow-worker, about a subject rarely discussed before:

PHILEMON

Episte of Paul — Written in Greek,   c. A.D. 62

Paul had a friend named Philemon whose slave, Onesimus, had long since robbed from him and escaped. Now in Rome, Onesimus has become a Christian, and is himself a missionary. Paul sends Onesimus back to Philemon with this gem of tact and wisdom, asking reconciliation as brothers in Christ, and possibly even . . . freedom?

Slavery has been a universally recognized, legal practice since time immemorial, and in the Roman Empire retribution is swift and terrible to those who tamper with it. While neither Jesus nor Paul have preached against it, their teaching is, of course, replete with the conviction of the equality of every person; and Paul's letter will someday play a large part in slavery's eradication in the West.

> . . . for love's sake I . . . appeal to you—I, Paul, an ambassador and now a prisoner also for Christ Jesus—I appeal to you for . . . Onesimus, whose father I have become in my imprisonment . . . I am sending back . . . my very heart . . . If he has wronged you at all, charge that to my account . . . I will repay it . . . greetings to you [from] Mark . . . and Luke, my fellow workers.   1:9–25

Nero, grown fat and slovenly from a life of excess, still fancies himself an athlete and has a driving desire to be an Olympic champion. So a trip is planned for him to attend and participate in the Olympic games in Greece. He will combine the trip with a concert tour and share his musical talents with everyone along the way. In Greece, Nero throws the discus; he boxes, wrestles, sings, plays the lyre and recites poetry (the latter three events included just for him) . . . and lowers the standards of the games to a point of almost wiping them out, for he never places lower than "first," and returns home with over a thousand gold medals.

[. . . his] incursions into the arts at Rome did not satisfy him, and he headed for Greece . . . [announcing] . . . "The Greeks alone are worthy of my efforts, they really listen to music." . . . his jealousy of rivals and his awe of the judges can scarcely be believed . . . [the other competitors he] insulted . . . to their faces; and if any were particularly good singers, he would bribe them not to do themselves justice.   Suetonius, THE TWELVE CAESARS, Nero:23

Nero's advisor and commander of the Praetorian Guard, Burrus, dies, ostensibly from a tumor growing in his throat, more likely from poison on a throat swab ordered by Nero to "ease the pain," and Nero appoints two new commanders. One is a popular choice, Tacitus says in his ANNALS OF IMPERIAL ROME, "for having managed the corn supply without personal profit," and the other a hoodlum cohort named Tigellinus, because Nero "found his unending immoralities and evil reputation fascinating . . . and in whose debaucheries he participated." His own well-being in jeopardy now, Seneca says to Nero, "It is nearly 14 years, Caesar, since I became associated with your rising fortunes, eight since you became emperor. During that time you have showered on me such distinctions and riches that, if only I could retire to enjoy them unpretentiously, my prosperity would be complete." Nero is only too glad to be rid of him, and Seneca goes into retirement to work on completing his writings.

In the years of his oversight Seneca had run the empire with wisdom, fairness and even brilliance. His stoic good sense, logic and indomitable fortitude held Nero in check—to a degree—as once, when he persuaded Nero out of a common massacre with one sentence: "Remember," Tacitus records him saying, "however many people you slaughter you cannot kill your successor." But Seneca has also been held in contempt, not only by enemies of his own generation, but critics to our very own, for preaching one thing and practicing another; for espousing the simple, sane and sensible stoic life and belief, and living like a king, having amassed a fortune in his years with Nero as large as Nero's own: 300,000,000 sesterces in the first four years alone. Seneca maintains that having money is not the issue, though, but the use one puts it to; whether it becomes a relentless master or charitable servant. And he writes, in a letter to his brother, Gallio, thoughts that hauntingly echo those of the Apostle Paul, himself . . .

The highest good is immortal: it knows no ending . . . but pleasure dies the moment when it charms us most . . . Whatever I possess, I will neither hoard it greedily nor squander it recklessly . . . I will do nothing because of public opinion, but everything because of conscience [at all times as though) the eyes of the Roman people are upon me . . . Whenever . . . Nature demands my breath again, or reason bids me dismiss it, I will quit this life, [with a] good conscience, and good pursuits; that no one's freedom, my own least of all, has been impaired through me . . . the philosopher['s] . . . wealth . . . must be obtained without wronging any man . . . it must be alike honorably come by and honorably spent . . . [then] he will have something to boast of, if he throw his house open, let all . . . come [in] . . . and say, "If any one recognizes here anything belonging to him, let him take it" . . . how excellently rich will he be, if after this speech he possesses as much as he had before!   Seneca, Book VII, MINOR ESSAYS, Of a Happy Life

62   Free, now, from bothersome restraints, Nero divorces his wife, Octavia, and marries Poppaea. Riots break out in Rome, for the Romans love Octavia for her goodness, and are loath to see her misused. Nero is not swayed, and Poppaea triumphs. Only 20 years old, a terrified Octavia is stabbed to death with the swords of a dozen centurions. Poppaea demands—and gets—Octavia's head as her own prize.

. . . While still in captivity in Rome, Paul writes to his church at Ephesus . . .

EPHESIANS

Epistle of Paul — Written in Greek,   c. A.D. 62

Even though a prisoner in Rome—an "ambassador in chains"—Paul knows only too well what is going on all around him . . . out in the world, and he writes, not only to Christians in Ephesus but throughout the empire—and the ages—to . . .

Look carefully then how you walk, not as unwise men but as wise, making the most of the time, because the days are evil. [So] . . . put on the whole armor of God, that you may be able to stand against the wiles of the devil. For we are not contending against flesh and blood, but against principalities . . . powers . . . against the world rulers of this present darkness . . ."   5:15 & 6:13–17

Ephesus

The whole armor of God, Paul says, is this: the breastplate of righteousness; the shoes, the gospel of peace, the shield of faith, the helmet of salvation, and the sword of the Spirit, which is the word of God. And he tells them it is all part of God's Great Plan. ". . . to me this grace was given . . . to preach to the Gentiles the unsearchable riches of Christ, and to make men see what is the plan of the mystery hidden for ages in God who created all things by Jesus Christ . . ."   3:7–9

This seems to have been a general letter, circulated to many churches, with the copy from Ephesus the only one preserved, hence its name, EPHESIANS. In it Paul explains in detail both the human and divine sides of the new-growing community, the church, which he calls the BODY OF CHRIST. Two hundred years from now a copy of this epistle will be written on papyrus manuscript, and remain in existence to this day, the oldest copy of Paul's letters.

Still under house arrest, Paul is alone in Rome, now, all his companions, even Luke ". . . left me to my fate—may God forgive them!" Their reason for leaving is not known but Paul's own words indicate some kind of personal friction. But still he has visitors, and some of them come from the royal household itself, which he tells about in his fourth "captivity" letter to the church at Philippi.

PHILIPPIANS

Epistle of Paul — Written in Greek,   c. A.D. 62

It is clear that by this time Christianity has won converts even in the royal house, itself, under the very nose of Nero; for Paul, in his glory, tells his "dearly loved brethren," at Philippi, ". . . what has happened to me has served to advance the gospel, so that it has become known throughout the whole praetorian guard and to all the rest that my imprisonment is for Christ; and most of the brethren have been made confident in the Lord because of my imprisonment, and are much more bold to speak the word of God without fear." 1:12–14 Paul's imprisonment has been long and hard but, he says, "Not that I complain . . . for I have learned, in whatever state I am, to be content. I know how to be abased, and 1 know how to abound. I can do all things in him who strengthens me." Philippi was the first church Paul had founded in Europe, and there is no trace of harshness in this letter, but rather warmth and love as he addresses his "brethren, whom I love and long for, my joy and crown." Chapter two contains Paul's great paeon to Christ's suffering and glory:

. . . have this in mind among yourselves [that] Christ Jesus, though he was in the form of god, did not count himself equal with God, but taking the form of a servant, being

> born in the likeness of men... humbled himself and became obedient unto death, even to death on the cross. Therefore God has highly exalted him and bestowed on him the name which is above every name, that at the name of Jesus every knee should bow . . . and every tongue confess that Jesus Christ is Lord, to the glory of God the father. [Therefore] . . . Rejoice in the Lord always; again I will say, Rejoice. And the peace of God which passes all understanding, will keep your hearts and your minds in Jesus Christ.
>
> PHILIPPIANS 2:5–11 & 4:4 & 7

But there are more, by far, who are against "the Word," then—and now—and Paul could have been talking about our present day when he wrote, "For many of whom I have often told you and now tell you even with tears, live as enemies of the cross of Christ. Their end is destruction, and they glory in their shame . . ." So, he reminds the Philippians—and us—that our duty is honor: "Finally brethren, whatever is true, whatever is honorable . . . just . . . pure . . . lovely . . . gracious, if there is any excellence . . . anything worthy of praise, think about these things. What you have learned and received . . . heard and seen in me do; and the God of peace will be with you." And he closes his letter with special greetings from the Christians in Rome: ". . . all the saints greet you . . . especially those of Caesar's household."

Philippians from a
3rd century Greek manuscript

62 Luke abruptly ends his history of the early church (the book of ACTS) with Paul's imprisonment in Rome: perhaps that is when he left Rome. How much longer Paul remained is unknown but there is good reason to believe that he underwent a trial of some sort, and for whatever reason was released. Perhaps he was, again, acquitted of wrong doing; or perhaps what amounted to a "statute of limitations" ran out, none of his accusers came forth to press charges against him, and so, he eventually was freed . . . to carry on his missionary work. The third century Christian historian, Eusebius, writes:

> There is evidence that, having then been brought to trial, the apostle again set out on the ministry of preaching . . . Listen to the testimony on this point [in Paul's own words]: "At my first trial nobody supported me . . . But the Lord stood by me and gave me strength, that through me the message might be fully proclaimed in the hearing of the whole pagan world. Thus I was rescued out of the lion's mouth." The reference (the lion's mouth) being apparently to Nero, because of his beastial cruelty.   Eusebius, HISTORY OF THE CHURCH, 22:5
>
> and II TIMOTHY 4:18

If Eusebius is correct, Paul may, by this time, be starting out on another missionary journey, this time to Spain . . . and maybe beyond.

. . . Those Jews in Jerusalem who had harassed Paul and had him arrested, have turned their animosity to James the Younger, brother of the Lord (which relation, says the historian, Origen, implies "not so much nearness of blood . . . as it does . . . agreement of . . . preaching.) The leading figure and first bishop of Jerusalem, James is so highly respected and revered for having "scaled the heights of philosophy and religion," according to Eusebius, that "he alone [is] permitted to enter the Holy place . . . He [only can] enter the sanctuary alone, and [is] often found on his knees beseeching forgiveness for the people . . ." Now calamity strikes, as the Roman governor of Judea, Festus, dies, who had been a fair judge of Paul, "leaving the province without a governor or procurator." Despite the indignation and protests of the fair-minded Jews of the city, according to both Eusebius and Josephus, James is seized and thrown down from the sanctuary parapet; and his attackers begin to stone him. Not dead yet, James pulls himself to his knees and prays, "I beseech thee, Lord God and Father, forgive them; they do not know what they are doing." One among them is a fuller with a cloth-beating club, which he brings down on James' head, killing the much-loved apostle instantly, whose only crime was that he loved the Lord. His murder will not go unavenged, and will bring terrible consequences in just a few years.

Nineteen hundred and forty years from now, a limestone ossuary, or bone box will come to the world's attention in Israel inscribed with the Hebrew words "Ya'akov bar Yosef akhui diYeshua" or, in English, "James, son of Joseph, brother of Jesus." It will make headlines worldwide, and instantly be called, by some, one of the most momentous archeological finds in history, dating to less than 30 years after Jesus' own death and with His name carved in stone. The ossuary—20" long, 10" wide and 12" high—was found by a so-called artifact looter, and so its contents and original site are unknown, and its authenticity is in question for, some say, there is evidence of modern tampering either in the patina, the inscription or the stone, itself. Where the ossuary of the High Priest Caiaphas, the instigator of Jesus' death had been elaborately ornate, as befitted one of so exalted a worldly position (See: A.D. 32), the ossuary of James is completely free of decoration. James was after all, the most humble and frugal of men, devoting his life, not to ostentation, but to prayer, fasting and serving his brother/his Lord.

With James' death do the Christians begin to understand and accept the knowledge that there will be no second coming during their life-times, and the epistles from here on will reflect that knowledge, encouraging life-styles for long lives: marriage, families, children. Among other instructions for church organization, Paul will now say that a man must "have many years of experience" before being named a bishop.

63   An earthquake strikes southern Italy and causes a volcano named Vesuvius to smoke and tremble. It will continue to rumble warnings for the next 16 years, but the Romans who live in nearby towns will just learn to live with it. Some of the nearby towns, or cities, are Stabia, Herculaneum and Pompeii, a sophisticated, cosmopolitan seaside resort area of luxurious villas, shopping centers, formal gardens and recreation areas which attracts tourists from far and wide. Vesuvius is one of the attractions.

64   The heavy hand of Imperial Rome is heaviest in Judea where the "stiff-necked" people just will not give up. Jewish zealots repeatedly revolt against Roman occupation. The Jewish historian, Joseph Ben Matthais, or Josephus, is now governor of Galilee and one of the Jews' ablest generals. He is also working on what will be a 20 volume history which he calls the ANTIQUITIES OF THE JEWS. It begins with the creation of the world and con-

tinues right up to this very time. Josephus will have much to write about in the next few years, for Judea is the only corner of the empire that the Romans cannot handle: the Jews can get upset over the smallest things, like setting a statue of the immortal god, Nero in that empty room they call the "Holy of Holies." The riot and bloodshed that incident brings about causes Josephus to travel to Rome to plead for the Jews and try to make the Emperor understand them.

Coin of Nero

But Nero doesn't bother himself too much with minor problems like that, though, because he is a very busy man. Not only is he an Olympic champion, now, but an actor and singer, and he plans great spectacles in the woods . . . but Tacitus says ". . . even at this pleasures . . . Nero took no vacation from crime." He has one of his advisors executed on a charge of keeping his great wealth too long by living to a "prolonged old age," and another because he could trace his family back to Augustus, himself. Then he revels in a "notorious banquet" given by Tigellinus on gold and ivory lakerafts "rowed by degenerates, assorted [by] age and vice."

> On the quays were brothels stocked with high-ranking ladies . . . Opposite them could be seen naked prostitutes, indecently posturing and gesturing . . . Nero was already corrupted by every lust, natural and unnatural . . . But now . . . he went through a formal wedding ceremony with one of the perverted gang . . . bridal veil . . . dowry, marriage bed, wedding torches, all were there.   Tacitus, ANNALS, 14:15:37

Twice he marries males, and Suetonius tells his story like this:

> Having tried to turn the boy Sporus into a girl by castration, he went through a wedding ceremony with him—dowry, bridal veil and all . . . [an] amusing joke is still going the rounds . . . [that] the world would have been a happier place had Nero's father . . . married that sort of wife.   Setonius, LIVES, Nero:28

Nero's delicate sensibilities are offended by the city of Rome: its dark, crowded streets and the filthy, teeming tenements with their shiftless rabble. The smell sometimes wafts up as far as his villa, and he wishes aloud that he could build a new Rome. And here, Tacitus says, simply, "Disaster followed."

64, July 19.   Fire breaks out in the shops and stalls that adjoin the Circus Maximus, so fierce and terrible (fanned by the wind) . . . "it swept the whole length of the circus . . ."

> Whether it was accidental . . . [or] criminal on the part of the emperor . . . It began in the Circus . . . Breaking out in shops selling inflammable goods, and fanned by the wind . . . the conflagration instantly grew and swept the whole length of the Circus. There . . . [was no] obstruction which could arrest it. First [it] swept . . . over the level spaces. Then . . . climbed the hills . . . The city's narrow winding streets . . . encouraged its progress. Terrified, shrieking women, helpless old and young, people intent on their own safety . . . [or] unselfishly supporting invalids . . . all heightened the confusion. When people looked

> back, menacing flames sprang up before them or outflanked them. Nobody dared fight the flames. Attempts to do so were prevented by menacing gangs. Torches . . . were openly thrown in, by men crying that they acted under orders. Perhaps they had received orders.
> Tacitus, ANNALS 14:15:38

Tacitus may not be certain that Nero started the fire, but Suetonius harbors no doubts at all:

> Pretending to be disgusted by the drab old buildings and narrow, winding streets of Rome, he brazenly set fire to the city; and though a group of ex-consuls caught his attendants, armed with . . . blazing torches, trespassing on their property, they dared not interfere. He . . . knocked down . . . walls with siege-engines [and] set the interiors ablaze . . . Suetonius, THE XII CAESARS, Nero:38

For five days the fire rages, swallowing the city up and killing thousands. The emperor, away at Antium, returns to Rome only when the fire reaches his own mansion—the Golden House—which it destroys. For the "relief of the homeless," he opens the Field of Mars, numerous public buildings and even his own gardens . . . and distributes food and aid. But even these measures "earn him no gratitude" for Nero is not able to silence the rumors going around that . . .

> . . . while the city was burning, Nero had gone on his private stage and, comparing modern calamities with ancient, had sung of the destruction of Troy.   Tacitus, ANNALS 14:15:40
>
> Nero watched the conflagration from the Tower of Maecenas, enraptured by what he called "the beauty of the flames"; then put on his tragedian's costume and sang THE SACK OF ILIUM from beginning to end.   *ibid.*

Just when the fire is "finally stamped out," it breaks out again, with less loss of life but even worse loss of property, temples, monuments and mansions, many of which had been built and stood since the days of the kings!

> . . . the terror lasted for six days and seven nights (altogether) . . . Nero's men destroyed not only a vast number of . . . mansions which had belonged to famous generals and were still decorated with their triumphal trophies; temples, too . . . dedicated by the kings . . . in fact, very ancient monument[s] of historical interest that had hitherto survived . . . Then he opened a Fire Relief Fund . . . which bled the provincials white and practically beggared all private citizens.   *ibid.*

This fire causes even more resentment and suspicion because it broke out on the estate of Nero's henchman, Tigellinus. Guilty or not, Nero needs a scapegoat and none is more convenient than the sect of "Christians," members of the new religion that have "infiltrated" right into Nero's own household.

> Nero fabricated scapegoats—and punished with every refinement the notoriously depraved Christians (as they were popularly called.) Their originator, Christ, had been exe-

cuted in Tiberius' reign by the governor of Judaea, Pontius Pilate. But in spite of this temporary setback the deadly superstition had broken out afresh, not only in Judaea (where the mischief had started) but even in Rome. All degraded and shameful practices collect and flourish in the capital.

First, Nero had self-acknowledged Christians arrested. Then, on their information, large numbers of others were condemned . . . Their deaths were made farcical. Dressed in wild animal skins, they were torn to pieces by dogs, or crucified, or made into torches to be ignited after dark as substitutes for daylight. Nero provided his gardens for the spectacle, and exhibited displays in the Circus, at which he mingled with the crowd—or stood in a chariot, dressed as a charioteer. Despite their guilt as Christians, and the ruthless punishment it deserved, the victims were pitied. For it was felt that they were being sacrificed to one man's brutality rather than to the national interest.   Tacitus, ANNALS 14:15:42–44

Mosaic from Pompeii

These reports by Tacitus are among the first written references to Christianity by a non-Christian historian, and the only reference in Latin literature to Pontius Pilate's role in Jesus' death. Tacitus' hostility to the Christian faith at least did not keep him from reporting the details of the fire and its aftermath. But the Christian historian, Eusebius, writing 200 years after Tacitus (and basing his work on earlier reports) tells it from a different perspective:

When Nero's power was . . . firmly established he gave himself up to unholy practices and took up arms against the God of the Universe. To describe the monster of depravity that he became lies outside the scope of [this work.] Many writers have recorded . . . his perverse and extraordinary madness . . . the senseless destruction of innumerable lives . . . he was the first of the emperors to be declared enemy of the worship of Almighty God.
Eusebius, HISTORY OF THE CHRISTIAN CHURCH, 25:1

To this the Roman/Christian historian Tertullian refers [thus]:

That such a man was author of our chastisement fills us with pride. For anyone who knows him can understand that anything not supremely good would never have been condemned by Nero.   Tertullian, DEFENSE OF THE CHRISTIAN FAITH, 5

The apocryphal EPISTLES OF PAUL AND SENECA portray Seneca's disgust and loathing for the man he had once served; and Paul's farewell to him:

Seneca: . . . my dearest Paul . . . I am extremely concerned and grieved that your innocence should bring you into suffering . . . the frequent burnings of Rome, the cause is manifest. The Christians and Jews are indeed commonly punished . . . but that impious miscreant who delights in murders and butcheries [is guilty] and disguises his villainies with lies . . .

> Paul: I am thereby assured that I sow the most strong seed in a fertile soil . . . which shall increase and bring forth fruit to eternity. Farewell . . . Seneca, who art most dear to us.
>
> The (probably not authentic) EPISTLES OF PAUL AND SENECA

The government building which held Jewish records is destroyed in the fire. It is, of course, not known whether there ever existed any official written documents concerning the birth, life or death of Jesus of Nazareth but, if there were, they probably were destroyed in this fire, thus preventing forever, any official Roman notice of *"Christus."*

. . . According to tradition, the Apostle Peter has been in Rome for some time, and is there now with his young companions John Mark and Silvanus (Silas), a Greek speaking Roman citizen, and frequent traveling companion of Paul. The horrors of Nero's persecutions are very real to Peter and make him all the more aware of persecutions in other places as well. The first letter of PETER is addressed to Christians in Asia Minor. It is generally (but not universally) believed to be Silas' highly literate rendering of Peter's dictation, and a true account of the faith of the old apostle.

I PETER

Epistle of Peter — Written in Greek,   c. A.D. 64

"Beloved, do not be surprised at the fiery ordeal which comes upon you to prove you," Peter says in his letter, ". . . But rejoice in so far as you share Christ's sufferings." Scholars believe that Peter dictated this letter to Paul's companion, Silas, because of his own statement in it and, also, because it is written in well educated Greek, far better than Peter, himself, would have known. He can see there are hard times ahead, and warns the "beloved brethren" not to be surprised at the "fiery ordeal" ahead . . . but to "maintain good conduct" so none can speak against them as wrongdoers, ". . . let none of you suffer

St. Peter

as a murderer, thief or mischief maker, yet if one suffers as a Christian, let him not be ashamed, but under that name let him glorify God. For," he adds, it "it is God's will that by doing right you should put to silence the ignorance of foolish men."   2:15, 4:12,13

In his letter the old apostle, he whom Jesus called "the Rock," exhorts his brethren to love, godliness, patience, obedience, and always hope in Christ, even while "your adversary the devil prowls around like a roaring lion, seeking someone to devour . . . Be subject for the Lord's sake to every human institution, whether it be the emperor . . . or governments . . . live as free men, yet without using your freedom as a pretext for evil but live as servants of God. Honor all men. Love the Brotherhood. Fear God." And as one last precaution, Peter adds, "Honor the Emperor."   2:17

The emperor already has grandiose plans for the building of the "new Rome," including ordinances on how homes are to be constructed, of what material, how far apart, where streets shall be and how wide, and where firewalls and water supplies shall be. His own palace, instead of a "Golden House," will, this time, be a spectacle of nature with woods, fields, lakes, canals and streams. With his "love of the impossible," as Tacitus calls it, he will outdo nature, itself.

. . . A second letter, using Peter's name as the title, is written, not at this time, but much later.

II PETER

Epistle of "Peter" — Written in Greek,   c. A.D. 150?

Ever since the time of Simon Magus, or "Magician," (A.D. 32 & ACTS 8:4–25) heresies have sprung up of all sorts, some saying that Jesus was not really "born," He just "appeared," some that He was just a mere man and not the Messiah, or, yes, the Messiah but not a real man; and yet others claim that there is no connection between Christianity and Judaism; it is a newly "invented" religion, totally apart. All these heresies, plus the constant turmoil between Jews and Romans are creating a bubbling cauldron just about ready to boil over; and the writer of II PETER warns of troubled times ahead. He could be—and in effect is—talking to our own age today:

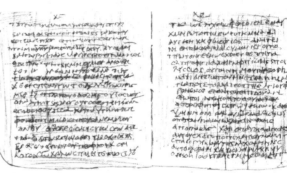

II Peter 1:16–22 ms. from AD 300

> . . . there will be false teachers among you, who will secretly bring in destructive heresies, even denying the Master who brought them . . . men will follow licentiousness, and because of them the way of truth will be reviled. They have eyes full of adultery, insatiable for sin. They entice unsteady souls . . . they promise freedom, but . . . are themselves slaves of corruption.   II PETER 2:1–3, 14,15

To "escape from the corruption that is in the world," II PETER says, "make every effort to supplement your faith with virtue, virtue with knowledge, knowledge with self-control . . . steadfastness . . . godliness . . . brotherly affection . . . [and finally] . . . love," a beautiful progression of virtues from a master writer. Although the salutation reads "Simon Peter," and the writer says that "this is the second letter . . . I have written you," II PETER is generally believed to have been written long after the apostle's death by a loyal disciple, to honor his name, an ancient and honorable practice.

The writer warns, also, against misinterpreting the letters of "our beloved brother Paul," as do the "ignorant and unstable" who twist them "to their own destruction." Just as the ancient prophets talked of the "Day of the Lord" so, also, does II PETER, and says

> it will be better for those who have never heard of "the Way" than for those who have known but turned away. (2:21) For, he says, the (gospels and epistles) are NOT "cleverly devised myths," but were written because "we were eye-witnesses to the majesty of Christ." And for those who despair of Christ's second coming, he reminds them of PSALM 90:4 ". . . do not ignore this one fact, beloved, that WITH THE LORD ONE DAY IS AS A THOUSAND YEARS AND A THOUSAND YEARS A DAY."

64   The venerable old apostle Simon Peter—Jesus' disciple from the very beginning 34 years ago—is killed, one of the hundreds of victims of Nero's vicious persecutions; and over

Peter's crucifixion from an ancient manuscript

the years much legend will grow up about his death. One ancient document called the *ACTA PETRI*, or ACTS OF PETER, although considered apocryphal and unauthentic, tells a touching story that has found a permanent place in Christian legend. Peter, the *ACTA* says, is in Rome during the terror, flees the city for safety from Nero's mad wrath and, on the Appian Way, is stopped by the Lord Jesus. Startled, Peter asks, "*Quo vadis, Domini?* Where are you going, Lord?" "To Rome, to be crucified again," the Master replies. Mortally ashamed at his weakness in betraying his Lord a fourth time, Peter returns to Rome, is arrested and (according, now, to Eusebius) asks to be hung head down on the cross because he is not fit to die the same way as did his Lord.

The letter to the HEBREWS is written.

HEBREWS

Epistle of unknown author — Written in Greek,   c. A.D. 64

"In many and various ways God spoke of old to our fathers by the prophets, but in these last days he has spoken to us by His son." Thus does the author of HEBREWS begin: and then his whole epistle explains what he means. Abraham, Joseph, Moses, all the fathers understood God by faith, he says, but Christ is greater than all. "What more shall I say?" he asks, "for time would fail me to tell of Gideon, Barak, Samson, Jephtha, of David and Samuel and the prophets [and their mighty deeds . . . their suffering . . . imprisonment, stoning, scourging, being sawn in two . . .] And by all these, though well attested by their faith, did not receive what was promised, SINCE GOD HAD FORESEEN SOMETHING BETTER FOR US."   11:40

Fragment of Hebrews 3–4 century

That something better is Jesus Christ, HEBREWS says, in a profound spelling-out of His superiority over all things: angels, prophets and Old Testament heroes and rulers; for in Jesus is Judaism brought to its perfect fulfillment. Higher than the angels, higher than Moses the mediator of the LAW, Jesus is now the High Priest, the only sacrifice God will accept, not animals or "things," but His own son. The great theme of HEBREWS is faith which echoes time and again. By faith did Abraham leave his home for an unknown land and offer up his son; by faith did Moses lead the Hebrews out of Egypt; Sarah, Rahab, Isaac, Jacob, all lived by their faith, but now that faith is to be in God's son, Jesus Christ, and the true Day of Atonement is, now, the day Jesus was crucified . . . the "mediator of a new covenant."   (12:24)

> But now hath he obtained a more excellent ministry . . . the mediator of a better covenant . . . established upon better promises. For if that first covenant had been fault-less, then should no place have been sought for the second.   HEBREWS 8:6,7
>
> Behold, the days are coming, says the LORD, when I will make a new covenant with the house of Israel . . . not like the covenant I made with their fathers . . . which they broke . . .   JEREMIAH 31:31,32 (See 605 B.C.)

Mosaic of Christ from Cefalù, Sicily

Some scholars think HEBREWS was written by a Hellenistic Jewish Christian because, read aloud, it sounds less like a letter than an oration in Greek philosophical style and, in fact, its authorship (but not its authenticity) has been questioned from earliest times. Clement of Alexandria thought it was written by Paul; Tertullian said Barnabas; while others named Clement of Rome or even Luke writing down Paul's thoughts. Centuries after its writing the German reformer, Martin Luther will attribute it to Apollos, one of Paul's friends, who Luke in ACTS called "an eloquent man . . . mighty in the scriptures." 18:24 But Origen of Alexandria summed it up by saying that the author is known only to God. Whoever he was, he wrote with great clarity and precision, his thoughts highly reasoned. On suffering, he said, "My son, do not regard lightly the discipline of the Lord nor lose courage when you are punished by Him. For the Lord disciplines him whom he loves, and chastises every [one] he receives." 12:5 His touching exhortation at the end reminds the Hebrews (and us, today) to ". . . let brotherly love continue. Do not neglect to show hospitality to strangers, for thereby some have entertained angels unawares."   13:2

65   The epistle of JUDE is written.

JUDE

Epistle of Jude — Written in Creek,   c. A.D. 65

Jude introduces himself at the beginning of his 25 verse letter as "a servant of Jesus Christ and brother of James," as authoritative a voice as can be. It may be a short letter, but it is powerful, with a monumental message that speaks directly to our Brave New 20th Century World, as well as his own. "Our Lord Jesus Christ gave us the faith ONCE FOR ALL TIME," Jude says, loud and clear. It is not to be changed through the years, tampered with, re-written or twisted to conform to modern mores or personal preferences . . . and Jude has good reason to worry . . .

> "Beloved," he writes, "being very eager to write to you of our common salvation, I found it necessary to write appealing to you to contend for the faith which was once for all delivered to the saints. For admission has been secretly gained by some . . . who pervert the grace of our God into licentiousness and deny our only Master and Lord, Jesus Christ . . . these men defile the flesh . . . Woe to them . . . you must remember, beloved, the predictions of the apostles . . . [who] said to you, 'in the last time there will be scoffers . . . following their own ungodly passions . . . and setting up divisions amongst the faithful.'" Jude says these "false teachers" are "fruitless trees . . . convince some, save some . . . and on some have mercy. It is these people who set up divisions, worldly people, devoid of the spirit," But, Jude says, "to him who is able to keep you from falling and present you without blemish . . . to the only God . . . our savior Jesus Christ . . . be glory, majesty, dominion and authority now and forever. Amen."

. . . Sixty-nine years old, now, Seneca has been living in virtual exile for three years, working on his writings, and knowing that his life is in danger from Nero's madness at any time. But he is not afraid to die. With his enormous fortune he may not have lived like a stoic, but he will certainly die like one.

> . . . you mustn't worry as if you were having to make a great decision. There's nothing so very great about living . . . the great thing is to die in a manner which is honorable, enlightened and courageous . . . [But] live as if you are on public view, as if someone could peer into our innermost heart . . . which someone can! For what is to be gained concealing things from man when nothing is barred from God? He is present in our minds, attendant in our thoughts. * Of this one thing make sure against your dying day—that your faults die before you do.   Seneca, LETTER FROM A STOIC

65   Nero has finally gone too far. The senate has kept quiet as long as it can and now, a conspiracy is organized. The senators will kill this Caesar at the capitol just as the first Caesar was killed; only this time the hatred of the emperor is universal and the number of conspirators is great. But the servant of one man, hoping for rich reward, reveals the plot to Nero, and thus begins a bloodbath that numbs the mind. So many men, and women, are betrayed and betray each other that, Tacitus says, they ". . . gave away their fellow conspirators wholesale . . ." and a thoroughly frightened Nero increases his guard to where ". . . the whole of Rome was virtually put in custody."

> Line after line of chained men were dragged to their destination at the gates of Nero's garden . . . [there] guilt was deduced from affability to a conspirator, or a chance conversation or meeting on entrance to a party or a show together.　Tacitus, ANNALS 15; 5 7

More blood is shed than in many battles, almost wiping out the aristocracy of Rome. One death that Nero had long wanted is that philosophical thorn in his side, Seneca, who obeys Nero's order with the same stoic calm he had believed and taught. Seneca opens his own veins but, being old and "lean from austere living," the blood runs slowly and he uses the time to dictate a treatise on morality to his secretaries . . . and to comfort his servants and friends. "Surely," he says, "nobody was unaware that Nero was cruel! After murdering his mother and brother, it only remained for him to kill his teacher . . ." He is given hemlock to drink—the same that killed Socrates—but it doesn't work, and to end his suffering. Tacitus says in his chilling account, is finally "suffocated in a vapor bath." His body is cremated "without ceremony in accordance with his own instructions . . . written at the height of his wealth and power." His brother Gallio—the apostle Paul's sympathetic judge—is not immune from Nero, either, and is ". . . denounced as a public enemy and patricide . . ." a strange charge by a man who murdered his own mother, brother and wife.

But Nero is unmoved by references to his bestial crimes: what really hurts him is being told he is a bad actor, singer or musician, and he has one nobleman executed, who fearlessly stands before him and says:

> . . . I was as loyal as any of your soldiers as long as you deserved affection. I began detesting you when you murdered your mother and wife and became a charioteer, actor and incendiary!　Subrius Flavus, quoted by Tacitus, ANNALS 15:67

And as the blood flows from his veins, another voices thoughts that echo those of Peter and Paul, themselves . . .

> . . . You have been born . . . into an age when examples of fortitude may be a useful support.　Thrasea Paius, *ibid.* 16:32

The conspiracy over and the danger past—so Nero thinks—he gets back to important matters, the five-yearly games, and he declares that there should be no favoritism: he will "compete on equal terms and rely on the conscience of the judges to award him the prize he deserves." For Nero, the artist, has come out of the Roman closet now, and he wants everybody to benefit from his genius. His playing on the lyre, singing, acting, recitation of poetry . . . and groveling for awards scandalizes conservative Romans and disgusts the liberals; but Nero doesn't see it that way, and so that no one be cheated of the pleasure of his talent, he makes attendance at his concerts compulsory!

> . . . absence was even more dangerous than attendance, since there were many spies . . . noting who was there—and noting whether their expressions were pleased [or not] . . . offenders received instant punishment.　Tacitus, ANNALS

Suetonius tells it like this:

> . . . no one was allowed to leave the theater even for the most urgent reasons [including] childbirth . . . some even feigned death . . . it was . . . a worse danger to be absent from the show, as many "informers" secretly . . . scrutinize names and faces . . . and note the delight or disgust of the company . . . Suetonius, THE HISTORIES, Nero 23

One whose face is scrutinized and observed to be dozing is hauled off to immediate execution, only to be saved by the "intercession of the well-disposed," is the famous general, Titus Flavius Vespasianus. In only five years Vespasian will become the ninth emperor of Rome.

. . . Still enamored of his wife, Poppaea, Nero is delighted even more that she is to bear him a child, an heir to the throne. But coming home drunk and in a foul mood from one of his infamous stage performances, Nero flies into a rage when Poppaea says the wrong thing to him, and he kicks her, and the baby inside her, to death. At Poppaea's funeral Nero speaks the eulogy, saying how fortunate she was to have carried his child.

Nero's next victim is his own "Arbiter of Good Taste," Petronius Arbiter, upon whom he had relied for so long for, as Tacitus says, ". . . to the blasé emperor nothing was smart and elegant unless Petronius had given his approval." Petronius opens his own veins, but not before he gets a little bit of revenge . . .

> Petronius wrote out a list of Nero's sensualities—giving names of each male and female bed-partner and details of every lubricious novelty—and sent it under seal to Nero. Then Petronius broke his signet ring. Nero could not imagine how his nocturnal ingenuities were known. He suspected (a senator's wife) who knew all his obscenities from personal experience . . . she was exiled. Tacitus, ANNALS 16:18

66   The apostle Paul returns from Spain and continues his missionary work in Rome. He writes his last three letters to his friends Titus (the first "bishop" of Crete) and Timothy (first bishop of Ephesus.) Of course, it should be remembered here that Paul may have died in Nero's first persecution of 64, and these letters would then have been written by someone else, in his name. Still, they are very "like him" in their warmth and concern, for his friends and "his" churches.

TITUS

Epistle of Paul — Written in Greek,   c. A.D. 66

Probably a Greek, Titus was a close friend of Paul's, who mentioned him often in his other letters. Paul gave the responsibility of organizing the church on the island of Crete to Titus, and he became its first bishop. Paul tells Titus, "This is why I left you in Crete, that you might amend what was defective . . . teach sound doctrine. Remind [the brethren] to be submissive to rulers and authorities, to be obedient, ready for any honest work; to be gentle and show perfect courtesy toward all men . . . I desire you to insist on these things."

Twelve years ago, when Paul wrote his first letter to the Corinthians, he—and the church—still expected the Lord's second coming at any time; and warned against making long term plans, including . . . marriage.

> . . . in view of the impending distress it is well . . . to remain as [one] is . . . Are you [married? Do not seek to be free. Are you free from [marriage]? Do not seek marriage. I mean, brethren, the appointed time has grown very short . . . I want you to be free from anxieties . . . and married [people] are anxious about worldly affairs . . . I say this, to secure your undivided devotion to the Lord.   I CORINTHIANS 7:25–35

Now, with James' and Peter's deaths and the grim reality of persecution from a hostile state, Paul, and the other elders understand that the church has a future . . . probably a long, hard one, and they had better prepare.

I TIMOTHY

Epistle of Paul — Written in Greek,   c. A.D. 66

Paul met Timothy on his first missionary journey in Timothy's hometown of Lystra in Galacia/Asia Minor, and they remained close friends. The son of a Greek father and Jewish/Christian mother, Timothy was already a Christian when he and Paul met, and he finished the first journey and the second, also, then being joined by Luke. In this letter Paul calls Timothy "my true child in the faith . . . my son. Great indeed," Paul says, "is the mystery of our religion, but believe . . . there is one God, and there is one mediator between God and men, the man Christ Jesus who gave himself as a ransom for all; and one household of God, which is the church of the living God, the pillar and bulwark of the truth."

Paul has come to accept that Jesus' second coming will not happen soon, and in this letter he changes his teaching on marriage and families. In A.D. 54 he had told the Corinthians that time spent on worldly concerns could better be spent preparing for eternity. But now that has changed, and Paul tells Timothy that he wants Christian families strong, so they "give no occasion to the adversary to speak reproachfully of them . . . if any provide not for his own, and especially for those of his own house, he hath denied the faith and is worse than an infidel. But thou, O man of God flee [the snares of lust, greed and evil and] follow after righteousness, godliness, faith, love, patience, meekness. Fight the good fight of faith. Lay hold on eternal life . . . in the sight of God . . . and before Jesus Christ . . ." And Paul talks of practical, day-to-day administration of the new churches: the qualifications for bishops, deacons and elders. Being a bishop is a "noble task," he says, "one that must be above reproach, the husband of one wife . . . who must manage his own household well [else] how can he manage a church?" Twice he warns of bishops falling into the condemnation/snares of the devil. As for the rich of this world, "charge them not to be haughty," Paul says, "for the love of money is the root of all evil, but to be rich in good deeds." Concerned for Timothy's health, he suggests, "a little wine for the sake of your stomach and frequent ailments."   3:6–6:11

Paul has often referred to the "sufferings" of "this present time," and now, A.D. 66, these sufferings are terrible—and about to get worse: official government persecution of the struggling young church by a hostile state; wars and rumors of wars being waged by a most un-military "leader" whose main talents are obscenity, sin and scandal, and has, through crime and corruption, brought low in just a few years the empire Claudius had tried to return to decency. Paul, now back in Rome for the last time—the very heart of worldly evil—writes a second letter to Timothy which almost could be called his "Last Will and Testament."

II TIMOTHY

Epistle of Paul — Written in Greek, c. A.D. 66

Paul addresses this, his last letter, to "Timothy, my beloved child," whose tears, at last parting, he remembers. "I long day and night to see you, that I may be filled with joy." He urges him to be steady, endure suffering, do the work of an evangelist, fulfill your ministry, and "do not be ashamed . . . of testifying to our Lord, nor of me, his prisoner. God did not give us a spirit of timidity but. . .of power [to] ". . . be strong in the grace that is in Christ Jesus. An athlete is not crowned unless he competes according to the rules." It seems almost as if Paul had precisely the 20th century in mind when he wrote these words about a "new age" to come:

> For the time is coming when people will not endure sound teaching, but . . . will accumulate for themselves teachers to suit their own likings, and will turn away from listening to the truth and wander into myths.   II TIMOTHY 4:3

Paul knows that his "time of departure" is almost come, that he is "already on the point of being sacrificed," and that he cannot escape the persecutions any more than Peter did; but he looks forward to the "crown of righteousness . . . that the Lord, the righteous judge, will award to me . . . and to all who have loved his appearing." Paul sounds anxious and lonely in this his last letter, and he entreats Timothy twice to ". . . do your best to come to me soon. All have deserted me. Luke alone is with me. Get Mark and bring him with you . . . bring the cloak I left . . . at Troas, also the books, and above all, the parchments . . ."   4:13

There is some very ancient—and some modern—scholarly speculation that the cloak, or wrap, for which Paul asked Timothy was not a garment to wear, but a wrapper, or carrying case, for his letters; and that his need for Mark was for Mark to take the then-wrapped books and parchments away from sure destruction in Rome . . . perhaps to John in Ephesus, who could begin to compile them into a "New" Testament.

Paul finishes his letter telling Timothy that while the Lord stood by him and gave him strength "at his first defense," and he was "rescued from the lion's mouth," the lion/Nero will have his way; and after sending greetings to his many friends, he asks Timothy, poignantly, to ". . . do your best to come . . . before winter."

66 to 70   There are more Jewish uprisings and revolts against the stern Roman occupation in Judea, and the repercussions are not just local, for there are Jews and Jewish partisans in many parts of the empire, and the rebellion is spreading with alarming speed. Finally realizing that it is not just another minor disturbance, Nero sends Vespasian and Titus, father and son, his two best generals, to the scene. Moving in their most powerful war machines, they surround the city and put it under siege. The siege of Jerusalem will continue for four long years! The Jewish historian, Joseph Ben Matthias, or Josephus, having been in Rome on an unsuccessful mission to plead for the Jews, returns with Titus, now, to act as his interpreter.

67   Just as he expected, <u>the Apostle Paul is arrested again in Rome . . . and beheaded, a martyr to his Lord, his faith and his church.</u> He is buried in a cemetery near the left bank of the Tiber River, but his body will later be taken to the catacombs under the Appian Way. Paul traveled well over 10,000 miles (and perhaps as many as 25,000) on his missionary journeys, and the church today would not be a universal church FOR ALL PEOPLE were it not for him. Its universality was one of the first doctrines Paul taught:

From an ancient manuscript

There is neither Jew nor Greek, bond or free . . . male nor female, for ye are all one in Christ Jesus.   GALATIANS 3:28

Where the Greek philosophers had passively approved slavery, sodomy, incest, infanticide and abortion, Paul preached LIFE . . . everlasting!

For the wages of sin is death, but the gift of God is eternal life through Jesus Christ our Lord.   ROMANS 6:23

Revenge is sweet, philosophy taught, but Paul, like Jesus, said, "Forgive . . ."

. . . be ye kind to one another, tenderhearted, forgiving one another, as God in Christ forgave you. EPH 4:32 You who were dead in sin, God made alive with him, having forgiven us our trespasses, having canceled the bond of legal demands; this he set aside, nailing it to the cross.   COLOSSIANS 2:13,14

And while philosophy advocated the supremacy of the "state" over individual freedom or rights, Paul preached LIBERTY from God's own Word:

Proclaim Liberty throughout all the land unto all the inhabitants thereof. LEVITICUS 25:10 *
Stand fast therefore in the Liberty wherewith Christ hath made us free.   GALATIANS 5:1

But with liberty comes responsibility and Paul warned:

> . . . only use not liberty for an occasion to the the flesh but by love [to] serve one another . . . Bear ye one another's burdens . . . [and] be not weary in well-doing [but] do good unto all men. GALATIANS 5:13, 6:2,9,10 . . . [and do it cheerfully, for] God loveth a cheerful giver.
> 2 CORINTHIANS 9:7

From these maxims, and from Paul's own "three cardinal virtues"—FAITH, HOPE and LOVE/CHARITY—will come the schools, hospitals, homes for the homeless and the fatherless, all the charitable foundations and institutions of Western Civilization, oases of care, compassion, healing and salvation through the religion of Jesus Christ. And when the day finally comes for slavery to be abolished, Paul's voice will be heard loud and clear:

> I am sending [your former slave] back to you . . . no longer as a slave, but as a beloved brother. PHILEMON 1:12

Wall fresco from
Rome 3rd century

It is a far cry from the reality of the degraded and depraved world all around him . . . and Paul's last gallant, noble words in his last letter have come ringing down the centuries, an inspiration to faith and dedication to Christians for all time . . . a glorious epitaph for the Apostle to the Gentiles:

> For I am already on the point of being sacrificed: the time of my departure has come. <u>I HAVE FOUGHT THE GOOD FIGHT: I HAVE FINISHED THE RACE. I HAVE KEPT THE FAITH.</u>
> Paul of Tarsus, II TIMOTHY 4:6–7

There is some evidence that Paul did, in fact, realize his missionary goal of visiting Spain, and possibly even Britain, where he could visit Christians already there. There are legends about him from Marsailles, France to Yngs Avalon in Britain; one that says he founded the great abbey at Bangor Iscod. Before the legends are dismissed as mere myth, Plato's admonission should be remembered that, "Every myth has its truth." Twenty-nine years from now Clement, Bishop of Rome, will write a letter to the church in Corinth (one of the first churches Paul founded) and say that Paul . . .

> . . . was the herald of the Gospel in the West as well as the East, and enjoyed the illustrious reputation of . . . teaching the whole world to be righteous. And after he had been to the extremity of the West, he suffered martyrdom before the sovereigns of mankind.
> Clement I, Bishop of Rome, EPISTLE TO THE CORINTHIANS, c. 5

Latter-day Biblical revisionists, seeking to "water down" the Holy Scriptures to suit personal political agendas and "isms" will say that Paul took the pure and simple teachings of the pastoral Jesus and corrupted them into a chauvinistic theology to suit himself. But

Paul's writings are now, in this Year of the Lord, A.D. 67, complete and in wide circulation, held in high esteem and lauded by other epistle writers. In the years ahead, when the Gospel writers and the early church fathers and historians all play their parts in this great drama, they will have every opportunity to declare Paul a heretic and reject his works as "un-Christian." But that will not happen. Instead, they will honor Paul as a true and faithful servant; treasure and revere the works of their "beloved brother" as authoritative and indispensable to the Faith, and warn the "unlearned and unstable" that they distort Paul's scriptures "unto their own destruction."

> And [consider] that the long-suffering of our Lord is salvation; even as our beloved brother Paul . . . according to the wisdom given unto him hath written unto you.　　II PETER 3:15

Just 30 years from now, before the first century ends, Clement I, the fourth bishop of Rome, will call Paul "heroic," a "noble example . . ."

Paul

> . . . the greatest and most righteous pillar [of the church, who] taught righteousness . . . to the whole world.　　Clement I, EPISTLE TO THE CORINTHIANS 5:2,7

Ignatius, bishop of Antioch, will call Paul a "real saint and martyr" and hope that . . .

> . . . when I come to meet God may I follow in [Paul's] footsteps.
> Ignatius, EPISTLE TO THE EPHESIANS 12:2, c. A.D. 107

Polycarp, bishop of Smyrna, who will be born just a few years from now and "know John," will write that.

> . . . the wisdom of the blessed and glorious Paul . . . when . . . present among you face to face . . . taught you accurately and firmly "the word of truth."　　Polycarp, EPISTLE TO THE PHILIPPIANS 3:2 c. A.D. 155

Peter & Paul from 1st century

And in far-away Gaul (today's France) Irenaeus, student of Polycarp and then bishop of Lyons, will write against the heresies of his day (c. A.D. 180) admonitions applicable to our own, about the . . .

> . . .tradition . . . founded and established . . . by those two most glorious apostles Peter and Paul . . . who wished their successors [to be] perfect and irreproachable, since their sound conduct would be a great benefit [to the church], and [their] failure . . . the greatest calamity.　　Irenaeus, AGAINST HERESIES, 3:1,2 c. A.D. 180

67   The Jewish/Roman war is producing, according to Josephus who is recording every detail, "inexpressible calamities." In Caesarea, alone, Herod's beautiful, modern sea-port city, over 20,000 Jews are killed in one hour's time; and Caesarea is not alone.

> It was . . . common to see cities filled with dead bodies, still lying unburied . . . old men, mixed with infants, all scattered about together; women also lay amongst them, without any covering for their nakedness.   Josephus, THE JEWISH WAR, 2:18:2

And the siege of Jerusalem continues. Thousands more Jews have already died there, if not by the sword, by starvation and disease. Those caught trying to escape are crucified or butchered. But the Jews will not surrender God's city.

68   The Romans take control of the desert outpost of the sect of Essene brothers at Qumran. It is not known, today, whether the brothers fled or were wiped out by the army, but their scrolls are hidden safely in caves in the wilderness by the Dead Sea. The Romans know nothing about them. There they will lie, quiet, forgotten and untouched for 2015 years, until A.D. 1947, when a little Arab boy searching for a lost goat, will throw a rock into a cave and hear, to his surprise, the sound of breaking pottery. The several hundred scrolls they find there are the oldest books of the Old Testament in existence. Before this find there were some very old copies in European churches, libraries and monasteries, but the Dead Sea Scrolls are a thousand years older than they, a most important archeological find for Bible scholarship; for word-for-word comparison of the scrolls with present-day texts has provided indisputable proof that the Old Testament has come down through 21 centuries virtually errorless.

. . . All Rome is finally in arms against Nero. Law and order have fallen to chaos throughout the empire; there is mutiny and insubordination in the army, riot and unrest in the streets. The *Pax Romana,* while far from dead, is taking a beating. In Spain the army proclaims General Galba emperor on his promise of rich reward to the legions, and Nero, hearing of it, faints dead away, then flees the city in terror. The Roman Senate condemns him to death *in absentia* and hearing of it, according to Suetonius, he "muttered through his tears . . .

> "Dead! And so great an artist!" While he hesitated a runner brought him a letter [wherein he read that] having been declared a public enemy by the Senate, he would be punished "in ancient style" when arrested . . . in terror he snatched up . . . two daggers . . . but threw them down again . . . moaning about his cowardice, and muttering: "How ugly and vulgar my life has become!"   Suetonius, THE XII CAESARS, Nero:49

But "at last," Suetonius says, "after nearly fourteen years of Nero's misrule, the earth rid herself of him." At age 31, on the anniversary of Octavia's murder Nero commits suicide and ". . . the line of Caesars became extinct."

69   Within months the army, feeling that (1) Galba (notable mainly for his excessive greed and cruelty) reneged on his promises, murders him, touching off what is known as the Year of the Four Emperors. Otho (2) (he who had shared Poppaea's favors with Nero and been

exiled to Spain for having locked Nero out of their mutual bedroom), is now proclaimed emperor, only to have his forces defeated by those of Vitellius (3) general of the legions on the Rhine River in Germany. Degraded toady to three emperors, his boyhood was spent as one of Tiberius' male prostitutes at Capri. (A notorious glutton, it was Vitellius who gave Rome the reputation for exotic—and disgusting—foods like peacock brains and flamingo tongues.) The empire is in a state nearing anarchy. Now the legions under the command of General Vespasian march on Rome: a march of horror, rape, pillage, looting and outrage. But Vespasian, himself, is 1500 miles away from Rome, the commander of the siege of Jerusalem. When his elite guard salutes him as Caesar and Augustus, Vespasian (4), an honorable Roman, decides to return to Rome. He will be its 9th emperor, and his son, Titus, will continue the siege of Jerusalem.

Vespasiam

. . . In the very midst of all of this social upheaval, a thoughtful, intelligent Jewish man in early middle age, living in Rome, decides to write a "book;" in fact, his friends have been begging him to do it. He knows the way times are nowadays, he may never live to see old age, and there are things that need to be put into writing, facts to be set straight. Too many false stories are going around told by people who do not have their facts right; nor have the position that is his. So, he begins to write his book; not a long book, to be sure, but a book that will tell the truth. He has been many places, seen much, known many people, but the book will not be about that. It will be about just one Man, whom he remembers coming to his mother's home when he, himself, was just a young lad. Paul's letters tell what to believe about the man, how to feel, think about Him and act because of Him. But they do not tell the story of His life, who He was, or where He came from or what He did or said. And if somebody who knows the truth doesn't put down in writing the real story of this Man's life soon, it may never be written down—correctly—at all. Thirty-nine years have gone by since Jesus of Nazareth was crucified in Jerusalem. In those 39 years His disciples have organized churches in His name all over the mid-east and in Europe, in Greece and here, in Rome. But now most of them are gone. Peter is dead, Paul is dead, as are most of Jesus' closest friends. But JOHN MARK is very much alive, willing and anxious to set down in writing everything about his Lord that he remembers himself, that he learned from his friend and mentor, the old apostle, Peter, and that which was revealed to him through the grace of God.

69   The book of MARK is the first Gospel—or, GOOD NEWS—written.

The Years

that write the

GOSPELS

and connect the
AGE OF THE APOSTLES
with the
EARLY CHURCH FATHERS
and the
GROWTH OF CHRISTIANITY

The Years that Write the GOSPELS

(and the remaining books of the New Testament)

It has long been thought that the evangelist Mark wrote his Gospel just before the destruction of Jerusalem by the Romans in A.D. 70, and that the remaining books of the New Testament were completed in the 20 years following, the last as late as A.D. 95. This view is being challenged by some modern scholars who believe that ALL the books of the New Testament were completed, and in circulation, BEFORE that event occurred. Surely, the argument goes, so devastating an event as Jerusalem's second destruction would not have gone un-noted by the Gospel writers had they written after the fact.

The new theories have found much support among Bible scholars, because they make good sense. However, this book will use the traditional dating because, first of all, the new theories have not been conclusively proved and, secondly, because the age-old traditions will much more clearly dramatize the events in the 30 years ahead. To simply "lump together" at 69 or before, the four Gospels and the remaining books would, necessarily, end the story now; and the coming years are far too important to the continuity of the Christian story, indeed, indispensable . . . to say nothing of exciting . . . to cut off at this point and not include. For, earth-shaking and world-changing events, both natural and man-made, are about to happen. But mostly, they are the years that bridge the span between the "Apostolic Age"—the years the New Testament was "lived" and the people who lived it—and the emergence of the "CHURCH" and the completion of the "CANON" of the Bible.

The last section of this book not only tells a story, but deals, also, with questions with which Christian apologists (and Sunday School teachers, like myself many years ago) are so often challenged. First of all, the whole thing is so ridiculous: a king born in a stable, who becomes an obscure carpenter, who turns the world upside down and is crucified as a criminal . . . and then RISES from the DEAD! How could anybody take a fairytale like that seriously? And why do the Gospels sometimes differ from each other and/or contain contradictions and omissions; how and why did they come to be written; and if Jesus really did live, die and rise again why didn't others of that time write about Him, also, besides the writers of the Bible?

Well, they did. Christ and Christianity are mentioned many times in secular writings of that age, usually—and understandably—in negative terms, and will feature in this book, and have, already . . . as in Tacitus and Suetonius. But there are also the pseudo-Christian writings often referred to as the "lost books of the Bible" which, if authentic, would re-write the faith, drastically. Modern-day revisionists, hoping to diminish the church and re-model Jesus to suit their own political agendas, use various of these "lost books of the Bible" to prove their own prejudices or "isms." They accuse the early church fathers and the church of knowingly losing them so that their "truths" would never be known. But while books such as the Gospel of Thomas and the heretical Gnostic gospels may have been lost for centuries and only recently found, they were NOT lost when the early church fathers decided them to be unauthentic and elected to keep them out of the Bible.

Then, they were not lost, they were REJECTED as not being the whole truth or as gross distortions of the truth, and are just as heretical today as they were 2000 years ago, and could, more aptly, be considered, the Rejected Books of the Canon.

To conclude this story, I have woven a simple narrative about the writing of the Gospels in the hope that it might suggest (without lengthy explanation or sermonizing) what MAY or COULD have happened. If I am wrong and the Gospels were, in fact, written before A.D. 70 (and in a far different manner than these pages will show) so be it. I stand corrected, but I truly believe that my error will do no damage to the Bible story. This book's narrative is only trying to dramatize possibilities for the different outlooks, opinions, experiences and aims of the four evangelists. It makes no claim to being definitive, but wants only to suggest what MIGHT or COULD have happened.

69   The Gospel of Mark is written.

MARK

Gospel of Mark — Written in Greek,   c. 69

"The time is fulfilled and the kingdom of God is at hand!" announces John the Baptist in MARK's first chapter; and to herald that event he returns almost 600 years to the ancient prophet Isaiah (40:3): "Behold I send my messenger . . . a voice crying in the wilderness . . . to prepare the way of the Lord . . ." Mark's "good news" opens with John in the wilderness, and continues a fast-moving, exciting narrative throughout, putting his thoughts down just as the inspiration comes to him. His writing is that of an intelligent, but unpretentious, ordinary man, telling a story with an unadorned, straight-forward honesty and clarity; a towering testimony to a firm faith. His Jewish nature comes through in his writing, but he actually wrote the book in the much-used dialect of Greek called Koine. Tra-

St. Mark from the Lindisfarne Gosphels @ 700 A.D.

dition says that Mark founded the church in Alexandria, Egypt, and was its first bishop.

Tradition also believes that John Mark was born into a wealthy family; the book of ACTS says that his mother was a devout follower of Jesus of Nazareth and suggests that the "last supper" was held in her home. Mark, himself, may well have been the "young man" MARK tells about (but does not name) who ran off into the night naked when guards grabbed for him and ripped off his garment as Jesus was arrested. (14:51) If so, he would have been, perhaps, 12 to 15 years old at the time; well old enough to remember that incident . . . and many others, as well.

Mark traveled with Paul and Silas on the first missionary journey, although to Paul's disappointment, he left them before long. No one knows what caused their falling out, but the two worked together much in later years and, in fact, in Paul's last letter, he asked Timothy to ". . . bring Mark with you when you come, for he is very useful to me . . ." Perhaps that request is why Mark would be in Rome at this time. Mark was a very close friend of Peter, also, and as he probably spoke both Greek and Latin (raised as he was in a wealthy family) was invaluable to Peter as an interpreter. His gospel reflects both the memories of what he learned from Peter and his own experiences and travels. His story of Jesus' great question to his disciples, "But who do YOU say that I am?" surely came directly from Peter, himself, and is one of the great dramatic moments in the New Testament, for, if the correct answer had been just a great teacher, a good and profound moral leader, His message and meaning could have been open to many interpretations. But MARK records that Peter answered, "Thou art the Christ, the son of the living God," and

Jesus replied that he, Peter, could not have known that had it not been REVEALED to him by "my father, which art in heaven." 8:27 Thus, Mark teaches that every human being who hears that question must, also, answer it one way or another, and those who answer as Peter did must, then, accept that what Jesus did, and said, and taught was right and good and TRUE: true then, true now, and true forever.

Mark wrote his book from Rome for the Christians in Rome, to explain to them the human nature of Jesus, the man, the Son of God. He portrays Jesus as he remembers Him, a real-life, flesh and blood man of action; doing things and getting things done "immediately," a word he uses many times. He shows (probably remembers) Jesus to be a man of such magnitude and authority that He had merely to say "Follow me" and men followed. Mark portrays Jesus' friendliness, firmness and goodness, His good humor, utter resolve and incredible courage with a vivid, majestic dignity, in an almost Latin literary style. It is not surprising that this short book should have had such a tremendous impact, not only on the early Christians, but on the very world, itself.

70   Just as Nero's death ended the dynasty of Julius Caesar—the "Julian" Caesars, now the accession of Titus Flavius Vespasianus begins the "Flavian" line. Born humbly, Vespasian

Vespasiam

worked himself up in both political and military careers and served as *praetor, aedile* and the highest office *consul*, and has been governor of Parthia, Syria and Africa, returning, according to Suetonius, "no richer than when he went." A blunt and able soldier and general, he has fought and commanded many battles, coming the closest to death only when he fell asleep at one of Nero's concerts. Now he intends to restore discipline in the army, govern to "ensure that the working classes earn enough money to buy themselves food," and to "shore up the state." Rome is still an ashen shambles after the great fire, and Vespasian begins to earn the Roman's respect right from the start when he carries away the first basketful of rubble on his own shoulders.

With Vespasian's return to Rome as emperor, his son Titus takes command of the siege of Jerusalem, and the Jewish general/historian Josephus remains with him to be his interpreter. When Josephus writes his HISTORY OF THE JEWISH WARS, he will record the number of Jews in Jerusalem at this time as 3,000,000; not all resident population, but mostly religious pilgrims in the city for Passover, Jews from all over Judea at what will prove to be the wrong place at the wrong time. Josephus tries earnestly to avoid catastrophe by talking the Jews into signing peace. Former governor of Galilee and general of the Jewish forces, Josephus is now considered a traitor by the Jews and they do not even listen to him. Titus wants to get the job over and done with, for he has no liking for this part of the world; desert, hot wind and sand. So he assembles his heaviest artillery: catapults and wheeled *ballistas* to encircle the city and hurl missles of rock and fire. Slowly the huge assault towers are rolled up to the city walls to wait, poised for the final attack. According to Josephus, though, it is the Roman soldier, himself, that is the empire's most dreaded weapon:

> . . . Romans fight like their weapons are permanently attached to them. Flavius Josephus, HISTORY OF THE JEWISH WARS

But it is the battering ram that drives the Jew to madness; day after day, never stopping, never quiet, for 139 days, thudding out its incessant message of doom. And inside the city a million Jews are starving . . .

> . . . and wrangling with each other who should be leader. Someone set fire to the town granaries . . . and left the ancient, dirty, high-walled city . . . without food . . . *ibid.*

Twice Josephus carries peace terms from Titus into the city, and twice the Jews refuse. They will not surrender the city for it is not their city to surrender; it is God's city.

> Thus did the miseries of Jerusalem grow worse and worse every day. And . . . the multitude of carcasses that lay in heaps one upon another was a horrible sight, and produced a pestilential stench . . . *ibid.* 6:1:1

But, Josephus says, even worse were the robbers who plunder the dead bodies, and the "seditious" Jews who were the cause of the whole thing in the first place, and continue to aggravate the Romans . . .

> So all hope of escaping was now cut off . . . Then did the famine widen its progress and devoured the people by whole houses and families . . . the children . . . wandered about the market-places like shadows, all swelled with famine and fell down dead wheresoever their misery seized them . . . as for burying them, those that were sick . . . were not able to do it, and those that [could] . . . were deterred . . . by the great multitude of . . . dead bodies . . . Nor were there any lamentations . . . or mournful complaints [for] . . . A great silence . . . a kind of deadly night, had seized upon the city . . . *ibid.* 5:7:3

After the final long summer with the starving Jews dying, rotting and stinking under the blistering sun, the city falls, and the battering rams . . . finally . . . cease . . .

> When . . . the Romans swarmed into the city . . . every alley, room and corner was choked with bloody corpses . . . Into the Temple court the soldiers dashed massacreing the thousands who had taken refuge there . . . [then the Jews'] . . . terror increased [and they] stormed out like ravenous demons, slashing, clawing, biting their way through . . . they staggered about in the alley ways in search of crusts, filthy hay, bits of old leather . . . offal . . . *ibid.*

As much of the city burns, some of Titus' commanders urge burning down the Temple, also, "because the Jews would never leave off rebelling while that house was standing . . ." but Titus "was not in any case for burning down so vast a work." But neither Titus' objections nor anything else could save the Temple, Josephus says, for . . . "God had for certain long ago doomed it to the fire; and now that fatal day was come . . ."

Prophesied: A day of wrath is that day, a day of distress and anguish, a day of ruin and devastation . . . a day of trumpet blast and battle cry . . . because they have sinned against the LORD . . . neither their silver nor their gold shall be able to deliver them on the day of the wrath of the LORD . . . ZEPHANIAH 1:15–18 (630 B.C.)   *   Behold the day of the LORD comes, cruel, with wrath and fierce anger, to make the earth a desolation and to destroy its sinners from it . . . I will make the heavens tremble, and the earth will be shaken out of its place . . . Thy holy people possessed thy sanctuary a little while: our adversaries have trodden it down. ISAIAH 13:9–13 and 63:18 (721 BC & 530 B.C.)   *   . . . their silver and gold are not able to deliver them in the day of the wrath of the LORD: they cannot satisfy their hunger or fill their stomachs with it. EZEKIEL 7:19 (570 B.C.)   *   Alas for the day! . . . Let all the inhabitants of the land tremble . . . a great and powerful people: their like has never been from of old, nor will be again after them through the years of all generations.   JOEL 1:15, 2:1,2 (500 B.C.)

Waiting until Titus "retires into the Antonia Fortress" the "seditious lay still for a little while, and then attacked the Romans again" . . . and finally the Temple, itself:

. . . one of the [Roman] soldiers without staying for any orders, and without any concern or dread upon him at so great an undertaking . . . snatched some[thing] out of the fire, and being lifted up by another soldier, he set fire to one of the Temple's golden windows . . .
Josephus, WARS 6:4:5

A horrified Titus does all he can to put out the fire but is too late. The Jews' holy house of God, Herod's Temple that Josephus calls "the most admirable of all the works that we have seen or heard of," is, like the first Temple—Solomon's—burned to the ground and reduced to ashes and rubble. It was renowned, Josephus says, "both for its curious structure and its magnitude, and also for the vast wealth bestowed upon it [and] the glorious reputation . . . for its holiness." 6:4:7 Jerusalem and its fabulous Temple are no more. Israel lies, as once before, a heap of rubble. The Sanhedrin is abolished, thousands of survivors are sold into slavery, and ***the JEWISH STATE, AFTER <u>1200 YEARS,</u> CEASES TO EXIST.***

Sixty-two years from now, in A.D. 132, during the reign of the Emperor Hadrian, a self-proclaimed "Messiah" named Shimeon Bar Kokhba will provoke another revolt against Rome by declaring that year as the "Year One of the Redemption of Israel," and himself as its "President." His futile, bloody war will go on for three years, and when he is finally defeated, and killed in battle, Rome will take cruel and extreme steps to guarantee that it never happens again. All Jews—every one of God's "stiff-necked" people—will be exiled from Jerusalem, forbidden ever to return, separated and scattered to all parts of the empire," never again to have a nation of their own . . . until the formation by the United Nations almost 2000 years later, of the modern state of Israel in A.D. 1948. Largely because of the Bar Kokhba revolt and the resulting "Diaspora," or "Dispersion of the Jews," are there Russian Jews, German Jews, Spanish Jews, Polish Jews, etc. And because of this, also, many scholars believe, did Judaism and Christianity, conclusively, go their separate ways: Judaism to centuries of quiet but valiant struggle to preserve itself and its faith from extinction, and Christianity to spread its message of sacrifice and redemption throughout the world.

> Prophesied: I saw in the night visions, and behold, with the clouds of heaven there came one like a son of man, and he came to the Ancient of Days and was presented before him. And to him was given dominion and glory and kingdom, that all peoples, nations and languages should serve him; his dominion is an everlasting dominion, which shall not pass away, and his kingdom one that shall not be destroyed.   DANIEL 7:13,14 (See: 533 B.C.)

Only one short length of Jerusalem's city wall remains standing called, to this day, the "Wailing Wall" by the countless generations of Jews who have mourned there. All religious landmarks, synagogues, libraries, records, documents and books are destroyed. Consequently any official documents there MAY have been about the birth, life or death of Jesus of Nazareth are gone . . . forever. God has sealed the fact that Jesus was the Messiah. From this time on no one can ever come forward and make that claim, or give evidence, for family lines can nevermore be traced. The destruction of Jerusalem has fulfilled Jesus' own prophecy, made 38 years ago:

The Wailing Wall

> But when you see Jerusalem surrounded by armies, then know that its desolation has come near . . . for these are days of vengeance, to fulfill "all that is written . . . For great distress shall be upon the earth and wrath upon this people; they will fall by the edge of the sword, and be led captive among all nations; and JERUSALEM WILL BE TRODDEN DOWN BY THE GENTILES . . .   Jesus of Nazareth, LUKE 21:20–24 (See: A.D. 32, Tuesday)

During the next centuries Jewish scholars in exile without nation, homeland or holy temple, will labor diligently to preserve their faith. Hundreds of civil and sacred written and unwritten laws, ethical and moral teachings, legal decisions, and commentaries, interpretations and amplifications on, and paraphrases of, the Hebrew scriptures will be gathered together into a Jewish literature called the (Palestinian/Babylonian) TALMUD (learning.) Held in esteem second only to the Torah, itself, the Talmud will help shape modern Judaism's manners, mores, customs and beliefs. And without meaning to it will, also, testify to the fact that there was, in truth, a man called Jesus who worked miracles, had a following and "was hanged on Passover Eve. . ."

> Jesus . . . practiced sorcery and led Israel astray and enticed them into apostasy . . . As nothing was brought forward in his defense, he was hanged on Passover Eve." The Babylonian
> Talmud, Sanhedrin 43a

Another non-Christian reference to Jesus is found in a manuscript from Syria in the British Museum, which asks what good it does to kill a good man? "The Athenians suffered famine and plague after Socrates' death, Samos was covered with sand and overwhelmed by the sea when Pythagoras was burned, and after the Jews executed their wise king . . .

> . . . their kingdom was abolished (and] ruined and, driven from their land, [they) live in complete dispersion. But Socrates lives on in Plato, Pythagoras in the statue of Hera; and the wise King of the Jews lives on in the teachings which he had given." The Mara bar
> Serapion, Syriac MS #14.658, The British Museum, London

70 Titus' triumphal procession back to Rome is enormous and grand; golden-eagled S.P.Q.R. standards gleaming in the sun, long trumpets and drums blaring and beating a cadenced step by measured step for the bronze-clad, victorious warriors, followed by the pathetic remnant of a once-proud people, chained, ragged and defeated. Once again whatever could be salvaged of the Temple's sacred vessels, censers, bowls and candlesticks are hauled away to a foreign country, this time never to return. Once again the Jews are led away into bondage.

> Titus . . . carried away the noblest of the zealots to . . . his triumphal procession . . . through Rome. Josephus, JEWISH WARS

Hated by the Jews, and rightfully so, Titus is heaped with honors, and his father, the Emperor Vespasian commissions the building of a gigantic triumphal arch in the center of the city, with figures of the Jewish captives carved on it, carrying to Rome the Temple's holy vessels and seven-branched Menorah. Like the Wailing Wall, the Arch of Titus still stands, to this day.

The Arch of Titus

From the Arch of Titus

In Rome, Vespasian's first priority is to make peace with the Senate and put the government back on a legal level. He is a good man for the job according to Suetonius, ". . . a man of great patience . . . not the sort to bear grudges or pay off old scores . . . no innocent party was ever punished [with his knowledge or acceptance] during his reign . . . his only fault avarice [exacting] heavy tribute from the provinces, and openly engaging in business dealings which would have disgraced even a private citizen." (Suetonius, LIVES 10:13–16) And yet Vespasian is generous with his wealth, however misbegotten, rebuilding earthquake-shattered cities, sponsoring the arts and sciences, paying rhetoric teachers' salaries, and encouraging food production ". . . by ordering great numbers of lavish dinners." And he begins a major "public works" project (that had been one of Augustus' ambitions): a gigantic sports arena, an "Amphitheater of Vespasian" a . . . Colosseum.

Planned on a "colossal" scale, the Colosseum will be built on the same site on which—until the fire—stood Nero's fantastic "Golden House," that of the revolving dome, the mile-long colonnade and the hundred foot statue of the tyrant/emperor. This new structure will be over 600 feet long and 500 wide, with outer walls four stories high, big enough to seat 50,000 spectators at its unbelievable games. It will be built of Italian limestone and cement, and be crowned with graceful Grecian columns. It will boast the most modern engineering expertise with such ingenious devices as elevators to raise up to arena level fantastic scenery and the participants, both human and animal, for its games from vaulted dens below ground; and a system of underground pumps that can flood the entire football-field-sized arena for mock sea battles. Admittance through numbered entryways will be gained for the huge mobs of spectators by similarly numbered tickets (a system used to this day.) The building of the Colosseum will employ thousands of people for the next 10 years: architects, engineers, stone masons and laborers, to say nothing of the merchants, seamen and traders for whom the training of gladiators and procurement of wild beasts from Africa and India will become big business.

73, Spring, the 15th of Nisan.   The Jews' last stand, their final resistance, comes on the fortified desert plateau outpost of Masada, that fortress King Herod had built for himself and stocked with enough provisions to last for years. According to the historian, Josephus, when the Roman 10th legion finally takes the fortress, it finds Masada's 960 defenders, men, women and children . . . dead, by their own hands.

Josephus, himself, is rewarded generously by Vespasian, for the help he was to both himself and Titus in the Jewish war. Hated as a traitor by the Jews, he is honored by the emperor, given a large estate near Rome by Vespasian and awarded Vespasian's own name, so that Joseph Ben Matthias now becomes Flavius Josephus.

Josephus

. . . By this time, the "book"—the Gospel or Good News—which Mark wrote of the life of Jesus has received a wide circulation, and is being read all over the empire. Mark wrote his Gospel for the Christians in Rome, but Christians everywhere are eager to read it or have it read in their churches. Many other "biographies" of Jesus have been written but many of them are of dubious value, gross exaggerations or outright falsehoods, and it is Mark's

"Good News" that everyone wants. After all, he actually knew Jesus, and is now one of the important church fathers. Everything he says in his book he learned first hand, inspired by God, Himself; or from Peter, and Peter knew Jesus from the very beginning. So now, churches in every country want copies, their congregations eager to learn more about Jesus the man, the Son of God, what He was like in life, what He did and what He said. So more scrolls are copied and carried to other parts of the empire . . .

. . . and *MAYBE* SOMETHING LIKE THIS HAPPENED NEXT . . .

c. 75   One copy of Mark's Gospel finds its way to Syria, 1500 miles away from Rome, where an old man lives, another father of the church, who has been preaching about Jesus throughout the mid-east for 45 years now. He reads Mark's book carefully and the memories come back like a flood. Long gone are the days when he was an arrogant, fire-brand tax collector for the Romans. He had that to live down, all right, just as Paul did his past. "Yes, the young man is right," Matthew thinks, "Mark told his story well. But he didn't tell it all. He couldn't. He was just a young lad when our Lord was alive. He doesn't know the things I know; it wasn't given to him as to me. He doesn't explain how Jesus fulfilled Jewish LAW and the PROPHETS. THAT'S a story that needs to be told . . . and I alone can tell it." Matthew knows no Greek, only Aramaic, so a Greek friend begins to write for him, as he dictates: "The book of the genealogy of Jesus Christ, the son of David, the son of Abraham. Abraham was the father of Isaac, and Isaac was the father of Jacob, and Jacob the father . . ."

Another copy of Mark's book makes its way to Antioch in Asia Minor, and comes to the attention of Theophilus, a high-born Greek administrator at the Roman consulate. Theophilus reads Mark's book and wonders if these things are true. "I will show it to my friend, Loukas," he decides. "He comes back to Antioch every once in a while and is here now. He will know." His friend, Loukas, is the well-loved doctor everyone knows as Luke, a man revered for his saintliness and respected for his wisdom and learning. Luke has already read the book, as he has others, including the "Q" document, as well. "Oh, yes, most excellent Theophilus," Luke responds. "Mark is right. I know him well and he speaks the truth—as far as he can. But there is much that he does not know. There are, in fact, things that no other person in the world knows . . . but me. Yes, my friend, I will write out the story for you, just as God revealed it to me; and not only that story but another, also, of the years I spent with Peter and Paul. And you shall read things nobody knows . . . but I." And so, in two separate corners of the empire, two men who may never even have met, nor probably ever will, begin working in their own ways and their own time, on their own Gospels of Christ.

77   The Roman naturalist Pliny (the Elder) finally publishes his encyclopedia, NATURAL HISTORY or *HISTORIAE NATURALIS,* on which he has been working for so many years. A man of many talents and abilities, including military, the Emperor Vespasian has appointed Pliny Admiral of the Fleet. "Now, as his ships sail the southern coast of Italy just offshore the beautiful resort city of Pompeii, Pliny stops to see the rumbling, smoking Mount Vesuvius, and study firsthand the effects of the earthquake 14 years ago.

. . . In the far north, General Gnaeus Julius Agricola is military governor of Britain, as far north as the edge of the Scottish Highlands. Having been born into the equestrian class, he rose through the ranks as *quaestor, praetor, censor* and *patrician*. A man of dignity, compassion and wisdom, he knows that allies are not won by force and coercion and so governs Britain with judicious humanity. In this year, 77, the promising young Roman orator and future statesman and historian, Cornelius Tacitus (whose later works this book quotes often) marries Agricola's daughter. He greatly admires his father-in-law as a man of character and nobility and someday will write about him that, more than anyone else ". . . Agricola deserves credit for civilizing the wild Britons."

79   The Emperor Vespasian dies at age 63 after ruling nine years, a reign of sanity and accomplishment, bringing Rome back to a semblance of law and order. Vespasian had a great sense of humor and the butt of his jokes was usually himself and his well-known weaknesses. He liked to tell the story of a favorite servant who asked for a loan for his poor brother, and admitted he would charge his brother a commission, but only so much. Vespasian bade him bring the brother to him, gave him the loan directly and then demanded the commission for himself. *Go find another brother," he told the servant. "The one you mistook for your own turns out to be mine." (Suetonius, LIVES 10:23) And at the end, knowing he was dying, Vespasian wryly observed, "Dear me, I must be turning into a god."

Titus

. . . Vespasian's son, now Emperor Titus, is a remarkable man. Much hated and feared before becoming emperor that he would be another Nero, he will in fact be, according to Suetonius, "universally loved" afterward for what proved to be noble and admirable qualities in a leader. Conqueror of Jerusalem, he fought in the front ranks, himself, having a horse shot out from under him and killing 12 Jewish defenders with 12 arrows in a row. Of medium height, he is handsome, sturdy and athletic, with an incredible memory. A musician and poet as well as soldier and statesman, he has a rare gift of being able to copy, exactly, anyone's handwriting and likes to say that he could have been the greatest forger in the world. Titus begins his reign in a spirit of justice and fairness, hoping to carry on his father's policies. But less than three months into his reign, disaster strikes, of terrible proportion . . .

Mt. Vesuvius

79, August 24.   After rumbling and smoking 16 years, Mount Vesuvius finally erupts, a gargantuan blast of 10 times the power the 20th century will witness at Mount St. Helen's; and the cities of Pompeii, Herculaneum and Stabiae are buried under 15 to 30 feet of lava and ash, instantly entombing 16,000 people. Admiral Pliny, in the flagship of his fleet, rushes to the scene with rescue operations, and to get another look at the volcano . . . this time a live volcano. He is suffocated by poisonous gasses rising from the crater. Pliny's nephew, 18 year-old Pliny the Younger (and his mother, the elder Pliny's sister) is almost 20 miles away at Misenum during the eruption, but even from there will describe ". . . the darkness of a sealed room." His uncle was not afraid to go near the volcano, young Pliny said, because . . .

| Fortune favors the brave. | Pliny the Elder |

Pliny the Younger and Cornelius Tacitus are good friends, write to each other often (much of their correspondence still in existence), and now Tacitus asks Pliny to describe the eruption. Pliny is only too glad to comply for he knows these letters will live for centuries, and they will be a fitting memorial to his uncle.

Your request that I . . . send you an account of my uncle's death . . . deserves my acknowledgments . . . about one in the afternoon, my mother desired him to observe a cloud . . . of . . . very uncommon appearance . . . likening it to that of a pine tree, for it shot up to a great height . . . This phenomenon seemed to a man of learning and research as my uncle . . . worth looking into. [On receiving word of imminent danger] . . . He ordered the galleys to be put to sea and went himself on board . . . Hastening then to the place from whence others fled with the utmost terror, he steered his course direct to the point of danger . . . with . . . much calmness and presence of mind . . . the cinders . . . grew thicker and hotter . . . fell into the ships . . . pumice stones, and black pieces of burning rock . . . vast fragments . . . rolled down from the mountain . . . broad flames shone out in several places from Mount Vesuvius . . . houses . . . now rocked from side to side with . . . violent concussions . . . It was now day everywhere else, but there a deeper darkness . . . than in thickest night . . . my uncle, laying himself down upon a sail cloth . . . called twice for some cold water, which he drank, when . . . the flames, preceeded by a strong whiff of sulphur . . . obliged him to rise. He raised himself up . . . and instantly fell down dead; suffocated . . . by . . . [the] noxious vapor . . . the third day after his body was found entire . . . looking more like a man asleep than dead.   Pliny the Younger, LETTERS LXV, to Tacitus

But Tacitus wants to know more: how the eruption affected him, Pliny the Younger and his mother, being 20 miles away, and Pliny replies that at first he continued with the studies which his uncle had assigned him earlier . . .

As I was at that time but eighteen years of age, I know not whether my behavior [was] courage or folly . . . the buildings all around us tottered [so my mother and I] resolved to quit the town. A panic-stricken crowd followed us [driving] us forward . . . we [were] in the midst of a most . . . dreadful scene . . . The sea seemed to roll back upon itself [leaving] several sea animals [ashore.] . . . a black and dreadful cloud, broken with rapid zigzag flashes, revealed . . . variously shaped masses of flame . . . like sheet lightning, but . . . larger . . . Soon afterwards, the cloud began to descend, and cover the sea. It already surrounded the [Isle of Capri] and . . . Misenum. My mother besought . . . me to . . . escape . . . as I was young . . . but . . . I . . . refused to leave her, and . . . compelled her to go with

> me . . . [all around were] the shrieks of women, the screams of children . . the shouts of men . . . It seemed that all mankind were involved in the same calamity, and that I was perishing with the world itself. Pliny the Younger, LETTERS LXV, to Tacitus

But what was tragedy for Pliny and Pompeii (and, incidentally, for the son of Felix, the procurator who heard Paul the Apostle's first trial) was a boon for posterity, for our knowledge of the Roman way of life would be infinitely poorer without the reality of those three cities preserved in an instant under their ashen tomb. When they are excavated almost 2000 years after the eruption, the lava blanket will reveal the terror-stricken, fleeing forms of people and animals; mothers clutching babies, wives clinging to husbands, children huddled together, and a little dog turning only long enough to scratch a flea. It will reveal fresh bread in an oven, food on tables and a dose of medicine by a sick boy in back of a shop; and it will reveal, also, a city of beautifully colonnaded homes and villas, with brilliant frescoed walls (one with a Christian symbol upon it) and mosaic-tiled floors. At the center of the city is the public forum and, as this was a famous resort area, down one dark, narrow street its pornographically painted red-light district.

The Colosseum

80 Begun by Vespasian, and 10 years in the building, the Colosseum at Rome is completed and dedicated by the Emperor Titus. The dedication is celebrated with 100 days of bloody games between man and man, man and beast, and even ships at "sea." Over 2000 men are killed in the 100 days and uncountable exotic animals of every description. Spectators come from all over the empire to see for themselves the wonders Rome has to offer, but they no longer come for the comedies and dramas of ancient Greece or Republican Rome that lifted the spirits, enlightened the mind or ennobled the soul. It is only blood, gore, viciousness and violence that matters now to most people; that and their hand-outs from the state. But the opening of the Colosseum is a matter of interest to Rome's literary young men-about-town, also, and one of them, Marcus Valerius Martialis, or Martial, devotes 33 of his EPIGRAMS to the "spectacles," or, DE SPECTACULIS LIBER. In awe of the building, itself, he compares it—favorably—to some of the "seven wonders of the world":

> Let not barbarian Memphis tell of the wonder of her Pyramids, nor Assyrian vaunt its Babylon; let not the soft Ionians be extolled for [Diana of Ephesus] . . . let not Carians exalt to the skies . . . the Mausoleum [of Hallicarnassus] . . . All labor yields to Caesar's Amphitheatre: one work in place of all shall fame rehearse. Martial, the SPECTACLES, I

One awesome aspect of the Colosseum, Martial says, is the flooding of its arena for live naval battles, to the death, for ships and men alike:

> Whoever you are who come from distant shores . . . that this naval battle with its ships, and the waters that represent seas, may not mislead, I tell you "here but now was land." Believe you not? Look on while the [sea-fight lasts]. Wait one moment—you will say "Here but now was sea."   Martial XXIV

Spectators come from *everywhere*, he says, Egypt, Ethiopia, Arabia and even such [faraway shores] as . . . Britain! He is in awe, also, of the animals used in the games: rhinoceros, bull, lion, elephant, a pair of steers, a buffalo, bison, a wild boar and "a mother sow" whose brood is born through her wounds. The horrors of the arena are not lost on Martial, though, and he tells of the end of one condemned criminal:

> . . . so Laureolus, hanging on [a] cross, gave up his vitals defenseless to a bear. His mangled limbs lived, though the parts dripped gore, and in all his body was nowhere a body's shape.   *ibid.* VII

The bloodthirstiness of the spectators is not lost on Martial, either, nor the moral depths to which Rome has sunk, and he sees a commentary even in the behavior of animals:

> . . . a tigress . . . savagely tore a fierce lion with maddened fangs; strange was the thing, unknown in any age! She ventured no such deed what time she dwelt in her deep woods: she is in our midst—[in Rome!]—and shows more fierceness now.   *ibid.* XVIII

Named for the month of his birth, Martial came to Rome from his birthplace, Spain, in the last year of Nero's reign, 69, and until his EPIGRAMS began to sell, lived the life of the stereotypical starving poet in a third floor attic. Now, at 41, he is one of Rome's most popular—and prosperous—poets, with a house in town, a villa in the country, and friends who number among Rome's most notable literati: Quintillian, Juvenal and Pliny the Younger. Years from now at Martial's death, Pliny will call him ". . . a man of genius, of subtle, quick intelligence . . . wit and pungency . . . [whether his writings last or not] he wrote as if they would."

Pliny's own writings, like those that describe the eruption of Mount Vesuvius, are a fascinating and vivid depiction of first century Rome. They are not poetry or epigrams, but a collection of his personal correspondence, to all sorts of people: his earliest boyhood friend, business and social acquaintances, and notable people from his fellow writer, Tacitus, to (20 years hence) his mentor, the Emperor Trajan. In one of his most historically significant letters, Pliny the Younger mentions a religious sect whose members . . .

> . . . addressed a form of prayer to Christ, as to a divinity . . .   Pliny the Younger, LETTERS XCVII

But, by this time, Christianity is no longer a sect, or minor cult, passed down by word of mouth, but a universal religion, known "throughout the world," mentioned in many writings, both sacred and secular. The Jewish writer Josephus, he who wrote the HISTORY OF THE JEWISH WARS, now writes in another history, THE ANTIQUITIES OF THE JEWS, about a ". . . Jesus, who was called the Christ and his brother, John . . ."

> Now, there was about this time, Jesus, a wise man, if it be lawful to call him a man, for he was a doer of wonderful works, a teacher of such men as receive the truth with pleasure. He drew over to him both many of the Jews, and many of the Gentiles. He was [the] Christ; and when Pilate, at the suggestion of the principal men amongst us, had condemned him to the cross, those that loved him at the first did not forsake him, for he appeared to them alive again the third day as the divine prophets had fortold these and ten thousand other wonderful things concerning him; and the tribe of Christians, so named for him, are not extinct at this day. Josephus, ANTIQUITIES OF THE JEWS, XVIII:3.3

The manuscripts of two other writers make their appearances at about this time, if long tradition is correct. No one knows where or how, but both are about the same man of whom Josephus wrote—Jesus of Nazareth, called Christ. One book is by a man who knew Him well, and the other by one too young to have known Him at all.

80   The Gospel of MATTHEW is written.

MATTHEW

Gospel of Matthew — Written in Greek,   c. A.D. 80

"Think not that I have come to destroy the LAW and the PROPHETS; I have not come to destroy, but to fulfill them!" Incredible words! Monumental message! Laws and prophecies made 500, a thousand years ago and a carpenter from Nazareth says he will fulfill them! "You have heard it was said of the men of old . . . but I say to you . . ." I say. Not the scribes, not the ancient scriptures, but I, Jesus of Nazareth! Here, in Matthew's book, is the mighty fulfillment of the religion of the Jews. A thousand years of prophecy and expectation are now incarnate in one man, Jesus of Nazareth, Jesus Christ. Son of God, yes, and the long-awaited MESSIAH of the Jews as well. No more is mere obedience to the letter of the Mosaic Law enough; fixed, stringent and looking to the past. Now, through love of Jesus Christ, it will

St. Matthew from a 9th century Gospel

come freely and gladly, for Jesus' injunctions are replete, not with retribution and punishment, but with love, forgiveness and welcome.

Matthew was that same tax collector to whom Jesus said, "Follow me," one of those *publicani* or publicans spoken of in the same breath as "sinners." What an enigmatic choice Jesus made in selecting a Roman collaborator for a disciple, a Jew with a practical, working knowledge of Roman ways. Matthew would be an old man by this time, widely traveled in the east, having preached the Good News in Syria, Ethiopia and possibly even Persia. His book was probably written in Greek, or even Aramaic, the language in which he and Jesus would probably have conversed. Matthew may have been familiar with Essene teaching for much of their thought is similar, and one of the Dead Sea Scrolls even clarifies one of Matthew's beatitudes: "Blessed are the poor in spirit . . ." The scroll reads: "Blessed are they who have remained poor for the spirit's sake."

Some scholars think that the Apostle, himself, may not have actually written MATTHEW, but all feel it is a very accurate record of his beliefs and teachings. It is obvious that the writer was well schooled in the Hebrew LAW and PROPHETS, and wrote his account specifically for Jewish Christians, to explain to them how Jesus fulfills the Old Testament prophecies. Matthew knew of Mark's book, which was written some 10 or 12 years earlier, and used it in writing his, borrowing, in fact, nearly 600 separate verses. Twenty years from now Papias, bishop of Hieropolis, Greece, will write that ". . . Matthew made a collection of the sayings of Jesus . . ." Matthew also used the document called "Q" and enlarged on them both to write the longest of the four Gospels. He begins with a long genealogy that goes back to the book of Ruth to show how Jesus was descended from king David, fulfilling a most important prophecy. Matthew does something else, though, without ever intending to. He proves the accuracy of his own book by being technically correct with Roman law: the "early in the morning" appearance before Pontius Pilate, Pilate's dismissal of the case after the first hearing and the gambling for Christ's clothes at the cross. All those things, and more, are totally compatible with Roman law of that time.

3rd century fragment of Matthew 21:13–19

If Mark was indeed, the young man mentioned, but not named, in his own book who ran off into the night when Jesus was arrested (MARK 14:51,52), then Matthew's path would have crossed his early and, in fact, probably often. But Matthew is the only evangelist to tell of the Magi, or Wise Men who visited the little boy Jesus with gifts, and of the horrors King Herod committed because of their visit. We have no way of knowing whether those incidents prompted his ministry in the east or whether he searched out the Magi while there, but it is a reasonable speculation.

Just as Moses taught from a mountain 1300 years before, so does Matthew tell how Jesus took His disciples to a mountain to talk privately with them and teach them, in a long discourse, or "sermon on the mount" what they must do. He taught them how especially blessed would be the meek, the merciful, the pure in heart, those who mourn and those who would be persecuted for His sake. And in that most beautiful, and perfect prayer, MATTHEW tells how Jesus taught them to pray, "Our Father, who art in Heaven, hallowed be thy name . . ."

80   The book of LUKE is written which, with the ACTS OF THE APOSTLES, makes up a two volume life of Christ and birth of the Christian church. Like Matthew, Luke knew of, and had read, Mark's book and incorporated some 350 verses from it into his own.

THIS book is assuming, with long tradition, that Luke was, in fact, Paul's "beloved physician," and a Greek, not a Jew. If so, things MAY have happened like this.

LUKE

Gospel of Luke — Written in Greek, c. A.D. 80

The cosmopolitan city of Antioch, in Asia Minor, was the birthplace of the Greek physician, Loukas or, as he is known in the Bible, Luke, the author of the book of LUKE and that wonderful journal of his travels, both spiritual and physical, known as the ACTS. Like his mentor, Paul, Luke was born into a cultured, Hellenistic society and had an excellent education, not only in Hippocratic medicine, but probably in the great Greek works of science, literature and philosophy as well, for his book is beautifully written, elegant of phrase, philosophically profound and meticulously crafted. No one knows when Luke became a Christian, but it was likely before he and Paul met. However, he must have greatly impressed the older man, for Paul took him along on two of his missionary journeys and made Luke's city of Antioch his headquarters for their travels, and they remained fast friends to the very end.

3rd century fragment of LUKE

Luke must have been a gentle man, kind, loving and understanding, for his book contains much that reflects that kind of nature. His is the only Gospel that tells the "parables of love": the Good Shepherd and the Prodigal Son. He alone records Jesus' words of forgiveness from the cross, "Father, forgive them for they know not what they do," and "This day thou shalt be with me in Paradise." Even the one seemingly harsh thing Luke records Jesus saying—"If any man come to me and hate not his father and mother he cannot be my disciple," is probably dramatic exaggeration and actually comes closer to meaning, "love me first, before all others." But the most beautiful part of Luke's book is the story that he, and he alone tells, the story of the first "Christmas."

Mary & Jesus from a
Roman Catacomb

At some time during his travels, Luke learned of and wrote about his Savior's birth in great detail, and it poses a most tantalizing puzzle. From whom did he learn the intimate, personal details that make up that touching tale: the message of the angel to Mary; her visit to her cousin Elizabeth, pregnant with John the Baptist; the journey to Bethlehem, shepherds in the fields and angels singing praises to the swaddling-clad baby lying in a manger? The other Gospel writers breathe not a word of it. Could Luke have met and talked with Jesus' mother, Mary? If Mary had been 16 at Jesus' birth (a not un-reasonable age) she would have been 66 at the time of Paul's second missionary journey, the first Luke traveled with him, and they could well have met. Mary had many things to "ponder in her heart" all these years, and she would have warmed easily to this kind and gentle young man. A strong bond would have sprung up between him and the older woman, a bond of love for the son to whom she gave birth and the Savior whom he worshipped but never knew as a man . . . who died before he was born.

An active imagination can conjure up a fascinating scene: an awed, respectful Greek doctor sitting in eager anticipation at the feet of a lovely, silver-haired lady, full of years, her face a vision of radiant peace. She is as fresh as a spring blossom and as old as all time. She looks at him with eyes that have seen eternity; the most sublime happiness and joy, and the most excruciating sorrow and pain. She tells him wonderful things of days long ago, how a mysterious visitor hailed her as "blessed amongst women" and "specially favored of God." Her face glows as she tells him of that starry night in Bethlehem after the long, hard journey from Nazareth, and how angels sang glorious hymns to shepherds in the field when her son was born. She remembers how bright he was as a boy, but how serious and profound; loving but distant . . . other worldly. Then pain shadows her face as she remembers the bad times. But, those are the things everybody knows. The good ones are her own private memories, to share only . . . with someone very special.

c. 80 Luke's second book, the ACTS OF THE APOSTLES, continues the narrative:

The ACTS of the APOSTLES

Book of History — Written in Greek, c. A.D. 80

St. Luke from a Byzatine manuscript

The book of ACTS is the second part of Luke's history of the Christian Church, and continues the story where the Gospel of LUKE left off. Luke wrote his history for a personal friend whom he addressed in his first book, LUKE, as "most excellent Theophilus," and about whom nothing more is known than that he may have been a Greco/Roman official of some rank. (However, Theophilus" in Greek means "all friends of God," so the books COULD have been written for a general audience.)

The role that Luke played in the formation of the new Christian church is extremely important, for without his account of the activities—or acts—of the apostles, we would know almost nothing about the history of the fledgling group. The histories of Josephus and the earliest Christian—and pagan—writers fill in some gaps but do not begin to tell the whole story. Paul's letters and the other epistles, and the gospels, lay out the *theology* of Christianity, but it is Luke's book of ACTS that tells of the people and events which formulated that theology in the years following Christ's resurrection.

The great, incredible day of Pentacost which changed a handful of uneducated fishermen into confident, enlightened leaders of a new faith, the exciting adventures of John and the newly emboldened Peter, the stoning of the new deacon, Steven, the importance of James as the head of the church in Jerusalem, the first great council which set Christianity apart from Judaism, the wise—but unheeded—warnings of the Rabbi Gamaliel, and especially the tremendous biography of the man Paul: none of these is told—first person—anyplace else. Of every one we would be ignorant, but for the diaries of Luke in his book of ACTS.

Luke wrote ACTS little by little during the missionary journeys he made with Paul, but probably compiled them later. Because of his excellent early education, Luke's Gospel and the ACTS were written in a highly literate Greek, and translate into an English that

is exciting, fast-moving and powerful. ACTS is a remarkable document, unlike any other book in the Bible, for while it is, of course, a magnificent statement of faith, it is, also a very human story, a wonderfully adventurous (and accurate) travel guide, a first person account by one who was there and took part. (The precise time and place when Luke joined Paul can be pinpointed in chapter 16, verse 10 when he stops referring to "them" or "they" and starts saying "we.")

The four Gospels that tell about Jesus take place in the bucolic, countryside atmosphere of rural Galilee that was, then, still an un-Romanized "free state," and are totally concerned with people, not places or things. They tell only of being "in the wilderness" or "in the fields," of "walking through the corn," "casting nets into the sea," of being "nigh unto the mountain," or "departed into a desert place." Only in the last week of Jesus' life (more often in the book of JOHN) does the outside world make an appearance, and that in Jerusalem. There the atmosphere is busy, colorful, raucous and . . . treacherous. There we read of the temple and the bustle about the temple, of money changers, scribes and priests, centurions and the Roman governor, Solomon's porch and buildings all around. Even a few foreign names and places enter the picture: Simon of Cyrene (in northern Africa) and, of course, Pontius Pilate of Rome.

But then comes the book of ACTS and it is a whole new world, a Roman world, to be sure, but much of it Hellenistic, more Greek than Roman. By chapter two it paints an international picture, speaking the tongues of Parthia, Media, Egypt, Asia, Crete and Arabia. With the appearance of the Apostle Paul, we are transported to the "street called Straight" in Damascus, Syria, that great, bustling hub of world trade; by sea to the island of Cyprus from which comes *cuprum,* copper; then up onto the south coast of Asia Minor through Galatia, so named by the Greeks for the invading Gauls 200 years ago. Traveling overland to Troas near the ruins of ancient Troy on the far west coast of that unique link between Asia and Europe, Paul crosses over the Aegean Sea into Macedonia, birthplace of Alexander the Great whose genius re-made the map of mid-and far-east. So much history is bound up in Paul's travels: Philippi, where the slayers of Caesar met their own fates: Thessalonica and 2000 year-old Corinth, burned by the Romans in 146 and rebuilt more beautiful than ever. Everywhere there are reminders of ages past and signs of the present age: busy, bustling streets and market places, colorful and raucous: theaters where the plays of Aeschylus and Sophocles are performed, and used for community assemblies as well. There are magistrates, mobs and Roman proconsuls like Sergius Paulus and Gallio, brother of the famous Seneca, for a while the power behind the throne of the emperor Nero, himself, in Rome. Finally beautiful, gleaming Athens, heart of Greece's Golden Age, but heart, too, of intellectual, art-loving self-centered Hellenism, a city, Paul says, "wholly given to idolatry." Here Paul "reasons" with his listeners for he is dealing with the philosophical mind, not the emotional/theological, and he speaks at the Areopagus and on Mars Hill, where He tells the Stoics and Epicureans that while God may have overlooked the times of ignorance when people worshipped gods of gold and silver, those times are past: Jupiter and Mercury, whom he and Barnabas are mistaken to be, no longer count, and the "UNKNOWN GOD" of the dedication on one of their own altars is, in fact, that God of whom he preaches.

Two of the Seven Wonders of the Ancient World appear in the book of ACTS (one named, one not): the gigantic temple of Diana at Ephesus, with its many-breasted goddess the source of great wealth for silversmiths selling copies . . . who riot against Paul for the threat he is to their incomes; and the "colossal" Colossus of Rhodes, which once towered astride Rhodes Harbor but, in Paul's time, already lay in ruins, leveled by an earthquake only 56 years after its completion. Paul sailed by Rhodes and the shattered Colossus three times on his travels, with a stop-over on his last journey back to Jerusalem. Then come Paul's two trials under Roman governors; his perilous, vividly-pictured sea journey sailing the "lee-side" of both Cyprus and Crete during the treacherous winter storm season; and their soul-wrenching shipwreck at Malta with its dramatic aftermath. Not until four months later does he arrive in Rome, traveling due north along the Appian Way, past the Forum of Appius 43 milestones from Rome; and at 33 milestones, the Three Taverns, where he/they are met by their Christian brethren. Here is high drama in an international setting. The supreme tragedy of Jesus' life, lived out in a rustic, pastoral countryside, is brought to universal status by the Apostle to the Gentiles and his young Greek protégé, Luke. To read the book of ACTS is to follow along on one of the most exciting, world-changing journeys of all time.

81 Throughout the Emperor Titus' entire two-year, two-month reign, his younger brother, Domitian, has never for a moment left off plotting against him, a fact of which Titus was well aware but too honorable to retaliate against. Now, with Titus' untimely death—or more probably, murder—at just 41, Rome does, again, have another Nero; not so colorful, perhaps, but every bit as cruel, his infamies un-celebrated only for want of a contemporary publicist. But we do have Suetonius, and he tells plenty.

> At Vespasian's death, Domitian toyed with the idea of buying the army's support from Titus and never once stopped plotting, secretly or openly against his brother. [He] would spend hours alone every day doing nothing but catching flies and stabbing them with a needle-sharp pen.   Suetonius, THE XII CAESARS. DOMITIAN 2,3

For the next 15 years Rome will again suffer a reign of terror, for Domitian is suspicious of everyone and willing to listen to any informer. Although he begins his reign with good intentions, passing laws and edicts for the betterment of the empire and its people, his capabilities are not up to being a competent ruler and his disposition too mean.

> He was not only cruel, but cunning . . . invited a palace steward to his bed and crucified him the next day . . . two officers saved themselves only by proving that they were too disgustingly immoral to do him any harm. He called himself "Lord and God," and "our Lord and God instructs you to do this" became regular.   *ibid.* 10, 11, 13

Domitian

Domitian's armies suffer a severe defeat in the northern province of Dacia (today's Romania) and for the first time, mighty—humiliated—Rome is forced to pay tribute to buy peace. Jealous of the famous General Agricola, Domitian recalls him home from his great successes in Britain . . . and has him murdered. He wipes out a revolt in Germany, but has become a vicious, raving madman and now no one is safe from his cruelties: Christians, Jews, the Senate or the army. Ironically, a monument still stands intact today in Rome partly built by Domitian, the commemoration of an act of infamy built by an infamous ruler . . . as Domitian completes the Arch of Titus in celebration of his brother's victory over the Jews and the destruction of Jerusalem.

c. 81   During this time of hardship and repression the Christian church is growing so rapidly and so faithfully, it has become almost "an empire within an empire." During these years the Jewish general, turned Roman collaborator, turned historian, Joseph Ben Matthias, or Josephus, is living in comfortable retirement in Rome, having been awarded a large country estate and the cognomen of the Emperor Vespasian's own Flavian family, the name Flavius Josephus. Josephus is despised by the Jews, however, who give him much of the blame for the destruction of Jerusalem, and for giving credence in his writings to that criminal about whom the new "Christian" religion revolves. While Josephus, himself, will never accept Jesus as the Christ, his writings do not even suggest a denial, and his inclusion of Christ into his Jewish histories will, in future years, be both refuted as latter-day additions, and defended by other scholars as authentic.

90   The aged apostle, John—he whom "Jesus loved," who, in his youth, had been one of the quick-tempered "sons of thunder," has been one of the church's leading figures all these

many years, the last of the original disciples and the only one to live to a ripe old age. Heeding Jesus' dying injunction to "behold thy mother," John cared for Mary while they were in Jerusalem and later took her with him to Ephesus where he is now head of its thriving church, the largest congregation in Christendom. One of his disciples is a young man named Polycarp, of whom more will soon be heard. John may have written many letters in his lifetime, but only three exist in the Bible.

I JOHN

Epistle of John — Written in Koine Greek,   c. A.D. 90

Many heresies of the faith have sprung up which could corrupt Jesus' mission and message, including the Gnostic, which blends Christian teaching with Creek and oriental mythology and mysticism. It denies that Jesus was a real, flesh and blood, human man; and John warns his "little children," ". . . so now many antichrists have come . . . [and] I write this to you about those who would deceive you." He opens his letter with a ringing affirmation of his own PERSONAL knowledge: "That which was from the beginning, which we have heard . . . seen with our eyes . . . touched with our hands concerning the word of life . . . made manifest . . . we testify to it . . . and proclaim also to you . . . that you (also) may have fellowship . . . with the Father and . . . His son Jesus Christ."

It is not known to what person or place John wrote this letter, but his writing makes clear that there was a strong bond between them, and he repeatedly assures his readers of his love, the love of Christ. "Beloved let us love one another," he says. "Everyone who believes that Jesus is the Christ is a child of God, and this is His commandment, that we should . . . love one another." John is stern, uncompromising and even threatening in this letter when he speaks of the uniqueness of Christ to salvation:

> Who is a liar but he that denieth that Jesus is the Christ? He is anti-Christ, that denieth the Father and the Son. Whosoever denieth the Son, the same hath not the Father. 2:22,23

But he is also at his kindest and most loving when he writes the lines known, down through the ages, as the . . . "Comfortable Words . . ."

> My little children, these things write I unto you, that ye sin not. [But] if any man sin, we have an advocate with the Father, Jesus Christ the righteous, And he is the propitiation for our sins: and not for our's only but also for the sins of the whole world. 2:1,2

Some of the "sins of the world" are the dread persecutions, which have taken so many Christians' lives, and John says "that as (Jesus] laid down His life for us . . . we ought to lay down our lives for the brethren." 3:16

II JOHN

Epistle of John — Written in Koine Greek,   c. A.D. 90

John wrote this short letter to a church in Asia Minor which he addresses as "the elect lady," and kept it very short as he "would rather not use paper and ink, but . . . hope to come to see you and talk with you face to face . . . that our joy may be complete." He stresses that in defending the faith he is not "writing you a new commandment, but the one we have had from the beginning, that we love one another."

III JOHN

Epistle of John — Written in Koine Greek,   c. A.D. 90

John kept this letter short, also, for the same reason as the first. He wrote it to a "beloved Gaius" who seems to have been an important person in the church, and tells of his concern over one Diotrophes who "put himself first . . . does not acknowledge my authority and refuses to welcome the brethren" Many times in these three letters, and in his Gospel, does John use the word "truth," so anxious is he to perpetuate the faith pure, whole and untainted; and he rejoices "No greater joy can I have than this, to hear that my children follow the truth . . . and you know that my testimony is true . . ."

While John in in Ephesus he has jurisdiction over the churches of "Asia" (Rome's name for western Turkey) and becomes particularly attached to six other cities which lie almost in a row north to south along its coast. Just south of legendary Troy is Pergamum, bustling hub of industry and trade where parchment was invented almost 300 years ago. Below it, Thyatira, another great commercial center founded in the 200's B.C. by the Ptolemies of Egypt. Then, Smyrna, as ancient as Homer, Pindar and Strabo and mentioned by all three in their works. Smyrna it was then and is now. Sardis is next, the capital of King Croesus' ancient Lydia . . . well acquainted with wealth and glory . . . and wickedness and vice. Philadelphia, the "city of brotherly love," is small in size but dear to John's heart for its constancy. One of eight cities so called in Asia Minor, Laodicea was named for the mother of King Seleucus who ruled here after the death of Alexander the Great. And finally, Ephesus itself, whose history goes back 1100 years. Proud and rich, it is the center of the worship of Artemis in her gigantic, wonder-filled temple, four times the size of Athen's Parthenon. Its theater is also one of the largest in the empire. Yet in spite of these pagan wonders Paul, and now John, have been immensely successful in Ephesus, and the Christian community flourishes. With Jerusalem destroyed and Rome not yet the—Christian—capital it will become, Ephesus, with Jesus' own beloved apostle, John, the only one still alive and living here, is a most important city. Now the aged apostle writes his book, that unique document that will become the fourth Gospel.

A great deal of scholarly debate revolves around the authorship of the Gospel of JOHN, the REVELATION TO JOHN, and in fact, even the three letters FROM JOHN. Although ancient tradition says John, the "beloved apostle; wrote them all, some biblical scholars believe it unlikely. The differences in style between them are too many, they say, and too dramatic, the content of each alien to the other: REVELATION'S Greek unlike any other Greek in the Bible. One man would not likely have written in such different ways. Some say JOHN'S—or REVELATION'S—author was a young disciple of the old apostle, also named John, who wrote for him (sort of like the argument against Shakespeare writing his own works.) Some also say the Gospel of JOHN was one of the earliest written, not this late at all. Even Lazarus has been named as the possible author, who would have seen Jesus with a perspective different from others.Whatever the answers, THIS writer will gladly leave the debate to others and present the conclusion of this book as many generations, and respected scholars, have believed, that the author is one man, and he Jesus' own apostle, grown old, now, the last surviving personal friend of Jesus and the only one who will die a natural, peaceful death . . . for whom, possibly, his long life was a heavier burden than an early martyrdom.

JOHN

Gospel of John — Written in Greek,   c. A.D. 90

"In the beginning was the WORD, and the Word was with God, and the Word was God. The same was in the beginning with God; all things were made by him; and without him was not any thing made that was made. In him was life; and the life was the light of men. And the light shineth in darkness; and the darkness comprehended it not . . . He was in the world, and the world was made by him, and the world knew him not. He came unto his own, and his own received him not. But as many as received him to them gave he power to become the sons of God, even to them that believe on his name . . . And the Word was made flesh, and dwelt among us (and we beheld his glory, the glory as of the only begotten of the father,) full of grace and truth."   JOHN 1:1–14

John

Here, in the incomparably beautiful and profound prologue to his gospel does John make his magnificent, exalted statement of belief in the Word of God, the *LOGOS*, which is manifest in Jesus, the carpenter of Nazareth. John's prologue is the door to a whole new world of insight, understanding and faith, for while the books of MATTHEW, MARK and LUKE told of Jesus the human man, how he lived and died in a Jewish/Greco/Roman world, here in the pages of JOHN does the Godly nature of the spiritual man shine forth as Jesus reveals Himself, His profoundest being, nature, person and meaning, in a rich kaleidoscope of colorful images:

> I am the way, the truth and the life: no one comes to the Father but by me. 14:6 * I and the Father are one. 10:30 * I am the light of the world, he who follows me will not walk in darkness, but will have the light of life. 8:12 * I am the bread of life; he who comes to me shall not hunger, and he who believes in me shall never thirst. 6:35 * Verily, I say unto you, before Abraham was, I am. 8:58 * I am the door . . . he who enters by the door is the shepherd of the sheep . . . I am the good shepherd . . . and I lay down my life for my sheep. 10:14 * Destroy this temple, and in three days I will raise it up. 2:19 * In the world you have tribulation; but be of good cheer, I have overcome the world. 16:33

Thus John illustrates over and over again the uniqueness of Christ to salvation, His being the culmination of thousands of years of spiritual growth, the fulfillment of the LAW of Moses and the Hebrew PROPHETS.

> You search the scriptures, because you think that in them you have eternal life, [but] it is they that bear witness to me. 5:39 * He that honoreth not the Son honoreth not the Father which hath sent Him. 5:23

And in chapter three, John sums up the whole matter, the entire meaning of Jesus Christ and the church He founded in another of His "Comfortable Words" . . .

> For God so loved the world that he gave his only begotten Son, that whosoever believeth in him should not perish, but have everlasting life. 3:16

And with these words does John put to rest the idea that Jesus was merely a great and profound teacher, for great teachers do not announce that "I and the Father are one; I am the bread of life," or "I have overcome the world." With these words must the reader of JOHN decide that Jesus was merely a madman, making ridiculous and laughable claims, and died for nothing, His followers all going to their deaths knowingly and willingly for a fraud and imposter—or, that He was what He said He was.

> I am the resurrection and the life; he that believeth in me, though he were dead, yet shall he live, and whosoever liveth and believeth in me shall never die. 11:25

To the "Great Commission" which Jesus gave His disciples (and Matthew recorded) to "Go and make disciples of all nations, baptizing them in the Father, Son and Holy Spirit, and teaching them all I have commanded you," John now adds authority for forgiveness of sins:

> Jesus said to them . . . As the Father hath sent me, even so I send you . . . Whosoever sins ye remit, they are remitted, and whosoever sins ye retain, they are retained. 20:23

John and his brother James, called the Greater, were those two sons of the fisherman, Zebedee, whom Jesus called "sons of thunder." The hot temper of his youth is gone now, though, and his book is called the "Gospel of love." John was the most faithful of Jesus;

friends and was with Him in every crisis. Indeed, it was he to whom Jesus entrusted His mother, Mary, when He hung on the cross (and local legend in Ephesus says that she lived out her life with him there.) John's complete and unqualified commitment to Jesus is touching and heartwarming from the very beginning to the last Passover supper; the agony in the Garden of Gethsemene; at the trial, and throughout the horrible long hours of crucifixion. And on Easter morning he was one of the first to learn the Good News at the tomb. Indeed, John closes his gospel saying that there were so many other things Jesus did that the world could not contain all the books that could be written, and he, more than anyone else, would know.

After the resurrection, John and Peter taught, preached, healed and were imprisoned together for a time. But his life and primary mission were devoted to Asia Minor, and primarily Ephesus, where he absorbed the Greco/Roman atmosphere that shows so vividly

Fragment of John
18:31–33 & 37
see page 404

in his writings, as he recalls Jesus' references to Himself as the Way, Truth, Life, the Water and Bread of Life, the Door and the Good Shepherd. "I am, I know, I speak," He says, and states unequivocally, "I and the Father are one. Only through me can men reach God." Using "Word" in a vivid portrayal of Jesus as the ultimate consummation of the "new" covenant, John paraphrases the lines that open the old: "In the beginning God created the Heavens and the earth," with profound eloquence: "In the beginning was the Word, and the Word was with God, and the Word was God."

"Verily, verily," John says time and time again, "truly, truly." In his summation, John the "beloved apostle," who loved the Lord, was Jesus' closest friend, with Him at every crisis and watched Him die like a criminal on the cross, betrayed and bereft, wrote of himself, John, that "He who saw it has borne witness; his testimony is true, and he knows he tells the truth . . . THAT YOU, ALSO, MAY BELIEVE."

The emperor Domitian is universally hated and feared for his extreme cruelty and erratic way of running the empire. He suspects everyone of plotting against him and says "the lot of all emperors is necessarily wretched, since only their assassination can prove that conspiracies are real." When a raven perches on the capitol roof, the people take it as an omen, and the following verse is surreptitiously circulated:

> There was a raven, strange to tell,
> Perched upon Jove's own gable, whence
> He tried to tell us, "All is well!"
> But had to use the future tense.

John's ministry and successes in "Asia" are widely known, even to Rome, and now he, too, falls victim to Emperor Domitian's mad persecutions, who has him exiled . . . to Patmos. Cast into chains, thrown into the dank hold of a Roman galley, the tired old man is given his own cross: slavery in the desolate stone quarries on a barren, rocky island. Here he labors under a Roman whip. But here, too, in the grotto of a sheltering cave he once again meets his Master; and receives the strange, marvelous visions that make up his book of REVELATION:

The REVELATION to St. John

Book of Apocalypse — Written in Greek, c. A.D. 95

"I am Alpha and Omega, the beginning and the end, the first and the last." Thus does REVELATION conclude the mighty drama. The Bible began with the creation of the world; and it closes, now, with the promise of a NEW heaven and earth. John (whichever "John" he was) wrote his book in Koine Greek sometime during the reign of the murderous Emperor Domitian, on the Greek island of Patmos, persecuted for his faith. In the years ahead when the early church fathers put together the "canon" of the New Testament (that is, decide which of the many books in existence are authentic and will be included and which not) REVELATION will almost be left out, for there will be strong feeling against it. To this day many churchmen agree, saying that no other book has been more misinterpreted and ill used. But there exist today, also, a vast wealth of beautiful poetry, powerful drama, gorgeous art work and glorious, inspiring music because of its inclusion.

REVELATION is an apocalypse; that is, "prophecy revealed": in this case revealed to John by an angel who "resembled the son of man." The strange, wonderful and frightening visions that were shown to John burst like fantastic fireworks from the pages of his book, and have been, for centuries, a source of awe and wonder. Some modern scholarship believes that early Christians would have had little trouble understanding John; that his cryptic allusions and symbols, his Hellenistic philosophy, oriental mysticism and pseudo-science were written in an elaborate, contemporary code, but that the "key" to that code has long ago been lost. After all, Christianity was, in John's time, an illegal, outlaw religion, practiced underground, and John's visions and symbols were things that his Christian brethren were all too familiar with: the Lamb of God seated on the Heavenly throne, opening the Seven Seals which let loose the terrible Four Horsemen of the Apocalypse: death, disease, war and judgment. They show dragons, beasts and angels; the war in Heaven between Michael and Satan, and the destruction of "Babylon."

Directly eastward across the water from his exile, lie the mainland and John's "Seven Cities of Asia;" and he writes to each one in turn: Sardis, whose "works are not perfect," and Thyatira, who "tolerates an adulteress." Laodicea, John says, is "neither hot nor cold,

3rd century ms.
fragment of Relevation

but lukewarm." Those three great, worldly cities always vying to be "first city of Asia"—Pergamum, Smyrna and John's own Ephesus, come in for much condemnation . . . but comfort, too, and are entreated not to fear what they are about to suffer. Only little Philadelphia is spared criticism, and told it will "escape the trial that is coming to the world."

John wrote his book using the fantasy-like imagery of the Middle-East, not the straight-forward, clean-cut classical Greek style, nor the "repetitive redundancy" of "Old Testament" Hebrew, and certainly not Elizabethan perfection nor the vulgar vernacular of 20th century English! Rather, he wrote REVELATION in a raw and cruel Roman age, a time of terrible persecution, where savage violence was NOT ONLY A DEPLORABLE ABBERATION OF ISOLATED CRIMINAL TYPES, BUT THE OFFICIAL POLICY OF THE WORLD'S LARGEST GOVERNMENT. Under the title "Caesar," cold-blooded killers occupied the most exalted throne in the world and could, with the nod of a head, commit any crime.

More likely, the telling of John's visions were meant to inspire faith, loyalty, trust and hope in an infant church that was reeling in a dizzy spin from assault on every side, persecuted by un-believers, heretics and anti-Christians together; and he used every means he could to bolster up his "little childrens'" spirits: he praised them, scolded them, badgered them, cajoled them . . . and even scared them. Although he calls it "Babylon," it was the Seven Hills of ROME upon which John based all his "sevens": seven churches, seven stars, seven lampstands. And the "beast" was NERO, or Nero incarnate, Domitian—whether one of his age or our own—who made Christians quake in fear. For the Hebrews, centuries ago, to have abandoned the God of Abraham and Moses for the fleshpots of Babylon was tragic and disastrous, but often more misguided than malicious. For latter-day Jews to be forced to worship the frivolous, capricious imaginings of the Greeks and the later Roman adaptations of them was an unacceptable affront not only to their faith but to their intelligence and integrity; and few felt compelled, by capitulation, to save their skins if not their souls. But now, for the Christians, whether Jewish convert or Gentile, to be forced to deny that One, True God's promised Messiah, whose only crime was compassion, healing, love and sacrifice—the greatest sacrifice of all time—to worship as gods such loathsome monsters of depravity as Claigula, Nero and, now, Domitian was blasphemous, degrading and degenerate beyond belief, and to resist that force, those demands for "emperor worship" was every bit worth dying for. Yes, death the "Roman way"—often in the arena by wild beast—was fearful, but life in this kind of Rome was even worse, and it is ROME'S DESTRUCTION REVELATION PROPHESIES, that ". . . mother of harlots . . . drunk with the blood of saints . . . and the martyrs of Jesus . . ."

. . . Fallen, fallen is [Rome] . . . for all nations have drunk the wine of her impure passion . . .   REVELATION 17:5,6 & 18:2,3 RSV

John was echoing Jeremiah's judgement against the first Babylon so long ago:

> Babylon hath been a golden cup in the Lord's hand, that made all the earth drunken. The nations have drunken of her wine, therefore all the nations are mad. JEREMIAH 51:7,
> see: 605 B.C.

John's promise of a new Jerusalem was not made just yesterday, but rather at the very time of the horrible destruction of the Old. The end of the world? For Christians and Jews, alike, that is exactly what the time seemed like. Earthquakes, floods, volcanoes? They are the growing pains of a living planet constantly in motion, not a portent of doom. Wars and rumors of wars? The pages of history are full of nothing but wars and rumors of wars from the beginning of time, every time some former or latter-day Nero decides that God is dead and sets himself up, instead. Whatever other fearful-sounding, dread-inducing, awe-inspiring, world-shaking, sin-scourging and/or soul-saving events John's revelations might prophecy and hold for us today and tomorrow, they are in reality, something much greater than that: for although they are cloaked in death, disease, destruction and damnation, his REAL message is this:

"The Lord God Omnipotent Reigneth . . . Hallelujah!

Worthy is the Lamb that was slain, to receive power and wealth and wisdom and might and honor and glory and blessing! For the kingdom of this world is become the kingdom of our Lord and of His Christ, and He shall reign

King of Kings and Lord of Lords for ever and ever. . . HALLELUJAH! AMEN!"

According to a second century historian named Tertullian (who will write a hundred years hence) the Emperor Domitian has a change of heart and releases some prisoners, including John, from bondage:

> . . . Domitian . . . who was a good deal of a Nero in cruelty . . . but being in some degree human . . . soon stopped what he had begun, and restored those he had banished.
> Tertullian, DEFENSE OF THE CHRISTIAN FAITH.

Tertullian, born Quintus Septimius Tertullianus of Carthage, North Africa, will become one of the great Christian apologists of the early church. A lawyer, an "eminent jurist" (according to Irenaeus), a man of great wit—and much sarcasm—he will tell, also, how he grew up a pagan, "a sinner of every brand, born for nothing but repentance." Tertullian will add a most intriguing footnote to the story of Jesus' crucifixion and resurrection:

This whole story of Christ was reported to Caesar (at that time it was Tiberius) by [Pontius] Pilate himself in his heart already a Christian.   Tertullian, DEFENSE OF THE CHRISTIAN FAITH

96, September 18.   To Rome's great relief, Domitian is assassinated (by a conspiracy that includes relatives and even his wife, and the senate moves quickly to restore sanity to the government. In full session it elects an aged, but honorable senator, Marcus Cocceius Nerva as emperor. He is the first of a succession who will be known as the "Five Good Emperors." He swears an oath that he will not put any senator to death . . . and keeps it, and pro-

Nerva

ceeds to undo as much as can be of the evil Domitian did. He melts down all of the many gold and silver idols of the would-be "Lord and God" for the public treasury, and permits no idols made of himself. He institutes many reforms, does nothing without the advice of the senate, "appoint[s] a commission . . . to reduce public expenditure," and even sells many of his own clothes and possessions, including houses and estates, to replenish the public coffers. And to ensure that his reforms continue he devises an effective method of arranging for a competent, able successor. He simply picks out the best man, adopts him, and makes him his legal heir. Pliny the Younger tells how . . .

. . . he took. . .laurels to lay . . . in the lap of Jupiter, and when he came out he said in a loud voice: "May good fortune attend the senate and people of Rome, and myself. I hereby adopt Marcus Ulpius Traianus."   Pliny the Younger, PANEGYRIC 8.2–3, LIVES OF THE LATER CAESARS

Although his heir Traianus, called Trajan, is not a relative and is a Spaniard, not an Italian, Nerva believes that his ability is more important than kinship or nationality, and so sets Rome on a path of good government that will last the next 32 years.

98, January 28.   Nerva is proud of his accomplishments as emperor and says (according to the historian Dio Chrysostom 68.3.1) "I have done nothing that could prevent me from laying down the imperial office and returning to private life in safety." But three months after the adoption, Nerva dies and Trajan becomes emperor, the second of the "Five Good Emperors." (The last three will be Hadrian, Antoninus Pius and Marcus Aurelius, who will reign after this book closes,) and who will be revered and respected by the Romans for their dedication to honor and duty, men who—despite Aurelius' persecution of Christians and Jews—will bring stability back to the empire . . . for a while.

As Trajan takes office, he presents a weapon to the *praefect* of the guard and says, "Take this sword, in order that, if I rule well, you may use it for me, but if ill, against me." Born at Italica, Spain, Trajan had a brilliant military career, rising to general, and in politics rising to consul, and now emperor. A long campaign in Dacia (today's Romania) over, with that nation now another Roman province, Trajan brings back a million pounds of silver and half million of gold, and celebrates the victory . . .

Trajan

> When Trajan, returned to Rome he gave spectacles lasting for one hundred twenty-three days, during which eleven thousand animals, both wild and tame, were slain, and ten thousand gladiators fought.   LIVES OF THE LATER CAESARS, Dio 68.15.1

He spends vast amounts on public works and games without "bleeding anybody dry," as Dio puts it. He restores the Circus Maximus, burned out in Nero's fire, builds libraries, baths and roads, and cuts a canal to drain the Tiber. To safeguard the corn supply he builds a new harbor at Ostia, a project so vast "he was said to have let the sea into the shore and moved the shore out to sea." And although he never loses his commanding military bearing, he also, never loses his sense of decency and humanity:

> He often went to call on his friends . . . accepted their invitations to dinner and invited them back in return. Often he would ride in their carriages. His association with the people was marked by affability and his relations with the Senate by dignity, so that he was loved by all and feared by no one. He joined others in the hunt and in banquets, as well as in their labours and plans and jokes . . . he would enter the houses of citizens, sometimes even without a guard, and enjoy himself there. His friends blamed him for being too accessible, but he replied that, as emperor, he behaved towards private citizens in the manner in which, as a private citizen, he had wanted emperors to behave towards him . . . by nature he was not at all inclined to duplicity or guile or harshness, but he loved, greeted and honoured the good, and the others he ignored. Moreover he became milder as he grew older.   LIVES OF THE LATER CAESARS, Eutropius 8.5.1 and Dio 68.5.3.

100   The first "Christian" century closes, as the Roman Empire reaches its greatest size and prosperity under the Emperor Trajan, the mightiest power the world has yet known. The Roman genius had always been that even in the worst of times they could learn from others, could incorporate the best of their enemies, win or lose, unto themselves. Thus, in the beginning, when Rome was only a small city, they learned government, legal codes and constitutions from other small Italian cities around them; art, architecture and ideas from Greece, and civil and military organization and technology from Carthage. Now supreme in the world, Rome seems immortal, but will, in fact, live only 300 more years before it finally expires; most of them years of calamity, terror and retreat from fierce barbarian hordes from the north, throwing Europe into its own "Dark Age." Future historians will cite many factors for Rome's fall: the cheapened value of citizenship, granted, now, even

THE ROMAN EMPIRE
AT ITS GREATEST EXTENT
c.100 A.D.

AT THE CLOSE OF
THE BIBLE

to "barbarians," chronic financial crises and the burden and expense of maintaining Rome's far-flung boundaries; over-zealous tax collectors and amoral, unethical business and social behavior; rampant immorality and vice; governmental cruelty and pandering to the blood lusts of its degraded people; and vain, murderous despots on the throne of Caesar to the final irony when the most exalted office in the world will be, literally, auctioned off to the highest bidder! Some will cite Christianity, itself, for having sapped the empire of its vitality and retreated inward upon itself. In spite of Rome's raping the world around it for its riches, for centuries now, the drain on the Roman economy has been far too lopsided due to the immense importation of goods, both necessities and luxuries, from foreign states. And especially, the fact that, under the emperors, the people have forgotten how to govern themselves, and not only forgotten, but don't want to: they would rather be taken care of than take care of themselves. And the drained Roman coffers will leave no funds . . . nor skills . . . to repair Rome's own crumbling cities, roads and aqueducts. Without water and transportation commerce will stagnate, farms lay waste, crops die and farmers starve. Neighbor will be cut off from neighbor, city from city and the empire from its government.

But Rome's death rattle is still far into the future. For now the empire flourishes and, for most people, these are good times; times of peace, prosperity and luxury. Centuries from now archeology will reveal Rome's presence and Roman ruins from Britain to Africa and from Spain to Asia, homes and public buildings of exquisite elegance and opulence, great cities of comfort and wealth. And for those with nothing, the government provides free grain and entertainment. Still, not everyone is happy, and the writer, Juvenal, is bitterly critical of the system which, he feels, is rank with corruption, injustice and abuse, with far too many of its people gripped in the bonds of slavery or locked into the public dole:

> We are suffering from the evils of protracted peace: more cruel than war, the hand of luxury has been laid upon us. No deed of lust or violence is lacking, now that poverty is dead in Rome. Soft wealth has corrupted the age with foul ease. Two things only the people anxiously desire . . . *PANEM ET CIRCENSES*—BREAD AND CIRCUSES!   Juvenal,
> SATIRE 10:80

Free food and games! And the bloodier the better. When their bellies are full and their blood lusts satisfied, they won't ask who's minding the state. The Circus Maximus, that gigantic race arena, planned out 700 years ago by the Tarquin, Rome's fifth king; begun by Julius Caesar, partly destroyed by "Nero's fire," and rebuilt by Trajan, now holds somewhere between two and 300,000 persons and is used by the government as a pacifier for the poor . . . as is Vespasian's Colosseum, gory death site of thousands. But it is not just the "poor" who wallow in

Rome's depravity. Proud wealth, royalty, nobility, all alike fall under the spell of vice, viciousness and immorality. Fabulous, gluttonous banquets at gilded town homes or luxurious country villas celebrate abomination and debauchery, unnatural perversions, incest, murder, anything and everything. Even a "good" emperor like Trajan can sponsor games that kill off

11,000 animals and 5000 human lives for sport. When Christianity does, indeed, turn in upon itself in monasteries, convents and abbies, it will not be a turning away from "life," or the "world," as its enemies charge, but from the decadence and degradation, immorality and inhumanity of life and the exploitation of the world. For the degenerate self-abasement by this time is the ultimate expression of the Hellenistic love of self-indulgence and "anything goes," and Christians are revolted, not by life, but by the excesses of life carried to base extremes. It will be another of history's great confrontations: between Christianity, founded and built upon faith, love, kindness, charity, brotherhood and sacrifice versus vicious, immoral Rome drowning in its own blood and gore; founded on law and justice, but swollen, over the years, with the pollution of butchery, treachery and greed.

— The writer Decimus Junius Juvenalis, or Juvenal, he whom those three words made immortal—BREAD AND CIRCUSES—despises the empire, sees no good in it at all and wishes for the return of the Republic. When asked why he writes satires he replies, "Why not? In this age how could I not write satires?" Very little is known of Juvenal's life except that he seems to have been poor but proud, a teacher badly treated and dishonestly paid. A man of genius, it is degrading and humiliating to him to have to earn a mean living off of the very society he deplores. Having been banished, once, to Egypt for aiming a barb at Domitian's "favorite," he has wisely not published his satires until after Domitian's death. But Juvenal's hatred of the empire is, at least, impartial. He hates its luxury and sloth just as much as its ugliness and vice; in short, anything that drives Rome further away from the ancient Roman values of honesty, dignity, honor, virtue, pride and self-respect.

Juvenal is not the only writer commenting on the world at this time. There are many others living and working now, in this "Silver Age" of literature, some whose works have lasted to this very day, and from whom this book, has quoted much. Their collective life spans range from A.D. 40 to 140 which means that they all grew up through childhood to manhood hearing dinner-table talk or school-boy gossip about this emperor bedding his sisters or that one murdering his mother, about these mass murders or those incestuous orgies, an incredible age where one historian could even record that one of the "good emperors" liked young boys . . . but that was all right, because he did it discretely, so it really didn't hurt anybody.

— Twenty year old Gaius Suetonius Tranquillus, born in Africa is now studying in Rome, and will become a lawyer, magistrate and someday, court archivist where he will have direct access to all state . . . and private . . . papers. Nobly born into the knightly *equestrian* class, Suetonius has easy access to the intimacies of the high-born; and his books, including the LIVES OF THE TWELVE CAESARS are full of anecdotes, gossip, and of course, scandal, for that and the Caesars walk hand in hand. From Augustus to Domitian, all come alive in his pages, as do the poets and writers Lucan, Horace, Terrance and Virgil . . . and Roman manners, mores, spectacles . . . and secrets. It is in his biography of Claudius that Suetonius makes mention of the founder of Rome's newest religion:

> Because the Jews at Rome caused continuous disturbances at the instigation of Chrestus (Christ) he expelled them from the city.　Suetonius, LIVES 1:25

— The Roman historian, Cornelius Tacitus, son-in-law and outspoken admirer of the murdered General Agricola, is now about 45 years old and working on his writings—much quoted in this book—the HISTORIES and the ANNALS OF IMPERIAL ROME. Whereas Juvenal lived a poor man's life amid the cast-off dregs of society and wrote about Rome's human refuse, Tacitus was born into wealth and position, and moves easily among the privileged few . . . and yet, he sees the end result the same; crime and corruption. His writings begin with the creation of empire under Augustus, follow through the degradations of those who succeeded him, and include, also, the miserable "year of the four emperors." It is Tacitus who tells of Nero's fire and how he made scapegoats of Christians, using them for human torches:

> Their originator, Christ, had been executed in Tiberius' reign by the governor of Judea, Pontius Pilate . . . Dressed in wild animals skins, they were torn to pieces by dogs, or crucified . . . Nero provided his gardens for the spectacle . . . Despite their guilt as Christians . . . the victims were pitied. For it was felt that they were being sacrificed to one man's brutality rather than to the national interest.　Tacitus, ANNALS 14:15:42–44

Orator and public official, *quaestor, aedile* and *praetor,* Tacitus is an ardent republican to the end, hopes for the Republic's restoration, and never reconciles himself to the empire.

> To plunder, to slaughter, to steal. These things they misname empire; and where they make a desert, they call it peace!   Tacitus, AGRICOLA

Some latter-day historians believe that Tacitus, like Suetonius with what they call his "malicious gossip," was far too vitriolic and one-sided in his accounts of the emperors he so detested, that most had good traits as well as evil; but we can never know, for, besides just a few other ancient histories and the emperors' own documents, the works of these two are all we have. And yet, "all we have" is a grave injustice, for these were great writers, Tacitus especially being called by a latter-day republican, Thomas Jefferson, "the first writer of the world without a single exception."

—   One writer sees Rome very differently from these three: to him it is the queen of cities, beautiful and exciting; but then he is not a Roman, he is a Greek and comes to Rome only once (or twice?) on "official business" for Athens. Lucius Mestrius Plutarchus, called Plutarch, is traveling, observing, learning and lecturing throughout Greece, Italy and Egypt, and greatly impresses those who hear him in Rome. Educated in Athens, Plutarch has a commanding knowledge of history and philosophy, and his most famous, and lasting, work (outside 300 others which are lost) is his monumental PARALLEL LIVES OF THE NOBLE GREEKS AND ROMANS, or PLUTARCH'S LIVES, from which this book has quoted much. From the founding of Rome nearly 800 years ago, to the "year of the four emperors" just past, 56 of the great Greeks and Romans come back to life again under Plutarch's pen. Themistocles, Pericles, Alcibides and Alexander; Pompey, Caesar, Cicero and Antony, in this book do we learn their stories. Fifteen hundred years from now, one William Shakespeare will study Plutarch's LIVES, move to Londinium and write plays based on those same lives. Then will Antony cry, once more, "Friends, Romans, countrymen . . . I come to bury Caesar, not to praise him!" Plutarch carefully explains that he is not writing "history," he is writing "lives" . . .

> . . . the most glorious exploits do not always furnish us with the clearest discoveries of virtue or vice in men, sometimes a matter of less moment, an expression or a jest, informs us better of their characters and inclinations, than the most famous sieges, the greatest armaments, or the bloodiest battles . . .   Plutarch, LIVES: ANTONY, I.

—   Marcus Valerius Martialis, called Martial, he who wrote those vivid descriptions of the Colosseum, its games, wonders . . . and horrors . . . is 60 now, rich, respected and famous, the first writer whose works are codex-bound like "books" rather than rolled scrolls. His books are, also, the first to be illustrated, not only with scenes from the text including the Colosseum, its thronged spectators, wild beasts, bloody arena and mock sea battles, but advertisements, as well, that tell where his books may be bought: ". . . at the bookstall of Secundus, behind the entrance to the temple of Peace and the Forum of Pallas."

— Gaius Plinius Secundus, or Pliny the Younger, who wrote so vividly to Tacitus about the eruption of Mount Vesuvius and his uncle (Pliny the Elder's) death is, today, a very important man. A lawyer at only 18, an orator without peer, inheritor of his father's and uncle's great fortunes, and close friend and confidante of the Emperor Trajan, he is also, not only a good man whose writings show that there was still some goodness left in Rome, but a generous man, who built, for his home town alone, a school, temple, public bath, children's home and library. Now, at 38, Trajan awards him another honor, and appoints him Consul of Rome. More will be heard from Pliny and Trajan, soon.

— Somewhere in the middle-east, a young lad is living now whose identity is, today, completely unknown. When he grows up he will become a Christian scribe, and labor for many years slowly, carefully and patiently copying out Christian manuscripts, in a town called Oxyrhynthus, far away from Rome, in Upper Egypt. About 20 to 30 years from now he will copy out the Gospel written by the Apostle John, who probably died just a few years ago. Depending on how old the scribe is now (if he is over, say, 10) his lifetime and John's could well have overlapped. Somehow or other, his manuscript will, in future years, become mixed in with some trash, abandoned in the desert, and forgotten. There the hot, exceedingly dry air will preserve some of it for 1900 years, when it will be found and sold, in a box of papyrus scraps and pieces to the John Rylands Library in Manchester, England, and much later identified as the oldest fragment of the "New Testament" in existence. It is just a small fragment containing only a few words, but they are clear and plain and easily recognizable as that portion of JOHN numbered 18:31–33 & 37 . . .

1st century fragment of John
18:31–33 & 37

> Then said Pilate unto them, take ye him, and judge him according to your law. The Jews therefore said unto him, it is not lawful for us to put any man to death: that the saying of Jesus might be fulfilled, which he spake, signifying what death he should die. Then Pilate entered into the judgement hall again, and called Jesus, and said unto him, Art thou the King of the Jews? . . . Jesus answered, Thou sayest that I am a king, To this end was I born, and for this cause came I into the world, that I should bear witness unto the truth. Every one that is of the truth heareth my voice.   JOHN 18:31–33 & 37

It is a spectacular find, for many reasons. It proves that JOHN was, indeed, not only written by this time, but (by 110–120) so widely circulated that it had traveled to an already active community of Christians in the farthest limit of Egypt. But, most of all, it is spectacular for what it does to arguments against Christianity. Consider. Nobody doubts that Julius Caesar lived when and where he did and did what he did, and yet, the oldest copy of his writings in existence dates to 900 years after he fought and wrote about his "Gallic Wars." The same goes for Rome's historian, Livy, except that the oldest copy of his works dates 1100 years after he wrote it; and to top them both, the oldest extant copies of Thucydides, Herodotus (from which so much of the history in this book is taken) and Plato (without whom Socrates would be unknown) who all lived at about 400 B.C. were copied out at about A.D. 1100, or FIFTEEN HUNDRED YEARS after they wrote their works. And this work of JOHN dates only nine DECADES, NINETY YEARS—not even ONE CENTURY—after the events it describes! Moreover, although this fragment of JOHN is the oldest New Testament document, it is by no means the only. There exist today not only fragments but books, and even some whole bibles that were copied out within only 200 years of John's death.

Some of these (Roman) writers are acquaintances, close friends and/or correspondents, and many of their letters still exist, on many subjects. In one letter, Pliny tells Suetonius not to worry about a bad dream, it might be a good omen; and in one to Tacitus he tells of the pleasures of a boar hunt . . . provided he remember to take along pen and paper, bread and a bottle of wine. Another says that he knows Tacitus' HISTORIES will be immortal and admits that he hopes to be mentioned in them; and, of course, there is his dramatic response to Tacitus' request to learn how Pliny the Elder died in the eruption of Mt. Vesuvius. Pliny, now Consul Pliny, and his closest friend, the Emperor Trajan, also carry on an enormous correspondence. Trajan appoints Pliny (in A.D. 110) governor of Bithynia, a large province in northern Asia Minor, and Pliny seeks out Trajan's advice about many matters: whether to restore or rebuild an "ancient bath now in a ruinous state," how to procure a shipment of corn, how long to keep a foreign ambassador waiting for word from Rome, how to collect some un-paid funds owed to the capital, whether he should use soldiers or slaves for a certain guard duty . . . and, especially . . .

Trajan

. . . *what to do with the Christians?*

For Christianity is already becoming a powerful influence in the empire and the age of the great Christian teachers, theologians and historians has begun. The "Apostolic Age" lasted through the lifetimes of Jesus' disciples-become-apostles, the "inner circle" who knew Him personally, to be followed, now, by the Age of the Early Church Fathers, some of whom knew THEM. The Fathers are the physical, intellectual, empirical link in the historical chain between Jesus, Himself, and the catholic-small-c (or universal) church that His life began, and that has spanned the centuries. It was through these early scholars that the church would grow to intellectual maturity, who would show how faith in the risen Christ is not unreasonable or irrational, but a comprehensible and deeply profound culmination of thousands of years of spiritual growth and development. Where pagan religious rites and rituals through the centuries had often been sadistic and dehumanizing with the "reading" of omens in animal entrails and weird incantations and initiations, orgiastic debauchery, cult prostitution and even human sacrifice, the Christian Fathers girded Jesus' message of faith, hope, love and charity, and His promise of forgiveness and salvation, with order, discipline, sanity, serenity, harmony and beauty of both rite and ritual. And these great scholars became, to the Christian faith, what Socrates, Plato and Aristotle were to Greek philosophy, and what Jefferson, Madison and Adams would someday be to American democracy, who the Bible could have been describing when it said; "There were giants on the earth in those days."   GENESIS 6:4

Giants, indeed, and heroes in an age of barbarism; they lived humbly, worked mightily and died heroically for their belief in Jesus the revealed truth, and were burned at the stake, beheaded, skinned alive and thrown to wild beasts in Roman arenas. Their stories can be found in few history books; modern, secular society prefers to forget they ever existed. But they did exist; heroes, every one, and their lives matter to us a great deal. They were philosophers, poets and doctors of both mind and soul, so prolific of genius some could write a hundred books with half an effort. To a world awash with blood, butchery, bondage and bestiality, they introduced a ritual of beauty, and taught Christians how to live lives of dignity, order, charity, humanity, equanimity and hope, and in so doing they became the . . .

. . . *founders of Western Civilization.*

— Clement of Rome, or Clemens Romanus, known as Clement I, the third bishop of Rome after the apostle Peter, is thought to have been consecrated by Peter, himself. In his one (undisputed) letter that has survived the centuries, he describes the organization of the early church and stresses the importance to Christians of "law and order," not the order imposed by a Roman whip, galley or cross, but that which is self-imposed willingly, with love, compassion, generosity, humility, moderation and always . . . charity. An Old Testament scholar, he wrote how the great heroes of ancient Israel—Abraham, Jacob, Moses, Aaron, Judith, Esther and Daniel—provided a pattern for Christian conduct; and he tells how the great Paul of Tarsus, the forerunner of the "early fathers," took the Good News or Gospel, of Christ to the "whole world." Paul, he says . . .

Latter-day coin of Paul

. . . was the herald of the Gospel in the West as well as the East, and enjoyed the illustrious reputation of . . . teaching the whole world to be righteous. And after he had been to the extremity of the West, he suffered martyrdom before the sovereigns of mankind.
Clement, bishop of Rome, EPISTLE TO THE CORINTHIANS, c. 5

— Ignatius, bishop of Antioch in Syria, was said in ancient legend to have been the child whom Jesus took in His arms then cured of epilepsy, or an "unclean spirit." He "saw the life of Christ continued in the Eucharist, the bread that is the flesh which suffered for our sins." Ignatius was, himself, at first a pagan and, like the great Paul, a persecutor of Christians; and he desires nothing more than to become a martyr himself, to be sacrificed for his faith and, in fact, at about A.D. 107–110, "ten soldiers" will escort him to Rome, allowing him to visit Polycarp on the way. There, after first begging the church of Rome NOT to deprive him of martyrdom by trying to intercede with the authorities on his behalf, he will be thrown to wild animals in the Colosseum:

> I fear your love, lest it do me an injury. If you intervene on my behalf . . . I shall have my course again to run . . . ye cannot do me a greater kindness than to suffer me to be sacrificed unto God, now that the altar is already prepared. Let fire and the cross, let the companies of wild beasts, let breakings of bones and tearing of members . . . [all] come upon me . . . I would rather die for Jesus Christ, than rule to the utmost ends of the earth.
> Ignatius, bishop of Antioch, EPISTLE TO THE ROMANS. (See also, Eusebius, HISTORY OF THE CHRISTIAN CHURCH, Ch. 1)

— Polycarp, bishop of Smyrna (one of John's "seven cities of Asia") was another "living link" between the people of the Bible and the later church fathers, for he KNEW Jesus' "beloved apostle," John, was John's disciple, wrote about and remembered him to his own disciples. Beginning with its mighty prologue, "In the beginning was the Word, and the Word was with God, and the Word WAS God . . ." John had drawn the *LOGOS* of Christ not as a "new truth," but of truth as old as all time and as eternal as the Father, himself. Now Polycarp, John's own disciple, is the first "Apostolic Father" to see the "newness" in a new conception of physics, ethics and logic of human development; that the revelation of Christ was a principle of understanding above and beyond that of the ancients or the classics. Polycarp's burden was a heavy one. Ever since the first "heretic," Simon the Magus or Magician, who tried to buy the gift of healing, there had been other heresies of all sorts. One sect said that Christianity was a new invention, independent and unrelated to Judaism; one that Jesus was not born of a woman, he simply "appeared" one day at the Synagogue at Capernaum; another says Jesus didn't really suffer, He only seemed to, didn't really die, but was rescued after He passed out. There are sects with a Great Mother goddess and a Primal Man, and one that says salvation comes only through wisdom (*sophia*) or "revelation," which only that sect's members could receive. For all these heresies, Polycarp (and others after him) applied one standard and one test: <u>Can it be found in, and is it based upon, HOLY SCRIPTURE?</u>

Seven years from now. Polycarp will receive "with great honor"—and kiss the chains of—the venerable teacher and historian, Ignatius, while being "escorted" by 10 soldiers on his way to martyrdom in the Roman Colosseum. And half a century from now a very old Polycarp will, himself, journey to Rome for discussions there about determining the dates for keeping the feast of Easter. On his return he will be seized during a pagan festival and, on February 23, A.D. 155, be burned at the stake for refusing to curse Christ, rejoicing in his ". . . 86 years of service to the Lord."

> . . . the proconsul repeated, "Swear by the genius of Caesar, revile Christ, and I will release you!" Polycarp replied, "Eighty and six years have I served Christ and he has done me nothing but good, how then can I curse him, my Lord and Savior?" . . . At this the whole multitude . . . clamored that he should be burned alive . . . and ran with all speed to fetch wood . . . The executioners would have nailed him to the stake, but he said, "He who gives me grace to endure the fire will enable me to remain at the pile unmoved." Then we saw a marvelous sight . . . The flames . . . like the sails of a ship, gently encircled his body . . . which . . . resembled, not burning flesh but bread that is baking or precious metal refined. And there was a fragrance like the smell of incense . . .   Eusebius, HISTORY OF THE CHRISTAIN CHURCH, 4:15

Polycarp's own disciple, Ireneaus, considered Polycarp THE man who held the church together through, not only the terrible Roman persecutions, but all these heretical speculations and pagan additions to the faith that were springing up all over. Polycarp's staunch, courageous opposition and unwavering commitment to pure, unadulterated scriptural doctrine . . . and his own person . . . will be fondly remembered by Ireneaus:

> . . . I can even now point out the place where the blessed Polycarp used to sit when he discoursed, and describe his goings out and comings in, his manner of life . . . personal appearance . . . how he used to speak of John . . . and the rest of those who had seen the Lord.   Ireneaus, bishop of Lyons. France

— Papias, bishop of Hieropolis, Greece, was also, a student of Polycarp and may, also, have "heard John." He tells, in his writings, how young John Mark had been interpreter to the old apostle, Peter. It was Peter's teachings, he says, that inspired the younger man to write his own book of MARK, the first written of the four Gospels and the model for MATTHEW and LUKE. Papias was a close friend and companion to . . .

— Justin Martyr, born the year this book ends, "Anno Domini," 100. He would come to believe that the Greek philosophy he very eloquently teaches is lacking too much to be complete, and that the Hebrew faith has much merit . . . as far as it goes. Reasoning, then, that Jesus Christ is the fulfillment of both, and being awed by Christian courage and undaunted commitment to Christ in the face of dreadful persecutions, he eagerly accepts the new faith and teaches it as the logical and reasonable fulfillment of both Greek and Hebrew beginnings. And that duality will extend not only into the FAITH of Christianity but into the PRACTICE of it as well. For, where the Greeks had taught the dignity of leisure (re: Aristotle, "The highest good for man is a life of contemplation,") the Romans, Virgil and Horace, taught the dignity of work, farming, good, honest labor. So, the Christian ethic, now, will teach the duality of labor and leisure: the two work together, one is not noble, the other base. Contemplation, prayer and leisure together with labor will make the Christian life.

All of these great Christian "Fathers" are living now, A.D. 100, aged from very old to very young, widely scattered throughout "the world" from Alexandria to Antioch and

Rome to Gaul. They are, with great struggle and sacrifice, preserving and passing down to future generations "the faith once for all delivered to the saints," just as the apostle JUDE had taught. They are painstakingly, little by little, drawing out a blueprint, so to speak, of the ORGANIZATION OF THE GOSPEL OF CHRIST into a worldly entity that will carry that "faith once for all delivered to the saints" forward for the next 2000 years, and beyond: a worldly entity strong enough, true enough and TOUGH enough to survive every human frailty, greed, graft, corruption and lust for both people and power; and still, generation after generation be able to renew itself cleansed of the impurities that are sure to come. Following them, now, will be the earliest great Christian HISTORIANS and APOLOGISTS or "Defenders of the Faith." These men aren't even born yet, are all in the future, near or far, and while this book could not begin to name them all, some are so vital to this story they must be included.

— Ireneaus, a student of Polycarp, and the next in the succession from Jesus to John to Polycarp, would have wonderful memories to pass on. A man of peace, not of fire, he became bishop of Lyons, and because of him Gaul/France would become Christian. He demonstrated how the Christian faith is, indeed the fulfillment of the Hebrew and helped, also, to set the date for Easter. Ireneaus will make the Gospel of JOHN a "living force" through his admiration for John's pupil, Polycarp. Ireneaus called Polycarp a "transmitter," not a "maker," for his heroic holding fast to the apostles' teachings and passing them on intact, staunchly opposed to new speculations, doctrines and heresies. Ireneaus' prodigious written work (only fragments of which still exist) including PROOF OF APOSTOLIC TEACHING, demonstrates how the Christian faith fulfills the Hebrew, using arguments solidly based on Holy Scripture. Ireneaus wrote of the Holy Communion, or *EUCHARIST*:

> As the bread, which comes from the earth, on receiving the invocation of God, is no longer common bread but Eucharist, and is then both earthly and heavenly; so our bodies, after partaking of the Eucharist, are no longer corruptible, having the hope of the eternal resurrection . . ."   Ireneaus,

— Clement of Alexandria, was born Titus Flavius Clemens about 150 in Athens of pagan parents, but lived in Alexandria, Egypt, where he taught the faith and became head of the Christian School of Instruction. He may possibly have been initiated into pagan rites, himself, before his conversion to Christianity, for he had a broad intellectual knowledge of pagan religious ceremonies, and used it to date the Hebrew scriptures as older, and therefore forerunners, of the Greek philosophic writings. He also had a penetrating knowledge of the Christian heresies and used them, also, to delineate and teach Christian orthodoxy. He saw Christianity as a philosophy, but far more advanced than the Greeks, who saw only fragments of the truth. In Jesus Christ, he said, was the truth absolutely and perfectly revealed.

But he still saw some value in all religions, as, for example, the Babylonian/Assyrian worship of the heavenly bodies in the cosmos, for being a "step in the right direction" to enable man to rise above the primitive worship of created THINGS to the CREATOR OF those things. Thus, Christ, Himself, was the ultimate form of philosophy, the LOGOS, the Reason. Clement's most famous student/become/church father, who would carry on—and surpass—his work, was . . .

— Origen of Alexandria, who would be called, by some, "The greatest teacher in the church after the Apostles." Born A.D. 185–6 in Athens to a Greek/Christian family, Origen was given an excellent Greek—and Christian—education, then took it upon himself to learn Hebrew so he could read the Old Testament in its original language. At 17 he saw his father dragged off in a Roman persecution to be killed for his faith, and was stopped only through the intervention of others, from offering himself to the same fate. That same persecution forced Clement of Alexandria to leave Egypt and his great Christian school, which opened the position to Origen who began—at the age of 18!—his long and illustrious teaching and literary career. In the next 52 years he would produce over SIX THOUSAND writings and teach multitudes of people from near and far; and his "fame spread throughout the Christian world." The major work of his life was written in these early Alexandrian years, a comprehensive study of Christianity of vast proportions, called ON FIRST PRINCIPLES. He overlooked no aspect of the faith, no doctrine, tenet, dogma or principle. With consummate wisdom and indefatigable energy he probed every question, every detail. Just a very few of his subjects were:

> God's Creation of All Things, and the Purpose of That Creation: the Transformation of the Universe, and the Truth Unveiled by Jesus; the Wonder of the Incarnation, and the Eternity and Omnipresence of the WORD: God's Plan for Holy Scripture, its True Meaning, Its Soul, Spirit and Chief Purpose, and How It Is Misunderstood. He talks of the New Human Race, and Its Conflict of Flesh and Spirit, its Key to Knowledge and the Varieties of Wisdom; of Man's Invisible Enemies, and his Attendant Angels, his Endowment with Reason, and with Free Will, and his affliction with Suffering, and Temptation. He tells How the Soul Chooses Freely, how and why Christ Appeals to Free Men, How Lives Can be Altered, but Healing is sometimes Deferred; why Rain Causes Both Fruits and Thorns, just as the Sun Both Binds and Loosens; what Evils are permitted by God, and Why there is No Good Apart from God.   Origen, ON FIRST PRINCIPLES

While still at Alexandria, Origen wrote (many!) COMMENTARIES on the books of JOHN, PSALMS, GENESIS, LAMENTATIONS, the Resurrection and . . . "Miscellany!" Excommunicated, for reasons unknown, in Egypt, Origen left Alexandria in 231 for Caesarea, where his fame and influence grew even greater . . . but (according to his student, Jerome) his "generosity, charm, sympathy and friendliness" never changed, and his deep and abiding love and reverence for Holy Scripture made his whole life a defense of ortho-dox doctrine against heresy. In his last 24 years at Caesarea he wrote COMMENTARIES on every book of the Bible, a TREATISE ON PRAYER and eight books AGAINST CEL-SUS (who had attacked Christianity 50 years before.) Hundreds of his extemporaneous lec-tures were published and, in 28 years and 50 volumes, he completed what he called his HEXAPLA: six versions of the Old Testament placed side by side for comparison. Tragi-cally, the HEXAPLA is long lost, but enough of Origen's works do exist to prove that there were, indeed, "giants on the earth in those days." In 250 there would be another bloody persecution of Christians by then Emperor Decius, and Origen would fall victim to it, im-prisoned at Tyre and cruelly tortured. Decius' timely death stopped the torture but broken, bloodied and crippled, Origen would linger two more years and die at 70, a martyr to his faith with spirit unbowed; the most influential and distinguished teacher of his time who honing, refining, enlarging and perfecting the work of others before him, reconciled Holy Scripture with Greek science and philosophy, and proved Christianity intellectually accept-able to persons of high culture and education, and left behind him, in the great seaport city of Caesarea, a thriving Christian school.

Rome has used King Herod's modern wonder-city of Caesarea as a capital city through-out its long occupation of Judea-now-Palestine. One of Herod's many construction tri-umphs, Caesarea was named for and dedicated to his friend the first Roman emperor, Cae-sar Augustus. An engineering marvel, an immense, bustling, busy seaport and hub of world trade and imperial bureaucracy, Caesarea has grown, over the years, into one of the most important cities in the east. Attracting people and ideas from far and wide, it is only natu-ral that the Christian Church should be drawn to it, also, and Origen's Christian library/school would grow to greatness and make itself, and Caesarea, world famous for Christian scholarship. Origen would spend the last years of his life in Caesarea and within just 10 years of his death another writer/scholar named Eusebius would be born in—and later become bishop of—Caesarea, who would also produce a monumental work, greatly influence the faith, and be called both "the Christian Herodotus" and the "Father of Eccle-siastical History":

— Eusebius Pamphili adopted his *cognomen* to honor his teacher and mentor, Pamphilus, who was a student and disciple of Origen and stew-ard of Origen's vast library. Together they wrote an "apology" or de-fense, of Origen's work (which still exists) and, when Pamphilus was slain in a persecution, Eusebius sought refuge from it in Egypt, only to be imprisoned there, but later released. As Bishop of Caesarea, Eusebius was, also, one of the churches' great scholars and wrote the first large scale, comprehensive history of Christianity (which exists to this day and from which this book has quoted often.) Eusebius' ECCLESIASTI-CAL HISTORY or HISTORY OF THE CHRISTIAN CHURCH is one of the church's priceless possessions, not only for his own scholarship and erudition (which were remarkable) but for the vast array of people, places and events he refers to and/or quotes who would be completely lost to history were they not in his book. Many fragments of other—long lost—works are preserved today only because they appear in Eusebius. The HISTORY covers the first 325 years of the church, beginning with Jesus Himself as the gospel of JOHN describes Him . . .

> In the beginning was the Word, and the Word was with God, and the Word was God . . .
> JOHN 1:1, quoted by Eusebius 1:2,4

. . . and continues through its years of incredible growth and expansion, the triumphs and terrors, glories and gore, those who defended the faith and those who would have destroyed it if they could . . . to Eusebius' own time, the time of the first Christian emperor, Constantine. Eusebius was a close friend, biographer and prolific "speech-writer" for Constantine, who "esteemed him highly," and when Constantine convened a great Christian Council in Nicea in 325, Eusebius was one of the 318 bishops in attendance. Constantine saw clearly that all the many heresies swirling about the faith by that time needed to be resolved and laid to rest, and that only a universal statement of belief could do that. When the debate on it became heated and contentious, he called on his friend, Eusebius, to offer the "confession of faith" he used in his own diocese, Caesarea, and so Eusebius did, in fact, present the first draft of the document which later became, with revisions, the "Nicene Creed," that Christians affirm to this very day.

> I believe in one God the Father Almighty, Maker of heaven and earth, and of all things visible and invisible: And in one Lord Jesus Christ, the only begotten Son of God, Begotten of his Father before all worlds, God of God, Light of Light, Very God of very God, Begotten, not made; Being of one substance with the Father, By whom all things were made: Who for us men and for our salvation came down from heaven, And was incarnate by the Holy Ghost of the Virgin Mary, And was made man: And was crucified also for us under Pontius Pilate; He suffered and was buried: and the third day he rose again according to the Scriptures: And ascended into heaven, And sitteth on the right hand of the Father: And he shall come again, with glory, to judge both the quick and the dead; Whose kingdom shall have no end. And I believe in the Holy Ghost, The Lord, and Giver of Life, Who proceedeth from the Father and the Son; Who spake
>
>
> Christ from an early mosaic
>
> by the Prophets: And I believe one Catholic and Apostolic church: I acknowledge one Baptism for the remission of sins: And I look for the Resurrection of the dead: And the life of the world to come. Amen.   The NICENE CREED as finally adapted and adopted by the Council of Nicaea

All these early fathers, from Syria to Spain and Egypt to England taught one Christianity, one faith, one common-ground of doctrine, tenets and principles. But the geographical area Christianity affected by this time was vast and diverse: three continents (Europe, Africa and Asia), many nations, traditions and languages (with two "official," Greek and Latin.) The Greek/eastern mind soared freely to heavenly heights by winding about, over and around, like mountain trails. The Roman/western mind was pragmatic and functional, direct and unbending like their roads, plowing straight through every obstacle. The eastern church sprang to life in the very heartland of Christianity's birth; eastern Christians trod the same territory and lived the same lives as Paul and Barnabas, Matthew, Mark, Luke and John; those in the west cringed from crazy Caesars who reigned Pontifex Maximus, high priest, over Rome's religions while they lined their Roman roads with crucified slaves. Born in the east when Christ was born, the faith had to be carried to the west and transplanted, the western understanding and propagation of the faith started from scratch, so to speak. To the east it was a part of their very existence, the truth the fathers taught orthodox, holy truth, Hagia Sophia, not to be argued about nor bargained for, absolute, for all time. When Roman west and Orthodox east, do, in fact, separate many centuries hence, it won't be the "beginning" of anything, just two equals going their separate ways, who don't see eye to eye. And while the Roman church in the years ahead will march missionaries across the world with the energy and drive of Roman legions, the Eastern will strive only to preserve its divinely delivered Orthodox faith for all time.

These early fathers will also record the remarkable growth of the new church, how pervasive it has become, and how wide-spread it was by their own time.

> . . . the church was extended by the Apostles to the utmost bounds of the earth. Irenaeus, c. A.D. 170 * . . . there is no race of men where prayers are not offered up in the name of Jesus. Justin Martyr, c. A.D. 150 * Christianity in Britain had penetrated even to those parts inaccessible to the Romans. Tertullian, c. A.D. 200

To Britain! That far away, and by 200! Well, its leading—Roman—community of Londinium, or London, is fast becoming one of the empire's important trading centers, its bustling Thames River dock-yards shipping tons of tin, lead, copper and wool to—and importing luxuries from—an eager world. When an exhausted, declining Rome withdraws its legions from Britain 300 years hence, much of the evidence of its long, pervasive presence will be covered over by time, and forgotten. Its lovely villas and palaces such as those (now uncovered) at Bath, Bignor, Fishbourne and Hinton St. Mary will burn or crumble and leave only their magnificent tile floors and some painted walls for future ages to marvel at. Then, exposed and undefended,

4th century wall tile
Hinton St. Mary
Dorset, England

the little island will lie easy prey to conquering Germanic Angles, Saxons and Jutes who will care nothing for Roman baths, temples, statues, Christian churches or the Christians, themselves, who will flee for their lives to Wales, Iona and Lindisfarne. Some refugees will bury their treasures, hoping to come back, as will a Christian family at Mildenhall, Suffolk, bury a magnificent silver table service, including a poignant memorial to their faith: three small spoons, engraved with names and Christian symbols, believed to have been Christening presents. One of the British Museum's proud possessions, the Mildenhall Treasure was unearthed by a farmer's plow in 1942 during World War II.

However Britain will be Christianized, and by whom, the faith will fall on fertile ground for, as Julius Caesar wrote 120 years ago, the Britons' "cardinal doctrine" already was that of a life after death, and the "good news" of Christ only fulfills their beliefs. More than 500 years from now the great Anglo-Saxon scholar named Baeda, once called "the candle of the church lit by the Holy Spirit," and remembered as the "Venerable Bede," will write that even a British king became Christian by 156:

> In 156 the British king, Lucius, sent a pious request to the emperor, Marcus Antonius Verus, brother of Commodus, asking to be made a Christian. The request was quickly granted . . . and the Britons received the Faith and held it peacefully in all its purity and fullness until the time of the Emperor Diocletian.   Venerable Bede, ECCLESIASTICAL HISTORY OF THE ENGLISH PEOPLE. 1.4

In his ECCLESIASTICAL HISTORY Bede will also tell how an English born Roman soldier named Alban became England's first Christian martyr and saint at about A.D. 225.

Alban, converted to the faith by a godly priest fleeing persecution, put on the priest's cloak and surrendered himself, instead. When his captors were unable to break him with torture, he was ordered decapitated. Seeing his faith and fortitude, his executioner begged to be slain with him . . . and was. (1:7) The church built on the site, and the city north-west of London, are today called St. Albans.

It is in his English HISTORY that the Bede divides time into B.C. (Before Christ) and A.D. (Anno Domini, In the Year of Our Lord), the first writer to do so, a system used to this day.

— When a newly consecrated bishop, whom we know today as Saint Patrick, takes the faith TO Ireland in 432, he will take it FROM England, un-Hellenized and un-Romanized, free from Hellenic philosophy and/or Roman authority, a Celtic Church of *Brittania*. Having been enslaved as a youth, his voice will be the first to speak out loud and clear against slavery. Born in 389 at either Daventry or Banwen on the Severn, Patrick's family long were Christians, his father a Roman *decurion* and Christian deacon, and his grandfather a Christian presbyter. In Ireland, Patrick will convert the Irish chieftans and Druids, found 300 churches, introduce the Latin mass and begin the institution of monasteries, which will become havens of peace and learning. Eventually, when Rome has fallen and the continent languishes in a "dark age," Patrick's monasteries will send missionaries BACK TO Europe to re-found European civilization.

Saint Patrick

— Christianity will even reach Scotland before the Romans pull out of England, when a young missionary from Strathclyde, named Ninian, will build a white-washed stone church on the Isle of Whithorn, 62 miles southeast of Dumfries, and proceed to convert the Scots. When he dies (Saint) Ninian will be buried in his church, that Bede will call Hvit-Aear, in Latin, *Ad Candidam Casam*, "the White House."

> The southern Picts . . . accepted the true faith through the preaching of Bishop Ninian a most reverend and holy man . . . Ninian's own episcopal see . . . famous for its stately church [is where] . . . his body and those of many saints lie at rest . . . The place . . . is commonly known as *Candida Casa*, the White House because he built [it] of stone, which was unusual among the Britons.   Bede, ECCLESIASTICAL HISTORY, 3.4

In spite of all of this, most secular (and even some church) history teaches that the earliest Christianity in England was brought by St. Augustine in 597, almost 200 years after the Roman legions pulled out of Britain and went home. If so, it would mean that one of the empire's most important territories, with one of its busiest sea ports, destination of travelers, traders, businessmen, emissaries, soldiers and diplomats was ignored by missionary Christians for more than 600 years after the church's founding! In reality, much tangible evidence, aside from the written records, of a very early Christian presence in England has been, and is still being, uncovered from Manchester to Galloway to Bath; and Christian symbols are being found which were used in Roman Britain some two and three hundred years before Augustine's arrival. A painted plaster wall from Lullingstone shows a young, clean-shaven Jesus with outstretched, praying hands was painted in Roman times; and a huge, beautiful floor mosaic showing, again, a clean-shaven Christ before a Chi-Rho, with Saints Matthew, Mark, Luke and John in its four corners, is called by its present home, the British Museum, "the earliest known representation of Christ executed on a floor from the [entire] Roman Empire."

Even as the Old Testament prophets had to teach that neither worldly power, wealth or influence could "buy" heavenly approval, which the destruction of Jerusalem proved, (righteousness alone could do that) so, now, do the New Testament church fathers have to teach that neither righteousness, piety nor faith will insure worldly well-being or social status; in fact, in a pagan world will very often bring suffering and sacrifice . . . but cannot take away the promise of Heaven. And they will have to learn that lesson well, for the years ahead are going to be rough ones. While persecutions now are sporadic, meant to punish certain individuals and actions, under future emperors Decius and Diocletian, the Roman Empire will attempt officially, to completely eradicate Christianity and issue executive edicts to close churches, confiscate Holy Scriptures, strip citizens of civil rights, imprison, enslave, torture and kill both clergymen and congregation, and force sacrifice to pagan idols on penalty of death.

Two of the most powerful pagan voices waging war on the new Christian faith in these early years are a Greek writer/critic named Celsus, to whose writings Origen addressed his

Christian defense, AGAINST CELSUS; and Syrian-born Roman philosopher Porphyry, who the future Emperor Constantine will call, ". . . the most learned of philosophers, although the fiercest enemy of the Christians." (CITY OF GOD 19:22) These men were not heretics within the church, but deadly enemies without. Neither man cared whether Jesus was made A god—lots of mortal men were made gods—but they didn't want Him to be THE God because, as Celsus said, "Jesus was just a low-grade magician, not a great hero, like the men of old." Celsus aimed his biting satire and wicked mockery at those "illiterate and bucolic yokels" called Christians who "created their revolutionary society, not on the worship of God, but of a corpse." (Cel. 7.68) "They say nothing in front of their elder . . . more intelligent masters, but let them get hold of children in private and some stupid women with them, they let out some astounding statements. (Cel. 3.55) His book, THE TRUE DOCTRINE, also mocked the cross as a Christian symbol:

Anti Christian grafitti.
3rd century from the Palatine Hill, Rome, reads: "Alexemenos worships his god."

> ". . . they speak of a tree of life, because their master was nailed to a cross and was a carpenter by trade. So that if he'd been thrown off a cliff, or pushed into a pit, or strangled . . . there would have been a cliff of life above the heavens or a pit of resurrection, or a rope of immortality . . ." Celsus, THE TRUE DOCTRINE, 6.34

But while Celsus hoped that Christianity could be eradicated if only it could be proven false, Porphyry, living 50–100 years later, knew by his time, that Christianity was here to stay, and hoped to deflate and diminish it by making Jesus just another pagan god in the vast Greco-Roman pantheon of gods, and was, therefore, the more dangerous of the two. Indeed, he was asked by the Emperor Diocletian to write a denunciation of Christianity, to begin a frontal attack, so to speak, for the official government persecutions he was planning. Porphyry would defend Rome's existing religions, including the worship of many gods and the sacrifice of animals to them, while condemning Christianity as "an unreasoning faith," and Christians as "polluted and contaminated and entangled in error . . . they worship the soul of Jesus because truth is a stranger to them." His strategy was to elevate Jesus to Greco-Roman godhood by condemning his followers:

> There is one God whom all men worship, and Jesus, like other pious men, worshipped this God and taught others to venerate him by his teaching. Jesus directed men's attention to the one God, but his disciples fell into error and taught men to worship Jesus. [Therefore] Christians should be persecuted because they "apostatized from the traditional worship and advocated destroying temples, ceasing animal sacrifice and shattering idols."
> (St. Augustine quoting Porphyry, CITY OF GOD 19.23)

In waging their personal vendettas against Christianity in its early days, enemy writers like Celsus and Porphyry inflicted enormous pain and havoc on the fledgling faith; but, unwittingly and unknowingly created a treasure trove of corroborative evidence for the truth and accuracy of the Gospels. When they alibied that Jesus' body had only been stolen, they were admitting that the tomb was empty. When Celsus accused Jesus of being a "low grade magician," he was admitting that Jesus worked miracles. When he condemned the "illiterate . . . yokels called Christians," he confirmed the existence of an early church; and when he mocked the cross as a Christian symbol, he confirmed the fact that a man called Christ was, in fact, crucified. Porphyry unwittingly gave Jesus credit for ending animal sacrifice and idol worship, and confirmed once more, that Christianity was, indeed, a healthy, thriving religion already wide-spread and influential within so few decades after its founder's life, death and resurrection. Celsus and Porphyry would be horrified to know it but, today, they are valuable friends of the faith.

But the unspeakable cruelties that these writers, and others, inspired in their own day is mind-boggling and heart-wrenching; for Diocletian did, indeed, issue imperial edicts throughout the empire, which were carried out only too eagerly. The great Christian historian, Eusebius (from whom this book has quoted often and to whom it is deeply indebted) was an eye-witness to many persecutions and recorded them in great detail in his HISTORIA ECCLESIASTICUS, or HISTORY OF THE CHRISTIAN CHURCH.

> The spectacle of what happened . . . after Diocletian [issued his official decrees] beggars description: By imperial command God's worshippers, perished wholesale . . . great numbers were locked up, and everywhere the jails built long before for murderers and grave robbers were crowded with bishops, presbyters and deacons . . . so that now there was no room for convicted criminals . . .   Eusebius, *Hist. Ecc.* 6.3

They were, Eusebius says, "flogged, racked and scraped, forced to disgusting, unholy sacrifices half dead than thrown away like corpses. They were mutilated by endless tortures, attacked by panthers, bears, wild boars and bulls goaded by red-hot irons . . . torments," he says, "too terrible to describe in endless variety . . . torn to bits with jagged potshards; women hung naked by one foot, a brutal and inhuman spectacle for all to see; others torn limb from limb by being tied to two bent trees which snapped back into position when ropes were cut; pointed reeds were driven under fingernails, molten lead poured on bare flesh, eyes gouged out, limbs maimed . . ." (*ibid.* book. eight, paraphrased) In brief, every effort was made to thwart the Christian belief in the resurrection, because no one could possibly be resurrected from mangled masses of torn flesh and shattered bones.

And yet, Eusebius says . . .

> I could tell of thousands who showed magnificent enthusiasm for the worship of the God of the universe . . . the unflinching courage of these noble people . . . One youngster not yet 20 standing without fetters, arms spread out as on a cross, praying unhurriedly to the Almighty . . . One little town in Phrygia encircled by fire and burnt to the ground, every

man, woman and child. Why? Because they one and all, mayor and magistrates included, declared themselves Christians and refused to commit idolatry. Eusebius, Book 8:3.4, 7.3 & 4, 10.10

Christian grafitti from the catacombs

Eusebius stresses that he was eye-witness to many of these events.

I was there myself and witnessed the ever-present divine power of Him to whom they testified, our Savior Jesus Christ, Himself . . . Inspired by the Holy Scriptures and looking with all earnestness towards the Almighty . . . they clung firmly to their vocation, the Christ-bearing martyrs endured . . . every outrage that iniquity could invent . . . In all these trials the splendid martyrs of Christ let their light to shine over the whole world that they everywhere astounded the eyewitnesses of their courage—and small wonder: they furnished in themselves unmistakable proof of our Savior's . . . divine and ineffable power . . . *ibid*. Book 8: 7.3, 10.1,12.3

One of the most powerful Christian voices on this subject of persecution, if not the most eloquent, was that of the North African-born lawyer and "eminent jurist," Tertullian of Carthage, the self-described "sinner of every brand, born for nothing but repentance." His conversion from paganism to Christianity was a cosmic event, and his *Credo Quia Absurdum,* "I believe because it is absurd," is quoted to this day:

The son of God was born, I am not ashamed of it because it is shameful. The Son of God died, I believe it because it is absurd, the Son of God was buried and rose again, I am sure of it because it is impossible."
Tertullian of Carthage, DEFENSE OF THE CHRISTIAN FAITH

Early mosaic from Greece

Tertullian's logical, legal mind and probing intellect are a challenge not only to Christianity's persecutors, but to his readers, as well. Why should not the God who created the universe and all things, who set in motion the immutable laws of physics that govern and order that universe, be able to suspend His own laws and for one time in history do the un-doable? Both Tertullian's defense of the Christian faith and his offensive arguments for it are done with a brilliant, compelling, penetrating insight, and a single-minded ferocity, for he is an angry man, hot-tempered, bitter and sometimes even coarse-mouthed. He exults that persecutors of Jesus will "liquefy" in fiercer flames than those they kindled against the Christians; and that all those who teach that there is no God and man has no soul shall go in "a single conflagration." In love with God the Father, Son and Holy Spirit, Tertullian hates equally everyone who teaches against them: teachers, writers, philosophers, actors; and his sharp wit and biting satire skewered the Romans' use of Christians as scapegoats for . . . everything.

> If the Tiber reaches the walls, if the Nile does not rise to the fields, if the sky doesn't move or the earth does, if there is famine, if there is plague, the cry is at once, "The Christians to the lion!" What, all of them to one lion? Did nothing ever happen before Christ?
> Tertullian, DEFENSE OF THE CHRISTIAN FAITH

They will even be accused of being "unprofitable" to the empire, to which Tertullian will reply:

> I will tell you truly who may complain that Christians are unprofitable: panders, pimps, assassins, poisoners, magicians, wizards, soothsayers, astrologers . . .   *ibid.*

And, in exultation, he will bid the Romans:

> Torture us, rack us, condemn us, crush us . . . nothing . . . is accomplished by your cruelties . . . it is the bait that WINS men for [Christ]. We MULTIPLY whenever we are mown down by you; the blood of Christians is SEED!   *ibid.*

But all these things, people and events are far into the future; two, three, four hundred years. Now, it is the Year of Our Lord 100, and this book ends at A.D. 100. The Roman Empire is at the greatest size it will ever reach, Trajan is its emperor, one of the "good emperors," and he has received another letter from the man he appointed governor of Bithynia, Pliny the Younger. Pliny and Trajan are close friends and carry on a constant and prodigious correspondence: Pliny has a problem in his province, just as every governor has in his, and he asks Trajan. . .

. . . *what to do with the Christians?*

"It is my invariable rule, Sir," Pliny says, "to refer to you in all matters where I feel doubtful: for who is more capable of . . . informing my ignorance?"

> Having never been present at any trials of the Christians, I am unacquainted with the method and limits to be observed either in examining or punishing them. Whether any difference is to be made on account of age . . . whether repentance admits to a pardon . . . whether the mere profession of Christianity . . . without crimes . . . are punishable . . .   Letter #97, Pliny to Trajan

Some of the Christians he has examined, Pliny tells Trajan, did indeed, recant their beliefs, repeat invocations to the Roman gods and "offered religious rites with wine and incense before your statue . . . some even reviled the name of Christ." Still, Pliny says, the only thing they would admit to being guilty of was . . .

Trajan

... that they met on a stated day before it was light, and addressed a form of prayer to Christ, as to a divinity, binding themselves by a solemn oath, not for the purposes of any wicked design, but never to commit any fraud, theft or adultery, never to falsify their word, nor deny a trust . . . after which it was their custom to separate, and then re-assemble, to eat in common a harmless meal.   LETTERS OF PLINY AND TRAJAN, #97

To test the truth of this statement, Pliny adds, he "had two female [Christians] put to torture . . . but all I could discover was evidence of an absurd and extravagant superstition." As to the others whom Pliny examined. . .

. . . if they confessed . . . I repeated the question twice again, adding the threat of capital punishment. If they still persevered, I ordered them to be executed. For whatever the nature of their creed might be . . . inflexible obstinacy deserved punishment. There were others also brought before me possessed with the same infatuation, but being Roman citizens, I directed them to be sent to Rome.   Pliny to Trajan, #97

Roman citizens, sent to Rome for trial! Just as Luke described the last journey of Paul in his book of ACTS 40 years ago! Another Biblical claim borne out by a secular source. And just as Christianity is widely accepted in Rome by this time, so is it here in Bithynia . . . and Pliny is worried.

. . . great numbers . . . [already are and are likely to be] involved . . . persons of all ranks and ages, and even of both sexes . . . In fact, this contagious superstition is not confined to the cities only, but has spread its infection among the neighboring villages and country.
Pliny to Trajan, #97

Pliny worries, also, about how to deal with the accusers of and accusations against the Christians: "A placard was put up, without any signature, accusing a large number of persons by name . . ." Trajan's reply is remarkable for its total lack of hostility or vindictiveness, its adherence to and respect for the law, and willingness to "co-exist . . ." "My dear Pliny," Trajan replies, "it is not possible to lay down any general rule . . . as a fixed standard . . ."

No search should be made for these people; when they are denounced and found guilty they must be punished; with the restriction, however, that . . . the party . . . shall give proof that he is not a Christian., by adoring our gods . . . shall be pardoned on the ground of repentance . . .   Emperor Trajan to Pliny the Younger, letter #98

And Trajan warns against anonymous informers . . .

Information's without the accuser's name subscribed must not be admitted in evidence against anyone, as it is introducing a very dangerous precedent . . . and is by no means agreeable to the spirit of our times.   Trajan to Pliny, letter #98

100   The "spirit of Trajan's time" will last only a short while. Under future emperors—even the "good" ones, Trajan's "leniency" will be abandoned, and thousands of persons who believe in Jesus Christ will die for their belief in the years ahead.

> *I am the resurrection and the life.*
> *He who believes in me, though he die,*
> *yet shall he live, and*
> *whoever lives and believes in me*
> *shall never die.*
>
> Jesus of Nazareth,   JOHN 11:25–26

Prophesied: He will swallow up death forever, and the Lord God will wipe away tears from all faces, and the reproach of his people he will take away from all the earth: for the Lord has spoken.   ISAIAH 25:8 (See: 739 B.C.)

5th Century mosaic from Ravenna, Italy
"I am the Way, the Truth & the Life."

An Afterword

This book ends "in the year of our Lord" (A.D.) 100 because the events of Bible times were completed by then; the persons' lives lived out, and the writings that tell their stories, completed. For Christians it was a bleak and desperate time. All those who had personally known Jesus were gone. His second coming, looked for so anxiously and lovingly, had not come about; and His followers were being persecuted and slaughtered in all parts of the empire.

But all was not lost. Indeed, could they then have known it, there was much to hope for; for although the persecutions were frightful, they were neither universal nor unceasing. While one emperor might be particularly severe, the next might ease off. And while the governor in one province might be vicious, the one in the next could be quite lenient . . . in fact, might even be a Christian, himself. For Christ's followers could be found as easily among the nobility, the military, the merchants and the bureaucracy as among the poor; and as far away as there was trade and travel, there were Christians.

In fact, within only 280 years more, persecution by the Romans would cease completely. For, in A.D. 312, the then Emperor Constantine, wavering on the brink of believing or not, saw a vision of the cross with the words on it: *In hoc signo vinces*—By this sign conquer!" . . . and did. On his death-bed this Roman emperor, the most powerful man in the world, ruler of the mightiest nation the world had ever known, himself worshipped as a god, received baptism in the name of Jesus Christ. Thus did Constantine set in motion the gears that would allow Christianity, the religion of a crucified "criminal," to become the official, state religion of the very empire which had put Him to death.

. . . The next stage was the spectacle prayed and longed for by us all—dedication festivals . . . and consecrations of [new churches] . . . ceremonies with full pomp . . . the sacraments and majestic rites of the church . . . singing of psalms and intoning of prayers given us from God . . . ineffable symbols of the Savior's Passion. [Then did all] lose fear of their former oppressors; day after day they kept dazzling festival, light was everywhere, and men who had once dared not look up greeted each other with smiling faces and shining eyes. They danced and sang in city and country alike giving honor first of all to God our Sovereign Lord . . . and then to the pious emperor . . . In every city [Constantine] published decrees full of humanity and laws that gave proof of munificence and true piety. Thus all tyranny [was] purged away . . . and by the things they did for all men to see, displayed love of virtue and love of God, devotion and thankfulness to the Almighty.

Eusebius, HISTORY OF THE CHRISTIAN CHURCH, 10.3.4 and 10.9.3

Index of
THE BIBLE AND THE WORLD TOGETHER
An Historical Guidebook

The OLD TESTAMENT

B.C. — THE LAW—Before Christ

??????? — "In the beginning . . ." The book of GENESIS takes place.

??????? — Stone age man

450,000 — 8000 Man can hunt, light fires.

20,000 — Cave paintings in France, Spain.

16,000 — Great Lakes formed. Persian Gulf and Caribbean show evidence of a great Flood? Mongol peoples into America?

12,000 — 10,000 Niagara Falls

10,000 — 8000 Bow and Arrow, pottery, beer.

8000 — 6000 Flax, domestic animals. Jericho oldest city? Spearpoints in America.

6000 — Painted pottery, oxen plows in Mesopotamia. Aztecs in Mexico grow cotton. Rice in Thailand.

5000 — Villages in Europe. Dug-out boats, mummies in Egypt. The COPPER AGE.

4500 — Egyptians calculate time. Mesopotamians make music, copper.

4000 — Archeological cultures widespread. Early governments.

3761 — Hebrew calendar, the year One.

3500 — Invention of the wheel, irrigation. Gold. City-states.

3100 — King Narmer (Menes) unites upper and lower Egypt.

3000 — THE BRONZE AGE—Beginning of RECORDED HISTORY. Cunieform. City-states of Sumer: mathematics, astronomy, medicine, business all written about. Also, Egypt. Heiroglyphic writing. Saluki dog. Musical instruments.Indus Valley Harappa. Mycenae, Knossos and Troy in Europe. Minoans on Crete. Yang-shao villages in China. Canaanites in Israel.

2740 — Djoser, Imhotep build "stepped" pyramid.

2700 — Gilgamesh rules 5th dynasty of Uruk in Sumer. The Gods of Gilgamesh. The remains of "the flood." Egypt's capital at Memphis. Egypt's gods.

2600 — Bristlecone Pine begins to grow. King Khufu (Cheops) builds Great Pyramid of Giza. (1st of 7 W of W) First quote in book from Herodotus. Great Sphinx built.

2500 — Ebla, Mari and Damascus thriving. The Enuma Elish found at Mari Ebla's library. The death pits of Ur. The Epic of Gilgamesh. The Ziggurat of Ur. Cedar wood from Phoenecia. Harappa flourishes. Canaanites settle Jerusalem.

2450 — Ptah-hotep and the Papyrus Prisse

2350 — End of Sumer with Sargon of Akkad. Tangun rules in Korea. China's advances.

2250 — Ebla destroyed by Naram-sin. The Ebla tablets naming names from the Bible.

2200 — The Sumerian King List with the flood account.

2000 — Hennu first explorer. Cheese. Incense and Myrrh. Incas. Mari code messages. Stonehenge.

1930 — Minoans/Knossos on Crete. Ship-wrecked Egyptian Sinuhe/Sinbad.

1900 — Mt. St. Helens erupts

1800 — "Golden Age of Babylon," Hammurabi's Law Code/Stele. Ur. Abraham leaves Ur. The COVENANT. THE AGE OF THE PATRIARCHS begins.

THE APOCRYPHA — 400 Years Between Old and New Testaments

Index

THE NEW TESTAMENT YEARS

A.D.

BIBLIOGRAPHY

(Including Classical Persons Quoted)

Most
frequently
cited
references:

AmHerMag = American Heritage Magazine
ANET = Ancient Near Easter Texts of James Pritchard
ArchOdys = Archeology Odyssey
BAR = Biblical Archeology Review
BartFamQuot = Bartlett's Familiar Quotations
BestWoCl = The Best of the World's Classics
BritMuPub = British Museum Publications
CamUniPr = Cambridge University Press
EnBritUC = Encyclopedia Britannica, University of Chicago
HarvUP = Harvard University Press
HornArMu/AnU = Horn Archeological Museum, Andrews University
LoebClLib = Loeb Classical Library
NatGeoSo = National Geographic Society
OriInstUC = Oriental Institute, University of Chicago
OxUniPr = Oxford University Press

Abercrombie, Thomas J., ARABIA'S FRANKINCENSE TRAIL, NatGeoSo, Oct. 1985

Adels, Jill Haak, THE WISDOM OF THE SAINTS, OxUniPr, 1987

Anderson, Bernard, UNDERSTANDING THE OLD TESTAMENT, Prentice-Hall, 1986

AESCHYLUS, Everyman's Library, J.M. Dent & Co. NY, Dutton & Co. 1906 (See also: Blackie, John Stuart)

Aesop, FABLES, (See: Jacob, Joseph)

Alcibiades,

AMERICA, GREAT CRISES IN OUR HISTORY TOLD BY ITS MAKERS, Veterans of Foreign Wars, Chicago, Ill, date ?

Anaxagoras,

ANCIENT EGYPT, NatGeoSo, ? ?

ANCIENT NEAR EASTERN TESTS, ANET (See: Pritchard, James B.)

Andronicos, Manolis, REGAL TREASURES FROM A MACEDONIAN TOMB (Seeking the Tomb of Philip of Macedon) NatGeoSo, July, 1978

Apicius, M. Gabius, COOKERY AND DINING IN ANCIENT ROME, Dover Pub. 1977

Aratus of Soli, Notes to: ACTS 17:28, OXFORD ANNOTATED BIBLE, OxUniPr, 1965

Archimedes, (ref: BartFamQuot)

Arden, Harvey, IN SEARCH OF MOSES, NatGeoSo., Jan. 1976

Aristophanes,

ARISTOTLE, THE WORKS OF, Great Books/Western World, EnBritUC, 1952

Asch, Sholem, THE APOSTLE. G.P. Putnams Sons, 1943

Asoka Maurya,

ATLAS OF THE BIBLE (See: Reader's Digest)

ATLAS OF THE BIBLE LANDS, G.S. Hammond, Co. 1959

Baeda, THE VENERABLE BEDE. trans. Leo Sherly-Price, Penguin Books, 1955
    BAEDAE, OPERA HISTORICA, trans. J.E. King, LoebClLib, HarvUP, (fp.1930) 1962

Barnabas, (See: Staniforth, EARLY CHRISTIAN WRITERS)

Barthel, Manfred, WHAT THE BIBLE REALLY SAYS. Wm. Morrow Co. Inc. NY 1982

Bartlett, John, FAMILIAR QUOTATIONS. Little, Brown & Co. 1955

Bass. George F., OLDEST KNOWN SHIPWRECK REVEALS SPLENDORS OF THE BRONZE AGE Nat-GeoSo. Dec, 1987

Batey, Richard A., SEPPHORIS—AN URBAN PORTRAIT OF JESUS, BAR, May/June 1992

Bede, Venerable (See: Baeda)

Bennett, Boyce M. and Scott, David H., HARPER'S ENCYCLOPEDIA OF BIBLE LIFE, Harper & Row, 1978

Bible, The (See: HOLY BIBLE)

BIBLE, THE, LIFE Mag. special double issue, Dec. 25, 1964, Vol. 57, No. 26
Managing Editor, George P. Hunt. Contributors: Ephraim A. Speiser, William F. Albright, Robert Wallace, Emil C. Kraeling, Robert Coughlan, Frederick C. Grant, John Knox, Frank M. Cross, Jr., G. Ernest Wright, David Noel Freedman, James B. Pritchard, Nahum M. Sarna, Seymour Siegel and Rabbi Shalom M. Paul.

BIBLICAL ARCHEOLOGY REVIEW Magazine (BAR), Hershel Shanks, Editor, Est. 1975
(Articles listed individually by author.)
(Missing stories re: Balaam's Ass ? ? - Crucified ankle bone. ? ?)

Biel, Jörg, TREASURE FROM A CELTIC TOMB, NatGeoSo, March, 1980

Biran, Avraham and Navah, Joseph, "DAVID" FOUND AT DAN. BAR, Mar/Apr 1994

Birley, Anthony, LIVES OF THE LATER CAESARS, Penguin Books, 1982

Blackie, John Stuart, THE LYRICAL DRAMAS OF AESCHYLUS, Dent/London, Dutton/NY, 1906

Bowra, C.M., CLASSICAL GREECE/GREAT AGES OF MAN, Time, Inc. 1965

Boyer, David S., JERUSALEM TO ROME ON THE PATH OF ST. PAUL, NatGeoSo, Dec. 1956

Brewer, The Rev. E. Cobham, CHARACTER SKETCHES OF ROMANCE, FICTION AND THE DRAMA, Selmer Hess, 1901

Brewer, E. Cobham, DICTIONARY OF PHRASE AND FABLE, Avenel, 1978

BRITISH MUSEUM AND ITS COLLECTIONS, THE. BritMuPub. 1976–87

Browne, Lewis, THE GRAPHIC BIBLE: FROM GENESIS TO REVELATION IN ANIMATED MAPS AND CHARTS. Macmillan, 1942

Brownrigg, Ronald. WHO'S WHO IN THE NEW TESTAMENT. Bonanza, 1980

Bruce, F.F., JESUS AND CHRISTIAN ORIGINS OUTSIDE THE NEW TESTAMENT, Eerdmans, 1974
—JESUS AND PAUL, PLACES THEY KNEW. Thomas Nelson, 1983

Bryant, Vaughn M. Jr., DOES POLLEN PROVE THE SHROUD AUTHENTIC? BAR, Nov/Dec, 2000

BUILDERS OF THE ANCIENT WORLD. NatGeoSo. 1968

Bullfinch, Thomas, BULLFINCH'S MYTHOLOGY, Spring Books, 1963

Caesar, Julius, COMMENTARIES ON THE GAELIC WARS, BestWoCl, Funk & Wagnalls, 1909
COMENTARII DE BELLO GALLICO, LoebClLib, HarvUP,

Caffery, Jefferson, FRESH TREASURES FROM EGYPT'S ANCIENT SANDS, NatGeoSo, Nov. 1955

Cahill, Thomas, HOW THE IRISH SAVED CIVILIZATION, Doubleday, 1995
—THE GIFTS OF THE JEWS, Doubleday, 1998

Cameron, George C., DARIUS CARVED HISTORY ON AGELESS ROCK. NatGeoSo. Dec, 1950

Cantor, George, THE GREAT LAKES GUIDEBOOK, Univ/Michigan Press, 1978

Capt, E. Raymond, THE TRADITIONS OF GLASTONBURY. Artisan Sales, 1983

Carpenter, Rhys, ANCIENT ROME BROUGHT TO LIFE, NatGeoSo, Nov. 1946

Casson, Lionel, ANCIENT EGYPT/GREAT AGES OF MAN. Time, Inc. 1965

Cato the Elder, DE RE RUSTICA, BestWoCl, Funk & Wagnalls, 1909
  —MARCUS PORCIUS CATO, ON AGRICULTURE, trans. Wm. Davis Hooper, LoebClLib, HarvUP, (1934) 1967

Cato the Younger,

Cerruti, James, DOWN THE ANCIENT APPIAN WAY, NatGeoSo, June, 1981

Churchill, Winston D., A HISTORY OF THE ENGLISH SPEAKING PEOPLES, Vol. 1, THE BIRTH OF BRITAIN, Barnes & Noble, 1993

CICERO, LETTERS OF MARCUS TULLIUS, The Harvard Classics, P.F. Collier, 1909

Clark, Lord Kenneth, CIVILIZATION, Harper & Row, 1969

Clement of Rome, (See: Staniforth, EARLY CHRISTIAN WRITINGS)

Cochrane, Charles Norris, CHRISTIANITY AND CLASSICAL CULTURE, OxUniPr, 1944

Coggins, Richard, WHO'S WHO IN THE BIBLE, Barnes & Noble, 1981

Comay, Joan, WHO'S WHO IN THE BIBLE: THE OLD TESTAMENT. Bonanza, 1980

COMMON PRAYER, THE BOOK OF, The Episcopal Church of U.S.A., 1945

COMMON PRAYER, THE BOOK OF, (1928 Commemorative Edition) Seabury Press, 1953

Confucious,

Coogan, Michael D. 10 GREAT FINDS, BAR, May/June, 1995 (Silver scroll, Hebrew mural)

Cooke, Jean; Kramer, Ann and Rowland-Entwistle, Theodore. HISTORY'S TIMELINE. Crescent Books, 1981

Cornell, George, EVENTS OF FIRST GOOD FRIDAY STILL BEING DEBATED, Chicago Tribune A. Apr. 13, 1990

Cornfeld, Gaalyah, ARCHEOLOGY OF THE BIBLE BOOK BY BOOK. Harper & Row, 1976

Cottrell, Leonard, THE HORIZON BOOK OF LOST WORLDS, Amer.Her.Pub. Co. (also see: Davidson, M)

Courtenay, William J., THE JUDEO-CHRISTIAN HERITAGE. Holt, Rinehart & Winston, 1970

Craig, Harden and Bevington, David, THE COMPLETE WORKS OF SHAKESPEARE, Scott, Foresman, 1973

Cressy, Sir Edward S., THE 15 DECISIVE BATTLES OF THE WORLD, Heritage Press, 1969

Cunliff, Barry, THE CELTIC WORLD, McGraw-Hill, (M.C. Library #936.4)

Davidson, Marshall, WITHER THE COURSE OF EMPIRE? (re: the paintings of Thomas Cole) AmHerMag, Vol. 8, No. 6, 1975 (see also: Cottrell, Leonard) THE HORIZON BOOK OF LOST WORLDS, Amer.Her.Pub. Co. (1962)

Davies, Graham I., KING SOLOMON'S STABLES STILL AT MEGGIDO? BAR, Jan/Feb, 1994

Davis, John D., THE WESTMINSTER DICTIONARY OF THE BIBLE, Westminster Press, 1944

Davis, Thomas W., FAITH AND ARCHEOLOGY, BAR, Mar /Apr, 1993

deCamp, L. Sprague, GREAT CITIES IN THE ANCIENT WORLD, Dorset, 1972

deGobineau, J.A., THE' WORLD OF THE PERSIANS, Minerva, 1975

Democritus of Thrace,

Dentan, Robert C., THE HOLY SCRIPTURES, Natnl. Council, Episcopal Church, USA, 1949

Desroches-Noblecourt, Christiane, TUTANKHAMEN. New York Graphic Society, 1963
  —TUTANKHAMEN'S GOLDEN TROVE, NatGeoSo, Oct. 1963

Dever, William G., ARCHEOLOGY AND THE BIBLE, Understanding Their Special Relationship, BAR, May/June 1990
  —SAVE US FROM POSTMODERN MALARKEY, BAR, Mar/Apr 2006
  —THE WESTERN CULTURAL TRADITION IS AT RISK, BAR, Mar/Apr 2006

DeWitt, William A., HISTORY'S 100 GREATEST EVENTS, Grosset & Dunlap, 1954

Dothan, Trade, LOST OUTPOST OF THE EGYPTIAN EMPIRE, NatGeoSo, Dec. 1982

Drummand, Henry, THE GREATEST THING IN THE WORLD. Collins. date ? (died 1897)

Durant, Will, THE STORY OF CIVILIZATION, CAESAR AND CHRIST, Simon & Schuster, 1935

Easton, Stewart C., THE HERITAGE OF THE PAST FROM EARLIEST TIMES TO 1500. Holt, Rinehart & Winston, 1965

Eban, Abba, HERITAGE, CIVILIZATION AND THE JEWS. Summit Books, 1984

EBLA TO DAMASCUS: ART AND ARCHEOLOGY OF ANCIENT SYRIA. Exhibition and publications, Detroit Institute of Arts, 1987

Edey, Mainland, LOST WORLD OF THE AEGEAN. Time, Inc. ?

EERDMANS' HANDBOOK TO THE HISTORY OF CHRISTIANITY. William B. Eerdmans, 1978

EGYPT'S PAST, THE MARVELS OF, LIFE Magazine five part series beginning April 5, 1968. Text by Tom Prideaux - Part I, Grant Pleasure Daily to My Heart, Apr. 5, 1968; II. Grandeur of Empire, Divine Order Radiating from Gods and Kings, May 31, 1968; III, A Miracle of Strength and Grace, Start at Sakkara . . . date ?; IV, The Might and Luxury of Empire ?; V, Magic Passage to Eternity, ?.

Ehrlich, Eugene & Scott, David H., MENE, MENE, TEKEL. Harper-Collins, 1990

Eilts, Hermann F., ALONG THE STORIED INTENSE ROADS OF ADEN. NatGeoSo, Feb. 1957

El-Baz, Farouk, FINDING A PHARAOH'S FUNERAL BARK, NatGeoSo, Apr. 1988

Elder, Isabel Hill, JOSEPH OF ARIMATHEA, Real Israel Press, 1979

Eliot, Alexander, THE STORIED WORLD OF RAMESES. LIFE Magazine, date ?

Ellens, J. Harold, THE DESTRUCTION OF THE GREAT LIBRARY AT ALEXANDRIA Archeology Odyssey, July/Aug 2000

Engnell, Ivan, "KNOWLEDGE" AND "LIFE" IN THE CREATION STORY. Leiden, 1965

ENCYCLOPEDIA BRITANNICA, Walter Yust, Ed-in-Chief; EncyBrit Inc./William Benton, pub. 1959

Epimenides of Crete. Notes to: ACTS 17:28, OXFORD ANNOTATED BIBLE, RSV, OxUniPr, 1965

Euclid, BartFamQuot, Little-Brown Co., 1955

Euripides,

Eusebius, THE HISTORY OF THE CHURCH, trans, G.A. Williamson, Penguin Books, 1989

Evans, M. Stanton, THE THEME IS FREEDOM, Regnery Pub. Inc. 1994

Eydoux, Henri-Paul, IN SEARCH OF LOST WORLDS. Hamlyn, 1975

FAMILIEN BIBEL, DIE NEUE ILLUSTRATE, A.J. Holman & Co. Phil, PA, 1891

Feldman, Steven (see also; Nancy E. Roth) THE SHORT LIST: N.T. FIGURES KNOWN TO HISTORY, BAR Nov/Dec 2002

Frontinus,

Furnish, Victor Paul, CORINTH IN PAUL'S TIME, BAR, May/June, 1988 (Erastus)

Gentili, Gino Vinicio, ROMAN LIFE IN 1,600 YEAR-OLD COLOR PICTURES. (Mosaics uncovered in Sicily) NatGeoSo, Feb. 1957

Gerster, Georg, THREATENED TREASURES OF THE NILE. NatGeoSo. Oct. 1963

GOLDEN HISTORICAL ATLAS: LANDS OF THE BIBLE. Simon & Schuster, 1975

Gonen. Rivka, BIBLICAL. HOLY PLACES. Collier Books, Macmillan Co. 1987

Gore, Rick, THE DEAD DO TELL TALES AT VESUVIUS (After 2000 Years of Silence) NatGeoSo. May, 1984
  —THE ETERNAL ETRUSCANS. NatGeoSo, June, 1988
  —THE MEDITERRANEAN, SEA OF MAN'S FATE. NatGeoSo, Dec. 1982

Grant, Michael, GREECE AND ROME, THE BIRTH OF WESTERN CIVILIZATION. Bonanza, 1986
  —JESUS, AN HISTORIAN'S REVIEW OF THE GOSPELS. Chas. Scribner's Sons, 1977

Grant, Robert M., AUGUSTUS TO CONSTANTINE, THE RISE AND TRIUMPH OF CHRISTIANITY IN THE ROMAN WORLD. Harper & Row, 1970

Gray, Andrew, ORIGIN AND EARLY HISTORY OF CHRISTIANITY IN BRITAIN, date & pub. ??

GREECE, THE MIRACLE OF, LIFE Magazine six-part series beginning Jan. 4, 1963,
—Part I, The Worth of Man, Jan. 4, 1963; II. Age of Gods and Heroes, date ?; III. The Birth of Reason, Feb. 8, 1963; IV. Golden Age of Athens, ?; V. The Two Wars of Destiny, Pride and Fall, April 5, 1963; VI. Alexander the Great, The Godlike Conqueror, May 3, 1963. Author(s?) unknown.

Greenhut, Zvi, BURIAL CAVE OF THE CAIAPHAS FAMILY. BAR, Sep/Oct, 1992

GRIFFITH OBSERVER (See: Mosely, John)

Groenewegen-Frankfort, H.A., and Ashmole, Barnard, ART OF THE ANCIENT WORLD, Prentice-Hall, date ?

Grollenberg, Luc H., SHORTER ATLAS OF THE BIBLE. Penguin, 1959

Grosvenor, Gilbert M., THE AEGEAN ISLES: POSEIDON'S PLAYGROUND, NatGeoSo, Dec. 1958

Grosvenor, Melville Bell, HOMEWARD WITH ULYSSES, NatGeoSo, 1973
—THE ISLES OF GREECE, AEGEAN BIRTHPLACE OF WESTERN CULTURE, NatGeoSo, Aug, 1972
—JOURNEY INTO GOLDEN GREECE AND ROME. NatGeoSo. Oct. 1968

Grun, Bernard, THE TIMETABLES OF HISTORY (from: Werner Stein, KULTURFAHRPLAN) Simon & Schuster, 1979

GUIDE TO THE ORIENTAL INSTITUTE MUSEUM, A. OriInstUC, 1982

Gurney, KINGDOMS OF EUROPE. Crown, 1982

Guterman, Norbert, THE ANCHOR BOOK OF LATIN QUOTATIONS, Doubleday, 1966

Hadas, Moses, IMPERIAL ROME/GREAT AGES OF MAN, Time, Inc. 1965
—and Thomas Suits, FLORILEGIUM LATINUM. Dover. 1991

Hadingham, Evan, EARLY MAN AND THE COSMOS. ? ?

Hale, William Harlan, THE HORIZON BOOK OF ANCIENT GREECE. AmHerMag, 1965

Hall, Alice J., EGYPT, LEGACY OF A DAZZLING PAST. NatGeoSo. March, 1977

Halley, Henry, HALLEY'S BIBLE HANDBOOK. Zondervan, 1965

Hamilton, Edith, THE GREEK WAY, Time. Inc. 1930
THE ROMAN WAY, Avon Books, 1932
THE ROMAN WAY, NatGeoSo, Nov. 1946

Hartt, Frederick, ART: A HISTORY OF PAINTING. SCULPTURE AND ARCHITECTURE. Prentice-Hall, 1976

Handel, George Frederick, MESSIAH, Autograph score, The Trustees.. British Museum, London, (Angel Records CL-3657) 1965

Hawkes, Jacquetta, THE ATLAS OF EARLY MAN. St. Martin Press, 1976
—THE FIRST GREAT CIVILIZATIONS/THE HISTORY OF HUMAN SOCIETY, ? ?
. . . and Wooley, Sir Leonard, PREHISTORY AND THE BEGINNINGS OF CIVILIZATION, ? ?

HERITAGE IN NEED OF HELP, A; NEW NILE DAM WILL DROWN FABLED MONUMENTS, author ? LIFE Mag. Oct. 29, 1965

Herodotus, THE HISTORIES, trans, Aubrey de Selincourt, Penguin Books, 1972

Hesiod, quote trans. J. Banks, BartFamQuot, Little, Brown & Co. 1955

Hinnels, John R. PERSIAN MYTHOLOGY. Hamlyn, 1973

HIPPOCRATES, trans. W.H.S. Jones, LoebClLib, HarvUP, (1923) 1952

THE HIPPOCRATIC WRITING, trans. Francis Adams, The Great Books, Ency Brit. 1952

Hoagland, Victor. THE BOOK OF SAINTS. Regina Press 1986

Hoffman, Michael A., EGYPT BEFORE THE PHARAOHS, A.A. Knopf, 1975

Holfelder, Robert L., HEROD'S CITY ON THE SEA. NatGeoSo, Feb. 1987

HOLY BIBLE, The, AUTHORIZED KING JAMES VERSION, Collier Clear-Type Press. 1957
—KING JAMES STUDY BIBLE #135, Thomas Nelson, 1988
—KING JAMES VERSION GIANT PRINT #893BG, Thomas Nelson, 1994
—KJ21, The TWENTY FIRST CENTURY KING JAMES VERSION, #2140B, Deuel Enterprises. Inc. 1994
—OXFORD ANNOTATED REVISED STANDARD VERSION, Eds., Herbert G. May & Bruce M. Metzger, OxUniPr, 1965
—PARALLEL BIBLE, THE NEW LAYMAN'S, (KJ, NIV, Liv, RSV), Zondervan, 1981
—(See also: Phillips, J.B., THE NEW TESTAMENT IN MODERN English, and . . . NEW TESTAMENT AND PSALMS, THE, AN INCLUSIVE VERSION.)

Homer, THE ILIAD, trans. A.T. Murray, LoebClLib, HarvUP, (1924) 1971
—THE ODYSSEY, *ibid.* (1919) 1966

Horace, COMPLETE ODES AND EPODES, The, trans, W.G. Shepherd, Penguin Books, 1983

HORIZON BOOK OF ANCIENT GREECE, (See: Hale, William Harlan)
—BOOK OF ANCIENT ROME, (See; Payne, Robert)
—HISTORY OF CHINA, ? ?

Horn, Siegfried, BIBLICAL ARCHEOLOGY AFTER 30 YEARS (1948–1978) HornArMu/AnU, 1982
—HESHBON IN THE BIBLE AND ARCHEOLOGY, *ibid.* 1978

House, H. Wayne, CHRONOLOGICAL & BACKGROUND CHARTS OF THE NEW TESTAMENT Zondervan, 1981

Hureau, Jean, IRAN TODAY: TRAVEL IN COLOUR. Iran Natnl. Tourist Org, brochure, ? ?

Huxhold, Harry N., TWELVE WHO FOLLOWED. Augsburg Pub. House, 1987

Ignatius, St. (See: Staniforth, EARLY CHRISTIAN WRITINGS.)

ILLUSTRATED BIBLE DICTIONARY, Inter-Varsity Press/Tyndale House Pub. 1986

Irenaeus, quoted in EUSEBIUS, THE HISTORY OF THE CHURCH, trans., G.A. Williamson, Penguin Books, 1965

Isocrates,

Jacobs, Joseph, THE FABLES OF AESOP. Macmillan Co. 1965

Johnston, Mary, ROMAN LIFE. Scott, Foresman. 1957

Josephus, Flavius. ANTIQUITIES OF THE JEWISH PEOPLE, William Whiston, Kregel, 1971
—HISTORY OF THE JEWISH WARS, *ibid.*

Judge, Joseph, A BURIED ROMAN TOWN GIVES UP ITS DEAD. NatGeoSo. Dec. 1982
—MINOANS AND MYCENAEANS, GREECE'S BRILLIANT BRONZE AGE. *ibid.* Feb. 1978

Jugurtha,

Justin Martyr, (See: Richardson, EARLY CHRISTIAN FATHERS)

Juvenal, JUVENAL AND PERSIUS, trans. G.G. Ramsev, LoebClLib/HarvUP, (1918) 1969

Kahn, David, THE CODE BREAKERS, THE STORY OF SECRET WRITING. Macmillan, 1967

Keith-Roach, Maj. Edward. THE PAGEANT OF JERUSALEM, NatGeoSo. Dec. 1927

Keller, Werner, THE BIBLE AS HISTORY. Bantam Books, 1982

Kemp, Peter, HISTORY OF SHIPS, THE, Orbis, 1978

Kennedy, D. James, WHAT IF THE BIBLE HAD NEVER BEEN WRITTEN? Thomas Nelson, 1998

Kenyon, Kathleen, THE BIBLE AND RECENT ARCHEOLOGY. BritMuPub, 1978

Knowles, Archibald Campbell, THE PRACTICE OF RELIGION. Morehouse, Gorham, 1957

Bibliography

Kramer, Samuel Noah, CRADLE OF CIVILIZATION/GREAT AGES OF MAN, Time, Inc. 1967

La Fay, Howard, EBLA, SPLENDOR OF AN UNKNOWN EMPIRE, NatGeoSo, Dec. 1978
—WHERE JESUS WALKED, NatGeoSo, Nov. 1967

Landis, Benson Y., AN OUTLINE OF THE BIBLE BOOK BY BOOK, Barnes & Noble, 1963

Langer, William L., AN OUTLINE OF WORLD HISTORY, Houghton-Mifflin, 1972

Leaky, L.S.B., FINDING THE WORLD'S EARLIEST MAN, NatGeoSo, Sep. 1960

Lind, L.R., TEN GREEK PLAYS IN CONTEMPORARY TRANSLATIONS, Houghton-Mifflin, 1957

Lemaire, Andre, PROBABLE HEAD OF PRIESTLY SCEPTER FROM SOLOMON'S TEMPLE SURFACES
IN JERUSALEM. BAR, Jan/Feb, 1984
—BURIAL BOX OF JAMES THE BROTHER OF JESUS, BAR, Nov/Dec 2002

Leonard, Jonathon Norton, ANCIENT AMERICA/GREAT AGES OF MAN, Time, Inc. 1967

Lewis, C.S., THE CASE FOR CHRISTIANITY, Macmillan, 1989
—MERE CHRISTIANITY, Macmillan, 1943
—THE SCREWTAPE LETTERS, Macmillan, 1961

LIFE Magazine special issues, see: The MARVELS OF EGYPT'S PAST; The MIRACLE OF GREECE; The
ROMANS; and special double issue, The BIBLE.

LINCOLN LIBRARY OF ESSENTIAL INFORMATION, THE. Frontier Press, 1967

Livy (Titus Livius), HISTORIA AD URBE CONDITIAE, LoebClLib/HarvUP, ? ?
—EARLY HISTORY OF ROME, Books I-V, trans. Aubrey de Selincourt, Penguin, 1971
—ROME AND ITALY, Books VI-X, tras. Betty Radice, *ibid.* 1982
—THE WAR WITH HANNIBAL, Books XXI-XXX, Aubrey de Selincourt, *ibid.* 1972
—ROME AND THE MEDITERRANEAN, Books XXXI-XLV, trans, Henry Bettenson, *ibid.* 1976

Lodge, Henry Cabot (Ed-in-Chief), HISTORY OF NATIONS (Many Vol.) P.F. Collier . . . ??
—THE BEST OF THE WORLD'S CLASSICS (BestWoCl), Funk & Wagnalls, 1909

LOST BOOKS OF THE BIBLE, THE. ? Bell Publishing Co. 1979

LE LOUVRE DES ANTIQUAIRES. 2 Place du Palais Royal, Paris ?

Luce, Henry, Ed-in-Chief, LIFE'S PICTURE HISTORY OF WESTERN MAN, Times, Inc. 1951

Ludwig, Emil, THE MEDITERRANEAN, SAGA OF A SEA. Whittlesey House, 1942
—THE NILE, THE LIFE-STORY OF A RIVER. Garden City Pub. Inc. 1939

Machlin, Milt, JOSHUA AND THE ARCHEOLOGIST. Reader's Digest, Sept. 1990

Magill, Frank N., MASTERPIECES OF PHILOSOPHY IN SUMMARY FORM. Salem Press, 1907

Martial, EPIGRAMS, trans. Walter C.A. Ker, HarvUP. (1919) 1968

Maier, Dr. Paul, THE FLAMES OF ROME, Doubleday, 1981
—JESUS, LEGEND OR LORD? Lecture on tape. Tobias Communications, 1999
—JOSEPHUS, THE ESSENTIAL WRITINGS, Kregel Pubs. 1988
—PONTIUS PILATE, A DOCUMENTARY NOVEL. Kregel Pubs. 1968

Maiuri, Amadeo, LAST MOMENTS OF THE POMPEIANS, NatGeoSo. Nov. 1961

Marinatos, Spyridon, THERA, KEY TO THE RIDDLE OF MINOS, NatGeoSo. May, 1572

Martin, Ernest L., THE BIRTH OF CHRIST RECALCULATED. Foundation/Biblical Research, 1980
—THE ORIGINAL BIBLE RESTORED. ASK Publications, 1991

Martin, William C., THESE WERE GOD'S PEOPLE. Southwestern, 1955

Maus, Cynthia Pearl, CHRIST AND THE FINE ARTS. Harper & Bros. 1938
—THE OLD TESTAMENT AND THE FINE ARTS. Harper & Row Pub. 1954

May, T.H. Delabere and Hadas, Moses, THE AENEID BY VERGIL, Bantam Books, 1961

May, H.G., (See: Ed. OXFORD ANNOTATED BIBLE)

Metzger, Bruce, GREAT EVENTS OF BIBLE TIMES. Doubleday, 1987
—(See: Ed. OXFORD ANNOTATED BIBLE)
—THE READER'S DIGEST BIBLE. READ. DIC. 1982

Millard, Alan, DOES THE BIBLE EXAGGERATE KING SOLOMON'S GOLDEN WEALTH? BAR, May/June 1989
—TREASURES FROM BIBLE TIMES. A Lion Book, 1985

Miller, Carl, LIFE 8000 YEARS AGO UNCOVERED IN AN ALABAMA CAVE NatGeoSo Oct 1956
—RUSSELL CAVE, NEW LIGHT ON STONE AGE LIFE, NatGeoSo Mar. 1958

Miller, Madeline S. and Miller, L. Land, HARPER'S ENCYCLOPEDIA OF BIBLE LIFE. Harper & Row, 1978

Morey, William C., OUTLINES OF ROMAN HISTORY, American Book Co. 1901

Morgan, The Rev. W., ST. PAUL IN BRITAIN/THE ORIGIN OF BRITISH CHRISTIANITY, Artisan Sales, 1984

Mosley, John, WHEN WAS THAT CHRISTMAS STAR? Griffith Observer (-atory), Dec, 1980

MOVING A 15,000 TON TREASURE, FEAT ON THE NILE TO SAVE THE TEMPLES OF ABU SIMBEL. Author ? LIFE Magazine, Oct. 29, 1965

McCrone, Walter C., THE SHROUD PAINTING EXPLAINED. BAR, Nov/Dec, 1998

McEvedy, Colin, THE PENGUIN ATLAS OF ANCIENT HISTORY, Penguin Books, 1986

NEW LAYMAN'S PARALLEL BIBLE (See: PARALLEL BIBLE)

NEW TESTAMENT AND PSALMS, THE, AN INCLUSIVE VERSION. The Editors, OxUniPr, 1995

Oracle at Delphi to Themistocles,

ORIENTAL INSTITUTE GUIDE (See: GUIDE TO . . .)

Origen, ON FIRST PRINCIPLES, trans, G.W. Butterworth. Peter Smith, 1973

Ovid, (Publius Ovidius Naso), THE EROTIC POEMS, Penguin Books, 1982

OXFORD ANNOTATED BIBLE WITH APOCRYPHA, RSV. Eds. Herbert G. May & Bruce M. Metzger. OxUniPr, 1965
—DICTIONARY OF THE CHRISTIAN CHURCH, THE. The Eds., OxUniPr, 1979
—DICTIONARY OF QUOTATIONS, ibid. 1979
—HISTORY OF THE CLASSICAL WORLD, ibid., date ? (M.C. Lib. #938)

PARALLEL BIBLE, THE NEW LAYMAN'S. The Publishers, Zondervan. 1981

Partridge, Eric, ORIGINS, A SHORT ETYMOLOGICAL DICTIONARY OF MODERN ENGLISH. Grenwich House, 1983

Payne, Robert, THE FATHERS OF THE EASTERN CHURCH, Dorset Press, 1989
—THE FATHERS OF THE WESTERN CHURCH, ibid.
—THE HORIZON BOOK OF ANCIENT ROME, American Heritage Pub. Co. date ?, Lib.Cong. #66-18667
—ROME TRIUMPHANT, BARNES & Noble, 1962

Peck, Harry T., HARPER'S DICTIONARY OF CLASSICAL LITERATURE & ANTIQUES (?) ?

Petronius Arbiter, THE SATYRICON, trans. Oscar Wilde, Dorset Press, 1992

Phillips, J.B., THE NEW TESTAMENT IN MODERN ENGLISH, Macmillan, 1962
—YOUR GOD IS TOO SMALL, Macmillan, 1969

Philo, THE WORKS OF PHILO JUDAEUS. trans. F.H. Carlson and The Rev. G.H. Whitaker, LoebClLib/HarvUP, (1929) 1949

PHYSICIAN, THE SECRET BOOK OF THE, (PAPYRUS EBERS) BartFamQuot, Little-Brown, 1955

Pigott, Stewart, THE DAWN OF CIVILIZATION, McGraw-Hill, 1961

Bibliography

Pindar, ODES

Pixner, Bargil, CHURCH OF THE APOSTLES FOUND ON MT. ZION. BAR, May/June, 1990

Plato, APOLOGY, CRITO, PHAEDO, SYMPOSIUM, REPUBLIC, THE Classics Club Ed. Walter J. Black N.Y. 1942

Plautus, EPIDICUS

Pliny the Elder,

Pliny the Younger, LETTERS OF GAIUS PLINIUS CAECILIUS SECUNDUS, The Harvard Classics P.F. Collier & Son, 1909

Plutarch, THE LIVES OF THE NOBLE GREEKS AND ROMANS, trans, John Dryden, Modern Library, Random House, no date.

Polycarp (See: Staniforth, EARLY CHRISTIAN WRITINGS.)

Potts, Dr. Timothy, CIVILIZATION: ANCIENT TREASURES FROM THE BRITISH MUSEUM. Australian National Gallery, 1990

Prideaux, Tom, (See: EGYPT'S PAST . . .) LIFE Mag. special

Pritchard, James B. ANCIENT NEAR EASTERN TEXTS RELATING TO THE OLD TESTAMENT (ANET) Princeton Univ. Press, 1955

Ptahhotep,

Pulak, Cemal, SHIPWRECK! RECOVERING 3000 YEAR-OLD CARGO, BAR, Sep/Oct, 1999

Pythagoras,

Rawlinson, H.G. INTERCOURSES BETWEEN INDIA AND THE WESTERN WORLD FROM THE EARLIEST TIMES TO THE FALL OF ROME. Cambridge Univ. 1926

Ray, Paul J. Jr., A NEW POMPEII DISCOVERED. Newsletter, Inst. of Archeology, HornArMu, Vol. 23;1, Winter, 2002

READER'S DIGEST ATLAS OF THE BIBLE. Ed. Joseph L. Gardner, Reader's Digest, 1981

READER'S DIGEST BIBLE. ED. BRUCE METZGER, 1982

READERS DIGEST, cont: see also:
  Machlin, Milt
  Schiller, Ronald
  Warshovsky, Kenneth

Reich, Ronny, CAIAPHAS'S NAME INSCRIBED ON BONE BOXES, BAR, Sep/Oct, 1992

Renfrew, Colin, ANCIENT EUROPE IS OLDER THAN WE THOUGHT, NatGeoSo, Nov. 1977

Richardson, Cyril, C. EARLY CHRISTIAN FATHERS, Collier, 1970

Robinson, John A.T., REDATING THE NEW TESTAMENT, Westminster, 1976

ROMANS, THE. LIFE Magazine six-part series, beginning _____ , 1966. (incomplete)
  Parts I and II, ? ?: Ill, Julius Caesar, text by Luigi Barzini, date ?; TV, The Busy, brawling City Life in Rome, Humming Life of a Country Town ?; V. The Caesars, Madmen, Statesmen and Saints. June 3, 1966; VI. The Whispers of Pompeii, Robin Espinosa ??

Rosen, Moishe, Y'SHUA, THE JEWISH WAY TO SAY JESUS. Moody, 1982
  —THE HOLOCAUST, FORGIVENESS & EVANGELISM. The JEWS FOR JESUS Newsletter, Vol. 6:5746, 1986

Roth, Nancy E. (see also: Feldman, Steven) THE SHORT LIST: N.T. FIGURES KNOWN TO HISTORY BAR Nov/Dec 2002

Rowley, H.H., THE GROWTH OF THE OLD TESTAMENT, Harper & Row, 1963

Ryken, Leland, HOW TO READ THE BIBLE AS LITERATURE AND GET MORE OUT OF IT. Academie Books, 1984

Sakellarakis, Yannis and Sapouna-Sakellaraki , Efi, DRAMA AND DEATH IN A MINOAN TEMPLE, Nat-GeoSo, Feb. 1981

Sandars, N.K., THE SEA PEOPLES, WARRIORS OF THE ANCIENT MEDITERRANEAN, Thames & Hudson 1978

Schiller, Ronald, THE CONTINENTS ARE ADRIFT. Reader's Digest, Apr. 1971

Schreider, Helen and Frank, IN THE FOOTSTEPS OF ALEXANDER THE GREAT, NatGeoSo, Jan. 1968

Schulberg, Lucille, HISTORIC INDIA/GREAT AGES OF MAN. Time, Inc. 1968

Scullard, H.H. and van deer Hayden, A.A.M., SHORTER ATLAS OF THE CLASSICAL WORLD, E.P. Dutton, 1967

Schulman, Edward, BRISTLECONE PINE, OLDEST KNOWN LIVING THING, NatGeoSo. Mar. 1968

Seneca, Lucius Annaeus, THE MINOR ESSAYS, BestWoCl, Funk & Wagnalls, 1909
—LETTERS FROM A STOIC, trans. Robin Campbell, Penguin Books, 1969

Severy, Merle, THE BYZANTINE EMPIRE, ROME OF THE EAST. NatGeoSo, Dec. 1983
—THE CELTS, EUROPE'S FOUNDERS. NatGeoSo, May, 1977

Shanks, Hershel, (See: BIBLICAL ARCHEOLOGY REVIEW, BAR)

Sherratt, Andrew, CAMBRIDGE ENCYCLOPEDIA OF ARCHEOLOGY. CamUniPr, 1980

Sherwin-White, Adrian Nicholas, ROMAN SOCIETY & ROMAN LAW IN THE NEW TESTAMENT. The SARUM LECTURES, OxUniPr, 1963

Sibylline Oracle, A.D. 6. (Pseudepigrapha ?) From a National Geographic Map ? ?

Speiser, E.A., ANCIENT MESOPOTAMIA: A LIGHT THAT DID NOT FAIL. NatGeoSo, Jan. 1951

Slavitt, David R. VIRGIL, Yale Univ. Press, 1991

SPLENDORS OF THE PAST: LOST CITIES OF THE ANCIENT WORLD. NatGeoSo, 1981

Socrates (See: Plato and Aristotle)

Solon,

Sophist on Truth,

Stager, Lawrence E., WHEN CANAANITES AND PHILISTINES RULED ASHKELON (silver calf) BAR. Mar/Apr, 1991

Staniforth, Maxwell and Louth, Andrew. EARLY CHRISTIAN WRITINGS. Penguin Books, 1968

Starr, Chester G., THE ANCIENT GREEKS. OxUniPr, 1971
—THE ANCIENT ROMANS. *ibid*.

Stein, Werner, KULTURFAHRPLAN (See: Bernard, TIMETABLES OF HISTORY)

Strelocke, Hans, POLYGLOTT TRAVEL GUIDE/EGYPT. Polyglott-Verlag, 1985

Strabo,

Strobel, Lee, THE CASE FOR CHRIST. Zondervan, 1998

Suetonius, Gaius Tranquillus, LIVES OF THE XII CAESARS, BestWoCl, Funk & Wagnalls, 1909
—THE TWELVE CAESARS, trans Robert Graves, Penguin Books, 1989

Tacitus, Publius Cornelius, (title?) BestWoCl, Funk & Wagnalls, 1909
—THE ANNALS OF IMPERIAL ROME, trans. Michael Grant, Penguin Books, 1989

Tamarin, Alfred, REVOLT IN JUDEA: THE ROAD TO MASADA. Scholastic, 1968

Terrance, (title?) trans, John Sargeaunt. LoebClLib/HarvUP, (1912) 1979

Tertullian, (Quintus Septimius Tertullianus) APOLOGY DE SPECTACULIS (DEFENSE OF THE CHRISTIAN FAITH) trans. T.R. Glover, HarvUP (1931) 1966

Thomas, D. Winton, DOCUMENTS FROM OLD TESTAMENT TIMES. Harper & Row, 1958

Thompson, Francis, THE HOUND OF HEAVEN, Pocket Books, 1940

Thycydides, HISTORY OF THE PELOPONNESIAN WAR. BestWoCl, Funk & Wagnalls, 1909

Topping, Audrey, THE FIRST EMPEROR'S ARMY, CHINA'S INCREDIBLE FIND. NatGeoSo, Apr. 1978

Trajan, Emperor, (Marcus Ulpius Traianus) CORRESPONDENCE WITH PLINY THE YOUNGER, Harvard Classics, P.F. Collier, 1909

Tushingham, A.D., THE MEN WHO HID THE DEAD SEA SCROLLS. NatGeoSo, Dec. 1958

van Loon, Hendrik Willem, THE ARTS. Simon & Schuster, 1937

Venerable Bede (See: Baeda)

Vester, Bertha Spafford, JERUSALEM, MY HOME, NatGeoSo, Dec. 1964

Viken, Gary, DEBUNKING THE SHROUD, BAR, Nov/Dec, 1998

Virgil, ECOLOGUES, GEORGICS, AENEID, trans. H. Rushton Faircloth, LoebClLib/HarvUP, (1918) 1966
—(See also: Slavitt, David)

Voegelin, Eric, ORDER AND HISTORY, Vol. I, ISRAEL AND REVELATION. Louisiana State Univ. Press, date ?

Wachsmann, Shelly, THE GALILEE BOAT. BAR, Sep/Oct, 1998

Walsh, Michael, BUTLER'S LIVES OF THE SAINTS. Harper San Francisco, 1984

Warshovsky, Fred, NOAH, THE FLOOD, THE FACTS, Reader's Digest, Sept. 1977

Weaver, Kenneth, ATHENS, HER GOLDEN PAST STILL LIGHTS THE WORLD, NatGeoSo, July, 1963
—THE MYSTERY OF THE SHROUD, *ibid.*, June, 1980

Wilken, Michael, THE CHRISTIANS AS THE ROMANS SAW THEM. Yale Univ. Press, 1984

Wilson, Bp. Frank E. FAITH AND PRACTICE. Morehouse-Barlow, 1939

Walker, Williston, A HISTORY OF THE CHRISTIAN CHURCH. Pub & date ? ?

Wallbank, T. Walter and Taylor, Alastaire M. , CIVILIZATION PAST AND PRESENT. Scott Foresman, 1960

Walton, John H. , CHRONOLOGICAL CHARTS OF THE OLD TESTAMENT. Zondervan, 1978

WEBSTER'S NEW TWENTIETH CENTURY DICTIONARY OF THE ENGLISH LANGUAGE. World Pubs. 1977

Whanger, Alan D., BOLSTERING THE CASE FOR THE SHROUD. Bar, May/Jun, 2000

Wines, Rev. B.C.. THE ROOTS OF THE AMERICAN REPUBLIC, Plymouth Rock Foundation, 1997

Wood, Michael, IN SEARCH OF THE TROJAN WAR. BBC, London, 1986

Wooley, Sir Leonard, see: Hawkas, Jacquetta

WORLD BOOK ENCYCLOPEDIA, Field Enterprises/ 1967

Wright, G. Ernest, BRINGING OLD TESTAMENT TIMES TO LIFE. NatGeoSo, Dec. 1957
—THE LAST THOUSAND YEARS BEFORE CHRIST, *ibid.*, Dec. 1960

Wright, Esmond, Gen. Ed. , HISTORY OF THE WORLD/PREHISTORY TO THE RENAISSANCE. Bonanza, 1985

Xenophon, ANABASIS, trans ? BestWoCl, Funk & Wagnalls, 1909

Yurco, Frank J., 3200 YEAR-OLD PICTURES OF ISRAELITES FOUND IN EGYPT. BAR, Sep/Oct, 1990